THE HEBREW BIBLE AND PHILOSOPHY OF RELIGION

Society of Biblical Literature

Resources for Biblical Study

Susan Ackerman, Hebrew Bible/Old Testament Editor

Number 70

THE HEBREW BIBLE AND PHILOSOPHY OF RELIGION

THE HEBREW BIBLE
AND PHILOSOPHY OF RELIGION

By

Jaco Gericke

Society of Biblical Literature
Atlanta

THE HEBREW BIBLE AND PHILOSOPHY OF RELIGION

Library of Congress Cataloging-in-Publication Data

Gericke, Jaco.
    The Hebrew Bible and philosophy of religion / Jaco Gericke.
        p. cm. — (Society of Biblical Literature resources for biblical study ; no. 70)
    Includes bibliographical references and indexes.
    ISBN 978-1-58983-707-2 (paper binding : alk. paper) — ISBN 978-1-58983-708-9 (electronic format)
    1. Philosophy and religion. 2. God (Judaism) 3. Jewish ethics—Philosophy. 4. Bible. O.T.—Criticism, interpretation, etc. I. Title.
    BL51.G45 2012
    221'.0601—dc23   2012041824

Printed on acid-free, recycled paper conforming to
ANSI/NISO Z39.48-1992 (R1997) and ISO 9706:1994
standards for paper permanence.

CONTENTS

Preface...vii

Acknowledgements..x

Abbreviations..xi

PART 1

1. A Philosophical Approach to Ancient Israelite Religion.....................3

2. Philosophical Approaches to the Study of Religion............................15

3. Philosophy of Religion and Hebrew Bible Interpretation:
   A Brief History of Interdisciplinary Relations....................................41

4. The Hebrew Bible in Philosophy of Religion.......................................81

5. Descriptive Currents in Philosophy of Religion for
   Hebrew Bible Studies...115

6. Possible Analogies for a Philosophy of Ancient
   Israelite Religion..155

7. Philosophical Criticism as Biblical Criticism....................................199

8. Toward a Descriptive Philosophy of Ancient Israelite Religion.......223

PART 2

9. The Nature of Religious Language in the Hebrew Bible....................243

10. The Concept of Generic Godhood in the Hebrew Bible....................259

11. Yhwh: A Philosophical Perspective 293

12. Natural A/theologies in Ancient Israel...343

13. Epistemologies in Ancient Israelite Religion 371

14. Religion and Morality in Ancient Israel...405

15. Summary and Conclusion 447

Bibliography...453
Index of Biblical References..487
Index of Modern Authors...489
Index of Subjects...497

PREFACE

I'm searching for the philosopher's stone
And it's a hard road,
It's a hard road daddy-o
When my job is turning lead into gold.[1]

When the young Friedrich Nietzsche's first book (*The Birth of Tragedy*) came out, it appeared to merit only one review. According to the critic who penned it, anyone who wrote a work of that sort was finished as a scholar. The book was subsequently rejected by Nietzsche's peers and only served to distance him from the academic establishment of the time. One reason for the work's bad reception was the fact that it undermined the traditional division between philosophical discourse and artistic expression so dear to western folk philosophy. Because Nietzsche's philosophical contribution to philology would not fit into the neat categories into which the academic discussions of his day were separated, he was a "problem philosopher" for many of his colleagues.[2]

---

1. From *The Philosopher's Stone* by Van Morrison. In the context of this foreword, I use the motif to symbolize a mad scientist seeking to achieve academic immortality with a Great Work that involves turning nonphilosophical biblical texts into a philosophy of Israelite religion. I have to say at the outset that I have no problem having recourse to Wikipedia entries, even though my doing so will scandalize many of my peers. In academic circles, Wikipedia has the reputation of being too superficial or unreliable for research purposes. As I see it, however, Wikipedia entries should be judged on their individual merit. While there are many entries in the field of theology that are patently filled with fundamentalist pseudoscholarship, there are also those that offer useful summaries of ideas otherwise difficult to explain to biblical scholars with little philosophical background. Furthermore, by making use of that resource I am making a statement about the supermodernist transgression this study represents.

2. See Laurence Gane and Kitty Chan, *Introducing Nietzsche* (Cambridge: Icon Books, 1999), 12.

This book has the potential to become Hebrew Bible scholarship's equivalent of Nietzsche's attempt to think beyond the established categories. Very few biblical scholars are ready to imagine an independent philosophical approach to ancient Israelite religion, one supplementing already extant interpretative methodologies. Even worse, biblical studies tends to be one of those fields where the discrediting of popular sentiments, rather than being welcomed as a sign of scientific progress, is dreaded as a possible precursor to a personal existential disaster. Perhaps, then, a tongue-in-cheek warning is required: readers who are comfortable in the belief that philosophical concerns, categories and concepts are the enemies of the biblical scholar may be in danger of being awakened from one of the oldest dogmatic slumbers in the business.

In the pages to follow I hope to demonstrate that certain types of descriptive varieties of philosophy of religion exist that are capable of aiding the clarification of meaning in the Hebrew Bible. Obviously, not everything written here is completely novel. Besides involving bits and pieces of ideas of many others before me, this study represents a continuation and marked revision of a chapter of methodological musings first put forward in my Ph.D. dissertation written during the period 2002–2003.[3] There I proposed the utilization of philosophy of religion as an auxiliary discipline in Hebrew Bible Studies. At the time I was staggering from a loss of faith from which I never recovered. My concerns were therefore largely evaluative and critical, that is, atheological.

However, readers familiar with stereotypical analytic philosophy of religion and hoping either for an attempted justification of biblical truth claims or seeking an atheological critique of ancient Yahwism are advised to turn elsewhere. The present work is motivated by a need for understanding and elucidation of the worlds in the text despite my essentially postrealist (i.e., atheist) interpretative paradigm. So while some readers will insist that it is impossible to come up with a theologically interesting and hermeneutically legitimate nonrealist and descriptive perspective on the Hebrew Bible, I believe I have done it. What the reader will encounter in the pages to follow is something unlike anything currently typical of mainstream biblical scholarship. To my mind it represents a pioneering

---

3. Jacobus W. Gericke, "Does Yahweh Exist? A Philosophical-Critical Reconstruction of the Case against Realism in Old Testament Theology" (Ph.D. diss., University of Pretoria, 2004), 10–25.

endeavor that has the potential of becoming the latest new form of interdisciplinary biblical scholarship.

Though my personal obsession is the possible role of and interest in the Hebrew Bible in a readerly context outside of faith-based scholarship (a topic debated on the *SBL Forum*), this study will enable biblical scholars of all persuasions to access levels of meaning that lie beyond the scope of linguistic, literary, historical and social-scientific perspectives on the text. It even opens up new avenues for more objective theological thinking, since I have no desire to make the text into an object of scorn, as is the case with the New Atheist hermeneutic (Richard Dawkins, Sam Harris, Christopher Hitchens, etc.). It is not a call for the end of biblical studies (Hector Avalos) but for the beginning of a new era therein, one in which both believer and skeptic can together read the ancient texts from a perspective as relatively neutral as that found in the study of any other ancient culture such as that of the Greeks.

If favorably received, this study therefore has the potential to revolutionize the way we think about ancient Israelite religion. Indeed, perhaps only die-hard biblical theologians of the older generation of biblical theology enthusiasts will be able to really appreciate the mind shift its central concern represents. The target reader, however, is the new generation, twenty-first-century biblical scholar with philosophical interests, unhampered by the hermeneutical and ideological baggage of the past. Both theistic and atheistic readers will find something to chew on and discover why philosophy bashing in biblical scholarship, I am sorry to say, now has to be considered as having been "so twentieth century."

In conclusion, I believe that, like life itself, biblical scholarship is but a game. This does not mean that one cannot take it very seriously. Yet for me the challenge is not winning, but figuring out how to make it more interesting than ever before. Of course, if the history of interpretation has taught us anything, it is that all our profound ideas are destined to become chaff in the wind. So rather than search for final answers, this study intends to initiate the quest for ultimate questions. In the end, it does not really matter which way the wind blows; and there is also no reason why one cannot learn to ride on its wings, like a god who is meditating, or wandering away, or on a journey, or perhaps asleep and in need of being awakened.

Jaco Gericke
Pretoria, December 2011

Acknowledgements

The writings of both biblical scholars and philosophers of religion have played a role in the development of my thoughts. Ghost mentors include biblical scholars such as James Barr, James Crenshaw, Robert Carroll, David Clines, and Rolf Knierim. In philosophy of religion, the thoughts of Don Cupitt and Keith Ward have greatly motivated my own endeavors. Many other scholars from a variety of fields have at one time or another influenced my thinking on issues addressed in this study and to all of them I am extremely grateful.

As for people closer to home, I would like to thank my colleague at the Vaal Campus of North-West University, Professor Hans van Deventer. Without him, I would simply have been deprived of the opportunity to undertake this study. Other supportive coconspirators include professors Dirk Human, Jurie Le Roux, Hendrik Bosman, and Dr. Christo Lombaard.

I am also very grateful to two wonderful women, Marlize and Charlotte, who each in her own way and time supported me kindly under the most complicated of circumstances.

Finally, I would like to thank Mrs. Isabelle Delvare for the proofreading of the manuscript. Many thanks also to Susan Ackerman, Bob Buller, and the SBL copyediting team for their painstaking and extended assistance in removing many shortcomings in the manuscript

I would also like to acknowledge my gratitude to the editors of the *Journal for Semitics*, *Old Testament Essays*, *Verbum et Ecclesia*, *Hervormde Teologiese Studies*, and *Scriptura* for permission to utilize selections from previously published articles in sections of this book

Without all of you, none of this would be possible. Well, technically it might still be possible, but it would not have been easy. Not that it was actually easy, but you know what I mean. I hope.

Abbreviations

AD	*Ars Disputandi*
APA	American Philosophical Association
BCP	Blackwell Companions to Philosophy
BCR	Blackwell Companions to Religion
BRMT	Blackwell Readings in Modern Theology
BTB	*Biblical Theology Bulletin*
BZAW	Beihefte zur Zeitschrift für die Alttestamentliche Wissenschaft
DDD	*Dictionary of Deities and Demons in the Bible*
ER	*Encyclopedia of Religion*
FAT	Forschungen zum Alten Testament
FRLANT	Forschungen zur Religion und Literatur des Alten und Neuen Testaments
HCPR	Handbook of Contemporary Philosophy of Religion
HUCA	*Hebrew Union College Annual*
HTS	*Hervormde Teologiese Studies*
IEP	*Internet Encyclopedia of Philosophy*
ISBE	*International Standard Bible Encyclopedia*. Edited by G. W. Bromiley. 4 vols. Grand Rapids: Zondervan, 1979–1988.
IJPR	*Internet Journal for the Philosophy of Religion*
JAAR	*Journal of the American Academy of Religion*
JBT	*Jahrbuch für Biblische Theologie*
JFR	*Jahrbuch für Religionsphilosophie*
JNABI	*Journal of the National Association of Biblical Instructors*
JNES	*Journal for Near Eastern Studies*
JPS	*Journal of Philosophy and Scripture*
JR	*Journal of Religion*
JSem	*Journal for Semitics*
JSOTSup	Journal for the Study of the Old Testament Supplement Series

LTT	Library of Theological Translations
NPNF	*A Select Library of Nicene and Post-Nicene Fathers of the Christian Church*. Edited by Philip Schaff and Henry Wace. 28 vols. in 2 series. 1886–1889.
NZSTR	*Neue Zeitschrift für Systematische Theologie und Religionsphilosophie*
OBT	Overtures to Biblical Theology
OTE	*Old Testament Essays*
OTL	Old Testament Library
PEW	*Philosophy East and West*
RCIP	Routledge Contemporary Introductions to Philosophy
REP	*Routledge Encyclopedia of Philosophy*
RelStud	*Religious Studies*
SBTS	Sources for Biblical and Theological Study
SemeiaSt	Semeia Studies
SEP	*Stanford Encyclopedia of Philosophy*
SJOT	*Scandinavian Journal of the Old Testament*
SJT	*Scottish Journal of Theology*
So	*Sophia: International Journal for Philosophy of Religion*
ST	*Studia Theologica*
TDOT	*Theological Dictionary of the Old Testament*. Edited by G. Johannes Botterweck and Helmer Ringgren. Translated by John T. Willis, G. W. Bromiley, and David E. Green. Grand Rapids: Eerdmans, 1974–.
ThWAT	*Theologisches Wörterbuch zum Alten Testament*
ThZ	*Theologische Zeitschrift*
TW	Theologische Wissenschaft
UF	*Ugaritische Forschung*
VE	*Verbum et Ecclesia*
VT	*Vetus Testamentum*
VTSup	Supplements to Vetus Testamentum
WTJ	*Westminster Theological Journal*
ZAR	*Zeitschrift für Altorientalische und Biblische Rechtsgeschichte*
ZAW	*Zeitschrift für die Alttestamentliche Wissenschaft*
ZTK	*Zeitschrift für Theologie und Kirche*

PART 1

A new scientific truth does not triumph by convincing its opponent and making them see the light, but rather because its opponents eventually die, and a new generation grows up that is familiar with it.*

---

* Max K. Planck, *Scientific Autobiography and Other Papers* (trans. Frank Gaynor; New York: Philosophical Library, 1949), 33–34.

1

A Philosophical Approach to Ancient Israelite Religion

The aspects of things that are most important for us are hidden because of their simplicity and familiarity. (One is unable to notice something—because it is always before one's eyes.) The real foundations of his enquiry do not strike a man at all. Unless that fact has at some time struck him.—And this means: we fail to be struck by what, once seen, is most striking and most powerful.[1]

1.1. The Philosophical Gap in Hebrew Bible Interpretation

Interdisciplinary research in the study of the Hebrew Bible is nothing novel.[2] In fact, it is impossible to do any other kind. All forms of biblical criticism have recourse to at least one auxiliary subject, be it linguistics, literary criticism, history, archaeology, anthropology, sociology, psychology, theology, philosophy, or another. In a pluralist hermeneutical context where different methodologies offer different insights, none of these auxiliary fields can lay claim to be *the* handmaid of biblical interpretation. All are equally useful aids in their own right, depending on what one wants to achieve in the reading of the text. The only essence in Hebrew Bible scholarship is thus not to be located in any particular approach to the text, but rather in the Hebrew Bible itself. (This is despite the well-known fact that the idea of a stable text is itself problematic.)

---

1. Ludwig Wittgenstein, *Philosophical Investigations* (trans. Gertrude E. M. Anscombe; New York: Wiley-Blackwell, 2001), §129.

2. Some ideas expressed here were first expressed in Jaco Gericke, "The Quest for a Philosophical Yahweh (Part 1): Old Testament Studies and Philosophy of Religion," *OTE* 18 (2006): 579–602.

Surveying the interpretative smorgasbord, the biblical scholar is confronted by an immense variety of reading strategies.[3] The extended family of biblical criticism include, *inter alia*, textual, source, tradition, redaction, form, historical, narrative, rhetorical, new, social-scientific, delimitation, feminist, ideological, canonical, psychological, mythological, composition, autobiographical and theological criticism. As for large scale approaches to the text, one can choose among biblical Hebrew linguistics, biblical geography, biblical archaeology, the history of Israel, the history of Israelite religion, comparative ancient Near Eastern studies, the sociology of Israelite religion, biblical theology, biblical ethics, biblical hermeneutics, cognitive perspectives, and so on.

From this overview, one might be tempted to conclude that Hebrew Bible scholars have at their disposal everything one could possibly need for the purposes of comprehensive and holistic research. In fact, one sometimes gets the impression that we have nearly exhausted possibilities for reading the text. All that is left is refinement, application, and keeping up to date with the latest trends in the auxiliary fields. Or so it seems. However, this conclusion is premature. From the perspective of religious studies proper, there is something seriously wrong with this picture. *Something is missing* as far as the multiplicity of approaches to ancient Israelite religion is concerned. For while we offer linguistic, literary, historical, theological, sociological, anthropological and psychological perspectives, there is to this day no officially recognized, independent and descriptive *philosophical* approach to the study of ancient Israelite religion.

1.2. The Involvement of Philosophy in Hebrew Bible Studies

To be sure, biblical scholars do make use of philosophy, in a number of ways:

1. For a long time in the history of biblical interpretation, philosophy was in fact the official handmaid of biblical commentary.
2. Every major era in biblical interpretation came about as a result of *philosophical* (especially epistemological) fashions that provided a hermeneutical justification for a particular

---

3. For discussion of the methods, see Richard N. Soulen and Kendall R. Soulen, *Handbook of Biblical Criticism* (Louisville: Westminster John Knox, 2001).

paradigm shift.[4] The epistemology of modernism lies behind the historical turn, while postmodern epistemologies provided the impetus for the creation and employment of a variety of socioliterary approaches.

3. A minimal acquaintance with ideas that have roots in philosophy is required when coming to terms with the theory underlying many forms of biblical criticism. Philosophy is always covertly present as something indelible and all forms of biblical criticism are only meaningful given a number of unspoken *philosophical* assumptions.[5]

4. Some fields in the study of the Hebrew Bible are by their very nature fundamentally linked to issues in related philosophical trends, e.g., biblical hermeneutics and biblical ethics.

5. Overviews of the history of biblical interpretation often note influential philosophical ideas in the makeup of notable biblical scholars. One cannot acquaint oneself with the history of biblical interpretation without becoming knowingly or unwittingly familiar with some of the popular assumptions in Platonism, Aristotelianism, rationalism, romanticism, idealism, historicism, personalism, positivism, Marxism, existentialism, postmodernism, and so on.

6. Biblical theologians have never really stopped worrying about the relation of philosophy to their subject. Even after the separation of biblical criticism and biblical theology from dogmatics, we find traces of dependence on ideas put forward by fashionable philosophers: Kant, Hegel, Kierkegaard, Marx, Wittgenstein, Foucault, Derrida, and so on.

A variety of philosophical subdisciplines are therefore indirectly still pulling some of the strings behind the scenes in research on the Hebrew Bible. Their influence is palpable, even in the writings of those scholars with no training in philosophy. Philosophical fields that are most clearly visible

---

4. On the influential role of philosophy in American theology, see Nancey Murphy, *Beyond Liberalism and Fundamentalism: How Modern and Postmodern Philosophy Set the Philosophical Agenda* (Valley Forge, Pa.: Trinity Press International, 1996).

5. On the philosophical assumptions in those dismissive of philosophy, see James Barr, *The Concept of Biblical Theology: An Old Testament Perspective* (Philadelphia: Fortress, 1999), 152.

include hermeneutics, ethics, philosophy of language, philosophy of literature, political philosophy, social philosophy and the philosophy of science.
It was the recognition of this state of affairs that once prompted a rare
retraction of earlier claims by none other than the late James Barr himself:

> In this respect, incidentally, I should perhaps make an amendment to my
> remarks in *The Concept of Biblical Theology*, ch. 10, in which I pointed
> out how far Old Testament scholarship was remote from philosophy.
> The judgment should perhaps have a temporal qualifier attached to it: it
> certainly applies up to my own generation. Judging from the influential
> hermeneutical philosophies, and from some of what is now written in
> biblical studies, a kind of philosophy, especially social philosophy and
> what is coming to be called critical-theory, is becoming more obvious
> and central in biblical study. But this is for the most part a new thing, an
> innovation as against what has been normal since the mid-nineteenth
> century. It may certainly change the air of biblical study. Philosophical
> claims or claims of critical theory, disquisitions about poststructural-
> ism, postmodernism and the like may take the place of what used to be
> called Hebrew Grammar or textual criticism. Derrida and Foucault will
> become more familiar than the Septuagint or Brown, Driver and Briggs.
> It certainly looks that way at the moment.[6]

Notwithstanding these overt and covert excursions to things philosophical, there is something that still does not make sense and that needs to be
examined more closely.

1.3. What about Philosophy of Religion?

It seems rather odd that Hebrew Bible scholars—whose main concern is
religious texts—have failed to make intensive and extensive use of the one
philosophical discipline actually exclusively devoted to the study of *religious* phenomena, i.e. *philosophy of religion*. To be sure, one does encounter isolated allusions to philosophy of religion in the works of biblical
scholars, that is, indirect references to philosophical debates on the nature
of religious language, the problem of evil and religious epistemology. Even
so, at present no dictionary or encyclopedia of biblical interpretation
includes entries such as *"philosophical criticism"* or *"philosophy of Israelite*

---

6. James Barr, *History and Ideology in the Old Testament: Biblical Studies at the
End of a Millennium* (Oxford: Oxford University Press, 2000), 27–28.

religion."[7] No wonder even James Barr felt that the prospect for interdisciplinary research looked bleak:

> It would be difficult to exaggerate the degree of alienation that the average biblical scholar has felt in relation to the work of disciplines like *philosophical theology or philosophy of religion.* Their modes of discussion and decision seem to him or her remote and unreal. The questions they discuss and the criteria they apply seem to be contrived and artificial, and the world of discourse in which they move seems to be quite a different world from the world of the Bible, to which the biblical scholar feels he has a sort of direct and empirical access.[8]

If this assessment is accurate, readers may be perplexed as to why anyone in their right mind would want to consider such an apparent mismatch as that between Hebrew Bible interpretation and philosophy of religion in the first place. One maxim of "theological engineering" in the current paradigm holds that the very different nature of the two subjects suggests that they cannot be fused into a hybrid form of inquiry. Biblical studies are descriptive and historical, while philosophy of religion is evaluative and normative. Past attempts to read the texts from a philosophical perspective—and there have been many—are now considered to have failed spectacularly. Philosophical concerns, categories, and concepts have severely distorted biblical thought. Characterized by nonphilosophical genres, the texts show no overt concern with philosophical issues. They contain neither philosophical definitions, nor formal arguments seeking to justify religious truth claims. The last two centuries of biblical criticism since the separation of biblical and dogmatic theology have therefore taught us, if anything, that the Hebrew Bible is not a philosophical textbook.

As for philosophy of religion, in the West the discipline tends to be equated with a critical appraisal of philosophical concepts in contemporary Judeo-Christian religious truth claims. In stereotyped formats it is difficult to distinguish the field from normative metaphysical speculation, Christian apologetics, Christian philosophical theology, and so on. Hence

---

7. To be sure, a word search on the internet will reveal entries concerned with a "biblical philosophy" of something in the vulgar sense of the term, as can be seen by doing a Boolean word search with "Bible" and "philosophy" on the Internet. Here one finds titles such as "A biblical philosophy of X" or "Biblical philosophy as X," but most of the time the term "philosophy" is used in the populist sense of "opinion."

8. Barr, *Concept of Biblical Theology*, 146, emphasis added.

belief revision in the history of Israelite religion, synchronic theological pluralism, narrative and poetic representation, as well as metaphorical god-talk all seem profoundly problematic to any reader of the Hebrew Bible with some historical consciousness. We look in vain for any overt philosophy of religion in the texts and cannot construct a unified contemporary relevant philosophy of religion from its contents.

But if we grant all this, which I do, why should anyone even want to consider the possibility of a philosophical approach to ancient Israelite religion in the first place?

1.4. Rationale for a Descriptive Philosophical Approach to Ancient Israelite Religion

For my proposal of a philosophical approach to the study of ancient Israelite religion to be taken seriously, it will have to satisfy two requirements. First, I will have to demonstrate the possibility of involving philosophy of religion in historical biblical interpretation without repeating the hermeneutical fallacies of the past. Second, I will have to show that a philosophical approach to ancient Israelite religion is worth our while and able to deliver insights into the meaning of the biblical materials that already existing approaches to the text are unable to offer. In this regard, I offer a number of reasons as to why a philosophical approach to ancient Israelite religion is not a luxury but a necessity.

First, there is the requirement to be *comprehensive* in our understanding of ancient Israelite religion. In the scientific study of religion, it is taken for granted that linguistic, literary, historical, anthropological, sociological, psychological, and theological perspectives must be supplemented by a *philosophical* approach to obtain a holistic understanding of the religion in question:[9]

> The study of religion, to be complete, needs to address basic philosophical questions about what exists (metaphysics), what can be known (epistemology), about what is valuable (value theory and ethics).... Phi-

9. Peter Connolly, ed., *Approaches to the Study of Religion* (London: Continuum, 1999). For a survey and discussion of approaches to the study of religion, see Robert A. Segal, ed., *The Blackwell Companion to the Study of Religion* (BCR; New York: Wiley-Blackwell, 2006).

losophy is hard to avoid. Even radical dismissal of philosophy involves a philosophy.[10]

One cannot begin to comprehend the fundamental structures of meaning even in the study of ancient prephilosophical religions without attending to their texts' basic assumptions regarding reality, knowledge, and value. It is therefore impossible to understand the conceptual backgrounds implicit in the Hebrew Bible without a descriptive philosophical clarification of the metaphysical, epistemological and moral presuppositions of its discourses.

Second, a philosophical approach can help us to avoid possible anachronistic *philosophical-theological* distortions in our research. Unless we are able to come up with a historical-philosophical clarification of the concepts, beliefs, and practices of ancient Israelite religion for its own sake, we are left with a scenario in which we have no formal means of controlling our tendency to project our own anachronistic Jewish or Christian philosophical-theological assumptions about religious language, religious epistemology, the nature of God, the existence of God, the problem of evil, and so on, onto biblical god-talk. Contrary to popular belief, therefore, we actually need *more*—not fewer—philosophical inquiries, precisely because the Hebrew Bible is not a textbook in the philosophy of religion.

Third, *descriptive* methods have been available in philosophy of religion for quite a while now. Not all types of philosophical analysis of religion are critical, speculative, systematic, or normative in nature. Certain methods in analytic, phenomenological, and comparative currents in philosophy of religion offer tools that can be utilized purely with the aim of clarifying meaning. These methods make a historical approach within philosophy of religion possible. In turn, descriptive philosophies of religion are suitable for use in biblical criticism with its historical agenda. Since philosophy of religion is no longer necessarily an endeavor whose concerns are limited to apologetics or natural a/theology, the popular objections to the involvement of it in biblical studies do not apply here.

Fourth, there exists a *yawning philosophical gap* in research on the Hebrew Bible. Neither philosophers of religion (including Jewish philoso-

---

10. Charles Taliaferro, "Philosophy of Religion," in Segal, *Blackwell Companion to the Study of Religion*, 123. The need for a philosophical approach to the concept of deity is also explained by Raimundo Panikkar, "Deity," *ER* 4:274–76.

phers) nor Hebrew Bible scholars have made much effort to come up with purely descriptive, in-depth philosophical accounts of the beliefs, practices and concepts of ancient Yahwism(s). On the one hand, philosophers of religion (and Jewish philosophers) focus mostly on contemporary or past *philosophical* traditions within Judaism and Christianity and do not have any desire to engage in a philosophical analysis elucidating ancient Israelite religion for its own sake. On the other hand, scholars of the Hebrew Bible who do study ancient Yahwism(s) have by default adopted all possible approaches in religious studies, except a *philosophical* one. So neither biblical scholars nor philosophers of religion study ancient Israelite religion descriptively from the perspective of issues on the agenda in philosophy of religion.

Taken together, these four points offer a cumulative argument as to why a philosophical account of biblical Yahwism is timely, sorely needed and, perhaps most important of all, possible.

1.5. Objectives of This Study

During the twentieth century, a debate has raged regarding the place and role of philosophy as such in Hebrew Bible studies in general, and within Old Testament theology in particular.[11] The contents of this book are not intended to contribute to that discussion and I leave it to biblical theologians to decide how they wish to operate in relation to philosophy per se. Instead, my aim is to argue in favor of the establishment of a new and independent interpretative methodology exclusively concerned with involving philosophy of religion in particular as an auxiliary subject. As such my goals overlap with, yet differ from, those of biblical theology; just as the objectives of philosophy of religion overlap with yet differ from those of systematic theology.

That being said, it is of paramount importance to note that the aim of this study is *not* to show how the Hebrew Bible can contribute to popular debates in contemporary Jewish or Christian philosophy of religion. Rather, the objective is to demonstrate how currents in descriptive philosophy of religion can be of use to biblical scholars concerned with the clarification of meaning in the Hebrew Bible. The findings of this type of historical-philosophical analysis may or may not be relevant to philoso-

---

11. See James Barr, *Concept of Biblical Theology*, 146–71.

phers of religion or biblical theologians proper. Whether they are can at best be an epiphenomenon of the descriptive philosophical enterprise. When philosophical-atheological relevance becomes a guiding principle it predisposes us to distortive readings.

My agenda, therefore, has nothing to do with a personal interest in either defending or criticizing Yahwistic religious beliefs to edify the ideological agenda of any religious or secular community of readers. I have no desire to read (Judeo-Christian) philosophy into the Hebrew Bible, nor any hope to construct a (Judeo-Christian) systematic philosophy of religion from its diverse contents. [12] I have no intention to *reinterpret*, actualize, or demythologize the text for existentialist theological purposes. Neither am I after a reductionist philosophical (e.g., naturalist) *explanation* of Israelite religion or a neo-Yahwistic philosophy of religion seeking to subvert current constructions of reality. All I seek to do is to pioneer a new approach within biblical studies aimed at a descriptive philosophical elucidation of the beliefs, concepts, and practices of ancient Israelite religion as represented in the Hebrew Bible.

1.6. OUTLINE OF CONTENTS

The presentation to follow is divided into two parts corresponding roughly to the theory and the practice of the new approach.

Part 1 consists of chapters 2 to 8, which provide the backdrop to, the justification for, and the details of the new methodology.

In chapter 2 we face our demons with the aid of metaphilosophy of religion and discover a plurality of answers to the question of what exactly a philosophical approach to the study of religion is supposed to be. Chapter 3 traces historical relations between Hebrew Bible interpretation and philosophy of religion, from the perspective of biblical studies. In chapter 4 we invert our point of view to look at relations between the disciplines from the perspective of philosophy of religion. Chapter 5 provides a discussion of relevant descriptive currents in the philosophical study of religion, and also refutes a number of popular objections against the involvement of philosophy in the study of the Hebrew Bible. In chapter 6, we consider a few possible analogies from both philosophy and biblical studies for imagining the presence of folk-philosophical assumptions in

---

12. On the suspicion of system as manic, see Don Cupitt, *Philosophy's Own Religion* (London: SCM, 2001), 170 n. 3.

the biblical discourse itself. In chapter 7 I introduce the theory behind "philosophical criticism" as new exegetical methodology and in chapter 8 look at the theoretical intricacies of involving and combining descriptive varieties of philosophy of religion on a larger scale.

As illustration of how the theory can be applied to operate in practice, we come to part 2, which consists of chapters 9 to 15. Here, loci on the agenda of philosophy of religion are descriptively brought to bear on the Hebrew Bible. This section shows some of the tangible results that can be achieved when we look at and clarify what we have in the Hebrew Bible from the perspective of descriptive currents in philosophy of religion.

Chapter 9 deals with the nature of religious language in ancient Israel via a philosophical reassessment of many popular ideas in biblical theology. In chapter 10, I offer an introductory philosophical analysis of the concept of generic godhood in ancient Israelite religion. In chapter 11, we consider some proposals and prospects for a philosophical theology of the Hebrew Bible. In chapter 12, we look at traces of natural a/theologies implicit in the biblical discourse and discuss some interesting issues in ancient Israelite ontology. The subject of chapter 13 is the epistemology of Israelite religion, while chapter 14 deals with the relationship between religion and morality in the Hebrew Bible (especially metaethics). Chapter 15 is the conclusion to the study.

1.7. A Supermodern Disclaimer

Books on the Hebrew Bible, whatever form they take, often tell readers as much about their authors as about their subject, if not more. This study's plea for a philosophical approach to the text does not naively operate with either precritical or positivist assumptions about the interpretative task. I know as well as anybody that Christian philosophical concerns are anachronistic and that pure historical description is a myth (in the pejorative sense of the word). I am quite familiar with and accept the hermeneutical insights of Gadamer and Ricoeur, who showed us the ways in which the exegete is and remains a historical animal, never totally abstracted from the local sociocultural matrix. I realize that my philosophical concerns are not transhistorical or perennial in any sense.

However, the context in which this study asks to be located is not so much postmodernism as *super*modernism. The term is lesser known in biblical hermeneutics and comes from anthropologist Marc Augé's book,

Non-places: Introduction to an Anthropology of Supermodernity.[13] While most biblical scholars appear to be modernists working on premodern texts in a postmodern world, I would like to imagine that this study is novel not only in terms of methodology but also in terms of its location within the "supermodern condition." Characterized by an excess of time, space and ego, all of which supervene on the present study in ways that distinguish its utilization of philosophy of religion from postmodern obsessions with social and literary philosophy, supermodernism can be introduced in the following manner:

> If distinguished from hypermodernity, supermodernity is a step beyond the ontological emptiness of postmodernism and relies upon a view of plausible truths. Where modernism focused upon the creation of great truths (or what Lyotard called 'master narratives' or 'metanarratives'), postmodernity is intent upon their destruction (deconstruction). In contrast supermodernity does not concern itself with the creation or identification of truth value. Instead, information that is useful is selected from the superabundant sources of new media. Postmodernity and deconstruction have made the creation of truths an impossible construction. Supermodernity acts amid the chatter and excess of signification in order to escape the nihilistic tautology of postmodernity. The Internet search and the construction of interconnected blogs are excellent metaphors for the action of the supermodern subject.[14]

In supermodernism it is not that the world or the text lacks meaning— rather, there seems to be too many possible meanings to discern from. It is in the recognition of this that the theoretical discussion in this study now commences.

---

13. Marc Augé, *Non-places: Introduction to the Anthropology of Supermodernity* (trans. John Howe; London: Verso, 1995).

14. "Hypermodernity," *Wikipedia, The Free Encyclopedia* [cited 16 January 2010]. Online: http://en.wikipedia.org/w/index.php?title=Hypermodernity&oldid=329598080.

2

PHILOSOPHICAL APPROACHES
TO THE STUDY OF RELIGION

The question "*What is philosophy?*" can perhaps be posed only late in life, with the arrival of old age and the time for speaking concretely. In fact, the bibliography on the nature of philosophy is very limited. It is a question posed in a moment of quiet restlessness, at midnight, when there is no longer anything to ask.[1]

2.1. WHAT IS A "PHILOSOPHICAL" APPROACH TO RELIGION?

Most Hebrew Bible scholars lack expert knowledge of philosophy of religion. Consequently, this chapter offers a basic introductory metaphilosophical overview of that subject in order to set the scene for the discussion to follow. For let us suppose that the agenda of Hebrew Bible interpretation is essentially historical and descriptive. Whether there can be a hermeneutically justified philosophical approach to ancient Israelite religion within biblical scholarship at all will depend on what we understand under the concept of "philosophy of religion" itself. And here lies the catch, if only because the meaning and use of every term of the concept are essentially contested.

One reason why there can never be a singular definition of philosophy of religion is that there are no essential properties of a philosophical approach to religion. Simply saying that it is "philosophical reflection on religion" or a given religion's philosophy will not do, for this still begs the question of what both "philosophy" and "religion" are actually supposed to be.

---

1. Gilles Deleuze and Félix Guattari, *What Is Philosophy?* (trans. Hugh Tomlinson and Graham Burchell; New York: Columbia University Press, 1994), 1, emphasis original.

Consider the way in which the word "philosophy" is sometimes used in ordinary language. From this one gets the impression that philosophy is simply "opinion" or "speculation"; hence, references to one's "philosophy of life," "philosophy of coaching," "philosophy of parenting," and so on. But the more of a philosophical background one has, the more the idea of what philosophy and its use are tends to alter. Ask an undergraduate student of philosophy or the average biblical scholar, and you can perhaps expect a more stereotyped definition—one that reveals a particular historical and ideological frame of reference. But ask a postmodern metaphilosopher, a historian of philosophy, or a comparative philosopher, and you are likely to encounter a somewhat more qualified, nuanced and antiessentialist view.

This state of affairs makes it impossible to offer an intentional definition of philosophy. Both historically and globally, the form and content of philosophical reflection on religion have never been completely homogenous or stable. Not surprisingly, then, ideas of what counts as a philosophical approach to religion have tended to conform to contemporary philosophical concerns.[2] During the premodern period, the main focus of philosophical inquiries was on metaphysics; during the modern era it was on epistemology; and during postmodern times there developed an interest in language (the so-called "linguistic turn"). Of course, these distinctions are essentialist stereotypes. For instance, ancient philosophical reflection was also concerned with language and the postmodern period has seen the revival of metaphysics in the form of post-Kripkean semantics. And many current philosophical debates show a larger representational turn that privileges the philosophy of *mind* (cognitive studies).[3] Yet there is no consensus, and representationalism is not the last word.[4]

From an interdisciplinary point of view the above-mentioned stereotypical historical shifts seem even more complex. Up unto the modern period it is impossible to specify a philosophical discipline exclusively concerned with religion as a distinct and only human cultural phenomenon.[5]

---

2. For an overview, see Mark D. Jordan, "Religion, History of the Philosophy of," in *The Oxford Companion to Philosophy* (ed. Ted Honderich; New York: Oxford University Press, 1995), 759–63.

3. For an introduction and critical overview of this debate, see Peter M. S. Hacker, "Beyond the Linguistic Turn," in *The Analytic Turn: Analysis in Early Analytic Philosophy and Phenomenology* (ed. Michael Beany; London: Routledge, 2007), 1–20.

4. See Cupitt, *Philosophy's Own Religion*, 91.

5. Jordan, "Religion," 760.

In the early Hellenistic period, philosophical approaches to religion were part of metaphysics. During the early Christian era, philosophies of religion were intertwined with "holy teaching" in many patristic and late medieval contexts, and came to be known as "natural theology" or "natural religion."[6] This intermingling of philosophical inquiries with religious themes is still apparent among early modern philosophers such as John Locke and George Berkeley until, gradually, we come to find philosophical texts devoted exclusively to religious topics. Not surprisingly, unitary histories of philosophy of religion up to this point are virtually unknown.[7]

The first use of the term "philosophy of religion" in English is said to come from the work of Ralph Cudworth.[8] For this reason, some locate the origins of philosophy of religion as a field in the mid-seventeenth century. In German literature, the first use of the term *Religionsphilosophie* as a philosophical discipline exclusively concerned with religion as phenomenon is first encountered in the work of Hegel.[9] At that stage, equivocation was very much the order of the day. When Hegel referred to *Religionsphilosophie*, the details of his writings show that he intended by it something entirely different from, say, what Schleiermacher meant.[10] In most histories of the subject its founding fathers are, aside from Hegel, also held to be earlier philosophers such as Hume and Kant. Others would like to go back even further to Butler, Pascal and Locke, and view the discipline as the Enlightenment's replacement for dogmatic theology.[11]

What seems to be undisputed is that since the latter part of the seventeenth century, we find the rising popularity of the evidentialist notion

---

6. Ibid.

7. Hence the popular alternative of publishing selections of popular essays from the primary literature, e.g., Charles Taliaferro and Paul Griffiths, eds., *Philosophy of Religion: An Anthology* (Oxford: Wiley-Blackwell, 2003). Louis Poijman and Michael Rea, *Philosophy of Religion: An Anthology* (5th ed.; London: Thomson/Wadsworth, 2008) is also very comprehensive.

8. Charles Taliaferro, "Philosophy of Religion" [cited 4 January 2010]. Online: http://plato.stanford.edu/archives/spr2009/entries/philosophy-religion/.

9. See William Wainwright, ed., *The Oxford Handbook of Philosophy of Religion* (New York: Oxford University Press, 2005), 3.

10. For a list of nineteenth-century works, see "Religionsphilosophie," *Wikipedia, Die freie Enzyklopädie* [cited 26 January 2010]. Online: http://de.wikipedia.org/w/index .php?title=Religionsphilosophie&oldid=68004693.

11. Cupitt, *Philosophy's Own Religion*, 7.

that one should accept religious beliefs as true only when proven true.[12] Two reactions followed. One involved a shift from theoretical (speculative) to practical (moral) reasoning—as in Kant, who thought one could neither prove nor disprove religious truth and held that belief is necessary as foundation for morality, a regulative ideal of sorts. Another reaction had Schleiermacher shifting philosophical attention away from belief and conduct to religious feelings and experience. Both these approaches became widely influential in the previous two centuries. Yet the first approach already began to wane as positivism replaced idealism early in the twentieth century. (It has, however, returned recently in different form.) The second reaction has continued to be attractive to many philosophers of religion to this day.[13]

Thus, according to the majority vote, a major cultural shift had taken place during the nineteenth century. The names to contend with were Schleiermacher, Hegel, Feuerbach, and Kierkegaard.[14] The idea of "philosophy of religion" and what it would involve, however, did not become clear until the mid-nineteenth century, when the subject "Philosophy of Religion" was first taught in the universities. Together with the phenomenology of religion and the history of religion, it subsequently coconstituted the curriculum of what became known as the "scientific study of religion" (*Religionswissenschaft*). In this context of the humanities, as opposed to a theological faculty, religion has come to be considered an all-too-human historically and culturally evolving phenomenon.[15]

It took a while before philosophy of religion emerged as a completely independent philosophical subject in philosophy departments, with its own agenda of specialized issues of interest.[16] At English universities the subject appeared in the curriculum only in the first decade of the twentieth century.[17] Yet philosophy of religion was still rather neglected during the first half of the century. Reasons for this included the widespread consensus that Hume and Kant had shown the traditional proofs for the existence of God to be bankrupt. There was also the demise of nineteenth-century

---

12. Wainwright, introduction to *Oxford Handbook*, 4.
13. Ibid.
14. Ibid., 3.
15. Cupitt, *Philosophy's Own Religion*, 15.
16. See George Pattison, *A Short Course in the Philosophy of Religion* (London: SCM, 2001).
17. Wainwright, introduction to *Oxford Handbook*, 3.

idealism, largely replaced in English-speaking countries by analytic philosophy. Notable events during this period included the impact of neoorthodox theologians (Barth, Brunner and others such as Tillich), the popularizing of existentialism (Kierkegaard, Marcel, Buber), the renewal of Thomism (Maritain, Gilson, etc.), the rise of phenomenology (Otto) and finally, antimetaphysical philosophers (e.g., Dewey). All of these contributed to the demise of ontological concerns in the field.[18]

By the mid-twentieth century, some analytic philosophers began to take a serious interest in questions of meaning in religious language. They began to wonder what kind of claims religious people were making in stating dogmas or reporting religious experiences. This led to a resurgence of philosophical theology from the 1960s to the present, especially in English-speaking countries. The result was a relative loss of interest in the question of cognitive meaningfulness. There was also the conviction that positivism and logical empiricism's objections to meaningfulness were logically and epistemologically susceptible to serious critique themselves. A further impetus was provided by the shy return of metaphysics and the implementation of the tools of modal logic and probability theory.[19]

Two developments resulted, which would end the clearcut separation between philosophy of religion and philosophical theology. First came a revival of interest in older scholastic and seventeenth- and eighteenth-century philosophical theology. This was the result of the increasing sophistication of reasoning and the personal religious commitment of a new generation of philosophers. Second was the increase in religious issues of interest to philosophers, such that by the 1980s philosophy of religion and philosophical theology were no longer wholly separate disciplines in practice. Particularly prominent in all this was a fundamentalist epistemological turn among Anglo-Saxon Christian philosophers, and the switch from trying to convince skeptics to the need for self-understanding and the clarification of dogma (or even devotional contributions).[20] At present, the modern origins of the discipline are readily apparent in representative definitions of the subject:

> Philosophy of religion is the philosophical examination of the central themes and concepts involved in religious traditions. It involves all the

---

18. Ibid., 4.
19. Ibid., 5.
20. Ibid., 6.

> main areas of philosophy: metaphysics, epistemology, logic, ethics and value theory, the philosophy of language, philosophy of science, law, sociology, politics, history, and so on. Philosophy of religion also includes an investigation into the religious significance of historical events (e.g., the Holocaust) and general features of the cosmos (e.g., laws of nature, the emergence of conscious life, widespread testimony of religious significance, and so on).[21]

Things are a little more complicated and definitions say as much about the particular philosopher's metaphilosophical context as about the subject itself. In fact, all definitions of the subject are stereotypes and, as we shall soon see, in contemporary practice there is no such thing as *the* philosophical approach to religion. It is thus important that as biblical scholars we see things in perspective, for instance, by noticing global academic trends. As the first decade of the twenty-first century has come and gone, there is major ambivalence toward the philosophy of religion as a discipline. This is the case in the context of both philosophy as a whole and society at large.

On the one hand, while the collapse of a rigid intellectual hegemony exerted by logical positivist epistemologies led to a demise of philosophical interest in religion during the first half of the twentieth century, the study of religion as such is no longer dismissed as a waste of time. Though as a research and teaching area religion is certainly less well funded in university budgets than the sciences, it has been increasingly recognized as playing a major role in human society. Signs of this are the strong fundamentalist streak in American and British analytic Christian philosophy of religion, and the New Atheist response to it. Despite increased secularization overall, religion cannot be ignored or trivialized. Not that religious belief has become more credible in mainstream philosophy. But the naïve belief, so popular in the sociology of religion during the second half of the twentieth century, that secularism would destroy religion, has vanished. Whatever its pros and cons are, religion seems to be here to stay.

On the other hand, while some philosophers of religion would like to imagine a proliferation of renewed interest in their subject, many people both inside and outside the academy have lost all interest in arguing over the philosophical intricacies of Christian theism. Not only is philosophy

---

21. See Charles Taliaferro, "Philosophy of Religion," in *SEP* [cited 16 January 2010]. Online: http://plato.stanford.edu/archives/spr2009/entries/philosophy-religion/.

as a human or social science itself becoming less and less relevant to many academic contexts where the natural sciences are calling the shots; where it is still accommodated, most philosophers pursue their work without any interest in philosophy of religion. So, while the basic suggestions of this study may interest a particular if not peculiar community of readers, I know very well that there will be many others who may just manage a yawn or two.[22]

2.2. Pluralism in Contemporary Metaphilosophy of Religion

According to Rob Fisher in his discussion of the study of religion in his "Philosophical Approaches,"

> Philosophical approaches to the study of religion are presently going through a crisis of identity. Two questions make the nature of this crisis clearer. First, where is a philosophical approach to the study of religion to be found? ... The question appears to have no straightforward answer. We find people adopting philosophical approaches to the study of religion in philosophy departments, religious study departments, theology departments, and in humanities departments.... The second question ... what is it that people who are adopting philosophical approaches to the study of religion are doing? Again it should be no surprise that there is no single answer forthcoming or in relation to which agreement can be reached.[23]

Today philosophical approaches to the study of religion are to be encountered in more than one academic location.

First, in many departments of philosophy proper, either philosophy of religion is a separate discipline, or some of its riddles are discussed as part of metaphysics. This is typical in English-speaking countries. The focus is still on the nature of religious language, arguments for and against the existence of God, the nature of divine attributes, religious epistemology, religion and morality, and so on.

---

22. An informative recent summary of philosophy of religion's current state is found in Victoria Harrison's "What's the Use of Philosophy of Religion?" in *God, Goodness and Philosophy* (ed. Harriet Harris; Oxford: Ashgate, 2011), 29–45.

23. Rob Fischer, "Philosophical Approaches," in Connolly, *Approaches to the Study of Religion*, 105.

Second, in departments of theology, philosophy of religion is often paired with philosophical theology in the context of systematic theology or theology proper. This is more typical of Continental Europe, and the focus tends to be on how ideas and concepts in the history of philosophy enable us to better understand a particular tradition's religious doctrines. In the conservative parts of the United States, philosophy of religion and apologetics are often intertwined in theological faculties, when theological research is limited to a defense of what is considered to be orthodox and unalterable beliefs.

Third, in the context of the humanities, we find philosophy of religion being taught in courses on religious studies. Here the focus in philosophical approaches pertains to the intellectual dimension of religion. The emphasis is more on describing and understanding the beliefs of the religious traditions in philosophical terms than on evaluating the merits of religious truth claims. Since no religious affiliation is required, it may be in this academic context, that is, biblical studies in a humanities faculty, that the philosophical approach to ancient Israelite religion as developed in this study is most at home.

Given this plurality of contexts, it should not come as a surprise that the very grammatical structure of the concept "philosophy of religion" is ambiguous. The idea that there is such a thing as "philosophy of religion" depends in large part upon the idea that there is something called religion, which it is reasonable to have a philosophy of; or upon the idea that the phenomenon of religion brings with it, or has involved in it, some philosophical problems. The first way of thinking construes the phrase "philosophy of religion" as an objective genitive: it understands religion (or the idea of religion) as the proper object of philosophy as done by philosophers of religion, much as law (or the idea of law) tends to be understood as the proper object of philosophy as done by philosophers of law. The second way of thinking construes the phrase differently, as containing a subjective genitive, and therefore as suggesting that the proper scope of philosophy of religion is those questions that arise out of religion as such, or out of some particular religion. On this construal, "philosophy of religion" indicates the philosophical questions or the philosophical activity that belongs to religion or to some specific religion.[24]

---

24. See Paul Griffiths, "Comparative Philosophy of Religion," in *A Companion to Philosophy of Religion* (2nd ed.; ed. Charles Taliaferro, Paul Draper, and Philip Quinn; BCP 9; London: Wiley-Blackwell, 2010), 718.

One can therefore make a distinction between a religion's own philosophical material and a philosophical perspective on (nonphilosophical) religion. It is the latter sense (a philosophical perspective on religion) that the study of the Hebrew Bible, which is itself not philosophical in contents, can make most use of. Moreover, in view of these distinctions, philosophy of religion is itself not the kind of field for which a stereotyped subject matter can be deduced. Not only has the concept's identity conditions changed over the centuries, but new contexts, perspectives, ideas, approaches, and objections are developing all the time.[25] At present, then, the metaphilosophical scenario is indeed a supermodern one, characterized as it is by an overabundance of possible meanings for "philosophy of religion." One of the reasons for this pluralism lies in the ways in which the relationship between philosophy and religion has been understood through the ages.

2.3. HISTORICAL PERSPECTIVES ON THE RELATIONSHIP BETWEEN PHILOSOPHY AND RELIGION

Already in 1972 Max Charlesworth asked:

> What is philosophy of religion? The short answer is that it is simply philosophising about religion; but, like most short answers, this does not get us much further forward since it is not at all self-evident what exactly is meant by "philosophy" and what by "religion" and how the one can be concerned with the other. For, first, we have to engage in philosophising in order to define what "philosophy" means, so that our view of what philosophy is itself involves taking up a philosophical position. In this respect, one's conception of the task of philosophy of religion will depend upon one's conception of the task of philosophy and this, as we have said, has to be argued for philosophically. And second, it is notorious that the definition of "religion"—what is and is not to count as a religion—presents formidable difficulties.[26]

---

25. See Jeremiah Hackett and Gerald Wallulis, eds., *Philosophy of Religion for a New Century: Essays in Honor of Eugene Thomas Long* (Studies in Philosophy and Religion 25; New York: Springer, 2004).

26. Max J. Charlesworth, *Philosophy of Religion: The Historic Approaches* (London: Macmillan, 1972), ii. Compare this with the discussion of multiple philosophical perspectives on religious issues as outlined in Charles Taliaferro's *Evidence and Faith: Phi-*

Charlesworth classically discerned four distinct views in the history of philosophy about the relationship between philosophy and religion. Further refinements of Charlesworth's ideas were provided by William Abraham,[27] David Pailin,[28] and Rob Fisher.[29] At least five views on the relationship between philosophy and religion are now commonly discerned.

The first view thinks of *philosophy as religion*, thus making a religion out of philosophy. Though there are intimations of this conception of the philosophy of religion among the pre-Socratic philosophers, it is above all with Plato and his heirs that it is made fully explicit. It also emerges in modern philosophy with Spinoza and, in a quite different context, with Hegel. In our own time, many Thomist philosophers of religion still see the subject as part of metaphysical reflection. According to this view, philosophy is religion.[30] Understandably, biblical scholars who assume this view will find no role for philosophy in the context of historical exegesis.

The second conception understands *philosophy as the handmaid of religion*. Past examples of people who held this view include Thomas Aquinas, who summed up a long tradition of thought that began with Philo of Alexandria and passed through thinkers as various as Origen, St. Augustine, Abelard and Moses Maimonides. For Aquinas and his predecessors, "the task of philosophy of religion is above all a defensive or apologetic one,"[31] justifying the preambles of religious faith and defending the "articles of faith" by showing their negative possibility or *prima facie* non-self-contradictoriness.[32] Biblical scholars who take this view for granted tend to involve philosophy of science and hermeneutics on the level of meta-commentary.

A third view sees philosophy as *making room for faith*. It is found in Kant, for whom philosophy has no positive justificatory role with regard to religion. Rather its function is to establish the conditions of the possibility of religion and, in a negative way, to make room for religious faith. With

---

losophy and Religion since the Seventeenth Century (New York: Cambridge University Press, 2005).

27. William J. Abraham, *An Introduction to Philosophy of Religion* (Eaglewood Cliffs, N.J.: Prentice Hall, 1985), ch. 1.

28. David Pailin, *Groundwork of Philosophy of Religion* (London: Epworth, 1986), 29–31.

29. Rob Fischer, "Philosophical Approaches," 116–17.

30. Charlesworth, *Philosophy of Religion*, 1–44.

31. Ibid., 7.

32. Ibid., 45–86.

Kant (at least according to one interpretation of his thought) the limitations of pure reason *vis-à-vis* religion come to be heavily emphasized. Philosophy's task is seen as that of pointing toward the possibility of religion by showing the inadequacies of pure reason. Kierkegaard and later Protestant thinkers (*reformed epistemology*) radically exploit this view.[33] Many fundamentalist biblical scholars and heirs to the Biblical Theology Movement who rage against philosophy in Old Testament theology will find this perspective to be most convenient to endorse.

The fourth conception sees the task of *philosophy as the analysis of religious language* and as involving a purely analytical or metalogical enterprise. For Wittgenstein and for the diverse currents of analytic philosophy concerned with conceptual analysis, it is not the business of philosophy to engage in metaphysical or transcendental speculation. Rather, one should seek to analyze the conditions of meaningfulness in religious language. Thus philosophy of religion becomes the clarification of religious concepts, in an attempt to better understand the function of religious language and what it means to hold certain religious beliefs and to engage in particular religious practices (e.g., prayer).[34] This particular perspective on the relationship between philosophy and religion is one of two adopted and adapted in this study.

The fifth and final view sees philosophy's role toward religion as *the study of reasoning used in religious thought*. This approach is concerned with a philosophical discernment of the influence of culture on the development and nature of particular beliefs. The underlying assumption is that historical context and cultural structures influence the nature and contents of belief, which is not a monolithic or static phenomenon but is instead polymorphic, pluralistic, and dynamic. Philosophers of religion working within this perspective are concerned with describing how the structures in individual and group thought condition what ordinary religious people believe. Philosophy's task is to describe the factors that influence beliefs, and the ways in which these factors affect the expression of those beliefs.[35] This view is the second approach this study will adopt and adapt for the sake of developing a descriptive philosophical approach to the study of ancient Israelite religion.

---

33. Ibid., 87–144.
34. Ibid., 145–74.
35. Pailin, *Groundwork of Philosophy of Religion*, 31.

2.4. Contexts and Currents in Contemporary Philosophy of Religion

2.4.1. The So-Called Analytic-Continental Divide

In philosophy proper, there are major disagreements regarding how the philosophical study of religion is best pursued, if at all. A great gulf separates the way in which Anglo-American analytic philosophers approach their subject from the approach (or approaches) taken by their Continental counterparts. So broad is the conceptual chasm that for many it seems as if there are two different ways in which philosophy is now studied—ways one might be forgiven for thinking really amount to two quite different subjects. Not surprisingly, by the end of the twentieth century, it had become commonplace among philosophers of religion to distinguish two contexts for philosophical approaches to the study of religion. The distinction is known as the so-called analytic-Continental divide.[36]

There is, first, the problem of defining analytic and Continental philosophy.

> I will work with a very rough and schematic definition along full the following lines: Analytic philosophy refers to the kind of philosophy that takes Gottlob Frege, G. E. Moore and Bertrand Russell as its founding fathers. It is usually practiced today in English-speaking philosophy departments. Continental philosophy describes the kind of philosophy that is derived from the European Continent, especially Germany and France, and is heavily indebted to the writings of the "three H's," Hegel, Husserl and Heidegger, as well as the "masters of suspicion," Marx, Nietzsche, and Freud.[37]

---

36. For an introduction to the analytic tradition, see James F. Harris, *Analytic Philosophy of Religion* (HCPR 3; London: Kluwer, 2002). For an introduction to the Continental tradition, see Philip Goodchild, "Continental Philosophy of Religion: An Introduction," in *Rethinking Philosophy of Religion: Approaches from Continental Philosophy* (Perspectives in Continental Philosophy 289; ed. Anthony P. Smith and Daniel Whistler; New York: Fordham University Press, 2002), 1–39. Another excellent overview of Continental traditions is Merold Westphal, "Continental Philosophy of Religion," in Wainwright, *Oxford Handbook*, 472–93.

37. Nick Trakakis, *The End of Philosophy of Religion* (London: Continuum, 2008), 33; see also idem, "Meta-Philosophy of Religion," *AD* 7 (2007): 4.

Of course, the opposition is itself neither watertight nor strictly geo-graphic. One finds analytic perspectives on mainland Europe and Anglo-American philosophers working in the Continental tradition. Moreover, neither side of the divide can be construed in static or essentialist terms. Even so, stereotypes are functional. Analytic philosophy, for example, is a highly specialized field, divided into various subfields, such as the philoso-phy of mind, the philosophy of language, and the philosophy of religion. These subfields are in turn divided into further subfields that have become the preserve of a select group of practitioners working on a standard set of research problems, with each problem carefully dissected into its parts so as to be amenable to eventual resolution.[38]

Continental philosophy, by contrast, is not characterized by any such division of labor, but is more integrative or synthetic in approach. The term "Continental" is not itself Continental, but is a word from the Anglo-Saxon context that is used to denote:[39]

1.   Thinkers, texts and traditions from France and Germany, in particular those since the time of German idealism;
2.   The works of Anglophone thinkers primarily engaged in the critical analysis and creative developments of Continental thinkers' ideas;
3.   Typical key figures representative of the trend, including nineteenth-century thinkers such as Hegel, Feuerbach, Marx, Kierkegaard and Nietzsche; and
4.   Twentieth-century ideas that come from thinkers such as Heidegger, Foucault, Ricoeur, Levinas, and Derrida; and that link up with currents in phenomenology, hermeneutics, ide-ology criticism, critical theory and deconstruction.

In Continental philosophy of religion, individual problems are usually dealt with in a systematic way, in the context of a larger and often interdis-ciplinary framework. There is no standard list of topics, and in most works one will look in vain for attempts to prove that God exists or an analytic discussion of the problem of evil and theodicy. It is therefore typical of Continental philosophers not to restrict themselves to strictly philosophi-

---

38. See Trakakis, "Meta-Philosophy of Religion," 5.

39. This point represents an adaptation of Westphal, "Continental Philosophy of Religion," in Wainwright, *Oxford Handbook*, 472–73.

cal concerns, let alone to a particular subdiscipline within philosophy, to disregard any such classificatory regimes, and to investigate a broad array of problems—from meaning and metaphysics to ethics and politics—as these surface in the writings of their predecessors and contemporaries. Strictly speaking, then, there is no "Continental philosophy of religion," though there obviously are plenty of Continental philosophers who have various things to say about religion and theology.[40]

A highly helpful introductory discussion of this particular "messy diversity" in philosophy of religion is found in Gwen Griffith-Dickson's *Philosophy of Religion*, a SCM core text.[41] She notes that in the United States, the divide is also evident in the different stereotypes of the American Philosophical Association (APA), which is more analytic, and the American Academy of Religion (AAR), which is more Continental (hermeneutic).[42] Those said to work on one side of the divide do seem to have very different assumptions regarding what counts as legitimate philosophical and religious concerns, styles, conceptions, and objectives. The problem of the divide also involves different mindsets, with results not unlike those that occur when immovable objects meet irresistible forces.

The analytic group tends to consist of professional philosophers who emphasize logical rigor and formalities in systematic argumentation, are conservative in their atheological preferences and think of the "other side" as guilty of sloppy reasoning. The Continental group is more hermeneutic in orientation, and tends to be derived from theology and religious studies, with its emphasis on social and historical contextuality. Its members tend to be more progressive and view analytic philosophers as lacking in historical and cultural consciousness.[43] Analytic philosophers of religion are usually trained and housed in departments of philosophy, and many have little if any training in theology or biblical criticism.

The differences in interest between the groups can be seen as particularly acute when one contrasts the focus on God, the religious object, and the rational credentials of claims in analytic philosophy with the tendency in Continental approaches to reflect on religion, the human subject, and

---

40. See Trakakis, "Meta-Philosophy of Religion," 5.

41. Gwen Griffith-Dickson, *The Philosophy of Religion* (London: SCM, 2005), 20–26.

42. Ibid., 24.

43. Ibid., 26–27.

the ethical implications of it all.[44] As Nick Trakakis also observes, however, for a long time philosophers of religion from both sides have tended to be somewhat averse to any kind of introspective reflection as demanded by metaphilosophical questions.

Many analytic philosophers of religion seem to suffer from a lack of historical consciousness, and naïveté regarding both the pervasiveness of ideology and the implications of a consistent hermeneutics of suspicion. This was pointed out in a rather theological manner by Merold Westphal, in his "Traditional Theism, the AAR and the APA."[45] A large contingency of so-called Christian philosophers of religion, especially in the United States, are analytic in orientation and still work with a naïve realist hermeneutic when it comes to the god-talk of the Hebrew Bible.

Many Continental philosophers, on the other hand, are alleged to ignore questions of truth. Analytic philosophers raise questions regarding the rational adequacy in Continental rhetoric. The latter often write in an unnecessarily complex manner while their evaluative judgments of what is supposedly false are based on self-refuting metaphysical, epistemological and moral presuppositions. The result is god-talk that oscillates between what can appear to be a mixture of selective crypto-fundamentalism and reconstructive mythology.

In some places, however, the situation is beginning to change.

> There is now an increasing willingness on the part of members of both philosophical traditions to take a step back from their daily philosophical routine. More attention is being paid to dialogue about the nature, methods and objectives of the work they engage in.[46]

Neither side of the analytic-Continental divide in philosophy of religion, therefore, is monolithic or static—a pluralism of philosophical approaches pervades both.[47] This study itself will not fit into either stereotype, but will

---

44. See also Wainwright, introduction to *Oxford Handbook*, 9.

45. Merold Westphal, "Traditional Theism, the AAR and the APA," in *God, Philosophy and Academic Culture* (ed. William Wainwright; Atlanta: Scholars Press, 1996).

46. Trakakis, "Meta-Philosophy of Religion," 7.

47. On contemporary perspectives, see Eugene T. Long, ed., *Issues in Contemporary Philosophy of Religion* (Studies in Philosophy and Religion 23; New York: Springer, 2002).

feature a hybrid approach that intends to avoid the methodological short-comings of either side of the so-called divide.[48]

2.4.2. Major Currents in Contemporary Philosophy of Religion

Several currents are operative in contemporary philosophy of religion.[49] During the last quarter of the twentieth century, at least five major trends have been discerned.[50]

The first happens to be *analytic philosophy of religion*, which is basically identical to the analytic side of the so-called analytic-Continental divide discussed in the previous section.[51] Contrary to what the name implies, however, it is not a uniform movement in terms of method, concerns, or ideology. Its historical precursors lie in neorealism and philosophical analysis. Assuming that religious language is at least meaningful, the primary focus is no longer natural theology but religious epistemology and the relation between faith and rationality. The cluster of issues of interest under its umbrella is quite broad and includes philosophical theology that focuses on the concepts of particular religious traditions (e.g., the trinity, incarnation, and atonement in Christian dogmatics). This current is the stereotypical face of philosophy of religion in the English-speaking West: while critical perspectives are present, much of the work associated with analytic philosophy of religion tends to be little more than a mixture of natural theology and Christian apologetics.[52] Even so, the interest in conceptual clarification in this current—as well as its topical skeleton—will be adopted and adapted for the development of a descriptive philosophical approach to the study of ancient Israelite religion.

The second current is associated with *hermeneutics* and *deconstruction*. It is associated with the Continental side of the divide noted above. This group has as forerunners earlier existential and phenomenological approaches and represents both moderate and radical developments

---

48. Trakakis, *The End of Philosophy of Religion*, 33.

49. To be sure, different ways of categorizing approaches are possible. See Griffith-Dickson, *Philosophy of Religion*, 25.

50. Eugene T. Long, *Twentieth-Century Western Philosophy of Religion, 1900–2000* (HCPR 1; Dordrecht: Kluwer, 2003), 388.

51. For a useful overview of this current, see Willam Hasker, "Analytic Philosophy of Religion," in Wainwright, *Oxford Handbook*, 421–45.

52. See Cupitt, *Philosophy's Own Religion*, 15.

of these earlier trends. While some philosophers of religion working in this current focus on presuppositions implicit in human understanding, others concern themselves with the indeterminacy of meaning and truth in religion.[53] Aside from utilizing elements in the phenomenology of religion, the methodology developed in this study will not make extensive use of this current and its concerns.

A third current is connected with *critical theory* and ideological criticism. It too represents a broad and diverse group, but its proponents have in common roots in Marxist social philosophy. This group also shows influences from earlier phenomenological and existential perspectives and much of its work focuses on social and political oppression, and concern for a better life. Some of its ideas have been influential in liberationist and public theologies, where the traditional boundaries between theology and philosophy have become blurred.[54] A number of biblical scholars who utilize philosophy look to this current as part of metacommentary. Since our concern is historical and descriptive even as it is philosophical, this current will not feature in any substantial manner in the methodological theorizing to follow.

The fourth current is *comparative philosophy of religion*. This cluster of approaches is motivated by religious pluralism and the diversity of symbols and religious experiences in the world, both past and present. It employs the findings of twentieth-century historians of religion and anthropologists of religion, and seeks to develop new conceptions and methods appropriate to analyzing religion in a pluralist comparative context. Some practitioners challenge the traditional problematic of Western philosophy of religion, calling for new definitions that break down the traditional boundaries between philosophy and theology.[55] Along with analytic philosophy of religion and the phenomenology of religion, elements of this current will be also utilized in the construction of a hybrid philosophical approach to the study of ancient Israelite religion.

Last, and certainly not least, is the fifth current, *feminist philosophy of religion*.[56] This represents the most recent addition to the field and as such is much younger than feminist theology.

---

53. Long, *Twentieth-Century Western Philosophy*, 389.
54. Ibid., 389.
55. Ibid.
56. For an excellent introduction and overview of this current, see Sarah Coack-

Four main reasons have been suggested for this. First, from the seventeenth to the nineteenth century, the perspective of white European males dominated the formative period of philosophy of religion to such an extent that it was hard to see how the distortions of this long tradition might be overcome. Second, in the twentieth century, once philosophy of religion was professionalized and gerrymandered within philosophy faculties at universities, it was insulated both from the old theology faculties and the new religious studies faculties created in the 1960s and 1970s; therefore, feminists interested in pursuing Ph.D.s had to choose between philosophy, where philosophy of religion was not regarded as "real" philosophy during the ascendancy of the analytic movement, and religious studies/theology, which took philosophical concerns seriously and thus provided a more welcoming location for feminist theorizing on religion. Third, many feminist philosophers themselves have harbored either suspicions of religion or impoverished understandings of it, and so have been slow to develop a significant body of scholarship in this area. Fourth, the entrenched bias and resistance to feminism within mainstream analytic philosophy of religion, combined with the myth that its own methods, norms, and content are gender neutral, has impeded recognition of the relevance of work appearing under the rubric of feminist philosophy of religion. Feminist theology, on the other hand, flourishes in an academic field that for nearly forty years has been hospitable to a variety of liberation theologies, death-of-god theologies, environmental theologies, and postcolonialist theologies.[57]

A more recent set of feminist perspectives, increasingly important since the 1960s, has sought to liberate human experience, thoughts, and ways of being from dominant patriarchal models. It is developing new approaches to philosophy of religion that seek to take seriously the insights of feminist philosophy. While some of these are reformist, others are radical and revolutionary, and therefore are important to feminist and nonfeminist philosophy alike for providing a critical understanding of various religious concepts, beliefs, and rituals, as well as of religion as a cultural institution that defines, sanctions, and sometimes challenges gender roles and gender inflected representations.[58] As with the other critical approaches not uti-

---

ley, "Feminism and Analytic Philosophy of Religion," in Wainwright, *Oxford Handbook*, 494–525.

57. Nancy Frankenberry, "Feminist Philosophy of Religion," *SEP* [cited 20 January 2010]. Online: http://plato.stanford.edu/archives/fall2008/entries/feminist-religion/.

58. Frankenberry, "Feminist Philosophy of Religion."

lized, while biblical scholars are free to make use of the agenda of this current, the present study will not be doing so for historical (as opposed to ideological) reasons.

2.5. STANDARD ISSUES OF INTEREST IN PHILOSOPHY OF RELIGION

Philosophers of religion also differ as to what are legitimate concerns to have for those engaged in philosophical reflection on religion. As the field has become more and more crosscultural and cosmopolitan in recent decades, so the number of issues of interest has grown enormously. Today the field of philosophy of religion includes a growing, ambitious range of projects. The main topics that have been at its heart since the mid-twentieth century—the meaning of religious belief, the existence of God, the relationship between religion and science—are still there. However, such issues are now considered alongside distinctive philosophical projects that are specific to individual religious traditions (philosophical theology). Consider the definition of the field in the Philosophy of Religion Section at the AAR:

> The philosophy of religion section analyzes the interface between philosophy and religion, including both philosophical positions and arguments within various specific religious traditions and more generalized philosophical theories about religion. The section includes in its purview not only traditional topics of Western philosophy of religion but also those arising from non-Western traditions and from the study of religion in a comparative context.[59]

This abstract reflects the fact that the second half of the twentieth century saw an expansion of the philosophical agenda.

> The expansion of philosophy of religion to take into account a wider set of religions, and to focus on issues deriving from within a specific religion, is related to expansion in terms of methodology. Philosophers of religion have rediscovered medieval philosophy, and new translations and commentaries of medieval Christian, Jewish, and Islamic texts have blossomed. There is now a selfconscious, deliberate effort to combine

---

59. See the definition offered at the bottom of the AAR website online: http://www.aarweb.org/Meetings/Annual_Meeting/Program_Units/PUinformation.asp?PUNum=AARPU045.

work on the concepts in religious belief with a critical understanding of their social and political roots. The work of Foucault has been influential on this point, and feminist philosophy of religion has been especially important in rethinking what may be called the ethics of methodology. This is, in some respects, the most current debate in the field.[60]

At present, however, a typical university course on the subject will tend to be Western, Christian, theistic and analytic, and therefore concerned with the philosophical perspective of ideas propounded in Christian theology.[61] Despite the pluralism of interests, at bottom many of the topics discussed are in themselves potentially generic and can be adopted and adapted for the purpose of studying other religious traditions. These may be presented in overlapping fashion and are now considered standard. I refer to these loci not because I assume that this is what philosophy of religion has to be concerned with, or because I agree with analytic philosophers about their projects' validity in philosophy of religion proper. I only wish to give a brief indication of the concerns that are in fact being attended to in mainstream scholarship.[62] It goes without saying that the typical university curriculum outlined below is exemplary of standard concerns in analytic Christian philosophy of religion, but is not necessarily of interest to all those engaged in philosophical reflection on religious matters (e.g., many Continental philosophers of religion).

The first locus of this type of course concerns *the nature of religion*, and problems with defining the concept.[63] Noting that different perspectives are available from anthropological, sociological, psychological, philosophical, and theological assessments, it typically offers a variety of definitions. It posits that religion as a phenomenon is polymorphic and polythetic, and that it is therefore essentially a contested concept. Following on from this, prototypical analysis focusing on family resemblances seems more apt than a classical approach that seeks individually necessary and jointly sufficient conditions for what count as instances of religious phenomena. Many writers have even disputed the usefulness and appropriateness of the

---

60. Taliaferro, "Philosophy of Religion."

61. Good introductions to multicultural philosophy of religion are Keith E. Yandell, *Philosophy of Religion: A Contemporary Introduction* (RCIP 5; London: Routledge, 1999); and Griffith-Dickson, *Philosophy of Religion.*

62. A brief topical introduction in English here is Philip Quinn, *Philosophy of Religion A–Z* (Edinburgh: Edinburgh University Press, 2006).

63. For a lively overview, see Griffith-Dickson, *Philosophy of Religion*, 60–108.

very concept of "religion" as a cross-cultural category, suggesting that it is a colonialist Western Christian superimposition on other cultures, whose spiritualities are cast into the mold of a system analogous to church structures and dogmas.[64]

In the study of the next locus, *the nature of religious language*,[65] it is noted that speaking about the Divine is somehow different from other ways of speaking. While the grammatical structures of religious discourse are the same as those of any other discourse, the logical structure may not be. A typical discussion may feature the tripartite distinction between religious language as univocal, equivocal, or analogical.[66] Much of the treatment of this topic is concerned with the charge of meaninglessness presented by logical positivism early in the twentieth century. So-called verification and falsification criteria or principles of meaningfulness have sparked a number of theories in the field that aim to show how religious language makes sense (or not). From this perspective, religious language can be studied from various perspectives and as having various characteristics: literal, analogical, symbolical, mythological, metaphorical, noncognitive, parabolical, and so on. Several versions of each view are available, and both realist and nonrealist understandings are attested.

In the third locus, the discussion of *the concept of revelation*, the question is typically whether revelation should be seen as propositional, nonpropositional or both. There are also philosophical issues concerning hermeneutics and the interpretation of sacred scriptures, the development of and changes in religious doctrines, questions concerning the nature of religious experience, the relationship between faith and history, the influence of culture on dogma, sources of revelation and also the forms and contents thereof.[67]

In the typical curriculum's discussions on *the nature and attributes of deity*, concern has traditionally lain with the classical concept of the divine

---

64. This view is eloquently argued in Timothy Fitzgerald, *The Ideology of Religious Studies* (Oxford: Oxford University Press, 2000).

65. For an introduction to the issues, see Dan R. Stiver, *The Philosophy of Religious Language: Sign, Symbol, and Story* (Oxford: Wiley-Blackwell, 1996).

66. For a useful electronic resource on the problematic, see "Religious Language," by Jennifer H. Weed, *IEP* [cited 11 November 2009]. Online: http://www.iep.utm.edu/.

67. A very good comparative and descriptive assessment of the subject can be found in Keith Ward, *Religion and Revelation: A Theology of Revelation in the World's Religions* (Oxford: Oxford University Press, 1994).

along the lines of "perfect being" theology.[68] The major foci are, first, the meaning of concepts for deity, and second, debating the logical coherency of concepts related to divine properties. Three divine properties in particular attract interest: omnipotence, divine knowledge, and deity's relation to time (divine eternity).

The topic of *arguments for and against the existence of deity* speaks for itself. Here a number of arguments are put forward and each comes in several versions, for instance ontological arguments, cosmological arguments, arguments from design, teleological arguments, arguments from religious experience, moral arguments, arguments from consciousness, and so on. Atheological arguments include perspectives from sociology, psychology, and natural science (cosmology, neuroscience, evolution), the problem of evil, logical arguments, challenges to meaningfulness, ontological disproof, and so on.[69] Many assert that arguments for and against the reality of deity prove nothing, and at most should be considered "useful," "interesting," or "edifying." Others think they are a waste of time and, focusing on epistemology, deny that the theological task is to prove that the divine exists. Also relevant is the debate on realism versus nonrealism regarding the ontological status of God, with its question: In what sense of the word can we say whether deity "exists" or not?

The problem of evil and theodicy,[70] while sometimes discussed solely as an atheological argument against the existence of the divine, is often considered separately. There are many versions of the problem, and distinctions are made between the logical, epistemological and evidential problems of evil. There are also distinctions between metaphysical, natural, and moral evil. Different conceptions of divinity also come into play, and in theodicy typical responses involve defenses appealing to free will,

---

68. For a good example of philosophical theology, see Thomas V. Morris, *Our Idea of God: An Introduction to Philosophical Theology* (Contours of Christian Philosophy; Oxford: Regent College Publishing, 2002). For an entertaining and delightfully humorous overview of what can otherwise become very complex philosophical issues, see Keith Ward, *God: A Guide for the Perplexed* (Oxford: Oneworld Publications, 2005).

69. One of the best introductions to this topic is Daniel Kolak, *In Search of God: The Language and Logic of Belief* (London: Wadsworth, 1993).

70. Few studies simply present the issues. Most try to solve the problem. A good introduction to the perspectives on offer in philosophy of religion, throughout the history of reflection on the issues, can be found in Mark J. Larrimore, *The Problem of Evil: A Reader* (Oxford: Wiley-Blackwell, 2001).

soul-making, divine limitations, human ignorance, possible worlds, illusion, and so on. Counterresponses include the falsification challenge and charges of trivialization and rationalization.

In *religious epistemology*,[71] the concern typically lies with the nature of belief and the justification of religious truth claims and appeals to religious experience. Classical foundationalism has fallen into disrepute and moderate to radical postfoundationalist views are now more in vogue. Issues typically discussed are the relation between faith and reason and the challenges posed by logical positivism and evidentialism. Many philosophers of religion now work in this area, preferring to demonstrate the rationality, or nonrationality, of belief over trying to prove that religion is true.

On the subject of *religion and morality*,[72] the relation between religion and morality is debated. Some appeal to morality to argue for the reality of God, while others appeal to morality to argue the opposite. There is the question of whether morality can stand without religious foundation, and a variety of theories on the relation between religion and morality have been proposed, including versions of so-called divine command ethics, theological voluntarism, moral realism, and so on. A popular problem is the Euthyphro dilemma, which revolves around the relation between deity and the moral order. Other discussions concern the ontological status of moral claims and moral epistemology.

A number of other topics are also discussed at random or as independent issues, including the relation between *religion and culture, religion and history,* and *religion and science.*[73] This last topic in particular is concerned with issues such as the concept of creation, creationism versus evolution, the history of the relations between religion and science, and the question of whether religion and science supplement, complement, or contradict each other. Then there is the issue of challenges posed by *religious pluralism*, where a distinction is often made between exclusivism, inclusivism, parallelism (pluralism), and interpenetration.[74]

---

71. A comprehensive introduction can be found in Douglas R. Geivett and Brendan Sweetman, *Contemporary Perspectives on Religious Epistemology* (Oxford: Oxford University Press, 1992).

72. See William J. Wainwright, *Religion and Morality* (Ashgate Philosophy of Religion Series; London: Ashgate, 2005).

73. A highly readable introduction to this is Pailin, *Groundwork in Philosophy of Religion.*

74. See Griffith-Dickson, *Philosophy of Religion*, 8. A useful overview of the issues

In some texts, *philosophical theology* also comes into play, and philosophers of religion become more specific, not hesitating to discuss *religious concepts* from within particular religious traditions. Many of these discussions have focused on religion-specific beliefs, for example creation, providence, trinity, incarnation, atonement, miracles, prayer, and life after death (and heaven/hell).[75]

All of the above issues have been typical loci on the agenda in Western analytic Christian philosophy of religion. In Continental approaches, these topics are not clearly demarcated, but are instead intertwined with social and theological concerns. On none is there universal consensus, and most philosophers of religion tend to specialize in only one or two topics. Continental philosophers also touch upon many of them, but in a very different manner, on the way to more constructive matters. In Jewish, Islamic, Hindu, Buddhist, Taoist, and Jain philosophy of religion, some adopt the loci of the analytic Christian agenda whilst adapting them to another religious tradition's issues. Some philosophers of religion seek to compare religious concepts in different traditions. Again, pluralism is the only reality.

2.6. Conclusion

Given the diversity and complexity of the scene within the metaphilosophy of religion, one thing should be readily apparent. There exists a pluralism of locations, assumptions, concerns, agendas, methods, and objectives. Thus a philosophical approach to religion, even though it is interested in certain types of problems, cannot be conceived of in an essentialist manner. This should be kept in mind alongside the popular objections to the utilization of philosophy of religion in the study of ancient Israelite religion.

Awareness of the plurality of possible philosophical approaches will be important when considering the viability of suggestions for interdisciplinary research made later on in this study. I shall not attempt to utilize phi-

---

can be found at David Basinger, "Religious Diversity (Pluralism)," *SEP* [cited 2 March 2010]. Online: http://plato.stanford.edu/archives/fall2009/entries/religious-pluralism.

75. Good recent introductions are found in Michael C. Rea, ed., *Trinity, Incarnation, Atonement* (vol. 1 of *Oxford Readings in Philosophical Theology*; ed. Michael C. Rea; Oxford: Oxford University Press, 2009); and in Michael C. Rea, ed., *Providence, Scripture, and Resurrection* (vol. 2 of *Oxford Readings in Philosophical Theology*; Oxford: Oxford University Press, 2009).

losophy of religion in any vague manner. I shall look only to those methods that allow for a hermeneutically legitimate descriptive philosophical account of the Hebrew Bible for its own sake.

However, before the new methodology can be introduced, we need to build a bridge between this chapter's discussion of philosophy of religion and the newly envisaged philosophical approach to the study of Israelite religion to be discussed later on. In the next two chapters we shall listen to and learn from the stories of past relations between Hebrew Bible interpretation and philosophical reflection on religion.

3

Philosophy of Religion and Hebrew Bible Interpretation: A Brief History of Interdisciplinary Relations[1]

Most work in biblical theology has tended to ignore philosophy and to depict philosophical work as a rival or enemy.[2]

3.1. Introduction

Many histories of biblical interpretation discuss general philosophical influences on prominent biblical scholars.[3] Conspicuously absent from these types of overview, however, is a discussion exclusively devoted to a historical account of the relationship between Hebrew Bible interpretation and *philosophy of religion*. When present in biblical-theological assessments at all, references to the philosophy of religion are few and far between.[4] In view of this gap in the research, this chapter seeks to offer a

---

1. This chapter represents a revision of Jaco Gericke, "Old Testament Studies and Philosophy of Religion: A Brief History of Interdisciplinary Relations," *OTE* 23 (2010): 652–87.

2. Barr, *Concept of Biblical Theology*, 155.

3. Gerhard F. Hasel, *Old Testament Theology: Basic Issues in the Current Debate* (3rd ed., Grand Rapids: Eerdmans, 1985); John Hayes and Frederick Prussner, *Old Testament Theology: Its History and Development* (Atlanta: John Knox, 1985); Ben C. Ollenburger, *Old Testament Theology: Flowering and Future* (2nd ed.; SBTS 1; Winona Lake, Ind.: Eisenbrauns, 2004); Magne Saebø, ed., *Hebrew Bible/Old Testament: The History of Its Interpretation* (2 vols.; Göttingen: Vandenhoeck & Ruprecht, 1996–2008); John Sandys-Wunsch, *What Have They Done to the Bible?* (New York: Liturgical Press, 2005).

4. For example, Robert C. Dentan, *Preface to Old Testament Theology* (New York: Seabury, 1963), 16–20; Hasel, *Old Testament Theology*, 25; Barr, *Concept of Biblical Theology*, 3, 146; Ollenburger, *Old Testament Theology*, 22; Christoph Bultmann,

cursory introduction to traces of philosophy of religion within Hebrew Bible interpretation.

In view of the conceptual complexities in writing a unitary history (given the intertwining of the disciplines before the modern period and their separation thereafter), all this chapter can offer is a selective and brief summary of nearly two and a half millennia of reception history. From the nineteenth century onward, the story in this chapter will be told wholly from the perspective of Hebrew Bible studies. By contrast, an account of the ways in which the Hebrew Bible has featured within modern philosophy of religion will be the topic of the next chapter. The last two centuries are characterized by, *inter alia*, the quest for independence on both sides, which is why at least two stories have to be told.

Given limitations of space, it goes without saying that it will be impossible to do justice to all the details and intricacies of the plot. The accounts to follow therefore barely scratch the surface and not all players can be mentioned. In addition, I am sure much more could be said with reference to the ideas of those individuals actually included in the narrative. Readers interested in more detail can consult the literature mentioned in the references.

3.2. From the Greeks to Gabler

But before we can begin with philosophical readings of the Hebrew Bible, we need to understand the background in philosophy that made those readings possible in the first place. Relatively long ago in the sixth century B.C.E., Western philosophical readings of religious texts became all the rage. The official scapegoat was Pherecydes of Syros,[5] who was alleged to have read some kind of new meaning into Homer.[6] Two philosophical perspectives were then introduced.[7] On the one hand, there was *ethical theory*.

"Early Rationalism and Biblical Criticism on The Continent," in Saebø, *Hebrew Bible/ Old Testament*, 2:896.

5. Dan C. McCartney, "Literal and Allegorical Interpretation in Origen's *Contra Celsum*," *WTJ* 48 (1986): 281.

6. As noted by Origen in his *Contra Celsum* 4.42. See Owen Chadwick, *Origen: Contra Celsum* (London: Cambridge University Press, 1980).

7. McCartney, "Literal and Allegorical Interpretation," 281–301; Folker Siegert, "Early Jewish Interpretation in Hellenistic Style," in Saebø, *Hebrew Bible/Old Testament*, 1.1:130.

As Greek moral values changed, the narrated actions of the Homeric gods became an embarrassment. So philosophical readings reinterpreted the old tales as profound metaphors of everyday spiritual truths. On the other hand, there was *epistemological justification*: allegorizing was necessary in order to be able to use ideas from ancient myths as part of an appeal to tradition in the justification of contemporary philosophical ideas.

Philosophical readings of Greek religion involved both figurative and literal types. On the one hand, we find the popularization of "allegorical" reading. Philosophical allegorizing looked for the truths of physics, ethics, and psychology in the myths, legends, and poems of Homer and Hesiod. Like conservative exegesis to this day, the aim was "reconciliation" between the older, cruder stories and whatever philosophical system the reader wanted to see exemplified therein.

Besides the critics of Homer and Hesiod, there were philosophers who shared with most other Greeks an ardor for Greek poetry and held classical poetry in honor. They were convinced that there was only an *apparent* antagonism between the epic tradition and their own knowledge. If the reader's own understanding of the truth did not conform to the literal statements in the *Iliad* and the *Odyssey*, then they must discover a more orthodox or credible meaning to assign to them.[8]

Allegory was not the only form of philosophical-critical analysis used in philosophical exegesis. Back then the discipline of "philosophy" also encompassed historical and literary criticism. Aristotle wrote philosophical works on the phenomena of rhetoric and poetry. He also reflected on the concept of metaphor with the aid of metaphysical jargon. Many other ancient Greek philosophers engaged in close readings of the Homeric epics with the historical-critical aims of analyzing internal inconsistencies within the epics, and of producing editions of the epics' authentic text that were free of interpolations and errors and that explained archaic words. Others simply sought to appreciate the epics as literature. There is little that is really novel under the exegetical sun.

The above-mentioned varieties of philosophical exegesis provided the backdrop for the first philosophical readings of the Hebrew Bible/Old

---

8. Henning Graf Reventlow, *From the Old Testament to Origen* (vol. 1 of *History of Biblical Interpretation;* trans. Leo G. Perdue; Atlanta: Society of Biblical Literature, 2009), 34.

Testament[9] in the centuries to follow.[10] Traces of philosophical heritage are already evident in the choice of Greek words in certain sections of early versions of the Septuagint (LXX). For example, the Septuagint translators of Gen 1–11 adopted basic Platonic philosophical concepts and refined forms of expression as part of a metalanguage created after philosophical reflection on linguistic and mental constructs in the Hebrew Bible.[11] Apparently, LXX translators wanted to communicate ancient Israelite beliefs in the contemporary Greek idiom.[12]

Philosophical reflection on ancient Israelite religion is also presupposed in the apocryphal and pseudepigraphic literature that arose during the Hellenistic and Roman periods.[13] A familiar example is the Wisdom of Solomon, a collection of theological essays written in Greek by an Alexandrian Jew in about 100 B.C.E. Purporting to be Solomon, the author both compared Jewish religion with the wisdom (philosophy) of the Greeks and insisted that ancient Israelite religious beliefs were in fact the highest form of wisdom. Chapters 12–15 even contain allusions to early theories on the origin of pagan religion. A second instance of philosophy in biblical literature can be found in the case of 4 Maccabees (first century C.E.), another text concerned with the interpretation of Jewish beliefs in terms of Greek philosophy. Its interest lies in the reasoning used in religion (the martyr incident), and its ideas prepared the way for subsequent attempted reconciliations between ancient Israelite religion and Greek philosophy.[14]

---

9. I shall refer to the "Hebrew Bible" as the "Old Testament" when discussing Christian interpreters whose writings did not focus on the Hebrew original.

10. See Siegert, "Early Jewish Interpretation in Hellenistic style," 130–98, for a detailed overview. From the above one might surmise that we are Greek and philosophical not only when practicing theology but also when carrying out historical and literary criticism.

11. See Evangelia Dafni, "Genesis 1–11 und Platos Symposion Überlegungen zum Austausch von hebräischem und griechischem Sprach- und Gedankengut in der Klassik und im Hellenismus," OTE 19/2 (2006): 584. Dafni wrote a number of philosophically related papers on the Septuagint, e.g., "Natürliche Theologie im Lichte des hebräischen und griechischen Alten Testaments," ThZ 57 (2001): 295–310. The discussion of philosophy of religion in relation to the LXX would be an entirely different subject on its own. This study is limited to the Hebrew Bible.

12. Dafni, "Genesis 1–11 und Platos Symposion," 584.

13. See Otto Kaiser, The Apocrypha: An Introduction (New York: Hendrickson, 2004), for an overview.

14. That is, linking Yahwism(s) with the ontology of Plato and the ethics of Stoicism; see Kaiser, Apocrypha, 107; and Robert A. Kraft, "Scripture and Canon in the

By the first century B.C.E., all the great philosophical trends of the day were those derived from the ideas of earlier philosophers such as Plato, Aristotle, Epicurus, and Zeno.[15] There was little difference between philosophy and exegesis. As John F. Procopé notes, "From the first century B.C.E., philosophy came increasingly to be an exercise in expounding canonical texts."[16]

The roots of philosophical readings of the Hebrew Bible/Old Testament[17] can be found in what one biblical scholar referred to as "Alexandrine philosophy of religion."[18] A number of Jewish and Christian philosophers from this time onwards went to great lengths to expound the beliefs of ancient Israelite religion in the language and concepts of Greek philosophy. The two incentives (ethical, epistemological) that had given rise to the philosophical exegesis of Homer centuries earlier provided these early biblical scholars with a means of extracting interesting philosophical lessons from the most unpromising of biblical materials.[19]

The first major well known individual personality usually associated with philosophical commentaries on the Hebrew Bible was Philo (ca. 30 B.C.E.–ca. 50 C.E.). As a Hellenistic Jewish philosopher born in Alexandria, Philo spoke of philosophizing "according to Moses" and used allegory to harmonize Greek philosophy and Judaism.[20] While Philo did not reject the historical dimension in ancient Israelite god-talk, he argued that the truth claims of ancient Yahwism were not intended to be read on the level of historical narratives, and sought to reinterpret crude mythological representations of the divine via nonliteral modes of exposition.[21]

Commonly called Apocrypha and Pseudepigrapha and in the Writings of Josephus," in Saebø, *Hebrew Bible/Old Testament*, 1.1:199–216 for a detailed overview.

15. See John F. Procopé, "Greek Philosophy, Hermeneutics and Alexandrian Understanding of the Old Testament," in Saebø, *Hebrew Bible/Old Testament* 1.1:459.

16. Ibid.

17. On the matter of terminology, see n. 9 above.

18. To be precise, it was the well-known nineteenth-century biblical theologian Hermann Schultz, in *Old Testament Theology: The Religion of Revelation in its Pre-Christian State of Development* (Edinburgh: T&T Clark, 1892), 434. It was called thus by Schultz because he discerned along Hegelian lines the influence of the "Greek spirit."

19. Procopé, "Greek Philosophy, Hermeneutics and Alexandrian Understanding," 415.

20. See Siegert, "Early Jewish Interpretation in Hellenistic style," 162–98.

21. See Procopé, "Greek Philosophy, Hermeneutics and Alexandrian Under-

An early example of a Christian philosophical perspective on the Old Testament is to be found in the writings of Justin Martyr (100–165 C.E.).[22] Justin had the dual intention of making biblical ideas seem philosophically credible and of showing that famous Greek philosophers were themselves dependent on biblical wisdom. Thus in section 59 of his *First Apology*, Justin wrote: "And that you may learn that it was from our teachers—we mean the account given through the prophets—that Plato borrowed [from] Moses."[23] In his belief that the Greeks got their philosophy from Moses, Justin was following ideas already embryonic in Philo. He was himself followed in the same line of thought by Clement of Alexandria (150–215 C.E.), who emphasized the permanent importance of philosophical reflection on the Old Testament for the fullness of knowledge of Scripture, and sharply criticized those who were unwilling to make any use of it.[24] For Clement, one portion of divine truth was to be found in revelation and the other portion in philosophy (thus providing a precursor to the later distinction between "natural" versus "revealed" theology). In attempting to show that the Old Testament was philosophically up to date (and more), Clement and others like him looked to Aristotle's apologies as a guide to literary criticism:

> In response to Plato's attack on poetry he [Aristotle] argued that poetry has its own function, which is not primarily to teach truth or sound morals, and that it must be judged by how well it carries out this function. *Literature has its own internal criteria. It must be understood on its own terms.*[25]

The same idea would return with a vengeance in our own time, albeit in the writings of scholars with antiphilosophical sentiments, who were bliss-

---

standing," 453–76, for a thorough overview of the influence of Middle Platonism on Philo's theological hermeneutics.

22. See Oskar Skarsaune, "The Development of Scriptural Interpretation in the Second and Third Centuries—Except Clement and Origen," in Saebø, *Hebrew Bible/ Old Testament*, 1.1:389–417.

23. See Richard J. Plantinga, ed., *Christianity and Plurality: Classic and Contemporary Readings* (BRMT; Oxford: Blackwell, 1999), 56.

24. According to the contributors to "Clement of Alexandria," in the Introduction to the *New World Encyclopedia* [cited 28 September 2009]. Online: http://www.newworldencyclopedia.org/entry/Clement_of_Alexandria?oldid=685482.

25. See Procopé, "Greek Philosophy, Hermeneutics and Alexandrian Understanding," 464, emphasis added.

fully ignorant of the philosophical roots of literary criticism. For the time being, the relationship between theological readings of the Hebrew Bible and philosophical reflection on ancient Israelite religion would remain ambivalent. A decidedly less enthusiastic assessment of philosophical exegesis comes from the writings of Tertullian (ca.160–225 c.e.):

> For it [philosophy] is the material of the world's wisdom, the rash interpreter of the nature and the dispensation of God. Indeed heresies are themselves instigated by philosophy.... The same subject matter is discussed over and over again by the heretics and the philosophers; the same arguments are involved. [The heretics and philosophers constantly ask:] Whence comes evil? Why is it permitted? What is the origin of man? ... Unhappy Aristotle, who invented ... dialectics, the art of building up and pulling down [by using argumentation]; an art so evasive,... so far-fetched in its conjectures, so ... productive of contentions— embarrassing even to itself, retracting everything, and really treating of nothing! Whence spring those ... "unprofitable questions," and "words which spread like a cancer"? From all these, when the apostle would restrain us, he expressly names *philosophy* as that which he would have us be on our guard against. Writing to the Colossians, he says, "See that no one beguile you through philosophy and vain deceit, after the tradition of men, and contrary to the wisdom of the Holy Ghost." He had been at Athens and had in his interviews [in Athens] become acquainted with that human wisdom which pretends to know the truth [philosophy], whilst it only corrupts it, and is itself divided into its own manifold heresies, by the variety of its mutually repugnant sects.... *What indeed has Athens to do with Jerusalem?* What has the Academy to do with the Church? What have heretics to do with Christians? Our instruction comes from the porch of Solomon, who had himself taught that the Lord should be sought in simplicity of heart. Away with all attempts to produce a Stoic, Platonic, and dialectic [*sic*] Christianity![26]

Despite this now famous outburst, it would not be valid to adopt Tertullian as the patron saint of antiphilosophical biblical theology.[27] His remarks should be read in the context of his other writings, which reveal that Ter-

---

26. The excerpt is drawn from a translation of Tertullian's *Heretics* 7, as quoted in James Stevenson, *A New Eusebius: Documents Illustrating the History of the Church to A.D. 337* (London: SPCK, 1987), 166–67, emphasis added.

27. As correctly pointed out by James Barr, *Old and New in Interpretation: A Study of the Two Testaments* (London: SCM, 1966), 41.

tullian's real pain was not in fact the use of philosophical categories and methods, but rather very specific philosophical ideas that gave rise to what he considered to be heresies. Tertullian himself used philosophical (e.g., Stoic) ideas in his biblical interpretation.

Origen (185–254 C.E.) is best known for having produced a corrected version of the Septuagint and for being the first Christian to construct a philosophical hermeneutics.[28] He wrote commentaries on most books of the Old Testament and as a philosopher of his time often justified his claims by resorting to allegory.[29] Origen's way of thinking was basically Platonist, yet the philosophy he read back into the Old Testament was no more incongruous than the Platonism that philosophers such as Porphyry extracted from Homer or "foisted onto foreign myths."[30] In this Origen was clearly an heir to the Hellenistic philosophical tradition, particularly in his belief that beyond quasihistorical details lay a depth of metaphysical mystery.

Augustine of Hippo (354–430 C.E.) wanted to pursue a philosophical way of life while coming to terms with the biblical materials. Troubled in the remembrance of the New Testament text's admonition: "Beware lest any man spoil you through philosophy and vain deceit, after the tradition of men, after the rudiments of the world, and not after Christ" (Col 2:8–9), Augustine lamented the fact that:

> When I then turned toward the Scriptures, they appeared to me to be quite unworthy to be compared with the dignity of Tully [i.e., Marcus Tullius Cicero]. For my inflated pride was repelled by their style, nor could the sharpness of my wit penetrate their inner meaning.[31]

While Augustine recognized important differences between Old Testament literature and Greek philosophical treatises, he nevertheless sought

---

28. James N. B. Carleton Paget, "The Christian Exegesis of the Old Testament in the Alexandrian Tradition," in Saebø, *Hebrew Bible/Old Testament*, 1.1:501.

29. Paget, "The Christian Exegesis of the Old Testament in the Alexandrian Tradition," 522.

30. See Procopé, "Greek Philosophy, Hermeneutics and Alexandrian Understanding," 477.

31. Augustine, *The Confessions of St. Augustine* (trans. Albert C. Outler; London: Courier Dover, 2002), 36.

to understand the biblical text via philosophical readings.[32] He therefore pursued philosophical reflection on Old Testament concepts such as "creation" and "time" and became convinced that Yhwh was in fact identical to Plato's Being. Like those before him, Augustine speculated that the philosopher must have known the book of Exodus:

> But the most striking thing in this connection, and that which most of all inclines me almost to assent to the opinion that Plato was not ignorant of those writings, is the answer which was given to the question elicited from the holy Moses when the words of God were conveyed to him by the angel; for, when he asked what was the name of that God who was commanding him to go and deliver the Hebrew people out of Egypt, this answer was given: "I am who am; and you shall say to the children of Israel, He who *is* sent me unto you;" as though compared with Him that truly *is*, because He is unchangeable, those things which have been created mutable *are* not—a truth which Plato zealously held, and most diligently commended.[33]

Because of his love for the classics, Augustine fully accepted the Greek and Latin translations of the Hebrew Bible. In this he would later be contradicted by Jerome (347–420 c.e.) who, like many a biblical theologian of a later age, insisted on the *Hebraica veritas*. Jerome's convictions were not, however, motivated by philological concerns as is popularly believed. The privileging of Hebrew thought was the result of an interest in pre-Aristotelian philosophy of language. However, because there was the need to make prephilosophical ancient Israelite religious language seem philosophically relevant, we find that:

> From that period the Old Testament opened the way to two new studies which could not but influence the way it was understood: the philosophy and history of religions. Between these two the Old Testament had in the course of time a lot of difficulty in maintaining its autonomy and *it could not resist the temptation to become a philosophy or history of religion.*[34]

---

32. David F. Wright, "Augustine: His Exegesis and Hermeneutics," in Saebø, *Hebrew Bible/Old Testament*, 1.1:701–30.

33. Augustine, *City of God* 8.11 (NPNF 1/2:152).

34. Edmund Jacob, *Theology of the Old Testament* (trans. Arthur Heathcote and Philip Allcock; London: Hodder & Stoughton, 1958), 16, emphasis added.

With the rediscovery of the ideas of Aristotle in the Middle Ages, Jewish scholars began to take an interest in providing a philosophical account of the biblical deity.[35] Abraham ibn Daud (ca. 1110–1180) was the pioneer in medieval Jewish philosophy of religion, and his philosophical treatise *ha-Emunah ha-Ramah* (*The Exalted Faith*, ca. 1160) constitutes the first systematic attempt to reconcile Aristotelianism and Jewish philosophical perspectives on the Hebrew Bible.[36] In the introduction to *ha-Emunah ha-Ramah* he stated that he had decided to write his book in order to solve the problem of free will. Ibn Daud noted that "the Scriptures failed to provide an unequivocal answer to this problem (i.e., biblical verses on this issue contradict one another)."[37] Yet because Ibn Daud assumed the Hebrew Bible to be unified divine revelation, he was convinced that philosophy could aid the theologian to distinguish between the verses that should be understood literally and those that are in need of philosophical explication. In his view, many who had begun to study the Bible failed to keep the lamps of philosophy and religion burning simultaneously, and therefore could not discover the harmony between the two modes of knowledge.[38]

Moses Maimonides (1135–1204) also hoped to reconcile philosophy with the teachings of the Torah.[39] In his *Moreh Nevuchim* (*Guide for the Perplexed*), he sought to clarify representations of Yhwh with the aid of Aristotle's metaphysics.[40] The "perplexed" whom Maimonides sought to guide were those who found contradictions between literal readings of the Hebrew Bible and the truths of philosophy. He also felt that members of the general public should not be exposed to metaphysics in its pure state as it could damage their faith. Since his concerns (for example, the problem of evil and the relationship between philosophy and religion) were relevant beyond the confines of Jewish philosophy, almost every philosophical

---

35. Keith Ward, *Concepts of God: Images of the Divine in Five Religious Traditions* (Oxford: Oneworld Publications, 1998), 61.

36. Resianne Fontaine, "Abraham Ibn Daud," *SEP* [cited 16 September 2009]. Online: http://plato.stanford.edu/archives/fall2008/entries/abraham-daud/.

37. Ibid.

38. For a comprehensive discussion, see ibid.

39. See Kenneth Seeskin, "Maimonides," *SEP* [cited 16 September 2009]. Online: http://plato.stanford.edu/archives/fall2008/entries/maimonides/.

40. On Maimonides's exegesis, see Sara Klein-Braslavy, "The Philosophical Exegesis," in Saebø, *Hebrew Bible/Old Testament*, 1.2:302–20.

work written during the remainder of the Middle Ages cited, commented on, or criticized Maimonides' views.[41]

Gersonides (1288–1344) was another relevant Jewish philosopher who, in the introduction to his book *Sefer Milhamot Ha-Shem* (*Book of the Wars of Yhwh*), sought to deal with many questions generated by philosophical reflection on the Hebrew Bible.[42] These include topics that would become standard philosophical concerns in later philosophy of religion, for example: What is the nature of prophecy? Does Yhwh know particulars? Does divine providence extend to individuals? And so on. Gersonides attempted to reconcile ancient Israelite beliefs with what he felt were the strongest points in Aristotle's philosophy. Since, however, pagan philosophy often won out at the expense of theology in Gersonides' work, many of his writings were rejected, especially those on astrology. In recent years, Gersonides' contributions have become a topic of renewed interest.[43]

In the footsteps of the Jewish philosophers followed several Christian thinkers who hoped to develop philosophical perspectives on many topics in the Old Testament.[44] Anselm of Canterbury (1033–1109) was a philosopher of the eleventh century who is best known for having concocted the ontological argument for the existence of God, expounded in chapter 2 of his *Proslogion*. Less known is the fact that Anselm also wrote three little treatises to introduce beginners to the Old Testament. In these he attempted to show, among other things, how some of the ideas presented by Augustine might be developed with the aid of new perspectives in contemporary logic (with reference to the nature of religious language in the Old Testament and the relation between the Old Testament and philosophical-theological reflection). For Anselm, the Old Testament, while not itself philosophy, generates philosophical questions.[45]

Thomas Aquinas (1225–1274) is known in philosophy of religion particularly for his five ways in which the existence of God may allegedly be inferred. In addition, however, he was also an "apprentice profes-

---

41. See Seeskin, "Maimonides," for a thorough philosophical discussion.

42. See Tamar Rudavsky, "Gersonides," *SEP* [cited 24 September 2009]. Online: http://plato.stanford.edu/archives/fall2008/entries/gersonides/.

43. See Rudavsky, "Gersonides," for a detailed discussion.

44. Karlfried Froehlich, "Christian Interpretation of the Old Testament in the High-Middle Ages," in Saebø, *Hebrew Bible/Old Testament*, 1.2:531–54.

45. For a detailed treatment, see Thomas Williams, "Saint Anselm," *SEP* [cited 22 September 2009]. Online: http://plato.stanford.edu/archives/fall2008/entries/anselm/.

sor (*baccalaureus biblicus*) instructing students on the books of the Old Testament."[46] Aquinas wrote philosophically motivated commentaries on Isaiah, Jeremiah and Lamentations.[47] Like many before him, he did not think of philosophy as distortive of biblical beliefs, and he linked Plato with Moses: "Moreover Plato is said to have known many divine things, having read the books of the Old Law, which he found in Egypt."[48] In his *Summa Theologica* Aquinas developed Clement's distinction between natural theology (natural philosophy, later called "science") and revealed theology (biblical revelation). Identifying philosophical reflection with the former, Aquinas set the agenda for philosophical reflection on biblical religion during the centuries to follow. For him, however, this involved something more than merely the philosophical clarification of canonical texts. Much of the philosophy that was aimed at justifying religion came to a point where divine revelation (and therefore the Hebrew Bible) could no longer be called upon to justify metaphysical arguments. The fallacies of appeals to tradition and authority in natural theology were recognized as such, so that philosophical apologetics had to make do with appeals to reason and empirical experience alone.[49]

During the Renaissance that followed, both Neo-Platonic ideas and Thomistic appropriations of Aristotle's scheme of education influenced Hebrew Bible interpretation.[50] From then, up to the era of the Reformation, the influence of Plato increased, although here we also see a more reserved application of Aristotelian traditions in the attempt to make philosophical sense of ancient Israelite religion.

Martin Luther (1483–1546) was one reformer who not only commented on the Old Testament but also taught a course on Aristotle at

---

46. "Thomas Aquinas," *Wikipedia, The Free Encyclopedia* [cited 1 August 2010]. Online: http://en.wikipedia.org/w/index.php?title=Thomas_Aquinas&oldid=505110646.

47. Froehlich, "Christian Interpretation of the Old Testament," 538–46.

48. Quoted in Taylor Marshall, "Thomas Aquinas on Plato Reading the Old Testament," in *Canterbury Tales* [cited 17 February 2010]. Online: http://cantuar.blogspot.com/2008/04/thomas-aquinas-on-plato-reading-old.html.

49. For a detailed treatment, see Ralph McInerny and John O'Callaghan, "Saint Thomas Aquinas," *SEP* [cited 16 September 2009]. Online: http://plato.stanford.edu/archives/fall2008/entries/aquinas/.

50. See Jeremy Catto, "The Philosophical Context of the Renaissance Interpretation of the Bible," in Saebø, *Hebrew Bible/Old Testament*, 1.2:106–33, for further details.

Erfurt.[51] The early Luther had a great affinity with Aristotelian philosophy, particularly the idea that all important truths have two characteristics: universality and consistency with one another. When contradictory statements were found in the Old Testament, Aristotle's logic was used to settle the problem. This was a very easy thing to do; all that was necessary was to assign a meaning to the words that would allow the student or professor to construct a logically consistent system.[52] In later life, however, Luther came to develop an aversion to much of Aristotle's metaphysics as interpreted by his scholastic predecessors. Like many biblical theologians ever since, he would choose to limit the philosopher's value for understanding the Old Testament to his philosophical theories of rhetoric and poetics.[53]

The eclectic use of philosophy continued in the era of early Pietism, in which philosophical reflection on Israelite religion was severely limited:

> The *Lectio logica* or *analytica, the last remaining use of philosophy for biblical studies,* sought to understand the structure and inner coherence of the texts of books of Holy Scripture and determine their principal theme.[54]

However, despite the bracketing of philosophical concerns, the Protestant principle of staying "biblical" and the principle of *scriptura … sui ipsius interpres* (interpreting Scripture with Scripture) had repressed its philosophical roots (Greek philosophers used to argue that one must interpret Homer only through Homer). The same scaled-down and ambivalent relationship between philosophy and Hebrew Bible interpretation can be observed in the writings of John Calvin (1509–1564). Unlike Luther, Calvin paid more attention to the Hebrew Bible, and his readings thereof often referred positively to parallels between ancient Israelite religion and classical philosophy. Unlike many biblical theologians, he did not feel ashamed to appeal to the authority of Plato; and his background in Renaissance humanist literary criticism made him wary of roping the Hebrew Bible into the service of a scholastic neo-Aristotelian philosophical-theo-

---

51. Joy F. Kirch, "Martin Luther: How One Man Responded," in *Western Philosophy* [cited 17 September 2009]. Online: http://www.tamuk.edu/mcpe/kirch.htm.

52. Kirch, "Martin Luther: How One Man Responded."

53. Ulrich Köpf, "The Reformation as an Epoch of the History of Theological Education," in Saebø, *Hebrew Bible/Old Testament*, 1.2:348.

54. See Johannes Wallmann, "Scriptural Understanding and Interpretation in Pietism," in Saebø, *Hebrew Bible/Old Testament*, 1.2:919, emphasis added.

logical system. In the end, he could not avoid doing something similar, and other classical philosophers and their theories became paradigms for consideration in studying the Hebrew Bible.[55]

With the arrival of the Enlightenment, the official reputation of overt philosophical reflection that depended upon divine revelation began to fall into greater disrepute. From the sixteenth century, the idea grew steadily that people could understand certain features of biblical religion by using unaided reason. This idea was designated "natural religion" or "natural theology," and the resulting view of the divine was "deism." The English deists are often credited with the invention of biblical criticism.[56] The tense relationship between their philosophy of religion and Old Testament theology (even though both terms are somewhat anachronistic here) is clearly evident. However, their need for historical criticism did not actually mean taking complete leave of philosophy in biblical interpretation. Rather, it meant exchanging premodern metaphysical assumptions for modern epistemological ones. The rise of historical criticism was philosophically founded and not unrelated to, *inter alia*, Cartesian rationalism, Lockean empiricism, Kantian idealism, Herder's romanticism, Hegelian dialectic, Von Ranke's historicism, Baconian commonsense philosophy, and Troeltschian social philosophy.

The strain of rationalism on theological reflection on the Hebrew Bible provoked countercultural extremes. The quintessence of ardent disputes of the time can be summed up in the words of Blaise Pascal (1623–1662). After an intense religious experience he coined the familiar phrase opposing the God of the Bible and the God of the Philosophers:

> *Memorial.* In the year of grace, 1654, on Monday, 23rd of November, Feast of St Clement, Pope and Martyr, and others in the Martyrology. Vigil of St Chrysogonus, Martyr, and others. From about half past ten in the evening until about half past twelve. *Fire! God of Abraham, God of Isaac, God of Jacob, Not of the philosophers and scholars.* Certitude. Certitude. Feeling. Joy. Peace.[57]

---

55. See the detailed discussion by R. Ward Holder, "John Calvin," *IEP* [cited 23 September 2009]. Online: http://www.iep.utm.edu/.

56. See Henning G. Reventlow, "English Deism and Anti-Deist Apologetic," in Saebø, *Hebrew Bible/Old Testament*, 2:851–74; and John W. Rogerson, *Old Testament Criticism in the Nineteenth Century: England and Germany* (London: SPCK, 1984).

57. Emphasis mine. The English translation comes from A. J. Krailsheimer, *Pensées: Blaise Pascal* (London: Penguin Classics, 1995), 285.

Taken out of context, Pascal's dichotomy between Yhwh and the "delicious monster" of philosophical theology would subsequently be misunderstood as though it meant Pascal dismissed philosophical reflection on ancient Israelite religion altogether. However, the fact of the matter is that after his conversion experience Pascal actually devoted himself all the more to both philosophy and theology.[58] Even so, in these words we find the seeds of what later came to be seen as a dichotomy between a history-related faith in a biblically revealed God versus a philosophically argued faith in a rational Deity (or traditional religion vs. natural religion).[59]

Contemporaneous to Pascal we find the views of Benedict Spinoza (1632–1677), who rebelled strongly against any attempt to make ancient Israelite religious beliefs agree with reason or Aristotelian philosophy as represented in the work of Maimonides.[60] In chapters 1–4 of his *Tractatus Theologico Politicus* we read the following piece, much of which would become a popular assumption in subsequent historical-critical Old Testament theologies:

> Now in the course of my investigation I found nothing expressly taught by Scripture which does not agree with our understanding and which is repugnant thereto, and as I saw that the prophets taught nothing, which is not very simple and easily grasped by all, and further that they clothed their teaching in the style, and confirmed it with the reasons, which would most deeply move the mind of the masses, to devotion towards God, *I became thoroughly convinced that the Bible leaves reason absolutely free, that it has nothing in common with philosophy, in fact, that revelation and philosophy stand on totally different footings.*[61]

In this manner, Spinoza wished to show that "philosophy and religion, reason and faith, inhabit two distinct and exclusive spheres, and neither should tread in the domain of the other."[62] From a proper historical reading of the biblical text, he believed it was clear that the prophets were not

---

58. For this information, see "Blaise Pascal," *Theopedia: An Encyclopedia of Biblical Christianity* [cited 25 September 2009]. Online: http://www.theopedia.com/index.php?title=Blaise_Pascal&oldid=19347.

59. Magne Saebo, "From the Renaissance to the Enlightenment—Aspects of the Cultural and Ideological Framework of Scriptural Interpretation," in Saebø, *Hebrew Bible/Old Testament: The History of Its Interpretation*, 2:43.

60. Hayes and Prussner, *Old Testament Theology*, 27.

61. Quoted in Hayes and Prussner, *Old Testament Theology*, 28, emphasis added.

62. Nadler, "Baruch Spinoza."

philosophers but pious individuals with vivid imaginations. They perceived what they took to be God's revelation through their imaginative faculties. This is what allowed them to apprehend what Spinoza believed lay beyond the boundary of the intellect. He argued that the prophets, inspired though they were, were not necessarily to be trusted when it came to questions of philosophy. Their pronouncements set no parameters on what should or should not be believed about the natural world on the basis of our rational faculties.[63]

Given what philosophical reflection on religion involved in Spinoza's day (a kind of speculative metaphysics without appeal to alleged divine revelation), it is no surprise that Spinoza could not see the possibility of a descriptive philosophy of religion in which the religion in question happened to be ancient Yahwism(s). However, a closer look at Spinoza's own philosophy of religion reveals that he was not actually dismissing the use of philosophy in biblical interpretation as such, but was simply applying many invisible contemporary insights in the philosophy of history and epistemology in arguing against outdated systematic philosophical-theological reflection.[64] Even so, Spinoza's seemingly absolute dismissal of philosophy would be all that was remembered by many Old Testament theologians, who would subsequently attempt to rid biblical theology of philosophical reflection altogether [65]

François-Marie Arouet (1694–1778), better known as Voltaire, was a French philosopher not particularly well known for his views on the Hebrew Bible. Voltaire's opinion of the biblical material is nonetheless interesting. According to him the Hebrew Scriptures represent an outdated legal and/or moral reference, by and large a "metaphor," but one that still taught some good lessons. It was clearly the words of Man [sic] rather than divine truth.[66] Shocking at the time, the notion of metaphorical reductionism would become quite commonplace in subsequent biblical theology. Yet Voltaire's own understanding of the Hebrew Bible should be seen in the context of his deism. He takes the text to make room for what he believes to be the truth of "natural religion" (i.e., philosophy of religion). For Voltaire, biblical criticism was not a mere academic exercise, as he

63. Steven Nadler, "Baruch Spinoza," *SEP* [cited 16 September 2009]. Online: http://plato.stanford.edu/archives/win2009/entries/spinoza/.

64. Hayes and Prussner, *Old Testament Theology*, 29.

65. Ibid., 29–30.

66. Bultmann, "Early Rationalism and Biblical Criticism on the Continent," 876.

believed that the contingent nature of ancient Israelite beliefs meant there was no need to look to Yahwism for a personal faith. This move beyond the biblical ideas was considered justified in view of pluralism and development in ancient Israelite religion itself, thus making for a paradigmatic synthesis between biblical criticism and philosophy of religion.[67]

Another relevant personality of the time before biblical theology was Gotthold Ephraim Lessing (1729–1781). In his research on the Pentateuch, Lessing was driven by two key concerns of eighteenth-century philosophy of religion.[68] First, Lessing appropriated from the Pentateuch's creation accounts the concept of a universal deity, which he believed was reemphasized in the Decalogue's prohibition against images. Second, his concern with ethics seemed to be paralleled by the prominence of laws in the biblical corpus. However, naïve realism with regard to the truth claims of ancient Israelite religion was out of the question since, for Lessing, metaphysical and moral ideas about God belong to one class of truths, persuasions of historical events to another. From the point of view of philosophy of religion, he concluded:

> If no historical truth can be demonstrated then nothing can be demonstrated by means of historical truths. That is: contingent truths of history can never become the proof of necessary truths of reason.[69]

This was Lessing's "garstige breite Graben." Inasmuch as philosophical reflection on religion during this time was concerned with the establishment of necessary truths, Lessing could not imagine the study of ancient Israelite religion as an end in itself in the context of a philosophy of religion proper.

I close this discussion of the period before independence in biblical theology with reference to the relevant ideas of Johann Gottfried Herder (1744–1803). In this regard, it is interesting to note that Herder's most intrinsically valuable contribution to the philosophy of religion concerns his interpretation of the Hebrew Bible.[70] In his philosophical reflection, Herder championed a strict naturalism and required that interpreters of

---

67. Ibid., 889.

68. As noted in ibid., 896.

69. Ibid., 896.

70. See Henning G. Reventlow, "Towards the End of the Century of Enlightenment," in Saebø, *Hebrew Bible/Old Testament*, 2:1041–50, for an overview.

the Hebrew Bible resist the temptation to resort to allegorical readings to make ancient mythological beliefs appear more theologically relevant than they actually were. Thus he finally severed the link between philosophy and allegorical exegesis. In addition, his romanticist opposition of Hebraic to Classical (Greek and Latin) cultural frames of reference, though mostly descriptive at the time, would later become the stimulus for an evaluative antithesis between biblical and philosophical thought.[71]

3.3. Relations since Gabler

3.3.1. Initial Positive Interaction

The first Old Testament theologies all adopted a philosophical framework.[72] Mediations of Kantian and Hegelian philosophies of religion played an influential role,[73] as did Enlightenment epistemology's turn to history in the flight from allegory.

When Johann Phillip Gabler bid biblical scholars to take leave of dogmatics in biblical theology at his inaugural lecture in 1787, he could have meant taking leave of philosophical reflection on Israelite religion as well. After all, philosophy was considered the handmaid of dogmatic theology; and putting aside the one might well have involved doing away with the other. While many biblical scholars would argue precisely along this line of *non sequitur* reasoning (as many still do), things were not so simple. Gabler himself was a professor of philosophy before his appointment in

---

71. Barr, *Old and New in Interpretation*, 43–44. For a critical assessment of Herder and his ideas and suggestions regarding a post-Herder approach, see Rolf Knierim, *The Task of Old Testament Theology: Substance, Method, and Cases* (Grand Rapids: Eerdmans, 1995), 51.

72. Ollenburger, *Old Testament Theology*, 5.

73. In discussing Hegelian and Kantian influence, biblical theologians have often focused only on metaphysics, epistemology, ethics, and philosophy of history without paying specific attention to either Hegel's or Kant's philosophy of religion with reference to ancient Israelite religion. For more on that subject, see David Kolb, *New Perspectives on Hegel's Philosophy of Religion* (New York: State University of New York Press, 1992); Raymond K. Williamson, *Introduction to Hegel's Philosophy of Religion* (New York: State University of New York Press, 1984), especially 49–51, 322, 341; Philip Rossi, "Kant's Philosophy of Religion," *SEP* [cited 15 April 2010]. Online: http://plato.stanford.edu/archives/win2009/entries/kant-religion/; and also the supplementary file dealing with the influence of Kant's philosophy of religion.

theology and, not surprisingly, his entire project of separating biblical and dogmatic theology was itself motivated by philosophical criteria:

> But let those things that have been said up to now be worth this much: that we distinguish carefully the divine from the human, that we establish some distinction between biblical and dogmatic theology, and after we have separated those things which in the sacred books refer most immediately to their own times and to the men of their own times from those pure notions which the divine wished to be characteristic of all times and places, *let us then construct the foundation of our philosophy upon religion* and let us designate with some care the objectives of human and divine wisdom.[74]

For Gabler, in other words, the ultimate aim of a historical biblical theology was to provide a more sure foundation for a normative philosophy of religion. Gabler adopted his agenda from the ideas of Samuel F. N. Morus, a classical philologist and philosopher.[75] The philosophical context for the earliest biblical theology is quite explicit in some of Morus's publications, which compare the process of eliciting universal truths of scripture with the process of eliciting universal truths from the particulars in philosophy.[76] For Gabler, the task of biblical theology was not finished after literary criticism and historical criticism had done their work—that gave us only "true biblical theology." What was further required was arriving at a "pure biblical theology," something made possible only by "philosophical criticism."[77] By this Gabler meant a rationalist sorting process of reconstructing universal elements from the history of Israelite religion, with the particularist nuances of sociocultural contingencies removed. The result of such "purification" was seen as a preliminary step on the way to a Christian philosophy of religion proper.

Johann Gottfried Eichhorn was another former philosophy professor who "converted" to Old Testament studies. Though interested in philosophical reflection on ancient Israelite religion, Eichhorn was a severe critic of the Kantian moral exegesis popular at the time. Eichhorn charac-

---

74. Quoted in Ollenburger, *Old Testament Theology*, 502. Emphasis mine.

75. Knierim, *Task of Old Testament Theology*, 531.

76. John Sandys-Wunsch and Laurence J. P. Eldredge, "Gabler and the Distinction between Biblical and Dogmatic Theology: Translation, Commentary and Discussion of His Originality," *SJT* (1980): 133–58.

77. See Hasel, *Old Testament Theology*, 17.

terized Kant's program as a relapse into an antiquated allegorical method that had originated in early philosophical interpretations of Homeric mythology and had entered Old Testament interpretation through what Eichhorn called "early Jewish Alexandrian philosophy of religion."[78]

In 1796, Georg Lorenz Bauer produced the first Old Testament theology and adamantly distanced himself from the philosophical *eis*egesis of those he referred to as "church fathers, allegorists and mystics." Severely opposed to the ways in which "every philosopher found his system enshrined" in the religious ideas of ancient Israel,[79] Bauer wanted to read the text only by way of grammatical and historical considerations. Yet Bauer himself could not avoid having recourse to concepts and categories popular in philosophy of religion, and he anachronistically referred to ancient Israelite god-talk as being concerned with the "eternity and immutability of God."[80] He even wrote of Yhwh as "the most rational (*vernünfstige*), highest, wise, self-subsistent cause of the world."[81] In this manner, Bauer's attempt at purely historical Old Testament theology was still dependent on an anachronistic "perfect being" theology.

For Christoph Friedrich von Ammon, as for Bauer, the task of Old Testament theology was indeed to produce a foundation for a more purely philosophical theology. This would be done by way of citing prooftexts and testing them according to criteria of rationality understood in a Kantian moral sense. Still, von Ammon's use of Kant was often cautious, and he regarded interpretation on the basis of pure practical reason as a philosophical *midrash* and as a "species of allegory."[82]

Another philosophical theology of the Old Testament is found in the writings of Wilhelm Martin Leberecht de Wette, who wrote under the influence of Kant as mediated through the anthropology of Jakob F. Fries. The latter revised Kant's idealism in the context of philosophy of religion, and de Wette aimed to translate ancient Israelite religious concepts into more contemporary philosophical terms based on their inner nature and not on their outer form.[83] In this way, philosophy in the form of Kantian idealism was believed to provide a means of merging histori-

---

78. Reventlow, "Towards the End of the Century of Enlightenment," 838.

79. Ollenburger, *Old Testament Theology*, 5.

80. Ibid.

81. Ibid.

82. Ibid.

83. Hasel, *Old Testament Theology*, 18.

cal and philosophical readings on the way to constructing a philosophy of religion proper.

Next was Gottlieb Philipp Christian Kaiser, who sought to provide a more Hegelian framework for Old Testament theology by subsuming the Hebrew Bible under the universal history of religion, and then ultimately under universal religion.[84] This was definitely more Hegelian than Kantian in terms of philosophical dependence, in that the diachronic development of ancient Israelite religion now came to be viewed as part of general historical dialectic.

Another Hegelian was Johann Karl Wilhelm Vatke. Hegel's philosophy of religion provided Vatke with what he considered to be a hermeneutical foundation for understanding Israelite religion. His desire was to relieve the methodological tension between history and philosophy via unity on a higher level.[85] In 1835 he wrote an extended philosophical preface to his treatment of Old Testament theology, in which he showed that philosophical and historical concerns are not necessarily incommensurable. Vatke is also distinguished by the fact that he himself wrote a fully fledged *Religionsphilosophie* (1888).[86]

Bruno Bauer, a student of Vatke more often remembered as a radical New Testament scholar, wrote an historical philosophy of Israelite religion along Hegelian lines in 1838, entitled *Das Religion des Alten Testaments in der geschichtlichen Entwicklung ihrer Principien*. In this work, we find a critique of Hegel's history of revelation and an attempt to discredit Hegel's subordination of the Hebrew faith to the philosophical religions of Greece and Rome.[87]

An interesting development during this time concerns the trend to conceive of ancient Israelite wisdom literature analogous to Europe's *Geistesgeschichte* (a trend that culminated a century later in von Rad's idea of a Solomonic "Enlightenment").[88] Already in Eichhorn we encounter the classification of ancient Israelite proverbial wisdom as "philosophical poetry," while de Wette opted for "practical philosophy" (contrasting it with

---

84. Ibid., 19.

85. Ollenburger, *Old Testament Theology*, 8.

86. Ibid.

87. Hayes and Prussner, *Old Testament Theology*, 105.

88. Rudolph Smend, "The Interpretation of Wisdom in Nineteenth-Century Scholarship," in *Wisdom in Ancient Israel* (ed. John Day, Robert P. Gordon, and Hugh R. Williamson; New York: Cambridge University Press, 1998), 265–67.

"speculative philosophy").[89] Heinrich Ewald came to identify ancient Israelite wisdom literature with philosophy, and by the end of the nineteenth century we come across discussions of biblical wisdom literature under headings such as "The religious and moral philosophy of the Hebrews" (for example in Eduard Reuss's translation of the Hebrew Bible). Even as late as 1914, Karl Kautsch could still entitle a small book *Die Philosophie des Alten Testaments*, by which he meant the biblical assumptions related to moral philosophy and philosophical anthropology. Also, for Johann F. Bruch, the key word for Israelite wisdom was neither humanism nor secularism (as became popular in the twentieth century), but "philosophy."[90]

Alongside the above-mentioned philosophical approaches were others that hoped to proceed more purely historically. One example was Daniel G. C. von Cölln's work, published in 1836, in which he attempted to argue against de Wette's alleged introduction of philosophy into biblical theology. In addition, during the mid-nineteenth century, antiphilosophical tirades began to multiply, particularly in conservative reactions against rationalist perspectives on Israelite religion.[91] This prepared the way for the antiphilosophical sentiments of the next century.

3.3.2. The Rise of Antiphilosophical Sentiment

The situation was still promising for interdisciplinary interaction in the early days of the twentieth century as interest in Old Testament theology returned after a period of decline following the dominance of the history of religion.[92] Because philosophy of religion became more prominent in the academic world during this time, part of the new methodological debate in biblical scholarship actually included discussions explicitly concerned with the relationship between Old Testament theology and a philosophical approach to religion. An early example of this trend is to be found in the writings of Rudolph Kittel, who argued that the history of religion must be expanded into Old Testament theology by way of a philosophy of religion in order to arrive at some higher essence or truth.[93]

---

89. Ibid., 266.

90. See ibid., 257–86, for a detailed discussion.

91. Hayes and Prussner, *Old Testament Theology*, 105.

92. Ollenburger, *Old Testament Theology*, 22.

93. Rudolf Kittel, "Die Zukunft der alttestamentlichen Wissenschaft," *ZAW* 39 (1921): 96.

In 1923, Willy Staerk raised the question of the relation between the history and philosophy of religion and biblical theology.[94] Staerk granted the history of religion its due, but called for philosophical reflection on the historical data from a phenomenological point of view, so that Old Testament theology might come to its fulfillment as a component of systematic theology.[95] Staerk also proposed a philosophical starting point, defining religion in terms of a transcendental unity of apperception in the experience of the unconditioned personal as a synthetic a priori.[96] Here we find a continuation of a Hegelian philosophy of ancient Israelite religion, attempting to locate Old Testament theology within the context of the historical development of religious consciousness.

A few years later, Carl Steuernagel[97] begged to differ with Staerk's views and proposed the systematic presentation of Old Testament theology in concepts drawn from purely historical analysis, without borrowing these categories from philosophy. (König had made a similar suggestion in 1922.) The idea became influential, especially after being expounded in the work of Walter Eichrodt. Eichrodt reasserted König's idea regarding the need for intratextual categories rather than systematic theological ordering principles.[98] Though the philosophical discipline of phenomenology could be selectively applied, the presence of descriptive philosophical concerns would be seen in a negative light and as theologically insufficient.[99] During this time, it became fashionable to point out differences between "biblical" (Hebrew) and "philosophical" (Greek) thinking in religion. According to Eichrodt, "*In striking contrast to the religious philosophy of Greece* we are dealing not with a timeless idea, a new state of the soul, an interpretation of the world which is independent of history but with a once and for all decisive event."[100] In later comments on Gerhard von Rad's problematic distinction between the history of Israelite religion and biblical history,

---

94. Willy Staerk, "Religionsgeschichte und Religionsphilosphie und ihrer Bedeutung für die biblische Theologie des Alten Testaments," *ZTK* 4 (1923): 289–300.

95. Ibid., 290.

96. Ibid., 292.

97. Carl Steuernagel, "Alttestamentliche Theologie und alttestamentliche Religionsgeschichte," in *Vom Alten Testament* (ed. Karl Budde; BZAW 41; Giessen: Töpelmann, 1925), 266–73.

98. Barr, *Concept of Biblical Theology*, 29–32.

99. Ibid., 31.

100. Walter Eichrodt, *Theology of the Old Testament* (trans. John A. Baker; 2 vols.; OTL; Louisville: Westminster John Knox, 1961–1967), 1:505, emphasis added.

Eichrodt would criticize the idea by concluding that "[o]ne cannot avoid characterizing it as a *religious philosophy*."[101]

Eichrodt also found it necessary to inform his readers that anyone trained in philosophical thinking would be "constantly scandalized" by biblical authors' anthropomorphic conceptions of God.[102] He also felt that ideas of "the heathen" and "philosophical theories" of creation *ipso facto* "carry within them the seed of pessimism."[103] Allegedly, it is only "heathen and philosophical thought that speak of the world as having no beginning."[104] Ancient Israelite conceptions of the world were therefore to be sharply distinguished from the "philosophical manipulation of the world as a rational institution."[105] Eichrodt also warned, "The living movement of God's dealing with men disappears when philosophical abstraction dictates the language to be employed."[106]

Along with a more cautious use of the history of religion, the bracketing of philosophy of religion explains why references to the latter subject in Old Testament theologies during that time remained few and far between. Notable instances include a sentence in Gerhard von Rad who, in his discussion of monotheistic tendencies in Deutero-Isaiah, had some or other axe to grind when he felt the need to point out the following otherwise trivial bit of information: "But with him [Deutero-Isaiah] there is no truth based on *philosophy of religion*; he believes rather than only those who confess Jahweh are able to make his solity as the Lord of history credible."[107] Interestingly, Von Rad had no problem thinking of the prophet as expounding a philosophy of *history*.[108] The inconsistencies in biblical theologies' relations with philosophy of religion now began to proliferate. One example of a remark that is not negative yet implies the context as anomalous is an admission by Ludwig Köhler who, in a discussion of the concept of spirit in the Old Testament (a topic in which the

---

101. Ibid., 1:514, emphasis added.

102. Ibid., 1:104.

103. Ibid., 2:108.

104. Ibid., 2:104.

105. Ibid., 2:111–12.

106. Ibid., 2:216.

107. Gerhard von Rad, *The Theology of Israel's Historical Traditions* (vol. 1 of *Old Testament Theology*; 2 vols.; OTL; Louisville: Westminster John Knox, 2001), 212, emphasis added.

108. William A. Dyrness, *Themes in Old Testament Theology* (Downers Grove, Ill.: Intervarsity Press, 1979), 219, 222.

dichotomy with Greek thought had tended to reach fever pitch), felt the need to inform his readers that "where the Old Testament speaks of spirit its language approximates more than anywhere else to the language of the *philosophy of religion* and spirit becomes something in terms of which God almost ceases to exist."[109] The assumption is that elsewhere in the Old Testament its language and that of philosophy of religion are far removed from each other. Notwithstanding such ambivalent dispositions, by mid-century relations between Old Testament theology and philosophy of religion really did take a turn for the worse. Many Old Testament theologians, unaware of their own philosophical assumptions (usually semiexistentialist and personalist)[110] came to think of all philosophical readings of the Old Testament as a priori hermeneutically illegitimate. The dismissal of the involvement of philosophy in attempts to understand ancient Israelite religion would soon be very aggressively promoted by adherents of the so-called Biblical Theology Movement, which saw itself as being overtly antiphilosophical in its orientation to ancient Israelite religion:[111]

> The biblical theology movement constantly opposed the influence of modern philosophy and its constructs as modes to understand biblical thought. It also tended strongly to reject an understanding of the Bible on the basis of Greek thought and its categories. In its rejection of the domineering effect of modern philosophy it shared once again a concern of neo-orthodoxy. The attempt was to understand the Bible outside certain modern or ancient philosophical norms and patterns of thought. It was argued that the Bible must be understood "in its own categories" (James Muilenburg) and the scholar must put himself "within the world of the Bible" (B. W. Anderson). The contrast between Greek and Hebrew thought (T. Boman and others) became rather important. Although the NT was written in Greek, the Hebrew mentality was common to both testaments. The idea of the Hebrew mentality led to significant studies of words in both testaments. The outlines of the Hebraic thought patterns were reflected in the words of the Hebrew language, and this Hebraic thought content was also communicated through the vehicle of language (Greek) of the NT.[112]

---

109. Ludwig Köhler, *Theology of the Old Testament* (trans. Andrew S. Todd; LTT; London: James Clarke & Co., 1957), 112, emphasis added.

110. According to Barr, *Concept of Old Testament Theology*, 168.

111. James Barr, *The Semantics of Biblical Language* (New York: Oxford University Press, 1961), 8–20.

112. This quotation comes from Gerhard F. Hasel's online discussion of the Bibli-

Examples of literature trying to divorce the biblical traditions from any and all relations with the philosophical are many. In 1949 Henry and Henriette Frankfort published their *Before Philosophy*, which distinguished the Hebrew Bible from both philosophy and myth. The work itself, however, utilized insights of the philosophy of mythology developed by Ernst Cassirer.[113] Then there is also George E. Wright's book, *The Old Testament against Its Environment* (1950), in which the author went to great lengths to distance biblical culture from, among other things, philosophical reflection. Wright considered it his duty to share the news that "Israelite monotheism was not derived from philosophical speculation."[114]

The ruling assumption of the time included the misconception that there was such a thing as "Hebrew thought" or a Semitic mindset (and by extension Hebraic/biblical logic), which stood over and against Greek/Hellenistic thought (or "philosophical/Aristotelian logic").[115] It was now quite popular to deny that Western logic and Aristotelian metaphysics were applicable to ancient Israelite religious language and epistemology. The idea of "Hebrew thought" led to the stereotyping of philosophical reflection on religion as a priori abstract, static, theoretic, and systematic, out of place in the context of biblical revelation, which was hailed as dynamic, practical, and historical.[116]

Interactive relations with philosophy of religion soon became virtually nonexistent. Very few Old Testament theologies written during the greater part of the second half of the twentieth century made any reference to that discipline at all. One example is found in the writings of Robert Dentan, whose Old Testament theology contains a very short section of no more than four pages entitled "The influence of the philosophy of religion."[117] No possibility of the auxiliary involvement of philosophical approaches to

---

cal Theology movement [cited 3 April 2010]. Online: http://mb-soft.com/believe/txn/bibtheol.htm.

113. Henry Frankfort and Henriette A. Frankfort, *Before Philosophy: The Intellectual Adventure of Ancient Man* (London: Penguin, 1949).

114. G. Ernest Wright, *The Old Testament against Its Environment* (Chicago: Regnery, 1950), 39.

115. Barr, *Old and New in Interpretation*, 42.

116. Ibid. The classic and most familiar outdated studies here are Johannes Pedersen, *Israel: Its Life and Culture* (4 vols.; London: Oxford University Press, 1926–1940); and Thorleif Boman, *Hebrew Thought Compared with Greek* (trans. Jules E. Moreau; 3rd rev. ed.; New York: W. W. Norton, 1970).

117. Dentan, *Preface to Old Testament Theology*, 16–20.

the study of Israelite religion was even imagined. Consequently, it should come as no surprise that we find in other writings during this time many sustained attempts to discredit philosophical reflection on theological grounds. Thus as Avery-Dulls wrote:

> Any number of supposedly biblical theologies in our own day are so heavily infected with contemporary personalist, existential or historical thinking as to render their biblical basis highly suspect.[118]

This is no marginal point of view. To this day, many biblical scholars rage against the Enlightenment or postmodernism. Additional swearwords include "rationalism," "idealism," "historicism," "positivism," "mysticism," "relativism," "nihilism," and so on, all of which are to them taboo.[119] Old Testament theologies after the middle of the century began to make a point of emphasizing that the Hebrew Bible is not philosophical in its concerns and that one looks in vain for neat philosophical definitions or systems in it. It was also endlessly insinuated that philosophical questions put to the text were hermeneutically illegitimate, and that philosophical reflection on ancient Israelite religion had no place in Old Testament theology: "Much has been said about the imposition of the categories of Greek philosophy on the Bible, and the consequent distortion of the Bible."[120]

Of course, there was a lot of inconsistent reasoning, and the god-talk of biblical theology remained enslaved to that of Christian philosophical theology. Admissions to the philosophical background of theology as such were only made reluctantly and with a sense of smug superiority, as in Van Imschoot, who claimed, "It is the honour of Greek philosophy to give us our technical vocabulary."[121] This is something that not many biblical theologians would like to be reminded of, namely that biblical theology itself is a concern derived from ancient Greek philosophy of religion.

---

118. Avery Dulls, "Response to Krister Stendahl's Method in the Study of Biblical Theology," in *The Bible in Modern Scholarship* (ed. J. Philip Hyatt; New York: Abingdon, 1965).

119. Walter C. Kaiser Jr., *Toward an Old Testament Theology* (Grand Rapids: Zondervan, 1991), 4.

120. John L. McKenzie, *A Theology of The Old Testament* (Garden City, N.Y.: Doubleday, 1976), 25.

121. Paul van Imschoot, *Theology of the Old Testament* (New York: Desclée, 1965), x.

3.3.3. A Philosophical Turn?

The final quarter of the twentieth century saw the slow and haphazard return of openness to philosophy in some quarters as a result of developments in both subdisciplines. At this point we encounter a growing number of often unintentional brief excursions to loci in philosophy of religion, appearing in the writings of many prominent biblical scholars. Earlier anomalies and forerunners are attested to, such as the discussion of Wheeler-Robinson (1938) on the "philosophy of revelation" in the Old Testament.[122] Another example is the subsection on predicting the future as a philosophical problem in Robert Carroll's *When Prophecy Failed*. Despite his interests in philosophy, Carroll later dismissed the value of philosophical theology, because of the alleged distortive influences it had had on the reading of the Hebrew Bible.[123]

One early instance of exceptional philosophical reflection on ancient Israelite religion was Arthur Gibson's extensive study on biblical semantic logic and the nature of religious language (1981).[124] Almost thirty years have gone by, and the book has not been given its due. It sought to show that the study of biblical and ancient Near Eastern languages and literatures can be established on a logical basis. In a recent new prologue for the second edition,[125] Gibson also demonstrated how the central areas of biblical usage (names, predicates, expressions of quantity, idioms) can be mapped employing some of contemporary philosophy, logic and linguistics.

Another notable (if indirect) contribution to interdisciplinary dialogue in the early 1980s was Dale Patrick's *The Rendering of God in the Old Testament*. Part 3, though primarily concerned with hermeneutics and rhetoric, does touch on the question of realism, and the discussion of Yhwh in the Hebrew Bible is related to arguments for the existence of God

---

122. Henry Wheeler-Robinson, *The Philosophy of Revelation* (Oxford: Clarendon, 1938).

123. Robert P. Carroll, *When Prophecy Failed: Reactions and Responses to Failure in the Old Testament Prophetic Traditions* (London: SCM, 1979), 29–33.

124. Arthur Gibson, *Biblical Semantic Logic: A Preliminary Analysis* (New York: St. Martin's Press, 1981).

125. Arthur Gibson, *Biblical Semantic Logic: A Preliminary Analysis* (2nd ed.; London: Continuum, 2001).

in philosophy of religion.[126] In a later study on *The Rhetoric of Revelation in the Hebrew Bible*, Patrick looked to the analytic philosophy of language of John L. Austin and applied it to biblical discourse, something which in itself borders on a philosophical approach to biblical god-talk.[127]

Another relevant publication that was almost philosophical in flavor is Terence Fretheim's *The Suffering of God*.[128] The study overcomes to some extent the anachronism of "perfect being" theology in the context of the Hebrew Bible, and comes as close as has hitherto been possible to a nondistortive quasiphilosophical theology of the biblical traditions. Its philosophical assumptions include the metaphysics of certain versions of process theism in general, and open theism in particular. Typically, philosophical (metaphysical) jargon pops up all over the place, and the concerns implicit in the headings align very closely with those of philosophy of religion, even if Fretheim did not intend to produce a philosophical theology. As can be expected, Fretheim did not manage to stay on the level of pure description. He also failed to incorporate the dark side of Yhwh in his discussion.

Aside from the aforementioned scholars, there are several Old Testament theologians who, despite the antiphilosophical sentiments of their peers, actually concerned themselves more extensively (albeit still not exclusively or wholly independently) with philosophical perspectives on aspects of ancient Israelite religion as represented in the Old Testament. I mention four of them in this regard.

The first example of this type of more extensive—albeit still somewhat reserved—interest in the kinds of questions one encounters in philosophy of religion can be found in the writings of James Crenshaw, whose entire career has been characterized by a fascinating obsession with biblical perspectives on the problem of evil.[129] His contributions to discussions on theodicy are even included in annotated bibliographies of philosophy

---

126. See Dale Patrick, *The Rendering of God in the Old Testament* (OBT 10; Minneapolis: Fortress, 1981), 117.

127. Dale Patrick, *The Rhetoric of Revelation* (OBT 22; Minneapolis: Fortress, 1999).

128. Terence E. Fretheim, *The Suffering of God: An Old Testament Perspective* (OBT; Philadelphia, Fortress, 1984).

129. As noted in James L. Crenshaw, *Defending God: Biblical Responses to the Problem of Evil* (Oxford: Oxford University Press, 2005).

of religion proper.[130] Besides the aforementioned interest, Crenshaw's research on biblical wisdom literature reveals an affinity for things philosophical (in the original sense of the word). In a recent paper he offered what might even be considered an example of an attempt at comparative philosophy of religion, in that ancient Near Eastern wisdom traditions are scanned for parallels with concerns in Greek philosophy.[131] Yet despite decades of Crenshaw's willingness to engage in philosophically relevant issues, in the end his philosophical interests seem to have been curbed by the antiphilosophical sentiment of his generation.

A second—more extensive—instance of engagement with philosophical issues in the context of Old Testament theology is encountered in the writings of Otto Kaiser. Kaiser's interests in philosophy in the context of Old Testament theology culminated in 2003 with his *Zwischen Athen und Jerusalem: Studien zur griechischen und biblischen Theologie, ihrer Eigenart und ihren Verhältnis.* The willingness of this publication to compare ancient Israelite religion and Greek philosophy with reference to commonalities is indeed a major advancement on what is traditional in Old Testament theology.[132] As in Crenshaw, it represents the first step toward a comparative philosophy of religion, even if it is not itself considered by its author as a *Religionsphilosophie* of the Hebrew Bible. Given the nature of philosophy of religion in the Continental tradition in which Kaiser operates, this is understandable. Kaiser views Old Testament theology as "the study of the human reflection of the experience of the Divine."[133] His three-volume theology of the Old Testament shows the influence of Hegel and Heidegger, and Kaiser was one of the few Old Testament theologians to have been an expert on both ancient (Plato, Aristotle) and modern (Kant,

---

130. See "Biblical Perspectives" in William Wainwright, *Philosophy of Religion: An Annotated Bibliography of Twentieth-Century Writings in English* (New York: Garland, 1978).

131. James L. Crenshaw, "Sipping from the Cup of Wisdom" in *Jesus and Philosophy: New Essays* (ed. Paul K. Moser; Cambridge: Cambridge University Press, 2009), 41–62.

132. Otto Kaiser, *Zwischen Athen und Jerusalem: Studien zur griechischen und biblischen Theologie, ihrer Eigenart und ihren Verhältnis* (BZAW 320; Berlin: de Gruyter, 2003).

133. "Otto Kaiser (Scholar)," *Wikipedia, The Free Encyclopedia* [cited 11 August 2009]. Online: http://en.wikipedia.org/w/index.php?title=Otto_Kaiser_(scholar)& oldid=495680177.

Hegel, Nietzsche) philosophy.[134] Thus we may concur with both Hans-Peter Müller and James Barr in their claim that Kaiser played a major role in braving the antiphilosophical sentiment of his generation.[135]

A third very important example is encountered in the writings of James Barr. In his earlier work, Barr discussed aspects related to the nature of religious language in the Hebrew Bible and noted the distinction between propositionalist and personalist approaches to the concept of revelation.[136] He also wrote on natural theology in Israelite religion[137] and admitted to having been influenced by the ideas of William J. Abraham, an analytic philosopher of religion working on the concept of revelation. Indeed, Barr spent much of his career trying to repair the damaged relations with philosophy that Barthian neoorthodoxy caused within Old Testament theology. In his *The Concept of Biblical Theology*, he included a chapter on the relation between biblical theology and philosophy.[138] However, Barr's noting of the absence of philosophy of *religion* as such remained marginal and his focus was more on issues in hermeneutics, philosophy of science, and trends in the general history of philosophy. Near the end of his career, Barr would note with some disdain that postmodern philosophy had begun to make inroads into biblical studies.[139]

Up until the end of the 1990s, there was reluctance in mainstream biblical scholarship to involve philosophy in interpretation. That is why David Clines, who had become skilled in postmodern philosophy of literature, could still lament the absence of poststructuralism in methodological reflection at international conferences:

---

134. Otto Kaiser, *Grundlegung* (vol. 1 of *Der Gott des Alten Testaments: Theologie des Alten Testaments;* 3 vols.; Göttingen: Vandenhoeck & Ruprecht, 2003).

135. Hans-Peter Müller, "Alttestamentliche Theologie und Religionswissenschaft," in *Wer Ist Wie Du, Herr, unten den Göttern?* (ed. Ingo Kottsieper and Otto Kaiser; Studien zur Theologie und Religionsgeschichte Israels; Göttingen: Vandenhoeck & Ruprecht, 1994), 20–31. Cited in Barr, *Concept of Biblical Theology*, 455.

136. James Barr, *The Bible in the Modern World* (London: Trinity Press International, 1973).

137. James Barr, *Biblical Faith and Natural Theology* (Oxford: Oxford University Press, 1994), 3.

138. Barr, *Concept of Biblical Theology*, 146–71.

139. Barr, *History and Ideology*, 27.

> It is a matter for regret that the principal speakers at congresses of
> the IOSOT have given the impression that they care nothing for these
> movements of thought, as was all too evident at the Paris meeting, for
> example, when the four great Parisian names of our time, Derrida, Fou-
> cault, Kristeva and Lacan, were never mentioned (I believe).[140]

The general situation soon changed with influences from the philosophy
of language (cognitive linguistics), the philosophy of literature (deconstruction, etc.), and social philosophy (critical theory). For the most part,
however, these were all incidental and brief excursions to philosophy on
the way to more pressing concerns, such as application and exegesis. In
stark contrast, we find one Old Testament theologian who not only recognized the *non sequitur* reasoning inherent in the evasion of a descriptive
philosophical approach, but actually did the unthinkable and suggested
the need for a "biblical philosophy." That was Rolf P. Knierim.

Curiously, James Barr left out Knierim's contribution in his discussion of relations between biblical theology and philosophy. Yet in my view
Knierim was perhaps the first and most capable scholar to envisage a full-
fledged philosophical approach in a hermeneutically justified manner. He
extended the rediscovery of metaphysical and epistemological assumptions in the text beyond the wisdom literature and, following Barr, suggested that we rethink the concept of "Hebrew thought" to a greater extent
than many would want to. Knierim went even further in recognizing that
all ordinary language (even nonphilosophical biblical Hebrew) contains
metaphysical and epistemological assumptions, and that religious reasoning is always implicit in Hebrew Bible polemics.[141] He therefore suggested
that it might be worth our while to ask about the meaning the concept
"God" had in ancient Israel, and this in the context of philosophical concerns (something more or less unheard of for an Old Testament theologian
to suggest). In his approach the parallels with conceptual analysis in analytic philosophy of religion are readily apparent, and Knierim shrewdly
anticipated the expected critique against his ideas as follows:

---

140. David J. A. Clines, "From Copenhagen to Oslo: What Has (and Has Not)
Happened at Congresses of the IOSOT," *On the Way to the Postmodern: Old Testament
Essays 1967–1998* (2 vols.; JSOTSup 292; Sheffield: Sheffield Academic Press, 1998),
1:194–223.

141. Knierim, *Task of Old Testament Theology*, 221.

> Someone may ask whether the reach into this dimension of the questions does not amount to a biblical philosophy or a philosophy of the biblical truth. Indeed! And what would be wrong with that? Would it not, while focusing on the Bible, be in contact with *philosophy of religion* and with philosophy in principle, as biblical philosophy's contribution to those fields? Would it not, together with these fields, be concerned with the questions of reality, world, facts, meanings, language and truth, including the Bible's own foci and position on these matters in each of the testaments?[142]

Curiously, though, Knierim himself never wrote a historical philosophical theology of the Hebrew Bible or came up with a descriptive philosophy of ancient Israelite religion outside of biblical theology. Ultimately, even he saw philosophy (of religion) as but a handmaid to biblical theology, not something worth pursuing for its ability to clarify the Hebrew Bible for its own sake.[143] Yet Knierim's positive assessment of philosophical reflection was a sign of the times and will be remembered as having been a much needed attempt at providing a corrective to the popular misconception that all philosophy by nature distorts the Bible's conceptual background. But few would listen, and Knierim, perhaps more than most, had to discover over years of endless debates and responses to peers how difficult it is to convince the establishment that philosophy is not an enemy.

By the end of the millennium it was recognized that philosophical perspectives were never wholly absent in the study of the Hebrew Bible. This is readily apparent in the histories of biblical interpretation written during this time and which now include major foci on relations with philosophy. Here one thinks both of certain contributions to recent large-scale edited works such as Magne Saebø's *Hebrew Bible/Old Testament: The History of Its Interpretation* (1996–2008) and of individual works such as Peter Addinall's *Philosophy and Biblical Interpretation: A Study in Nineteenth-Century Conflict*.[144] Secondly, as in biblical theology, there is a covert interest to

---

142. Ibid., 492, emphasis added.

143. See the discussion of Knierim's ideas related to this issue (ibid., esp. 410, 492). See also Wonil Kim et al., eds, *Theological and Hermeneutical Studies* (vol. 2 of *Reading the Hebrew Bible for a New Millennium: Form, Concept, and Theological Perspective*; 2 vols.; Studies in Antiquity and Christianity; London: Continuum, 2000), 103. In my view, Knierim's work is not given its due.

144. Peter Addinall, *Philosophy and Biblical Interpretation: A Study in Nineteenth-Century Conflict* (Cambridge: Cambridge University Press, 1991).

be discerned in various issues and currents in philosophy of religion. Leo Perdue's *The Collapse of History* and his *Reconstructing Old Testament Theology: After the Collapse of History* both note a variety of philosophical influences on biblical scholars.[145] The contributions of Hans-Peter Müller and Manfred Oeming should also be noted.[146]

A good example of the "return of the repressed" is found in the writings of Walter Brueggemann. Although Brueggemann may claim to bracket ontology and rage against irrelevant philosophical obsessions, no Old Testament theologian before or since has tried to be so philosophically fashionable, nor commented more frantically on the ontological status of Yhwh. But Brueggemann does not himself trace his own ideas to their philosophical roots. Much of his metalanguage comes from Continental philosophy of religion, and he is explicit about leaning heavily on theories on the supposed "metaphorical" nature of all religious language, as attested in the philosophy of religion of Paul Ricoeur and Sallie McFague. There are also numerous references in his theology to philosophical ideas, including the hermeneutics of Hans-Georg Gadamer, Paul Ricoeur, Emmanuel Levinas, and Jacques Derrida. At other times he fails to mention his indebtedness to analytic philosophers such as Gilbert Ryle, from whom the notion of "thick description" is borrowed via Clifford Geertz.[147] Elsewhere Brueggemann, like those before him, both bashes philosophy (except for the Sophists and the postmodernists), but like von Rad and others since had no problem with speaking of an Israelite "*philosophy* of

---

145. Leo G. Perdue, *The Collapse of History: Reconstructing Old Testament Theology* (Minneapolis: Fortress, 1994); idem, *Reconstructing Old Testament Theology: After the Collapse of History* (OBT; Minneapolis: Fortress, 2005).

146. Hans-Peter Müller, "Bedarf die Alttestamentliche Theologie einer philosophischen Grundlegung," in *Alttestamentlicher Glaube und biblische Theologie* (Stuttgart: Kohlhammer, 1994), 342–51; idem, "Alttestamentliche Theologie und Religionswissenschaf," 20–31; idem, *Glauben, Denken und Hoffen: Alttestamentliche Botschaften in den Auseinandersetzungen unserer Zeit* (Berlin: LIT, 1998); and Manfred Oeming, *Gesamt biblische Theologien der Gegenwart* (Stuttgart: Kohlhammer, 1985).

147. See Ollenburger, *Old Testament Theology*, 377. For a related discussion, see also Brian D. Ingraffia, *Postmodern Theory and Biblical Theology: Vanquishing God's Shadow* (Cambridge: Cambridge University Press, 1995), which is less informative on biblical theology than the title suggests and actually little more than Christian apologetics against Nietzsche, Heidegger, and Derrida, and the relationships between their thought and biblical theology.

history."[148] At one point he even speaks of a "complete prophetic philosophy of history"[149] in the Hebrew Bible. As a result, Brueggemann's dismissals of the concerns of Greek and modern philosophy (at times taken to be representative of philosophy as such) cannot be taken seriously. After all, Brueggemann himself shows in the ways he uses the categories of postmodern thought in the construction of his biblical theology that philosophy as such is no problem.

Another radical yet interesting, if idiosyncratic, view around the turn of the millennium can be found in the writings of Thomas L. Thompson. In his infamous work on biblical "history," Thompson argues that, although the biblical concept of Yhwh is essentially to be thought of as post-Platonic, the Hebrew Bible itself is actually a product of Hellenism.[150] Going against the grain of everything the Biblical Theology Movement held dear, Thompson tries to deconstruct the notion of Greek versus Hebrew (or philosophical versus biblical) thinking. He does this by tracing the development of philosophy from oriental wisdom literature and finds no great originality in Greek philosophy—Aristotle only collated what is already present in Sumerian and Egyptian texts. However, for Thompson (as for von Rad and Brueggemann), the Hebrew Bible contains a "philosophy of history" rather than a philosophy of religion. On one occasion, however, he does suggest that the Hebrew Bible "also provides us with avenues of approach to such Western concepts as the personally divine. It also opens us to the critical development of a *philosophy of religion*."[151]

The Hebrew Bible in a philosophical context is thus seen as a means to an end, a halfway station on the way to contemporary theorizing, and not a body of discourse, the philosophical analysis of which can be a legitimate concern for biblical scholars. One uses the Hebrew Bible for constructive purposes rather than philosophy of religion for historical inquiry. An example of this would be Seizo Sekine's *Transcendency and Symbols in the Old Testament: A Genealogy of the Hermeneutical Expe-*

---

148. Walter Brueggemann, *An Introduction to the Old Testament: The Canon and Christian Imagination* (Louisville: Westminster John Knox, 2003), 123.

149. Walter Brueggemann, *Isaiah 40–66* (IBC; Louisville: Westminster John Knox, 1998).

150. On this see Thomas L. Thompson, *The Bible in History: How Writers Create a Past* (London: Jonathan Cape, 1999).

151. Ibid., 388, emphasis added.

riences.[152] This work looks at various encounters with transcendence through an interpretation of Old Testament texts as symbols. As such, it represents an attempted fusion of philosophical hermeneutics and traditional historical-critical exegesis. Ultimately it is also constructive rather than purely descriptive, as it builds upon the views of Paul Tillich, Hans-Georg Gadamer, and Paul Ricoeur.

Further traces of a warming towards philosophy during the next decade include Robert Gnuse's recourse to Whitehead's process philosophy of religion as foundational for Old Testament theology,[153] and Mark Brett's analysis of Childs via an eclectic and critical use of philosophical scholarship.[154] The work of John Barton on Old Testament ethics and theology also includes discussions that are not all that different from what a comparative philosophy of religion would do in a discussion of the relationship between religion and morality in ancient Israel. Barton often exposes the anachronism of Christian philosophical theological assumptions without deploring philosophical concerns altogether.[155]

In his *Understanding Old Testament Ethics*, Barton could point to the fact that, while the Old Testament is not "philosophy" in any sense we are familiar with, its moral assumptions can still be clarified by philosophical concepts, categories, and perspectives.[156] In another publication, *The Original Story: God, Israel and the World*, Barton, along with Julia Bowden, offers an entire section on "Major themes in the Old Testament" that in many details approximates a comparative philosophical-theological perspective on the Hebrew Bible. Barton discusses, *inter alia*, the difference between a divine watchmaker and a living God; Israelite perspectives on the human condition; the nature of biblical morality; and religious experience in ancient Yahwism.[157]

---

152. Seizo Sekine, *Transcendency and Symbols in the Old Testament: A Genealogy of the Hermeneutical Experience* (BZAW 275; Berlin: de Gruyter, 1999).

153. Robert Gnuse, *The Old Testament and Process Theology* (St. Louis: Chalice, 2000).

154. Mark Brett, *Biblical Criticism in Crisis? The Impact of the Canonical Approach on Hebrew Bible Studies* (London: Cambridge University Press, 2001).

155. John Barton, "The Basis of Ethics in the Hebrew Bible," *Semeia* 66 (1995): 11–22; idem, "Alttestamentliche Theologie nach Albertz?" *JBT* 10 (1995): 25–32.

156. John Barton, *Understanding Old Testament Ethics: Approaches and Explorations* (Louisville: Westminster John Knox, 2003), 55 and *passim*.

157. John Barton and Julia Bowden, *The Original Story: God, Israel and the World* (Grand Rapids: Eerdmans, 2004), 39–119.

A related theological approach drawing on the current of critical theory in philosophy of religion is found in the recent theology of the Old Testament by John Rogerson. Rogerson makes use of the Frankfurt School's social-philosophical approach to religion to show the relevance of the Hebrew Bible for today's world.[158] He does this by drawing on the insights of critical philosophers, including Benjamin and Bloch, Adorno and Horkheimer, Assmann and Habermas. For Rogerson the remarkable thing about the text is the persistence of its visions of a better humanity and a better world. Rather than seeking to establish what people may or may not once have believed in ancient Israel, he addresses the human condition in today's world, asking what interpreters are doing today when they invoke the biblical texts.

When it comes to explicitly engaging with the text on philosophical terms, the most prominent philosophical approaches to Israelite religion remain discussions of ancient Israelite wisdom literature. This involves description and elucidation of worldview via philosophical categories. An early example of such philosophical clarification of the text is Michael Fox's brief discussion of Qoheleth's epistemology, using a term such as "empiricism" to characterize the way the sage's biblical persona operated.[159] A more recent folk-philosophical description of wisdom ethics and cosmology can be found in some of the writings of Leo Perdue, who did relevant research on conceptions of reality in ancient Israelite wisdom literature.[160]

Other studies involving philosophy in this context include Rainer Braun, *Kohelet und die Frühhellenistische Popularphilosophie*;[161] Ran-

---

158. John W. Rogerson, *A Theology of the Old Testament: Cultural Memory, Communication, and Being Human* (Philadelphia: Fortress, 2010).

159. Michael Fox, *Qohelet and his Contradictions* (JSOTSup 71; Sheffield: JSOT Press, 1989).

160. Leo G. Perdue, "Cosmology and the Social Order in the Wisdom Tradition," in *The Sage in Israel and the Ancient Near East* (ed. John Gammie and Leo G. Perdue; Winona Lake, Ind.: Eisenbrauns, 1990). See also Tomas Frydrych, *Living under the Sun: Examination of Proverbs and Qoheleth* (VTSup 90; Leiden: Brill, 2002). The study carries out comprehensive comparison of the worldviews represented by Proverbs and Qoheleth, and the worlds that these reflect, looking at the aims and methods of their quest, their epistemologies, their theological and cosmological perspectives, and their anthropological and social views.

161. Rainer Braun, *Kohelet und die Frühhellenistische Popularphilosophie* (BZAW 130; Berlin: de Gruyter, 1973).

hilo C. Aquino, "Existential Pessimism and the Affirmation of God: A Philosophical Reading of Qoheleth";[162] Peter Kreeft, *Three Philosophies of Life: Ecclesiastes—Life as Vanity, Job—Life as Suffering, Song of Songs—Life as Love*;[163] William H. U. Anderson's "Philosophical Considerations in a Genre Analysis of Qoheleth";[164] John T. Wilcox's recent philosophical studies on Job, *The Bitterness of Job: A Philosophical Reading*;[165] and (especially) the section on "A Philosophical Analysis of Job" in Robert Sutherland's *Putting God on Trial: The Biblical Book of Job.*[166]

More philosophical perspectives on the Hebrew Bible (aside from religious-philosophical ones) appear in Leon Kass, *The Beginning of Wisdom: Reading Genesis*;[167] Martin Sicker, *Reading Genesis Politically: An Introduction to Mosaic Political Philosophy*;[168] and Thomas L. Pangle, *Political Philosophy and the God of Abraham.*[169] There was also recently a work by Mary Healy and Robin Parry, *The Bible and Epistemology: Biblical Soundings on the Knowledge of God*, which features contributions on the Hebrew Bible.[170] The concern with epistemology in Ryan O'Dowd in the aforementioned volume and elsewhere also deserves a mention.

On the whole, however, the use of philosophy in the study of ancient Israelite religion still tends to be reserved for metacommentary. A classic example of this is Megan Bishop Moore, *Philosophy and Practice in*

---

162. Ranhilo C. Aquino, "Existential Pessimism and the Affirmation of God: A Philosophical Reading of Qoheleth" (master's thesis, Saint Thomas Aquinas University, 1981).

163. Peter Kreeft, *Three Philosophies of Life: Ecclesiastes—Life as Vanity, Job—Life as Suffering, Song of Songs—Life as Love* (San Francisco: Ignatius Press, 1989).

164. William H. U. Anderson, "Philosophical Considerations in a Genre Analysis of Qoheleth," *VT* 48 (1998): 289–300.

165. John T. Wilcox, *The Bitterness of Job: A Philosophical Reading* (Ann Arbor, Mich.: University of Michigan Press, 1994).

166. Robert Sutherland, *Putting God on Trial: The Biblical Book of Job* (Victoria: Trafford, 2004), 141–57.

167. Leon Kass, *The Beginning of Wisdom: Reading Genesis* (New York: Free Press, 2003).

168. Martin Sicker, *Reading Genesis Politically: An Introduction to Mosaic Political Philosophy* (Westport, Conn.: Praeger, 2002).

169. Thomas L. Pangle, *Political Philosophy and the God of Abraham* (Baltimore: Johns Hopkins University Press, 2003).

170. Mary Healy and Robin Parry, eds. *The Bible and Epistemology: Biblical Soundings on the Knowledge of God* (Colorado Springs: Paternoster Press, 2007).

Writing a History of Israel.[171] The context is the debate between so-called minimalists and maximalists, where recourse to philosophy of science seems to be in high demand. Moore therefore deals with a number of related topics, including empiricism, objectivity, representation and language, subject, explanation, truth, evidence, and evaluation. Organizing around these concepts, Moore sought to situate the study of ancient Israel and Judah in the broader intellectual context of academic history in general.

Last and least, we find what is perhaps the first attempt to pioneer the establishment of an independent philosophical approach to the study of ancient Israelite religion. In my unpublished doctoral dissertation,[172] I proposed the utilization of philosophy of religion as auxiliary discipline both in exegesis and on a larger scale. The methodological intricacies were further developed in a series of articles entitled *The Quest for a Philosophical Yhwh.*[173] Specializing in this type of interdisciplinary research, my interests have changed from critical atheology and the deconstruction of biblical truth claims (2003–2007) to a more historical and descriptive type of philosophy of religion more focused on a clarification of the folk philosophical assumptions in the biblical texts themselves (2008–2011). The present study is from this later phase in my work and represents my own contribution to the story of interdisciplinary research between Hebrew Bible studies and philosophy of religion told in this chapter.

3.4. Conclusion

The historical relationship between Old Testament theology and philosophy of religion is more complex than can be ascertained from many currently available summations in histories of Old Testament interpretation. Relations with philosophy of religion have changed over time, from an early active involvement when biblical theology was seen by some as

---

171. Megan Bishop Moore, *Philosophy and Practice in Writing a History of Israel* (London: Continuum, 2005).

172. Gericke, "Does Yahweh Exist?"

173. Jaco W. Gericke, "The Quest for a Philosophical Yahweh (Part 1)"; idem, "The Quest for a Philosophical Yhwh (Part 2): Philosophical Criticism as Exegetical Methodology," *OTE* 19/3 (2006): 1178–92; and idem, "The Quest for a Philosophical Yhwh (Part 3): Towards a Philosophy of Old Testament religion," *OTE* 20/3 (2007): 669–88.

having a preparatory task (most of the nineteenth century), through a hostile rejection of philosophical perspectives on Yahwism by many (most of the twentieth century), to a more fruitful if partly reluctant involvement of philosophy for the understanding of the Old Testament and Old Testament scholarship (around the beginning of the twenty-first century). In the next chapter we take a step back and look at the last few centuries from the perspective of the auxiliary subject.

4

THE HEBREW BIBLE IN PHILOSOPHY OF RELIGION

Some dialogue among these specialists, especially between biblical scholars and philosophers of religion, is unquestionably long overdue.[1]

4.1. INTRODUCTION

In this chapter we pick up the story from the parting of the ways late in the eighteenth century. The plot represents an inversion of the scenario sketched in the previous chapter: our concern lies not with the way philosophy of religion has featured in Hebrew Bible studies, but with how the Hebrew Bible has featured in modern philosophy of religion. Once more it is beyond the scope of the discussion to provide a thorough treatment and evaluation of everything that could be said on the Hebrew Bible in philosophy of religion. It is impossible to note everything philosophers of religion have written since the discipline's independence and with reference to ancient Israelite religion. I therefore offer only the briefest idiosyncratic selection of representative examples to show what has, and has not, been forthcoming in this regard. The aim is to briefly note examples of the Hebrew Bible in the work of major figures.

The discussion to follow is limited mostly to Christian philosophy of religion. The only reason for this is that, until relatively recently, philosophy of religion as an official academic discipline has been mostly Western and Christian. Perspectives on the Hebrew Bible in mainstream Jewish philosophy of religion, though even more directly relevant to our own ultimate theoretical concern, will be offered at a later stage.

---

1. Eleanor Stump, "Modern Biblical Scholarship, Philosophy of Religion and Traditional Christianity," *Truth Journal* 1 (1985) [cited 8 October 2009]. Online: http://www.leaderu.com/truth/1truth20.html.

4.2. The Hebrew Bible in Modern Philosophy of Religion

As noted earlier, Western philosophy of religion in the strict sense is a modern development first clearly discernible in the work of philosophers such as Hume, Kant, and Hegel. It is in their writings that we first observe an autonomous philosophical subdiscipline devoted to the kinds of issues that arise in Western monotheistic traditions.[2] The question concerns what they and subsequent philosophers of religion have thought about and done with the Hebrew Bible. As with the topic in the previous chapter, no such highly specific history of interdisciplinary relations currently exists. What follows provides an idea of how it might look.

4.2.1. Early Days

Our first figure is David Hume (1711–1776), who mixed philosophy of religion with reflection on the history of religion in ways that affected the study of the Hebrew Bible itself. Following his *Enquiry Concerning Human Understanding* (1748), Hume's thoughts culminated in his *The Natural History of Religion* (1757) and *Dialogues Concerning Natural Religion* (1779). His eclectic concern with the Hebrew Bible is most apparent in his philosophical reflection on the development of religious beliefs and in his analysis of the concept of miracles. Let us briefly consider each in turn.

In his *Natural History of Religion*, Hume postulated the absence of philosophical reflection in the ancient world by arguing that the origin and foundations of religious belief did not rest with reason or philosophical argument.[3] Instead, Hume speculated, fear and ignorance first gave rise to polytheism, which by the same psychological forces was transformed into monotheism. On this view theism is itself a product of conflicting tendencies in human nature, which result in an unstable oscillation between anthropomorphism and mysticism in representations of deity. Given such instability, there is a natural tendency for theism to revert back into polytheism via the postulating of "demigods" (e.g., Jesus), in order to satisfy the iconic need in the representation of divinity.[4]

---

2. Long, *Issues in Contemporary Philosophy of Religion*, 6.

3. This discussion on Hume is indebted to Paul Russell, "Hume on Religion," *SEP* [cited 6 December 2009]. Online: http://plato.stanford.edu/archives/win2008/entries/hume-religion/.

4. Ibid.

Hume's view on miracles also had some bearing on biblical materials. While accounts of miracles presented in the Hebrew Bible were previously assumed to confirm the authenticity of the tradition and establish divine revelation as fact, Hume argued that this line of reasoning is logically and epistemologically suspect. According to Hume, a miracle supposedly involves the transgression of a "law of nature" by way of divine fiat. But if this is the case, it follows "that no testimony can ever be sufficient to establish a miracle, unless the testimony is of such a kind that its falsehood would be more miraculous than the fact it endeavors to establish."[5] This view of miracles would contribute to the legitimating of naturalism in subsequent historical-critical readings.

Though he was a philosopher, Immanuel Kant (1724–1804) is familiar to historians of biblical theology.[6] Discussions of the influence of Kant on biblical interpretation, however, tend to focus primarily on Kantian epistemology and ethics, with little if any attention to the influence of his philosophy of religion. The latter was extensive and decisive, and included critical evaluations of arguments concerning the existence of God, the attributes of God, the immortality of the soul, the problem of evil, the relationship of moral principles to religious belief and practice, and so on. These discussions included allusions to the Hebrew Bible.[7]

On the whole it might be said that Kant did not like the Hebrew Bible very much. Reasons frequently given for this include his pietistic background and the antihistorical bias of his idealist philosophy.[8] Yet the effect of the Hebrew Bible on Kant's moral philosophy in particular cannot be denied, and his distinction between the foundations of biblical morality and those of his own presupposes a degree of informal, unwritten prior comparative philosophical reflection on certain motifs from the text:

> I confess gladly that I cannot allow charm to accompany the concept of duty, precisely owing to its dignity. For it contains unconditional necessitation which stands in flat contradiction against charm. The majesty of the law (like that on Sinai) evokes reverence ... which arouses the respect

---

5. Ibid.

6. For the former, see Henning G. Reventlow, "Immanuel Kant: The Impact of His Philosophy on Biblical Hermeneutics," in Saebø, *Hebrew Bible/Old Testament*, 2:1034–40.

7. Rossi, "Kant's Philosophy of Religion."

8. Walter A. Kaufmann, *Discovering the Mind: Kant, Goethe, Hegel* (Brunswick, N.J.: Transaction, 1991), 126.

of the subordinate for his commander. But in this case, since the commander is to be found within ourselves, a feeling of the sublimity of our own calling, which enraptures us more than anything beautiful.[9]

Kant obtained not only the background for his concept of "law" in part from the Hebrew Bible, but also its content. The assumption of his moral philosophy was the idea that humanity is "special" and above the rest of nature (Gen 1:26), and thereby Kant sought to justify human dignity and rationality. Even his appeal to purpose in the context of history and nature was clearly rooted in an Israelite philosophy of history—with its compatibilist notion of providence vis-à-vis the will of autonomous individuals, who still have to act freely and obey the commands in order for events to materialize. For the most part, however, Kant was very selective in admitting overt recourse to ideas rooted in ancient Israelite religion.[10]

Georg W. F. Hegel gave his first lectures on the philosophy of religion "in the summer semester of 1821 at the University of Berlin, lectures that he was to repeat on three occasions, in 1824, 1827, and 1831."[11] His interest in religion was already evident from his days as a theological student in Tübingen, and after that at Frankfurt, Jena, and Nuremberg. After the idea of "deity as transcendental signified" had been rendered problematic by Enlightenment philosophy, history, and science, Hegel set out to develop a new philosophical theology that would reestablish the conceptual foundations of religion by offering a postmetaphysical and postcritical way of thinking about God.[12]

Hegel saw ancient Israelite religion as but "one of the temporary phases through which the knowledge of God passed in the course of its evolution into the absolute religion, Christianity."[13] He divided religious consciousness into natural and spiritual religions. In the latter category Hegel placed ancient Israelite religion as a religion of sublimity in contrast

---

9. Quoted in ibid., 126.

10. Ibid., 136–37.

11. Peter C. Hodgson, "Hegel's Philosophy of Religion," in *The Cambridge Companion to Hegel and Nineteenth-Century Philosophy* (ed. Frederick C. Beiser; Cambridge: Cambridge University Press, 2009 [cited 17 December 2009]. Online: http://cco.cambridge.org/extract?id=ccol9780521831673_CCOL9780521831673A010.

12. Ibid.

13. Emil G. Hirsch, "Hegel, Georg Wilhelm Friedrich," *Jewish Encyclopedia* [cited 19 August 2010]. Online: http://www.jewishencyclopedia.com/articles/7477-hegel-georg-wilhelm-friedrich.

to Greek religion (a religion of beauty) and Roman religion (a religion of utility). In thus characterizing the Hebraic legacy, Hegel disliked Yahwism for its alienation of humanity from divinity, from the beginning in Eden onwards. He found the character of Abraham deficient on the grounds that the patriarch had allegedly set up a world-denying and world-alienating system, which later came to fruition in what Hegal regarded as Jewish legalism.[14] He saw Moses as an agent of liberation who led the ancient Israelites into a confrontation with the Infinite. Yet as a lawgiver he too was lacking, since he set up an infinite Object over and against the people on the one hand and since he alienated the people from the rest of the human race on the other. Hegel thus thought it a weakness that the deity was a "Master" or a "Lawgiver."[15]

In this manner, Hegel's philosophy of Israelite religion was as much evaluative as it was descriptive. Yet, unlike his predecessors, Hegel did not consider the Hebrew authors incapable of abstract thoughts. He saw ancient Yahwism as highly developed, though opposed to healthy subjectivity, so much so that it had to become rigid and restrictive.[16] Hegel also discerned a struggle against infinity in biblical faith, in that the entire history of Israelite religion seemed to him to have been a battle against *Schicksal* by a people thrown into the maelstrom of history without a proper sense of transcendence. Here Hegel used, for the first time with reference to religion, Fichte's concept of *synthesis* and *antithesis*, and saw Mosaic Yahwism as the beginning of a movement, the end of which would culminate in a unity of the human and divine in the *Religionsphilosophie*. The same infinite qualitative *difference* between deity, humanity and the world/nature eventually became the central obstacle that Hegel's later philosophy of religion sought to overcome.[17]

Our next example,[18] Sören Kierkegaard, wrote commentaries on selections of texts from the Hebrew Bible. These were creative philosophical

---

14. See Erich M. Dale, "Hegel, Jesus, and Judaism," *Animus* 11 (2006): 6.

15. Hirsch, "Hegel."

16. Dale, "Hegel, Jesus, and Judaism," 7.

17. Ibid.

18. I have not incorporated a discussion of Continental thinkers such as Karl Marx as left-Hegelian in this section, even though he had much to say about the Hebrew Bible. According to one anecdote, Marx even recommended that his wife read the prophets rather than go to church (see Andrew N. Wilson, *God's Funeral: The Decline of Faith in Western Civilization* [London: Abacus, 1999], 113). However, Marxist readings are more sociological than philosophical in orientation and have

readings that recently became the topic of discussion in a publication entitled *Kierkegaard and the Bible*. There the publisher describes Kierkegaard's
interest in the Old Testament in this way:

> Although Kierkegaard certainly cited the Old Testament much less
> frequently than he did the New, passages and themes from the Old Tes-
> tament do occupy a position of startling importance in his writings. Old
> Testament characters such as Abraham and Job often play crucial and
> even decisive roles in his texts. Snatches of Old Testament wisdom figure
> prominently in his edifying literature. The vocabulary and cadences of
> the Psalms saturate his expression of the range of human passions from
> joy to despair. The essays in this first tome seek to elucidate the crucial
> rhetorical uses to which he put key passages from the Old Testament,
> the sources that influenced him to do this, and his reasons for doing so.[19]

Kierkegaard commented on a number of Hebrew Biblical stories
and motifs, as the contents of the publication show: Part 1—"Individual
Texts and Figures": (1) "Adam and Eve: Human Being and Nothingness,"
by Tim Dalrymple; (2) "Abraham: Framing Fear and Trembling," by Tim
Dalrymple; (3) "Moses: The Positive and Negative Importance of Moses
in Kierkegaard's Thought," by Paul Martens; (4) "David and Solomon:
Models of Repentance and Evasion of Guilt," by Matthias Engelke; (5) "Job:
Edification against Theodicy," by Timothy H. Polk; (6) "Psalms: Source
of Images and Contrasts," by Matthias Engelke; (7) "Ecclesiastes: Vanity,
Grief, and the Distinctions of Wisdom," by William Williams; (8) "Nebu-
chadnezzar: The King as Image of Transformation," by Matthias Engelke;
Part 2—"Overview Articles": (9) "Kierkegaard's Rewriting of Biblical Nar-
ratives: The Mirror of the Text," by Iben Damgaard; (10) "Kierkegaard's
Use of the Old Testament: From Literary Resource to the Word of God," by

---

been discussed in depth in sociological approaches to the Bible (e.g., Roland Boer,
Marxist Criticism of the Bible [London: Sheffield Academic Press, 2003]. Also, the
work of Ludwig Feuerbach, though important in philosophy of religion proper, was
more focused on explaining the New Testament and Christian theology than on
describing ancient Israelite religion. Although these two important thinkers are not
discussed here, a full-fledged history of interdisciplinary relations would do well to
include both.

19. Preface in *The Old Testament* (vol. 1 of *Kierkegaard and the Bible*; ed. Lee
C. Barrett and Jon Stewart, 2 vols.; Kierkegaard Research: Sources, Reception, and
Resources 1; Surrey, England: Ashgate, 2009), xi.

Lori Unger Brandt; (11) "Kierkegaard's Use of the Apocrypha: Is It 'Scripture' or 'Good for Reading?'" by W. Glenn Kirkconnell.[20]

This sort of discussion by philosophers was also evident in biblical scholarship, where it was common to examine various philosophers' readings or understanding of certain biblical motifs. Yet such philosophical commentaries were not limited to theistic philosophers of religion. We also encounter reflections on ancient Israelite religion and the Hebrew Bible in famous nineteenth-century atheist philosophies. Here we see radically incommensurable ideas on the value of Yahwism for contemporary philosophy of religion. I offer one example of both negative and positive perspectives below.

On a decidedly negative note, Arthur Schopenhauer was not fond of the Hebrew Bible, and quoted from Greek and Latin translations of the text instead. Schopenhauer denied legitimate existence to philosophy of religion—in the form in which he knew that discipline.[21] He did, however, offer bits and pieces of philosophical description of Israelite religion. On occasion, he found it necessary to describe and compare what he took to be the Hebrew Bible's own metaphysical assumptions:

> The basic character of Judaism is realism and optimism, which are closely related and the preconditions of actual theism, since they consider the material world absolutely real and life as a pleasing gift made expressly for us. The basic character of Brahmanism and Buddhism, on the contrary, is idealism and pessimism, since they allow the world only a dreamlike existence and regard life as a consequence of our sins.[22]

Not that Schopenhauer's ideas differed from everything in the Hebrew Bible. (Qoheleth would probably agree with him on everything, except the need for idealism and atheism.) Overstating his aversion to Yahwism, Schopenhauer noted that his favorite motif was exactly that which many theologians in his own day found most problematic:

---

20. Ibid., v–vi.

21. Arthur Schopenhauer, *The World as Will and Representation* (trans. Eric F. J. Payne; 2 vols.; New York: Courier Dover Publications, 2005), 2:168.

22. Arthur Schopenhauer, *Essays and Aphorisms* (trans. Robert J. Hollingdale; London: Penguin, 1970), 190.

> The myth of the Fall of man ... is the only thing in the Old Testament to which I can concede a metaphysical, although only allegorical truth; indeed, it is this alone that reconciles me to the Old Testament.[23]

Whatever we make of this, it seems that Schopenhauer's assessments stand in stark contrast to our example of a positive atheist perspective. This comes from the writings of Friedrich Wilhelm Nietzsche. The prospective theology student turned classical philologist turned philosopher came to appreciate the Hebrew Bible in ways quite contrary to those of his Christian German idealist philosophical predecessors:

> In the Jewish "Old Testament," the book of divine justice, there are men, things, and sayings on such an immense scale, that Greek and Indian literature have nothing to compare with it. One stands with fear and reverence before those stupendous remains of what man was formerly, and one has sad thoughts about old Asia and its little out-pushed peninsula Europe, which would like, by all means, to figure before Asia as the "Progress of Mankind." To be sure, he who is himself only a slender, tame house-animal, and knows only the wants of a house-animal (like our cultured people of today, including the Christians of "cultured" Christianity), need neither be amazed nor even sad amid those ruins—the taste for the Old Testament is a touchstone with respect to "great" and "small": perhaps he will find that the New Testament, the book of grace, still appeals more to his heart (there is much of the odour of the genuine, tender, stupid beadsman and petty soul in it). To have bound up this New Testament (a kind of Rococo of taste in every respect) along with the Old Testament into one book, as the "Bible," as "The Book in Itself," is perhaps the greatest audacity and "sin against the Spirit" which literary Europe has upon its conscience.[24]

The same idea was later repeated:

> I do not like the "New Testament," that should be plain; I find it almost disturbing that my taste in regard to this most highly esteemed and over-estimated work should be so singular (I have the taste of two millennia *against* me): but there it is! "Here I stand, I cannot do otherwise"—I have the courage of my bad taste. The Old Testament—that is something

---

23. Schopenhauer, *World as Will and Representation*, 2:580.
24. Friedrich W. Nietzsche, *Beyond Good and Evil* (trans. Helen Zimmern; Project Gutenberg) [cited 8 August 2010]. Online: http://www.gutenberg.org/etext/4363.

else again: all honour to the Old Testament! I find in it great human beings, a heroic landscape, and something of the very rarest quality in the world, the incomparable naïveté of the *strong heart*; what is more, I find a people. In the New one, on the other hand, I find nothing but petty sectarianism, mere rococo of the soul, mere involutions, nooks, queer things, the air of the conventicle, not to forget an occasional whiff of bucolic mawkishness that belongs to the epoch (and to the Roman province) and is not so much Jewish as Hellenistic.[25]

The above assessments require qualification; Nietzsche admired only the older forms of robust Yahwism:

What an affirmative Semitic religion, the product of the ruling class, looks like: the law-book of Mohammed, the older parts of the Old Testament.... What a negative Semitic religion, the product of an oppressed class, looks like: the New Testament (—in Indian-Aryan terms: a chandala religion).[26]

Interestingly, Nietzsche believed that the removal of Yhwh's dark side was a grave theological error. For him, greatmaking properties (in the context of the notion of maximal greatness in philosophy of religion) were not those of omnibenevolence and "perfect being" theology. What made a God like Yhwh worthy of worship had little to do with user-friendly attributes:

How can we be so tolerant of the naïveté of Christian theologians as to join in their doctrine that the evolution of the concept of god from "the god of Israel," the god of a people, to the Christian god, the essence of all goodness, is to be described as progress?[27]

According to Nietzsche, the decline of monistic Yahwism and the introduction of metaphysical dualism in Israelite religion led to a sickly, subservient

---

25. Friedrich Nietzsche, *On the Genealogy of Morality* (ed. Keith Ansell-Pearson; trans. Carol Diethe; Cambridge: Cambridge University Press, 1995), 114. For the German original, see the resource at Friedrich Nietzsche, "Dritte Abhandlung: Was bedeuten asketische Ideale?" in *Zur Genealogie der Moral* (Projekt Gutenberg), §22 [cited 8 August 2010]. Online: http://gutenberg.spiegel.de/buch/3249/5.

26. Friedrich Nietzsche, *The Will to Power* (trans. Gordon Kaufman and Reginald Hollingdale; London: Vintage Books, 1968), 75.

27. Nietzsche, *The Anti-Christ* (trans. Henry Louis Mencken; London: Nu Vision, 2007), 15.

herd morality and suffocated the quest for human excellence. Worst of all, it replaced a life-affirming naturalness with an otherworldly, life-denying negativism. He therefore offered the following evaluative moral assessment of the history of Israelite religion: "The history of Israel is invaluable as a typical history of an attempt to *denaturize* all natural values: I point to five facts which bear this out."[28] At first, the situation looked promising and was characterized by vitality:

> Originally, and above all in the time of the monarchy, Israel maintained the right attitude to things, which is to say, the natural attitude. Its Jahveh was an expression of its consciousness of power, its joy in itself, its hopes for itself: to him the Jews looked for victory and salvation and through him they expected nature to give them whatever was necessary to their existence—above all, rain. Jahveh is the god of Israel, and *consequently* the god of justice: this is the logic of every race that has power in its hands and a good conscience in the use of it. In the religious ceremonial of the Jews both aspects of this self-approval stand revealed. The nation is grateful for the high destiny that has enabled it to obtain dominion; it is grateful for the benign procession of the seasons, and for the good fortune attending its herds and its crops. This view of things remained an ideal for a long while, even after it had been robbed of validity by tragic blows: anarchy within and the Assyrian without. But the people still retained, as a projection of their highest yearnings, that vision of a king who was at once a gallant warrior and an upright judge—a vision best visualized in the typical prophet (i.e., critic and satirist of the moment), Isaiah.[29]

Eventually, however, things took a turn for the worst:

> But every hope remained unfulfilled. The old god no longer *could* do what he used to do. He ought to have been abandoned. But what actually happened? Simply this: the conception of him was *changed*—the conception of him was *denaturized*; this was the price that had to be paid for keeping him. — Jahveh, the god of "justice"—he is in accord with Israel *no more*, he no longer visualizes the national egoism; he is now a god only conditionally.... The public notion of this god now becomes merely a weapon in the hands of clerical agitators, who interpret all happiness as a reward and all unhappiness as a punishment for obedience

---

28. Ibid., 21.
29. Ibid.

or disobedience to him, for "sin": that most fraudulent of all imaginable interpretations, whereby a "moral order of the world" is set up, and the fundamental concepts, "cause" and "effect," are stood on their heads. Once natural causation has been swept out of the world by doctrines of reward and punishment some sort of *un*natural causation becomes necessary: and all other varieties of the denial of nature follow it. A god who *demands*—in place of a god who helps, who gives counsel, who is at bottom merely a name for every happy inspiration of courage and self-reliance.[30]

Aside from this assessment, Nietzsche drew on bits and pieces from the Hebrew Bible in many and varied ways. On some occasions, he simply enjoyed being creative with humorous, if blasphemous, comments.

4.2.2. The Rise of an Academic Discipline

None of the figures mentioned thus far were philosophers of religion in the exclusive or professional sense, since the subject became a reality at university level only late in the nineteenth century. Only then did there appear many papers, articles, chapters in books, and sections in textbooks in philosophy of religion (or a related field in theology or philosophy) that incidentally dealt with linked issues in the Hebrew Bible. Not all can be mentioned here, but one example from the German literature is *Zu Bibel und Religionsphilosophie*, by the German psychologist Heymann Steintahl. The work is not so much a philosophy of Israelite religion as a text that views the biblical traditions as a source of materials for reflection. Another example of interdisciplinary interaction is Klaus Hemmerle's "Wandern mit deinem Gott—Religionsphilosophische Kontexte zu Mi 6, 8."[31] Further such instances exist, but need not be mentioned here—for now the plot thickens.

During the first half of the twentieth century, Hegelian German personal idealism and neo-Kantianism began to dwindle as earlier positivism led to a turn to empirical science as a paradigm for philosophy. Thereafter came the turn to language and logical positivism. This seemed to spell

---

30. Nietzsche, *The Anti-Christ*, 21 §25.

31. Klaus Hemmerle, "Wandern mit deinem Gott—Religionsphilosophische Kontexte zu Mi 6, 8" [cited 18 June 2012]. Online: http://www.klaus-hemmerle.de/cms-joomla/download/Wandern%20mit%20deinem%20Gott%20-%20religionsphil-osophische%20Kontexte.pdf.

the end for philosophy of religion as normative enterprise.[32] Equated with natural theology, philosophy of religion was nearly devastated by the positivist challenge, the verification criteria of which suggested that religious language was not so much either true or false as essentially meaningless.

An example of the Hebrew Bible in the afterlife of its theological use is found in elements of Ludwig Wittgenstein's later philosophy of religion. Interesting perhaps is the way in which his familiarity with the Hebrew Bible influenced his *Philosophical Investigations*. Wittgenstein believed he had departed from what he took to be a Greek visualist paradigm of reality to return to the "Hebraic" dynamism of the spoken word. As he told his friend Maurice O'Connor Drury, "Your religious ideas have always seemed to me more Greek than biblical. Whereas my thoughts are one hundred percent Hebraic."[33]

Wittgenstein insisted that the motto for the whole of his later philosophy came from a phrase in Goethe's *Faust*, "in the beginning was the deed," and reliance upon the double meaning (both "word" and "deed") of the Hebrew term *davar*. He sincerely believed that this "Hebraic" formulation enabled him to make the radical philosophical moves he made, which were ignored in most philosophy and theology departments in what Wittgenstein called the "darkness" of that time. As for the overt presence of the Hebrew Bible in *Philosophical Investigations* itself, it is found in the form of the imagery through which philosophical problems are illustrated:

> Consider this example. If one says "Moses did not exist," this may mean various things. It may mean: the Israelites did not have a single leader when they withdrew from Egypt or: their leader was not called Moses or, there cannot have been anyone who accomplished all that the Bible relates of Moses. We may say, following Russell: the name "Moses" can be defined by means of various descriptions. For example, as "the man who led the Israelites through the wilderness," "the man who lived at that time and place and was then called "Moses," "the man who as a child was taken out of the Nile by Pharaoh's daughter" and so on. And according as we assume one definition or another the proposition "Moses did not exist" acquires a different sense, and so does every other proposition about Moses. And if we are told "N did not exist," we do ask: "What do you mean? Do you want to say ... or ... etc.?" But when I

---

32. Long, *Twentieth-Century Western Philosophy of Religion*, 7.

33. Maurice O'Connor Drury, "Conversations with Wittgenstein," in *Recollections of Wittgenstein* (ed. Rush Rhees; New York: Oxford University Press, 1984), 161.

make a statement about Moses, am I always ready to substitute some one of these descriptions for "Moses"? I shall perhaps say: By "Moses" I understand the man who did what the Bible relates of Moses, or at any rate a good deal of it. But how much? Have I decided how much must be proved false for me to give up my proposition as false? Has the name "Moses" got a fixed and unequivocal use for me in all possible cases?[34]

This is not exactly philosophical biblical criticism; it is rather philosophy of language using the biblical contents as an illustration. Yet it shows that even a philosopher who was not typically religious was able to employ the Hebrew Bible to see all things from a religious perspective. Wittgenstein's use of the Hebrew Bible for illustrative purposes was a sign of the times and of the seeming end of its direct relevance to philosophy.

By mid-century, philosophy of religion seemed poised to end. But it did not, and the tide turned. As Nicholas Wolterstorff argued in his essay "How Philosophical Theology Became Possible in the Analytic Tradition of Philosophy,"[35] three developments in particular can be discerned as having contributed to the renewal of philosophy of religion:

1. The demise of *logical empiricism* during the 1960s, and thus the end of antimetaphysical bias in analytic philosophy and an openness to religious topics;
2. A reduction of interest in the question of the origin of concepts and the limits of thought, which plagued and still plagues the Continental traditions;
3. The proliferation of *metaepistemology* and new theories of knowledge, during which classical foundationalism was left behind and the rationality of belief affirmed.

These developments in the analytic tradition have turned philosophy of religion into one of the more vibrant areas of Anglo-American philosophy. Attention to the Hebrew Bible took various forms during this time. An influential contribution to the revival was the anthology *New Essays in*

---

34. Wittgenstein, *Philosophical Investigations*, 42.
35. Nicholas Wolterstorff, "How Philosophical Theology Became Possible in the Analytic Tradition of Philosophy," in *Analytic Theology: New Essays in the Philosophy of Theology* (ed. Oliver D. Crisp and Michael C. Rea; Oxford: Oxford University Press, 2009), 155–69.

Philosophical Theology, edited by Alasdair MacIntyre and Anthony Flew.[36] The main concerns of the study were the meaningfulness of religious language, and whether religious beliefs, even if neither provable nor capable of disproof, are at least rational to hold. And so the stage was set for a new round of discussions in analytic philosophy of religion, one that would last for several decades.

Textbooks in philosophy of religion during this period did not as a rule feature the Hebrew Bible as their exclusive concern. Yet there are exceptions to this rule, and while many biblical scholars of the day debated the existence of Old Testament theology, one creative individual actually dared to involve the history of Israelite religion in what he conceived of as Old Testament *philosophy*. In 1934, Charles H. Patterson wrote an article entitled "The Philosophy of the Old Testament,"[37] which two decades later would be extended to the length of a book.[38] In the introduction to this ambitious work, Patterson revealed his historical and descriptive philosophical agenda as

> an attempt to present impartially the significant ideas expressed in the various parts of this literature. It is not written as an apology in support of all or any of these ideas; neither is it intended to discredit any of the views found in the Old Testament. The aim of the book is to aid the reader in understanding the materials which are there. The evaluation of these ideas ... must be left to each individual.[39]

Patterson then goes on to say:

> There are difficulties which must be overcome if the Old Testament is to be approached in the spirit of philosophy. For one thing, no fixed or final conclusions about any of its teachings can be in advance. The ideas which one finds expressed in the literature must be evaluated in each

---

36. Alasdair MacIntyre and Anthony Flew, eds., *New Essays in Philosophical Theology* (London: SCM, 1955). For an introduction to these and other developments, see Thomas P. Flint and Michael C. Rea, eds., *The Oxford Handbook of Philosophical Theology* (New York: Oxford University Press, 2009), 3.

37. Charles H. Patterson, "The Philosophy of the Old Testament," *JNABI* 2 (1934): 60–66.

38. Charles Patterson, *The Philosophy of the Old Testament* (New York: Ronald Press, 1953).

39. Ibid., 11.

instance on the basis of the evidence which can be found to support it. This is not an easy goal to attain, for biblical literature has often been presented from a sectarian point of view and one's prejudices concerning matters of vital importance are not easily set aside.[40]

Patterson's aim was to explain to students of philosophy the Hebraic contribution to the Western intellectual tradition, especially given that most presentations of the history of philosophy tended to focus primarily on Greek influences. There was something unforgettable about this collection of scrolls in Western society.[41] Patterson's book is technically not a philosophy of Israelite religion so much as a historical introduction to the Hebrew Bible, specifically aimed at and tailored for students of philosophy. What is quite refreshing, however, is that the author displays none of the antiphilosophical sentiment of mid-twentieth-century biblical theologians. He too is aware that his philosophical approach might raise a few hermeneutical eyebrows:

We are not accustomed to think of the Old Testament as a book of philosophy. There are some respects in which this attitude is correct, for the book is primarily religious rather than philosophical. Its teachings are presented not from the point of view of logical argumentation but as a part of the religious instruction which was given for the admonition of the Hebrew people and through them to the rest of the world. Even so, the book has its philosophical implications and they are important for anyone who wants to construct a world view of his own that will be adequate to deal with the many problems which arise in connection with his own experience.[42]

He continues:

---

40. Ibid.

41. Cf. Robert P. Carroll, *Wolf in the Sheepfold: The Bible as Problem for Christianity* (London: SPCK, 1991), 31; Don Cupitt, *The Meaning of the West: An Apologia for Secular Christianity* (London: SCM, 2008), *passim*.

42. Patterson, *Philosophy of the Old Testament*, 20. Other books in the twentieth century feature the concept of the "philosophy" of the Hebrew Bible. Yet the term there is used not in its technical sense but in its populist folk-philosophical sense, to refer simply to the "ideas" of the Bible, for example in David Neumark's study, *The Philosophy of the Bible* (Cincinnati: Ark, 1918), which is simply a retelling of the findings of historical criticism as opposed to traditional views.

> When we speak of the philosophy of the Old Testament, we have in mind
> the world view that is implied in the various writings which it contains.
> This does not mean there is a world view of which all of the different
> authors were conscious but, rather, that each one of them had his own
> understanding of the nature of the universe and it was from that particu-
> lar point of view that each of the respective writings was produced. It is
> the world views of these authors which we have in mind when we speak
> of the philosophy of the Old Testament.[43]

In his historical and philosophical account of some of the basic metaphysical, epistemological, moral and other assumptions in the Hebrew
Bible, Patterson sought to work mainly descriptively, despite his philosophical concerns:

> Since the literature of the Old Testament includes a wide variety of literary
> forms, it is to be expected that the philosophy of the book will be expressed
> in many different ways. Each group of writers follows a unique pattern for
> expressing those ideas which are believed to be most important.[44]

Patterson did not limit his concerns to "moral philosophy" but went further, making sobering inferences such as the following:

> Although the problems of ontology and epistemology are not discussed
> directly in the Old Testament, it would be a mistake to suppose the vari-
> ous writings do not imply a conception of reality or specific methods for
> arriving at truth. It is with reference to these two problems that the Old
> Testament makes some of its most important contributions to philosophy.[45]

Yet his book is not as purely descriptive as it claims to be. At times, Patterson's developmentalist ideas are reminiscent of some of the Hegelian
theologies of the Old Testament in the nineteenth century. At least the
author does not bracket the history of religion in his philosophy of religion. In its concern with the Hebrew Bible, this was an anomaly at a time
when philosophy of religion tended to be equated with natural theology
and apologetics for normative purposes.

---

43. Patterson, *Philosophy of the Old Testament*, 20–21.
44. Ibid., 21.
45. Ibid., 22.

During this period, many philosophical theologians also commented on issues in the Hebrew Bible. They include especially conservative scholars of the Protestant traditions, who at times tried to give a philosophical account of bits of Hebraic biblical faith. Many texts in doctrinal theology and historical theology also include philosophical sections on biblical materials, the contents of which are recast in philosophical language.

One example is Paul Tillich's *Biblical Religion and the Search for Ultimate Reality*.[46] This work begins by defending a philosophical approach to the biblical materials, against those writers influenced by Barth to deny philosophy of religion any involvement with the study of Scripture. Tillich meant for biblical religion and philosophy to connect at a personal level. Despite the contrast between philosophical and biblical language, he believed it neither necessary nor possible to separate them wholly from each other. Tillich clearly felt that the God of the Philosophers was the same as the God of the Bible.

Another example is Langdon Gilkey's penetrating philosophical analysis of concepts in Old Testament theology as popularized by biblical theology in his article "Cosmology, Ontology, and the Travail of Biblical Language."[47] For Gilkey the problem with the use of the Bible in the type of theology Barth inspired was that it had no clear concept of the "act of God." Though not purely historical, the essay contains descriptive philosophical accounts of elements in biblical ontology. One frequently overlooked aspect of Gilkey's contribution was the implication that bracketing philosophical concerns actually makes one more (not less) prone to anachronistic philosophical eisegesis.

4.2.3. The Contemporary Situation

Over the last few decades, reluctance to involve the Hebrew Bible in philosophy of religion has partly diminished. As will become clear in the discussion to follow, some philosophers of religion still retain a definite interest in particular and specific aspects found within ancient Israelite religious traditions. We shall see how a few of them are actually calling for closer interaction between philosophers of religion and biblical scholars.

---

46. Paul Tillich, *Biblical Religion and the Search for Ultimate Reality* (Chicago: University of Chicago Press, 1964).

47. Langdon Gilkey, "Cosmology, Ontology, and the Travail of Biblical Language," *JR* 41 (1961): 194–205.

One example of this tendency is Eleanore Stump, who writes the following:

> Partly because it requires a set of highly specialized skills, the research generated by this historical approach has not received much critical scrutiny either from professional historians or from philosophers, even those with a professional interest in the study of religion. And some dialogue among these specialists, especially between biblical scholars and philosophers of religion, is unquestionably long overdue. No doubt philosophers of religion can benefit greatly from biblical scholars by learning about the historical foundations of Christianity and Judaism. Surely some detailed acquaintance with biblical criticism is crucial for understanding the religion one is attacking or defending, and the philosophical examination of Judaism and Christianity will not be done well without some attention to the best contemporary understanding of the biblical texts on which those religions are founded.[48]

As they stand, there is nothing obviously problematic about these remarks. However, a clearly fundamentalist agenda is to be found in the rest of the discussion, where the author rages against biblical criticism and the "unorthodox" findings of historical critical research. Stump qualifies the need to learn from biblical scholars with the insinuation that they themselves should first take cognizance of what philosophers of religion are doing; which in turn will allegedly render historical-critical research defunct. According to Stump, the final judgment regarding historical authenticity may turn out very differently if biblical scholarship is subjected to analysis and questioning by philosophers. She believes that much of biblical scholarship cannot survive philosophical scrutiny, and bringing philosophical analysis to bear on biblical criticism will alter the historical conclusions that can be justified by that discipline.[49]

Stump's fundamentalism is not an isolated instance. Other prominent analytic Christian philosophers of religion, for all their philosophical sophistication, cling to similar hermeneutical assumptions. To be sure, these philosophers may wish to justify their conservatism by appealing to the implications of the development of postfoundationalism and anti-evidentialism in the epistemology of religion. However, the philosophical superstructure of complex philosophical arguments they use tends to be

---

48. Stump, "Modern Biblical Scholarship." See n. 1 above.
49. Ibid.

a smokescreen for the weakness of the biblical-theological base structure. This is particularly evident in the writings of Alvin Plantinga who, on the one hand, is perfectly capable of talking the talk of sophisticated philosophy. On the other hand, when Plantinga ventures across disciplinary lines in "When Faith and Reason Clash: Evolution and the Bible" (1991) and "Two (Or More) Kinds of Scripture Scholarship," his rhetoric is typical of the kind of fundamentalist discourse that brackets the problems grappled with over the last two centuries of biblical criticism:

> Scripture is inerrant: the Lord makes no mistakes; what He proposes for our belief is what we ought to believe. Scripture is a wholly authoritative and trustworthy guide to faith and morals. God is not required to make a case. The principal Author of the Bible—the entire Bible—is God himself, not so much a library of independent books as itself a book with many subdivisions but a central theme: the message of the gospel. "Interpret Scripture with Scripture." One can't always determine the meaning of a given passage just by discovering what the human author intended.[50]

These are the words of a philosopher of religion some consider the best of his generation. Yet there is nothing here in the way of critical historical consciousness or any trace of a real understanding of what critical biblical scholarship is actually all about.[51] Neither is there an understanding of the philosophical implications of literary and social-scientific criticism. As a result, all of Plantinga's philosophical concerns with the Hebrew Bible are susceptible to the critique James Barr presented when he discussed the "philosophical roots" and naïveté of lay fundamentalists in his book *Fundamentalism*.[52] Interestingly, Barr himself once referred to the collection of essays entitled *Hermes and Athena: Biblical Exegesis and Philosophical Theology*, pointing to some of the hermeneutical oddities therein.[53] How-

---

50. Alvin Plantinga, *Warranted Christian Belief* (New York: Oxford University Press, 2000), 385.

51. For additional evidence, see, for example, Alvin Plantinga, "Advice to Christian Philosophers," in *Christian Theism and the Problems of Philosophy* (ed. Michael D. Beaty; Notre Dame, Ind.: University of Notre Dame Press, 1990).

52. James Barr, *Fundamentalism* (London: SCM, 1977), 270–77.

53. Stump, Eleanore, and Thomas P. Flint, eds., *Hermes and Athena: Biblical Exegesis and Philosophical Theology* (Notre Dame: Notre Dame University Press, 1993). See Barr, *History and Ideology in the Old Testament*, 28.

ever, as its online blurb explains, this publication was focused more on New Testament studies:

> Intended as a pioneering venture in dialogue between the fields of contemporary philosophy of religion and biblical studies, this volume addresses many central issues: Christology, resurrection, miracles, moral development, authority, and the nature of historical-critical inquiry. Several essays engage overarching questions concerning the methodology of contemporary historically oriented biblical scholarship, the importance of such scholarship to ordinary believers, and the gradual acceptance of such scholarship within the Catholic Church. Other essays focus on particular topics, such as the empty tomb stories in the Gospels, the connection between knowledge and morality in the letter to the Colossians, and the place of miracles in Luke and the Acts.[54]

Whatever the hermeneutic aspects of the concern with the New Testament, a closer look into the way some analytic Christian philosophers of religion work with the biblical texts makes one wonder what would happen if they really took the findings of biblical criticism more seriously. Fundamentalism has also been a topic in philosophy of religion itself, as in the case of the Oxford expert on the subject, Harriet Harris.[55] But perhaps the best critical assessment of fundamentalism that is operative within philosophy of religion was offered by Michael Levine, when he pointed out that:

> Contemporary philosophy of religion now is, and for the past 30 years has been, dominated by the religious agendas of Christian conservatives. Far from "now becoming recognized once again as a mainstream philosophical discipline"—as a catalogue blurb (Philosophy 2000) announcing a new *Ashgate Series* in the philosophy of religion falsely proclaims—not only has mainstream philosophy long ignored such philosophy of religion, but so has the study of religion generally (e.g., biblical scholarship, theology and religious studies).[56]

---

54. This summary comes from the online reference at http://undpress.nd.edu/book/P00171.

55. See Harriet Harris, *Fundamentalism and Evangelicals* (Oxford: Oxford University Press, 2008).

56. Michael P. Levine, "Contemporary Christian Analytic Philosophy of Religion: Biblical Fundamentalism, Terrible Solutions to a Horrible Problem, and Hearing God," *IJPR* 48 (2000): 89.

Besides Eleanore Stump and Alvin Plantinga, well known fundamentalist philosophers of religion include William Lain Craig, Stephen T. Davis, John Frame, Norman Geisler, Richard Swinburne, Peter van Imwagen, Nicholas Wolterstorff, and many others. Their beliefs regarding the text/ reality relationship are often naive-realist, notwithstanding individual idiosyncrasies and varying degrees of dogmatism and hermeneutical sensitivity between them. In the end, for all their jargon and philosophical sophistication, these scholars' popular variety of philosophical theology's biblical hermeneutics is ultimately little more than "fundamentalism on stilts."[57]

Of course, fundamentalist Christian philosophers have their supposed epistemological justification to show that even when belief cannot be proven true, it is at least not totally irrational. But the real problem with this kind of Christian philosophy of religion is that it brackets the history of Israelite religion. Conservative philosophers show a general lack of appreciation of the major problems that twentieth-century Old Testament theology had to come to terms with: theological pluralism, history as a problematic locus of revelation, the anachronism of classical philosophical-theological categories, mythological parallels and comparative religion, the question of a *Mitte*, the absence of Jesus from all allegedly christological Old Testament discourse, evaluative versus descriptive ways of reading, and so on.

If this judgment sounds harsh, consider the ways in which some philosophers of religion still read the Hebrew Bible. Relatively recently, a conference took place at the University of Notre Dame. The the theme was: "My ways are not your ways: the character of the God of the Hebrew Bible." Unfortunately, as could be expected from an institution from which Plantinga and similar thinkers hail, the program schedule shows that many of the participants mistook philosophy of religion for conservative Christian apologetics:

Thursday, September 10, 2009:
Mike Rea: Welcome and Introduction
Louise Antony: Does God Love Us?

---

57. Jaco Gericke, "Fundamentalism on Stilts: A Response to Alvin Plantinga's Reformed Epistemology," *VE* 30/2 (2009): 1–5.

Friday, September 11, 2009:
Edwin Curley: The God of Abraham, Isaac, and Jacob
Evan Fales: Satanic Verses: Moral Chaos in Holy Writ
John Hare: Animal Sacrifices
Mark C. Murphy: God Beyond Justice
Eleonore Stump: The Problem of Evil and the History of Peoples:
     Think Amalek

Saturday, September 12, 2009:
Richard Swinburne: What does the Old Testament Mean?
Nicholas Wolterstorff: Reading Joshua
Gary Anderson: What about the Canaanites?
Christopher Seitz: Canon and Conquest: The Character of the
     God of the Hebrew Bible
Concluding Remarks: Howard Wettstein
Panel Discussion: Gary Anderson, Paul Draper, Daniel Howard-
     Snyder

The general idea behind an event such as this shows that philosophical reflection on the Hebrew Bible is not in principle considered impossible. There is no reason a conference on the Hebrew Bible cannot have a similarly philosophical albeit more historical section. The trouble, however, with looking to philosophers of religion for how this is to be done is that the same fundamentalism is evident all over the Anglo-Saxon world. This can be seen in many of the remarks related to the Hebrew Bible in *The Oxford Handbook of Philosophical Theology* or *Oxford Readings in Philosophical Theology.*[58] A quick look at the hermeneutical fallacies committed by contributors to these core texts will convince any mainstream biblical scholar that whatever philosophical competence might be possessed is rendered void by the lack of appreciation of the philosophical implications of biblical criticism.

Fundamentalism of a different sort is also present in the process philosophy of some neo-Thomists and evangelical Christian philosophers

---

58. See Stephen T. Davis, "Revelation and Inspiration," in *The Oxford Handbook of Philosophical Theology*, 30–53; Michael C. Rea, ed., *Providence, Scripture, and Resurrection* (vol. 2 of *Oxford Readings in Philosophical Theology*; 2 vols.; Oxford: Oxford University Press, 2009). Crypto-fundamentalist contributions are those of William Lane Craig, Richard Swinburne, and Nicholas Wolterstorff.

known as "open theists." The latter approach is a quasifundamentalist offshoot of process philosophy of religion (which tends to be more liberal), and its interest for us lies in the fact that it too is philosophy concerned with the Hebrew Bible. Open theism has been a significant topic in conservative philosophy of religion, for example in the writings of David Basinger, William Hasker, Clark Pinnock, Richard Rice, and John Sanders. Philosophers of religion such as Peter Geach, Richard Swinburne, and Richard Purtill also advocated open theism in their writings. [59]

In process philosophy of religion, the Hebrew Bible is once again read without adequate attention to theological pluralism or heterodoxy, and features mainly as a source for *dicta probanta*. While the philosophers are willing to admit the presence of texts that contradict classical theist orthodoxy, their philosophical readings of the Hebrew Bible are simply the other side of Calvinist fundamentalism—in that they seek to harmonize everything in the opposite direction. In addition, while they accept the fact that texts assume cognitive limitations on the part of Yhwh, process philosophy of religion in the form of open theism seems blissfully ignorant of the dark side of the deity in relation to the actualization of evil and the frequent overriding of human free will.

An altogether different, yet still somewhat hermeneutically suspect, interest in the Hebrew Bible is found in the work of Continental philosophers of religion. There had been some tension between them and the fundamentalist analytic philosophers discussed above, as is evidenced in a debate that took place between 1989 and 1995 in the journal *Faith and Philosophy*, initiated by the liberal theologian Gordon Kaufman. The topic for discussion was whether theologians should take any notice of, or show any interest in, the work of philosophers of religion such as Plantinga, Wolterstorff and Swinburne. The latter philosophers were criticized for simply presupposing traditional theistic conceptions and formulations; and for lacking sensitivity to the significance of religious pluralism, and to the symbolic and culturally relative nature of all talk about the mystery of deity.[60]

Whatever we make of this critique, Continental philosophy of religion does seem to exhibit greater historical consciousness than is displayed in many analytic approaches. Yet the biblical scholar will note that this is

---

59. From the philosophical overview by James Rissler, "Open Theism," *IEP* [cited 10 February 2010]. Online: http://www.iep.utm.edu/.

60. See Brian Hebblethwaite, *Philosophical Theology and Christian Doctrine* (Oxford: Wiley-Blackwell, 2005), 3.

often coupled with curious generalizations about conceptions of Yhwh in the texts. There appear to operate both an overly optimistic selectiveness in what counts as relevant god-talk and a repression of unbelief in the wake of the collapse of realism in biblical theology. On the one hand, Continental philosophers seem to know that there are serious differences between the stereotypical God of the Philosophers and the God of Abraham, Isaac, and Jacob; and that Yhwh does not fit into the Perfect Being Theology of classical theism, something which analytic philosophers of religion often seem to forget (or do not wish to know).

As John Caputo wrote:

> That very finite Hellenistic creature called "God" is a being cut to fit the narrow needs of Greek ontology, of Parmenides and Plato, who were scandalized by time and motion and change, and of Aristotle, who did the best he could to make the name of matter and motion respectable among the Greeks. But from a biblical point of view, this highly Hellenic *theos* was an imperfect—may I say a pathetic, or better an apathetic?—way to think of God. It had nothing to do with Yahweh who was easily moved to anger and jealousy, who was a God of tears and compassion, who suffered with his suffering people, who was moved by their sighs and lamentations, who was angered by their meanness of mind and had a well-known and much respected temper, who had, in short, a short fuse.[61]

Often liberal systematic theologians, many Continental philosophers of religion tend to work in ways that are essentially reconstructive. With reference to the Hebrew Bible some repression and selectiveness is clearly evident. In the end many of them like to think of God as love, thereby taking leave of the dystheistic elements in the conceptions of Yhwh in ancient Israel. A good example here—with which Hebrew Bible scholars will be very familiar—is that of Paul Ricœur in his role as philosopher of religion. To be sure, philosophy of religion was not Ricœur's only interest. He did not limit himself to the Hebrew Bible, and his work is popular in the areas of Hebrew Bible hermeneutics, narrative theory, the role of the imagination, the prevalence of metaphor, and the second naiveté rather than for the phenomenological-type philosophy of religion with which he read a number of biblical texts. Nevertheless, Ricœur treated the Hebrew

---

61. John D. Caputo, *The Prayers and Tears of Jacques Derrida: Religion without Religion* (Bloomington: Indiana University Press, 1997), 336.

Bible in many of his writings before his death in 2005. One example is his treatment of characters like Adam and Job in his *Symbolism of Evil*.[62]

An even better example is *Thinking Biblically: Exegetical and Hermeneutical Studies*, written with André LaCocque and originally published in 1997.[63] In this study the authors try to show that the Hebrew Bible consists of vibrant, philosophically consequential, and unceasingly absorbing discourse. They know very well that philosophy brings concepts, arguments, and theories that were forged outside the biblical field of thought. Yet this does not stop them from undertaking philosophical readings and the volume takes the form of parallel essays on what they call "strong texts": Gen 2–3, Ps 22 ("My God, my God, why have you forsaken me?"), the Song of Songs, Exod 3:14 ("God said to Moses, "I am who I am"), the story of Joseph in Gen 44, and others. In doing so Ricœur assumes that the subsequent history of the biblical text within Jewish and Christian traditions should be a factor in its interpretation. Because Ricœur's agenda is ultimately Christian, canonical (i.e., panbiblical, also involving the New Testament), and normative, he uses revamped bits from the Hebrew Bible for contemporary philosophy of religion rather than philosophy of religion for the historical clarification of ancient Israelite religion.[64]

A second Continental philosopher whose work has some bearing on the Hebrew Bible is Emmanuel Levinas.[65] As in the case of Ricœur, some circles in biblical scholarship have taken a shine to Levinas for his new ways of looking at the Hebrew Bible. This is unsurprising given the unlikely

---

62. Paul Ricœur, *Symbolism of Evil* (trans. Emerson Buchanan; New York: Harper & Row, 1967).

63. André LaCocque and Paul Ricœur, *Thinking Biblically: Exegetical and Hermeneutical Studies* (trans. David Pellauer; Chicago: University of Chicago Press, 2003).

64. See the assessment by Kevin Vanhoozer, *Biblical Narrative in The Philosophy of Paul Ricœur: A Study in Theology and Hermeneutics* (New York: Cambridge University Press, 1990). The third section of Carsten Pallesen's "Philosophy of Reflection and Biblical Revelation in Paul Ricœur," in *ST* 62/1 (2008): 44–62, examines the antagonism between natural and revealed theology that marks the range and limits of Ricœur's hermeneutic philosophy. It is argued that the kind of dependency or heteronomy implied in religion, especially in the biblical idea of the absolute as an external truth event, presents a genuine challenge to both phenomenology and hermeneutics, and that this problem is addressed in Ricœur's theories of revelation and testimony.

65. Levinas is included in Long's discussion in his *Twentieth Century Philosophy of Religion*, 440.

match between philosophy and ancient Israelite religion in his work.[66] He too was not exclusively a philosopher of religion, and the tension between the Hebrew Bible and Western philosophy in his work resulted in a distinction between his writings on philosophy and his texts on Judaism. Still, one cannot read much of his work without encountering direct and indirect allusions to the biblical materials.

Writing as a philosopher, Levinas rejected Pascal's distinction between the God of Abraham, Isaac, and Jacob, and the God of the philosophers. According to Levinas, philosophical discourse should be able to include the Yhwh of whom the Hebrew Bible speaks. He argues that what biblical theologians refer to as Greek as opposed to Hebrew mentality is recommended by the biblical texts themselves.[67] He believes—somewhat anachronistically—that the God of Israel was assumed to be transcendent and beyond the language and thinking of being. Levinas also seems more interested in reinterpreting the biblical traditions for the sake of constructing a contemporary philosophical perspective than in using philosophy descriptively for a better historical understanding of the Hebrew Bible from a purely descriptive perspective. His concern is therefore not limited to the Hebrew Bible for its own sake. Like other Jewish philosophers, he seeks to go beyond it to include talmudic and later Jewish philosophical traditions.

Our next example of a philosopher of religion in the Continental tradition with connections to the Hebrew Bible is Jean-Luc Marion. In *God without Being*, Marion challenges the tradition of metaphysical theology and claims that God must no longer be thought of in terms of the traditional category of Being. Marion introduces the concepts of the idol and the icon—which are two modes of apprehending the divine in reality. The distinction is highly reminiscent of Barth's distinction between reason and revelation. According to Marion, the idol and the icon belong to two distinct and competing historical movements. The idol is negative and Greek

---

66. See Tamara Cohn Eskenazi, Gary Allen Phillips, and David Jobling, eds., *Levinas and Biblical Studies* (SemeiaSt 43; Atlanta: Society of Biblical Literature, 2003). This volume is the first in English to show how Levinas's ideas can also transform the ways in which we read biblical texts. The essays collected here introduce Levinas to those not familiar with his work and exemplify how his approach to texts illuminates new and significant possibilities for reading the Bible afresh.

67. See Claire E. Katz and Lara Trout, *Emmanuel Levinas and The Question of Religion* (London: Routledge, 2005), 1, 121–52.

(philosophical) while the icon is positive and Hebraic (biblical). Marion thus invokes the old Hebrew–Greek distinction, somewhat differently from Levinas and more in the current of the older illusionary binary opposition between Hebrew and Greek thinking that privileges the Hebraic. In short, like Levinas before him, Marion was not so much interested in a philosophical clarification of ancient Israelite religion as in the use of motifs derived from it on the way to a more normative and constructive contemporary philosophy of religion.[68]

Next to be mentioned is the Cambridge philosopher of religion, Don Cupitt. Though not so much concerned with ancient Israelite religion for its own sake, in several contexts Cupitt reads the Hebrew Bible in a very creative manner for the sake of producing a contemporary philosophy of religion. In doing so, he often combines philosophical and historical modes of interpretation. In *Sea of Faith*, for example, he provides a brief philosophical summary of the Hebrew Bible's worldview.[69] In *After God: The Future of Religion*, Cupitt combines the history of Israelite religion with philosophy of religion in remarks such as the following:

> As we see in the Hebrew Bible ... the dispute with God becomes the classic arena in which selfhood is elaborated and human subjectivity is produced. Nowhere else do we find such psychological riches. The psalmist moves from ecstatic adoration to bitter reproach to penitent submission and then to joy and gratitude. Prayer was the classic method of investigating and exercising the self, opening speculative thought and stretching the soul, and the relationship to God thus developed became a resource utilized in the construction of many other human relationships.[70]

Cupitt is one of the few philosophers of religion who actually takes cognizance of the theological pluralism and diachronic diversity in ancient Israelite religion:

> And Nietzsche was right to describe the Hebrew Bible as the best book in the world, because it is the book of the one religion that above all others

---

68. Jean-Luc Marion, *God without Being* (Chicago: University of Chicago Press, 1991), 16. For the source of this summary see Long, *Twentieth-Century Western Philosophy of Religion*, 447–50.

69. Don Cupitt, *Sea of Faith* (London: SCM, 1984), 61–64.

70. Don Cupitt, *After God: The Future of Religion* (London: Basic Books, 1997), 32.

is not just a system of worship but something far greater—an argument with itself.[71]

What is most refreshing is Cupitt's refusal to panel-beat the God of the Bible to conform to the "perfect being" theology of analytic Christian philosophy of religion. At one point Cupitt poignantly remarks on Harold Bloom's view regarding the nature of Yhwh in a way that shows one can describe the text in philosophical terms without bracketing the history of religion or explaining away conceptual heterodoxy:

> This God, the Yahweh of the J writer in the Hebrew Bible, is … like a powerful uncanny male child, a sublime mischief maker, impish and difficult. He resembles Lear and the Freudian superego in being a demonic and persecuting father; entirely lacking in self-knowledge and unwilling to ever learn anything. Like the human characters he interacts with, he has a continually changing consciousness. He manifests the pure energy and force of becoming. He is Nietzschian will-to-power, abrupt and uncontrollable, subject to nothing and nobody.[72]

Aside from this, Cupitt frequently remarks on various interesting aspects in the text from a philosophical perspective, even though it is never his exclusive concern but merely part of his argument concerning something else. One thinks of his discernment of nonrealist tendencies in ancient Israelite tradition history.[73] In one discussion, Cupitt writes regarding the philosophical implications of biblical criticism for how we think of ancient Israelite god-talk in the biblical text, "The Old Testament can now be seen as profoundly voluntaristic and expressive in its use of religious language."[74]

Among other things, Cupitt has also written on fictionalism in biblical narrative art;[75] the folk philosophy of language implicit in Gen 1–3 (and the creation myths' "discursive idealism" as mythological truth about the language/reality relation);[76] traces of Greek dualist metaphysi-

---

71. Ibid., 42–43.

72. Don Cupitt, *Sea of Faith* (3rd ed.; London: SCM, 2003), 247.

73. Don Cupitt, *Taking Leave of God* (London: SCM, 1980), which offers a philosophical reflection on the denial of sacrificial tradition in Amos 5:25 and Jer 7:33.

74. Cupitt, *After God*, 36.

75. Don Cupitt, *What's a Story?* (London: SCM, 1991).

76. Don Cupitt, *Philosophy's Own Religion*, 65–67, 103, and *passim*.

cal assumptions;[77] the concept of generic divinity; the politics of wisdom literature; and the folk psychology of the psalms. In his later writings, he came to rely much on the biblical scholar Thomas L. Thompson's fiction-alist approach; and in the end was interested in providing a postmodern theory of religion in general, in which reflections on ancient Israelite reli-gion featured relatively marginally.

Another figure is Keith Ward, who comfortably straddles the analytic-Continental divide with his phenomenological, historical and compara-tive approach to philosophy of religion. Ward has written a number of philosophical discussions of aspects of ancient Israelite religion; and his reflections on Judaism vis-à-vis other faiths include descriptive philosoph-ical treatments of the Hebrew Bible's concepts of "revelation," "creation," "human nature," and "God."[78] He recognizes the gap in research when it comes to a philosophical perspective on ancient Israelite religion for its own sake:

> *There is need for a philosophical account of the nature of this God*, which might clarify the way in which other peoples might relate to him, or come to understand what he is. There is no such account in the Bible itself, which confines itself to revelations given to the patriarchs and prophets of Israel. Both the Upanishads and the Buddhist Pali Canon contain sections which may fairly be regarded as philosophical or doc-trinal, exploring views of the nature of ultimate reality in a reflective and meditative way. In the Old Testament there are virtually no passages of that sort. *Philosophical* reflection on the nature of Jahweh, the god of Abraham, Isaac and Jacob is almost entirely absent. It is accordingly very difficult to know what the Hebrews thought about God; that is, how they themselves interpreted the words they used about God. I rather suspect

---

77. Don Cupitt, *Jesus and Philosophy* (London: SCM, 2009). The inner/outer dis-tinction in 1 Sam 16:7 ("But Yahweh [God] said to Samuel, 'Do not look on one's appearance or on the height of one's stature ... for I do not see as mortals see. They look on the outward appearance, but I look on the heart.' ") is said to be "Platonic." Another example that comes to mind is the idea of Moses making the tabernacle according to a blueprint from heaven (see Exod 25–40). However, prior to Plato many ancient Near Eastern myths already contained notions of heavenly counterparts to earthly things, and it is therefore impossible to say with certainty that any given instance of dualism in biblical metaphysics was derived from Platonic ontology.

78. See the relevant chapters in Ward, *Religion and Revelation*, 111–33; *Religion and Creation* (Oxford: Oxford University Press, 1996), 3–36; *Religion and Human Nature* (Oxford: Oxford University Press, 1998), 159–85; *Concepts of God*, 81–98.

they thought as many different things about God as different philosophers do. But we do have enough material to construct a fairly clear idea of the Biblical God, though its interpretation cannot be decisively established.[79]

Note that the absence of a philosophical account of Yhwh in the biblical texts, far from being seen as providing any sort of rationale for avoiding philosophical reflection, is in fact implied to be precisely the reason why it is so sorely needed. Working with phenomenological and comparative concerns, Ward's writings are more historically conscious than those of many purely analytic philosophers of religion. Yet even for Ward, whose writings at times come very near to a descriptive philosophical reading of biblical texts, the Hebrew Bible is not his sole concern, and he remains a Christian philosopher of religion. Biblical scholars, however, might well look to Ward's work to see how traces of a descriptive philosophical approach to Israelite religion might look when combined with a sense of humor, self-critical acumen, and creativity, all of which make the analysis easy to follow and always a pleasure to read, even when one disagrees with him.

Our next example on the Continental side is the work of Merold Westphal, who specializes in post-Kantian philosophy, and has often concerned himself with issues that are at home in the philosophy of religion. In his discussion of philosophers such as Kant and Kierkergaard, Westphal has not hesitated to comment in philosophical terms on elements in Israelite religion in the Hebrew Bible that are currently relevant.[80] His approach to the text commonly adopts a phenomenological perspective in the form of a descriptive type of philosophy of religion. Like that of the other philosophers of religion discussed, Westphal's concern with ancient Israelite religion is still relatively marginal and never purely descriptive or historical in orientation. Yet his work also suggests that the Hebrew Bible and its contents can be philosophically interesting, and that if one does it properly there can be no hermeneutical objections to a philosophical account of the text's beliefs and practices.

---

79. Ward, *Concepts of God*, 81–82, emphases added.

80. See especially the relevant sections in Merold Westphal, *God, Guilt, and Death: An Existential Phenomenology of Religion* (Studies in Phenomenology and Existential Philosophy; Bloomington: Indiana University Press, 1984), 107–13, 122–28, 226–31; and in his *Kierkegaard's Critique of Reason and Society* (Macon, Ga.: Mercer University Press, 1987), 62–85.

Other examples of philosophical interest in the Hebrew Bible exist. There are mainstream Continental philosophers who do not specialize in religion but who do touch on the Hebrew Bible from time to time. Names such as Jacques Derrida (on the secret of Abraham, the hospitality of Elijah) and Slavoj Žižek (e.g., on Moses and on God in the Book of Job) come to mind. In addition to these individual philosophers, a specific variety of the Continental habit is also evident in some German introductions to philosophy of religion that include a historical precursor to the philosophical discussion proper. These usually feature a section that shows the ancient Near Eastern background to philosophical thought about religion.

One example is Hermann Deuser's *Religionsphilosophie*, which contains a chapter entitled "Biblische, antike und scholastische Tradition."[81] As is common in this kind of historical background, the concern is not so much a philosophical account of ancient Israelite religion as a historical discussion of how the Hebrew Bible represents a turn away from myth and a philosophy of history; and of how ideas of monotheism and critical wisdom prefigure a number of later Greek philosophical ideas. In Deuser's publication, for example, Deuteronomistic and Joban theology are touched on and compared with related ideas elsewhere (e.g., Job with Socratic dialogue). The author, rather than offering a philosophical description, is satisfied with repeating the ideas of biblical scholars (von Rad, Otto Kaiser). No more than twelve pages are devoted to the biblical context before the author moves on to more interesting materials from Western philosophy.

Finally, over the last decade, attempts at interdisciplinary engagement can be found in the recent *Journal of Philosophy and Scripture,* an electronic journal edited by graduate students in philosophy at Villanova University:

> *The Journal of Philosophy and Scripture* is an e-journal dedicated to reading scripture in light of philosophy and to examining philosophy in light of scripture. The Journal's task is informed by three primary aims: (1) to encourage philosophical discussions of religion to attend to the primary sacred texts (e.g., the Bible, the Qur'an, the Bhagavad-Gita) that fundamentally shape the religions under discussion, (2) to encourage a process of mutual reflection by means of which both philosophy and scripture may be more clearly illuminated, and (3) to do the above

---

81. Herman Deuser, *Religionsphilosophie* (Berlin: de Gruyter, 2008), 56–62, 75–82.

with a keen eye to possible effects on the ways in which we practice philosophy and religion.[82]

The journal has since ceased publication. It had a Continental flavor, and while it is not exclusively devoted to the Hebrew Bible and Israelite religion, it may be noted as an example of the ways in which philosophers have shown a concern for establishing links for the purpose of interdisciplinary research.

A final genre in which Israelite religion appears in philosophical writings is the history of Western philosophy. Good examples are the relevant sections in Bertrand Russell's *History of Western Philosophy* or, more recently, Richard Tarnas' *Passion of the Western Mind*.[83] To be precise, the genre usually features a short overview of the history of Israelite religion and certain ideas therein, presented with the aid of philosophical terms. This is typically given as part of the background for a discussion of the relationship between philosophy and Christianity. Alternatively it is found when Greek philosophical thought is distinguished from the mythic period before it. Thus the Hebrew Bible and its elements also feature as part of a historical introduction to certain problems in Christian philosophy of religion, such as divine command ethics.

4.3. Conclusion

In this chapter it was shown that Christian philosophers of religion do at times have recourse to the Hebrew Bible. No generalization is possible, since the role the texts play in the writings of both analytic and Continental philosophers varies in relation to the ideological concerns of the author in question. In relatively recent times many significant scholars on the analytic side of the divide have exhibited marked traces of fundamentalist hermeneutics (Plantinga, Craig). On the other side, when they involve the biblical materials at all, Continental traditions have tended to be strangely selective if interestingly overly optimistic (Caputo, Ricœur, Levinas). In some cases, interesting perspectives on the text have been provided that

---

82. James Wetzel (editorial adviser), *Journal of Philosophy and Scripture* [cited 10 April 2010]. Online: http://www.philosophyandscripture.org/index.html

83. Bertrand Russell, *History of Western Philosophy* (rev. ed.; London: Allan & Unwin, 1961), 311–24; Richard Tarnas, *The Passion of the Western Mind: Understanding the Ideas that Have Shaped Our World View* (New York: Ballantine, 1991), 91–170.

biblical scholars might themselves need to engage with (Ward, Cupitt, Ricœur, Westphal, Deleuze, and Guattari). They are united in being more interested in looking to the Hebrew Bible as a background to discussions in contemporary philosophy of religion, than in using descriptive philosophy of religion to clarify the concepts, beliefs and practices of ancient Israelite religion for its own sake.

Whatever one may think of this state of affairs, Hebrew Bible scholars interested in a philosophical approach and in more extensive interdisciplinary relations should take cognizance of what philosophers of religion have done with, and to, the text. If the metaphilosophical assessment of this chapter seems evaluative, it is because this is indeed the case. My concern with a purely descriptive philosophy of religion only pertains to the methodology I wish to develop for the study of ancient Israelite religion, not to the discussion of ideological trends in contemporary philosophy of religion. Hence I point out where I think philosophers distort the contents of the biblical texts.

It is now time to consider which currents in philosophy of religion might actually be of use to the exegete of the Hebrew Bible seeking to work both historically and philosophically in the quest for a better understanding of the concepts, beliefs and practices of ancient Israelite religion.

5

DESCRIPTIVE CURRENTS IN PHILOSOPHY OF
RELIGION FOR HEBREW BIBLE STUDIES*

The philosophy of religion is not necessarily or absolutely linked with natural theology. For example, one might pursue a philosophical approach to religion while denying natural theology altogether.[1]

5.1. INTRODUCTION

Biblical scholarship is for the most part a historical and descriptive enterprise. Stereotypically, philosophy is thought to be evaluative. However, descriptive varieties of philosophy of religion do exist and some of their methods can be used for the clarification of concepts, beliefs, and practices in ancient nonphilosophical religions. In other words, there are subcurrents on both sides of the analytic-Continental divide that, when adopted and adapted through a shrewd bit of "theological engineering," offer the biblical scholar hermeneutically legitimate forms of philosophical analysis. In this chapter we take a closer look at those philosophical traditions.

5.2. THREE DESCRIPTIVE PHILOSOPHICAL CURRENTS

Descriptive or elucidative philosophy is different from theoretical or therapeutic philosophy.[2] Three currents in particular come to mind:

---

* This chapter represents a extension of the general ideas of my article "Descriptive Currents in Philosophy of Religion for Hebrew Bible Studies," *HTS Teologiese Studies/Theological Studies* 67.3 (2011). Online: http://www.hts.org.za/index.php/ HTS/article/view/855.

1. Barr, *Biblical Faith and Natural Theology*, 3.

2. On descriptive philosophy, see Daniel Hutto, "Philosophical Clarification: Its Possibility and Point," *Philosophia* 37 (2009): 629–52.

1. *Analytic traditions* of the type concerned with conceptual clarification (allowing one to work descriptively with nonphilosophical materials);
2. *Phenomenological approaches* and the method of *reduction* (bracketing), which allow for a descriptive type of philosophy of religion (allowing one to work historically without the need for justification or critique); and
3. *Comparative philosophy*, which is able to deal with non-Western conceptual frameworks and is comfortable with religious pluralism (allowing one to deal with the multiplex nature of the Hebrew Bible through the use of extrabiblical concepts and categories).

5.2.1. ANALYTIC TRADITIONS

If we look at what many analytic Christian philosophers of religion are involved in—Christian apologetics of the fundamentalist variety—one cannot imagine that analytic philosophy could be of much use for biblical interpretation. Yet not all analytic philosophy is of that sort:

> Although there are many similarities in methodology, interests, emphases, and results among various philosophers who are commonly regarded as belonging within the analytic tradition, analytic philosophy is not and has never been monolithic. There are also widespread and significant differences among analytic philosophers concerning their methodology, interests, emphases, and results. In all, analytic philosophy is a very heterogeneous "movement." Although there are some common themes, there is also much variety among analytic philosophers in their fundamental philosophical commitments and positions as there has been among idealists or realists or theologians; consequently, it is misleading to talk about "analytic philosophy" as a single movement in philosophy without recognizing the significant differences among analytic philosophers.[3]

In its narrower sense, "analytic philosophy" is often used to refer to a specific philosophical program that is ordinarily

---

3. Harris, *Analytic Philosophy of Religion*, 3.

dated from about 1900 to 1960, and commenced with the work of English philosophers Bertrand Russell and George E. Moore in the early
twentieth century. They turned away from dominant forms of Hegelian-
ism (objecting in particular to its idealism and purported obscurity) and
began to develop a new sort of conceptual analysis, based on new developments in logic.[4]

Furthermore,

> Today analytic philosophy (sometimes called "analytical" philosophy)
> has become a generic term for a style of philosophy that came to domi-
> nate English-speaking countries in the twentieth century. In the United
> States, United Kingdom, Canada, Scandinavia, Australia, and New Zea-
> land, the overwhelming majority of university philosophy departments
> identify themselves as "analytic" departments.[5]

Initially analytic philosophy of religion was closely associated with
positivism. "Positivism" may be a pejorative term in biblical scholarship,
but it involves the useful realization that even in philosophy *the question
of meaning is epistemologically more fundamental than, and prior to, the
question of truth*. This insight formed part of what Gilbert Ryle called "the
revolution in philosophy"[6] and Richard Rorty regarded as "the linguistic
turn"[7] heralding the "age of analysis."[8] This had implications not only for
conceptions of philosophy in general but also for how one viewed the task
of philosophy of religion as such. The clarification of meaning has become
a necessary philosophical endeavor, and the analytic philosophy of religion is not limited to propositional justification and critical evaluation of
religious truth claims.

At midcentury Western analytic philosophy of religion appeared to
be gasping for breath. The logical positivists and the positivists of revela-

---

4. "Contemporary Philosophy," *Wikipedia, The Free Encyclopedia* [cited 12 July
2010]. Online: http://en.wikipedia.org/w/index.php?title=Contemporary_philo-sophy
&oldid=501804754.

5. "Analytic Philosophy," *Wikipedia, The Free Encyclopedia* [cited 3 August
2012]. Online: http://en.wikipedia.org/w/index.php?title=Analytic_philosophy&oldid
=502358950.

6. See Gilbert Ryle, *The Revolution in Philosophy* (London: Macmillan, 1957).

7. See Richard Rorty, *The Linguistic Turn: Essays in Philosophical Method* (Chicago: University of Chicago Press, 1992).

8. See Morton White, *The Age of Analysis* (New York: Mentor Books, 1955).

tion cooperated in challenging the legitimacy of natural theology and the philosophy of religion. Soon after, however, new approaches in philosophy with roots in the early twentieth century began to flourish, leading to renewed interest in philosophy of religion. Neo-Thomists and process philosophers breathed new life into metaphysics, and analytic and existential philosophers opened up new avenues for philosophical reflection on the meaning and truth of god-talk. These discussions often reflected an empirical and historical mindset that was quietly calling into question the classical foundations of Western philosophy and philosophy of religion. The last quarter of the century saw the blossoming of this empirical and historical approach, and an accompanying enormous change of climate in philosophical reflection on religion. The period has been characterized by pluralism in human experience and diversity in philosophical method. It is a period in which many of the traditional foundations and methods of philosophy of religion have been called into question.[9]

Biblical scholars who are heirs of the Biblical Theology Movement's aversion towards philosophy have missed this revolution and do not realize that analytic philosophy of religion now offers descriptive methods of philosophical analysis. Especially relevant for biblical scholars are those perspectives in analytic philosophy that sought to reject sweeping philosophical systems in favor of close attention to detail, common sense, and ordinary language.[10] A classic example of this view is found in the earlier Ludwig Wittgenstein, who wrote in his *Tractatus Logico-Philosophicus* that:

> Philosophy aims at the logical clarification of thoughts. Philosophy is not a body of doctrine but an activity. A philosophical work consists essentially of elucidations. Philosophy does not result in "philosophical propositions," but rather in the clarification of propositions. Without philosophy thoughts are, as it were, cloudy and indistinct: its task is to make them clear and to give them sharp boundaries.[11]

---

9. See Eugene T. Long's HCPR outline in James Harris, *Analytic Philosophy of Religion*, vi.

10. For an introduction to this philosophical current and its role in philosophy of religion, see the collection of essays in Harriet Harris and Christopher Insole, eds., *Faith and Philosophical Analysis: The Impact of Analytical Philosophy on Philosophy of Religion* (London: Ashgate, 2005).

11. See Ludwig Wittgenstein, *Tractatus Logico-Philosophicus* (trans. Gertrude Elizabeth Margaret Anscombe; New York: Wiley-Blackwell, 2001), 51.

I am not claiming that Wittgenstein is correct here—only that his view is useful in that it allows biblical scholars to utilize philosophy descriptively in a hermeneutically legitimate manner. There is no need for a philosophical approach to justify or criticize biblical truth claims or to harmonize the pluralism of ancient Israelite religion. One can also limit the aim to the understanding and elucidation of what is there. The "later" Wittgenstein further elaborated on the descriptive task in his *Philosophical Investigations* as follows:

> A philosophical problem has the form, "I don't know my way about." Philosophy may in no way interfere with the actual use of language; it can in the end only describe it. For it cannot give it any foundation either. It leaves everything as it is.[12]

The clear insistence on taking account of the contexts and practice in life of what we say has been enormously influential on the philosophy of religion. Yet our interest is not identical to Wittgenstein's agenda, which sought to make metaphysical problems disappear. Instead, what is interesting in Wittgenstein from the perspective of biblical scholarship is simply the idea that philosophy can concern itself with the clarification of concepts. One example of this in the context of philosophy of religion is in Wittgenstein's response to James Frazer's *The Golden Bough*. Wittgenstein suggested that magic rituals were not to be understood anachronistically as useless and superstitious primitive science. Rather, he argued, one should attempt to show the ways in which ideas made sense in their sociohistorical context (as part of what he calls "forms of life" or "language games"). One can also show how remnants of such ways of looking at the world survive even in today's scientific worldviews.

A philosophical approach to ancient Israelite religion might learn from Wittgenstein's critique of Frazer. Not for the sake of attempting to salvage the alleged credibility of Hebraic cultic rituals, but inasmuch as Wittgenstein's approach offers us the opportunity to do philosophy while concerning ourselves solely with understanding their meaning against the backdrop of their use in particular contextual conceptual backgrounds:

> The proper aim of anthropology and religious studies should be description, to understand and describe the fundamental concept functionality,

---

12. Ludwig Wittgenstein, *Philosophical Investigations*, 42.

the metaphysical properties, of a specific ritual language game by observing the thought and activity of ritual practitioners. The aim should be to provide Wittgenstein's *übersicht*, to provide a perspicuous presentation of what goes on and why, to prevent Frazer's kind of confusion and mischaracterization regarding the elements of ritual activity.[13]

Much attention is given to the "how" of belief, and not only to the "what" that is believed. The way in which the ancients believed in Yhwh is surely as important as, or even determinative of, how we understand the contents of their beliefs. Ultimately, Wittgensteinianism's relation to contemporary analytic philosophy of religion is itself a complex matter, especially when it comes to the relation with analytic philosophy of religion. The use of "analytic" in this context is not the same as in the label used for the Cambridge and Oxford movements that Wittgenstein influenced. Whereas those movements were antimetaphysical, contemporary analytic philosophy of religion tends too often to take metaphysical realism for granted. Analytic debates about religion in the early days involved both believers and nonbelievers among leading philosophers. Wittgenstein's methods are therefore not central in analytic philosophy of religion today, even if he is associated with this current.[14]

A second cluster of analytic approaches that allow us to give more substance to what we borrow from the analytic traditions comes from a time somewhat later than Wittgenstein's heyday. After the First World War, in the late 1940s and the 1950s, analytic philosophy took a turn towards ordinary-language analysis. This movement followed in the wake of Wittgenstein's later philosophy, which had departed dramatically from his earlier work. In contrast to earlier analytic philosophers (including the early Wittgenstein), ordinary language philosophy emphasizes the use of language by people in nonphilosophical contexts and therefore has more of a sociological grounding.

The influence of the later Wittgenstein pushed common discourse front stage, and ordinary language philosophy pushed earlier analytic formality into the wilderness. The focus came to be on the elimination of confusions that sometimes arise. The diversity of language was

---

13. Felicia DeSmith, "Frazer, Wittgenstein and the Interpretation of Religious Practice," *Macalester Journal of Philosophy* 14 (2005): 58–73.

14. See Dewi Zephaniah Phillips, "Wittgensteinianism: Logic, Reality and God," in Wainwright, *Oxford Handbook of Philosophy of Religion*, 448.

emphasized, and language was shown to have purposes other than that of describing reality. Philosophy was no longer assumed to be special, and philosophers were no longer seen as obliged to deliver a priori or analytic truths, which came to be regarded with suspicion. Systematic theories were no longer needed.[15]

One of the most prominent ordinary language philosophers of the 1950s was Gilbert Ryle, who made the following interesting remark pertaining to the possibility of descriptive philosophy:

> Philosophy must then involve the exercise of systematic restatement. But this does not mean that it is a department of philology or literary criticism. Its restatement is not the substitution of one noun for another or one verb for another. That is what lexicographers and translators excel in. Its restatements are transmutations of syntax, and transmutations of syntax controlled not by desire for elegance or stylistic correctness but by desire to exhibit the forms of the facts into which philosophy is the enquiry.[16]

On Ryle's account, a good analogy for the task of the descriptive philosopher comes from cartography. Competent speakers of language such as the ancient Israelites are to a philosopher what an ordinary villager is to a mapmaker:

> A local villager knows his way by wont and without reflection to the village church, to the town hall, to the shops and back home again from the personal point of view of one who lives there. But, asked to draw or to consult a map of his village, he is faced with learning a new and different sort of task: one that employs compass bearing and units of measurement. What was first understood in the personal terms of local snapshots now has to be considered in the completely general terms of the cartographer. The villager's knowledge by wont, enabling him to lead a stranger from place to place, is a different skill from one requiring him to tell the stranger, in perfectly general and neutral terms, how to get to

---

15. Roger B. Jones, "Varieties of Philosophical Analysis," *History of Philosophy Overview* [cited 12 May 2009]. Online: http://www.rbjones.com/rbjpub/philos/history/his003.htm.

16. Gilbert Ryle, "Systematically Misleading Expressions," in Rorty, *The Linguistic Turn*, 85–100.

any of the places, or indeed, how to understand these places in relation to those of other villages.[17]

Moreover,

> The ordinary villager has a competent grasp of his village and is familiar with its inhabitants and geography. However, when asked to consult a map relating to the same knowledge he has practically, the villager will have difficulty until he is able to translate his practical knowledge into universal cartographic terms. The villager thinks of the village in personal and practical terms while the mapmaker thinks of the village in neutral, public, cartographic terms. By "mapping" the words and phrases of a particular statement, philosophers are able to generate what Ryle calls "implication threads." In other words, each word or phrase of a statement contributes to the statement in the sense that, if the words or phrases were changed, the statement would have a different implication. The philosopher must show the directions and limits of different implication threads that a "concept contributes to the statements in which it occurs." To show this, one must "tug" at neighboring threads, which, in turn, will also be "tugging." Philosophy, then, searches for the meaning of these implication threads in the statements in which they are used.[18]

As biblical scholars, we are not concerned to assess whether this is the correct way of doing philosophy. We only note that ordinary language philosophy can offer a useful analogy for a philosophical method or approach capable of dealing with the nonphilosophical language of the Hebrew Bible. One philosopher of religion who recognized how ordinary language contains all the data needed to discover the philosophical assumptions of people who themselves are not particularly philosophical is Don Cupitt. In a little book called *The New Religion of Life in Everyday Speech*, Cupitt—who is actually more Continental than analytic—discerned philosophy of religion within ordinary language and picked out all the phrases people use that are religiously or philosophically important and interesting. Taking stock of his own related work, Cupitt explains

---

17. Julia Tanney, "Gilbert Ryle," *SEP* [cited 16 March 2010]. Online: http://plato.stanford.edu/archives/win2009/entries/ryle/.

18. "Gilbert Ryle," *Wikipedia, The Free Encyclopedia* [cited 13 July 2010]. Online: http://en.wikipedia.org/w/index.php?title=Gilbert_Ryle&oldid=501683042.

how his philosophical analysis of ordinary language can help us better to understand religious beliefs:

> I decided to take up an idea from Wittgenstein and try to find out what philosophical and religious ideas belong to us all because they are built into the ordinary language that we all share.... Taking up the phrases that are the most provocative and that incorporate the boldest metaphors, and therefore cry out the most insistently for analysis and interpretation, we start to unpack them. It turns out that they often make complex philosophical points in a nutshell. If we then take the next step ... we soon find a complex metaphysics of ordinariness.[19]

For Cupitt, then, the philosophical contents of "religion" are built into the ordinary language that religious and nonphilosophical people actually use. Thus philosophy of religion can work even with ancient Israelite religious language, even though it is not explicitly philosophical:

> At least since Plato, ordinary language's way of thinking has been regarded as low, confused, and simply mistaken.... But the notion that the thought of ordinary people might be intellectually interesting, and might have a logic of its own quite different from the "academic" or "platonic" style of thinking traditional in high cultures of the west developed only slowly.... Considerations such as these have prepared us very slowly for the idea that there really is an interesting philosophy and set of ways of thinking embedded in ordinary language, and that it is about time for us to dig it all out and take a good look at it. When post-Nietzschean philosophers such as Wittgenstein, Dewey and Heidegger came along telling us that we must now learn to think in a post-Platonic, post-metaphysical way, then clearly the time had come for the philosophy that is in ordinariness to emerge. But even at this late date it is proving a difficult birth. Really, very difficult—and nowhere more so than in philosophy of religion.[20]

Indeed, many still imagine ordinary language analysis to be unsuited to philosophy of religion.[21] Cupitt shows that this is far from the case. Biblical scholars who find no philosophical arguments in the Hebrew Bible's ordinary language would do well to take cognizance of this. In fact, one

---

19. Don Cupitt, *The Way to Happiness* (London: Polebridge, 2005), 2.
20. Ibid., 14–15.
21. Craig Vincent Mitchell, *Charts of Philosophy and Philosophers* (Grand Rapids: Zondervan, 2007), 68.

wonders what the contents of bits of ancient Israelite religion might look like when reconstructed in philosophical terms and derived from the ordinary language of characters in the biblical texts.

Another relevant figure in the Wittgensteinian tradition is Dewi Zephaniah Phillips. Phillips was able, from early on, to argue for clarification as a proper philosophical activity. In his study on the concept of prayer, he often suggests that philosophical clarification need not focus on philosophical problems but can be used with reference to nonphilosophical language and literature.[22] This kind of descriptive philosophy of religion seeks to attain a clearer understanding of religious phenomena—of the language, belief and actions into which they are woven—and attempts simply to try to make sense of the whole thing. In this sense philosophical clarification results not so much in the dissolution of philosophical puzzles as in a new understanding of the subject under investigation. Thus clarification leaves everything as it is, yet allows the contents of a text to be transformed in the eye of the analyst. In this view, philosophical clarification is simply conceptual analysis that pays attention to the depth grammar of discourse, thus bringing out criteria of meaning that are internal to it and revealing what it means to engage with it.

Another interesting and relevant notion in Phillips's work comes to us in the notion of "contemplative philosophy."[23] Phillips wanted to go beyond Ricoeur's dichotomy of the hermeneutics of recollection (apologetics) and the hermeneutics of suspicion (atheology). Instead, he opts for a descriptive option he calls the "hermeneutics of contemplation."[24] For Philips, philosophy is an activity based on "family resemblance," with some forms of the discipline having little (if anything) in common with other forms. Practitioners engaged in one of the other different philosophical methodologies might not accept descriptive work as "real philosophy." Yet according to Philips it is perfectly possible to limit one's philosophical concerns

---

22. Dewi Zephaniah Phillips, *The Concept of Prayer* (2nd ed.; Oxford: Blackwell, 1981), *passim*.

23. For an introduction, see the summary at "Analytic Philosophy," *Wikipedia, The Free Encyclopedia* [cited 23 February 2010]. Online: http://en.wikipedia.org/w/index.php?title=Analytic_philosophy&oldid=345825297.

24. Phillips explored this position in his *Religion and the Hermeneutics of Contemplation* (Cambridge: Cambridge University Press, 2001). He suggested that intellectuals need to see their task not as being for or against religion, or as explaining religion away, but as understanding it.

to clarification. From this perspective, the urge to press on to adjudication can be viewed as a result of our culture's functional obsessions. There is no reason why "understanding" religion cannot be as important an end in itself as is defending or criticizing religion in the context of another language game.[25]

In these brief remarks on the analytic philosophy of people such as Wittgenstein, Ryle, Cupitt, and Phillips, we see the possibility of descriptive options in the analytic current for biblical scholars. The four authors were discussed simply to provide a foretaste of this alternative way of thinking. There are others who see things along similar lines, and more will be said on the value of philosophical analysis in the discussion to follow. Note, however, that none of the agendas of these philosophers needs to be adopted *en bloc*. Neither do I mean to say that the analytic traditions are "where it's at." I am well aware of the fact that analytic philosophy is currently a cluster of problematic currents in the English speaking word, and that analytic philosophy of religion is a breeding ground for fundamentalist thinking. I also know that we find ourselves in the context of developing postmodern, postanalytic and postempiricist approaches. Even so, analytic philosophy of religion remains a respectable current in the discipline within the English-speaking world; and conceptual clarity and rigor in argumentation are virtues that are always well worth adopting in biblical scholarship.

5.2.2. Phenomenological Approaches

Second, we can also look for ideas from so-called *phenomenological* perspectives. The *phenomenology of religion* is in its broadest sense a descriptive approach to the philosophy of religion. "It seeks to understand religious experience in terms consistent with the orientation of the worshipers."[26] It assumes that, however one may debate the existence of the gods, religion itself is a reality—a phenomenon that can be observed and analyzed. But rather than try to evaluate religious truth claims or explain religious beliefs and practices, it seeks only to describe them care-

---

25. See Peter F. Bloemendaal, *Grammars of Faith: A Critical Evaluation of D. Z. Phillips's Philosophy of Religion* (Leuven: Peeters, 2006), 159.

26. "Phenomenology of Religion," *Wikipedia, The Free Encyclopedia* [cited 3 February 2010]. Online: http://en.wikipedia.org/w/index.php?title=Phenomenology_of_religion&oldid=504926076.

fully, so as to help us see them clearly, irrespective of how we may personally or subsequently seek to think of them or judge their relevance to our own contexts. This means that phenomenological description can focus either on the intentional act, or on the horizon, the life world or language game of the believer from which the belief emerged. Or it can focus on the intentional act, for instance, a god, the holy, and so on.[27] One sets aside all questions regarding what is real or not and concentrates entirely on describing what is given to consciousness along with the acts by which intentional objects are grasped.

Phenomenology of religion is a type of philosophy of religion that "views religion as being made up of different components. It studies these components across religious traditions so that a more objective understanding of them can be gained."[28] The scholar need not be a believer and what is perhaps of greatest use is not the phenomenology as such but the so-called phenomenological reduction or *"epoché"* as explicated in the work of Edmund Husserl. Husserl was himself not a philosopher of religion, but once stated that the problem of "God" is philosophy's greatest mystery.[29] Phenomenological approaches to religion do not pretend to study "God" *in re* but rather concern themselves with human representations of deity as an intentional object of consciousness. Husserl's work indirectly provided the foundation for a descriptive philosophical approach to the intentionality of religious consciousness. A classic early representative who applied the method was Gerhardus van der Leeuw, in his *Religion in Essence and Manifestation* (1933).[30]

Perhaps the most familiar name in phenomenology of religion for biblical scholars is that of Rudolf Otto. In his *The Idea of the Holy: An Inquiry into the Non-rational Factor in the Idea of the Divine and Its Relation to the Rational*, Otto wrote a chapter on "The Numinous in the Old Testament."[31] Many biblical scholars would agree that his variety of descriptive philoso-

---

27. Merold Westphal, "Phenomenology of Religion," in *The Routledge Companion to Philosophy of Religion* (ed. Chad Meister and Paul Copan; London: Routledge, 2007), 661.

28. "Phenomenology of Religion," *Wikipedia*.

29. Long, *Twentieth-Century Western Philosophy of Religion*, 143.

30. Ward, *Concepts of God*, vii.

31. The original was, of course, in German. For the English translation, see Rudolph Otto, *The Idea of the Holy: An Inquiry into the Non-rational Factor in the Idea of the Divine and Its Relation to the Rational* (Galaxy Books 14; Oxford: Oxford University Press, 1968).

phy of religion did help to clarify the biblical texts in some respects. Many have also been using Otto's philosophical jargon, thereby showing that philosophy of religion is not really the enemy: the problem lies only in the use of the distortive currents.

A more recent and excellent defense of phenomenology of religion *qua* descriptive philosophy of religion can be found in Merold Westphal's *God, Guilt and Death: An Existential Phenomenology of Religion*.[32] Westphal argues for an alternative to philosophical approaches to religion that limit themselves to evaluation and explanation. Not that these aims are wrong in themselves, but inasmuch as the question of meaning precedes the question of truth, one must also recognize the legitimacy, and even the priority, of a purely descriptive approach. Phenomenology of religion in this sense asks us not to speculate anew on actual reality, but to get better acquainted with what is familiar yet still unknown. Descriptive philosophy is still philosophy, and the few excursions to the Hebrew Bible by Westphal show that the phenomenological approach is hermeneutically sound despite being philosophical.

In a chapter entitled "Prolegomena to Any Future Philosophy of Religion That Will Be Able to Come Forth as Prophecy," Westphal argues that a phenomenological approach is the most scientific of methods:

> The phenomenology of religion, however, is a descriptive enterprise. It is concerned with truth, but not with the truth of religious assertions; and it brackets questions of transcendence in order to describe the form and content of religion as an observable phenomenon. Phenomenology of religion discusses God, but it does so by describing various forms of belief in God rather than debating the truths of these beliefs. It is systematically uncommitted regarding the latter question. Therefore the fundamental difference between natural (a)theology and phenomenology of religion is not about God but about religion. Rather, one is normative, the other descriptive.[33]

A little further on, Westphal goes on to explain why descriptive philosophy of religion has now replaced normative approaches in phenomenological contexts:

---

32. For descriptive approaches and several sections touching on the Hebrew Bible, see Westphal, *God, Guilt and Death*, 1–15.

33. Westphal, *Kierkegaard's Critique*, 3.

> This is the point at which phenomenologists of religion argue that phi-
> losophy of religion can be a science. They have taken Kant seriously. They
> have heard him argue that metaphysics cannot be possible as a science in
> the transcendent sense, giving objective truth about God, freedom and
> immorality; and they have also heard him explain that metaphysics can
> be possible as an immanent science describing the structure of human
> experience. *This is the key to their withdrawal from normative to descrip-
> tive philosophy of religion.*[34]

Westphal realizes that no descriptive philosophical analysis is wholly dis-
interested and that the *epoché* remains an ideal. But that is what makes it
interesting for him, given philosophy's major challenge in understanding
the God of the philosophers vis-à-vis the God of Abraham, Isaac and Jacob.

Another phenomenological approach in philosophy of religion (combined with the comparative perspective to be discussed in the next section) can be found in the writings of Keith Ward. In his discussion of
the concept of God in several religious traditions (including the Hebrew
Bible), Ward writes:

> In this book I have adopted, as far as I can, a phenomenological method.
> That is, I have tried to look at five major religious traditions as sympa-
> thetically as I can, using terms acceptable to those traditions themselves.
> I have tried to bracket my own beliefs, or at least not let them intrude
> judgmentally upon the tradition I am considering. Where I have criti-
> cized, I have sought to let the criticisms arise from within the traditions
> themselves, so that they rather pose difficulties within a tradition than
> reasons for rejecting the tradition altogether.[35]

These two elements—bracketing one's own religious-ideological assumptions and, when doing descriptive work, allowing only for critique from
inside the traditions to clarify pluralism—are important catalysts for
imagining a descriptive philosophical approach to ancient Israelite religion aimed only at clarification. In opting to utilize these particular elements of a phenomenological approach I am not the first biblical scholar
to make use of reduction. The following is an example of something similar in David Steinberg's take on the history of Israelite religion:

---

34. Ibid., 7, emphasis added.
35. Ward, *Concepts of God*, vii.

> In observing the culture of ancient Israel it is first of all necessary to bracket out all (theological) notions of deity that are post-Kantian, or that are derived even indirectly from Neo-Platonism and Neo-Aristotelianism. Ancient Israelite thinking was prescholastic and pre-Aquinas and pre-Christian and pre-Jewish. As a consequence, certain distinctions between categories of being and of thought shared by most contemporary scholars, heirs of Western philosophic developments since the thirteenth century c.e., distinctions that fill this chapter, cannot be ascribed to Israelite thought.[36]

In other words, the problem lies not with adopting a philosophical perspective on ancient Israelite religion. Steinberg himself goes for a phenomenological approach. Rather, it is about reading distortive, anachronistic philosophical-theological conceptions of deity into biblical god-talk. We find something similar in Old Testament theology in the writings of Eichrodt, who was accused by Vriezen that his way of doing things was not a theology at all, but was instead a phenomenology of Israelite religion.[37] Whether this is true or not is not presently our concern. I am also well aware that there is more to phenomenological approaches (which are also plural and changing) than phenomenological reduction. However, it is this element of phenomenological analysis that is most relevant for the development of a descriptive philosophical approach to Israelite religion. Irrespective of its philosophical merits or problems, the basic attitude behind phenomenological reduction may be functional as a corrective tool in combining historical and philosophical analyses of the Hebrew Bible. It allows us to bracket both the concern with any supposed extra-textual truth and anachronistic theological (dogmatic) beliefs about what the texts are saying.

Besides the possible value for biblical scholarship of elements in the analytic and the phenomenological approaches, there is still the need for a third dimension. This is because we need a descriptive approach that allows us to do justice to the theological pluralism and historical change in Israelite religion. Scholars of the Hebrew Bible, should they turn philosophical, are likely to be historical philosophers of religion who have to deal with non-Western cultural conceptions of deity that show marked

---

36. David Steinberg, *Israelite Religion to Judaism: the Evolution of the Religion of Israel* [cited 19 July 2009]. Online: http://www.adath-shalom.ca/israelite_religion.htm.

37. Barr, *Concept of Biblical Theology*, 82.

differences from ideas about "God" in classical Christian philosophical theology. And so we come to *comparative* philosophy of religion, the third and final ingredient in our methodological recipe.

5.2.3. COMPARATIVE PERSPECTIVES

Late in the nineteenth century, anthropologists did significant research on ancient non-Western religions and there developed an interest in the history and plurality of religions. The comparative philosophical approach then suffered a setback during the first half of the twentieth century, when neo-orthodox theologians began to popularize their idea of the discontinuity between revelation and reason in the context of Christian dogmatics. Though this attitude still prevails in many circles today, the tide began to change soon after the middle of the century, so that during the last quarter of the twentieth century we saw the birth of a whole new type of philosophy of religion.[38]

Comparative philosophy of religion in its new format represents a third relevant perspective for this study, especially elements of approaches that stem from the late 1960s. Over the last few decades, many philosophers of religion have begun to challenge the assumption that one may not discuss issues outside contemporary varieties of philosophical theism. This trend coincided with an increasing awareness of global issues and postcolonialism, with technological advancements and multicultural societies. The sharp boundaries between philosophy of religion and the history of religion are no longer justifiable.[39] Conceptions of what philosophy of religion is or could be have changed dramatically, and it is now possible to study any issue in any religion or religious tradition, present or past, with the aim of understanding different conceptual frames of reference.

Perhaps the most sustained and fruitful attempt to facilitate comparative philosophy as such has come from *Philosophy East and West*—an international, interdisciplinary academic journal that seeks to promote literacy in non-Western traditions of philosophy in relation to Anglo-American philosophy. Philosophy defined in terms of cultural traditions broadly integrates literature, science, and social practices into the professional discipline. Special issues of the journal have been devoted to topics

---

38. Long, *Twentieth-Century Western Philosophy of Religion*, 474.
39. Ibid., 475.

as diverse as "Problems of the Self," "Existence: An East-West Dialogue," "Philosophy and Revolution," and "Environmental Ethics."[40]

Until recently, the impact of all this on philosophy of religion has been limited in scope. Most philosophy departments remain concerned with contemporary Western culture. Philosophers of eastern or ancient religions therefore are rare, and operate instead in the context of religious studies, where there has been an explosion in philosophical approaches to religion. One instance of the proliferation of perspectives and topics is the series of books, *Toward a Comparative Philosophy of Religions*, published by the State University of New York Press. This is the first collection to include contributions not only by philosophers proper but also by philosophically orientated scholars in theology, the history of religions, and anthropology.

One comparative philosopher of religion whose work shows the possibility of a philosophical approach to ancient Israelite religion is Ninian Smart. Smart lamented that philosophy of religion as conventionally practiced had ignored the history of religion and comparative religion. He therefore went on to suggest a three-tiered prolegomenon for the philosophy of religion, structured around the comparative analysis of religions, the history of religions, and the phenomenology of a range of (religious) experiences and actions. He has also raised concerns about the parochialism of contemporary "analytic" philosophy of religion, which has led virtually to its marginalization within philosophy. More controversial is his suggestion that philosophy of religion—along with the history of religions and anthropology—should "go wild," "implying exegetical hermeneutics and intratextual morphology more than redactive dogmatics."[41]

Smart thinks that it is impossible to define religion in such a way as to do justice to the idiosyncrasies of individual traditions. Yet all religions are riddled with propositions that acquire their meaning in the context in which they are used. No religious idea should be divorced from the larger conceptual background of which it was part. This form of philosophy of religion is thus itself descriptive, historical and actually devoted to pluralist conceptions of deity. As such, and because comparative philosophy of religion is not about constructing normative unified systematic theories

---

40. "Philosophy East and West," *Wikipedia, The Free Encyclopedia* [cited 28 March 2010]. Online: http://en.wikipedia.org/w/index.php?title=Philosophy_East_and_West.

41. Purushottama Bilimoria, "What Is the 'Sub-Altern' of the Comparative Philosophy of Religion?" *PEW* 53 (2003): 340.

or concerned with natural theology and apologetics, it is ideal for studying intra- and interreligious diversity, also with reference to ancient Israelite religious traditions in their own contexts and reception history.

According to Michael Levine in his review of a recent text by Ninian Smart:[42]

> In "The Philosophy of Worldviews, or the Philosophy of Religion Transformed" … Smart … calls for an overhaul of the philosophy of religion that would have it abandon its traditional focus on Western (mostly Christian) theism, along with its focus on the problems of natural theology (evil, immortality etc.) as conceived and treated in the context of Western theism. The changes Smart envisions are so radical that he calls for the "extension" of the philosophy of religion in favor of what he terms the "philosophy of worldviews." What, if anything, remains of the philosophy of religion as traditionally conceived is unclear. But as he sees it, this extended philosophy would be "the upper story of a building which has as its middle floor the comparative and historical analysis of religions and ideologies, and as a ground floor the phenomenology not just of religious experience and action but of the symbolic life of human beings as a whole."[43]

In other words, one of Smart's major arguments is that philosophy of religion should become a philosophical approach to worldview analysis.[44] What this implies is that comparative religion, the history of religion, and philosophy of religion can now be combined on an interdisciplinary level as a crosscultural philosophy of religion aimed primarily at awareness and mutual understanding. In making this suggestion I do not wish to get drawn into the debate as to the pros and cons of Smart's views in the context of philosophy of religion proper. Instead, I would simply like us to

---

42. Ninian Smart, "The Philosophy of Worldviews, or the Philosophy of Religion Transformed," in *Religious Pluralism and Truth: Essays on Cross-Cultural Philosophy of Religion* (ed. Thomas Dean; Albany: State University of New York Press, 1995), 22–39.

43. Michael P. Levine, "Ninian Smart on the Philosophy of Worldviews," *Sophia* 136 (1997): 11. Levine aptly (as usual) notes that the parochialism of contemporary "analytic" Christian philosophy of religion is regrettable. Furthermore (and perhaps more than Smart), he regards it as a moribund and isolated field within philosophy as such.

44. Ninian Smart and John T. Shepherd, *Ninian Smart on World Religions: Selected Works* (Oxford: Ashgate, 2009).

consider some of the possibilities that elements of Smart's revisionist prolegomenon offer for a philosophical approach to the pluralist theologies within the Hebrew Bible, when compared with philosophical beliefs from their reception history.

Since comparative philosophy of religion is motivated by the diversity of religious experiences and symbols in world religions, our own new descriptive philosophical approach to the Hebrew Bible is also motivated by taking cognizance of the intrareligious diversity within the multiplex traditions of the Hebrew Bible. It is also motivated by the alienness of some of the ancient Israelite beliefs when contrasted with ideas in modern Jewish and Christian philosophical theology. Thus, because our concern is description, looking to comparative philosophy of religion means that the pluralism in biblical theology, though a problem for any constructive systematic philosophical perspective, is no longer such for our purpose. Neither is the fact that our descriptive metalanguage comes from a cultural context different from that of the Hebrew Bible. This can be seen from a short overview of the conceptual challenges recognized in comparative philosophy proper.[45]

According to Ronnie Littlejohn,[46] several potential pitfalls await the comparative philosopher of religion, the recognition of which many biblical scholars will appreciate

1. *Descriptive chauvinism* involves reading a text from another tradition and assuming that it asks the same questions as, or constructs responses or answers in a similar manner to, the tradition with which one is most familiar.
2. *Normative chauvinism* is the belief that one tradition is best and that insofar as the others are different, they are inferior or in error. A common form of normative chauvinism is the

---

45. See, for example, Taliaferro, Draper, and Quinn, *A Companion to Philosophy of Religion*. For the challenges of comparative philosophy as world philosophy, see Ninian Smart, *World Philosophies* (ed. Oliver Leaman; New York: Routledge, 2008). For some of the challenges of eastern versus Western perspectives, see David Wong, "Comparative Philosophy: Chinese and Western," *SEP* [cited 12 June 2010]. Online: http://plato.stanford.edu/archives/win2009/entries/comparphil-chiwes/.

46. Ronnie Littlejohn, "Comparative Philosophy," *IEP* [cited 10 January 2010]. Online: http://www.iep.utm.edu/.

belief that unless philosophy is done in a certain way, then it cannot properly be considered philosophy.

3. The problem of *incommensurability arises when it is* impossible to translate some concepts of one tradition into those of another. Alternatively, traditions may differ on what counts as evidence and grounds for decidability, thus making it impossible to adjudicate between them.

4. There is the illusion of *perennialism which involves* overlooking historical change. As those who study any religion in depth know very well, all traditions are plural, complex, and evolving. They do not only have tensions with other traditions: they also display internal conflict.

The aim of comparative philosophy of religion is not a synthesis of traditions but a different sort of philosophical analysis. One does not inhabit the different standpoints represented by the traditions as developing an emerging standpoint and a new way of understanding the human condition.[47]

5.3. A Parallel: Conceptual Clarification in Philosophical Theology

The task of a descriptive philosophical approach to Israelite religion as represented in the Hebrew Bible can also be compared to the task of clarification in philosophical theology. But what exactly is philosophical theology, and what exactly is the relation between it and the philosophy of religion? Currently there is no longer any real answer, as the two fields have for all practical purposes become virtually identical:

> Philosophy of religion is sometimes divided into philosophy of religion proper and philosophical theology. This distinction reflects the unease of an earlier period in analytic philosophy, during which philosophers felt that reflection on religion was philosophically respectable only if it confined itself to mere theism and abstracted from all particular religions; anything else was taken to be theology, not philosophy. But most philosophers now feel free to examine philosophically any aspect of religion,

---

47. Ibid.

including doctrines or practices peculiar to individual religions. Not only are these doctrines and practices generally philosophically interesting in their own right, but often they also raise questions that are helpful for issues in other areas of philosophy. Reflection on the Christian notion of sanctification, for example, sheds light on certain contemporary debates over the nature of freedom of the will.[48]

This proliferation of topics and the fact that "anything goes" as far as topics for philosophical discussion are concerned is part of the reason why a philosophical approach to ancient Israelite religion is now a live option. But what has all this to do with the suggested philosophical approach to ancient Israelite religion as represented in the traditions of the Hebrew Bible? Four relevant considerations come to mind that will be illustrated in this section:

1.   Philosophical theology is one way of doing *philosophy of religion*.
2.   Philosophical theology studies a *specific* religious tradition.
3.   Philosophical theology is able to concern itself with *any topic*.
4.   Philosophical theology includes the *descriptive* task of clarification.

In these ways, the concept of descriptive philosophical theology offers a parallel to what this study is seeking to promote as a philosophical approach to ancient Israelite religion. But what is the difference between such a discipline and biblical theology on the one hand, and philosophical theology proper on the other? A philosophical theology of the Hebrew Bible is different from biblical theology as philosophical theology proper is different from systematic theology. As systematic and philosophical theology have overlapping concerns but exist as warranted separate disciplines within theology, so too biblical theology and a philosophical theology of the Hebrew Bible, while having some interests in common, are in the end two different fields.

On the other hand, a philosophical theology of the Hebrew Bible is also different from philosophical theology proper, as biblical theology is different from doctrinal theology. Thus, as biblical theology is different

---

48. Eleanore Stump, "Religion, Philosophy Of," *REP* [cited 12 November 2009]. Online: http://www.rep.routledge.com/article/K113.

from systematic theology and can allow for descriptive approaches aside from more evaluative ones, so too a philosophical theology of the Hebrew Bible will be more historically orientated than philosophical theology proper. This means that, just as biblical theology had to create its own questions, concerns, concepts, and categories, and had to avoid borrowing uncritically from systematic theology, so too a philosophical theology of the Hebrew Bible cannot merely adopt loci from philosophical theology proper, but must also adapt them.

But how is philosophical theology also philosophy of religion? After all, many metaphilosophies of religion still equate the essential task of philosophical approaches to religion with natural a/theology as either justifying or offering critique of religious truth claims. Some philosophical theologians, however, now consider propositional justification as being preceded by a more descriptive task, that of clarification. An excellent overview and defense of the validity of the clarifying role in philosophical theology in general (as opposed to its confinement to natural theology) can be found in Scott MacDonald, "What is Philosophical Theology?"[49] MacDonald shows the fallacy inherent in the belief that philosophy without evaluation is not "real" philosophy. As he notes with reference to natural theology and the obsession with normativity:

> The sheer weight of this tradition in philosophy since the seventeenth century and the negligence of other models for philosophical theology make it natural to assume philosophical theology is coextensive with this kind of natural theology. If we give in to this temptation we implicitly agree to two kinds of limitations on philosophical theology, one limiting the kinds of philosophical activity open to the philosophical theologian, the other limiting the range of issues she can legitimately pursue.[50]

In defense of making room for clarification, MacDonald continues:

> It is not the case that all philosophical activity is concerned primarily with the truth or epistemic justification of a particular theory or set of propositions or beliefs. In order to have a handy way of referring to the sorts of philosophical reflection I want to call attention to here I will borrow a phrase from Aquinas's philosophical theology "clarification"

---

49. Scott MacDonald, "What Is Philosophical Theology?" in *Arguing about Religion* (ed. Kevin Timpe; New York: Routledge, 2009), 17–29.

50. Ibid., 17.

(*manifestatio*). A great deal of philosophical activity is concerned not with justifying but with clarifying propositions or theories.[51]

In other words, there is room for description in philosophy, and it is just as much part of "doing" philosophy as the critical evaluation of truth claims or the proposal of ideas about what is absolutely the case. Biblical scholars who have not been able to imagine a philosophical approach to the Hebrew Bible in the context of historical work might have overlooked this descriptive option. Moreover, one has to understand just how important the descriptive task actually is, as MacDonald further explains by way of an analogy:

> I propose to explain what clarification is simply by describing a case in which an ordinary philosopher engages in what I take to be the clarification of a philosophical theory. Imagine a philosopher who works in ethics and is interested in moral realism…. She does not think that realism is true (perhaps she doesn't think it is false either), but finds it intriguing and worth investigating…. Her philosophical agenda includes various kinds of projects, three of which are worth specific mention. First, she gives some attention to analyzing concepts central to moral realism…. Second, she is interested in the internal coherence or consequences of moral realism…. Third, she also takes an interest in moral realism's external relations: how does it square with a theistic view of the world?[52]

Thus lest there be any suggestion that what I am proposing is not philosophy but only linguistics (lexicography) or anthropology (social-scientific worldview description), I refer the objector to MacDonald's own arguments showing clarification as a philosophical activity independent of epistemic justification and just as fully entitled to be considered philosophical inquiry. In this manner, clarification in philosophical theology shows how a descriptive philosophical approach to the Hebrew Bible might operate in historical biblical scholarship, for it both allows us to work with concepts particular to ancient Yahwism and warrants limiting the inquiry to a concern with meaning rather than truth. Not that as historical philosophical theologians we would be totally unconcerned with natural theology and propositional justification. However, our concern is

---

51. Ibid., 23.
52. Ibid., 23–24.

historical and descriptive, even in these matters. Thus it is not our concern to argue for the existence of Yhwh without appealing to the Hebrew Bible. But we are interested in describing and clarifying the traces of natural theology and propositional justification implicit in or presupposed by the Hebrew Bible itself.

5.4. Doing Philosophy of Religion in the Context of Hebrew Bible Studies

Typically, then, while philosophy of religion working in the contemporary Christian tradition is indeed a normative enterprise reflecting on the truth of religious beliefs,[53] I conceive of the task of a philosophical approach to ancient Israelite religion in the context of biblical studies as involving something a little different. We shall become biblical scholars utilizing philosophy of religion to understand the Hebrew Bible historically, not philosophers of religion seeking to have the Hebrew Bible contribute to contemporary philosophical debates or hoping to prove its truth claims wrong. Here lie the fundamental differences between the two contexts involved in this interdisciplinary research, and they can be summed up as follows:

Philosophy of Religion (Christian)	Philosophical Approach to the Hebrew Bible
Christianity/Judaism	Ancient Israelite Yahwism(s)
Philosophical concepts	Folk-philosophical assumptions
Mainly evaluative	Mainly descriptive
Concepts from systematic theology	Concepts from biblical theology
Apologetic/atheological	Historical/phenomenological
Mainly justification/critique	Clarification only
World outside the text	Worlds inside the text

---

53. See Merold Westphal, "Phenomenology of Religion," *REP* 7:353.

From this it should be readily apparent that a descriptive philosophical approach to Israelite religion finds a parallel in all descriptive philosophical subdisciplines. One example is descriptive philosophy of science, which attempts to describe in philosophical terms what science actually does and assumes about the world, as opposed to what science should do or what reality consists of. Another instance is the philosophy of art, which seeks to understand the aesthetic phenomenon rather than merely to defend or criticize art.

5.5. DIFFERENCES FROM THISELTON'S "PHILOSOPHICAL DESCRIPTION"

The concept of "philosophical description" was introduced by Anthony Thiselton in his *The Two Horizons: New Testament Hermeneutics and Philosophical Description with Special Reference to Heidegger, Bultmann, Gadamer and Wittgenstein.*[54] In this work Thiselton famously suggested employing linguistic and hermeneutic philosophy in understanding the New Testament.[55] The author's discussion begins with the question: "Why should the interpreter of the New Testament concern himself with philosophy?" Following this, he argues for the need to take philosophy seriously in New Testament studies. Chapter 1 starts with: "Why philosophical description?" After dealing with two objections (concerning fashion and distortion), Thiselton spells out why he thinks philosophical description is useful:

1. New Testament scholars use philosophical categories in their work. Thus any kind of dialogue with or critique of such scholars has to involve philosophical considerations, if that dialogue is to be taken seriously.
2. Philosophy is helpful in describing the nature of, and in appraising, the hermeneutical process (that is, the fusion of two horizons articulated by Gadamer).
3. Philosophical hermeneutics bears on a host of issues directly relevant to biblical interpretation, and interpretation inevi-

---

54. Anthony Thiselton, *The Two Horizons: New Testament Hermeneutics and Philosophical Description with Special Reference to Heidegger, Bultmann, Gadamer and Wittgenstein* (Grand Rapids: Eerdmans, 1980).

55. Ibid., 3.

tably carries with it philosophical issues (as shown by Paul Ricoeur).

A powerful example of the way in which philosophy shapes biblical inter-pretation is philosophy of language, another philosophical discipline that Thiselton invokes. As Old Testament scholar Craig Bartholomew tells us:

> Thiselton has rightly alerted us to the important relationship between philosophy and biblical interpretation, as this is focused in hermeneutics. In all theoretical work epistemological, ontological and anthropological presuppositions provide, as it were, the scaffolding for our theory con-struction. Such scaffolding is not neutral, and it can only help if we are conscious of the philosophical presuppositions and theories informing and shaping our scholarship.[56]

The postmodern turn has, of course, gone a long way toward exposing hidden scaffolding. I welcome this. But the myth of neutrality in Hebrew Bible scholarship remains widespread. So although Thiselton's two major texts on biblical hermeneutics have been widely reviewed, there has been surprisingly little thorough interaction with his work. Bartholomew again says:

> And would this affect our handling of the OT? This is not to suggest that OT scholars should become philosophers and theologians. It is to suggest that OT scholarship requires solid philosophical (and theologi-cal) input if it is not to work with hidden philosophies shaping it. Thus, I suggest, we desperately need scholars like Thiselton who will do the hard philosophical work, and biblical scholars need regular dialogue with such people. Especially in the USA in recent years there has been a renaissance of Christian philosophy under the leadership of scholars like Alvin Plantinga and Nicholas Wolterstorff. The growing corpus of work that this "movement" is yielding, and the work of scholars like Thiselton, provide a ready starting point for such dialogue.[57]

---

56. Craig G. Bartholomew, "Three Horizons: Hermeneutics from the Other End—An Evaluation of Anthony Thiselton's Hermeneutic Proposals," *European Jour-nal of Theology* 5 (1996): 131.

57. Ibid.

In view of what I wrote in the previous chapter on fundamentalism in analytic Christian philosophy of religion, the reader will understand why I am sorry to say that this type of response is exactly what I cannot agree with. Even if pluralism is the name of the game and everyone should have his or her say, we can do better than the cryptofundamentalism of Reformed Epistemology. But how does the agenda of the present study differ from Thiselton's? Thiselton is here not so much interested in descriptive philosophy of religion as such. His focus is almost wholly on hermeneutics. I suppose—given the hermeneutical current in philosophy of religion itself—that one could make a case for overlap, but Thiselton himself does not do so in the book. Moreover, given the focus on hermeneutics, Thiselton's primary concern lies with a philosophical description of the exegetical context rather than with a philosophical description of the meaning of the texts themselves. Finally, Thiselton's concern is limited to the New Testament, where philosophy is less of a problem given the partly Hellenistic historical-cultural context. In these ways, then, Thiselton's contribution differs from my own.

5.6. Fallacies in Possible Objections to a Philosophical Approach to Ancient Israelite Religion

As we saw earlier, there is a long tradition in biblical interpretation that considers philosophy to be a distortion of religion.[58] The usual suspects include, inter alia, Paul's derision of Greek wisdom (1 Cor 2:6); the pseudo-Pauline warning of believers not to let themselves be spoiled by philosophy (Col 2:8); Tertullian's claim that Athens and Jerusalem have nothing in common; Thomas Aquinas's distinction between truths from reason and revelation; the later Martin Luther's dismissal of Aristotelian metaphysics and logic; Benedict de Spinoza's denial that philosophy and a historical approach to the Bible can peacefully coexist; Blaise Pascal's distinction between the God of Abraham, Isaac, and Jacob and the God of the Philosophers; Johann Philip Gabler's differentiation between biblical and dogmatic theology; Johann Gottfried Herder's stereotype of Hebrew poetry; Karl Barth and his followers' aversion to natural theology; Walter Eichrodt's view that extrabiblical concepts and categories were a priori distortive; the Biblical Theology Movement's concept of "Hebrew thought"

---

58. Charlesworth, *Philosophy of Religion*, 87.

vis-à-vis Greek thinking (from Boman); and Brueggemann's antisubstantive ontological concerns. The cumulative influence of such antiphilosophical sentiments in the history of interpretation has led to a state of affairs in which Old Testament theologians always find it necessary to point out that philosophy has no place in biblical scholarship at the level of exegesis.

In order to prevent latent antiphilosophical sentiment in biblical scholarship from becoming an obstacle in the communication of the new ideas to follow, it is of paramount importance to anticipate possible objections to involving philosophy of religion in the study of the Hebrew Bible. On this point, three categories of possible critique may be distinguished: (1) objections appealing to the nature of the Hebrew Bible; (2) objections appealing to the nature of the philosophy; and (3) objections appealing to the nature of biblical scholarship. In this section I intend to show cognizance of, and to reply to, several possible objections to a philosophical analysis of the beliefs, concepts and practices of ancient Israelite religion.

The first objection against a philosophical approach to ancient Yahwism(s) might be based on the belief that the Hebrew Bible contains no philosophy of religion. Thus, according to Horst D. Preuss, "Israel had no philosophical conception of God."[59] Erhard Gerstenberger reinforces the point, saying, "Yhwh became not only the personal God but the exclusive Lord of the whole world, and *this view did not develop out of philosophical considerations*."[60]

If this truism were to be used as an argument against a philosophical approach to ancient Israelite religion, we have a clearcut case of *non sequitur* reasoning. It simply does not follow that philosophical inquiry requires the object of its analysis to be itself philosophical in nature. As the philosophical theologian Morris reminds us:

> The Bible is not a textbook of philosophical theology. Its texts on God are thus neither as complete nor as specific as the philosophical theologian needs in order to be able to answer fully his conceptual, or philosophical questions. Are these questions then illegitimate from a biblical standpoint? I see no reason to think so at all. From the fact that the biblical documents, written as they were to deal with burning practical questions

---

59. Horst D. Preuss, *Old Testament Theology* (2 vols.; OTL; Louisville: Westminster John Knox, 1996), 1:245.

60. Erhard Gerstenberger, *Theologies in the Old Testament* (London: Continuum, 2002), 224, emphasis added.

of the greatest personal significance, do not address all the possible philosophical questions, which can also, in their own way, be of the greatest personal significance, *it does not follow at all that these more theoretical questions are illegitimate.*[61]

Indeed not. For philosophical analysis does not require the contents of its inquiry (or the methods behind the thinking under scrutiny) to be itself philosophical in nature in order to clarify its meaning from a philosophical perspective. The reason is simple. Though not philosophical in the Western sense of the concept, the Hebrew Bible does contain metaphysical, epistemological and moral assumptions that can be described in philosophical terms. A philosophy of Israelite religion is therefore possible, not because the Hebrew Bible is philosophy *but because it is religion* and because religious language of necessity contains presuppositions about the nature of reality, knowledge and morality which can be described in philosophical terms.

The second objection involves the frequently heard claim that philosophical questions are out of place and anachronistic because the biblical authors are not concerned with them. This seems to be the gist implicit in the words of James Orr:

> There is no speculative philosophy in the Old Testament, nor any certain trace of its influence. Its writers and actors never set themselves to pursue knowledge in the abstract and for its own sake. They always wrought for moral purposes. But moral activity proceeds on the intellectual presuppositions and interpretations of the experiences within which it acts. Hence, we find in the Old Testament accounts of the origin and course of nature, a philosophy of history and its institutions, and interpretations of men's moral and religious experiences. They all center in God, issue from His sovereign will, and express the realization of His purpose of righteousness in the world.[62]

The same assumption—that one should stick to the concerns of the biblical authors themselves—is found in the words of Barton:

---

61. Morris, *Our Idea of God*, 31.

62. James Orr, "Philosophy," *ISBE* [cited 30 April 2010]. Online: http://www.bible-history.com/isbe/P/PHILOSOPHY/.

The study of Hebrew Bible ethics has sometimes suffered from an unwillingness on the part of scholars to contemplate "philosophical" questions at all, on the grounds that people of ancient Israel simply were not interested in, or could not have understood, questions of such a kind. A case could undoubtably be made in favour of such a belief but it needs to be made: it should not be asserted as though it were obvious.[63]

The main problem with any objection against a philosophical approach to Israelite religion appealing to the concerns of the authors is that it tends to operate with double standards. This soon becomes apparent once one realizes *that all our concerns are anachronistic by default* (they are *ours*). For example, none of biblical authors were interested in or concerned with the kinds of questions biblical scholars ask when engaged in linguistics, historical criticism, literary criticism, sociology or theology. Yet if this objection were consistently incorporated into biblical hermeneutics (itself an anachronistic cluster of concerns), it would follow that none of the traditional and popular approaches to the Hebrew Bible is hermeneutically valid either. So why are they tolerated? In the end, philosophical concerns per se are no more anachronistic than any other contemporary concerns, and the problem is not about being anachronistic. Instead, the trouble lies with the application and type of philosophical method given that there might be a distortion of meaning. Philosophical concerns and approaches that read into the text what is not there are obviously distortive. But those which simply seek to bring out what is there yet unarticulated cannot possibly be considered a problem.

The third objection points to the possession of philosophical assumptions by the exegete as an obstacle to understanding. When one wishes to show what is wrong in another's interpretation, one simply accuses them of being blind to their *philosophical* presuppositions. [64] But is this really a valid objection? Only in the sense that philosophical-theological assumptions can lead one to see meanings in the text which are not there. However, having philosophical presuppositions per se is no scandal since these are omnipresent, as Barr notes: "Biblical theologians have theological presuppositions but they (like historians) have philosophical presuppositions as well."[65]

---

63. Barton, "Basis of Ethics," 20.

64. Barr, *Concept of Biblical Theology*, 168.

65. Ibid. The omnipresence of philosophical assumptions in theology was shown

All the theological ideas of antiphilosophical biblical scholars are riddled with Western folk-philosophical assumptions. Even those who rage against philosophical assumptions have, upon closer scrutiny, simply exchanged one stereotype of philosophy for another more antisystematic variety, whether they realize it or not.[66] Moreover, one eventually comes to learn that the concern is not with philosophical assumptions as such but with certain philosophical methods and schools of thought. The reality is that the problem is not the biblical theologian's philosophical assumptions but philosophical-theological presumption. In order to know whether we are being presumptuous or not, however, we actually need a philosophical clarification of the Hebrew Bible's own folk-philosophical assumptions to compare these with our own.

The fourth objection goes one step further and holds that philosophical categories are distortive, being forced as they are onto the discourse from the outside, rather than having been taken from the biblical contents itself. This was Walter Eichrodt's main objection to the use of extrabiblical categories in biblical theology. This idea is also implicit in Hasel, who reflects as follows on the debate on the role of philosophy within biblical theology:

> The biblical theologian neither takes the place of nor competes with the systematic theologian or dogmatician. The latter has and always will have to fulfill his own task in that he endeavors to use current philosophies as the basis for his primary themes and categories. For the systematic theologian, it is indeed appropriate to operate with philosophical categories because his foundations are on a base different from that of the biblical theologian. The biblical theologian draws his categories, themes, motifs and concepts from the biblical text itself. The biblical theologian stands in danger of surreptitiously introducing contemporary philosophy into his discipline. But he must be careful to guard himself against this temptation.[67]

---

by Nancey Murphy in *Beyond Liberalism and Fundamentalism*. Murphy argues that the philosophy of the modern period is largely responsible for the polarity of Protestant Christian thought, even though the modern philosophical positions driving the division between liberals and conservatives have themselves been called into question.

66. Barr, *Concept of Biblical Theology*, 168.

67. Hasel, *Old Testament Theology*, 195.

Since then, we still quite often encounter this insistence on sticking to intrabiblical frames of reference, as expressed by Preuss:

> While there are inferences that may be drawn from the Old Testament's understanding of the nature of God, one should be careful about the use of later philosophical, theological categories of thought to set forth the Old Testament's view of reality.[68]

Moreover, according to Brueggemann, "the Old Testament does not readily conform to ... the categories of any Hellenistic perennial philosophy."[69]

Such claims are usually simply asserted in view of how the intrusion of dogmatic theology (which utilizes philosophical categories) into Old Testament theology have distorted the biblical data. The basic idea here, that philosophical categories can be distortive, is valid. However, the fallacy in this line of thought is that of essentialism and non sequitur. It does not follow that if some philosophical categories are distortive that all philosophical categories are such by necessity. Hence, as was aptly pointed out by Anthony Thiselton, the problem is not philosophical categories per se but the tendency to opt for poorly chosen ones.[70] He mentions James Barr, who compared "purist" or "internalist" perspectives with externalist ones, arguing that the fundamental error in purist thinking is the supposition that by taking an internal viewpoint we somehow guard against error.[71] In discussing the problematic opposition of Hebrew and Greek thought in the question of distinctiveness, Barr recognized the fact that "the issue is not between philosophy and theology but between a proper historical-cultural study and an unhistorical use of philosophical categories."[72]

Barr thus realized (unlike many of his contemporaries) that the problem with philosophy lies not with the use of philosophical categories per se but rather with the uncritical and unhistorical superimposition of philosophical-theological frameworks on conceptual backgrounds in the Hebrew Bible where they are distortive of metaphysical assumptions in the textual data.[73]

---

68. Preuss, *Old Testament Theology*, 1:239.
69. Brueggemann, *Old Testament Theology*, 117.
70. Thiselton, *The Two Horizons*, 3–4.
71. Barr, *Old and New in Interpretation*, 171–92.
72. Ibid., 40.
73. Ibid., 34–64.

The fifth objection follows from the fourth and stems from a concern that philosophy works with a *metalanguage* which gets tends to get super-imposed on the text's own vocabulary. Again, however, the argument fails as an objection to the use of philosophical language which is no more "metalanguage" than a history or sociology of religion, as Mark Smith recognized:

> First order discourse is discourse expressed in religious experience, such as prayer; second order discourse involves discourse representing intellectual reflection about the contents of that experience, as in theology, or philosophy of religion, or history of religion or comparative religion.[74]

The fact is that terminology and jargon not explicitly attested in biblical Hebrew are not necessarily distortive. I mean, why are biblical theologians not bothered by metalanguage such as "morphology," "metaphor," "rhetoric," "narration," "context," "character," "structure," "history," "redaction," "gender," "monotheism," "religion," "theology," "culture," "morality," "experience," "hermeneutics," and so on?[75] Not only do these terms ultimately derive from early philosophical backgrounds, but none of them is found in the Hebrew vocabulary of the biblical texts. And yet they are considered perfectly proper. This shows that the real problem was never the use of nonbiblical terms per se. Rather, it comes in with distortive extensions relative to presumptuous agendas.

The sixth objection concerns the nature of the biblical language, which is prose and poetry filled with metaphor and myth, and as such is considered to be problematic for philosophical reflection. The argument is implicit in a remark by Robert Carroll:

> Theology operates with abstract philosophical notions whereas much of the language in the Bible is highly metaphorical. In philosophical talk, God is abstract.... In biblical language, God is a character in a narrative, a player in a story.[76]

---

74. Mark Smith, *God in Translation: Deities in Cross-Cultural Discourse in the Biblical World* (FAT 57; Tübingen: Mohr Siebeck, 2008), 18.

75. The same point was made by Mark Smith in *The Memoirs of God: History, Memory, and Experience of the Divine in Ancient Israel* (Augsburg: Fortress, 2004), 2.

76. Carroll, *Wolf in the Sheepfold*, 37.

If the aesthetic literary qualities of the Hebrew Bible are taken to be problematic for philosophy, then the notion of what philosophy is and can be concerned with has been utterly oversimplified. Philosophy itself cannot be reduced to its scholastic-systematic or normative-contemporary varieties of speculative metaphysics. It has from the beginning included a concern with literature, fiction, and art. In fact, much of the standard jargon in biblical literary criticism (e.g., narrative, metaphor, rhetoric, myth) ultimately derives from early Greek philosophy (e.g., from Aristotle's poetics and rhetoric). Literary criticism itself was born in philosophical reflection. What is more, while an attempt to construct a normative systematic metaphysics from the Hebrew Bible may be challenged by its literary ontology, the use of descriptive philosophy of religion to clarify the concepts, beliefs, and practices of the world in the text has no such obstacles.

The seventh possible objection concerns the assumption that the theological pluralism of the Hebrew Bible is unsuited to doing philosophy. This idea was voiced by Carroll, again most eloquently, in a remark that basically advises one to forget about a philosophical-theological reflection on its contents:

> Reflecting on what you read may not be as conducive to systematic theology as you might have wished. The book is too untidy, too sprawling and too boisterous to be domesticated and tamed by neat systems of thought. If you want neatness, then close the book and turn to theology. But if you can tolerate contradiction and contrariety, if you can handle hyperbolic drive and chaotic manipulation of metaphor, then the Bible will burn your mind. We humans have produced few things like it. Oh, and a final word of warning: "the things you're likely to read in the Bible … ain't necessarily so!" [77]

One can agree with everything here, yet still question the assumption that pluralism is problematic for all philosophical reflection. After all, descriptive philosophy aimed at clarification has no problem in simply elucidating the nature of diachronic variation and synchronic variability. Since a descriptive philosophical analysis as found in the analytic, phenomenological, and comparative traditions in philosophy of religion has nothing to do with the construction of a unified systematic normative philosophy of religion—in which case the Hebrew Bible would be immensely prob-

---

77. Ibid., 147.

lematic—the objection seems irrelevant. Theological pluralism in the Hebrew Bible is for us not a problem but is instead precisely that, and the nature of this pluralism can and should be described and clarified in philosophical terms.

The eighth objection holds that philosophy is irrelevant in the sense that, even if it could be utilized in a hermeneutically legitimate manner, it cannot contribute to the kind of historical clarification of meaning that biblical scholars are interested in. According to Barr:

> Philosophy does not seem to solve biblical questions. So much in biblical scholarship depends on knowledge of a different kind…. A knowledge of Kant will not enable the scholar to distinguish between the *piel* and *hiphil* of the Hebrew verb and a reading of Hume will not explain why the Greek versions of Jeremiah and Job are substantially shorter than the present Hebrew text.[78]

Hopefully this view is not representative of the views of all biblical theologians, as the fact of the matter is that it involves fallacies of irrelevance and oversimplification. It all depends on what one means by philosophy. To be sure, knowledge of Kant will not teach anyone Hebrew grammar, but neither will knowledge of von Rad; for this was not the purpose of either's writings. And a reading of Hume may not settle the problem of the differences in length between the Hebrew and Greek versions of Job and Jeremiah, but neither will a reading of Barr's metatheology, for that was not his concern.

The fact is that a descriptive philosophical approach will aid our understanding of the Hebrew Bible if it is aimed at clarifying the metaphysical, epistemological, moral, and other assumptions in the text. Without a philosophical analysis of what the Hebrew Bible's worldviews took for granted about issues on the agenda in philosophy of religion, biblical scholars have not made a beginning in coming to terms with the basic conceptual content of ancient Israelite religion.

The ninth objection involves pointing out that philosophy is of necessity concerned with normative claims (like systematic theology), whereas biblical scholarship has a purely historical and descriptive interest of the kind that is not philosophical at all. It is assumed that mere descriptive philosophical clarification of religious concepts is not philosophy of reli-

---

78. Barr, *Concept of Biblical Theology*, 146.

gion proper, which is supposedly distinguished by its being concerned with the rational and critical evaluation of truth claims. In response to this objection, then, the now familiar reply follows. Not all philosophy is interested in critique or justification of truth claims, or in turning the object of its analysis into a normative system of ideas about the way things are. Descriptive philosophical approaches offer the possibility of historical clarification of the Hebrew Bible. A closer look at what philosophers actually do in practice shows that much of their philosophical task is actually not concerned with putting normative claims on the table. Students of the history of philosophy are used to *historical philosophical* research that seeks to translate ideas into philosophical language.[79]

The tenth objection is related to the previous one. It involves the claim that biblical scholars cannot do philosophy of religion because philosophers assume nothing, and bracket alleged instances of divine revelation to which they cannot appeal since they rely on the light of reason only. This objection, while in itself correct about how natural theologians have often operated, involves a category mistake. Of course, if we were natural theologians who assumed that the theological status of the Hebrew Bible was that of divine revelation, then indeed the text would have to be bracketed in our philosophical inquiries. However, since we operate in the context of biblical scholarship in which the concept of revelation pertains not to the Hebrew Bible itself but to the extension of that concept in the worlds in the text, the objection fails. Biblical scholars will not be using the Hebrew Bible to do philosophy of religion in the form of natural a/theology—they will be utilizing descriptive varieties of philosophy of religion to clarify the meaning of the biblical texts.

The eleventh objection comes from Continental philosophy. It claims that philosophical theology is impossible given the history of religion, and after Kant, and that as a result a theoretical understanding of God is simply hopeless. Here again the objection is presumptuous, since as biblical scholars our concern is not God as *noumenon,* but with representations of deity in the Hebrew Bible. The critique is invalid, moreover, in the same sense as the previous objection—it fails to take cognizance of the possibility of a descriptive philosophy of religion and of a phenomenological approach, both of which were in fact born in recognition of Kant's ideas. In summary, then, a philosophical approach to ancient Israelite religion

---

79. Hebblethwaite, *Philosophical Theology and Christian Doctrine*, 6.

is not concerned with arriving at a theoretical understanding of any transcendent realm or God *in re*: it is simply aimed at a better understanding of what the Hebrew Bible assumed about these matters, whether these assumptions are true or not.

The twelfth objection follows from the previous two and concerns the claim that biblical scholars are not philosophers. As Barr noted:

> And in this respect the biblical scholar, at least in the English speaking world, has felt himself closer to the atmosphere of the church and the practical work of the average clergyman, who (it is supposed) is more anxious to get to grips with the Bible and its message than to discuss such apparently theoretical matters as being and becoming, the nature of knowledge, or the subject-object relationship. Relief from the unrealities of philosophical theology has been an unquestionable part of the motivation of those attracted to biblical theology.[80]

Note that in the course of his argument, Barr has shifted the goalposts. His reference to philosophical topics in the second-to-last sentence of the quoted section concerns issues in metaphysics and epistemology proper, whereas his last sentence makes a claim about philosophical theology. These disciplines are not identical. Moreover, none of them is irrelevant. To be sure, the topics in their philosophical contexts might seem dry to some biblical scholars, but the argument from disinterest or boredom just doesn't cut it. Many biblical scholars are bored by linguistic or historical approaches, which are not for that reason rendered dysfunctional or irrelevant. So there is no reason why we cannot attempt to describe in philosophical terms what the texts took for granted about being and becoming, the subject-object relationship, the nature of knowledge, and so on.

The thirteenth objection suggests that biblical scholars should leave philosophy to philosophers proper. Again, however, double standards are at work, readily apparent from the fact that we do not leave historical inquiries to historians proper or biblical theology to theologians proper. So why should we feel compelled to leave biblical philosophy to philosophers proper? There are good reasons not to do so. First, it is impractical, since philosophers of religion proper have normative concerns with contemporary beliefs and do not have the luxury of becoming exclusively concerned with a descriptive clarification of ancient Israelite religion for

---

80. Barr, *Concept of Biblical Theology*, 146–47.

its own sake. Second, many philosophers of religion have no knowledge of classical Hebrew or training in biblical criticism, both of which are pre-requisites for anyone seeking to engage in a hermeneutically legitimate philosophical approach to ancient Israelite religion as encountered in the Hebrew Bible. If biblical scholars do not develop and engage in a descriptive philosophical approach to the text aimed at historical clarification, no one will.

A fourteenth and final possible objection might come from someone who concurs with the claim that a philosophical approach is possible, but imagines it to be redundant. After all, other disciplines are already concerned with the Hebrew Bible and philosophical issues (some forms of biblical theology, systematic theology, Jewish and Christian philosophy of religion). However, while many other disciplines do indeed discuss the kinds of issues that philosophers of religion are interested in, and do so with reference to the Hebrew Bible, none uses a purely descriptive approach that actually involves doing philosophical analysis rather than just hermeneutical metacommentary. Jewish philosophy and biblical theology may investigate related concerns such as the nature of Yhwh or biblical theodicy or ethics, yet no other discipline is really concerned with purely descriptive philosophy of religion.

In addition, any possible overlap with already extant agendas does not mean that a philosophical approach to Yahwism is redundant, for such overlap is present in all subjects of all disciplines. Just because historians and sociologists share many common concerns does not render either of their disciplines superfluous—even when there is often little distinction between historical sociology and social history. Literary criticism in the study of the Hebrew Bible is not considered unnecessary just because some literary critics proper have at times written on the biblical text. Via analogy, therefore, just as biblical theology is not made redundant by overlapping discussions in historical, systematic, and philosophical theology, so too a philosophical approach to ancient Israelite religion is not invalidated if some of its concerns overlap with those in biblical/systematic theology or Jewish philosophy.

In summary, then, we have identified and rebutted a number of popular objections to a philosophical approach in the study of ancient Israelite religion as represented in the Hebrew Bible. None of these can any longer be considered to hold water in any absolute sense. Though much in the critique of philosophical *eise*gesis carries within it a valid point of concern and was probably brought to the fore owing to legitimate hermeneutical insights and historical consciousness, it should now be admitted that, when used as generalizations, the objections are fallacious. Since any weight they carry is based purely on essentialist presuppositions or views regarding the nature of the Hebrew Bible, philosophy of religion and biblical scholarship, they now need to be rethought in terms of absolute normativity.

In some ways the fourteen objections discussed above now seem so "twentieth century." Times change, so perhaps the moment has come to rethink the relations between Athens and Jerusalem.

5.7. Conclusion

In this chapter I have discussed a number of currents in descriptive philosophy of religion that might be of interest to scholars of the Hebrew Bible, many of whom errantly imagine that historical and philosophical concerns are incommensurable. None of these currents or trends has been claimed to be right or the only one possible: it has only be said that they are useful in as much as they offer descriptive tools biblical scholars might use for the clarification of meaning in the biblical texts. Moreover none of the traditional objections against involving philosophy in a study of the Hebrew Bible has validity, even if it may have made a worthwhile point in the context in which it was originally. The approach to be developed in this study will therefore be a descriptive enterprise that combines elements from analytic, phenomenological and comparative perspectives considered to be functional for the study of ancient Israelite religion. But before I introduce the new methodology, a few analogies can help us to get our heads around what *prima facie* seems like an outrageous idea: philosophy *in* the Hebrew Bible.

6

POSSIBLE ANALOGIES FOR A PHILOSOPHY OF
ANCIENT ISRAELITE RELIGION

We go more outside the usual realm of biblical studies when we turn
to *the renewed effect of philosophy on our subject.* The typical biblical
scholarship of modern times has been rather little touched by philosophy—certainty much less than it has been touched by theology.[1]

6.1. INTRODUCTION

In the previous chapter we looked at three descriptive philosophical currents that offer tools for the clarifying of concepts, beliefs, and practices in
religion. The objective was to get biblical scholars' heads around the idea
that we engage in descriptive philosophy of religion that limits itself to the
elucidation of meaning. Now we go one step further than theorizing about
a philosophical perspective *on* Israelite religion (the objective genitive) by
imagining the presence of philosophical assumptions *in* Israelite religion
(the subjective genitive). In order to do this we shall be broadening the
very concept of "philosophy" via possible analogies to the new methodological approach to be introduced in the next chapter.[2]

6.2. FOLK PHILOSOPHY IN ANCIENT ISRAELITE RELIGION

Biblical scholars tend to view the concept of "philosophy" in stereotypical forms and, not finding any such discourse in the Hebrew Bible, deny
the presence of philosophical data altogether. The stereotypes absent from

---

1. Barr, *History and Ideology in the Old Testament,* 27, emphasis added.
2. The concept of this chapter and the fruitful employment of analogy was
inspired by Barr's notion of "Historical Theology—A Possible Analogy?" in Barr, *Concept of Biblical Theology,* 209–21.

biblical discourse include Greek substantive philosophy, critical secular thought, scholastic metaphysics and formalized analytic arguments. However, the tendency to deny the Hebrew Bible anything philosophical when its rhetoric does not conform to Western varieties of philosophical systems actually involves a colonialist ethnocentric hermeneutical fallacy. Metaphilosophers with historical consciousness and crosscultural awareness know that the question of what makes philosophy philosophical does not have a single answer.

> For Plato it was a critical wisdom about both the ultimate realities and this world. For Plotinus it was a religious worldview. For Aristotle it was systematic knowledge indistinguishable from science. For Aquinas it was greatly implicated with theology. For the later Wittgenstein it was a method of examining language in ways that would dissolve previous metaphysical problems. All this without considering the slants provided by, say, Chinese and Indian philosophy.[3]

In the ancient world, there were indeed no absolute differences between wisdom literature, theology, science, and philosophy (the love of wisdom). Ethics was *moral philosophy* and scientific thinking just *natural philosophy*. Aristotle's philosophy comprised not only his metaphysics and logic but also his *Poetica* and *Rhetorica* (literary criticism). So when it comes to philosophical concerns, we would do well to remember that the concept of a philosophy of x (where x can be language, science, religion, mind, law, art, mathematics, literature, culture, etc.) is a product of the modern era, conceivable only when philosophy and a given domain of discourse had already parted ways). The whole idea of a professional philosopher whose concerns are limited to metascientific reflection is a very recent phenomenon.

So is there philosophy in the Hebrew Bible? Well, that depends on what one understands by the concept. If by philosophy one understands a concern with traditional Western philosophical questions, arguments and speculation, the answer is "no." However, though one would not speak of philosophy in this sense in the Hebrew Bible, one can easily speak of *folk philosophical presuppositions* in the texts. In other words, the biblical texts contain metaphysical, epistemological, and ethical assumptions about the nature of reality, existence, life, knowledge, truth, belief, good and evil,

---

3. Smart, *World Philosophies*, 2.

value, and so on. What is more, the biblical texts also contain presuppositions about the issues that are of interest to philosophers of religion, for instance the nature of religious language, the concept of revelation, the nature of deity, and the existence of deity. But if this is the case, then surely the Hebrew Bible contains data that a descriptive philosophy of religion can clarify, irrespective of whether or not the contents are relevant and true.

The concept of "folk philosophy" has in recent years become an accepted idea in comparative philosophy, area philosophy, and world philosophy, especially in fields dealing with ancient and/or non-Western cultural worldviews. With the aid of this concept, philosophers are now able to work historically and descriptively to clarify the unsystematic and unarticulated worldviews of ancient cultures traditionally branded as unphilosophical in the Western sense (e.g., the Aztecs).[4] It has also been recognized that folk philosophies come to expression in different ways in different cultural contexts. So from a multicultural, postcolonialist perspective we will have to rethink and qualify our understanding of the absence of philosophy in the Hebrew Bible. In the remainder of this chapter I wish to show by way of several analogies how we can begin both to see folk philosophy in the text and to recognize the need for a purely descriptive philosophical approach to ancient Israelite religion.

6.3. ANALOGIES FROM PHILOSOPHY

6.3.1. HISTORICAL INTRODUCTIONS TO JEWISH PHILOSOPHY

A first field that offers an analogy directly relevant to our concerns and where the presence of folk philosophy is recognized in the Hebrew Bible is Jewish philosophy. To be sure, most Jewish philosophy is not aimed at providing a purely descriptive philosophical clarification of ancient (especially preexilic) Yahwism(s). The analogy from Jewish philosophy is therefore not perfect, particularly since in Jewish philosophy the Hebrew Bible is mostly a controversial resource for contemporary philosophical reflection, so that the clarification of the biblical text is seldom an end in itself. Still, the presence of folk philosophical assumptions is definitely granted.

---

4. James Maffie, "Aztec Philosophy" [cited 25 August 2010]. Online: http: //www .iep.utm.edu.

Is the Bible a source for philosophical reflection? A natural reaction is that it is. The Bible depicts the character of God, presents an account of creation, posits a metaphysics of divine providence and divine interventions, suggests a basis for morality, discusses many features of human nature, and frequently poses the notorious conundrum of how God can allow evil. Surely then it engages questions that lie at the heart of Jewish philosophy and religious philosophy generally. Yet the categorization of the Bible as philosophy must be qualified. For the Bible obviously deviates in many features from what philosophers (and especially those trained in the analytical tradition) have come to regard as philosophy.[5]

The authors' statement is motivated by a number of stereotypical hermeneutical considerations aimed at showing how the Bible differs from philosophy:

First, the Bible contains, at its very core, a great deal of material that is not necessarily philosophical: law, poetry, narrative. Second, we expect philosophical truth to be formulated in declarative sentences. The Bible yields few propositional nuggets of this kind. Third, philosophical works try to yield conclusions by means of logical argumentation. The Bible contains little sustained argument of a deductive, inductive or practical nature and attempts to impose the structure of rational argument on the biblical text yields little benefit. Fourth, philosophers try to avoid contradicting themselves. When contradictions appear, they are either a source of embarrassment, or a spur to developing higher order dialectic to accommodate the tension between theses. The Bible, by contrast, often juxtaposes contradictory ideas, without explanation or apology.... Fifth, much of what the Bible has to say of subjects of manifest philosophical importance seems primitive to later philosophical sensibilities.[6]

Most biblical scholars would agree with the above. However, rather than make the acceptance of these statements a reason to shun philosophy, some Jewish authors read the Hebrew Bible in relation to philosophical thought and thereby allow the text to function in the context of comparative philosophy of religion:

5. Shalom Carmy and David Shatz, "The Bible as a Source for Philosophical Reflection," in *History of Jewish Philosophy* (ed. Daniel H. Frank and Oliver Learnman; Routledge History of World Philosophies 2; London: Routledge, 2003), 13.

6. Ibid., 13–14.

In the remainder of this chapter we hope to illustrate the possibilities for a meaningful encounter between Bible and philosophy, one that will accord the Bible its rightful place among the sources of Jewish philosophy without exaggerating its analytical character and without blurring the lines between its formulations of certain problems or approaches and the formulations of later philosophers.[7]

Examples of attention to the use of the Hebrew Bible in philosophical reflection include "The Bible and Philosophical Exegesis," which is discussed in the section on foundations and first principles in *The Jewish Philosophy Reader*.[8] For the new approach to be developed in this study, we find a good analogy within some contemporary historical introductions to Jewish philosophy, where the authors discuss biblical "roots," "foundations," "first principles," "origins," and "(re)sources" in philosophical terms. Thus, according to one historian of Jewish philosophy: "We begin the story of Jewish philosophy with the Hebrew Scriptures."[9]

This is a typical assessment,[10] and many contemporary historians of Jewish philosophy are not reluctant to admit and clarify some of the folk philosophical ideas implicit within the biblical materials. Another good example comes from Norbert Samuelson's *Jewish Philosophy: An Historical Introduction*, in which the author deals with the history of Jewish philosophy from the formation of the Hebrew Scriptures to the present time.[11] Writing on the topic of "On the Hebrew Scriptures Being Jewish and Philosophical," Samuelson remarks, "Implicit within the words of the biblical text is a world and life view that is itself philosophical, because it includes claims about all the central topics of philosophical inquiry.[12] We can also see how philosophy of religion is mixed with the Hebrew Bible in Samuelson's *Revelation and the God of Israel*.[13] The book combines a descriptive

---

7. Ibid., 16.

8. See Daniel H. Frank, Oliver Leaman, and Charles H. Manekin, eds., *The Jewish Philosophy Reader* (London: Routledge, 2000), 3–38.

9. Norbert M. Samuelson, *Jewish Philosophy: An Historical Introduction* (London: Continuum, 2006), 11–78.

10. See also the use of philosophy in the popular sense in Neumark, *Philosophy of the Bible*; or a more specific focus in Israel I. Efros, *Ancient Jewish Philosophy: A Study in Metaphysics and Ethics* (Detroit: Wayne State University Press, 1964).

11. Samuelson, *Jewish Philosophy*, 11–78.

12. Ibid., 16.

13. Norbert M. Samuelson, *Revelation and the God of Israel* (Cambridge: Cambridge University Press, 2002), 11–21.

clarification of ideas in the Hebrew Bible with a combined philosophical and historical interest, showing what can be done. Another rather good analogy of descriptive Jewish philosophy that biblical scholars might be able to relate to is David Schatz's discussion of ancient Israelite philosophical assumptions about divine providence and free will in the Joseph narrative and in the story of the hardening of Pharaoh's heart.[14] Whereas many Christian philosophers have wanted to try to salvage a belief in human freedom through reinterpretation, Schatz casually (and correctly) notes that free will is not much of a concern in many biblical stories. He also discusses the form the problem of evil takes in the Hebrew Bible and is careful to distinguish it from the ways in which it is treated in Christian "perfect being" theology. In Yahwism, the problem of evil is not related to arguments against the existence of God.[15]

Finally there is the Bible-Philos project of "Jewish Philosophical Theology." It is run by the Department of Philosophy, Political Theory and Religion (PPR) at the Shalem Center in Jerusalem and is part of a larger program in "Analytic Theology" initiated by the John Templeton Foundation in 2010. The project shows recognition of a gap in the research that I have tried to point out since 2003:[16]

> The Hebrew Bible occupies an anomalous position on the contemporary academic landscape. The field of biblical studies produces a steady stream of works on the compositional history, philology, and literary character of the biblical texts. But the *ideas* that find expression in the Hebrew Scriptures—the metaphysics, epistemology, ethics, and political philosophy of the biblical authors—have seldom been explored by the field of biblical studies in a systematic fashion. At the same time, philosophers, who see the study of ideas as the principal purpose of their work, tend to assume that the biblical texts fall outside the scope of their discipline. The result is that despite general agreement that the Bible has had an unparalleled significance in the history of the West, its ideas have remained, until recently, largely beyond the reach of sustained academic investigation.[17]

---

14. David Schatz, "Judaism," in Meister and Copan, *Routledge Companion to Philosophy of Religion*, 56.

15. Ibid., 60.

16. See Gericke, "Does Yahweh Exist," 10–24.

17. The statement was found online [cited 10 February 2012]: http://www.bible-andphilosophy.org/project-overview.

Preference is therefore given to research that can be of obvious interest to contemporary philosophy and theology. Quoting from the website, these are the following:

1. Are there distinct biblical or talmudic concepts of *truth, being, justice,* or *love*?

2. Do the texts of the Hebrew Bible, Talmud, and Midrash have a distinct approach (or approaches) to familiar questions in ontology, epistemology, philosophy of language, or hermeneutics?

3. Do the Bible or classical rabbinic sources have a distinct approach (or approaches) to philosophical and/or scientific topics such as human nature, the nature of the mind, or the nature of the spoken word? To what do the biblical or talmudic concepts of the *soul* refer?

4. What are the biblical or talmudic views of reason and argument? Of the search for wisdom, knowledge, and truth? Of conscience? Of science? Of prophecy?

5. To what do the biblical or talmudic concepts of *God* refer? Is God to be understood as *perfect being*? And if not, then what?

6. Are there distinctive biblical or talmudic approaches to morals? To self-improvement and virtue? To law? How does the classical Jewish concept of *holiness* differ from its meaning in other traditions, and how is it related to goodness?

7. Does the central narrative sequence of the Bible (Genesis to Kings), if considered as a whole, raise questions of philosophical significance? What about the corpus of the later prophets (Isaiah to Malachi)? The biblical compilation as a whole? Is there a distinctive biblical approach to history? To narrative? To time?

8. Do particular biblical stories or books of the Bible, Talmud, or Midrash advance philosophically significant teachings or points of view? What about the "biographies" of particular biblical or talmudic figures?

9. What do the various genres by means of which the biblical or talmudic authors express their ideas (narrative, law, prophetic oration, etc.) tell us about the content of those ideas?

10. How do biblical or classical rabbinic concepts, issues, and viewpoints compare with those of ancient Greece? Of the

ancient Near East and India? Of later Western philosophy, including modern philosophy?[18]

One example of this type of Jewish philosophical theology is Yoram Hazony's *The Philosophy of Hebrew Scripture*.[19] Hazony proposes a new framework for reading the Bible and argues that the biblical authors used narrative and prophetic oratory to advance universal arguments about ethics and political philosophy, metaphysics and theory of knowledge. Hazony's book, as well as the larger project and its concerns with the Hebrew Bible, can all be seen as part of this analogy to what is envisaged by my study. However, as a biblical scholar my focus is more historical and descriptive, and my first concern is not to show the relevance of the text for today's world. Moreover, the project's alliance with some fundamentalist Christian philosophers of religion (e.g., from Notre Dame) is sure to give part of it a lack of appreciation for the problems of Old Testament theology. Nevertheless, its existence is worthy of note.

These examples from historical Jewish philosophy show how we as biblical scholars might begin to imagine both a descriptive philosophical approach to ancient Israelite religion and the presence of folk philosophy in the texts themselves. More examples could be given, yet the ones mentioned here suffice to illustrate at least an acknowledgement of the possibility of mixing historical and philosophical concerns in the interpretation of the Hebrew Bible.

6.3.2. Varieties of Ancient Near Eastern Philosophy

Most histories of Western philosophy continue to equate the love of wisdom with a Greek philosophical tradition that began inexplicably in the sixth century b.c.e. as though in isolation and without precursor. Yet history is more complex than this. Philosophy was not an original Greek invention, but actually comes from ancient Near Eastern precursors.[20] This

---

18. See http://www.bibleandphilosophy.org/project-overview [cited 10 February 2012].

19. Yoram Hazony, *The Philosophy of Hebrew Scripture* (New York: Cambridge University Press, 2012).

20. Walter Burkert, "Prehistory of Presocratic Philosophy in an Orientalizing Context," in *The Oxford Handbook of Presocratic Philosophy* (ed. Patricia W. Cord and Daniel W. Graham; New York: Oxford University Press, 2008), 60.

origin is attested in Aristotle's *On Philosophy* and his pupils discussed the *barbaros philosophia* as they took account of Egyptian, Chaldean, Iranian, and Jewish sages. One of them, Damascius, in his book on first principles, quotes from the first lines of *Enuma Elish*. More recently, scholars such as Simo Parpola have argued that the origins of many aspects of Greek philosophy lie in ancient Near Eastern (specifically Assyrian) religion and mythology.[21] Interestingly, then, we encounter in contemporary comparative metaphilosophical discussions the recognition of a variety of ancient Near Eastern folk philosophies which can serve as possible analogies to folk philosophies in ancient Israelite religion.

First, there is so-called "Babylonian philosophy," a folk philosophy commonly traced back to early Mesopotamian wisdom literature. It is embodied in certain philosophies of life, particularly wisdom ethics implicit in dialectic, dialogues, epic poetry, folklore, hymns, lyrics, prose, and proverbs. Its concerns extend to the natural folk philosophy that today we call scientific inquiry. "These different forms of literature were first classified by the Babylonians, who also developed forms of reasoning both rationally and empirically."[22] Historians of ancient philosophy also know that Babylonian philosophy had an influence on Greek philosophy. *The Dialogue of Pessimism*, well known to many scholars of the Hebrew Bible, "contains similarities to the agonistic thought of the sophists, the Heraclitean doctrine of contrasts, and the dialogues of Plato."[23] It also represents a precursor to the Socratic method. Less well known is that the official father of Greek philosophy, Thales, was a Phoenician who once studied in Babylonia.[24]

Our second example of ancient Near Eastern folk philosophy is Egyptian philosophy. Egyptologists have not shied away from discussing what they believe to be philosophical issues encountered in ancient Egyptian religion. An interesting example comes from the proceedings of a 1989

---

21. Simo Parpola, "The Assyrian Tree of Life: Tracing the Origins of Jewish Monotheism and Greek Philosophy," *JNES* 52 (1993): 161–208.

22. "Akkadian Literature," *Wikipedia, The Free Encyclopedia* [cited 6 July 2010]. Online: http://en.wikipedia.org/w/index.php?title=Akkadian_literature&oldid=504505499.

23. "Philosophy," *Wikipedia, The Free Encyclopedia* [cited 6 August 2010]. Online: http://en.wikipedia.org/w/index.php?title=Philosophy&oldid=504148515.

24. "Assyro-Babylonian literature," *Wikipedia, The Free Encyclopedia* [cited 1 February 2010]. Online: http://en.wikipedia.org/w/index.php?title=Assyro-Babylonian_literature&oldid=335903264.

seminar hosted by the Department of Near Eastern Languages and Civilizations at Yale University and published as *Religion and Philosophy in Ancient Egypt*. As is evident in the titles of some of the essays, for instance "The Cosmology of the Pyramid Texts" (James P. Allen), "State and Religion in the New Kingdom" (Jan Assmann), and "The Natural Philosophy of Akhenaten" (James P. Allen), this work was considered philosophical, as it arose from philosophical interests.[25]

On a more individual level, a descriptive philosophical approach to Egyptian religion and mythology is found in the writings of Jan Assmann. Assmann has engaged at times in what can only be described as a distinct variety of comparative philosophy of religion. He sees no problem in using the concept of "philosophy" with reference to some of the religious beliefs in ancient Egyptian culture. Recently, in his *The Price of Monotheism*,[26] he even suggested that ancient Israelite religion (the Moses of the Hebrew Bible) introduced the world to the true-false philosophical distinction in a new, permanent and revolutionary form. He also compared the moral philosophy of pagan (Egypt) with what he calls "the philosophy of justice" in the Hebrew Bible. Whether or not one is convinced by the use of terms in Assmann's arguments, his philosophical account of Egyptian and biblical ideas provides a useful analogy for imagining the presence of folk philosophical notions in ancient Israelite religion.[27]

Third, Persian philosophy can be traced back to Old Iranian philosophical traditions and related literature with ancient Indo-Iranian roots.[28] The tradition of philosophy in the Persian-speaking world is extraordinarily rich, creative, and diverse. A recent anthology was completely dedicated to its historical and philosophical clarification.[29] The term "philosophy" is here used in its widest sense to include implicit critical theological reasoning, and to extend over a period of more than two millennia. It

---

25. James P. Allen, ed., *Religion and Philosophy in Ancient Egypt* (New Haven: Yale University Press, 1989).

26. Jan Assmann, *The Price of Monotheism* (trans. Robert Savage; Stanford, Calif.: Stanford University Press, 2009).

27. For critique of Assmann, see Eckart Otto, *Mose: Geschichte und Legende* (Munich: Beck, 2006), 105; and Smith, *God in Translation*, 323–27.

28. "Iranian philosophy," *Wikipedia, The Free Encyclopedia*. Cited 1 February 2010. Online: http://en.wikipedia.org/w/index.php?title=Iranian_philosophy&oldid=340828427.

29. Seyyed Hossein Nasr and Mehdi Amin Razavi, eds., *From Zoroaster to Omar Khayyam* (vol. 1 of *An Anthology of Philosophy in Persia*; London: Tauris, 2008).

comes in many forms and during the pre-Islamic period was intertwined with religion in Zoroastrian texts such as the Gathas, the Dēnkard, and the Bundahishn. The dominant philosophical concerns include metaphysics, cosmology, and eschatology. Much of Persian philosophy is typically associated with the teachings of Zarathustra (Zoroaster), in which we encounter folk philosophical treatments of the problem of evil. The ideas stemming from this tradition would later have a significant influence on Greek philosophy, some exponents of which (e.g., Eudoxus of Cnidus) held that Zoroastrian thought was the best known and most useful of all philosophies.

Many elements of Persian philosophy are now indelibly inscribed in Western folk philosophy, and not only as a result of the Persian influence on Israelite religion in the postexilic period. For example, Plato himself learned Zoroastrian philosophy and incorporated much of it into his own Platonic realism. In his writings in the *Republic* he was even accused of plagiarizing parts of Zoroaster's *On Nature*, for instance the *Myth of Er*. Another interesting example is the way in which Zarathustra's ideas were communicated via the Persian philosopher Osthanes to his most famous student, the Greek philosopher Democritus, the man famous for having invented the idea of the "atom." In 2005 the *Oxford Dictionary of Philosophy* ranked Zarathustra's legacy as number two in the chronology of philosophical events.

Taken together, these brief remarks on ancient Near Eastern folk philosophy provide an analogy for how to think of folk philosophy in ancient Israelite religion from a cultural context that is close to that of the Hebrew Bible itself. If one can speak of Babylonian, Egyptian and Persian philosophy, it need not be difficult to conceive of ancient Israelite philosophy.

6.3.3. African Philosophy

Another very interesting possible analogy in the controversy regarding the validity of speaking of folk philosophy in ancient Israelite religion comes to us in the form of African philosophy.[30] Like ancient Israel, Africa is not typically associated with the Western philosophical tradition. The very

---

30. The idea of an analogy between my concept of a philosophical approach to ancient Israelite religion and a previous generation of African philosophy was suggested to me by the South African philosopher Ernst Wolff.

idea of African philosophy remains an essentially contested concept.[31] A great deal of debate concerns the question of whether there is such a thing at all:

> African philosophy is used in different ways by different philosophers. Although African philosophers spend their time doing work in many different areas, such as metaphysics, epistemology, moral philosophy, and political philosophy, a great deal of the literature is taken up with a debate concerning the nature of African philosophy itself.[32]

This heated debate began officially in 1945, when the Belgian missionary Father Placide Tempels published the first work in this genre, *La philosophie bantoue*.[33] Tempels was reacting to a prevailing belief about Africans, argued for in earlier works by anthropologists such as Lucien Lévy-Bruhl and by some Catholic theologians, that Africans were incapable of philosophical thought. Temples asserted that the people of Sub-Saharan Africa have a distinctive philosophy. Though writing in colonialist fashion, as a child of his own time, he attempted to describe its underpinnings:

> We do not claim, of course, that the Bantu are capable of formulating a philosophical treatise, complete with an adequate vocabulary. It is our job to proceed to such systematic development. It is we who will be able to tell them, in precise terms, what their inmost concept of being is. They will recognize themselves in our words and will acquiesce, saying, "You understand us: you know us completely: you 'know' in the way that we 'know.' "[34]

---

31. Introductions to the issues can be found in Kwasi Wiredu, ed., *A Companion to African Philosophy* (Oxford: Blackwell, 2004); Lee M. Brown, *African Philosophy: New and Traditional Perspectives* (Oxford: Oxford University Press, 2004); Richard H. Bell, *Understanding African Philosophy: A Cross-Cultural Approach to Classical and Contemporary Issues in Africa* (New York: Routledge, 2002); and Barry Hallen, *A Short History of African Philosophy* (Bloomington: Indiana University Press, 2002).

32. "African Philosophy," *Wikipedia, The Free Encyclopedia* [cited 12 April 2010]. Online: http://en.wikipedia.org/w/index.php?title=African_philosophy&oldid=336249387.

33. Placide Tempels, *Bantu Philosophy* (trans. A. Rubbens; Paris: Présence Africaine, 1959).

34. Ibid., 36.

Tempels tried to show that African philosophical categories can be identified through the categories inherent in African languages and that the primary ontological category in African metaphysics is not Being but Force.[35] In non-African philosophy, so the argument goes, Being is conceived of as something distinct from Force (that is, beings may have Force or may not), or Force is thought to be part of Being (that is, Being is more than Force, but dependent upon it). By contrast, noted Tempels, in African metaphysics reality is dynamic to the extent that Being equals Force. In a debate that biblical theologians might find reminiscent of the controversy about the uniqueness of "Hebrew thought," Tempels argued that owing to difference in conceptual categories, the African mind is structured in a way that sharply contrasts with the Western enterprise of understanding and defining Being. "Yet for all Tempels's efforts, *Bantu Philosophy* was rightly criticized on the ground of its gross generalizations concerning the thought of an entire continent."[36] "Tempels responded by insisting that there was a coherent and interesting philosophy among the Bantu (more specifically, the tribes of the inner Congo, where he worked)."[37] His work, though controversial, nevertheless inspired further discussions of the possibility of imagining an African philosophy.

"While Tempels's book has been seen by many as the starting point for the academic study of African philosophy, questions of African identity began long before his work."[38] Over the course of several decades in the twentieth century, African-born scholars trained in Western philosophy have busied themselves with a metaphilosophical debate over whether there exists an African philosophy and, if so, what its nature is. This debate regarding the nature and existence of African philosophy has culminated in two camps, the universalists and the particularists.[39] The universalists

---

35. It is hard to overlook the parallel found in Mark Smith's suggestion that ancient Israelite metaphysics was concerned with power rather than being. On this, see the next chapter.

36. "Bantu Philosophy," *Wikipedia, The Free Encyclopedia* [cited 9 August 2010]. Online: http://en.wikipedia.org/w/index.php?title=Bantu_Philosophy&oldid =434518056.

37. Bruce B. Janz, "African Philosophy." [cited 4 February 2010]. Online: http:// pegasus.cc.ucf.edu/~janzb/ papers/37AfPhil.pdf.

38. Ibid.

39. Sources for this outline are Polycarp Ikuenobe, "The Parochial Universalist Conception of 'Philosophy' and 'African Philosophy,'" *PEW* 47 (1997): 189–90; Kwasi Wiredu, "On Defining African Philosophy," in *African Philosophy: The Essential Read-*

argue that the conceptual content of "philosophy" should be the same in both the Western and the African contexts. The particularists in turn suggest that different cultures have different ways of explaining reality, and hence, African philosophy is essentially different from other philosophies. A third view argues for a combination of universalist and particularist elements in African philosophy, in the sense that although there are culturally determined philosophical ways of constructing meaning, these ways are not necessarily always incommensurable. As a result of these debates, there developed what Henry Odura Oruka initially distinguished as four trends in African philosophy, two of which can be mentioned as useful analogies for a philosophical approach to ancient Israelite religion, since they are more descriptive and historical in origin.[40]

The first is so-called *ethnophilosophy*. It involves the recording of the beliefs found in African cultures. The concept has also been used in the context of Japanese and Mesoamerican philosophy.[41] This line of thinking treats African philosophy as consisting in a set of shared beliefs, values, categories, and assumptions that are implicit in the language, practices, and beliefs of African cultures. African thought is regarded as a communal philosophy rather than as being the philosophical thought of an individual. There is also the concept of Negritude promoted by Leopold Senghor who, like a biblical theologian concerned with "Hebrew thought," argued that "the distinctly African approach to reality was based on emotion rather than logic, worked itself out in participation rather than analysis, and manifested itself through the arts rather than the sciences."[42]

Ethnophilosophy thus regards the collective traditional wisdom, or the generally held ontological assumptions and worldview of African ethnic groups or tribes, as having the same status as Continental philosophy.

---

ings (ed. Tsenay Serequeberhan; New York: Paragon House, 1991), 87–110; Dismas A. Masolo, *African Philosophy in Search of Identity* (Edinburgh: University of Edinburgh Press, 1994).

40. Henry Odera Oruka, "Four Trends in Current African Philosophy," in *Philosophy in the Present Situation of Africa* (ed. Alwin Diemer; Wiesbaden: Steiner, 1981), 1–7.

41. Fidelis U. Okafor: "In Defense of Afro-Japanese Ethnophilosophy," *PEW* 47 (1997): 363–81.

42. "African Philosophy," *New World Encyclopedia* [cited 12 April 2012]. Online: http://www.newworldencyclopedia.org/p/index.php?title=African_philosophy&oldid=684750.

[A] part of ethnophilosophy's stimulating power can perhaps be traced to the ambiguity of Tempels's approach: on the one hand, it could easily be dismissed as paternalism or the attempt to force African philosophy into the straightjacket of European concepts, while on the other hand the expressed desire to give "ethnic" philosophy a new role within the international hierarchy of the philosophies was immensely attractive. Some claimed that ethnophilosophy is no philosophy at all, because it remains indifferent toward individually critical, that is, typically philosophical, approaches. Related debates touch upon fundamental questions concerning the nature of philosophy as such.[43]

To the outside observer from an Anglo-Saxon analytic background, ethnophilosophy indeed appears to be a kind of philosophical anthropology (the premises of which it continues to share). It is ethnography incorporating interest in a culture's metaphysical questions. Its opposite is "conventional" Western philosophy, which persistently explores truth with the help of a single, individual mind, aiming at the crystallization of a truth relevant for everyone. What matters for ethnophilosophy is the truth that is brought forward by the way of life of a group of people and is found on the "inside" of a culture. This truth supposedly exists independently of any consideration of those things that exist on the outside. Ethnophilosophy is therefore radical in the sense that opposes being dictated to by any intruding variety of "international" philosophy.[44]

In spite of the intensive critical evaluation and transformation that ethnophilosophy has suffered in Africa since the 1960s, it has never attracted much attention from those who have no academic link with the specific domain of African philosophy. It seems, however, that through recent confrontations with globalization, ethnophilosophy has started to expand its field of influence. In 1997, Fidelis Okafor published an article in *Philosophy East and West* with the slightly curious title, "In Defense of Afro-Japanese Ethnophilosophy." In it Okafor reevaluates qualities such as "folkness" and "communal mind" as characteristics of a philosophy that takes a people's *Weltanschauung* as simultaneously a point of departure and an objective. He suggests that ethnophilosophy is "the reasoning or thinking that underlie the existential outlook, the patterns of

43. Thorsten Botz-Bornstein, "Ethnophilosophy, Comparative Philosophy, Pragmatism: Toward a Philosophy of Ethnoscapes," *PEW* 56 (2006): 153.

44. Ibid.

life, belief system, aesthetic and moral values, [and] customary laws and practices of a particular people" as primary constituents of philosophy.[45]

The question biblical scholars might ask is whether this form of philosophical anthropology might not be a useful analogy for a descriptive philosophical approach to ancient Israelite religion.

The second variety of African philosophy is so-called *philosophical sagacity.* It represents an individualist version of ethnophilosophy that pertains to the beliefs of certain special members of a community. These include the thoughts of sages, some of which may not be philosophical in the strict sense yet constitute raw data for technical philosophical reflection by professional or trained philosophers. Someone like Henry Odera Oruka used the concept of sagacity to point out that there is and was indeed philosophy, in the fullest sense of the word, implicit in the discourses of the sages of Africa. It was a philosophy that concerned itself with daily problems and issues common to every human being, for instance the Deity's existence, life, knowledge, and death. Odera Oruka argued that such issues were usually best addressed by those sages who could to some extent "transcend" the communal way of thinking.

Though commentators have often equated "sage philosophy" with "philosophic sagacity," Odera Oruka did not. He distinguished between two wings of sage philosophy: (1) folk or popular sagacity and (2) philosophic sagacity. While the former is associated with "communal maxims, aphorisms and general commonsense truths, the latter involves the thoughts of wise men and women that transcend popular wisdom and attain a philosophic capacity."[46] Hence, whereas philosophic sagacity can be located within sage philosophy, not every instance of sage philosophy constitutes philosophic sagacity. The novelty of Odera Oruka's project lies in philosophic sagacity, since the folk sagacity dimension is commonly considered to be a fallback on ethnophilosophy.

Toward the end of his life, Odera Oruka added two more trends to the four he initially listed.[47] One was called *literary/artistic philosophy* and involved the work of literary critics who reflected on philosophical issues

---

45. Ibid., 154.

46. This summary of the complexities of the concept of sagacity comes from "Henry Odera Oruka," *Wikipedia, The Free Encyclopedia* [cited 3 February 2010]. Online: http://en.wikipedia.org/w/index.php?title=Henry_Odera_Oruka&oldid=336553021.

47. This section is entirely indebted to the outline provided by Bruce B. Janz, "Afri-

within African prose and poetry. The other was what Odera Oruka called a *hermeneutic philosophy* (also called historical-hermeneutic), which consists of a philosophical analysis of African languages for the sake of finding and clarifying philosophically relevant content implicit therein. Also associated with analytic Anglophone approaches, it relates to the work of scholars such as Barry Hallen, whose work will be mentioned shortly. The term "hermeneutic" has also been used by a number of other philosophers to mean the philosophy of interpretation, in an African context. Amid these contrasting perspectives or types of African philosophy, not all of which are incommensurable, the perennial issue of the foundation of African philosophy takes several forms:

> First, it is a question about sources. Are there texts, and what counts as a text? Do cultural forms such as proverbs, songs, tales, and other forms of oral tradition count as philosophy in themselves, or are they merely the potential objects of philosophical analysis? Does the wisdom of sages count as philosophy, or is that wisdom at best merely the object of philosophical analysis? Is African philosophy African because it draws on tradition in some way? To take another line of inquiry, if we think of African philosophy as a discipline, where does disciplinarity come from, and what is its justification? Is African philosophy really a form of anthropology? Does it have more in common with literature, religion, or politics than with Western philosophy?[48]

By analogy, biblical scholars will ask the same questions with reference to folk philosophy in ancient Israelite religion. Moreover, we can look at the task of the hypothetical descriptive philosopher of ancient Israelite religion as comparable to that of an African philosopher working in the analytic tradition.[49] I wish to illustrate this point via reference to the ideas of Barry Hallen and Kwasi Wiredu.[50] Odera Oruka assigned Hallen

---

can Philosophy" [cited 4 February 2010]. Online: http://pegasus.cc.ucf.edu/~janzb/papers/37AfPhil.pdf.

48. Ibid., 12.

49. For specific philosophical approaches to African traditional religion, see John S. Mbiti, *African Religions and Philosophy* (rev.; ed. London: Heinemann, 1990).

50. Barry Hallen, "Does It Matter Whether Linguistic Philosophy Intersects Ethnophilosophy?" *APA Newsletters* 96 (1996): 136–40; "Analytic Philosophy and Traditional Thought: A Critique of Robin Horton" in *African Philosophy: A Classical Approach* (ed. Parker English and Kibujjo M. Kalumba; Upper Saddle River, N.J.: Prentice Hall, 1996): 216–28; "Academic Philosophy and African Intellectual Libera-

to the category of being concerned with philosophical sagacity, but then with first-order descriptive folk sagacity rather than with second-order critical philosophical sagacity. Hallen is an Anglophone analytic ordinary language philosopher working along "hermeneutical" lines. His work is concerned with the philosophical analysis of concepts in a given African language to help clarify their meaning.

According to Hallen, the question may be asked whether it is appropriate to use alien methods as well as technical words and meanings that are foreign to African languages, to analyze and clarify concepts in these languages. Hallen himself used ordinary language philosophy in which there is an emphasis upon *ordinary, common,* and *collective* uses of language; and upon philosophical *description* rather than critique. Since ordinary language is a medium through which a people's beliefs, thoughts, traditions, and customs can be known, every word, every concept, and every sentence of a language is important, and can be subjected to philosophical analysis, explication, and clarification (narrow analysis) within the context of its use. Whether or not Hallen is doing African philosophy as many think it should be done is, for the present, beside the point.[51] I simply note Hallen's philosophical analysis of African thought as an analogy to how a philosophical approach to ancient Israelite religion might be conducted by a biblical scholar interested in the clarification of meaning of what is stereotypically thought to be nonphilosophical cultural conceptual content.

My second example of an African philosopher of religion whose work features research that might represent a plausible analogy for the type of discussion that might be undertaken by a philosopher of ancient Israelite religion working descriptively and comparatively is Kwasi Wiredu. In a number of papers, Wiredu clarifies African conceptions of the divine in philosophical terms and compares them with Western philosophical conceptions of God, to show the fundamental metaphysical differences between the two.[52] One example is his "African Religions from a Philo-

---

tion," *African Philosophy* 11/2 (1998): 93–97; *The Good, the Bad, and the Beautiful: Discourse about Values in Yoruba Culture* (Bloomington: Indiana University Press, 2000); and *A Short History of African Philosophy.*

51. For a critical overview, see Gbenga Fasiku, "African Philosophy and the Method of Ordinary Language Philosophy," *The Journal of Pan African Studies* 2/3 (2008): 1–17.

52. Kwasi Wiredu, "African Philosophical Tradition: A Case Study of the Akan," *The Philosophical Forum* 24/1–3 (1992–1993): 41.

sophical Point of View," which appeared in a textbook in comparative philosophy of religion.[53] Biblical scholars working with the conceptual challenges of ancient Israelite religion might examine elements in Wiredu's approach to African philosophy of religion. His contributions are recognized in introductions to philosophy of religion, suggesting that if one can speak of African philosophy of religion, the idea of ancient Israelite philosophy of religion might not appear as absurd as it does *prima facie*.

The point of this extended analogy is this: if African philosophy is conceivable, then so too is a philosophical approach to ancient Israelite religion. If Hallen and Wiredu can use philosophy to clarify African traditional religion, biblical scholars can do the same with ancient Yahwism. I can therefore imagine the task of a philosopher of ancient Israelite religion as being like that adopted by those ordinary language African ethnophilosophers who limit their research to descriptive clarification, and who no longer tend toward generalization or the systematizing of ideas into one unitary "African" perspective. Nonphilosophical data and pluralism can be admitted and analyzed in African philosophy in the absence of attempts to harmonize historical and ideological diversity. One can simply work with smaller cultural complexes and then describe in philosophical terms all the differences of nuance in and between traditions. For example, rather than discussing the "African" concept of this or that, most African philosophers settle for a minimalist approach in which issues of interest might include, *inter alia*:[54]

1. The Yoruba concept of "person"
2. The concept of cause in African thought
3. The relation of soul and body in Akan thought
4. The concept of time in Yoruba thought
5. Self as a problem in African philosophy
6. The problem of knowledge in divination
7. The concept of truth in the Akan language
8. The concept of the good man in Hausa
9. The problem of evil: An Akan perspective

---

53. Kwasi Wiredu, "African Religions from a Philosophical Point of View," in Taliaferro, Draper, and Quinn, *A Companion to Philosophy of Religion*, 34–55.

54. These topics approximate the contents in Emmanuel Chukwudi Eze, *African Philosophy: An Anthology* (Blackwell Philosophy Anthologies; Oxford: Blackwell, 1998).

To imagine the possibility of an ancient Israelite philosophy, substitute "ancient Israel" for "Africa," and "Yahwistic," "Priestly," "Deuteronomistic," or other more specific individual biblical traditions for "Akan," "Igbo," "Yoruba," "Hausa," "Zulu," and others. If African ethnophilosophy is theoretically possible even when ancient African thought is pluralist, dynamic, and only folk philosophical in the Western sense, so is a philosophy of ancient Israelite religion. Both involve a philosophical anthropology that neither looks for professional Western philosophy in the texts nor tries to construct a systematic unified philosophy from it, but that instead merely translates the folk philosophical assumptions implicit in ordinary religious language into nondistortive philosophical terms. Consider therefore the following, and substitute "ancient Israelite" for "Diola" and "Senegalese."

> It may be … that there is no Diola philosophy in the rigorous sense understood by Western thought, because the Senegalese peasant hardly reflects exhaustively on being, on the value or conditions of action and has great difficulty in dealing with abstraction or logical dialectics. But if, by *philosophy*, one means the original synthesis of knowledge, an attitude vis-à-vis the world and life's problems, even if the elaboration is only implicit, rather confusedly felt than a clearly expressed cosmology, there unquestionably exists a Diola philosophy inscribed not only in dogma, myth, rites and symbols, proverbs and enigmas, songs and dances but also in the banal, daily gesture of the rice grower or the millet grinder, in the organization of the habitat or the curious division [*découpage*] of the paddy fields.[55]

One might say the same about Israelite "philosophy," which is without question a folk philosophy or compendium of folk philosophies implicit in the text. From such a postcolonialist perspective, biblical theologians' denials of the philosophical in ancient Israelite religion once again seems like a curious and unwitting variety of Western colonialist reasoning that denies the existence of any philosophy not created in the Greek or analytic image. Granting the absence of overt stereotypical critical philosophy in the Hebrew Bible, antiphilosophical sentiment in exegesis in the name of theological or historical-hermeneutical consciousness is therefore noth-

---

55. Louis Vincent Thomas, quoted in Issiaka P. Leleye, "Is There an African Philosophy in Existence Today?" in *Philosophy from Africa: A Text with Readings* (ed. Pieter H. Coetzee and Andre P. J. Roux; Cape Town: Oxford University Press, 2003), 86.

ing more than having cast the text into an alien philosophical mold and found it wanting. Consequently, methodological and conceptual debates in African philosophy are things that biblical scholars can learn from when seeking to address the controversy regarding the relationship between the Hebrew Bible and philosophy.

6.3.4. PHILOSOPHY IN LITERATURE

The presence of folk philosophy in the Hebrew Bible can also be demonstrated with reference to the analogy of philosophy in literature.[56] This is not the same as the philosophy *of* literature, but instead refers to how philosophy is present in literary works that are usually classified as being other than philosophical. The basic idea of this section is that philosophical data is not only found in the writings of philosophers but is also encountered in all folk philosophical assumptions. In some cases, therefore, philosophy also comes to us in the form of prose and poetry.

The first example comes from Chinese philosophy.[57] One common portrait of the difference between Chinese and Western traditions posits a radical incommensurability in the very nature of their philosophical inquiry. Western philosophy in its analytic format is, stereotypically, systematic argumentation and theory; whereas Chinese "philosophy" is "wisdom" literature, composed primarily of stories and sayings designed to move the audience to adopt a way of life—or to confirm its adoption of that way of life.[58] Moreover, the latter is pluralistic and without essence, and involves diverse currents or trajectories, such as Taoism and Confucianism, as well as subcurrents that are analogous to the various perspectives in the Hebrew Bible (Priestly, Deuteronomistic, Chronistic, and other).

Like the Hebrew Bible, Chinese philosophy is different from a discursive rationality in that it instructs by way of high-level generalizations. Inspired by the achievement of insight or wisdom in particular cases, narratives create general rules that one believes will work for many

---

56. See the relevant subsection discussed in an easily accessible manner at "Philosophy and Literature," *Wikipedia, The Free Encyclopedia* [cited 24 February 2010]. Online: http://en.wikipedia.org/w/index.php?title=Philosophy_and_literature&oldid=336960814.

57. For an introduction, see Wong, "Comparative Philosophy."

58. Ibid.

other cases in the future. The readers are expected to obtain philosophical insight from stories, and Eastern philosophy is generally more invitational and prescriptive than Western philosophy, which is overall more speculative and argumentative. Of course, this difference between Eastern and Western philosophical styles is more a matter of degree than an absolute contrast.[59] Even in the Western tradition philosophy comes in many forms: "Philosophy expresses itself in a variety of written forms. One thinks of Plato's dialogues, Aristotle's treaties, Augustine and Rousseau's Confessions, Descartes and Marcus Aurelius' Meditations, Heraclitus and Nietzsche's aphorisms."[60] Can philosophy be found in prose and poetry? Indeed, it can. Despite his insistence on the centrality of argumentation in philosophy, Plato dispatched the short analytical arguments presented in book 1 of *The Republic* in favor of lengthy expository portraits of the ideal city-state and the harmonious soul for the rest of the work. "These portraits sometimes present only the thinnest of arguments for crucial premises, and at other times no argument at all."[61] Aristotle likewise believed that discussions about the good in human life were best expressed in stories, because otherwise the lessons could not be properly assimilated by the young, who lacked experience of life. Philosophy was not only found in overt philosophical arguments.

It is in fact hard work to find an acknowledged figure in the Western tradition to whom exceptions to the rule do not apply, at least to some degree. "It is true that much Western philosophy, especially of the late modern variety, and most especially that emanating from the United Kingdom and North America, attempts to establish its claims through rigorous argumentation that does not appeal to experience or explanatory power in the broad sense."[62] However, differences in the ways philosophy is conceived simply reflect differences in the interests philosophy is meant to satisfy.[63]

Prose and poetry can be seen as applied folk philosophy. Some philosophers have indeed undertaken to write philosophy in the form of fic-

---

59. Ibid.

60. Frank, Leaman, and Manekin, "Bible and Philosophical Exegesis," 3.

61. Wong, "Comparative Philosophy."

62. Ibid.

63. "Philosophy and Literature," *Wikipedia, The Free Encyclopedia* [cited 1 February 2010]. Online: http://en.wikipedia.org/w/index.php?title=Philosophy_and_literature&oldid=336960814.

tion, including novels and short stories. In doing so, they have resorted to narrative to get their teachings across.[64]

> Other philosophers have resorted to narrative to get their teachings across. The classical 12th century Islamic philosopher, Abubacer (Ibn Tufail), wrote a fictional Arabic narrative *Philosophus Autodidactus* as a response to al-Ghazali's *The Incoherence of the Philosophers*, and then the 13th century Islamic theologian-philosopher Ibn al-Nafis also wrote a fictional narrative *Theologus Autodidactus* as a response to Abubacer's *Philosophus Autodidactus*. The German philosopher Friedrich Nietzsche often articulated his ideas in literary modes, most notably in *Thus Spoke Zarathustra*, a re-imagined account of the teachings of Zoroaster. Marquis de Sade and Ayn Rand wrote novels in which characters served as mouthpieces for philosophical positions, and act in accordance with them in the plot. George Santayana was also a philosopher who wrote novels and poetry; the relationship between Santayana's characters and his beliefs is more complex. The existentialists include among their numbers important French authors who used fiction to convey their philosophical views; these include Jean-Paul Sartre's novel *Nausea* and play *No Exit*, and Albert Camus's *The Stranger*. Maurice Blanchot's entire fictional production, whose titles include *The Step Not Beyond*, *The Madness of the Day*, and *The Writing of Disaster*, among others, constitutes an indispensable corpus for the treatment of the relationship between philosophy and literature. So does Jacques Derrida's *The Postcard*.[65]

To be sure, the Hebrew Bible might not have been intended to communicate this kind of philosophy. Yet the fact is that it cannot but contain folk philosophical assumptions that are implicit in its discourse. Terrence Fretheim has shown how the biblical authors also imparted ideas about divine nature in a story.[66] Thomas Thompson saw a glimpse of this when, in his introduction to general historiographical issues, he remarked on the trouble of confusing stories with historical evidence. He realized that the ways in which the biblical narrators go about reflecting on the past should not be equated with modern notions of history: "The Bible's language is not an historical language. It is a language of high literature, of story, of

---

64. Ibid.

65. Ibid.

66. Partly because theology itself is riddled with philosophical concerns; see Fretheim, *Suffering of God*, 24–25.

sermon and of song. It is a tool of philosophy and moral instruction."[67] He also noted: "Much like the poet of Deuteronomy 32, who sends his audience to the past for his teaching, Aristotle creates a philosophical past to ground the fundamental elements of his philosophy."[68] Whether we agree with Thompson or not, the biblical texts as literature cannot but contain folk philosophy.

We see this best when we turn to discussions of philosophy in popular culture (e.g., films). Perhaps the movie that has invited the greatest amount of philosophical explication is *The Matrix*, a 1999 American science fiction-action film.[69] Several books are now available that discuss the philosophical assumptions and problems implicit in the narrative of the trilogy. Examples include *The Matrix and Philosophy: Welcome to the Desert of the Real*, which appeared in the Popular Culture and Philosophy series, Matt Lawrence's *Like a Splinter in Your Mind: The Philosophy behind* The Matrix Trilogy, and Christoper Grau's *Philosophers Explore* The Matrix.[70] Philosophical accounts of the film seek to familiarize readers with key issues implicit in the fictional narrative: metaphysics, epistemology, ethics, philosophy of mind, race, gender, existentialism, Taoism, and mysticism.

To be sure, the authors of the script of *The Matrix* had a philosophical background and intentionally worked explicit allusions to philosophical problems into their narrative. Yet while I have chosen *The Matrix* in view of its popularity, other less overtly philosophical scripts and narratives have also been explored for their philosophical assumptions in the *Popular Culture and Philosophy* series: *Seinfeld, The Simpsons, Harry Potter, The Lord of the Rings, Star Wars*, and even *James Bond, Baseball* and Mel Gibson's *Passion of the Christ*.[71] As to the concept of philosophy in popular culture, the editor of the series had the following to say:

---

67. Thompson, *Bible in History*, 99.

68. Ibid., 288.

69. "The Matrix," *Wikipedia, The Free Encyclopedia* [cited 2 March 2010]. Online: http://en.wikipedia.org/w/index.php?title=The_Matrix&oldid=346564179.

70. William Irwin, ed., The Matrix *and Philosophy: Welcome to the Desert of the Real* (Chicago: Open Court Publishing, 2002); Matt Lawrence, *Like a Splinter in Your Mind: The Philosophy behind* The Matrix Trilogy (Oxford: Wiley-Blackwell, 2004); Christoper Grau, *Philosophers Explore* The Matrix (New York: Oxford University Press, 2005).

71. In the series Popular Culture and Philosophy, Open Court Publications, edited by William Irwin and others.

Since its inception in 2000, Open Court's Popular Culture and Philoso-
phy® series has brought high-quality philosophy to general readers. The
volumes present essays by academic philosophers exploring the meanings, concepts, and puzzles within television shows, movies, music and
other icons of popular culture.... Most PCP volumes are not about entire
genres in popular culture. They focus on specific television programs, hit
movies, books, video games or trends. Proposals for titles such as "Video
Games and Philosophy" or "Action Movies and Philosophy," are much
less appealing than (for example) "Grand Theft Auto..." or "Kill Bill and
Philosophy." While many items in popular culture have identifiable philosophical content, that does not guarantee that "X and philosophy" will
appeal to fans. (By X, I mean the topic in question, not the highly under-
rated Los Angeles punk band of the 1980s!) In many cases, fans would
probably rather rewatch the movie or reread the book than open a book
of scholarly essays about it. But when most fans think the movie or rock
band in question is misunderstood or underappreciated, PCP volumes
are just the thing—especially when the philosophers writing about the
concepts and arguments in question are fans themselves.[72]

If philosophical discussions of these stories are possible, there is no reason
why a philosophical commentary on the Hebrew Bible *qua* folk philosophical script(s) is out of place. Do we dare to imagine titles such as *Abraham and Philosophy, Moses and Philosophy, David and Philosophy, Jeremiah and Philosophy*; or *Genesis and Philosophy, Leviticus and Philosophy,
Judges and Philosophy,* and *Daniel and Philosophy*? Is there any reason why
we should not?[73]

6.3.5. Philosophical Approaches to Myth

Our final analogy from philosophy for imagining the presence of folk
philosophy in the Hebrew Bible (and a philosophical approach to ancient
Yahwism) comes to us from philosophical approaches to the study of
mythology. While the ancient distinction between *mythos* and *logos* is still
maintained in biblical theology to the extent that it considers philosophy
and religion distinct categories operating with different criteria of rationality, philosophers still use and analyze myth as part of doing philoso-

---

72. Message retrieved online on 10 April 2010 from http://www.opencourtbooks
.com /categories/pcp.htm.
73. See Knierim, *Task of Old Testament Theology*, 490.

phy. But if myth can be studied philosophically, or contains philosophical truths, why is a philosophical approach to ancient Israelite religion so hard to imagine?

There was no smooth transition from myth to philosophy in ancient Greece, and much of philosophy and the concern with reason, knowledge and justice is basically depersonalized solar mythology. Plato himself was of the opinion that myth could express philosophical truths. Philosophers of religion since Hegel, and also phenomenologists of religion (e.g., Nathan Söderblom), believed that one could write a philosophy of religion on the basis of the history of religion.[74] And so, contrary to popular belief, applying philosophy to myth does not presuppose a mistake in category.

Within biblical interpretation itself, philosophical approaches to myth are best known in the form of existential/existentialist biblical interpretation.[75] These are associated mostly with New Testament scholarship and with the hermeneutics of Bultmann based on Heidegger's philosophy. According to the popular distinction, philosophy speaks on the level of ontology while the Bible at best offers only an ontic perspective. However, Bultmann recognized that any ontic interpretation of human existence presupposes a generally hidden ground in ontology. On this program, one can understand the ontic aspects in the biblical text only if one first considers the ontological-existentialist structures of human being in general through the aid of philosophy. Interestingly, Hebrew Bible interpreters have shown less of an interest in this approach than scholars studying the New Testament.[76]

But there is much more to philosophical approaches to myth than existentialist perspectives. Particularly notable here is the second part of Ernst Cassirer's *Philosophie der symbolischen Formen*.[77] Characteristic of Cassirer's philosophy of mythology is his concern for the more "primitive" forms of world presentation—a concern for the ordinary perceptual awareness of the world expressed primarily in natural language.[78] Above all, he is inter-

---

74. On this see Otto, *Idea of the Holy*, 74.

75. Soulen and Soulen, *Handbook of Biblical Criticism*, 57.

76. One example in the study of the Hebrew Bible is Alexander DiLella, "An Existential Interpretation of Job," *BTB* 15 (1985): 49–55.

77. Ernst Cassirer, *Mythical Thought* (vol. 2 of *The Philosophy of Symbolic Forms*; New Haven: Yale University Press, 1955).

78. "Ernst Cassirer," *SEP* [cited 5 March 2010]. Online: http://plato.stanford.edu/archives/fall2008/entries/cassirer/.

ested in the mythical view of the world lying at the most primitive level of all. For Cassirer, the most basic and primitive type of symbolic meaning is expressive meaning. Religious language itself is therefore seen as expressive (emotive) rather than descriptive (referential). According to him, this type of meaning underlies mythical consciousness. It also explains its most distinctive feature—the absence of any Platonic distinction between appearance and reality. This is true in the sense that "there was sometimes not believed to be any essential difference in efficacy between the living and the dead, between waking experiences and dreams, between the name of an object and the object itself, and so on."[79] Appearance was accepted as reality (e.g., when the objects of dreams are taken to be as real as those in waking life). However, this view has been criticized on the grounds that Plato's two-world dualism is but a depersonalization of the mythological distinction between the sacred and the profane realms.

A second illustration of a philosophical approach to myth (and vice versa) comes to us in a book entitled *Philosophy in a New Key: A Study in the Symbolism of Reason, Rite and Art* by the American philosopher Susanne K. Langer (1895–1985).[80] In it she declared that "[s]ymbolism was the 'new key' to understanding how the human mind transformed the primal need to express oneself."[81] Langer's early philosophical work in the 1920s can be situated in the tradition of Anglo-American logical philosophy.[82] "She was particularly influenced by the Whitehead and Russell of the *Principia Mathematica*, the Wittgenstein of the *Tractatus* and her own mentor at Harvard, Professor Henry M. Sheffer, who interested her in the 'unlogicized' areas of mental life."[83] Under Sheffer's influence she came to question the relations between the complicated conventional symbols of mathematical logic and other areas of human symbolization, such as ordinary language, myth, ritual, and art. In the preface to the second edition, Langer wrote:

---

79. I shall exploit this unity with a surrealist analogy in a later chapter.

80. Susanne K. Langer, *Philosophy in a New Key: A Study in the Symbolism of Reason, Rite, and Art* (3rd ed.; Cambridge: Harvard University Press, 1942).

81. "Philosophy in a New Key," *Wikipedia, The Free Encyclopedia* [cited 24 March 2010]. Online: http://en.wikipedia.org/w/index.php?title=Philosophy_in_a_New_Key&oldid=192485418

82. Ibid.

83. Richard M. Liddy, "Symbolic Consciousness: The Contribution of Susanne K. Langer," *Proceedings of the American Catholic Philosophical Association* 44 (1971): 94–110. Online: http://www.anthonyflood.com/liddysymbolicconsciousness.htm.

The process of philosophical thought moves typically from a first, inadequate, but ardent apprehension of some novel idea, figuratively expressed, to more and more precise comprehension, until language catches up to logical insight, the figure is dispensed with, and literal expression takes its place. Really new concepts, having no names in current language, always make their earliest appearance in metaphorical statements; therefore the beginning of any theoretical structure is inevitably marked by fantastic inventions. There is an air of such metaphor, or "philosophical myth," in the treatment of musical "meaning," which I think I could improve on were I given another fling at it today.[84]

Ordinarily, the conventional wisdom of the day relegated myth to the nonphilosophical side of human thought. Rudolph Carnap, for example, "had held that poetry was merely an emotional catharsis of the poet aiming at the stimulation of the percipient's immediate emotion."[85] But contrary to such positivist views, Langer vindicated the properly intellectual character of the nondiscursive "presentational" symbols of myth.[86] Under the influence of the neo-Kantian Ernst Cassirer Langer pointed in particular to the highly "formal" character of nonphilosophical literature: "Myth is primitive philosophy, the simplest presentational (anschauliche) form of thought, a series of attempts to understand the world, to explain life and death, fate and nature, gods and cults."[87] Literalism regarding ultimate issues lies at the origin of the discursive thought of early philosophy. Prior to that, according to Langer, myths, symbolic images, and stories were indeed the only materials capable of symbolizing humans' fundamental orientation in the universe. The early philosophers' distinction between the myth and its meaning amounted to the "breaking" of myth. Philosophy made various attempts to state the ultimate meaning of life and the universe literally, whereas myth had expressed it through its symbols. Philosophy knows, however, that myth as serious symbol begins to wane as soon as the literal question of its factual content is raised and metaphysical distinctions are made.[88] On this view, therefore, the task of philosophical reflection on myth is to clarify rather than critique.

---

84. Langer, *Philosophy in a New Key*, x.
85. Liddy, "Symbolic Consciousness," 96.
86. Ibid., 94–110.
87. Langer, *Philosophy in a New Key*, 177.
88. Ibid., 202.

A third example of the philosophical study of myth is found in *Myth and Philosophy from the Presocratics to Plato*, by Kathryn A. Morgan.[89] The author is not interested in providing a philosophical account of myth or in a philosophical theory to explain what myth really is. Rather, she engages in a discussion of how myth functioned in the thought of early Greek philosophers themselves. The concern with myth is thus postphilosophical. Morgan explores the dynamic relationship between myth and philosophy in the Presocratics, the Sophists, and Plato—a relationship that is found to be more extensive and programmatic than has been recognized. The idea that myth was considered "irrational'" in philosophy ignores the important role played by myth also within philosophy, not just as a foil, but also as a mode of philosophical thought. The case studies in this book reveal myth deployed as a result of methodological reflection, and as a manifestation of philosophical concerns.

What is becoming ever more apparent in the postmodern philosophical study of myth is that philosophy did not come from nowhere; much of it is depersonalized religion and mythology. This is especially seen in comparative Continental philosophy of religion, as in Frank Reynolds and David Tracy's *Myth and Philosophy*, in which many stereotypes are deconstructed.[90] Their later work, *Religion and Practical Reason: New Essays in Comparative Philosophy of Religions*, showed that philosophy of religion is especially useful amid the deconstruction.[91]

In a very real sense, the lines have blurred. "The concept of pure and neutral rationality is an ideal of modern philosophy rather than a reality, and it met with serious objections during the nineteenth and twentieth centuries."[92] Schopenhauer and Nietzsche taught us that underneath rational discourse, human reason has unnoticed irrational drives. "The distinction between philosophy and mythology, reason and belief, and poetic intuition and critical reasoning, can therefore be justified only in a

---

89. Kathryn A. Morgan, *Myth and Philosophy from the Presocratics to Plato* (New York: Cambridge University Press, 2000).

90. Frank Reynolds and David Tracy, *Myth and Philosophy* (New York: State University of New York Press, 1990).

91. Frank Reynolds and David Tracy, *Religion and Practical Reason: New Essays in Comparative Philosophy of Religions* (New York: State University of New York Press, 1994).

92. "Pre-Socratic Philosophy," *New World Encyclopedia* [cited 8 June 2010]. Online: http://www.newworldencyclopedia.org/p/index.php?title=Pre-Socratic_philosophy&oldid=795024.

limited sense."[93] It should not then come as a surprise that a recent publication in mythological criticism proper should have been entitled *Thinking through Myths*. This study offered philosophical reflections on myths[94] and brought together essays that use many philosophical tools—including phenomenology, metaphysics, semiotics and moral philosophy—to study mythical worlds and to think philosophically through myths. Such a philosophical approach to mythology focuses on investigating the cognitive dimension of myths. One asks what it might mean to say that myths are rational, in what sense myths are a permanent feature of our culture, and what happens when we reject the idea that myths belong to a primitive stage of human thought.

In the book, Robert Segal discusses Edward Taylor's conception of myth as primitive philosophy, and gives other views of the relationship between myth and philosophy—from James Frazer to Karl Popper, Rudolph Bultmann, and Hans Jonas.[95] Hebrew Bible scholars might take note of Milton Scarborough's comparative phenomenological analysis of Gen 1:1–2:4 and Plato's *Timaeus*.[96] His interpretation of myths deals with the kind of "being in the world" that they disclose. On the basis of the existential turn of phenomenology, the author shows that myths use prereflective, operative intentionality in their description of aspects of the lived world. A publication such as *Thinking through Myths* thus provides an example of the philosophical study of myths from the perspectives of Anglo-Saxon philosophy.

The bottom line for our purposes is that myth and philosophy can, and do, mix; and that the popular attempt to divorce the two in the context of biblical theology is an anomaly caused by academics who do not seem to have the same qualms or hermeneutical problems when it comes to asking philosophical questions concerning mythological discourse. In view of the possibility of philosophical reflection on mythology and the use of myth in philosophy, we may therefore begin to conceive of the relation between myth in the Hebrew Bible and philosophy in a similar way. We can learn from the many and varied philosophical perspectives used to

---

93. Ibid.

94. Kevin Schilbrack, ed., *Thinking Through Myths: Philosophical Perspectives* (London: Routledge, 2002).

95. Robert Segal, "Myth as Primitive Philosophy: The Case of E. B. Tylor," in Schilbrack, *Thinking Through Myths*, 18–45.

96. Milton Scarborough, "Myth and Phenomenology," in Schilbrack, *Thinking Through Myths*, 46–64.

look at mythology, as these offer us a precedent for why and how this can be done in the context of biblical studies. It also means that biblical scholars who dismiss philosophy because ancient Israelite religion comes from mythical prephilosophical times might themselves be guilty of buying into the ancient philosophical stereotype of the relation between *mythos* and *logos*—something which is a postmodern world is no longer tenable.

This latter point—a collapse of the distinction between mythos and logos—was also an issue of consideration in Derrida's text "Plato's Pharmacy." In a close reading of Plato's dialogue, *Phaedrus*, Derrida tried to show that although Plato had attempted to construct a number of hard and fast distinctions—such as the distinction between philosophy and mythology—those distinctions were actually undermined by their own logic and rhetoric. Greek philosophy and Egyptian mythology are, everything considered, not all that different. But if this is the case, then biblical scholars should again be asking themselves whether they are really historically conscious and pro-Hebraic, or whether once again in denying folk philosophy in mythological texts they are actually promoting a colonialist stereotype of philosophy vis-à-vis mythology.

6.4. Analogies from Biblical Scholarship

In this section I will argue that Hebrew Bible scholars have actually already acknowledged the presence of folk philosophy in the text, even as they decry the intrusive and distortive effects of philosophy in biblical interpretation. The forthcoming examples, therefore, demonstrate the ways in which biblical scholars have by implication shown that there is nothing in principle wrong with a philosophical agenda in the context of research on ancient Israelite religion. The cases in point can therefore be seen as already operative and acceptable analogous precursors to a philosophical approach proper.

6.4.1. Worldview Research

The concept of worldview will be a familiar one to most biblical scholars.[97] In popular religious discourse these days, it is most commonly encoun-

---

97. See recently Bernd Janowski, "Das biblische Weltbild: Eine methodische Skizze," in *Das biblische Weltbild in seine altorientalischen Kontexte* (ed. B. Janowski and B. Ego; FAT 32; Tübingen: Mohr Siebeck, 2001), 3–26.

tered in two contexts. On the one hand it is all the rage in conservative Christian apologetics, which is currently obsessed with religious episte- mology; and is bent on proving to its own satisfaction the rationality of its system and explaining why people on the outside can't see the truth of that system.[98] Its proponents are concerned because they feel that one should have what they call a "biblical" worldview rather than one associated with taboos such as secularism, naturalism, evolutionism, humanism, existen- tialism, Marxism, atheism, postmodernism and nihilism—all of which are supposed to be demons in disguise. The fad is predictably fundamentalist and ahistorical. It involves a great deal of stereotyping and caricaturing, revealing a lack of any real understanding of what is being rejected. It is also anachronistic and willfully ignorant of myth and pluralism in the bib- lical materials, with the result that these "biblical" Christians are not as biblical as they think.

On the other hand, the concept of worldview itself is relatively young and actually comes from philosophy. In 1820, Wilhelm von Humboldt connected the study of language to the German national romanticist pro- gram by proposing the view that language is the very fabric of thought, and that thoughts are produced as a kind of inner dialog using the same grammar as the thinker's native language. "This view was part of a larger picture in which the worldview of an ethnic nation (its *Weltanschauung*) was seen as being faithfully reflected in the grammar of its language."[99]

---

98. Recent apologetic literature includes, *inter alia*, David Noebel and Chuck Edwards, eds., *Thinking Like a Christian: Understanding and Living a Biblical Worldview* (New York: B & H, 2002); David K Naugle, *Worldview: A History of the Concept* (Grand Rapids: Eerdmans, 2002); John Macarthur, Richard L. Mayhue, and John J. Hughes *Think Biblically! Recovering a Christian Worldview* (Wheaton, Ill.: Crossway, 2003); Allan N. Moseley, *Thinking against the Grain: Developing a Biblical Worldview in a Culture of Myths* (Grand Rapids: Kregel, 2003); Nancy Pearcey, *Total Truth: Liberating Christianity from Its Cultural Captivity* (Wheaton, Ill.: Crossway, 2005); Francis Schaeffer, *How Should We Then Live? The Rise and Decline of Western Thought and Culture* (Wheaton, Ill.: Crossway, 2005); and Mark J. Bertrand, *Rethink- ing Worldview: Learning to Think Live and Speak in This World* (Wheaton, Ill.: Cross- way, 2007).

99. "Linguistic Relativity," *Wikipedia, The Free Encyclopedia* [cited 10 May 2012] Online: http://en.wikipedia.org/w/index.php?title=Linguistic_relativity&oldid =506157660. For an online introduction, see "World View," *Wikipedia, The Free Encyclopedia* [cited 14 January 2010]. Online: http://en.wikipedia.org/w/index. php?title=World_view&oldid=337697815.

In this view, in other words, the language of a people reflects the *Welt-anschauung* of that people in the form of its syntactic structures and its untranslatable connotations and denotations. While in this line of thought the concept of worldview is most prominent in linguistics and anthropology, virtually any social science can incorporate it into its discussions. Philosophy in general and philosophy of religion in particular are no exception,[100] partly because having a worldview involves having philosophical assumptions:

> A comprehensive world view (or worldview) is the fundamental cognitive orientation of an individual or society encompassing natural *philosophy*, fundamental existential and normative postulates or themes, values, emotions, and ethics. The term is a loan translation or calque of German *Weltanschauung* composed of *Welt*, "world," and *Anschauung*, "view" or "outlook." It is a concept fundamental to German philosophy and epistemology and refers to a *wide world perception*.[101]

The *Oxford English Dictionary* defines "world view" as a "particular philosophy of life; a concept of the world held by an individual or a group."[102] In *Types and Problems of Philosophy*, Hunter Mead defines *Weltanschauung* as "a somewhat poetic term to indicate either an articulated system of *philosophy* or a more or less unconscious attitude toward life and the world."[103] In its article on the philosopher Wilhelm Dilthey, *The Encyclopedia of Philosophy* notes that "there is in mankind a persistent tendency to achieve a comprehensive interpretation, a *Weltanschauung*, or philosophy, in which a picture of reality is combined with a sense of its meaning and value and

---

100. Kai Nielsen, "Philosophy and '*Weltanschauung*.'" *Journal of Values Inquiry* 27 (April 1993): 179–86; Peter Riordan, "Religion as *Weltanschauung*: A Solution to a Problem in the Philosophy of Religion." *Aquinas* 34 (1991): 519–34; Ninian Smart, "The Philosophy of Worldviews: That Is, the Philosophy of Religions Transformed," *Neue Zeitschrift fur Systematische Theologie und Religionsphilosophie* 23 (1981): 212–24; Anfinn Stigen, "Philosophy as World View and Philosophy as Discipline," in *Contemporary Philosophy in Scandinavia* (ed. Raymond E. Olson and Anthony M. Paul; Baltimore: Johns Hopkins University Press, 1972).

101. "World View," *Wikipedia*.

102. *Oxford English Dictionary*, 2nd ed., s.v. "World View."

103. Hunter Mead, *Types and Problems of Philosophy* (New York: Holt, 1962).

with principles of action."[104] Any worldview has philosophical assumptions on the following topics:[105]

1. *Ontology*: assumptions about what exists.
2. *Metaphysics*: assumptions about the fundamental structures of reality.
3. An *epistemology*: assumptions about knowledge, belief and truth.
4. *Anthropology*: assumptions about the human condition.
5. An *etiology*: an account of its own origins and construction.
6. *Teleology*: assumptions about the meaning and purpose of life.
7. *Axiology* (values): assumptions about good and evil.
8. A *praxeology*: a methodology or theory of human action and conduct.

Assumptions regarding these matters are present even in the Hebrew Bible. "These basic beliefs cannot, by definition, be *proven* (in the logical sense) within the worldview itself, precisely because they are axioms and are typically argued *from*, rather than argued *for*."[106] However, their coherence can be explored philosophically and logically, and one can concern oneself with a philosophical clarification of any culture's worldview by identifying the ontological, metaphysical, epistemological, moral, and other assumptions of its religion. Ancient pre- or nonphilosophical cultures had worldviews too (and therefore philosophical assumptions) which, even when unarticulated, contradictory and mythological, can be reconstructed and described in philosophical terms. Indeed, the philosophical study of worldviews is of particular interest to philosophers of religion since the latter discipline is one where all other philosophical fields come together.

The first thing to take into consideration in light of the above is that worldview research is *already* being conducted in biblical scholarship. The most familiar example comes from Hebrew linguistics (often cognitive linguistics) and Bible translation studies. It is part of the hermeneutics of crosscultural communication, where worldview analysis is supposed to overcome the problem of conceptual distortion given the indeterminacy

---

104. Hans Peter Rickman, "Wilhelm Dilthey," in *Encyclopedia of Philosophy* (ed. Paul Edwards; New York: Macmillan, 1967), 2:403.
105. "World View," *Wikipedia*.
106. Ibid.

of conceptual extensions. However, up to now most of the focus has been on linguistic, literary, social-scientific, anthropological or theological perspectives rather than philosophical ones. Yet even these nonphilosophical discussions are riddled with philosophical (metaphysical and epistemological) jargon.

A second example of worldview analysis in biblical studies can be found in research on ancient Israelite wisdom. As noted earlier, biblical wisdom literature has been called "philosophical" in the sense of involving an implicit practical or ethical "philosophy of life." As such it is often contrasted with the stereotype of Greek philosophy as speculative and abstract, although the link between the two is recognized in the presence of natural theology (as in John J. Collins, "Epilogue: From Hebrew Wisdom to Greek Philosophy").[107] Theological discussions of wisdom literature also include references to a belief in cosmic and moral orders, deed-consequence causality, anthropology, assumptions about knowledge, etc.[108] Many commentaries on Qoheleth in particular border on the philosophical, both when it comes to remarks on content and in terms of the commentary's structure (cosmology, anthropology, epistemology, ethics, etc.). In many instances, however, the concern with worldview in wisdom is mingled with *theological* reflection.[109] Even so, this is enough to show that a philosophical concern with worldviews in the wisdom literature is legitimate.[110]

---

107. See, for instance, Norman Whybray, *Ecclesiastes* (Grand Rapids: Eerdmans, 1989); and John J. Collins, *Jewish Wisdom in the Hellenistic Age* (Louisville: Westminster John Knox, 1997), 222–32.

108. See, for example, Perdue, "Cosmology and the Social Order." See also Frydrych, *Living under the Sun.*

109. For example, Ronald Simkins, *Creator and Creation: Nature in the Worldview of Ancient Israel* (Peabody, Mass.: Hendrickson, 1994); Robert Gnuse, *Heilsgeschichte as a Model for Biblical Theology: The Debate concerning the Uniqueness and Significance of Israel's Worldview* (Lanham, Md.: University Press of America, 1989); Andrew D. H. Mayes, "Deuteronomy 14 and the Deuteronomic World View," in *Studies in Deuteronomy: In Honour of C.J. Labuschagne on the Occasion of His 65th Birthday* (ed. F. García Martínez; Leiden: Brill, 1994), 165–81.

110. Take, for instance, Ferdinand Deist, "Genesis 1:1–2:4a: World Picture and World View," *Scriptura* 22 (1987): 1–17; Alan Richardson, *Genesis 1–11: The Creation Stories and the Modern Worldview* (London: SCM, 1953); Michael L. Barré, " 'Fear of God' and the World View of Wisdom," *BTB* 11 (April 1981): 41–43; Raymond C. Van Leeuwen, "Liminality and Worldview in Proverbs 1–9," *Semeia* 50 (1990): 111–44; Carl H. Shank, "Qoheleth's World and Life View as Seen in His Recurring Phrases," *WTJ* 37 (1974): 57–73.

A third context of quasiphilosophical discourse on biblical worldviews comes from research on the prophetic literature. In this context scholars of the Hebrew Bible have shown that philosophical concerns are perfectly legitimate, as when Robert Carroll, in his *When Prophecy Failed*, not only incorporated theories of social psychology but also asked metaphysical questions regarding the nature of time, the future, and causality in the prophetic literature.[111] Another example of acknowledging the presence of folk philosophy in prophecy is David Stacey, who in his discussion of the phenomenon of prophetic drama in the Hebrew Bible remarked that "[i]t would be foolish to pursue this kind of discussion without recogniz- ing that in Israel, as in all other societies, there were different levels of perception in ... metaphysical matters."[112] If one can admit the presence of worldviews in the text, then one must grant both the presence of folk philosophical elements in the discourse and the validity of a philosophical approach in the clarification of such data. Even social-scientific studies dealing with biblical worldview are descriptive moral philosophy and axi- ology in disguise, thus already showing how a philosophical clarification of biblical worldviews is possible, that is by reconstructing the folk philo- sophical assumptions in the text and by describing what they amount to in philosophical language. So the fact is that few biblical scholars have a problem with the claim that there is a worldview (or rather several world- views) implicit in the Hebrew Bible. But if there are worldviews implicit in the religious language of ancient Yahwism(s), then folk philosophy is also present.[113] This means that if we can imagine worldview articulation in research on ancient Israelite religion, then by analogy we can imagine a descriptive philosophical approach to ancient Israelite religion.

6.4.2. "Hebrew Thought"

In some circles it is popular to discuss what tends to go under the con- cept of "Hebrew thought." The quantity of scholarly literature and popu- list internet resources directly and indirectly influenced by the subject is vast and it is beyond the scope of this section to justify or criticize the

---

111. See above in chapter 3.

112. David Stacey, *Prophetic Drama in the Old Testament* (London: Epworth, 1990), 252.

113. Compare this with, for example, Peter Kreeft, *The Philosophy of Tolkien: The Worldview behind* The Lord of the Rings (San Francisco: Ignatius Press, 2005).

idea in any of its many and varied forms. The "usual suspects" in the academia are Pedersen's *Israel*, Boman's *Hebrew Thought Compared to Greek*, Barr's *Semantics of Biblical Language*, Tsevat's *An Aspect of Biblical Thought: Deductive Explanation*, and, more recently, Carasik's *Theologies of the Mind*.[114] All of these works attempt to describe how ancient Israelites thought (about thought). Yet over time the notion of Hebrew thought changed and antiphilosophical sentiment is no longer as rife as when it was once stereotyped and fallaciously compared with Greek thinking. The following example is a classical instance of the latter.

> The Greek mind is abstract, contemplative, static or harmonic, impersonal; it is dominated by certain distinctions—matter and form, one and many, individual and collective, time and timelessness, appearance and reality. The Hebrew mind is active, concrete, dynamic, intensely personal, formed upon wholeness and not upon distinctions. Thus it is able to rise above, or to escape, the great distinctions which lie across Greek thought. Greek thought is unhistorical, timeless, based on logic and system. Hebrew thought is historical, centered in time and movement, based in life.[115]

The delicious irony of descriptions such as these, which oppose philosophical and biblical thinking and deny that philosophy can be relevant to understanding ancient Israel, is that they are themselves examples of descriptive folk philosophical analysis. If we understand philosophical enquiry as a second-order activity that has concepts, theories and presuppositions as its subject matter, then surely biblical theology's obsession with "thinking about (Hebraic) thinking" was itself a descriptive and comparative variety of philosophical clarification all along, even as it raged against all things philosophical. So while there are differences between biblical and philosophical concerns and modes of analysis, the early antiphilo-

---

114. Johannes Pedersen, *Israel: Its Life and Culture* (trans. Auslag Moller and A. I. Fausbell; 4 vols.; Oxford: Oxford University Press, 1926–1940); Mattitiahu Tsevat, "An Aspect of Biblical Thought: Deductive Explanation," *Shnaton* 3 (1978): 53–58 [Hebrew with English summary]; and Michael Carasik, *Theologies of the Mind in Biblical Israel* (Studies in Biblical Literature 85; New York: Lang, 2006).

115. Barr, *Old and New in Interpretation*, 34. For an excellent example of how Boman's fallacies are still popular on the Internet to this day, see Jeff A. Brenner, "Ancient Hebrew Thought" [cited 27 April 2010]. Online: http://www.ancient-hebrew.org/12_thought.html.

sophical agenda could only operate by becoming a historical philosophy of mind itself.[116]

The very notion of "Hebrew thought" can mean both the way of reasoning and the contents of belief, but either way, the findings of research thereon have the potential of being renamed "Hebrew *philosophy*." The trouble with the idea of "Hebrew thought" was never so much the concept per se as the attempt to stereotype and oppose it to Greek thought (and to pretend that these two were the only types of thinking possible). Contemporaneous studies have been more keen to show that Hebrew thought was just as capable of abstract and analytical reasoning as Greek philosophy, and that alleged differences in logical capabilities between the two are nothing of the sort. But here also, far from the distancing of biblical scholars from philosophy, we encounter an exercise in descriptive and comparative philosophy of mind, suggesting that historical philosophical concerns are quite commensurable with exegesis.

In other words, comparative and descriptive philosophical concerns are indelible in any attempt to show how the thought world of the Hebrew Bible differs from ancient Greek, medieval Christian or modern secular philosophical ideas. Anyone who seeks to deny the possibility of a philosophical approach to ancient Israelite religion must first demonstrate the anachronistic or distortive nature of a particular philosophical idea or concept. Yet they can do this only by first identifying the Hebrew Bible's folk philosophical assumptions and by philosophically clarifying the biblical contents. Thus antiphilosophical scholars have to translate the Hebrew Bible's own ideas into philosophical terms and compare them with anachronistic philosophical perspective in order to deny any similarity or explain the differences. In doing so, they clearly deconstruct their entire project of keeping philosophy out of the field. They must imply that the text's contents can be translated into philosophical terms, even as they repeat the warning of how distortive philosophical concepts and categories are.[117]

6.4.3. OLD TESTAMENT THEOLOGY

The Hebrew Bible/Old Testament is not a theological textbook or a systematic theology. It contains no overt unified theology—all is fragmented

---

116. Barr, *Old and New in Interpretation*, 42.
117. See Thiselton, *Two Horizons*, 3–4.

and implicit. The biblical authors were not interested in discussing the issues contemporary Old Testament theologians worry about, for instance pluralism, history, center, ancient Near Eastern parallels, relations to the New Testament, and so on. The word "theology" does not appear in biblical Hebrew and much of the jargon Old Testament theologians use is not found in the texts themselves. The discipline, though theological, is ideally also historical and descriptive, and seeks to reconstruct what the Old Testament texts assumed about theological issues. A great danger is reading Christian theology and its concerns back into ancient Israelite religion. It is analogous to historical theology in that it seeks to reconstruct and clarify theological assumptions in the writings of past authors rather than put forward normative theological conceptions for today; and is thus a good analogy for biblical theology.[118]

By analogy, the Old Testament is not a textbook of philosophy of religion or philosophical theology. It contains no overt philosophy of religion—all is implicit. Ancient Israelites were not interested in discussing the issues contemporary philosophers of religion worry about. The word "philosophy" does not appear in biblical Hebrew and much of the jargon philosophers of religion use is not found in the texts themselves. The discipline, though philosophical, is ideally historical and descriptive. It seeks to reconstruct what the Old Testament texts assumed about issues on the agenda in philosophy of religion. Historical philosophy that seeks to reconstruct and clarify ideas of past authors rather than put forward normative philosophical conceptions for today is a good analogy for biblical philosophy.

What needs to be said is that when some biblical theologians called for the purging of Greek philosophy from biblical theology, unless they were referring to specific ideas about and concepts of the deity, they were really calling for the end of the discipline itself, though they may not have realized it.[119] This is evident when biblical theologians discuss the nature of Yhwh in the Hebrew Bible. The very topic, whatever the contents of the data, is already philosophical in its roots, given the notion of Yhwh as a being with a nature and attributes. They already use abstract terms such as "transcendent" and "personal," and other notions that are hardly biblical

---

118. The best examples of relevant metatheological discussions for this section are Barr, *Concept of Biblical Theology*; and Knierim, *Task of Old Testament Theology.* Parts of Kohler's *Old Testament Theology* also come close to conceptual analysis.

119. See Allen, *Philosophy for Understanding Theology,* 5.

categories. But if it is possible to use such Greek philosophical jargon without distortion, why then rage against Greek philosophy as such? Surely the problem lies with certain anachronistic perfect being concepts of God in Christian philosophical theology, and not with a descriptive philosophical approach to biblical theology per se.

In addition, many of the topics Old Testament theologians discuss are also issues of interest in philosophy of religion. Old Testament theologians are already discussing the divine attributes, the nature of biblical god-talk, the nature of Israelite religion, theodicy, the concept of revelation and the relation between religion and morality. The legitimacy of these inquiries implies the legitimacy of parallel descriptive philosophical discussions. In this sense, then, biblical "philosophy" is implicit in Hebrew thought in the same way as biblical theology is implicit therein, and both are anachronistic without necessarily being distortively such. There is no biblical theology without philosophical concepts. All biblical theology presupposes the presence not only of the philosophical assumptions of its practitioners, but also of folk philosophy in the text.

The concern with doing justice to, and describing, Hebrew thought in biblical theology itself is therefore a useful analogy for imagining where the philosophy in the Hebrew Bible is supposed to come from. By doing biblical theology and describing what the ancient Israelites believed in theological terms, we have already made a beginning on the way to a descriptive philosophy of Israelite religion. All that is required thereafter is a philosophical analysis of biblical theological concepts, translating the findings of biblical theology into philosophical language and bringing these translations to bear on loci on the agenda in philosophy of religion.

6.4.4. OLD TESTAMENT ETHICS

In his study on Old Testament ethics, John Barton has suggested that biblical scholars should not be as quick to completely bracket philosophical issues as the Biblical Theology Movement's influence has led us to take for granted.[120] Biblical scholars who would deny a philosophical approach to Israelite religion in the context of the Hebrew Bible, yet take the hermeneutical validity of a discipline such as biblical ethics for granted, are applying double standards. The very subject of ethics is already an exam-

---

120. John Barton, *Understanding Old Testament Ethics*, 54 and *passim*.

ple of a philosophical approach that managed to get into the study of the Hebrew Bible, for it is easy to forget that ethics is one of the main branches of philosophy along with metaphysics, epistemology and logic. Moreover, the distinctions between these philosophical subjects are useful but not watertight. If a piece of literature contains ethical assumptions, it contains metaethical assumptions as well, and by default also metaphysical and epistemological assumptions. So if one is allowed to speak of ethics in the Hebrew Bible, then one has already granted the legitimacy of speaking of metaphysics and epistemology in the text as well. If we are consistent, all of this presupposes the presence of biblical "philosophy."

Inasmuch as biblical scholars engage in ethics, they are therefore partly already descriptive philosophers of religion since they are discussing the relation between religion and morality in the Hebrew Bible. It must therefore now be admitted that there has been a false dichotomy evident in writings on the involvement of philosophical concerns in biblical ethics. As John Barton recognized:

> Ancient Israel possessed nothing that could be described as "moral philosophy"—the attempt to work out systematically the basis on which ethics rests and to clarify why it is that moral imperatives or norms have the binding character people attribute to them.... In this sense the OT is not speculative or philosophical. Nevertheless, it does make sense to ask what in ancient Israel was thought or felt (perhaps at a fairly inarticulate level) to be the underlying basis of morality.[121]

In the last part, Barton recognizes that one can distinguish between moral philosophy (which is stereotyped according to Western scholastic types of philosophy) and moral folk philosophical assumptions. Insofar as there are any moral convictions in the Hebrew Bible, such folk philosophical assumptions are inevitably present, whether the ancient Israelites were conscious of these or not. This fact is what seems to be unwittingly admitted by William Dyrness in another context:

> Before we turn to this vision of the future in the next chapter, two things call for comment: the philosophy of history and the question of foretelling versus forthtelling. First, do the prophets present a philosophy of history? The fundamental conflict in the prophets is one of a moral battle

---

121. John Barton, "Approaches to Ethics in the Old Testament," in *Beginning Old Testament Study* (ed. John W. Rogerson et al.; St. Louis: Chalice, 1998), 119.

between God and the forces of evil, but the arena in which this struggle is carried on is human history. The moral struggle is not carried out with some cosmic inevitability (as in the Hindu doctrine of karma).[122]

So if one can envisage ethics in the Hebrew Bible and not consider philosophical terms such as "deontological," "casuistic," "apodictic," "theodicy," and so on as being *ipso facto* distortive, then we are already on the way to admitting the presence of philosophical assumptions in general and the usefulness of philosophical concepts and categories to describe them. So if a descriptive ethics of the Hebrew Bible is possible, then so is a descriptive biblical philosophy of religion.

6.4.5. COGNITIVE APPROACHES

Over the last two decades, a new method has been introduced to religious studies, one that can bring fresh insights to the study of biblical literature also. "Scholars who work on biblical literature using cognitive science approaches study literary sources in the context of religious beliefs, emotions, rituals, and social networks."[123]

One example among many of this trend in Hebrew Bible studies can be found in the research of Ellen van Wolde. She has been managing a research project with the intention of developing—for biblical scholarship—an integrated cognitive approach in which brain activities, individual sensations and experiences, and social and cultural routines are studied as intimately intertwined.[124] Inasmuch as we are dealing here with conceptual analysis and a worldview analysis of metaphysical and epistemological assumptions in ancient Israelite culture, an acceptance of the hermeneutical legitimacy of the enterprise implies an acceptance of the possibility of a descriptive philosophical approach to Israelite religion.

In this way, cognitive scientific discussions in biblical studies also provide an analogy for a descriptive philosophical approach despite the explanatory differences. It is simply philosophical anthropology in action,

---

122. Dyrness, *Themes in Old Testament Theology*, 222.

123. István Czachesz, "The Promise of the Cognitive Science of Religion for Biblical Studies" [cited 10 December 2010]. Online: http://religionandcognition.com/publications/czachesz_cssr.pdf.

124. Ellen van Wolde, *Reframing Biblical Studies: When Language and Text Meet Culture, Cognition, and Context* (Winona Lake, Ind.: Eisenbrauns, 2009).

so that a cognitive approach stands midway between philosophy of religion and the sociology and history of religion.

6.5. Conclusion

In this chapter we have looked at possible analogies for imagining the presence of folk philosophy in the Hebrew Bible, and for enabling the conceivability of a philosophical approach to ancient Israelite religion. We have done this by way of looking at examples from already operative extant disciplines in both philosophy and biblical scholarship. These analogies allow us to realize that philosophical reflection on ancient Israelite religion is already hinted at as a distinct possibility. They show us that there are definitely philosophically relevant data in the Hebrew Bible; and that our objections to coming up with philosophical perspectives on Israelite religion deconstruct themselves. We can only compare the Hebrew Bible with alien philosophical ideas by casting the biblical materials into equally alien (but nondistortive) philosophical terms, thereby engaging in comparative philosophy of religion. In view of this, I will now proceed to introduce a few descriptive philosophical methods for the study of the Hebrew Bible. In the next chapter my focus will be on utilizing descriptive philosophy of religion on the level of exegesis. Following this, the last chapter of part 1 will look at a large-scale approach.

7
PHILOSOPHICAL CRITICISM AS BIBLICAL CRITICISM

Philosophy does not seem to solve biblical questions. So much in biblical scholarship depends on knowledge of a different kind.[1]

7.1. INTRODUCTION

In this chapter I shall attempt to show how currents in descriptive philosophy of religion can be combined and adapted to create a form of philosophical exegesis that can be employed fruitfully as a new type of biblical criticism. In doing so I hope to offer what could become an independent and officially recognized form of textual interpretation that supplements already extant linguistic, historical, literary, and social-scientific perspectives. Bringing together insights from previous chapters, the new interpretative methodology aims to be both philosophical and historical and, because it has as its focus the clarification of meaning only, to bring to the table a hermeneutically legitimate way of involving philosophy of religion in the reading of ancient texts without distorting their contents. I call it philosophical criticism, and if all goes well, the reader will recognize the potential value of what could become the latest trend in biblical scholarship.

7.2. WHAT IS PHILOSOPHICAL CRITICISM?

Forms of biblical criticism usually take as identification marker the name of the auxiliary field or method utilized in the particular approach, for instance historical criticism (history), literary criticism (literature studies), social-scientific (sociology/social psychological) criticism, and so on. The concept of "philosophical criticism" is therefore ideal as a name for the

---

1. Barr, *Concept of Biblical Theology*, 146.

new exegetical method explained in this chapter. My concern is not with philosophy as such but with philosophy of religion. Matters are complicated by the fact that the concept is already in use and denotes different things in different contexts.

In philosophy proper, the concept "philosophical criticism" can refer to a philosophical critique of epistemological or moral assumptions (as in Kant or Nietzsche) or to the critical evaluation of truth claims with the aid of philosophy (as in critical philosophy of religion). It can also denote a philosopher's criticizing of specialists in another field, for their outdated or problematic philosophical ideas or the logical form of their arguments. Thus, according to one popular view:

> In philosophy, which concerns the most fundamental aspects of the universe, the experts all disagree. It follows that another element of philosophical method, common in the work of nearly all philosophers, is philosophical criticism. It is this that makes much philosophizing a social endeavor. Philosophers offer definitions and explanations in solution to problems; they argue for those solutions; and then other philosophers provide counter arguments, expecting to eventually come up with better solutions. This exchange and resulting revision of views is called dialectic.[2]

In this sense, philosophical criticism as I intend it should not be confused with what biblical scholars understand by the concepts of metacommentary and *Sachkritik*, where one tries to discredit the author's views by exposing the shaky philosophical assumptions in the discourse. Neither will I be using the concept in the way it functions in the writings of Gabler, who wrote of "philosophical criticism" as signifying "pure biblical theology," which involved a preparation of the biblical materials for the construction of a systematic philosophy of religion.[3] Gabler placed philosophical criticism alongside historical criticism in order to go beyond mere exegesis. For him philosophical analysis was not part of historical interpretation

---

2. "Philosophical Method," *Wikipedia, The Free Encyclopedia* [cited 14 July 2010]. Online: http://en.wikipedia.org/w/index.php?title=Philosophical_method&oldid=367114388. An early example relevant to our theme is that of Andrew S. P. Pattison, *Essays in Philosophical Criticism* (New York: Longmans, Green, 1883).

3. To be sure, the term "philosophical criticism" is used here with reference to Gabler; see Otto Merk, *Biblische Theologie des Neuen Testaments in ihrer Anfangszeit* (Marburg: Elwert, 1972), 68–81.

proper. This is also the case when one encounters sporadic references to "philosophical criticism" in contemporary biblical scholarship and philosophy, where it may simply mean bringing to bear philosophical ideas on the text, or reading the text as a philosophical parable.

In this chapter, however, I shall use the term in another, altogether novel, sense. I am not concerned with bringing philosophical perspectives to bear as much as I am with *doing* philosophy. Philosophical criticism in this sense is also different from the evaluative, critical and atheological connotations ascribed to it by myself in the agenda of an earlier article.[4] In the context of this study, then, philosophical criticism is understood as a descriptive type of philosophical analysis aimed at the clarification of meaning in the biblical texts. Its aim is to look at the biblical discourse from the perspective of loci on the agenda of philosophy of religion, with an interest in discovering what, if anything, a given passage assumes or implies on these matters and in translating the findings of the analyses into philosophical terms. In this way the folk philosophies of ancient Yahwism can be identified, reconstructed and elucidated.

7.3. Philosophical Analysis

According to Scott Soames,

> *Philosophical analysis* is a term of art. At different times in the twentieth century, different authors have used it to mean different things. What is to be analyzed (e.g., words and sentences versus concepts and propositions), what counts as a successful analysis, and what philosophical fruits come from analysis are questions that have been vigorously debated since the dawn of analysis as a self-conscious philosophical approach. Often, different views of analysis have been linked to different views of the nature of philosophy, the sources of philosophical knowledge, the role of language in thought, the relationship between language and the world, and the nature of meaning—as well to more focused questions about necessary and apriori truth. Indeed the variety of positions is so great as to make any attempt to extract a common denominator from the multiplicity of views sterile and not illuminating.[5]

---

4. This chapter represents a complete revision of Jaco W. Gericke, "The Quest for a Philosophical Yhwh (Part 2): Philosophical Criticism as Exegetical Methodology," *OTE* 19 (2006): 1178–92.

5. Scott Soames, "What Is Philosophical Analysis?" *Encyclopedia of Philosophy*

Moreover,

> Analysis has always been at the heart of philosophical method, but it has been understood and practised in many different ways. Perhaps, in its broadest sense, it might be defined as a process of isolating or working back to what is more fundamental by means of which something, initially taken as given, can be explained or reconstructed. The explanation or reconstruction is often then exhibited in a corresponding process of synthesis. This allows great variation in specific method, however. The aim may be to get back to basics, but there may be all sorts of ways of doing this, each of which might be called "analysis."[6]

Among the many ways of doing "analysis" on the way to getting back to basics are the following three:

1. *Regressive* conceptions of analysis. These involve working back from "what is sought," taken as assumed, to something more fundamental by means of which it can then be established.
2. *Decompositional* conceptions of analysis, which entail breaking a concept down into simpler parts.
3. *Transformative/interpretative* types of analysis, which involve translating the statements to be analyzed into their "correct" logical form.[7]

These three conceptions should not be seen as competing with one another. In actual practices of analysis, which are invariably richer than the accounts that are offered of them, all three conceptions are typically reflected, though to differing degrees and in differing forms.[8] Ultimately no consensus has formed concerning the role and importance of analysis in philosophy. There is no agreement on what "analysis" means. Wittgen-

---

[cited 12 August 2010]. Online: http://www-rcf.usc.edu/~soames/sel_pub/Philosophical_Analysis.pdf. For a more extensive discussion, see his *The Dawn of Analysis* (vol. 1 of *Philosophical Analysis in the Twentieth Century*; Princeton: Princeton University Press, 2003).

6. Michael Beaney, "Analysis," *SEP* [cited 22 July 2010]. Online: http://plato.stanford.edu/archives/sum2009/entries/analysis/.

7. Ibid.

8. Ibid.

stein's later critique of analysis and Quine's attack on the analytic-synthetic distinction, for example, have led some to claim that we are now in a "postanalytic" age. Such criticisms, however, are only directed at particular conceptions of analysis. In the context of biblical studies, our concern is simply pragmatic. Even if certain types of philosophical analysis eventually become outdated in philosophy proper, it might still be of use to biblical scholars in accessing levels of meaning in the text that are not available to other traditional, nonphilosophical exegetical methods.[9]

7.4. Functional Types of Descriptive Philosophical Commentary

Roland Boer distinguished two types of "philosophical commentary." On the one hand, there is the reading featuring a host of philosophical witnesses, with biblical criticism taking a backseat. On the other hand, there is interpretation that keeps the text in the foreground while sometimes visiting with philosophers for a "smoke and a chat."[10] In this study I opt for the latter, since my interest is not in using the Hebrew Bible for the construction of a contemporary Jewish or Christian philosophy of religion but instead in using issues in philosophy of religion as a lens through which to make sense of what the texts assume on those matters, purely for historical interest.

What follows represents my own hybrid adaptation of elements from regressive, decompositional, and transformative types of philosophical analysis, respectively. In order to avoid any misunderstanding of what this will deliver, I wish to state that philosophical criticism of the type envisaged here is a form of textualist hyperdescriptivism. By this I mean that not only do we bracket the question of truth in favor of the question of meaning, but our concern also lies completely with clarification as opposed to justification or critique. In addition, we shall be first and foremost concerned with the world *in the text* alone. The world *behind* it (historical background) and the world *in front of* it (our world and those of earlier

---

9. Ibid.

10. See, for example, "philosophical commentary" in the discussion by Roland Boer in Antonio Negri, *The Labor of Job: The Biblical Text as a Parable of Human Labor* (Durham, N.C.: Duke University Press, 2009), 113–18. Here the concern is reading the Bible for the sake of its possible contemporary relevance, not as part of a quest for a better understanding of the world in the text for its own sake.

reception history) are of relevance only to the extent that the meaning of folk philosophies in the text can be elucidated thereby.

The concept of "the world in the text" is well known in biblical scholarship, coming as it does from the hermeneutical philosophy of Paul Ricoeur. It refers to that set of assumptions and actions that are conducted in the text itself, without checking to see if these assumptions are possible in the world outside the text.[11] However, in order to do descriptive philosophical justice to the variable pluralism of conceptions of Yhwh and of reality in the biblical discourse itself, I have decided to adapt Ricoeur's terms to the context of modal fictionalism, so as to be able to speak of "the worlds (plural) in the text." By this I mean to denote what philosophers of post-Kripkean metaphysics understand by all actual, possible, and impossible worlds, which I locate in the transworld domains of intratextual pluralism. The focus will be on presuppositions, conceptual structures, and Gricean implicature, and to this end I offer three new related concepts to reveal the locations of the philosophically relevant data:

1. the worlds *under* the worlds in the text (presuppositions);
2. the worlds *inside* the worlds in the text (concepts); and
3. the worlds *above* the worlds in the text (implications).

I limit the philosophical description to these domains, which will be the targets of regressive, decompositional, and transformative analyses, respectively. How they relate to the worlds in front of and behind the text may be interesting, but historical referentiality and theological relevance in this sense are not my concern. Let us now look briefly at each type of analysis in turn.

7.4.1. Presupposition Reconstruction: The Worlds under the Worlds in the Text

Inception is a 2010 film directed by Christopher Nolan and starring Leonardo DiCaprio. The main character makes a living from extracting information from the subconscious mind of his subjects while they dream. The aim is to explore dream space and to share a dream. Yet to do so one must first have the ability to access the unconscious mind, and be fully aware of

---

11. Brueggemann, *Old Testament Theology*, 57–58.

the difficulties involved in navigating not only the first-level dream world but also dreams within dreams, and all the way down to "limbo"—the sea of the subconscious popularly expressed as primordial chaos in mythical cosmogonies.[12]

In this section I would like us to explore something analogous to what can be called the "subconscious" levels of ancient Yahwism(s)—the invisible building blocks from which the worlds in the texts were created and that hold it all together. Philosophical-religious exegesis of the Hebrew Bible will have to begin with regressive analysis aimed at identifying and reconstructing ancient Israelite religion's most general and fundamental assumptions about the nature of reality and human life—insofar as these are implicit in the biblical text. According to Don Cupitt:

> In the long period dominated by Plato (roughly 350 B.C.E. to 1800 C.E.), when there was a sharp distinction between the sensuous world below and the eternal purely intelligent world above, it was usually thought that while science was concerned with the lower world of the senses and empirical fact, philosophy is concerned with the higher world of a priori, eternal truth. To do philosophy you raised your sights. A modern version of the old doctrine would have to say something rather different, like this: in philosophy, many of the toughest and most interesting philosophical questions have to do with matters that are very hard to get hold of because we are so deeply immersed in them all the time. We can't distance ourselves from them so as to get a cool detached and "scientific" view of them. Examples are time, being, consciousness and language. Philosophy is nowadays very often not about things that are too high up and far off for us, but about things that are always presupposed, too close to us, so that we can't easily get them into focus. To find philosophy's space, don't climb *up*: step *back*.[13]

This process of "stepping back" is known by many names. What we are looking for is to expose presuppositions about topics in philosophy of religion in the text. On this point, it is interesting to note that there is such a thing as "expository philosophy." In *Thinking Philosophically*, Rich-

---

12. A worst-case scenario for the explorer of the dream world was succinctly summarized by the philosopher Gilles Deleuze, who famously said: "If you're trapped in the dream of the other, you're fucked."

13. Don Cupitt, *Above Us Only Sky: The Religion of Ordinary Life* (Santa Rosa, Calif.: Polebridge Press, 2008), 33.

ard Creel discussed seven activities philosophers engage in: they exposit, analyze, synthesize, describe, speculate, prescribe, and criticize. [14] Among these, what he calls "expository philosophy" is relevant to biblical scholars with descriptive philosophical agendas. Expository philosophy aims to get into the worlds "under" the worlds in the text: "Expository philosophy endeavors to lay bare what is covered up, to make conscious the unconscious, to make explicit the implicit."[15]

Expository philosophy helps to bring to the fore people's (any people's) assumptions about reality, value, and knowledge. Most of these are unarticulated and unsystematic folk philosophical "theories" that go without saying, and which they have absorbed from their environment and their intellectual traditions. Since few of these theories are consciously held, they are philosophical prejudices, as they are not subjected to critical examination. They are philosophical, nevertheless, inasmuch as they are about metaphysical, epistemological, moral, and other related assumptions. Expository philosophy is the effort to become aware of, identify, and reconstruct these assumptions for the sake of elucidation.

In the context of a philosophical approach to the Hebrew Bible, "stepping back" and concern with presuppositions will be immensely informative. It will expose the folk philosophical questions presupposed in every text.

Where, then, do we find the data with which we are to work in nonphilosophical biblical discourse? Here we come to the metaphor of expository philosophy and Ricoeurian notions of the world in the text, and we fine tune it to introduce the concept of "the world(s) *under* the worlds in the text." By this is meant nothing more than the totality of folk philosophical presuppositions in the text. Because these were operative in the minds of the biblical authors and are not necessarily shared by us, they provide a context for meaning, the ignorance of which ends up predisposing us to distort the meaning of the text itself. The presence of these assumptions can be illustrated with reference to the four philosophical categories.

First, there is metaphysics: the Hebrew Bible is not a metaphysical treatise, yet its discourse does contain assumptions about metaphysical issues. Included here are presuppositions in the texts about the nature of

---

14. Richard E. Creel, *Thinking Philosophically: An Introduction to Critical Reflection and Rational Dialogue* (Oxford: Wiley-Blackwell, 2001).

15. Ibid., 54.

existence, reality, being, substance, mereology, time and space, causality, identity and change, objecthood, and relations (e.g., subject and object), essence and accident, properties and functions, necessity and possibility (modality), order, mind and matter, free will and determinism, and so on. What the biblical scholar is interested in, however, is not just any sort of metaphysical reflection. If our aim is a more comprehensive understanding of fundamental assumptions in the text, a descriptive approach is warranted, to describe the most general features of the Hebrew Bible's conceptual schemes, that is, reality as it was assumed to manifest itself to ancient Israelite understandings. This is opposed to revisionary metaphysics, which in the history of philosophy has attempted to revise the traditional ways of thinking in order to provide an intellectually and morally preferred picture of the world via a well organized system. The latter variety of metaphysics is out of place in historical biblical studies, but there is nothing hermeneutically wrong with a descriptive approach which asks the following questions:

1. What does a text in the Hebrew Bible assume about cause and effect?
2. What does a text in the Hebrew Bible assume about the whole and the parts?
3. What does a text in the Hebrew Bible assume about generality in relation to specific individuals?
4. What does a text in the Hebrew Bible assume about properties and substance, and their relation and inherence?
5. What does a text in the Hebrew Bible assume about the relation between power and the possessor thereof?

The possibility of discerning the metaphysical assumptions of ancient Israelite religion is becoming more and more obvious in the writings of some biblical scholars who do happen to think that one can talk about metaphysical assumptions in ancient Israelite religion. Walter Eichrodt could speak of "metaphysical" statements in Deutero-Isaiah but did not mention that they are implicit elsewhere.[16] According to Rolf Knierim, we find in the Hebrew Bible folk metaphysics of a rather specific kind:

---

16. Eichrodt, *Theology of the Old Testament*, 1:191.

It is the so-called dynamistic ontology which says that reality is a dynamic process from beginning causes to their corresponding ends. The fact that the ontology had in the Old Testament already become subject to contestation, modification and complementation means neither than it has been abandoned in the wake of the historical development of philosophical discourse, nor that it is not also, alongside complementary alternative propositions, empirically verifiable, then and today.[17]

Another reference to biblical metaphysics is found in the remark by Mark Smith:

For the ancient Israelites their texts contain an ancient form of metaphysics. To be sure, these texts do not use the ontological language of "being" found in the works of the great metaphysicians of later ages such as Thomas Aquinas. Instead, a fundamental ontology used in the ancient world is embodied in language about power.[18]

Smith goes on to speak of different metaphysical "paradigms" and of alternative ontologies and metaphysics in the Hebrew Bible. Another example comes to us from the paper read at the 2007 IOSOT conference by Zioni Zevit entitled "Seeing Yhwh in Shamayim: A Problem in Ancient Israelite Metaphysics." All three examples given here are concerned with Yahwistic "metaphysics." Their use of this concept is a long way from the older biblical-theological idea that the Hebrew Bible has nothing in common with philosophy. The possibility of a philosophical rendering was recognized by Smith in a later publication on the translatability of religious language.[19]

However, even if Smith is right and the ontological language differs from medieval metaphysics, this does not rule out a philosophical approach to ancient Israelite religion. On the contrary, research to determine the difference between the Hebrew Bible's views on a given matter and those of Greek philosophical perspectives is actually already a form of descriptive comparative folk philosophy of religion. One cannot even know whether or how biblical perspectives differ from any other perspective (or in themselves) unless one actually describes the folk philosophical metaphysical assumptions of the Hebrew Bible. In doing so, one grants

---

17. Knierim, *Task of Old Testament Theology*, 410; cf. 89, 115, 253, 430.

18. Smith, *Memoirs of God*, 161–62.

19. Smith, *God in Translation*, 21. Smith recognizes that philosophy of religion is a second-order discourse, just like comparative religion (18).

the legitimacy of a descriptive philosophical account of Yahwism and the presence of folk philosophy in the text.

Contra someone such as Walter Brueggemann, who claims we should bracket ontology (although he means prescriptive as opposed to descriptive varieties),[20] and more in line with the ideas of Rolf Knierim, then, there is a place for ontology in the study of ancient Israelite religion. This not in the sense of a concern with what is really real (which Brueggemann deplores), but in the sense of asking what texts in the Hebrew Bible themselves assumed is really real, and in what sense, whatever that may be (what even Brueggemann allows).

Second, there is *epistemology*. The Hebrew Bible is not an essay in epistemology, yet its discourse does contain assumptions about the nature of knowledge, belief, truth, interpretation, understanding, and cognitive processes. The language of the Hebrew Bible is bound to contain implicit content on the following: what knowledge was assumed to be; how it was thought to be acquired; what types of knowledge there were assumed to be; how knowledge was assumed to be justified; what its limits were assumed to be; what it was thought to amount to; what its purpose was assumed to be, and so on. Such folk philosophical presuppositions are certainly present in the text. Here again pluralism is the norm, so that no unified epistemology can be reconstructed. A relevant concept in philosophy is ethnoepistemology,[21] which is related to the concept of *ethnophilosophy* derived from African philosophy and discussed earlier.

---

20. See Brueggemann, *Old Testament Theology*, 118.

21. James Maffie, "Ethnoepistemology," *IEP* [cited 29 January 2010]. Online http://www.iep.utm.edu/. "Indeed, the customary use of the terms 'ethnophilosophy' and 'ethnoepistemology' by Western philosophers is objectionable: it assumes that Western philosophy is the standard by which all other cultures' philosophies and reflective activities are to be understood and measured, and that Western philosophy is philosophy simpliciter, rather than one among many ethnophilosophies. The more broadly ecumenical and nonethnocentric use of the term 'ethnoepistemology' employed here, however, avoids this shortcoming since it includes all epistemological activities, whether they be African, East Asian, European, or Latin American. In this spirit it examines the entire gamut of human epistemological activities, ranging from those of ordinary folk and cognitive specialists (diviners, shamans, priests, magicians, and scientists) to those of epistemologists themselves. Ethnoepistemology includes both domestic and nondomestic epistemological practices, and accordingly regards Western epistemological practice as simply one among many alternative, contingent epistemological projects advanced by, and hence available to, human beings" (ibid.).

Admitting epistemology in the text and allowing epistemological perspectives on the text are certainly not a novelty. To be sure, instances of such approaches are rare, yet there is no reason why it cannot be done. For example, an excellent recent study with a concern somewhere between epistemology and psychology, and focused on ancient Israelite conceptions of the mind, is that by Michael Carasik, which thoroughly debunks the idea of the structures of Hebrew thought as *sui generis*.[22] By contrast, a conservative and rather superficial approach to ancient Israelite assumptions about knowledge—motivated by the same fundamentalist concerns that drive the epistemological obsession in philosophy of religion—is evident in some contributions to the study, *The Bible and Epistemology: Biblical Soundings on the Knowledge of God*.[23] Still, the latter is to be commended for its willingness to engage with epistemological concerns at all.

Third, there is *ethics*. On this subject as analogy, more will be said below. Suffice it here to note that ethics is itself a philosophical subject that somehow managed to sneak into Hebrew Bible interpretation without too much fuss. But we need—and the texts contain—more than substantive ethics. The Hebrew Bible is not an ethical treatise, yet its discourse does contain assumptions about *metaethical* issues such as the meaning of good and evil, the nature of right and wrong, criteria for moral discernment, valid sources of morality, the origin and acquisition of moral beliefs, the ontological status of moral norms, moral authority, cultural pluralism, and so on. There are also axiological and aesthetic assumptions in the text about the nature of value and beauty. These ideas will be implicit in the text, and the theological pluralism in ancient Israelite religion may well presuppose moral pluralism.

Fourth, there is *logic*. The Hebrew Bible is not a textbook on logic, yet its discourse does contain assumptions about valid arguments, the nature of language and its relation to reality, the nature of reasoning in religious thought, the warranting of beliefs, the justification of religious experience, strategies in polemical arguments, the nature of rational thinking, and the logic of belief revision. These are implicit in the text. Whatever we make of them in view of contemporary ideas on the matter, they can and should be described for what they were. Moreover, if it could be shown that the Hebrew Bible has a logic that differs from, say, Aristotelian logic, this is no

---

22. Carasik, *Theologies of the Mind*.

23. Mary Healy and Robin Parry, eds., *The Bible and Epistemology: Biblical Soundings on the Knowledge of God* (Colorado Springs: Paternoster, 2007).

reason to avoid philosophy. On the contrary, this would be all the more reason to describe biblical logic as folk philosophy, and engage in a philosophical clarification of ancient Israelite folk philosophical assumptions on the matter.

7.4.2. Conceptual Analysis: The Worlds within the Worlds in the Text

Regressive analysis, attending to assumptions, is not enough. The next step is conceptual clarification, or decompositional analysis. This too can be a purely descriptive philosophical activity that will allow the biblical scholar to approach the text both philosophically and historically. Indeed, the most popular form of philosophical analysis is *conceptual analysis*. No biblical scholar interested in understanding Israelite religion and bracketing possible anachronistic Christian philosophical-theological distortions can avoid it. For example, one cannot fully understand the expression "Yhwh lives" unless and until there is some philosophical analysis of the sentence "Yhwh lives," and there is no way to do such an analysis apart from providing a conceptual clarification of the language games in which it occurs. Here our evaluative point of view will be the same as the curious and neutral stance adopted by Wittgenstein in his remarks on Frazer's *The Golden Bough*.

Biblical scholars often use the term "concept" in a nonphilosophical sense, without realizing that in philosophy it is a technical term and that concepts have been primary targets for philosophical analysis. At the outset, however, a distinction should be made between the philosophical theory of conceptual analysis and the historical movement. Conceptual analysis as movement became defunct in the 1970s, yet conceptual analysis as such (also called philosophical analysis) is as old as philosophy itself. Much of twentieth-century analytic philosophy of religion has focused on linguistic analysis for the purpose of conceptual analysis.

If we can agree that there are concepts in the Hebrew Bible and in biblical theology, then we have to admit that those concepts can be subjected to philosophical analysis and clarification. This should not be difficult, given the fact that research concerned with conceptual analysis is not altogether absent from biblical scholarship.[24] What should be done in

---

24. This is evident from doing a word search using "conceptual analysis" on the SBL website, e.g., Randall Argall, *1 Enoch and Sirach: A Comparative and Conceptual Analysis of the Themes of Revelation, Creation, and Judgment* (Atlanta: Scholars Press,

this section is to gather the loose strings into an independent and officially recognized method, with philosophical interests beyond merely linguistic ones. Something very much like this can be found in one of the sessions headed by Won W. Lee at the 2010 SBL International meeting in Tartu, Estonia, entitled "Concept Analysis and the Hebrew Bible":

> **Description:** The unit examines concepts that unify particular textual units or books in the Hebrew Bible and the interrelationship of competing concepts within the same book or corpus in the Hebrew Bible (e.g., God's love and hate; peace and violence; wealth and poverty).
>
> **Call for papers:** The unit calls for papers addressing one of the following two areas: 1) methodological considerations (what constitutes "concepts" in a given text or book? How to compare different concepts within textual units? What contributions that this method makes in the contemporary landscape of biblical interpretation? What roles does a particular culture and societal ethos play in conceptualization and production of texts); and 2) interpretations of concepts that unify particular textual units or books in the Hebrew Bible and the interrelationship of competing concepts within the same book or corpus in the Hebrew Bible (e.g., divine justice and mercy, election and non- or/and anti-election, covenant and suffering).[25]

Those participating here may not view the matter from a philosophical-religious perspective, since conceptual analysis is most familiar from the context of linguistics and cognitive studies, which have already had a great impact on research in biblical scholarship. However, a more specifically philosophical interest is not altogether absent. This is found in the work of Christine Helmer:

> One key task of biblical theology is the clarification of its key concepts. If biblical theology leaves unexamined its philosophical presuppositions or its theological categories, then it is prone to the charge of "dogmatic" imposition still haunting the discipline.[26]

1995); or Deborah L. Ellens, *Women in the Sex Texts of Leviticus and the Hebrew Bible: A Comparative Conceptual Analysis* (New York: T&T Clark, 2008).

25. Online: http://www.sbl-site.org/meetings/Congresses_ProgramUnits.aspx?MeetingId=16.

26. Christine Helmer, "Open Systems: Constructive Philosophical and Theological Issues in Biblical Theology," *SBL Forum* [cited 15 September 2004]. Online: http://sbl-site.org/Article.aspx?ArticleID=310.

With refreshing lucidity, she continues:

> The clarification of concepts is a task that must be constantly checked with the empirical determination of these concepts if it is not to be divorced from the very data that it is called to conceptualize. By admitting the significance of this task, biblical theology underlines the essential historicity of its procedure. Paradoxically, conceptual clarification highlights historicity, rather than flying away from it.... Furthermore, an orientation to the concepts highlights the essential hermeneutical determination of biblical theology. Concepts serve as transhistorical bridges facilitating the understanding of ancient texts and communicating results to one's contemporaries. Although these concepts are determined at some minimal definitional level and must be kept open as to possible revision, they function to mediate a transhistorical "something" that matters to both author and reader/hearer. Whether studied in terms of the philosophical question concerning reality, or the religious studies question concerning religion, or the theological question concerning the particular configuration of the self/world/God relation, the "something" of which the biblical texts make claims can be debated and discussed.[27]

And then:

> If biblical studies can be sensitized to conceptual-theological or philosophical issues integral to the text, then the close proximity to biblical scholarship by systematic theology is one that might prove to be enlivening for this field.[28]

Though potentially philosophical, there is nothing sinister or potentially distortive in a conceptual analysis of the Hebrew Bible's religious concepts. Decompositional analysis is a philosophical tool that can be utilized and adapted for purely historical and descriptive purposes, for example to analyze an author's or corpus's use of the concept of truth or holiness or wisdom. Of course, zeal without knowledge tends to be a dangerous thing, and if we are to concern ourselves with conceptual analysis as philosophical analysis in the narrow sense of clarification, we would do well to acquaint ourselves with the history of related concerns in philosophy proper.[29] The biblical scholar interested in conceptual analysis must be

---

27. Ibid.
28. Ibid.
29. Convenient philosophical introductions to conceptual analysis as philosophi-

able to know the pros and cons of the different views of conceptual structure, for example classic theories, neoclassic theories, prototype theories, exemplar theories, theory theories, atomism, proxy type theories, dualist theories, pluralist approaches, and so on.

I am well aware of the fact that by the third quarter of the previous century conceptual analysis had become extremely unfashionable in philosophy, following the flight from intensions, the death of analycity, the paradox of analysis, the scientific essentialist critique of propositions, and the critique of transcendental arguments.[30] Since then, different opinions indeed rule the field, and the 1990s revealed a whole spectrum of views. Some philosophers have argued that the method of conceptual analysis is endlessly problematic. Others have said that while analysis is largely a fruitful method of inquiry, philosophers should not limit themselves to using only the method of analysis.[31] Yet others feel strongly that conceptual analysis still defines what philosophy is supposed to be about.[32]

Biblical scholars would do well to take note of this history, and to become acquainted with all the pros and cons of conceptual analysis dealt with in these debates. However, whether philosophy proper finds a use for conceptual analysis, or whether the approach can deliver the results philosophers wish to achieve, is irrelevant. All that biblical scholars need to know is that conceptual analysis represents a functional tool that can be employed for the clarification of meaning in biblical interpretation. Not that it will be able to deliver all possible meaning. One should not make a fetish of it. However, perhaps it can provide insights not available through other forms of exegesis. Every little bit helps.

cal analysis are found online at Dennis Earl, "Concepts," *IEP* [cited 12 April 2010]; online: http://www.iep.utm.edu/; and at Eric Margolis and Stephen Laurence, "Concepts," *SEP* [cited 12 April 2010]; online: http://plato.stanford.edu/archives/fall2008/entries/concepts/.

30. Robert Hanna, "Conceptual Analysis," *REP* 2:518.

31. "Philosophical Analysis," *Wikipedia, The Free Encyclopedia* [cited 12 February 2010]. Online: http://en.wikipedia.org/w/index.php?title=Philosophical_analysis&oldid=332404756.

32. Ibid.

7.4.3. Philosophical Translation: The Worlds above the Worlds in the Text

Presupposition reconstruction and conceptual analysis find their completion in philosophical translation (the transformative phase of analysis). However, our concern is not so much logical form as metaphysical entailment. The aim of this final philosophical task is transformative and involves biblical scholars translating the nonphilosophical language of the Hebrew Bible into philosophical terms. However, this will be a descriptive and historical exercise quite different from what happens when theologians do something similar to make the text seem relevant.

In other words, one has to try to state what would strike a philosopher (or an ancient Israelite with a philosophical vocabulary) who looks at the text and tells us what it seems to say when the discourse is put into philosophical wording. Ideally, what happens in this task is the explanation of what someone with an extensive knowledge of the findings of linguistic, historical, literary, and social-scientific research, and also an extensive philosophical vocabulary and competence, would "see" in the text. Our question is: what would the texts on their own terms be "saying" to such a person, in philosophical terms?

One thus leaves everything as it is, but gives a philosophical account of what is there. This type of philosophical translation is sorely needed precisely because the Hebrew Bible is not philosophy, and the most fundamental ideas about reality and human existence are not spelled out for us. Doing so is the task of the philosophical translator. We need to translate the biblical discourse into nondistortive philosophical language, where one simply repeats the idea of a verse with reference to what is implied as regards a particular issue in philosophy of religion. The object language is that of the Hebrew Bible and the target language is transacted in philosophical concepts. What this reading offers is a running commentary that reveals the worlds above the worlds in the text.

Of course, this type of analysis requires fluency in "philosophese" and a little creativity to discern multiple possible philosophical translations from the perspective of a variety of philosophical areas, disciplines, and loci. Thus one might say that in the language of metaphysics, the texts seem to be saying x, y, and z regarding the relation between religion and morality (for example); that from an epistemological perspective they appear to be saying p, q, and r; and so on. What we look for must be determined by the text itself and not be superimposed from the outside in a distortive manner. It concerns the art of finding appropriate philosophical terminology to describe the implication threads of the metaphysical, epistemological, moral, and other assumptions in the discourse about issues on the agenda in philosophy of religion.

The idea is not to make the text philosophically relevant, but merely to give a philosophical account of its meaning and to repeat what the text is saying in philosophical terms for its own sake. What makes this a philosophical rather than a purely linguistic exercise is the exclusive concern with the translation of biblical words into philosophical terms. Consider, for example, the following philosophical description by Georg Fohrer of the concept of Yhwh in a history of Israelite religion during the Mosaic period:

> According to the only Israelite explanation, that found in Exod. 3:14, the name means that this God is one of whom *hāyâ* can be fully predicated. Since this verb in the Hebrew refers not merely to static existence, but to dynamic and effectual presence, the name ascribes dynamic, powerful and effectual being to Yahweh. Yahweh's nature, as expressed by his name, is a union of being, becoming and acting—an effectual existence that is always becoming and yet remains identical with itself.[33]

This is typical Biblical Theology Movement talk—contrasting abstract, static and speculative Greek thinking with concrete, dynamic, practical Hebrew thought. Note also the "anachronistic" philosophical concepts used by Fohrer as he speaks of Yhwh being "predicated" and as having a "nature" (Aristotelian notions) or when he talks about Yhwh's "existence," "being," and "becoming" (Platonic concepts). These terms are not found in the Hebrew Bible itself, yet there is nothing a priori distortive in their use. Though philosophical, these terms can be applied purely descriptively— and what is wrong with that? Surely it is wrong to think that historical and philosophical concerns are mutually exclusive. Does such a philosophical description not create the kind of awareness of metaphysical assumptions in the text that other approaches tend to bracket?

Of course, we may well deny that Fohrer's philosophical translation is wholly correct, but then the problem lies with his particular description and not with the fact that his account of Yhwh happens to be philosophical. But

---

33. Georg Fohrer, *History of Israelite Religion* (trans. David E. Green; Nashville: Abingdon, 1972), 77.

if Fohrer can venture even a short philosophical analysis, what would be wrong with extending it to a book's length (while pointing out diachronic changes in the conceptual background)? Is Fohrer not already unintentionally actually doing philosophical analysis? Was not the denial that the LXX is correct in suggesting that Exod 3:14 is an ontological claim itself only possible as a result of prior unwritten philosophical translation, the details of which were left out with only the (alleged) bottom line being communicated? What else besides unwritten clandestine philosophical analysis has the Biblical Theology Movement been doing to be able to know that certain philosophical concepts are in fact not appropriate to begin with?

In sum, what we need then is a running commentary about what, if anything, the text is asserting when translated into metaphysical, epistemological, moral and logical terms, but with reference to each of the issues on the agenda in philosophy of religion. And while the idea of philosophical words replacing biblical ones may send many biblical theologians running for cover, the whole process will involve nothing more than "translating" (not reinterpreting) the Hebrew Bible's own ideas into something with a richer theoretical system. Any distortive philosophical vocabulary in any analysis says more about the philosophical analyst's incompetence than about philosophical translation being distortive per se. It is all a matter of finding the right concepts in the metalanguage, and if one philosophical cluster of jargon does not do the job well enough, we should not dismiss philosophy, but rather look to other currents. Philosophy and its history are rich with terms, and it is all a matter of going in search for the best description.

7.5. ISSUES ON THE AGENDA

The distinction between the three types of worlds discussed above blur when they all come together in the world in the text. As can be expected, the issues of interest in philosophical criticism will parallel those on the agenda of philosophy of religion as well as new ones prompted by the Hebrew Bible itself (e.g., Sheol). It includes a concern with the nature of Israelite religion; the nature of the Hebrew Bible's religious language; the concept of revelation; the nature and attributes of the divine; implicit reasons for believing or disbelieving in the reality or activity of Yhwh and the gods; varieties of the problem of evil; the nature of religious experience; the relation between religion and morality; religious epistemology; and so on. Not that data for these loci will be present everywhere in the discourse—one should not read philosophical issues into the text that are not there. Hence some adaptation and modification of the structure of popular philosophical-religious questions and topics might be necessary, as well as openness to the fact that a given text might presuppose notions utterly at odds with what is taken for granted in postbiblical Jewish and Christian philosophy of religion (e.g., the "problem of evil" as a result of "perfect being" theology). The interest here is purely historical and phenomeno-logical. Of course, since the loci typical in philosophy of religion represent many topics and subtopics, and since both the Hebrew Bible and the phil-osophical questions it could give rise to are virtually infinite, many types of discussions of virtually all texts in the Hebrew Bible are possible. The following are merely a few examples of such possibilities; they are couched in the rhetoric of the titles of journal articles:

- The Natural Theology behind Genesis 1
- The Axiology of the Concept of the "Good" in Genesis 1
- A Comparison of Perspectives on the Meaning of Life in Gen-esis 1 and 2
- The Metaphysical Assumptions of the Prediction of Genesis 15:12–16
- Genesis 18 versus "Perfect Being" Theology
- Traces of Moral Realism in Genesis 18:25
- Divine Providence, Free Will, and Determinism in the Joseph Narrative
- Problems Related to Yhwh's Personal Identity in Exodus 3:6
- A History of Philosophical Translations of Exodus 3:14
- Yhwh and Natural Evil in Exodus 4:11
- Yhwh and Pharaoh's Heart—Perspectives from the Philoso-phy of Action
- A Wittgensteinian Perspective on Ritual in Leviticus 16
- Religion and Science in Judges 1:12
- Evidentialism in the Religious Epistemology of 1 Kings 18
- Necessary and Sufficient Conditions for Godhood in Isaiah 41:21–24
- The Justification of Religious Experience in Jeremiah 23
- Religion and Morality in Hosea 1
- Fideism in Habakkuk 3
- Abductive Argumentation for the Existence of Yhwh in Psalm 94:7–12

- The Relation between Yhwh and Time in Isaiah 43:10
- Varieties of Atheism and the Nature of Unbelief in Psalm 14
- Assumptions Regarding the Nature of Religious Language in Psalm 18
- Natural Theology in Job 38–41
- Proverbs and Folk Philosophy
- The Problem of Divine Hiddenness in Qoheleth
- The Epistemology of Dream Interpretation in Daniel 2

As should be clear from these examples, the only limits to the kind of questions to be asked and the texts to which these could be put may well lie not so much in methodological restrictions as in the imagination and creativity of the exegete himself or herself. And though part of the discussion may overlap with what has been said in other disciplines (theological exegesis, ideology criticism, etc.), the overall interpretation of the individual texts from a philosophical-critical perspective will provide a unique reading of the text in question.

7.6. Pros and Cons

Philosophical criticism as envisaged in this study is a descriptive tool for biblical scholars rather than an evaluative one for philosophers of religion proper. The ideal philosophical critic qua biblical critic will need the basic exegetical training, and will be comfortable with reading Hebrew and making informed decisions about the findings of other forms of biblical criticism. Of course, the relation is paradoxical-dialectical: in a sense, being concerned with the foundations of biblical worldviews, the findings of philosophical criticism are conceptually prior to many other inquiries—in the Aristotelian sense of a first philosophy as the study of assumptions about reality (in the text). Philosophical criticism therefore both complements and supplements other forms of biblical criticism. It does not seek to degrade or replace any of them.

However, there are a few pros and cons that all those who intend to engage in the approach should pay heed to. On the one hand, several factors could prove limiting in the actual practice of philosophical criticism:

1. The interpreter has a deficient knowledge of philosophy in general and philosophy of religion in particular.

2. He or she tries to read the Hebrew Bible as though it contains ready-made philosophical discourse.
3. The interpreter misunderstands the nature, content, and purpose of philosophical criticism, attributing to it an evaluative as opposed to a descriptive function.
4. He or she seeks to use the method for the sake of religious apologetics or a/theology rather than an understanding of the folk philosophical ideas of the Hebrew Bible for their own sake.
5. The interpreter lacks the creativity and logical skills to discern possible topics of interest in the ordinary language of the biblical traditions.
6. He or she superimposes distortive Jewish or Christian philosophical-theological concepts, categories or concerns onto the text.
7. The interpreter falls prey to the fallacy of panbiblical generalization and extrapolates from one passage to the entire Hebrew Bible.
8. He or she ignores the challenges posed for philosophical exegesis by the history of Israelite religion and the findings of other forms of biblical criticism.
9. He or she is constrained by expectations provided by his or her own atheological ideology and personal expectations of what the text could or could not possibly mean.

These are but some examples of what might go wrong and earn the method a bad name. Of course, if the exegete does not intend to stick to descriptive philosophy of religion, they are free to opt for another current and none of these matters apply. On the other hand, the value of descriptive philosophical-critical exegesis can be seen being virtually synonymous with the value of philosophical-critical analysis in general. The following may be seen as potential benefits that may be derived from utilizing philosophy of religion as auxiliary discipline on the level of exegesis in Hebrew Bible studies:

1. Philosophical criticism fills a gap in biblical exegesis as the only independent and exclusively philosophical approach to ancient Israelite religion as encountered in the Hebrew Bible.

2. Philosophical criticism enables descriptive philosophy of religion to play the role of a primary auxiliary discipline in Hebrew Bible interpretation.
3. Philosophical criticism is the only platform from which to discuss the kinds of issues that are of interest to philosophy of religion and are bracketed by other approaches.
4. Philosophical criticism is the only method concerned with a philosophical clarification of the foundations of biblical worldviews.
5. Philosophical criticism enables the Hebrew Bible specialist to utilize a philosophical discipline in exegesis without the hermeneutical dilemmas generated by the traditional attempts in systematic and philosophical theology to read the texts from a philosophical perspective.
6. Philosophical criticism allows for a reconstruction of the folk philosophy of ancient Israelite religion for its own sake.
7. Philosophical criticism can act as a supplement and complement to other types of biblical criticism.
8. Philosophical criticism can be seen as worthwhile in its own right, or as a necessary precursor to larger scale philosophical-critical analysis, that is, philosophy of ancient Israelite religion (see the next chapter).
9. Philosophical critical exegesis may assist in closing the communication gap so often experienced by biblical scholars and their colleagues from other disciplines where philosophy is also utilized.

These are only some of the advantages of the establishment of a new, independent and officially recognized form of biblical criticism that concerns itself solely with reading the Hebrew Bible from the perspective of philosophy of religion.

7.7. Conclusion

In this chapter I have attempted to spell out the theory of philosophical criticism as an interpretative methodology concerned with a philosophical analysis of the Hebrew Bible aimed at a historical-philosophical clarification of ancient Yahwisms from the perspective of concerns in descriptive varieties of philosophy of religion. Three locations of data were discussed: the worlds below, inside and above the world in the text. The three approaches involved—presuppositional reconstruction, conceptual analysis, and philosophical translation—allow for a comprehensive philosophical approach concerned with the elucidation of meaning in biblical folk philosophy of religion. As such, philosophical criticism represents the most recent addition to the family of biblical criticism, featuring a type of exegesis concerned exclusively with reading individual Hebrew Bible from the perspective of loci on the agenda in philosophy of religion. It represents the first and micro-component in philosophical-critical analysis. In the next chapter we turn our attention to the second type or macrocomponent of philosophical-critical analysis, that is, a larger-scale discipline I call philosophy of Israelite religion.

8

Toward a Descriptive Philosophy of Ancient Israelite Religion[1]

Someone may ask whether the reach into this dimension of the questions does not amount to a biblical philosophy or a philosophy of the biblical truth. Indeed! And what would be wrong with that? Would it not, while focusing on the Bible, be in contact with *philosophy of religion* and with philosophy in principle, as biblical philosophy's contribution to those fields?[2]

8.1. Introduction

In traditional interpretations of the Hebrew Bible, a distinction is usually made between involving auxiliary disciplines on the level of exegesis versus involving them in a larger-scale approach:

Auxiliary Subject	Biblical Criticism	Large-Scale Approach
history	historical criticism	history of Israelite religion
sociology	social-scientific criticism	sociology of Israelite religion
theology	theological exegesis	Old Testament theology

In this chapter we make the following distinction:

---

1. This chapter represents a complete revision of my "The Quest for a Philosophical Yhwh (Part 3): Towards a Philosophy of Old Testament Religion," *OTE* 20 (2007): 669–88.

2. Knierim, *Task of Old Testament Theology*, 492, emphasis added.

Auxiliary Subject	Biblical Criticism	Large-Scale Approach
philosophy of religion	philosophical criticism	philosophy of Israelite religion

Philosophical criticism as discussed in the previous chapter is therefore the precursor to what I discuss in this chapter as the philosophy of Israelite religion. By this latter concept I mean the philosophical clarification of larger clusters of folk philosophies of religion (plural) in books, sources, traditions, and redactions within the Hebrew Bible. We are no longer simply doing exegesis of a particular passage; we are interested in how larger trajectories relate to issues on the agenda in philosophy of religion. This is not in order to create a unified systematic philosophy of religion based on the entire Hebrew Bible, or to offer something contemporary philosophers of religion should believe or judge. We are not using the Hebrew Bible to offer contemporarily relevant religious philosophy; we are simply utilizing philosophy of religion to understand the folk philosophies of religion unarticulated but nascent on a larger scale in the Hebrew Bible.

But what will a large-scale approach look like? As with philosophical criticism, the aim is the unpacking and clarification of meaning in the text itself, not a justification/grounding or explanation/deconstruction of biblical ideologies. In the discussion to follow in this chapter, a few remarks will be made regarding the possibility of utilizing descriptive philosophy of religion on a large scale. However, the theory of the current chapter will take practical form mostly in Part 2 of this study, when we look at what a philosophy of ancient Israelite religion could consist of.

8.2. Assumptions of a Large-Scale Inquiry

The primary assumptions of the discipline of philosophy of Israelite religion are the following:

1. The Hebrew Bible is not a textbook of philosophy of religion.
2. Because of the theological pluralism of biblical god-talk, one cannot construct a coherent normative philosophy of religion from its contents.
3. Ideational clusters exist in the text that relate to issues on the agenda of philosophy of religion.

4. A descriptive philosophical perspective on these larger complexes in ancient Israelite religion in the Hebrew Bible is possible.

5. The aim is not to harmonize these complexes or to make the text seem relevant to contemporary concerns—it is purely to clarify the complexes' meaning in their own contexts.

6. Following such clarification one worthwhile concern would be intrabiblical comparative philosophy of religion, with different complexes of thought juxtaposed to elucidate similarities and differences.

7. Another possible concern involves comparing biblical folk philosophical perspectives with postbiblical views on similar topics in Jewish and Christian philosophy of religion.

8.3. Loci on the Angenda

The traditional agenda of mainstream philosophy of religion—the primary auxiliary discipline for the present approach—has been rightly criticized for being a little more than a watered down version of Christian apologetics.[3] Be that as it may, however, such criticism is applicable only to attempts at normative reflection for contemporary thinking. Much of the syllabus and its concerns are general and universal enough to warrant adoption and adaptation in the context of almost any religion. In other words, even a historical and descriptive philosophical analysis of Yahwism can concern itself sooner or later with the standard repertoire of topics in the analytic tradition. As a result, the following might be fruitful loci on the agenda (where "x" is a source, tradition, book, or the Hebrew Bible as a whole):

1. The nature of religion in x
2. The nature of x's religious language
3. The concept of revelation in x
4. The nature and properties of Yhwh (and the gods) in x
5. Implicit or nascent arguments in x for or against the existence of deities
6. Religion and morality in x

---

3. Don Cupitt, *Philosophy's Own Religion*, 16.

7. Religious experience in x
8. The relation between religion and history in x
9. The relation between religion and culture in x
10. Religious epistemology in x
11. Religious concepts in x
12. Religious practices (prayer, sacrifice, prophecy, war, etc.) in x
13. Postmortem existence (Sheol) in x
14. Intra- and interreligious pluralism, in x_1 versus x_2, versus ... x_n, and so on.

This list of loci is not exhaustive, for the range of possible issues cannot be limited. Even a genealogical list can be discussed for its metaphysical assumptions. Legal texts contain metaethical beliefs. Poetry exhibits epistemological ideas. In short, anything and everything in the Hebrew Bible can be an object of philosophical reflection. It is a belated realization in contemporary mainstream philosophy of religion that not only the deity or religious language in general but also all intrareligious phenomena and practices can in themselves generate immensely interesting new philosophical puzzles. The aim is not to generalize but to summarize, however complex and variable the whole may be.

A philosophy of Israelite religion is therefore also a philosophical theology of the Hebrew Bible, inasmuch as it is concerned with a better understanding of issues in this specific religion, that is, biblical Yahwisms. For by analogy, just as philosophical theology is possible for Christianity despite the many different traditions, the conceptual pluralism and the differences in nuances and understanding of a single doctrine (e.g., the Trinity), so too it is possible with ancient Israelite religion, despite the different perspectives within the Hebrew Bible.

In addition, we shall attend not only to the intellectual dimension of Israelite religion as represented in the Hebrew Bible. Our descriptive philosophical interest also concerns the practical aspects, since they presuppose the intellectual dimension. No absolute distinction between these is possible. There is no religious rite, practice, or action that does not presuppose a host of folk philosophical assumptions about reality, knowledge, and morality, and that does not presuppose something or other on issues on the agenda in philosophy of religion. Though the focus is mostly on the worlds in the text, in a large-scale approach the comparative dimension means that the worlds behind and in front of the text must also come into play to some extent. Moreover, the focus is most definitely on the many actual and possible worlds (plural) in the text rather than merely on the world (singular) in the text. More on this will be said below.

Since our agenda is descriptive and historical, our primary concern cannot lie with whatever we may personally wish to believe is the case on any given question. Phenomenological reduction requires that our readerly religious, agnostic, or atheistic ideologies should be bracketed as much as possible, and that interest should ideally lie with the Hebrew Bible's own folk philosophical assumptions, whatever they may be. We should not be bothered by unorthodox conclusions, contradictions, outdated conceptions, or irrelevant discoveries. To be sure, in practice the prevalence of religious and secular commitments among biblical scholars means that this objectivity will remain only an ideal, but there is no other way about it and this is where ahistorical elements in an analytic approach should welcome the historical and social consciousness of Continental (e.g., phenomenological) perspectives.

8.4. Philosophy of Israelite Religion and the History of Israelite Religion

Philosophy of Israelite religion should not bracket the history of Israelite religion. We do need to engage in philosophical clarification without falling prey to the seduction of looking for a static system. But let us not fall into clichés, for we need not avoid systems altogether. We simply need to exchange unified Christian dogmatic systems for complex and chaotic Yahwistic biblical ones. The question now pertaining is how a philosophical consideration of the entire Hebrew Bible can happen if conceptual pluralism is both diachronic and synchronic.

With regard to Israelite religion, we may note that the word "religion" does not occur in biblical Hebrew. There was never such a thing as "Israelite religion" in the sense of a linear orthodox and coherent belief system endorsed by all ancient Israelites. It is impossible to give a unified philosophical account of ancient Israelite religion's beliefs, concepts or practices along the lines of Christian dogmatic presentations. Even the meaning of similar religious concepts, beliefs and practices changed over time and was multiple in any given period. So what we have in Israelite religion (which we distinguish from its manifestations in the Hebrew Bible) is a polymorphous entity comprised of clusters related only by way of family resemblances.

The Hebrew Bible came later and represents only the tip of the iceberg. Yet our focus will be on Israelite religion as represented in the text of the Hebrew Bible, not because it is assumed to be historically factual or theologically sound but for the sake of allowing philosophical analysis to clarify the meaning of the text. A philosophical approach must start with the acknowledgement that the texts have no center and offer no set of core beliefs. They were not written for us and none of the initial authors knew of any canonical context. The belief system is complex and polythetic, and its logic of belief revision fuzzy and dynamic. Notwithstanding the absolutist claims in the propositions of individual traditions, the text and its interpretation are fluid, multiple, and relative. Attempts at philosophical synthesis or harmonization are out of place. Neither is it our task to think in terms of evolution or progress by grading and evaluating the beliefs found in different texts.

In trying to get our heads around how Israelite religion is both a unity and a multiplicity, we can think of it as something analogous to a rhizome. This is a botanical term that became a philosophical concept when developed by Gilles Deleuze and Félix Guattari in their *Capitalism and Schizophrenia* (1972–1980).[4] It denotes an image of thought that apprehends multiplicities—an acentered, nonhierarchical, nonsignifying system without an organizing memory or central automation.[5] In a rhizome, everything is connected to everything else despite the many dead ends and the lack of rootedness of the whole. The same can be said of Israelite religion as represented in the Hebrew Bible.

Another interesting analogy would be to think of the Hebrew Bible in its reception history as what chaos theory calls a "strange attractor." The traditions of the Hebrew Bible provide the foci around which Israelite religion came to be understood and around which later patterns of religiosity evolved and continue to be maintained. The pluralism in the biblical discourse is often differentiable in a few directions, and exhibits great detail and complexity. Eventual developments were highly sensitive to initial conditions (the so-called "butterfly effect"). In the history of Israelite religion, small differences in these conditions yielded widely diverging trajec-

---

4. "Rhizome (philosophy)," *Wikipedia, The Free Encyclopedia* [cited 14 April 2010]. Online: http://en.wikipedia.org/w/index.php?title=Rhizome_(philosophy)&oldid=352345273.

5. Gilles Deleuze and Félix Guattari, *A Thousand Plateaus* (vol. 2 of *Capitalism and Schizophrenia*; trans. Brian Massumi; London: Continuum, 2004), 23.

tories, rendering long term prediction impossible. This would account for how the same religion can begin with exodus traditions and end up with both Daniel and Qoheleth, and lead to both Judaism and Christianity.[6]

Given the analogies of rhizomes and chaos for modeling pluralism from synchronic and diachronic perspectives, we may look to comparative philosophy of religion with the aim of a twofold philosophical clarification of theological pluralism: (1) intrareligious dynamic pluralism; and (2) interreligious dynamic pluralism. With regard to the former objective, the philosophical critic will have to negotiate the terrain of many worlds in the text, which present different conceptual complexes. The aim is to identify similarities and differences between them. There is no need to resolve contradictions, and their detection is part of the analysis. In addition, since the aim is not to construct a normative unified theory or a contemporary systematic philosophy of religion from the Hebrew Bible, there is no need to be selective, reductive, harmonizing or distortive of the conceptual or folk philosophical pluralism at hand. On the contrary, this approach will be aimed at determining and revealing the actual nature and extent of this pluralism. Hence the essentialist fallacy is avoided, since we know it is impossible to speak of the "biblical" view (unified and singular) on any given locus on the agenda in philosophy of religion.

So much for intrareligious pluralism. One may also distinguish interreligious pluralism, both sideways and forwards (or backwards) in time. Working sideways, the biblical scholar compares the folk philosophical assumptions about issues on the agenda in philosophy of religion with those of other ancient Near Eastern contexts. Looking forward, he or she may be interested in comparing what a given conceptual complex in the text assumes with how later traditions interpreted or misinterpreted it, and agreed with or differed from it. Thus one might look at Jewish or Christian philosophy of religion, and show how ancient Israelite religion displays similar or different ideas. The ultimate aim is not to say that either the older or the newer is better or worse; it is simply, and for interest's sake, to compare stages within the *Wirkungsgeschichte* of a biblical motif from a philosophical point of view.

With the latter form of comparative philosophy of religion, that is, comparing the Hebrew Bible's folk philosophical assumptions with later

---

6. "Chaos Theory," *Wikipedia, The Free Encyclopedia* [cited 10 May 2010]. Online: http://en.wikipedia.org/w/index.php?title=Chaos_theory&oldid=355572126.

Jewish and Christian philosophy of religion, we come to the historical and receptionist task of the method. Seen in this way, our philosophical analysis becomes a way to prevent anachronistic philosophical distortion and a means of uncovering it. There is no need to argue that any Israelite or biblical view on any given matter is more pure, or normative, or outdated, than any other. Nor is there a need to prove later views as biblical on the assumption that this makes them true. By contrast our concern, being descriptive, involves our attempting to understand what is there, for its own sake. And we can use comparative philosophy of religion to allow the biblical traditions' own intra- and interreligious distinctiveness to become more readily apparent. In this way a comparative approach also allows for appreciating what makes the Hebrew Bible both similar to and different from everything else. The connection with intrareligious comparison should, however, prevent one from speaking of the biblical vis-à-vis other views, since one has to be specific about which biblical view one is referring to.

One example of how this kind of interreligious comparative work might look is *When Gods Were Men*, by Esther J. Hamori.[7] She begins this text by distinguishing the phenomenon of Yhwh's appearing in concrete human form from several other types of anthropomorphism, such as divine appearance in dreams. This "'*iš* theophany*," as she terms it, is then viewed in relation to appearances of angels and other divine beings in the Hebrew Bible, and in relation to anthropomorphic appearances of deities in Near Eastern literature. Hamori then goes on to discuss philosophical approaches to anthropomorphism, tracing the development of opposition to the phenomenon from Greek philosophy through Avicenna, Averroes, Maimonides and Aquinas, and into the work of later philosophers such as Hume and Kant. In the end the author suggests that the work of others—for instance Wittgenstein's language games—can be applied fruitfully to the problem of divine anthropomorphism.

Of course, this is only an example and not exactly the way in which the present study would approach the same issue. We may also differ from Harmori in terms of the philosophical categories and the details in her findings. However, as an illustration of what has been done it shows what could be done, and thus what biblical scholarship has already accepted

---

7. See Esther J. Hamori, *When Gods Were Men: The Embodied God in Biblical and Near Eastern Literature* (Berlin: de Gruyter, 2008).

as perfectly permissible. We may therefore distinguish among at least four different categories[8] of philosophical states of affairs obtaining in the Hebrew Bible when the history of religion is taken seriously:

1. Philosophically interesting issues one tradition in ancient Israelite religion shares with other intra- and extrabiblical traditions, such as "the nature of God."
2. Philosophical interesting issues more or less unique to one tradition in Yahwism, such as the problem of divine hiddenness as manifested in Qoheleth.
3. Philosophical interesting issues that play a major role in some of the biblical traditions but a minor role outside these, such as prophetic conflict.
4. Philosophical interesting issues that play a minor role in the biblical traditions but a major role outside it, such as the logical problem of evil.

It is important to avoid generalizations as well as appeals to any one "biblical" view of anything, because there is no such thing. Philosophy of Israelite religion should not bracket the history of Israelite religion through sweeping statements.

8.5. Large-Scale Philosophical Method

Many bits and pieces of philosophical perspectives on the Hebrew Bible are today scattered across a range of methodologies, for example cognitive approaches, biblical ethics, deconstruction, and biblical hermeneutics. As noted above, however, the methodology of a philosophy of Israelite religion will be unified in a standard form of philosophical analysis but with a historical agenda. This means that it will have to work from the findings of philosophical criticism and to put these together so as to be able to compare and describe in philosophical terms. In a large-scale approach, the scope of the data complex to be considered is expanded from verses and chapters to sources, traditions, and books, and ultimately to the Hebrew Bible as a whole. An example of this kind of large-scale research would

---

8. See Arvind Sharma, "Hinduism," in Meister and Copan, *Routledge Companion to Philosophy of Religion*, 7.

be a series of commentaries that takes entire biblical books and analyzes the contents topically, as in the following list with reference to the book of Judges.

1. The nature of religion in Judges
2. The nature of religious language in Judges
3. The concept of revelation in Judges
4. The nature and properties of Yhwh in Judges
5. Implicit arguments for and against realism regarding gods in Judges
6. The relation between religion and morality in Judges
7. The nature of religious experience in Judges
8. The relation between religion and history in Judges
9. The relation between religion and culture in Judges
10. Religion and science in Judges
11. Religious epistemology in Judges
12. Religious pluralism in Judges

This can be part of a commentary whose main body consists of remarks of philosophical criticism, with the above as a sort of synthesis in the beginning or end. Also, if the particular concept is not attested in the given biblical book (e.g., the concept of God in Esther), or if it seems problematic in the context of the book (e.g., the concept of revelation in Qoheleth), or if the book contains multiple contradictory ideas on the specific locus (the attributes of Yhwh in the Psalms), this is not a problem. Since our goal is not the construction of a unified and systematic normative philosophy of religion, but simply a philosophical clarification of what is already implicit in the text from a literary-historical perspective, we leave everything as it is. The task is only to describe in philosophical terms whatever complexity, pluralism, and diversity the texts exhibit. This not to "solve" or "harmonize" anything but to "understand" what we are dealing with, whatever it may be. We leave everything as it is. We only clarify meaning.

8.6. Adoption and Adaptation of Issues in Christian Philosophy of Religion

Though a descriptive philosophy of Israelite religion will adopt much of its agenda from mainstream philosophy of religion, the loci listed above also represent an adaptation of the stereotypical Judeo-Christian *capita selecta*.

For looking at the issues of interest and the theories they generate within Christian philosophy of religion, the hermeneutically sensitive Hebrew Bible scholar will have some serious reservations about what the proposals for the utilization of that agenda would involve. After all, it would definitely be heuristically illegitimate to simply adopt the agenda of stereotypical Christian philosophy of religion *en bloc*, since many of the traditional loci pertain to philosophical questions generated by the dogmas of postbiblical systematic and philosophical theology and were not derived from a critical philosophical analysis of the religious traditions of Hebrew Bible Yahwism(s). In this, as discussed earlier, we can learn much from debates in African philosophy of religion as to the conceptual and interpretative challenges that awaits us. The examples that follow are worth considering in this regard.

When it comes to the nature of religion, we have already noted more than once that there never was, nor is there, any such thing as Israelite religion coming to us as a unified body of doctrine, even if individual Israelite traditions assumed as much. Israelite religion cannot, as is common in many types of Christianity, be described by a core list of dogmas. When in this study I refer to "Israelite religion," I do not mean to imply that all Israelites believed such things, or that it was all about holding to certain beliefs. I do not assume that the Hebrew Bible represents Israelite religion in a historically factual manner. Neither do I assume that everything is fiction. I do not assume either essentialism or perennialism, and I do not consider it appropriate to reconstruct Israelite religion on the model of Christian systems with a list of doctrines to be believed. I know that biblical Hebrew has no word for "religion"; and that whatever we understand by the category in the Hebrew Bible is not to be separated from a secular sphere, or set up as theological beliefs over and against political, economic, or social frames of reference.

The nature of religious language in the Hebrew Bible is multifaceted. The popular assumption among many biblical scholars that all religious discourse in biblical god-talk is metaphorical is the result of an uncritical adoption of the theory of the supposed metaphorical nature of religious language constructed with reference to postbiblical Christian dogma by modern philosophers of the Christian religion. As such, it cannot be taken for granted when analyzing the biblical discourse; if utilized as a working hypothesis it should first be tested to see if it really does justice to all of the details of the texts in their precritical and prephilosophical historical and literary contexts. To be sure, the Hebrew Bible's god-talk is often metaphorical, but the claim that it is always so borders on neo-allegorizing and often represents little more than a sorry attempt to immunize the discourse against criticism or to alleviate the embarrassment of crude anthropomorphisms.

In Christian philosophy of religion, the Hebrew Bible is considered to be a part of divine revelation. But within biblical studies, one cannot use that perspective as a working hypothesis, because when the philosopher of Israelite religion studies biblical Yahwism(s), the religion in question is no longer biblical Christianity but ancient Yahwism(s). There the traditions had nothing comparable to a canonical Hebrew Bible it considered as divine revelation. Instead, the texts speak of alien phenomena such as theophany, verbal communication and divine providence in socio-historical events. This state of affairs in turn implies that when one discusses the concept of revelation in ancient Israelite religion philosophically, the subject matter will be differently nuanced than in postbiblical Christian philosophy of religion.

When one has to deal with the nature and attributes of God in Christian philosophy of religion, concepts such as monotheism, omnipotence, omnipresence, omniscience, perfect goodness, and so on, have to be analyzed philosophically.[9] Perfect being theology tends to be very popular, while notions of maximal greatness include the great making properties of classical theism. Within the context of the Hebrew Bible these concepts are sometimes out of place, or have a very different content. Yhwh as depicted in the worlds in the text is often not assumed to be omnipotent, omniscient, omnipresent. or wholly loving in the traditional orthodox Christian sense. Even notions of perfection and maximal greatness for generic godhood differ from those modern philosophers of religion may take for granted. One therefore has to focus on the properties of Yhwh, and on their nature in specific worlds in the text. Philosophical analysis of biblical god-talk has to reckon with theological pluralism. In addition, given the concept of generic divinity in the Hebrew Bible, there arises the need for the philosopher of Israelite religion not only to ask what the properties of Yhwh, were but also what, according to the text, a god is, why Yhwh was called a god, and what, according to the text, was assumed by divinity.

---

9. See William Wainwright, "Monotheism," *SEP* [cited 12 May 2010]. Online: http://plato.stanford.edu/archives/win2009/entries/monotheism/.

Arguments concerning the existence of God, such as the ontological argument, the cosmological argument, and the argument from design, are based on attempts to correlate a modern worldview with an orthodox concept of the Christian deity. In the Hebrew Bible, since both the nature of the deity and the worldview(s) are different, these arguments are useless and out of place in ancient Israelite religion concerned with Yhwh as the living God. The Hebrew Bible offers no explicit, well formulated, and comprehensive arguments for or against the reality of specific deities; these have to be reconstructed from what is implicit in the folk philosophy. Our concern with natural theology and propositional justification is therefore limited to what is implicit and taken for granted in the text itself. Thus we are not concerned with natural theology proper, or with arguing for the existence of God as in philosophy of religion proper. Our task is not to prove that Yhwh does or does not exist. What the biblical scholar must do is to reconstruct what the texts presuppose with regard to the reasons for belief and unbelief in the reality of Yhwh and the gods implicit in the worlds in the text, whether these are valid or not. This also means that we will have to start not only with descriptive natural theologies but also with reconstructing atheologies of the Hebrew Bible (antagonist arguments against Yhwh and protagonist arguments against other gods) as these are implicit in polemics against idols.

Though evil may in some sense be problematic for ancient Israelite religion, one therefore cannot speak of the problem of evil in the same sense as it features in Christian philosophy of religion. In the context of Hebrew Bible Yahwism(s), not all texts have a problem reconciling the idea of an omnipotent and purely good deity with the presence of evil in the world, as in Christian philosophy of religion. Sometimes in the Hebrew Bible the ability to cause evil is assumed to be a great-making property for Yhwh. That is, the ancient Israelite idea of maximal greatness at times includes the power to do evil. In such texts there is the assumption or assertion that Yhwh is behind some of the metaphysical, moral and natural evil in ways that are anything but stereotypically orthodox from a popular Christian perspective. One therefore cannot consider the argument from evil to be arguing against the existence of Yhwh in the biblical traditions. The argument is also useless when Yhwh is depicted as being neither omnipotent nor omnibenevolent. In this case the problem is not evil, but the failure of divine justice. This means that not even the theodicy of process theology can be uncritically transposed into the context of the Hebrew Bible, for though it recognizes divine finitude as does the Hebrew Bible, the differences in worldview and benevolence factor make it anachronistic. The same goes for the free-will theodicy, which is also anachronistic in those contexts where Yhwh is depicted as overriding human free will.

In Christian philosophy of religion, the issue of religious experience is dealt with from the frame of reference of postbiblical Christian spirituality, which assumes that such experience represents a *sui generis* doxastic context. But there is a huge difference between philosophically analyzing, let us say, subjective Christian mysticism or conversion experiences, and doing the same with objective religious experiences in the worlds in the text, for instance, theophany, revelatory dreams, prophetic experiences, auditions, divination rituals, and so on. In analyzing the Hebrew Bible's variety of religious experiences, philosophers of ancient Israelite religion will, as always, have to pay close attention to issues such as form, content, textual intent, cultural factors influencing the presentation, rhetorical strategies, literary conventions, and so on. There is no need to explain anything away or to argue for any reality behind the text. We simply adopt a standpoint of observation from within. And while it has been popular to deny mysticism in Old Testament theology, the intermingling of divine and human properties in states of spirit possession, kingship, or ecstatic prophetic experience, should not be overlooked.

With regard to the relation between religion and morality, the pluralism of the Hebrew Bible and also its pre-Christian ethics provide altogether different materials for scrutiny than do contemporary Christian ethics. Biblical scholars have indeed discussed this locus, but mostly in the context of descriptive and applied ethics, while bracketing metaethical issues. By contrast, a philosophical approach to ancient Israelite religion's assumptions about morality will be primarily concerned with metaethical assumptions in the text. However, even here one need not reinvent the wheel. Plato's Euthyphro's dilemma concerning the relationship between the gods and morality is still relevant, and it might be interesting to read the Hebrew Bible with the problem in mind, so as to discover whether Yhwh as depicted in a particular text is the determiner of the moral order or himself subsumed thereto. Under this rubric one will also have to attend to ancient Israelite perspectives on the meaning of life and other axiological issues (value theory). Yet once again, there may be no one unified "biblical" view on the matter, which means that the possibility of theological pluralism also with regard to the relationship between the divine and morality as assumed in the Hebrew Bible must be reckoned with.

When it comes to the relation between religion and culture, one cannot use the format and frame of reference of Christian theology and Western culture if one wishes to understand the issue in the context of Hebrew Bible Yahwism(s). Here the ancient Near Eastern cultural context must provide the frame of reference via the findings of history of religion and comparative religion, rather than those of systematic theology or Christian missiology. The ideal result is analogous to some of the writings of Friedhelm Hartenstein, who is able to combine systematic theological and religio-historical concerns, for instance in his discussion of the "Personalität Gottes im Alten Testament."[10] So when the concepts of deity, the good, love, power, belief, and such are discussed, this must be done taking into account what social-scientific approaches to the Hebrew Bible have discovered on these matters. One cannot discuss a concept such as divine goodness without attending to how goodness was conceived of in the specific form of life in the historical and cultural context of the text in which it appears. It cannot be discussed as a free-floating concept, the associative meaning of which is burdened with anachronistic modern religious assumptions. In this way, philosophical analysis that shows historical and linguistic sensitivity actually becomes a way of preventing philosophical distortion in other approaches.

Religion and science seems to be the one locus in analytic philosophy of religion too anachronistic a topic for the study of ancient Israelite religion, but is it? Rolf Knierim has written interesting bits on "science" in the Hebrew Bible,[11] while research on the material culture of the time also provides data in this regard.[12] There is no reason why, with a little creativity, it cannot be applied to asking how creation accounts compared and conflicted with the science of the day, how wisdom literature and science related, and how technological developments influenced conceptions of deity. The remark in Judg 1:12 about iron chariots being a problem despite the presence of Yhwh comes to mind. Surely Job 38–42 contains some primitive science. Also, the rituals in the Pentateuch can be related to ancient Near Eastern science. Here, too, the concern is descriptive and

---

10. Friedhelm Hartenstein, "Personalität Gottes im Alten Testament," in *Personalität Gottes* (ed. Wilfried Härle and Reiner Preul; Marburg Jahrbuch, Theologie 19; Leipzig: Evangelische Verlagsanstalt, 2007), 19–46.

11. Knierim, *Task of Old Testament Theology*, 400–416.

12. See Ferdinand Deist, with Robert Carroll, *The Material Culture of the Bible* (London: Continuum, 2000).

one cannot simply superimpose later cosmological or creation/evolution controversies onto the text. Yet a study of biblical views of astronomy, biology, and psychology, and how these were affected by and affected religious language, would certainly be worth our while.

Religious epistemology in the Hebrew Bible can also be at odds with what is taken for granted in this topic in contemporary Christian philosophy of religion. With regard to the problems of verification and falsification, the situation is more complex than in postbiblical theology, since the characters in the worlds in the text did not, as modern philosophers of religion tend to do, see religious beliefs as belonging to a set of doxastic practices different from those of everyday empirical affairs. Foundationalist and evidentialist assumptions may be unfashionable these days, but the worlds in the text assume both in many scenarios. Also, it is quite important to determine what error theories the Hebrew Bible offers to account for belief and disbelief in the context of allotheism.

A philosophical analysis of the religious practices of the Hebrew Bible contains the same pitfalls and prospects as those mentioned in connection with religious concepts above. Once again, care must be taken when analyzing ancient Yahwistic religious rites such as prayer, sacrifice, divination, and other forms of worship and religious practices from a philosophical perspective. One might take a cue from what the biblical authors themselves by implication thought about, and examine, for example, the metaphysical assumptions of sacrifice as a problem in ancient Israel. A good analogy would be the manner in which Wittgenstein approached religious rites—not as primitive science but as embedded in specific forms of life. The philosopher of ancient Israelite religion must approach his or her inquiry in dialogue with anthropological, historical and biblical theological studies, rather than simply take for granted the applicability of what has been said about parallel activities in postbiblical Christian spirituality in mainstream philosophy of religion. However, unlike in Old Testament theology, for instance, the philosopher of ancient Israelite religion must ask whether the naturalist/supernaturalist dualism in modern Christian worldviews is not a false dichotomy in the Hebrew Bible, where neither the concepts nor their reference may always be operative in texts that presume a more holistic and continuous relation between the divine and the human realms. Moreover, the philosopher of ancient Israelite religion, unlike the Old Testament theologian, will not only ask how Yhwh was worshiped,but should at some point begin to wonder why Yhwh and the gods wanted to be worshiped in the first place.

On the topic of religious pluralism, we may note that some monotheistic trajectories in the Hebrew Bible assume exclusivism while other mono-latrist parts seem to allow for parallel perspectives on the Most High. The common stock of mythological motifs shows interpenetration, although the ideology of the Hebrew Bible seldom admits such mutual influence. Hence there is no "biblical" view on any religious matter; and philosophers of Israelite religion are different from philosophers of Christianity in that as biblical scholars they do not seek to prove one tradition truer to the facts (they bracket the question of what is really real along phenomenological lines). They cannot harmonize the pluralism in a fundamentalist or any other fashion (e.g., via schemes of progressive revelation or via a *Mitte*), as many systematic or philosophical theologians still do. Biblical scholars must seek only to describe the pluralism in philosophical terms, by leaving everything as it is and then elucidating it in philosophical wording, simply out of curiosity. Their desire is to see what is there for the sake of understanding it better on its own terms, even if not in its own terms.

Finally, with regard to an issue such as postmortem existence, it is quite clear that the Christian vocabulary of eternity, immortality, souls, heaven and hell, and so on are out of place in the context of the Hebrew Bible. The concept of Sheol exhibits an extension that blurs many contemporary boundaries and allows for multiple possible interpretations. And if the thanatological and anthropological concepts change, so do the format and contents of the philosophical problems to be identified, reconstructed, and discussed. For though the Hebrew Bible has no concept of the Christian heaven or hell, the idea of Sheol (and everything related to it) gives rise to interesting philosophical questions, the answers to which were taken for granted in ancient Israelite folk philosophies. These were not spelled out not because the ancient Israelites lacked curiosity or were incapable of critical or abstract speculation, but because many of the beliefs went without saying. In other words, we are dealing here with a topic that has not been sufficiently addressed in any philosophy of religion currently concerned with postmortem existence. We still have too limited an idea of how Yhwh was assumed to relate to the dead and their ontological status within ancient Israelite cosmographies. The Yahwistic concept of a person, personal identity, and what was thought to constitute a self, might also be discussed here. Collective and transgenerational identities make for interesting metaphysical questions.

These are but some of the loci and challenges that will be encountered in the envisaged process of adoption and adaptation. The list of possible topics can be limited only by lack of creativity in finding philosophical themes. As examples of such, one might decide to look at the metaphysics of causation in ancient Israelite religion; acts of Yhwh from the perspective of the philosophy of action, the concept of prayer, or even something quite different, such as erotic metaphors for Yhwh seen from the perspective of the philosophy of sexuality. There really is no limit, and neither does one have to be interested in only what Jewish or Christian philosophers of religion are concerned with at any given time. However, if one is to do a good job, one must have one's feet sturdily planted in both biblical studies and philosophy of religion, and know what is being discussed in both disciplines. A little knowledge of the auxiliary subject can be a dangerous thing, and biblical scholars should be competent enough to be able to read papers at conferences on philosophy of religion.

8.7. Conclusion

In this chapter we have discussed the possibility of a philosophy of religion, where the religion in question is ancient Israelite religion in all its complexity and the approach is historical and descriptive in its agenda. With the theory behind us, it is time to put it into practice. Now comes part 2 of the study, in which everything said in this chapter will be illustrated by way of actual philosophical perspectives on Israelite religion. Each of the chapters to follow will be dealing with a different locus.

PART 2

We are all agreed that your theory is crazy. The question that divides us is whether it is crazy enough to have a chance of being correct.*

---

* Quantum physicist Niels Bohr's alleged words to Wolfgang Pauli following the latter's presentation of Heisenberg's and Pauli's nonlinear field theory of elementary particles at Columbia University (1958), as quoted in Dael Lee Wolfle, ed., *Symposium on Basic Research* (American Association for the Advancement of Science 56; Washington D.C., 1959), 66.

9

THE NATURE OF RELIGIOUS LANGUAGE
IN THE HEBREW BIBLE[1]

It has been rightly stated that all language used in the Bible to refer to God is metaphorical.[2]

9.1. INTRODUCTION

The words "religious language" (henceforth RL) do not occur in the Hebrew Bible. In philosophy of religion, the concept refers to statements or claims made about divine beings. In that sense the RL of the Hebrew Bible denotes the god-talk of ancient Israelite religion. Most approaches to biblical god-talk in contemporary philosophy of religion have tended to be evaluative, either trying to make biblical god-talk seem philosophically credible or attempting to prove it nonsensical. Few philosophical inquiries are actually interested in the provisioning of a purely descriptive analysis of the RL of the Hebrew Bible for its own sake. This chapter, however, will attempt to demonstrate the following:

1. Popular notions regarding the nature of divinity in classical theism are anachronistic in the context of ancient Israelite religion, where exactly the inverse appears to have been taken for granted in the metatheistic assumptions of the biblical authors.

---

1. Much of the content of this chapter derives from a revised version of "The Nature of Religious Language in the Hebrew Bible: A Philosophical Reassessment," *JSem* 19 (2009): 78–97.

2. Fretheim, *Suffering of God*, 5.

2. What ultimately gave rise to the philosophical problem of RL in Judaeo-Christian philosophy of religion was not so much medieval Aristotelian-based notions of divine simplicity but rather the eclectic diachronic transmutations of polytheistic conceptual categories into monotheistic conceptual metaphors found in ancient Yahwism(s).

3. The popular view according to which god-talk in the Hebrew Bible is essentially metaphorical is philosophically a noninformative means of classifying the nature of religious language in the text.

4. Many of the present obsessions with viewing RL as metaphorical happen to proceed from a number of anachronistic assumptions involving false metaphysical dichotomies with regard to the supposed deity/reality relation in the Hebrew Bible.

5. It is possible to ask what theories of reference in religious language are operative in the text.

6. There are traces of nonrealist fictionalism in the ontology of the relation between language and reality in the text in the evaluative point of view of some implied authors.

The discussion commences, however, with an introduction to what philosophers of religion proper have been saying about the nature of religious language.

9.2. PHILOSOPHICAL THEORIES OF RELIGIOUS LANGUAGE

Three studies on biblical Hebrew are relevant for our concerns and have to be reckoned with in philosophical thinking. The first is James Barr's *Semantics of Biblical Language*, followed by Arthur Gibson's *Biblical Semantic Logic* and Enio R. Mueller's "The Semantics of Biblical Hebrew: Some Remarks from a Cognitive Perspective."[3] However, this is but the preliminary background to a philosophical analysis proper, which should go on to deal with the issues of interest to philosophers of religion in par-

---

3. The relevance of this study is that it points out the outdated nature of some of James Barr's philosophical assumptions about language and referentiality. See the electronic resource at http://www.sdbh.org/documentation/EnioRMueller_Semantics BiblicalHebrew.pdf.

ticular. And in analytical philosophy of religion many theories are attested with reference to the supposed nature of god-talk in the Judeo-Christian religious traditions. Discussions of the different views tend to present the research in two different formats—and sometimes confusingly so, especially given the overlapping of conceptual categories.

On the one hand, we find a *thematic-relational* presentation, which locates particular perspectives within one of the three classical (actually medieval) categories: univocal; equivocal; and analogical. The three categories may be understood as follows:

1. *RL is univocal* (i.e., words that refer to the deity and to humanity have exactly the same meaning).
2. *RL is equivocal* (i.e., human language cannot properly refer to divinity, and the same concepts mean different things in the religious context and in ordinary usage).
3. *RL is analogical* (i.e., one can postulate that there is some sort of relational similarity between what a word means when it applies to humanity and what it means when it applies to gods).[4]

On the other hand there is the *historical-genetic* type of presentation, which names and discusses the views of the pioneering individuals who have had something noteworthy to say on the subject. Interestingly, while many biblical theologians use the concepts of "analogy," "metaphor," and "symbol" interchangeably, in philosophy of religion these terms denote quite distinct options. A typical discussion in this format might include references to:

1. Philo and Greek exegetes of Homer, who think of RL as allegorical;
2. Thomas Aquinas, who argued that RL is analogical;
3. Immanuel Kant, who thought of RL as primarily morally regulative;
4. Paul Tillich, who thought of RL as symbolic;
5. Alfred Ayer, who suggested that RL is utterly meaningless;

---

4. Weed, "Religious Language."

6. Ludwig Wittgenstein and others who suggest that RL is non-cognitive;

7. Rudolph Bultmann and D. F. Strauss, for whom RL is mythological;

8. Ricoeur, McFague, Soskice, and others for whom all god-talk is metaphorical;

9. Donald Evans, who views RL as parabolic;

10. William Alston, who argues that RL is literal.[5]

Many of the concepts used here, for instance metaphor and analogy, overlap in certain writings. Of course, the above-mentioned types are simply convenient generalizations, and many discussions also focus on epistemic issues related to RL. For example, many would involve metalevel assessments such as Richard Hare's theory of "Bliks," Ian Ramsey's notion of "Models and Quantifiers," Thomas McPerson's idea of "Holy Silence," and so on.[6] In the end, however, the important fact from the perspective of anyone interested in a philosophical analysis of the RL of the Hebrew Bible is that all of the above philosophical theories of the nature of RL were constructed with reference to the propositions found in Jewish and Christian philosophical theology. As such, they are not the result of historical and descriptive biblical exegesis—a fact nowhere as evident as in the habit of philosophers of religion of mentioning the Hebrew Bible only for its place as part of the historical backdrop to the real problems. As Weed notes:

> The problem of religious language is generated by the traditional doctrine of God in the Abrahamic traditions. Since God is thought to be incorporeal, infinite, and timeless, the predicates we apply to corporeal, finite, temporal creatures would not apply to God.[7]

Surveying the philosophical research with some bearing on the biblical discourse, however, reveals that by "traditional doctrine" is actually meant the concept of God in "classical theism" and not the conceptions of Yhwh as reconstructed in the history of Israelite religion. This is readily apparent when Weed further states:

---

5. See Harris, *Analytic Philosophy of Religion*, 28–76.

6. Ibid.

7. Weed, "Religious Language."

> The problem of religious language is also generated by the medieval doctrine of divine simplicity, which claims that God does not have any intrinsic accidental properties.[8]

In other words, many philosophers of religion conceive of the biblical God as basically a prephilosophical form of the God of the Philosophers. This is evident from the errant belief that the so-called "Doctrine of Divine Simplicity" represents an adequate reflection of the profile of Yhwh in the Hebrew Bible. The basic idea is that God is radically unlike creatures in that he is devoid of any complexity or composition, whether physical or metaphysical. The belief is that "besides lacking spatial and temporal parts, God is free of matter/form composition, potency/act composition, and existence/essence composition. In this view there is also no real distinction between God as subject of his attributes and his attributes."[9]

As we shall see in a forthcoming chapter on the prospect of a descriptive philosophical theology of the Hebrew Bible, the philosophical descriptions listed above are seriously anachronistic inasmuch as the history of Israelite religion knows of many instances in which exactly the opposite profile of divinity was taken for granted in many of the (particularly preexilic) traditions of biblical Yahwisms. In other words, from a historical and descriptive perspective, the problem of RL in the Hebrew Bible is not generated by a belief in divine simplicity, as the problem of RL in contemporary Christian philosophy of religion may be. As a result, the question now facing us concerns the ultimate reason as to why the need arose in the first place to invert the dictums of biblical god-talk, and to move from a univocal to equivocal and analogical understandings of the Hebrew Bible's RL.

9.3. An Error Theory of Selective Diachronic Conceptual Reconfigurations

In what ways were ancient Near Eastern religious language games a problem in the more monotheistic trajectories in ancient Israelite religion? Alternatively, why might the authors of the Hebrew Bible consider their

---

8. Ibid.

9. Ilkka Pyysiäinen, "God: A Brief History with a Cognitive Explanation of the Concept," 1–35 [cited 12 November 2009]. Online: http://www.talkreason.org/articles/god.pdf. See also William F. Vallicella, "Divine Simplicity," *SEP* [cited 12 November 2009]. Online: http://plato.stanford.edu/archives/fall2008/entries/divine-simplicity/.

own religious language problematic? Why would they have to reflect on the nature of religious language if they had the concepts and the interest? In this regard, the hypothesis of this section is that the selective transmutation of polytheistic conceptual categories on the way to monotheistic conceptual backgrounds lies at the source of many philosophical problems for the meaningfulness and explanatory power of biblical discourse. For while many philosophical and biblical theologians might think of monotheism as an elegant unified theory that represents the most efficient and simplest account of the whole of reality, things are not so straightforward. Already in the Hebrew Bible we find that the idea of a single God who is before everything else, self-sufficient and nearly perfect, actually creates as many conceptual dilemmas as it solves.

First, there is the problem of *derivation*. In stereotypical ancient Near Eastern polytheism the structured world could be accounted for by divine design, so that if intelligence and order required an explanation the existence of the gods themselves *a fortiori* required a template on the next level. This could be achieved with the chaos material hypothesis, which itself has no order and on this line of reasoning therefore had no elements of design that need to be accounted for. In ancient Israelite religion, religious language became problematic because the notion of chaos matter was retained, and yet the divine was placed chronologically prior to it. With only cosmogony and no theogony, the biblical worldviews are able to account for the order in the world but unable to explain either the existence of chaos matter (why would a god create chaos?) or the order represented by the god itself.

Second, there is the problem of *classification*. In polytheism it made sense to refer to the gods in the generic sense because the term denoted a natural kind or type of being; and to think of a god as gendered, and as a parent or child, because both sexes were represented and gods had families. In monotheistic trajectories within Israelite religion, by contrast, the generic classification of Yhwh along folk taxonomic lines was retained, but now without any real conceptual warrant. In addition, the idea of a male deity with sons was retained while the idea of a wife was dropped in canonical theologies, thus making the rationale for their being a gendered god and sons of this god conceptually problematic and in need of metaphorization.

Third, one encounters the problem of *limitation*. In polytheism, there are many needy and imperfect deities whose frailties explain why they might want a world and humans to serve them. Their moments of impotence and the plurality of opposing wills among various deities explain why the world is itself not perfect, and why life is riddled with suffering and problems. Moreover, the many gods explain why different nations have different gods, while their limited cognitive abilities make clear why they have to meet as a council. Their subordination to the moral order and to fate elucidates why they can be classified as moral agents and are slaves to their divine natures. Their corporeality explains divine bodies, organs (e.g., divine hearts) and the need for sacrificial meals, and why they need to move about and require messengers. In certain theologies in the Hebrew Bible the divine has far fewer limitations, yet there is uneasiness as a result of the selective discarding of some motives along with the retention of others. The deity is supposedly self-sufficient, with nothing being impossible for him, yet he also needs to rest, wants to be served, requires sacrifices, has to meet in council, is be called "good" with reference to a universal standard, is able to move about, and exists in tense relation to chaos and an underworld. This results in selective metaphorization and the bracketing of certain problematic questions that were taken up only as time went on.

That these three conceptual problems are not the creation of contemporary anachronistic and evaluative philosophical judgment, but are based on a historical genealogy of the collapse of literal god-talk in the Hebrew Bible itself, is evident from within the pluralism and diachronic changes in ancient Israelite religion. What is interesting is that the genealogy seems to reveal the conceptual origins of virtually all the philosophical problems plaguing contemporary Christian philosophy of religion. It explains the problematic nature of issues such as religious language (given literalism's problems), the act of creation, the attributes of divinity and their logical coherence, the problem of evil, religion and morality, and religious pluralism.

In the end, then, the problem of RL in biblical theology has nothing to do with the anachronistic dilemma of expressing the Infinite in finite terms. Thus, while many philosophical theologians consider ancient polytheism to be conceptually crude and hail monotheism as a more elegant conception of reality, monotheistic metaphysics is actually conceptually more problematic than theogenetic polytheism. The fact is that the Hebrew Bible's record of selective transmutations of polytheistic concepts into monotheistic conceptual metaphors generated more conceptual dilemmas than it solved. This insight also provides an error theory capable of accounting for the attraction of allotheism (the worship of foreign gods) in a monolatrist set-up. There never was a clean break between the two conceptual categories. A historical genealogy of the loci of Christian philosophy of religion will show that the entire field is basically a coming to terms with, and fighting the fires kindled by, the conceptually eclectic monotheistic turn away from polytheism in ancient Israelite religion.

9.4. THE PANMETAPHOR BANDWAGON IN BIBLICAL THEOLOGY

In biblical theology it is ironic that those who would deny philosophy a place tend to be obsessed with metaphor, and use it as a reason for bracketing philosophical issues even as their theory of metaphor is philosophically informed. Biblical theologians have attempted to come to terms with the collapse of a univocal understanding in biblical god-talk by classifying it as metaphorical through and through. Thus it has become fashionable since the early 1980s to concur with ideas like those of Fretheim,[10] who claimed that all biblical god-talk (except perhaps the word "God") is metaphorical. Carroll[11] opines that whereas theology operates using abstract philosophical notions, much of the language of the Bible is highly metaphorical. Brueggemann[12] insists that metaphor is a central element in the articulation of Yhwh. Mills[13] imagines "God" to be a metaphor for a hidden deity/the divine.

The examples could be repeated ad infinitum, but the popular consensus is readily apparent.[14] It is common knowledge that ideas of biblical god-talk as involving equivocal and analogical representations of divinity are attested throughout the history of interpretation. A specifically "metaphorical turn" in biblical theology has therefore been underway for some time now. The influential precursors lie scattered from Aristotle and Philo, through Maimonides and Aquinas, but ultimately and more immediately are to be found in the more recent past in the ideas of linguists,

---

10. Fretheim, *Suffering of God*, 5–13.

11. Carroll, *Wolf in the Sheepfold*, 37.

12. Brueggemann, *Old Testament Theology*, 70.

13. Mary E. Mills, *Images of God in the Old Testament* (New York: Glazier, 1998), 146.

14. For a survey of the literature, see Pierre Hecke, *Metaphor in the Hebrew Bible* (New York: Peters, 2005), 1.

philosophers, and theologians such as Max Black,[15] Paul Ricoeur,[16] Lakoff and Johnson,[17] Sallie McFague,[18] and Janet Soskice.[19]

Unfortunately, whatever might be the merits of the metaphor theory for philosophy of religion proper, from the perspective of ancient Israelite religion understood descriptively there is something seriously wrong here. A recent assessment by a philosopher of religion, though informative, still does not seem to recognize the problem. In a paper entitled "Metaphor, Religious Language, and Religious Experience," Victoria Harrison asks whether it is possible to talk about God without either misrepresentation or failing to assert anything of significance.[20] "The article begins by reviewing how, in attempting to answer this question, traditional theories of religious language have failed adequately to sidestep both potential pitfalls. After arguing that recently developed theories of metaphor seem better able to shed light on the nature of religious language, it considers the claim that huge areas of our language and, consequently, of our experience are shaped by metaphors. Finally, it considers some of the more significant implications of this claim for our understanding of both religious language and religious experience."[21]

The assessment is fine as it goes and probably the most lucid one yet. My question is whether it might not be time for a paradigm shift— at least in historical perspectives on ancient religion. It is fine if contemporary philosophers of religion are able to salvage something by seeing everything as metaphor, but the real question is whether this adequately describes ancient Israelite folk philosophies of religious language. We need

---

15. Max Black, *Models and Metaphor* (Ithaca, N.Y.: Cornell University Press, 1962).

16. Paul Ricoeur, *The Rule of Metaphor: Multi-disciplinary Studies in the Creation of Meaning in Language* (trans. Robert Czerny with Kathleen McLaughlin and John Costello; London: Routledge, 1978).

17. George Lakoff and Mark Johnson, *Metaphors We Live By* (Chicago: University of Chicago Press, 1980); and later: *Philosophy in the Flesh: The Embodied Mind and Its Challenges to Western Thought* (London: Basic Books, 1999).

18. Sally McFague, *Metaphorical Theology: Models of God in Religious Language* (Philadelphia: Fortress, 1982).

19. Janet M. Soskice, *Metaphors and Religious Language* (Oxford: Oxford University Press, 1985).

20. Victoria S. Harrison, "Metaphor, Religious Language, and Religious Experience," *Sophia* 46/2 (2007): 127–45.

21. Ibid., 127.

to determine how ancient Israelites would have understood their god-talk, whether or not we find this believable or relevant. So rather than refining our theory of metaphorical religious language, perhaps we need to ditch the metaphorical approach altogether. This should be done for a number of reasons that are covered below and that boil down to the following fact: it is not so much that the theory of metaphorical representation is totally wrong; it is just that it actually explains nothing.

First, the notion that the RL of the Hebrew Bible is metaphorical is philosophically noninformative as it does not show what makes religious language different from any other language. On the level of metaphor as linguistic phenomenon, Nietzsche, Derrida, and Lacan have demonstrated that all language is essentially riddled with metaphors. Therefore classifying RL as such represents a form of nonessential predication.[22] If all language is metaphorical, saying that religious language is such is not informative. Moreover, in a very real sense the opposition between religious and ordinary language might itself be questioned as anachronistic in biblical god-talk because in those times religion was not opposed by a secular sphere. The fact that religious language is metaphorical still prompts the question: What is a metaphor for, exactly? If one can say, why bother with metaphor? If one cannot, how does one know the target domain exists? Hans Blumenberg, a contemporary philosopher who approaches metaphor historically and pragmatically, shows that its function is regulative—structuring and guiding thinking about the world rather than being a verifiable description of reality.[23] On the level of metaphor as literary phenomenon the god-talk of the Hebrew Bible is no more metaphorical than any other kind of talk about any other kind of entity; and the same metaphors applied to the deity are also applied to humans in other social contexts. Thus the king also was called a lord, father, shepherd, judge, and warrior. He, too, hid his face. His hand symbolized his power. So it is not, as is popularly believed, that "king" was a metaphor for Yhwh. Yhwh was seen as literally a king and that is why all the parallels exist. Ideas of a divine palace, throne, rule, army, and so on were not, in most cases, and as far as we can tell, assumed to be metaphorical only.

Second, the notion that the RL of the Hebrew Bible is metaphorical involves a sweeping generalization. It does so by ignoring nonmetaphori-

---

22. For a short overview, see Griffith-Dickson, *Philosophy of Religion*, 76.

23. Hans Blumenberg, *Paradigm zu einer Metaphorologie* (Frankfurt: Suhrkamp, 1999), 8, 25.

cal representations in the narrative. The theory does well in the context of poetic descriptions. Yet a large number of biblical prose texts contain many elements in the depiction of Yhwh that are not understood metaphorically by the narrator. While much of the biblical discourse is indeed metaphorical, a naïve literalism is also present in many instances.[24] For example, it would make nonsense of the stories to insist that Moses only desired to see Yhwh's metaphorical face, or that Yhwh reminded Moses that his metaphorical face would kill all mortals, or that Yhwh only showed Moses his metaphorical backside, or that the seventy elders only saw Yhwh's metaphorical human form on a metaphorical throne with metaphorical sapphire beneath his metaphorical feet. The presence of some literalism in the Hebrew Bible must therefore be acknowledged, and the reductionism inherent in panmetaphorical interpretations of its religious language must be seen for what it is: dogmatic eisegesis based on repression and anachronistic generalizations. This means that anyone claiming that the Hebrew Bible is all metaphorical commits the fallacy of hasty generalization.[25]

Third, the notion that the RL of the Hebrew Bible is metaphorical appears to be motivated by an anachronistic philosophical-theological agenda by the very scholars who decry the intrusion of philosophical concerns, but who themselves have taken for granted the anachronistic metaphysical dichotomies noted in the next section below. From an evaluative perspective this makes it unclear whether one is dealing with intended monarchic metaphor or unintentional sociomorphic projection. Many biblical theologians simply assume the former, while nontheistic readers will have experienced a *Gestalt* shift to recognize the likelihood of the latter. Our concern, however, is historical and descriptive. From this point of view it seems that the use of metaphors was not assumed to be anthropomorphical and that all human designations were modeled on already extant heavenly scenarios and were thus theomorphic. Especially since Feuerbach, modern theology has inverted the relationhip, but here more than ever ancient Israelite religion approached Platonic metaphysics, with its idea of earthly things being a copy of heavenly ones (although technically Plato did not assume this).

In the Hebrew Bible, Yhwh was often literally assumed to be a king because he was assumed to have literal land and a literal people, and so

---

24. Eichrodt, *Theology of the Old Testament*, 2:61.
25. Jaco W. Gericke, "Yahwism and Projection—A Comprehensive A/Theological Perspective on Polymorphism in the Old Testament," *Scriptura* (2007): 407–24.

on—and because the universe was seen as a hierarchy and as a literal monarchy. Thus, from the perspective of the hermeneutics of suspicion of the reader at least, in some cases panmetaphorism with reference to the classification of biblical god-talk almost appears to be motivated by apologetic concerns. These seem, moreover, not dissimilar to what once drove philosophically inclined readers to resort to an allegorical interpretation of Homer, that is, the desire to salvage realism and relevance in what might otherwise seem absurd, crude, or all-too-human representations of the divine. Moreover, Greek philosophy has never been left behind by biblical scholars; inter alia, they have simply exchanged one part of Aristotle's philosophy (the *Categories* and logic) for another (his *Rhetoric*). What was overlooked was the fact that Aristotelian theories of metaphor are inextricably intertwined with his metaphysics as metaphors are linked with the concepts of *genus* and *species*.[26]

In sum, then, while reading biblical god-talk as metaphor through and through might make the texts more user-friendly for contemporary theology, a panmetaphorical approach has no place in a purely descriptive historical philosophical analysis. Those who see metaphor everywhere and cry out against imposing philosophical grids are doing just that. Panmetaphorism is simply neoallegorism in a postmodern guise. What we really need is a new historical philosophical theory regarding the nature of religious language in the Hebrew Bible—one from which the dualism of postbiblical metaphysical assumptions is absent.

9.5. ANACHRONISTIC METAPHYSICAL ASSUMPTIONS IN BIBLICAL THEOLOGY

Much of the obsession with trying to show the alleged presence of metaphor in biblical god-talk stems from anachronistic dualist metaphysical assumptions in readers. These include, inter alia, a number of oppositions that are constantly being read into biblical god-talk by well-meaning biblical theologians:

1. *Religious versus secular*: In ancient Israelite religion the religious sphere was for the most part not something over and

---

26. Christof Rapp, "Aristotle's Rhetoric," *SEP* [cited 2 October 2010]. Online: http://plato.stanford.edu/archives/win2008/entries/aristotle-rhetoric/.

against the secular realm. Talking about Israelite religion as though it were something separate from history or society is artificial. To be sure, sacred and profane dimensions were distinguished, but the fact remains that the Hebrew Bible does not distinguish religious from secular language in an absolute sense.

2. *Infinite versus finite*: The concept of divinity in the Hebrew Bible often had little in common with the theological notion of Infinity. Yhwh was not assumed to be absolutely "Other" or "ineffable," and the texts show no indication that the use of finite human terms for the divine was in any way considered to be seriously inadequate.

3. *Transcendent versus immanent*: Technically, the text does not assume the existence of a transcendent realm. According to the ancient Israelite cosmography everything, including the divine realm, is actually immanent within the cosmos, notwithstanding spatial separation and structural distinctions. The distinction is anachronistic.

4. *Supernatural versus natural*: The text does not assume that divinity is supernatural in the modern sense, in other words that it can be situated vis-à-vis the "merely natural." In ancient Near Eastern folk taxonomy, the gods are a natural kind and divinity is a secondary substance. Our philosophical-ecological concept of "Nature" is not attested in the Hebrew Bible. It shares many overlapping domains in the semantic field of what many Hebrew Bible texts assume with reference to the concept "god."

5. *Spiritual versus physical*: The text does not assume a spiritual/physical dichotomy in the metaphysical sense (only in a comparative monistic sense). While the concept of "spirit" did denote insubstantiality, it was still assumed to refer to something as natural, elemental and "empirical" as wind or breath.

6. *Reality versus appearance*—Many biblical theologians like to speak as if Yhwh were depicted as having only *appeared* in human form with some ineffable divine reality lying behind all such "accommodation." Yet a less dogmatic (and Platonic) reading reveals that the human form in which Yhwh appears was believed to be his true form (even in visionary contexts otherwise filled with symbolism). The immensely popular

notion of "anthropomorphism" is therefore essentially anachronistic in this context. From a descriptive historical perspective, it represents an inversion of what the texts take to be
"theomorphism" in humans.[27]

Inasmuch as biblical theologians have taken these assumptions for granted
owing to critical realist ontological assumptions, they have imported Platonic dualism into ancient Israelite metaphysics.

9.6. Religious Language and Reference in Ancient Yahwism

Many philosophers of religion tend to assume that expressions within
religious language that are supposed to refer to divine beings pose special difficulties, since it is not easy to point to or identify the referents of
those referring expressions within ordinary experience.[28] As a result, two
accounts of how referring is supposed to take place have been forthcoming: *descriptivist* and *causal* theories of reference. Both have advantages
and disadvantages. One way these have been illustrated is by means of the
name and stories concerning the character of Moses in the Hebrew Bible.
Let us use Yhwh instead, and ask which of the two views was presupposed
in the biblical texts.[29]

According to descriptivist theories of reference the proper name
"Yhwh" refers because certain predicates or characteristics possessed by
Yhwh are contained in the name or description. If this was assumed to
be the case in ancient Israel folk philosophy of language, it would mean
that the god-talk in the text presupposed empiricism, realism, and a cor-
respondence theory of truth. On this view, since Yhwh had certain properties in the world in the text that made him who and what he was, it
was possible to know who one was talking about by speaking of Yhwh.
Yhwh was the proper name of an individual who possessed certain properties and of whom it could be said that certain descriptions were true.
Therefore, ancient Israelite god-talk presupposing a descriptivist theory of
reference would be those instances that recount certain qualities of Yhwh

---

27. Hamori, *When Gods Were Men.*

28. See Harris, *Analytic Philosophy of Religion,* 73.

29. Much of the basic structure of the theories as explained here is derived from
James F. Harris, "The Causal Theory of Reference and Religious Language," *IJPR* 29
(1991): 75–86.

(mercy and graciousness) or tell of the ways in which Yhwh acted (e.g., the God who led his people out of Egypt). In other words, by using the principle of identifying expressions, one can identfy Yhwh as the individual about whom the essential descriptions are true.

By contrast, if the causal theory of reference were taken to apply in ancient Israelite God talk, there would not be any reliance on predicates, characteristics, or descriptions to explain how one could refer to Yhwh. Instead, Yhwh would be assumed to be the individual who occupied the proper place in a historical account of how the people came to use the name or description to refer to the deity. This means that to determine the referent of a referring expression using the causal theory of reference, a story must be available that recounts the causal connection between the God and the use of a particular name or description to refer to that God. This view does not assume the principle of identifying propositions. Moreover, successful reference is possible independently of any set of properties of the referent. A causal theory thus explains the reference of the name "Yhwh" by tracing the name back through its long history of use within ancient Israelite religion. It has to be noted that this does not mean that historicity is required for any acts of Yhwh. The name refers to the same entity also should different traditions and representations in different periods ascribe different properties to Yhwh. This view, if present, could explain the possibility of modifying earlier representations, and would not be jeopardized by any lack of historicity or by misrepresentation.[30]

It is difficult to show which of the two theories is presupposed in any given text, if either. Aside from the causal and descriptive theories, there are other, hybrid perspectives, which together constitute the so-called positive theories of reference. Negative views of reference include those of philosophers such as Quine, who thought that reference is inherently indeterminate, and Davidson, who argued that it is a theoretically vacuous notion. Then there are the deflationists, who base their theories of reference on deflationary theories of truth to suggest that to say a statement is true is just to assert the statement itself.[31] Whatever we make of all this, the problem of reference in language continues to be one of the most vigorously debated issues in the philosophy of language. Since religious language cannot be excluded from the discussion, it might be interesting

---

30. See Saul Kripke, *Naming and Necessity* (Oxford: Basil Blackwell, 1972), 94–98.

31. See Marga Reimer, "Reference," *SEP* [cited 12 October 2010]. Online: http://plato.stanford.edu/archives/spr2010/entries/reference/.

if biblical scholars could provide an account of some folk philosophical assumptions about reference in ancient Israelite Yahwism(s). This will also be of relevance later when we consider the concepts of religious experience and religious epistemology.

9.7. Conclusion

In this chapter I have offered a prolegomenon to a more complete philosophical account of the nature of religious language in the Hebrew Bible. We have seen that, even when biblical theologians have decried the use of philosophy, they have not succeeded altogether in avoiding the superimposition of anachronistic philosophical categories onto the text. It was also demonstrated that biblical theologians need not uncritically adopt popular perspectives prevalent in philosophy of religion. Instead, they should opt for a historical-philosophical approach to ancient Israelite religious language and dare to come up with their own creative descriptive philosophical account of the RL of the Hebrew Bible—one that proceeds from the folk philosophical assumptions in the text itself.

10

The Concept of Generic Godhood in the Hebrew Bible[1]

The question of what a god is is absolutely central.[2]

10.1. Introduction

In the Hebrew Bible there is a phenomenon that, for want of a better word, was called an אל. But what is an אל? Interestingly, purely in terms of grammatical form, this question is not only linguistic, historical, literary, sociological, psychological, anthropological or theological in nature. Questions that take the form "What is X?" (where X is a concept, as in "What is knowledge?"/"What is justice?"/"What is a person?"/"What is an אל?") are also typical of philosophy (conceptual analysis) in general and of *philosophy of religion* in particular.

> The question "What is God?" is sometimes also phrased as "What is the meaning of the word *God*?" Most philosophers expect some sort of definition as an answer to this question, but they are not content simply to describe the way the word is used: they want to know the essence of what it means to be *God*. Western philosophers typically concern themselves with the God of monotheistic religions ... but discussions also concern themselves with other conceptions of the divine. Indeed, before attempting a definition of a term it is essential to know what sense of the term is to be defined. In this case, this is particularly important because there

---

1. This chapter is based on a revised version of Jaco W. Gericke, "What Is an אל? A Philosophical Analysis of the Concept of Generic Godhood in the Hebrew Bible," *OTE* 22 (2009): 21–46.

2. Mark Smith, *The Origins of Biblical Monotheism: Israel's Polytheistic Background and the Ugaritic Texts* (New York: Oxford University Press, 2001), vi.

are a number of widely different senses of the word "God." So before we try to answer the question "What is God?" by giving a definition, first we must get clear on which conception of God we are trying to define.[3]

In view of this we may ask the question of what a god was assumed to be in the most basic sense in which the word אל was used in the Hebrew Bible—that is, the *generic* sense.

We begin our inquiry with Wittgenstein's insight that questions of definition should make way for an examination of how the concept was used.

10.2. The Generic Sense

The generic sense is an oddity in monotheism, given a class with a singleton. Still, from the history of Israelite religion, we know that words such as אלהים, אל, and אלוה are used not only in the *absolute* sense as proper names for Yhwh but also in the *generic* sense as common nouns or appellatives indicating the type of being Yhwh and other related entities and phenomena were assumed to be. In a way, one may say that the distinction between the absolute and generic senses presupposes a distinction between *who* and *what* a divine being was assumed to be. This distinction is obfuscated with reference to Yhwh in virtually all English translations of the Hebrew Bible in that they render אלהים, אל, and אלוה with a capital "G," even on those occasions when the noun is clearly not used as a proper name. Instances of this trend include all of the following examples:

1. where אלהים, אל, and אלוה are part of *indefinite descriptions*, for example: *a* God who saves; *a* God of great wisdom; (there is) *a* God in Israel.
2. where אלהים, אל, and אלוה appear with the definite article, for example: *the* God of Israel; *the* God of Abraham, Isaac and Jacob.
3. where אלהים, אל, and אלוה appear extended with a pronominal suffix, for example: *my* God; *your* God; *our* God.
4. where אלהים, אל, and אלוה appear with a preceding adjective, for example *holy* God; *mighty* God; *jealous* God.

---

3. "Philosophy of Religion," *Wikipedia, The Free Encyclopedia* [cited 7 December 2009]. Online: http://en.wikipedia.org/w/index.php?title=Philosophy_of_religion&oldid=329379371.

The very possibility of using the generic sense with reference to Yhwh is in itself conceptually and ideologically contrary to the conceptions of God in contemporary Jewish and Christian philosophy of religion. These days (and notably since Thomas Aquinas) God is not considered to belong to a genus. Yet many texts in the Hebrew Bible assume as much. In much of the Hebrew Bible's generic אל-talk, the nature of generic divinity is assumed to be inclusive of—but not exhausted by—the nature of Yhwh *qua* "God."

First, Yhwh is often referred to (and worshiped as) a specific *kind* of אל (merciful, just, jealous, hidden, saving, etc.), implying that other kinds are conceivable in theory (see Deut 32:4; Pss 5:4, 68:20; Isa 30:18, 45:15; Jer 51:56, et al.). In other words, in theory Yhwh himself can instantiate a different set of properties or grades of the same properties without for that reason being considered less of an אל (e.g., if he is less, or not, merciful). The very possibility of (or need for) pointing out that Yhwh is an x kind of אל (or "an אל of x") implies that ancient Israelite generic אל-talk assumed a distinction between essential and accidental properties of divinity. This accounts for the conceptual possibility of theological pluralism in the representations of Yhwh himself and suggests the presence of modalities.

Second, a host of other entities and phenomena besides Yhwh are also called אלהים in both a realist and nominalist generic sense. These include, among others, foreign אלהים (e.g., Judg 11:24), sons of the אלהים (e.g., Gen 6:1–4), the divine council members (e.g., Ps 82:1, 6), divine messengers (e.g., Zech 12:8), stars (e.g., Judg 5:20), unidentified celestial entities (e.g., Ps 8:6), household spirits (e.g., Exod 21:20), *teraphim* (e.g., Gen 31:30), theriomorphic idols (e.g., Exod 32:8), anthropomorphic statues (e.g., Isa 44:17), demons (e.g., Deut 32:17), the king (e.g., Ps 45:7), dead ancestors (e.g., 1 Sam 28:17; Isa 8:19), human representatives (e.g., Exod 7:1), powerful humans (e.g., Gen 23:6), and the phenomenon of power (e.g., Hab 1:11). Certain phenomena in a superlative state are also classified as divine (e.g., a mountain [Ps 68:16], a garden [Ezek 28:13], trees [Ps 80:11], a wind [Gen. 1:2], a city [Jon 3:3], and the emotion of fear [1 Sam 14:15]. In sum, the extension(s) of the generic terms אל, אלהים, and אלוה in the Hebrew Bible were sometimes characterized by conceptual "theodiversity" (cf. "biodiversity").

In this regard, it is important for the purposes of this study to note that the claim that Yhwh (or another entity) is an אל expresses the *proposition* that Yhwh (or another entity) "is an אל." The proposition in turn expresses the *concept* of *being an* אל. In this sense the descriptive predication of אל, אלהים, and אלוה in the generic sense suggests that in the generic אל-talk of the Hebrew Bible we encounter the *concept* of generic אל-*hood* (i.e., the state or condition of being an אל). Several other givens in the data suggest as much.

First is the abstract nature of the reference of the generic terms themselves. If we let $א_a$ stand for אל, $א_b$ for אלהים, and $א_c$ for אלוה and we let $א^A$ and $א^B$ stand for the absolute (God) and the generic (god) senses of the three terms respectively, consider the denotation of the underlined words below:

$(א^B_a)$ לפני לא נוצר אל   Before me no <u>god</u> was formed (Isa 43:10c)

$(א^B_b)$ אלהים   אמר נבל בלבו אין   The fool says in his heart, there are no <u>gods</u> (Ps 14:1b)

$(א^B_c)$ ואשם זו כחו לאלהו   The guilty whose strength is his <u>god</u> (Hab 1:11)

In a, b, and c the word translated as "god" does not denote any particular or specific concrete instance of a divine being *qua* individual. Instead, "god" here is an undefined *abstract object* (i.e., אל as a general idea). This is only to be expected, since in itself the use of generics presupposes a prior process of abstraction from particular individual (and often variable) instances of the phenomenon in question. Different אלהים may have little in common with regard to properties instantiated, but via generalization they can all be called אלהים. What they have in common is then the property of "generic אל-hood."

A second indicator of the presence of the concept of generic אל-hood is the fact that the utilization of the generic terms in the Hebrew Bible appears to meet all the criteria for concept possession. To be sure, there are different views on what it means to possess a concept, but on assuming the functionality of the so-called "concepts-as-abilities" model,[4] a relatively clear cut case can be made, based on the following: while the notion of generic אל-hood seems somewhat abstract, and while the term "אל-hood" is not attested in the Hebrew Bible *verbatim*, the concept it

---

4. See Eric Margolis and Stephen Laurence, "Concepts," *SEP* [cited 12 April 2010]. Online: http://plato.stanford.edu/archives/fall2008/entries/concepts/.

signifies is implicitly present nevertheless. For example, according to the particular view of concept possession, the concept of generic אל-hood is verifiably present just as long as we can provide evidence in the text regarding the following:

1. the presupposed ability to *recognize* א[B] things;
2. the presupposed ability to *compare* them with non-א[B] things;
3. the presupposed ability to be able to *think* about א[B] things; and
4. the presupposed ability to be able to *talk* to others about א[B] things.

Examples of the assumption of the abilities mentioned above are not difficult to find, particularly when it comes to generic אל-talk in polemical discourse:

קנאוני הם בלא אל	They made me jealous <u>with what is no god</u> (Deut 32:21)
ונתנו את־אלהיהם בא כי לא אלהים המה	They have cast their gods into the fire; <u>for they were no gods</u> (2 Kgs 19:18)
ההימיר גוי אלהים והמה לא אלהים	Has a nation changed its gods <u>even though they are no gods</u>? (Jer 2:11)
היעשה־לו אדם אלהים והמה לא אלהים	Can man make for himself gods? <u>such are no gods</u>! (Jer 16:20)
חרש עשהו ולא אלה	A workman made it; <u>it is not a god</u> (Hos 8:6)

These texts come from various historical, literary, and ideological contexts, but they share a serious concern with concept application. No one would bother to deny that an entity worshiped as an אל is in fact such unless they had specific and definite ideas about what it meant to call something an אל. The reason why אל in the generic sense is never defined or discussed by the biblical authors, however, is clearly not the result of a lack of interest (or ideas) on their part with regard to what it meant to call something an אל. Nor is the absence of explanations to be accounted for by an appeal to

the supposed ontological mystery involved, or the supposed antiphilosophical mindset of the Hebrew culture (both conceptions are anachronistic).
What it meant to call something an אל could be taken for granted, even if
the concept's actual worlds extension was essentially contested.

Because the meaning was assumed by the biblical authors to be
common knowledge, any elaborate explanations would have seemed
superfluous. The realization of this brings us to the question of what
exactly it was about the "divine condition" (cf. the "human condition")
that went without saying—a question which cannot be answered, however,
via a biblical-theological approach that merely describes the attributes of
Yhwh. For in the texts above it is clearly assumed that the nature of generic
divinity was inclusive of, but not exhausted by, the nature of Yhwh—the
entities in question were dismissed as pseudo members of generic terms'
extension, not because they were not more like Yhwh but because they
were not אלהים.

In other words, the texts presuppose that ideally the entities in question should instantiate an unspecified list of necessary and essential
generic properties required for them to be legitimately classified as אלהים
(in more than a *nominal* sense). What these properties are—even though
they are not equated with the accidental properties of the kind of אל-ness
Yhwh himself instantiated—we are not told. The texts assume that the
answer can go without saying. Recognition of this requires us to try to
look beyond the concept of generic אל-hood itself, in order to determine
the relevant presuppositions implicit in its use.

Since the nature of divinity in the generic sense is assumed in the
Hebrew Bible to be *inclusive* of the nature of divinity in the absolute sense
(as demonstrated earlier), the nature and attributes of Yhwh are not irrelevant to our discussion. Yet unlike discussions on generic divinity in the
Hebrew Bible in the past, the concern in this chapter is not Yhwh but the
type of entity he (and others) are assumed to be. In other words, our concern lies with the class, not with individual members; with the type, not
the token; with the kind, not the instance; with the universal/trope, not
the particular; with the category, not the beings; and with the *genus*, not
the *differentia*.

10.3. What Is an אל?

Up to now, research on the concept of deity in ancient Israelite religion
has involved a concern with linguistic, historical, literary, social and theo-

logical perspectives on absolute Godhood (God), and with the question of what, according to the Hebrew Bible, the god Yhwh was assumed to be like. What is lacking is a philosophical analysis of the generic terms that is exclusively concerned with conceptual clarification (narrow analysis), and that involves taking a step back and asking what, according to the Hebrew Bible, is an אל? This question sounds very profound, but we are not interested in what a god actually or ultimately may be (i.e., in explanation). We are interested in presuppositions in the text, so our question may well be stated as: What, according to the Hebrew Bible, does it mean to call something an אל?

The two questions above pertain to the nature of generic godhood (the state or condition of being a god). Alternatively stated, they concern the metatheistic assumptions in the Hebrew Bible, or the presuppositions in the text about the divine condition. Generic godhood in ancient Israelite religion is not a novel concern in itself, although it becomes as much when asked in the context of philosophical analysis. The philosophical question itself may moreover be broken down into several subqueries, the formulation of which may seem rather abstract:

1. Is it possible to define the concept of generic אל-hood intensionally?[5]
2. What, according to the Hebrew Bible, makes an אל divine?
3. What are the necessary and/or sufficient conditions for being an אל?
4. What are the essential and accidental properties of אלהים?
5. How can one determine whether something is an אל or not?

Ideally the answer would have the following logical form: For any entity x, x is an אל if and only if a, b, c, and so on. Of course, the intention to answer the initial question and the subquestions might sound presumptuous. On the one hand, the Hebrew Bible is not philosophical theology, and the superimposition of philosophical concerns, concepts, and categories onto the world in the text is both distortive and anachronistic. On the other hand, biblical criticism has taught us, if anything, that given the

---

5. As opposed to extensionally or ostensionally. The word should not be confused with "intension" in popular jargon or with "intention" (with a "t") in phenomenology, which is concerned with conceptual content. Intensions here pertain to individually necessary and jointly sufficient conditions.

historical variation, theological pluralism, literary diversity, and conceptual complexity in the discourse, the Hebrew Bible is not likely to offer
us any clearcut or simple single answer to our question. That means that,
inasmuch as there is an answer to be inferred at all, it might be more than
one answer. The answers might not cohere, and whatever they are, there
is no guarantee that they will seem orthodox by the standards of what is
taken for granted in many modern philosophical theologies. Many biblical
scholars might therefore consider the asking of these questions as hermeneutically fallacious.

Whatever we may think in this regard, we have to consider the fact
that as a result of bracketing philosophical questions with reference to
generic godhood in the text, we actually know very little about Yhwh's
divine nature (and this not a logical necessity due to "mystery"). This is
evident when we consider the fact that the following questions are seldom
if ever raised in biblical theologies:

1. Why, according to the Hebrew Bible, is Yhwh called an אל?
2. What is it about Yhwh that makes the classification obvious
    and justified?
3. What is it about the אלהים that makes it meaningful and
    appropriate?
4. If Yhwh is a specific kind of אל, what variation in אל-ness is
    conceivable?

One can also extend the above questions to any entity or phenomenon in the
Hebrew Bible for which the generic term is used in whatever sense. However,
again popular philosophical-theological assumptions might make many of
these questions seem inappropriate or conceptually problematic. The primary reason the reader might feel cognitively challenged is the denial in
Jewish and Christian philosophical theologies that God is a member of a
species or genus. If that is the case, it is the objection that is anachronistic
rather than the questions. So the use of generic terms for the divine in the
Hebrew Bible presupposes something not unlike what later philosophers
engaged in metaphysics would call "secondary substances," "natural kinds,"
"quiddity," "universals/tropes," "sortals," "types," "classes," and so on.

Moreover, while the Hebrew Bible does not answer any of these questions in so many words, it cannot be denied that אל-like beings are associated with the states of affairs presupposed in the questions above. Moreover, the principle of sufficient reason suggests that there must be some or

other assumed grounds on which to associate the phenomenon of divinity with particular properties, functions, and relations. If that is the case, and given the fact that answers to these questions may only be implicit on the level of metatheistic assumptions underlying the use of the generic terms in the text, it follows that the questions are not as conceptually out of place as prima facie impressions suggest. So what have we already discerned about the meaning of the concept of generic אל-hood in the Hebrew Bible?

10.4. Gaps in Related Research

Curiously, the generic אל-talk of the Hebrew Bible and the metatheistic assumptions underlying it have never been the subject of a deep descriptive philosophical analysis exclusively devoted to the topic for its own sake. To be sure, there is nothing new under the sun, and many studies have been concerned with the Hebrew Bible's generic terms for divinity and their extension, and with the attributes of Yhwh *qua* divine being. However, the question is whether any of these studies has answered our question of what an אל is assumed to be in the sense reconstructed in the previous section.

First, relevant word studies found in typical Hebrew and Aramaic dictionaries and lexicons are almost exclusively concerned with linguistic issues, none of which provide the information we are looking for. Typical concerns involve root identification, statistical data pertaining to the occurrences of words for generic and absolute Godhood, morphological and syntactic intricacies, and so on. Also offered are various translation possibilities that have been utilized in the rendering of Hebrew into modern languages (with modern theological ideology not altogether absent). Though interesting in itself as background data for the present inquiry, such lexical-semantic analysis is not sufficient to enable us to answer our questions concerning the biblical concept of generic אל-hood.

Somewhat more directly related to the present inquiry, yet still not sufficiently adequate in terms of its scope, are discussions found in theological dictionaries of the Old Testament. Representative in this regard are entries under "God" (for some reason again under the discussion of אלהים rather than אל) in, *inter alia*, Ringgren, Schmidt, and van der Toorn.[6] In most of these studies one basically encounters a theological

---

6. Helmer Ringgren, "אֱלֹהִים," *TDOT* 1:267–84; Werner H. Schmidt, "אֱלֹהִים," *TLOT* 1:115–26; Karel van der Toorn, "God (1)," *DDD*, 911–19.

elaboration on the linguistic data. There are a few remarks on theories on the etymology of the generic terms, some attention to the grammatical oddities characterizing the use of the words, a few notes on the extension of the generic terms and on their use and role in the history of Israelite religion in comparison with other ancient Near Eastern conceptions of divinity (e.g., the Mesopotamian *DINGIR*, the Egyptian *Netjer*). The type of research data presented by Ringgren and by van der Toorn is most relevant for present purposes, as they exhibit an interest that overlaps with that implicit in our questions. Ultimately, however, the concern in these studies tends not to be exclusively with the generic concept for its own sake and, as a result, the inquiries do not answer the questions that form the basis of our research problem.

The same state of affairs pertains in the case of Old Testament theologies. Only some of these—biblical theologies of the systematic type, for example those of Eichrodt, Jacob, Köhler, Preuss, Rowley, and Vawter—deal in any notable manner with אלהים *qua* generic concept.[7] However, none of these discussions is deep and here too there is no exclusive concern with generics for its own sake as the real concern pertaining to the nature of absolute Godhood (with the generic sense as something simply to be noted). Other, more philosophy related, studies such as those of Föhrer, Kaiser, and Oeming are no more informative as they show little interest in providing a thorough analysis of the generic concept.[8] A noteworthy albeit unfortunately cursive remark is found in Knierim,[9] who wants us to ask "What is 'God'?" in the sense of considering what the Hebrew Bible meant by the word "God." He briefly suggests that we inquire as to what function the word "God" had in the worldview of ancient Israel and what difference it made to them:

> What did it mean for the Old Testament to say "God"? We use the word "God" because we have inherited it from a linguistic tradition thousands of years old. It was not coined by … the early Israelites…. It belonged to the common linguistic repertoire for deities by which the ancient

---

7. Eichrodt, *Theology of the Old Testament*; Jacob, *Theology of the Old Testament*; Köhler, *Theology of the Old Testament*; Preuss, *Old Testament Theology*; H. H. Rowley, *The Faith of Israel: Aspects of Old Testament Thought* (London: SPCK, 1956); Bruce Vawter, "The God of Hebrew Scriptures," *BTB* 12 (1982): 3.

8. Fohrer, *History of Israelite Religion*; Kaiser, *Grundlegung*; Oeming, *Gesamtbiblischen Theologien*.

9. Knierim, *Task of Old Testament Theology*, 491.

Near Eastern cultures expressed their world view. The ancient Israelites adopted it. Without it they would not have known the word "God." But while they must have known what it meant to say "God" we ourselves continue to use the word without knowing what their idea was. While their usage of the word was a linguistic expression generated by and imbedded in their understanding of its meaning, our usage of it rests on the tradition of the word alone, transmitted to and adopted by us, regardless of and even apart from an understanding of its meaning. One of the most self-evident or startling questions we may ask is, "What does the Bible mean, or what do you mean, when saying 'God'?"[10]

This is indeed the kind of question one would expect in analytical philosophy of religion and philosophical theology. Yet ultimately Knierim also is concerned with "God" *qua* Yhwh rather than with the Hebrew Bible's metatheistic assumptions about generic divinity as such or for its own sake. Moreover, Knierim never attempts to answer his own question but instead simply mentions the need for the particular inquiry.

A few papers on related issues published in academic journals also have some bearing but tend to be equally superficial.[11] Metatheologies such as those of Barr, Hasel, Hayes and Prussner, Ollenburger, Reventlow, and Stendahl show no evidence that the generic concept was ever a major concern in biblical theologies.[12] This again partly reveals the intrusion of dogmatic concerns upon historical and descriptive reconstructions.

Yet another scenario of partially related concerns is to be found in a few sociological perspectives on the concept of divinity in the Hebrew Bible. Probably the best known example is the study of Gottwald,[13] who in the latter part of his book attempts to provide a perspective from the sociology of religion on the symbolic function of deity in ancient Israel in

---

10. Ibid.

11. Thomas Krueger, "Einheit und Vielfalt des Göttlichen nach dem Alten Testament" [cited 12 February 2010]. Online: http://www.theologie.uzh.ch/faecher/altestestament/thomaskrueger/ Krueger_1998_Einheit_und_Vielfalt.pdf.

12. Barr, *Concept of Biblical Theology*; Hasel, *Old Testament Theology*; John H. Hayes and Frederick Prussner, *Old Testament Theology: Its History and Development* (Atlanta: John Knox, 1985); Ollenburger, *Old Testament Theology*; Henning G. Reventlow, *Problems of Old Testament Theology in the Twentieth Century* (London: SCM, 1985); Krister Stendahl, "Biblical Theology, Contemporary," in *Interpreter's Dictionary of the Bible* (ed. G. A. Buttrick; 4 vols.; Nashville: Abingdon, 1962), 1:418–32.

13. Norman K. Gottwald, *The Tribes of Yahweh: A Sociology of the Religion of Liberated Israel, 1250–1050 B.C.E.* (Maryknoll, N.Y.: Orbis, 1979).

its ancient Near Eastern context. Via sociological reductionism Gottwald offers us an interesting evaluative assessment of what he takes to be the actual referent of the Hebrew Bible's conceptions of absolute Godhood. What he does not offer us is any sort of explanation of the meaning of the concept of generic אל-hood elucidating descriptively the Hebrew Bible's own metatheistic assumptions about the divine condition. Thus we learn about what generic divinity is from a modern sociological perspective, but not what it was assumed to be according to the Hebrew Bible itself.

Literary-critical approaches to Yhwh (God) as a character in the narratives of the Hebrew Bible show a similar lack of interest in the generic concept of deity and metatheistic assumptions in the Hebrew Bible. David Clines seems to presuppose that we already know exactly what an אל was assumed to be when he discusses "God in the Pentateuch."[14] Those interested in an answer to our questions will, however, not learn anything from such a presumption. The same scenario is found in the publication of Jack Miles who, in his "biography" of God, asks the question "What makes God godlike?"[15] However, though this seems *prima facie* related to the concern of this study (cf. what makes an אל divine?), on closer inspection it turns out to be little more than a discussion of the distinguishing features of Yhwh *qua* Yhwh and not Yhwh as an אל (or an אל *qua* type). As with the study by Clines, this is not in itself a problem, but we should take cognizance of the fact that in these and other related inquiries an in-depth presupposition analysis of the generic concept apparently lies beyond the scope of the method.

Things do not change much as one crosses over from Old Testament theology to studies on deity in the history of Israelite religion. To be sure, the writings of Albertz, Föhrer, Keel and Uehlinger, Miller, Oesterley and Robinson, Ringgren, and Schmidt have much to offer with regard to the historical development of ideas about specific deities and biblical conceptions of Yhwh.[16] But none gives even a diachronic account of

---

14. David J. A. Clines, "God in the Pentateuch," in *Interested Parties: The Ideology of Readers and Writers of the Hebrew Bible* (Sheffield: Sheffield Academic Press, 1995), 187–211. Cf. idem, "Yahweh and the God of Christian Theology," *Theology* 83 (1980): 323–30.

15. Jack Miles, *God: A Biography* (New York: Knopf, 1995), 85–88.

16. Rainer Albertz, *A History of Israelite Religion in the Old Testament Period* (2 vols.; Louisville: Westminster John Knox, 1994); Fohrer, *History of Israelite Religion*; Othmar Keel and Christoph Uehlinger, *Gods, Goddesses, and Images of God in Ancient*

the metatheistic assumptions underlying the generic concept of divinity in the Hebrew Bible. In more specifically comparative religious studies, however, the studies of Saggs and Mark Smith are noteworthy, especially the latter.[17] Smith notes in his introduction that his research for the book was inspired by the question "What is an *ilu*?" He notes three traditional approaches to the study of generic divinity and also suggests a fourth approach:[18]

1. *Taking inventory*, that is, making a list of entities classified as divine.
2. *Explicating etymology*, that is, noting the root meanings of terms for "god."
3. *Atomistic comparative description*, that is, comparisons among ancient Near Eastern gods.
4. *Large-scale comparative description*, that is, offering a typology of divinity.

Ultimately, even Smith's study is not identical to what the present inquiry is looking for, since Smith's primary interest was the development of monotheism in ancient Israelite religion, so that the concept of generic divinity was not his exclusive concern. In fact, the material on generic divinity that relates to the present study is limited to part 2 of Smith's book, where he discusses what he calls the traits of deity or divine characteristics. According to Smith, these are: (1) size and strength; (2) body and gender; (3) holiness; and (4) immortality. Though conceptually useful, there are several reasons why this particular choice of properties will not suffice as an answer to what an אל is assumed to be; and why it cannot be adopted *en bloc* in the present inquiry.

Israel (Minneapolis: Fortress, 1998); Patrick D. Miller, *The Religion of Ancient Israel* (Louisville: Westminster John Knox, 2000); William O. E. Oesterley and Theodore H. Robinson, *Hebrew Religion: Its Origin and Development* (London: SPCK, 1952); Helmar Ringgren, *Israelite Religion* (trans. David E. Green; Philadelphia: Fortress, 1966); Werner Schmidt, *The Faith of the Old Testament: A History* (trans. John Sturdy; Philadelphia: Westminster, 1983).

17. Hallo W. Saggs, *The Encounter with the Divine in Mesopotamia and Israel* (London: Athlone Press, 1978); Smith, *Origins of Biblical Monotheism*, 83–102.

18. Smith, *Origins of Biblical Monotheism*, 6–9.

First, Smith purports to discuss the nature of generic divinity, but in the end, most instances discussed still concern Yhwh, the אל of Israel. This is problematic, since the four divine attributes listed above do not apply to all members of the extension of the generic terms (e.g., the deified dead, *rephaim,* were not particularly noteworthy for their size or strength.

Second, given that Smith's list is not applicable to all entities and phenomena in the extension of the generic terms, it follows that he did not adequately distinguish between essential and accidental properties of generic אל-hood. To be sure, the terms "essence" and "accident" may sound too philosophical for the taste of some biblical theologians because they are not attested *verbatim* in the Hebrew Bible itself. Yet neither are Smith's uses of the words "body" and "gender" or the biblical theologian's application of cherished terms such as "personal" or "transcendent." Clearly, the use of philosophical terminology is conceptually problematic only if applied in a constructive and speculative sense. When used in a descriptive and analytical sense, such terminology may well elucidate what the Hebrew Bible itself assumed yet did not bother to formulate.

Third, the intensional (in the technical semantic sense and not to be confused with "intentional") mode of meaning is yet again neglected. Smith's list does not tell us what the necessary and/or sufficient conditions for being an אל were assumed to be. For example, other entities and phenomena in the Hebrew Bible were also assumed to exhibit some of these attributes without for that reason being considered divine (e.g., humans and animals are also gendered and embodied). In other words, none of these properties was assumed sufficient for being an אל (the Hebrew Bible knows of holy, powerful and immortal substances that were not assumed to be divine). The reason Smith chose these particular traits or attributes rather than other possible ones is therefore not that his choice represents what the ancient Israelites themselves would have pointed out. Rather, he chose them because they happen to link up to, and seem relevant or interesting from the perspective of, metatheistic assumptions in traditional philosophical conceptions of divinity. This is despite the fact that Smith's list is surely less anachronistic than the perfect being theologies still presented in the writings of biblical theologians.

Ultimately, Smith's provision of a typology of divinity as vantage point, though certainly representing an improvement in the discussion of generic אל-hood in the Hebrew Bible, is ultimately (as can be expected) a look at kinds of divine beings rather than at divinity as kind. For this reason, perhaps, the study never really answers the question of what an

אל was assumed to be. For this reason the present study, whose aim is to answer such questions, must seek to build on, yet ultimately go beyond, Smith's pioneering contribution as a supplemental extension, though not as a replacement.

When one turns one's attention away from biblical studies proper to related research in the scientific study of religion proper (i.e., *Religionswissenschaft*), discussions are forthcoming that are partially more informative though not quite adequate. On the one hand, several studies provide us with research on the concept of generic divinity.[19] Pyysiäinen in particular actually asks the question, "What is it, in fact, that makes an entity a god?" Yet in this field of research, several tendencies complicate the use of the data for answering the question with reference to the metatheistic assumptions of the Hebrew Bible.

First, the historical and conceptual scopes of the inquiries mentioned above are too big as they are not limited to the concept of generic divinity in ancient Israelite religion. Second, even in this discipline the primary concern lies with the biblical conceptions of divinity in the absolute sense (i.e., God as individual divine being), rather than with the Hebrew Bible's concept of generic divinity for its own sake (i.e., the use of the generic term אל to indicate a genus). Third, the discussions that involve the Hebrew Bible tend to depend heavily on what biblical scholars have already discovered. This means that they contain the same gaps as mentioned above in connection with research in biblical studies. Fourth, because the discussions do not involve deep engagements with the textual data, oversimplification, selectivity, and generalization are common. Fifth, in the end those studies that do provide answers to the kinds of questions asked in this book are not sufficiently specific, resulting in uncertainty as to whether they are *en bloc* applicable to the metatheistic assumptions of ancient Israelite religion.

Under this category, I would include the study of religions of specific cultures that nevertheless appear to have *prima facie* relevance for our own inquiry. The seminal study of Jacobson on the concept of divinity in Mesopotamian religion is in a sense closer to what we are looking for, but in

---

19. T. M. Ludwig, "Gods and Goddesses," *ER* 6:67–78; Huw P. Owen, *Concepts of Deity* (New York: Macmillan, 1971); Raimundo Panikkar, "Deity," *ER* 6:274–76; Ilkka Pyysiäinen, "God: A Brief History with a Cognitive Explanation of The Concept" [cited 10 January 2010]. Online: http://www.talkreason.org/articles/god.pdf; L. E. Sullivan, "Supreme Beings," *ER* 6:166–81.

terms of contents is not always applicable to Israelite religion and does not analyze the generic concept in depth.[20] Then there are other studies whose titles seem relevant in the *verbatim* sense, but whose contents are either not related, or specific, or analytical enough. They include, for example, Haught's, *What Is God? How to Think about the Divine,* which deals with divine whatness, not with reference to the Hebrew Bible, but in a most general sense (the author considers possibilities for contemporarily credible conceptions of absolute Godhood).[21] Then there is the study edited by Lloyd that asked what God is with reference to the nature of Greek divinity.[22] The work by Dunand and Zivie-Coche seems directly relevant given the title of the first chapter, namely, "What Is a God?"[23] Ultimately, however, the study is limited to the nature of divinity in Egypt between 3000 B.C.E. and 395 C.E., again meaning that the cultural context is not specific enough. The same may be said of the study by Assmann.[24] In each case there is little concern for thorough analysis of the generic concept (and no study is exclusively focused thereon for its own sake). There is also the recent study edited by Porter published with reference to the Mesopotamian context.[25]

A final field of research to which this study will be closely connected is philosophy of religion. Under this rubric, I include systematic and philosophical-theological writings related to our topic. A few examples of a concern with the concept of "God" include Ramsey, Durrant, Morris, Ward, and especially Cupitt.[26] Philosophers of fame also had something

---

20. Thorkild Jacobsen, *The Treasures of Darkness: A History of Mesopotamian Religion* (London: Oxford University Press, 1979).

21. John F. Haught, *What Is God? How to Think about the Divine* (New York: Paulist Press, 1986).

22. Alan B. Lloyd, ed., *What Is a God? Studies in the Nature of Greek Divinity* (London: Duckworth, 1997).

23. Francois Dunand and Christiane Zivie-Coche, *Gods and Men in Egypt: 3000 B.C.E. to 395 C.E.* (trans. David Lorton; New York: Cornell University Press, 2004).

24. Jan Assmann, "Primat und Transzendenz: Struktur und Genese der Ägyptischen Vorstellung eines 'Hochsten Wesens,'" in *Aspekte der spätägyptischen Religion* (ed. Wolfhart Westendorf; Wiesbaden: Harrassowitz, 1979), 117–36.

25. Barbara N. Porter, ed., *What Is a God? Anthropomorphic and Non-anthropomorphic Aspects of Deity in Ancient Mesopotamia* (Transactions of the Casco Bay Assyriological Institute 2; Winona Lake, Ind.: Eisenbrauns, 2009).

26. Ian Ramsey, *Religious Language* (London: SCM, 1957); Michael Durrant and Peter Geach, "The Meaning of 'God,'" in *Religion and Philosophy* (ed. Martin Warner;

to say on the topic. Martin Heidegger, would-be theologian, wrote: "Only from the truth of Being can the essence of the holy be thought. Only from the essence of the holy is the essence of divinity to be thought. Only in the light of the essence of divinity can it be thought or said what the word 'God' is to signify."[27] Unfortunately, even the discussions of the concept of God in analytical (not to mention Continental) philosophy of religion turn out on closer inspection to be only of relative value for the present inquiry. This is because philosophers of religion proper tend to:

1. focus on concepts in Judaism and Christianity rather than those in ancient Israelite religion;
2. concentrate on overt propositions rather than on metatheistic assumptions;
3. focus on absolute Godhood (God) rather than on generic godhood (divinity *qua* genus);
4. work with the neat, systematic confessional data of the postbiblical traditions rather than with the complex, pluralist, dynamic, diverse and mythical discourse of biblical Yahwism(s); and
5. concern themselves with analysis that is evaluative rather than descriptive. In other words, they are usually concerned with truth claims (what things mean) rather than with historical assessment (what things meant).

To be sure, the above comments are generalizations based on stereotypical tendencies among mainstream philosophers of religion, and apply only inasmuch as philosophers of religion have shown any interest at all in the Hebrew Bible. Moreover, I do not intend to imply that they should not have been doing what they did do or should have paid more attention to the kind of interests that concern us in the present study. I just wish to make the point that no one can properly appeal to research in mainstream

---

Royal Institute of Philosophy Supplements 31; Cambridge: Cambridge University Press, 1992), 71–90; Morris, *Our Idea of God*, 27–46; Ward, *God: A Guide for the Perplexed*; Don Cupitt, *Taking Leave of God*; idem, *After God*; and idem, *New Religion of Life.*

27. Martin Heidegger, *Pathmarks* (ed. and trans. William McNeil; Cambridge: Cambridge University Press, 1998), 253.

philosophical approaches to the study of religion in order to claim that this study is superfluous because past authors have "been there, done that."

Many more examples of related research could be listed here, from a variety of related disciplines, but it would not make the point any clearer: the basic issues regarding relevance and problems are the same. The concerns of this study, its issues, and its interests have not, to my best knowledge, been dealt with sufficiently anywhere else in the format to be found in the discussion to follow. Of course, noting the gap in the research is one thing. Suggesting an appropriate research methodology with which to close that gap is another thing altogether.

10.5. Properties of Generic Godhood and Metatheistic Assumptions about the Divine Condition

Underlying the Hebrew Bible's use of the concept of generic אל-hood, we encounter what may be called "metatheistic assumptions."[28] By "metatheistic assumptions" I mean those presuppositions regarding the divine condition, a term that encompasses the totality of the experience of being divine. The Hebrew Bible often implies that there is a series of events that are common to a god's life as a finite and immortal entity, and that some of these events are inevitable. The ongoing way in which a god such as Yhwh was assumed to react to or cope with these events is the divine condition. However, understanding the precise nature and scope of what was meant by the concept "divine condition" is itself a philosophical problem.

The divine condition is a term I use in a metaphysical sense also, to describe the joy, anger, disappointment, concern, jealousy, and other feelings or emotions associated with being a god. Deities, to an apparently superlative degree among all living things, are assumed in the Hebrew Bible to be aware of the passage of time, the need for control, and the need to stay on top of things. They can remember the past (which cannot be changed) and imagine the future (whether because it is fixed or because the god causes it to be something is unclear). They are aware of their own limited control over reality as a whole and of the need for relations—no god exists just on its own. Yet reality is assumed to be a system that resists the eradication of all anomalies. Gods therefore, as if instinctively, wants

---

28. Jaco W. Gericke, "What's a God? Preliminary Thoughts on Meta-theistic Assumptions in Old Testament Yahwism(s)," *VE* 27 (2006): 856–57.

to create, rule, command, impress, and judge, and to harbor and reveal secrets. The divine struggle to satisfy the will to life and power defines the divine condition.

Metatheistic assumptions also relates to the principle of sufficient reason as postulated by Leibniz and Schopenhauer.[29] These presuppositions include the reason why something (anything) is called an אל in the first place and why it makes sense to believe that the properties of divinity are instantiated in relation to the human condition. After all, the phenomenon of divinity did not have to be called אלהים (the particular word), so why were these generic terms chosen for designating what it was that they were talking about? In this regard, consider what turns up when we retranscribe $א^B_a$, $א^B_b$ and $א^B_c$ back into (possible) pictographic form.[30]

$א^B_a$ [אל = ox, staff]

$א^B_b$ [אלהים = ox, staff, shout, hand, water]

$א^B_c$ [אלוה = ox, staff, hook, shout]

The precise denotations and connotations of each pictograph are a matter of debate. In addition, any associative assessment of the choice of pictographs might well be wishful thinking on the part of the esoteric and semantically overcreative exegete. Yet it is surely valid to ask whether any relation was taken for granted at some point in the earliest history of ancient Israelite religion between the choice of pictographs and the meaning of the generic concept (following a preexisting Northwest Semitic trend, of course). Is it merely coincidental that the imagery appears to represent what seems like a coherent micronarrative expressing a pasto-

---

29. "Principle of Sufficient Reason," *Wikipedia, The Free Encyclopedia* [cited 10 February 2010]. Online: http://en.wikipedia.org/w/index.php?title=Principle_of_sufficient_reason&oldid=342069553.

30. This was done using pictographs obtained from http://www.ancient-hebrew.org.

ral motif (particularly in view of the fact that pastoral metaphors were immensely popular in representing the divine condition)?

Unfortunately, there is little in scholarly research to fall back on, and probably for good reason. The subject of the relation between etymology and meaning is immensely controversial. The belief in a necessary relation is a familiar fallacy of the recent past. Usually meaning is not to be derived from the components or the root of a word, and the failure to pay attention to specific literary and historical contexts in which a given occurrence of the generic term is actually used in the Hebrew Bible itself will lead the reader potentially to commit any number of related semantic fallacies. Examples of such are the lexical fallacy, the root fallacy, the etymological fallacy, the one meaning fallacy, the fallacy of essentialism, the fallacy of definition by cognates, the fallacy of semantic anachronism, and the fallacy of illegitimate totality transfer. Meaning lies in use and context, not in etymology.[31]

Be that as it may, biblical scholars have not been altogether uninterested in the subject of roots and original meanings. Linguistic approaches often mention that for $\aleph_b$ there are basically two possibilities, also noting a host of alternatives of greater or lesser plausibility (though many have fallen into disuse as functional suggestions).

1. אלהים ($\aleph_b$) as plural (p) derivative ($\vdash$) of אל ($\aleph_a$) with root ($\sqrt{x}$} and possible ($\lozenge$) meanings ($=_{df}$) as <x, y, z>
   a. $\aleph_b$ (p) $\vdash \aleph_a \vdash \sqrt{}$ איל $\lozenge =_{df}$ <ram, first, in front>
   b. $\aleph_b$ (p) $\vdash \aleph_a \vdash \sqrt{}$ אלה $\lozenge =_{df}$ <terebinth>
   c. $\aleph_b$ (p) $\vdash \aleph_a \vdash \sqrt{}$ אלה $\lozenge =_{df}$ <to bind, swear, curse>
   d. $\aleph_b$ (p) $\vdash \aleph_a \vdash \sqrt{}$ אול $\lozenge =_{df}$ <strength, might, power>
   e. $\aleph_b$ (p) $\vdash \aleph_a \vdash \sqrt{}$ אל $\lozenge =_{df}$ <to, towards>
   f. $\aleph_b$ (p) $\vdash \aleph_a \vdash \sqrt{}$ (x)l$\lozenge =_{df}$ <other cognate root>

2. אלהים ($\aleph_b$) as plural (p) derivative ($\vdash$) of אלוה ($\aleph_c$) with root ($\sqrt{x}$) and possible ($\lozenge$) meanings ($=_{df}$) as <x, y, z>
   a. $\aleph_b$ (p) $\vdash \aleph_c \vdash \sqrt{}$ אלה $\lozenge =_{df}$ <to be fearsome>
   b. $\aleph_b$ (p) $\vdash \aleph_c \vdash \sqrt{}$ אלה $\lozenge =_{df}$ <to fear, seek refuge>

---

31. For some of these fallacies, see Barr, *Semantics of Biblical Language*; and the conservative but nevertheless readable apologetic by D. A. Carson, *Exegetical Fallacies* (Grand Rapids: Baker, 1984).

In theory there are many more possible root derivations, yet the alternatives given above represent those that have been most commonly proposed. Most scholars appear to consider the options 1a and 1d most likely and conclude that the idea of "power" or "leadership" represents the essential or core meaning of the generic concept. Now while from a diachronic perspective it might be interesting to try to determine what might have been the original associative meaning attributed to the terms for generic divinity, a less controversial way forward would rather be concerned with a reconstruction of the metatheistic assumptions underlying the actual use of the generic terms in the context of individual texts. Three classic instances of more forthcoming generic אל-talk may be mentioned for illustrative purposes, namely, Gen 3, Isa 41, and Ezek 28 (with detailed analysis following later in parts 3 and 4).

In the context of the second creation narrative, we encounter the following ambiguous and obscure reference in Gen 3:5 (if the translation is correct):

והייתם כלאהים	You will be <u>like gods</u>:
ידעי טוב ורע	knowers (plural) of good and evil

Aside from all the possible exegetical issues this verse might involve, what is relevant for present purposes is to consider the fact that, if the generic rendering is correct, then a prominent metatheistic assumption in this text involves the idea that "knowledge of good and evil" is considered an individually necessary condition for being divine. Later, in Gen 3:22, this is repeated and juxtaposed with another supplementary idea—being immortal—as a second individually necessary condition:

ויאמר יהוה אלהים	And Yhwh God said,
הן האדם היה <u>כאחד ממנו</u>	"Look, the human has become <u>like one of us</u>,
לדעת טוב ורע	to know good and evil
ועתה פן־ישלח ידו	and now, in case he puts forth his hand
ולקח גם מעץ החי	and take also of the tree of life,
ואכל וחי לעלם	and eat, and live forever...."

In Gen 2–3 then, the two trees in the garden in Eden appear to symbolize what is understood to be two quintessential properties of divine beings, namely (moral? axiological?) knowledge and immortality. Eating from one of the trees is apparently not believed to be sufficient for apotheosis; yet eating from both trees seems to represent a sufficient condition for becoming a divine being.

A second example of generic אל-talk where the metatheistic assumptions are readily apparent is found in Isa 41:21–24:

הראשנות מה הנה הגיד	Tell us the former things
ונשימה לבנו	that we may consider them,
ונדעה אחריתן	that we may know their outcome;
או הבאות השמיענ	or declare to us the things to come
הגידו האתיות לאחור	Tell us what is to come hereafter,
ונדעה כי אלהים אתם	<u>that we may know that you are gods</u>.

The metatheistic assumptions in this text also presuppose two allegedly essential properties of a deity. On the one hand, there is the presupposition that an entity alleged to be an אל is in fact an אל if and only if it has superior knowledge. The nature of this knowledge involves the god as epistemic agent (a) being cognizant of and able to reveal the contents and significance of the first events; and (b) being able to foretell what will happen in the future. On the other hand, the text assumes that an entity is an אל if and only if it is also powerful to the extent of (a) possessing the ability to actualize events and cause modifications in the structure of reality for good or ill; and (b) being able to verify possessing this ability by manifesting it. Exhibiting these kinds of knowledge and power are therefore presupposed in the text to be individually necessary and jointly sufficient conditions for being classified as a divine being in more than just the nominal sense. Perhaps the reason why entities that are not really such can be called gods is that the text assumes a radical polymorphism within the generic term's conceptual core.[32]

In this regard, it is interesting to note that different texts in the Hebrew Bible might contain different (and even incommensurable) metatheistic assumptions. From the examples above it is clear that whereas Gen 3

---

32. For the notion of conceptual cores, see Sharon Lee Armstrong, Lila R. Gleitman, and Henry Gleitman, "What Some Concepts Might Not Be," in *Concepts: Core Readings* (ed. Eric Margolis and Stephen Laurence; Cambridge: MIT Press, 1999), 248.

assumes immortality and knowledge of good and evil as being the proto-typical properties of divine beings, Isa 41 by contrast considers knowledge of temporal realities and the power to modify present states as typical. Clearly the identity conditions in the two texts are not exactly the same, which means that the dual prototypical properties presupposed are not identical. However, whether and to what extent the knowledge of good and evil (Gen 3) is of the same kind as, only overlaps with, or is radically different from, the knowledge of the past and future (Isa 41) might well be a matter that only a detailed analysis can determine.

Our third and final example, from Ezek 28:2–3, 9, adds yet additional ambiguity to the picture:

כה־אמר אדני יהוה	So says my lord Yhwh
יען גבה לבך	because your heart is high,
ותאמר <u>אל</u> אני	and you have said, "I am <u>a god</u>,
מושב <u>אלהים</u> ישבתי בלב ימים	(In) the abode of <u>gods</u> I sit in the seas."
ואתה אדם ו<u>לא־אל</u>	But you are but a man, and <u>no god</u>
ותתן לבך כלב <u>אלהים</u>	yet you set your heart as that of <u>gods</u>
האמר תאמר <u>אלהים אני</u>	Will you still say, "<u>I am a god</u>,"
לפני הרגך	in the presence of those who slay you,
ואתה אדם ו<u>לא־אל</u>	as you are but a man, and <u>no god</u>
ביד מחלליך	in the hands of who will wound you

In this text we again encounter what appear to be explicit assumptions about essential properties of generic אלהים. However, whereas in Gen 3 the necessary properties mentioned are immortality and knowledge of good and evil, and while Isa 41:21–24 refers to knowledge of the past and future and great power, in this text great *wisdom* and immortality are pro-totypical. Again we have two properties apparently necessary and essential for divine status, and again we are confronted with fuzzy data and no deep discussion of the nature and scope of the properties in question. In only one of these texts (Isaiah) do we encounter the popular view that "power" appears to be assumed a necessary property of generic divinity (as many scholars claim), while the only property to appear on all three counts is superior cognition.

Of course, the discussion above barely touches on the intricacies and depths of the three texts in question. Yet for the present it seems warranted to conclude that there are instances of texts in the Hebrew Bible where some of the metatheistic assumptions of a given trajectory within the traditions of ancient Israelite religion can be discerned—even if not fully appropriated. Together with the use of generic אל-talk and the concept of generic אל-hood, the presence of metatheistic assumptions in the discourse constitutes the background for appreciating the validity and relevance of the research problem stated in this chapter.

10.6. Generic Godhood as a Property

In this regard I would like offer a description of generic divinity in ancient Israelite religion that is not so much focused on intensions (necessary properties of generic אל-hood in the Hebrew Bible) as on looking at generic אל-hood as itself a property of sorts. After all, perhaps it is this property that is the only thing members in the extension of the generic term has in common, seeing that no other single quality is shared by all. The discussion to follow is based on selected subtopics in the philosophical treatment of properties.

In modern philosophy,

> a property is an attribute of an object; thus a red object is said to have the property of redness. The property may be considered a form of object in its own right, able to possess other properties. The concept of property differs from the logical concept of class by not having any extensionality; and from the philosophical concept of class in that a property is considered to be distinct from the objects that possess it. ... In classical Aristotelian terminology, a *property* (*proprium*) is one of the Predicables. It is a nonessential quality of a species (like an accident), but a quality that is nevertheless characteristically present in members of that species (and in no others).[33]

For example, generic godhood may be considered a special characteristic of divine beings. However, in the ancient Israelite framework this is not an *essential* quality of the species אל, as the biblical texts could also refer to

---

33. For an introduction to the topic, see "Property (Philosophy)," *Wikipedia, The Free Encyclopedia* [cited 12 April 2010]. Online: http://en.wikipedia.org/w/index .php?title=Property_(philosophy)&oldid=342508633.

manmade idols that lack the property as gods. Thus, in the classical frame-work, *properties* are characteristic, but nonessential, qualities.

> Interest in properties has ebbed and flowed over the centuries, but they are now undergoing resurgence. Just a few decades ago many philoso-phers concurred with Quine's dismissal of properties as "creatures of darkness," but philosophers now widely invoke them without guilt or shame. The last twenty-five years have seen a great deal of interesting work on properties, although when we turn to the recent literature on properties we find a confusing array of terminology, incompatible stan-dards for evaluating theories of properties, and philosophers talking past one another.[34]

In this section I offer a descriptive philosophical clarification of generic godhood as a property. I do this in recognition of the fact that meaning inevitably invites the question "meaning for whom?" In view of our objective to understand the biblical concept in its own contexts, irre-spective of whether it is considered credible or meaningful in the contexts of contemporary philosophical theology.

In the Hebrew Bible, generic אל-hood was assumed to be a *first-order property*. Given a hierarchy of properties, first-order properties and rela-tions are those that can only be instantiated by *individuals*. For example, in ancient Israel generic אל-hood was instantiated by Yhwh, Ba'al, the king, or the deified dead. Yet the property אל-hood did not itself have generic אל-hood as a property. That is, the property of אל-hood was not assumed to be itself an אל in the generic sense.

Generic אל-hood was also believed to be a *generic* property, that is, a property typically held in common by entities in the extension but not necessarily in each case. This fact accounts for the differences in onto-logical status within generic divinity and for nominal generic אל-hood, meaning the way in which many biblical authors could deny that the property of generic אל-hood was instantiated in an entity yet still call the entity an אל. It also accounts for how it was possible to, on the one hand, call both Yhwh and other gods אלהים—thus creating a class אלהים with many members—only to empty the same class by insisting that Yhwh

---

34. Chris Swoyer, "Properties," *SEP* [cited 19 July 2009]. Online: http://plato. stanford.edu/archives/fall2008/entries/properties/. The background to this discussion makes use of Swoyer's overview.

is greater than all אלהים (assigning a supraclass of ultimate divinity) and that the other אלהים are not really אלהים (assigning a subclass of pseudo-divinity). Such yes-and-no descriptions of foreign deities in particular were typical instances of fuzzy conceptualization in which generic אל-hood was itself assumed to have been a generic rather than an absolute property.

Generic was also assumed to be a *multigrade* or *variably polyadic* property. That is, generic אל-hood was predicated of various numbers of things. For example, the *predicate* "being an אל" was true of all the entities in the extension, who nevertheless were otherwise not the same kind of entities. That is why a host of other entities and phenomena besides Yhwh could also be called אלהים (or אלהים-like) in both a realist and a nominalist generic sense.

Moreover, generic אל-hood was a *compound property*, as it had a structure that involved or incorporated simpler properties (the properties of אל-hood). Given the changing conceptions not only of Yhwh but also of generic אל-hood in the history of Israelite religion, from the perspective of pluralism in biblical theology one should note that as compound property, generic אל-hood in the Hebrew Bible had a variable structure that differed in different contexts. The texts contain not only many possible world (in-the-text) extensions of polythetic classes but also multiple intensions specifying membership in supra, sub, and infra classes.

Generic אל-hood was a *determinable property*, since it was a property that could get more specific. For example, generic אל-hood could be qualified by identifying the kind of אל involved or the particular member of the extension and its share of the generic properties of generic אל-hood, which was not necessarily identical to that of other members. The very possibility of (or need for) pointing out that Yhwh is an x kind of אל (or "an אל of x"; where x denotes an accidental property, function or relation of generic אל-hood) implies that ancient Israelite generic אל-talk assumed a distinction between essential and accidental properties of generic divinity. This accounts for the possibility of theological pluralism in the representations of Yhwh himself.

Generic אל-hood in the Hebrew Bible was also *qua* generic concept a *natural kind property*. In the Hebrew Bible, in contrast to what is popular in contemporary thought, there was no natural/supernatural dichotomy. In this sense (and by definition in generics) generic אל-hood (as opposed to absolute Godhood) was designative of a genus and therefore of something very much like a natural kind in as much as the אלהים were folk-taxonomically seen as the highest ranking taxonomic type. There were אלהים as there were humans, animals, birds, fish, and plants (the denial of genus in divinity is a philosophical anachronism).

In the Hebrew Bible the concept of generichood was also assumed to be indicative of a purely *qualitative property* (being an אל) that could be represented in a generic and abstract sense without referring to a particular אל. "The distinction between properties that are purely qualitative and those that are not is usually easy to draw in practice, but a precise characterization of it is elusive."[35] In other words, whatever one may assume about the concept/reality relation with reference to absolute Godhood, technically the concept of generic אל-hood—as all generic terms—denoted an abstract object (hence had a nominal ontological status as universal). It referred not to any particular deity but to the category "divinity" as secondary substance in a purely abstract sense.

In being denotative of an abstract object, generic אל-hood was also assumed to be a *fictional property*. This can be seen in at least two contexts. First, when the author calls an entity an אל when it is presupposed or denied that the entity is in fact an אל. Included are those polemical texts that ascribe properties even to אלהים the texts deny existed, for instance being weak, frightened, or even nothing. Second, when the generic concept was used in such an abstract sense, though meaningful, it was not assumed to denote anyone—neither an actual individual אל nor a merely possible one. The concept of generic אל-hood *qua* property therefore fails to denote concrete phenomena. A good example is the אלהים in Jotham's fable (Judg 9). In a sense, since the generic concept classified and designated a type yet represented an abstract object with no particular referent, generic אל-hood was *ipso facto* a fictional property.

In some texts in the Hebrew Bible, the property of generic אל-hood was also assumed to be an *essential property* inasmuch as something was an אל if and only if it existed in the state or condition of being an אל. If an entity lacked אל-hood it could not be an אל in a realist sense—only in a nominalist one. However, because many texts distinguished between real and nominal generic אל-hood (between what is really an אל and what is called such but is in fact not such), real generic אל-hood could also be thought of as being an accidental property in that it is not assumed to be present in every possible circumstance in which something is called an אל.

---

35. Ibid.

So as with אל-hood itself, real generic אל-hood as property was assumed to be essential or accidental depending on the context.

Generic אל-hood was also assumed to be a *maximal property* in that not everything part of an אל was itself assumed to be אל-like. Thus the robe Isaiah saw on Yhwh or the medium on Samuel was not itself considered to exhibit the property of generic אל-hood. Moreover, in many contexts the breath of Yhwh, which vitalizes living creatures was not assumed to be אל–like, which is why being able to breathe was not assumed to be a sufficient condition for being an אל (Gen 2). The same applies to abstract albeit substantial parts of אלהים such as their glory which, though inextricably a necessary part of the state and condition of being a אל, did not in itself exhibit the property of generic אל-hood. In biblical categorization, particularly superlative phenomena such as an אל-like mountain or a divine garden could contain non-אל-like mereological constituents, animals, plants, and so on.

In yet another contrast to modern notions, generic אל-hood in the Hebrew Bible was a purely *relational property*. While many philosophers of religion might think of אל-hood as something an entity (אל) has even if there is nothing else in existence, some texts in the Hebrew Bible seem to presuppose that generic אל-hood is a relational property (analogous to parenthood). Just as the notion of being a parent is meaningless and inconceivable without the accompanying idea of children, so too the notion of prototypical generic אל-hood makes no sense for many biblical authors without a relation to a nation or at least an individual which acknowledges it as its אל. In the Hebrew Bible divinity was not assumed to exist in isolation. In this sense generic אל-ness was conceived of as a relational property ontologically dependent on the existence of others in relation to whom it could instantiate אל-hood.

The above observation links imply that in the Hebrew Bible generic אל-hood was often assumed to be an *extrinsic property*. An extrinsic property is exactly an attribute that exists only in relation; and generic אל-hood was assumed to be extrinsic *qua* property in as much as it was believed to exist only in this manner. The theological oddity of this biblical *noumenon–phenomenon* distinction in which an אל does not exist *qua* אל by itself is not always recognized. In short, for many texts in the Hebrew Bible, a necessary condition for being an אל was being somebody's אל.

In view of the above two aspects, generic אל-hood, being a relational and extrinsic property, was also believed to be a *secondary property*, since it was seen as depending on there being relations for it to be that kind of

thing. These relations were assumed to be contingent and as having originated at some point in time, hence the idea of generic אל-hood as having
been assumed to be a secondary property (in this context, not to be confused with the notion in Lockean epistemology). This explains why, for
example, Yhwh can promise to be an אל (generic sense) to Israel or deny
that he is an אל to them any longer (see Hos 1:9).

If אל-hood was a secondary, extrinsic, and relational property in the
above senses, it was also an *emergent property*. In philosophy, emergence
refers to the way in which complex systems and patterns arise out of a multiplicity of relatively simple interactions. As an emergent property, generic
אל-hood was thought to "arise" out of more fundamental entities (entities
called אלהים in view of their function and relation) and yet to be "novel"
or "irreducible" with respect to them. As a result, אל-hood was assumed to
be metaphysically primitive; and was considered to be a systemic feature
of complex systems governed by true, law-like generalizations.

Generic אל-hood in the Hebrew Bible was therefore also assumed
to be a *supervenient property* since possessing or instantiating it implied
having other properties as a result. Generic אל-hood as property super-
vened on the properties of generic אל-hood. That is why in the Hebrew
Bible some texts assume that if any entity has generic אל-hood as property it will also exhibit the properties of generic אל-hood (Isa 41:21–24;
Ezek 28:1–9). Failing the latter leads to the suspicion that the generic
אל-hood *qua* property was not itself instantiated in the entity in question.
Herein lay the criteria and rationale for the polemics against false אלהים
to begin with.

Being a supervenient property, generic אל-hood was also considered
to be a *complex property*. In contrast to the postbiblical philosophical conceptions of אל-hood and the notion of "divine simplicity," the property
of generic אל-hood was not assumed to be identical to the properties of
generic אל-hood. No אל's existence was assumed in the Hebrew Bible to
be the same as its essence—which is why the nature of generic divinity
was assumed to be instantiated but not exhausted in the nature of absolute Godhood (Yhwh). This also explains why Yhwh could both be called
"God" in the absolute sense (denoting a primary substance) and be folk-
taxonomically classified as belonging to the genus אלהים in the generic
sense (denoting his secondary substance, again in contrast to later philosophical-theological ideas).

Generic אל-hood as property was also a *nuclear property* in that it
denoted the nature of the object to which the concept referred and not an

extranuclear property that was supposed to be external to its nature. Being an אל was the nuclear property that entities with the property generic אל-hood instantiated.

Finally, being a nuclear property, generic אל-hood was also assumed to be a *constitutive property* since it tended to be mentioned explicitly in a description used to pick out the object that was called an אל. By contrast, the properties of generic אל-hood are its consecutive properties, as they are somehow included or implied by the אל's constitutive property.

10.7. Generic Godhood as a Fuzzy Concept

Something can now be said on the fuzziness of the concept of generic אל-hood in ancient Israelite religion as represented in the pluralistic traditions of the Hebrew Bible. While individual texts may allow for a classical conceptual analysis (definitionism), a panbiblical perspective that takes synchronic and diachronic pluralism seriously will have to reckon with a concept that is essentially fuzzy. The fuzziness concerns both the extension and the intension of the generic terms. These are fuzzy to the extent that their meaning can never be completely and exactly specified through logical operators or objective terms, and can have multiple interpretations, which are in part exclusively subjective.

We can therefore say that generic divinity was a fuzzy concept, since

> the content, value, and boundaries of application varied according to context or conditions, instead of being fixed once and for all. Usually this meant that the concept was vague and lacked a fixed, precise meaning, but without being meaningless altogether. It did have a meaning, or multiple meanings (it has different semantic associations) which, however, could become clearer only through further elaboration and specification. In logic, a fuzzy concept may in fact offer more security of meaning because it provides a meaning for something when an exact concept is unavailable.[36]

The biblical concept of generic אל-hood, being fuzzy, operated with a fuzzy logic.

---

36. "Fuzzy Concept," *Wikipedia, The Free Encyclopedia* [cited 10 February 2010]. Online: http://en.wikipedia.org/w/index.php?title=Fuzzy_concept&oldid =335905642.

The term "fuzzy logic" emerged in the development of the theory of fuzzy sets in the 1960s. A fuzzy subset A of a (crisp) set X is characterized by assigning to each element x of X the *degree of membership* of x in A (for example, X is a group of people, A the fuzzy set of *old* people in X). Now if X is a set of propositions then its elements may be assigned their *degree of truth*, which may be "absolutely true," "absolutely false," or some *intermediate* degree of truth: a proposition may be truer than another proposition.[37]

In a fuzzy conceptual analysis of the concept of generic אל-hood, one will have to specify a given biblical text's meaning for the generic concept without, however, having the liberty of placing restrictions on a different use of the concept in other biblical contexts. A dual theory combining classical and prototype/exemplar concerns might therefore be the most functional for a pan-biblical perspective, since the concept did exhibit multiple intensions and extensions across possible worlds in the text. Its meaning can therefore not be completely and exactly specified through logical operators (or objective terms), and has multiple interpretations (which may be only partly subjective).

10.8. Philosophical Definition

Now it is time to show what is involved in the task of definition. The quest for analysis via definitions has interested philosophers since ancient times.

Plato's early dialogues portray Socrates raising questions about definitions (e.g., "What is piety?" in the *Euthyphro*), questions that seem at once profound and elusive. The key step in Anselm's "Ontological Proof" for the existence of God is the definition of "God," and the same holds for Descartes's version of the argument in his *Meditation V*. More recently, the Frege-Russell definition of number and Tarski's definition of truth have exercised a formative influence on a wide range of contemporary philosophical debates. In all these cases—and many others can be cited—not only have particular definitions been debated, but the nature of, and demands on, definitions have also been debated. Some of these debates can be settled by making requisite distinctions, for definitions are not all of one kind: they serve a variety of functions, and their gen-

---

37. Petr Hajek, "Fuzzy Logic," *SEP* [cited 1 November 2009]. Online: http://plato.stanford.edu/archives/fall2010/entries/logic-fuzzy.

eral character varies with their function. Other debates, however, are not so easily settled, as they involve contentious philosophical ideas such as "essence," "concept," and "meaning."[38]

As a popular view has it, "a definition is a formal passage describing the meaning of a term (a word or phrase)."[39] In conceptual analysis, the idea of "definition" is strongly related to the classical theory of concepts, which is riddled with problems. Even without critiques on the theory, philosophers disagree about what it means to define, although most of them agree that defining is notoriously difficult. One cannot assume that there is some neat, fixed mental "something" that corresponds to the generic terms for divinity just because the biblical authors used these terms successfully; or that biblical scholars doing philosophical analysis can simply analyze the concept to arrive at its full definition. Different philosophers also specify different criteria for definitions, sometimes depending on the context in which the concept occurs or given the many types of definition available,[40] each with their own objectives.

In the past, most linguistic and theological perspectives in biblical scholarship have offered only what is commonly called extensional or denotative definitions of the concept of generic אל-hood. By this is meant that they have considered it satisfactory to list and discuss every entity called a אל. But this does not tell us what an אל was assumed to be or why each of these entities were classified as such. For that, we need an intensional (or connotative) definition aimed at trying to specify what was assumed to be individually necessary and jointly sufficient conditions for an entity or phenomenon to be a member of the extension of the generic terms for deity. Any definition that attempts to set out the essence of something, such as that by genus and differentia, just is an intensional definition.[41]

---

38. Anil Gupta, "Definitions," *SEP* [cited 11 November 2009]. Online: http://plato.stanford.edu/archives/spr2009/entries/definitions/.

39. "Definition," *Wikipedia, The Free Encyclopedia* [cited 18 February 2010]. Online: http://en.wikipedia.org/w/index.php?title=Definition&oldid=340659790.

40. Besides a host of other definitions, we can isolate the lexical, stipulative, precising, descriptive, operational, real, nominal, ostensional, theoretical, recursive, and persuasive types of definitions.

41. "Definition," *Wikipedia*.

What will be important in the quest for an intensional definition of generic divinity is something philosophers do agree about, that is, two intuitive criteria: conservativeness and use.[42]

1. The conservativeness criterion states that the definition should not enable us to establish essentially new claims for a given textual context.
2. The use criterion suggests that the definition should fix the use of the concept (in our case, generic אל-hood) in a given textual context.

An additional criterion for (useful) definitions can be derived from Quine's notion of ontological relativity. An ontological question in the form "What is an אל?" seems problematic not so much for being universal as for being circular. It becomes meaningless when regarded absolutely. If one asks what an אל was assumed to be, the answer depends on what was meant by the concept, which is precisely what one wants to determine in the first place. Yet how will one be able to recognize the correct answer on discovering it, unless one already knows it? So the question, it seems, cannot be answered by answering that "An אל is an X," as this implies all biblical texts' acceptance of "X." Any analysis, therefore, begs the question: hence the paradox of analysis.

Ultimately, philosophers of Israelite religion are not Hebrew lexicographers.[43] When analyzing the concept of generic אל-hood, we cannot content ourselves simply with reporting on how the generic terms were conventionally used. A philosophical approach can go beyond a merely linguistic one and offer very sophisticated "reconstructions" of the concept of generic אל-hood. While a Hebrew lexicographer may typically use about a dozen words (and sometimes even a few hundred) in defining, for example, אל, in contrast a philosopher of Israelite religion engaged in conceptual analysis may offer a lengthy book.[44] The philosopher's "analysis" (often called "explication") contains a very substantial element of pro-

---

42. See Gupta, "Definitions."
43. This discussion of the difference between philosophical and lexical concerns is indebted to Norman Swartz, *Definitions, Dictionaries, and Meanings* [cited 18 November 2009]. Online: http://www.sfu.ca/~swartz/definitions.htm.
44. My next publication is of this type.

posal: it is, in effect, a theory of how we might profitably conceive of some particular concept or of some set of interrelated concepts.

Unfortunately, although not unexpectedly, there will be no agreed-upon way of "balancing, or even of measuring, the various 'dimensions' (desiderata)" in philosophical analysis aimed at a definition of generic אל-hood.[45] What one biblical scholar offers as an analysis of the particular concept, another may think departs too far from, or is too closely wedded to, the ordinary use of that concept. What one finds overly precise, another finds too imprecise. What one finds too simple, another finds not simple enough. And so it goes. It should be clear by now that any desire to define generic אל-hood from a pan-Hebrew Bible perspective will shipwrecked by the conceptual pluralism inherent in multiple possible worlds intensions and extensions for the concept in the history of Israelite religion. A minimalist approach is therefore advisable, one that works with the data implicit in individual texts and is careful not to generalize from the results. The best way of making sense of the whole would then be a comparative perspective, as opposed to a systematic one.

10.9. CONCLUSION

In the current state of research, the nature of the conceptual structure of generic אל-hood from a pan-biblical perspective remains undetermined. In this chapter, we have barely scratched the surface of the concept's complexity. The intensional dimension of the conceptual system operative in ancient Israelite religion was, after all, quintessentially fuzzy and indelibly polythetic. In the next chapter, the discussion becomes more specific as we concern ourselves with what the Hebrew Bible took for granted about absolute Godhood, that is, about the nature of Yhwh himself.

---

45. Swartz, *Definitions, Dictionaries and Meanings.*

11

YHWH—A PHILOSOPHICAL PERSPECTIVE[1]

There is need for a philosophical account of the nature of this God, which might clarify the way in which other peoples might relate to him, or come to understand what he is.[2]

11.1. INTRODUCTION

In the previous chapter we looked at the concept of generic divinity in the Hebrew Bible. In this chapter, our concern lies with the Hebrew Bible's conceptions of absolute Godhood, that is, with a descriptive philosophical theology aimed at clarifying textual representations of the God Yhwh.

Commenting on previous related research, James Barr once stated, "Most biblical scholars have no time for the philosophical theologian's, 'It depends on what you mean by "God."'"[3] As we saw in the previous chapter, one biblical theologian who apparently made time was Rolf P. Knierim, when he wrote that "one of the most self-evident yet startling questions that we may ask ... is, 'What does the Bible mean, or what do you mean, when saying "God."'"[4]

Both Barr's and Knierim's references to the question concerning the meaning of "God" in the Hebrew Bible presuppose an interest with something more than semantic explication of the generic concept. Indeed, what is envisaged is nothing less than a descriptive philosophical theology of the Hebrew Bible. So what are the issues under consideration in such

---

1. The contents of this chapter represent a revised version of my paper, "Brave New World: Towards a Philosophical Theology of the Old Testament," *OTE* 22 (2009): 321–45.

2. Ward, *Concept of God*, 82.

3. Barr, *Concept of Biblical Theology*, 147.

4. Knierim, *Task of Old Testament Theology*, 490.

an approach? In his introduction to Christian philosophical theology, Thomas V. Morris notes that:

> The aim of philosophical theology is to employ philosophical methods and techniques for the purpose of gaining as much clarity as possible concerning the content of major concepts, presuppositions and tenets of theological commitment as well as the many connections that exist among them. In doing philosophical theology we ask questions such as these: Can a logically coherent conception of God be articulated? What is the ultimate source for our idea of God? What can be said about the range of God's power? How can we understand the nature of his knowledge? What is divine creation? How is God related to time? These are the sorts of questions typically investigated in philosophical theology.[5]

Of course, as Morris notes:

> The enterprise of philosophically reflecting on basic questions concerning God could, in principle, be pursued in any theistic religious tradition, any tradition affirming the existence of a divine being.[6]

Note that by implication the religion which is the object of philosophical analysis does not itself have to be philosophical before philosophical clarification can take place. Morris, though wishing to be "biblical," does not have purely historical and descriptive concerns limited to the biblical data, but ultimately seeks to involve the entire biblical tradition along with Christian systematic theology. The biblical scholar has the luxury of limiting the inquiry a bit more. So the biblical scholar can ask historical philosophical questions such as: Can a logically coherent conception of Yhwh in a given biblical text be articulated? What does a given biblical text assume regarding the ultimate source for humans ideas of the divine? What does a given text presuppose or imply about the range of Yhwh's power? How does a given text understand the nature of his knowledge? According to a given creation account, what is divine creation assumed to be? How, according to a given text, is Yhwh assumed to be related to time?

These are the sorts of questions that could typically be investigated in a philosophical theology of the Hebrew Bible. What this means is that while a typical textbook in Christian philosophical theology is organized

---

5. Morris, *Our Idea of God*, 16.
6. Ibid.

around concepts from Christian systematic theology, a philosophical theology concerned with Yahwism must be organized around concepts from Old Testament theology. The different agenda of concerns in Christian and Old Testament philosophical theology can be seen in the following example. On the one hand, the *The Cambridge Companion to Christian Philosophical Theology* has the following *capita selecta*:[7]

Christian Philosophical Theology
Part I *God*
1 Trinity
2 Necessity
3 Simplicity
4 Omnipotence, omniscience, and omnipresence
5 Goodness
6 Eternity and providence
Part II *God in relation to creation*
7 Incarnation
8 Resurrection
9 Atonement
10 Sin and salvation
11 The problem of evil

On the other hand, when adapted to the Hebrew Bible, a possible (but not necessary) set of *capita selecta* might involve the following concepts:

Philosophical Theology of the Hebrew Bible
Part I *El-hood*
1 Absolute divinity
2 Modality/typology
3 Complexity
4 Power, wisdom and glory
5 Holiness
6 Time and *torah*
Part II Yhwh in relation to creation
7 Theophany and dreams

---

7. Charles Taliaferro and Chad Meister, eds., *The Cambridge Companion to Christian Philosophical Theology* (Cambridge: Cambridge University Press, 2010), vii–viii.

8 Sheol
9 Word and wisdom
10 Evil and the cult
11 The value and problem of divine hiddenness

This agenda is not cast in stone, it is just a thought, and the possibilities are endless. The fact that the biblical scholar will be interested in a historical philosophical theology means that a philosophical analysis of, for example, the concept of "prayer" will be different from related discussions in Christian philosophical theology. Our concern will be with the concept of prayer in the Hebrew Bible (or in a given text) and what the Hebrew Bible (or this or that text) assumes the ancient Israelites are doing when they pray. It is thus a historical exercise, but what makes it philosophical is that we describe what is presupposed and implied in the biblical texts in nondistortive philosophical terms. The study of the philosophical theology of the Hebrew Bible must be historical, analogous to the study of ancient Greek philosophical theology.[8]

11.2. THE ANACHRONISM OF "PERFECT BEING" THEOLOGY

Ironically, the same biblical theologians who decry the use of philosophical concepts show no end to displaying their own addiction to the distortive anachronism known as "perfect being" theology. On this view, one counts a being as divine only if it is maximally great. That is to say, only if this being possesses the greatest array of possible great-making properties. The term "great-making properties" is generally used in the literature to signify those properties that it is intrinsically better to have than to not have. "Anselm had something like this in mind when he said of God that he is whatever it is better to be than to not be."[9]

The problem here, as every biblical theologian should know, is that what counts as great-making properties in ancient Israelite religion were not stable throughout the history of religion: different conceptions of Yhwh in the Hebrew Bible have incommensurable ideas on the matter. More-

---

8. See Kevin L. Flannery, "Ancient Philosophical Theology," in Taliaferro, Draper, and Quinn, *A Companion to Philosophy of Religion*, 83–98.

9. For an introduction to the topic online, see *Summa Philosophiae: Symposium of Philosophy, Theology and Scripture* [cited 10 February 2010]. Online: http://summaphilosophiae.wordpress.com/2007/03/15/perfect-being-theology/.

over, many of these differ radically from conceptions of deity in classical theism.[10] In this regard many an Old Testament theologian has assumed, asserted, or implied that Yhwh is believed to instantiate what philosophical theologians refer to as "maximal greatness," in other words, that Yhwh is believed to be omnipotent, omniscient, omnipresent, omnibenevolent, and so on. The fact of the matter is that these terms are part of a metalanguage that is completely out of place in many biblical narratives.[11] While some texts in the Hebrew Bible may endorse something vaguely approximating these attributes as they are popularly understood, there are many textual contexts in which this is by implication not the case.

For example, no one can show that a text such as Gen 18 presupposes or implies "perfect being" theology. In the narrative, Yhwh is depicted as moving about on his way (i.e., as not omnipresent) to verify a report regarding an alleged state of affairs (i.e., as not omniscient); as eating with Abraham (i.e., as not spiritual or incorporeal); and as taken to task by Abraham to ensure that he does the right thing (presupposing moral realism and not divine command ethics). In this text, then, Yhwh's profile simply does not satisfy the necessary and sufficient conditions for godhood taken for granted by many Christian philosophical theologians.

This—the relative absence of "perfect being" theology in the Hebrew Bible—has been pointed out in the past. An excellent example is that of Fretheim,[12] who actually tries to show that many texts depict Yhwh in ways that contradict almost every essential property of divinity proposed by "perfect being" theologians.[13] Fretheim's presentation stands over against conservative Christian readings that tend to be fundamentalist, anachronistically reading into Hebrew Bible god talk modern ideas of maximal greatness and attempting to produce a "biblical" view of God. In doing so these approaches fail to take cognizance of theological pluralism in ancient Israelite religion and tend to settle arguments to their own satisfaction by quoting and elaborating *ad hoc* on supposed proof texts that are understood to support classical theistic readings. This strategy "works" only by reinterpreting discourse that doesn't comply with preconceived dogmatic expectations. Such people are less interested in taking the

---

10. As argued with refreshing lucidity by Carroll, *Wolf in the Sheepfold*, 37.

11. Jaco W. Gericke, Yhwh and the God of Philosophical Theology," *VE* 27 (2006): 677–99.

12. Fretheim, *Suffering of God*.

13. Or "church theology," as Walter Brueggemann calls it.

Bible on its own terms than in defending their particular theory of biblical inspiration, reinterpreting the text to appear theologically orthodox relative to particular Christian dogmas.

However, Fretheim's exposition itself suffers from the drawbacks inherent in the kind of "open theistic" hermeneutics he seems to endorse. These approaches accept limitations on the part of the deity but tend to overemphasize cognitive limitations (reinterpreting ones about presence and power). In addition they ignore contrary readings supporting classical theism, anachronistically see everything as metaphor (except the word "God," although ironically its etymology is also metaphorical), and paint the deity in absolutely adorable terms by ignoring distheistic elements in the discourse that implicate Yhwh in the actualization of natural and moral evil.[14]

A more openminded and, in my view, honest assessment is that of Barton, who notes the "ambiguity" between the biblical material and the theological utterances of later times.[15] What we find in many texts of the Hebrew Bible does not fit well with what later counted for monotheism, omnipotence, and omniscience in both Jewish and Christian theologies. Barton offers the example of Yhwh's choosing Saul only to reject him later. According to Barton, anyone who, because of philosophical assumptions, assumes that Yhwh is omniscient while choosing someone he is going to reject anyway misses the point made by the biblical author, who did not share the assumptions of "perfect being" theology. Barton is certainly correct in his observation, but I fear that the antiphilosophical establishment of biblical theologians will make the wrong inferences.

Barton did not mean to imply that all philosophical questions are invalid simply for being philosophical. What he meant was that philosophical questions miss the point when they are presumptuous and arise from reading anachronistic philosophical-theological conceptions of God into biblical texts where the particular ideas are not present. The danger of philosophical thinking lies in projecting our own philosophical-theological assumptions about the nature of God onto biblical god talk, and not in philosophical analysis or the asking of philosophical questions per se.

---

14. As recounted in James Crenshaw, *Prophetic Conflict: Its Effect upon Israelite Religion* (BZAW 124, Berlin: de Gruyter, 1971), 77–88. See also the "problem" of evil in the Hebrew Bible later on in this study.

15. Barton, "Alttestamentliche Theologie," 25–34.

Without descriptive philosophical analysis, there is no way of preventing such philosophical-theological distortions.

In this regard, one of the most interesting and most challenging tasks of clarification is to become aware of what is taken for granted. This involves identifying something that is always present but goes without saying, and coming to perceive it as arbitrary. In this regard, when it comes to biblical god talk, a lot is taken for granted even by philosophers of religion who, immersed in more orthodox popular Jewish-Christian conceptions of deity, do not seem to be aware of deepseated, value-added metatheistic assumptions in the construction of Yhwh's stereotypical profile. These include binary oppositions,[16] in which one term is always privileged above another when it comes to biblical representations of divinity:

1. The empirical is better than the ideal.
2. Being alive is better than being dead.
3. Singleness is preferable to plurality.
4. Maleness is more apt than femaleness.
5. Anthropomorphism is superior to theriomorphism.
6. Power is better than weakness.
7. Knowledge is superior to ignorance.
8. Wisdom is better than foolishness.
9. Spiritual substance is better than fleshly substance.
10. Immortality is superior to being mortal.
11. Independence is better than dependence.
12. Seriousness is more fitting than a sense of humor.
13. Height is a more appropriate than depth.
14. Mystery is more proper than intelligibility.
15. Obscurity is more worthy than transparency.
16. Extraordinariness is preferable to ordinariness.

---

16. "Binary Opposition," *Wikipedia, The Free Encyclopedia* [cited 10 February 2010]. Online: http://en.wikipedia.org/w/index.php?title=Binary_opposition&oldid =341852180: "In critical theory, a binary opposition (also binary system) is a pair of theoretical opposites. In structuralism, it is seen as a fundamental organizer of human philosophy, culture, and language. In poststructuralism, it is seen as one of several influential characteristics or tendencies of western and western derived thought in which, typically, one of the two opposites assumes a role of dominance over the other. The categorization of binary oppositions is 'often value-laden and ethnocentric,' offering an illusory order and superficial meaning."

17. Glory is more apt than dullness.
18. Light is more suitable than darkness.
19. Ambition is better than resignation.
20. Creativeness is better than unproductiveness.
21. Self-assertion is better than self-negation.
22. Narcissism is more fitting than self-denial.
23. Prescription is more apt than permission.
24. Action is superior to passivity.

To be sure, exceptions to these notions are found time and again, but they only prove the rule. Looking at the above list of assumptions from the perspective of possible-world modality metaphysics (things could have been different), the conceptual oddity of such a scheme of things becomes a philosophical riddle. There is no logical necessity why the nature of deity and its relation to the world must be expressed like this. To be sure, theologically it may seem more appropriate to conceive of the divine in this fashion, yet we need to clarify why this particular way of representing absolute Godhood is considered to go without saying and what metaphysical, epistemological and moral assumptions underlie the privileging of particular properties, functions and relations.

11.3. The Doctrine of Divine Complexity

An interesting albeit conveniently overlooked example in which the use of Aristotelian metaphysical notions is indeed utterly distortive concerns the tendency of biblical scholars to bring to the text classical theism's so-called doctrine of "divine simplicity." In philosophical theology:

> The doctrine of divine simplicity says that God is without parts. The general idea of divine simplicity can be stated in this way: the being of God is identical to the attributes of God. In other words, such characteristics as omnipresence, goodness, truth, eternity, etc. are identical to his being, not qualities that make up his being.[17]

---

17. "Divine Simplicity," *Wikipedia, The Free Encyclopedia* [cited 18 December 2010]. Online: http://en.wikipedia.org/w/index.php?title=Divine_simplicity&oldid=340771152.

The doctrine is itself motivated by "perfect being" theology and by philosophical problems in conceiving of God as a necessary being if he is not also a simple being. Of course, the problem in this form is anachronistic in the context of ancient Israelite religion as expressed in the Hebrew Bible. Whether we believe this about God (or consider the description appropriate for Godhood) is not currently relevant. The fact is that whereas some texts in the Hebrew Bible may represent Yhwh in ways that by philosophical translation might be commensurable with some of divine simplicity's axioms, a substantial number of passages presuppose exactly the opposite. Recognizing this, a philosophical theology of the Hebrew Bible would therefore do well to take leave of ideas in Christian philosophical theology and instead opt for a doctrine that might even be dubbed "divine complexity." In the Hebrew Bible:

1. Yhwh is often assumed to have a body (theomorphism in humans).
2. Yhwh is often assumed to be composed of matter and form ("spirit" was believed to be a natural elemental substance such as wind).
3. Yhwh's properties are often not assumed to be identical with the divine essence or nature (absolute Godhood $\leq$ the extension of generic godhood).
4. Yhwh's essence is often not assumed to be identical to his existence (generic godhood $\geq$ absolute Godhood).
5. Yhwh is often assumed to be in a genus as a species (generic "god" is assumed to be something analogous to a natural kind or a folk taxonomic type).
6. Yhwh is often assumed to exhibit accidental properties (presupposed in Hebrew Bible modalities within typologies of divinity).
7. Yhwh is often not assumed to be wholly one (the deity is manifested in mereological parts, e.g., spirit, glory, name, word, etc.)
8. Yhwh's secondary substance is often assumed to be able to combine with something (cf. spirit possession/superlative states).

Many philosophical problems arise with such a conception of deity, but this is not our concern. Our task is a philosophical clarification of the Hebrew

Bible's own conceptions of Yhwh, whatever these are. To be sure, I cannot say that these axioms represent the "biblical" view of Yhwh, as there is no singular unified conception of the God of Israel in the text. What I can do is to point to the fact that, while Aristotelian concepts of deity might be distortive, the doctrine of divine complexity uses Aristotelian concepts and categories in a nondistortive manner to verbalize in philosophical language what the text itself often presupposes. We must distinguish Aristotelian philosophical theology (which is anachronistic and distortive) from Aristotelian categories (which can be adopted for functional, descriptive, and clarifying purposes).

11.4. From Attributes of God to Properties of Yhwh

A primary task in philosophical theology is the conceptual clarification of the attributes of God.[18] By contrast, the philosophical theologian of the Hebrew Bible will be interested in the attributes, or rather the properties, of Yhwh in his various depictions in the biblical discourse. Biblical theologians often talk about Yhwh's attributes or characteristics in a loose manner lacking nuance, and without any attention to the kinds of properties distinguished in the philosophy of properties.

My own concern here is not the philosophical debate on properties. I bracket the question of which theory of properties is correct and whether the concept of properties is philosophically justified at all. In my view property theory in philosophy may prove illuminating for a philosophical theology of the Hebrew Bible inasmuch as traditional biblical theologies of the systematic type (such as Eichrodt's) often contain a section on the "attributes" of Yhwh. Here it has been said that Yhwh is single, personal, and spiritual, to which might be added discussions of his power, presence,

---

18. See Gijsbert van den Brink and Marcel Sarot, eds., *Understanding the Attributes of God* (Contributions to Philosophical Theology 1; Frankfurt: Lang, 1999). In recent years, God's nature and attributes have been the center of numerous attempts at conceptual clarification and critical reflection. This volume contains, besides an introduction to the method of philosophical theology, essays on God's love, immutability, omnipresence, omniscience, simplicity, (im)possibility, and omnipotence. *Understanding the Attributes of God* is a highly readable survey of recent developments in philosophical theology and the authors all belong to the so-called "Utrecht school" in philosophical theology, whose approach is characterized by the cross-fertilization of Anglo-Saxon and Continental, philosophical and theological, and traditional and recent thinking. This volume offers a programmatic sample of their work.

knowledge, love, wrath, and holiness, and so on.[19] Such a description, at times bordering on an exercise in homiletics, might be considered sufficient for traditional biblical theologies, yet a philosophical theology of the Hebrew Bible worthy of its name will wish to determine what kind of property each of these attributes is assumed to be.

In this regard several different kinds of properties have been identified by philosophers, involving distinctions that may be functional for any philosophical account of the nature of Yhwh.[20] To be sure, the Hebrew Bible does not itself actually make these philosophical distinctions in any explicit manner, yet it presupposes and implies (or at least allows) them all the same. Not wishing to sound presumptuous, however, I shall introduce each type of property distinction with a question.

11.4.1. ESSENTIAL VERSUS ACCIDENTAL PROPERTIES

Does the Hebrew Bible show a distinction between essential and accidental properties in Yhwh? The distinction between essential and accidental properties has been characterized in various ways, but it is currently most commonly understood in modal terms, along these lines: an essential property of Yhwh is a property that a Hebrew Bible text assumes Yhwh must have, in order to be the kind of thing or individual that he is believed to be. By contrast, an accidental property of Yhwh is one that Yhwh is thought to have but that he can lack without ceasing to be the kind of entity he is thought to be. In other words, the basic modal characterization of the distinction between essential and accidental properties of Yhwh can be formulated with reference to Yhwh in the text.[21]

X is assumed to be an essential property of Yhwh in a given text if the narrator assumes it is necessary that Yhwh have X. By contrast, X is also assumed to be an accidental property of Yhwh. This is if it is assumed in

---

19. See the discussion in Eichrodt, *Theology of the Old Testament*, 1:206–27. A more recent example is found in Preuss's *Old Testament Theology*, 1:239–46.

20. Interestingly, many philosophical theologians neglect or fail to have recourse to the philosophy of properties, instead seeking to clarify properties traditionally ascribed to the deity by showing what they might involve, rather than what kind of properties they are assumed to be.

21. The following formulations are adapted from Teresa Robertson, "Essential vs. Accidental Properties," *SEP* [cited 12 January 2010]. Online: http://plato.stanford.edu/archives/fall2008/entries/essential-accidental/.

the text that Yhwh is believed to have X. But it implies that it is possible for Yhwh to be Yhwh without X. Putting this into the language of possible worlds in the text, X is assumed to be an essential property of Yhwh if a text assumes that in all possible worlds Yhwh has X. Alternatively, X is assumed to be an accidental property of Yhwh if it is implied that there can be a possible world in which Yhwh lacks X yet retains his identity.

While Christian philosophical theology with its notion of divine simplicity dislikes the notion of accidental properties in God, prima facie assessments suggest that in the Hebrew Bible Yhwh is indeed assumed to exhibit accidents, such as mercy. Though texts such as Exod 34:6–7 assume mercy to a property of Yhwh, it would appear that lacking mercy is not assumed to be something that would disqualify Yhwh from being considered a god or even from being Yhwh—it would only have implications for the *kind* of god he is assumed to be (cf. Ps 77, where the possibility that such change has actually occurred is entertained).

11.4.2. INTRINSIC VERSUS EXTRINSIC PROPERTIES

In the Hebrew Bible, are certain properties of Yhwh assumed to be extrinsic while others are seen as intrinsic?[22] This question can be answered in the affirmative if it can be demonstrated that some properties are instantiated by Yhwh because of the relations they bear to other things, while others are not.[23] In this sense, Yhwh's absolute (as opposed to his generic) godhood is assumed to be an intrinsic or nonrelational property that Yhwh has, quite independently of relationships to other things. This explains why the concept of absolute Godhood is not applied to other entities, for instance the king, messengers, spirits of the dead, abstract objects, lesser heavenly beings, superlative phenomena, and so on. Two interesting questions arise as a result: first, whether any text of the Hebrew Bible assumes that there are any other philosophically interesting intrinsic properties of

---

22. For a detailed philosophical discussion, see Brian Weatherson, "Intrinsic vs. Extrinsic Properties," *SEP* [cited 12 January 2010]. Online: http://plato.stanford.edu/archives/fall2008/entries/intrinsic-extrinsic/.

23. For a shorter introduction and this brief explanation, see "Intrinsic and Extrinsic Properties (Philosophy)," *Wikipedia, The Free Encyclopedia* [cited 12 January 2010]. Online: http://en.wikipedia.org/w/index.php?title=Intrinsic_and_extrinsic_properties_(philosophy)&oldid=295677194.

Yhwh; and second, how the text's own ideas of what is intrinsic and what is extrinsic are to be restated in philosophical terms.

11.4.3. PRIMARY VERSUS SECONDARY PROPERTIES

Does the Hebrew Bible assume a distinction between primary and secondary properties of divinity? If so, which properties of Yhwh are assumed to be primary and which secondary? Two intuitive ideas are at play here: first, that primary properties are objective features of the world and on many accounts are also fundamental properties that explain why things have the other properties they do, and second, that secondary properties are, by contrast, qualities that somehow depend on perception and interpretation. The question is what, if anything, the texts of the Hebrew Bible take for granted on this matter. The task of the philosophical theologian of the Hebrew Bible is to give a philosophical description of this. Again, pluralism in the texts should be left as it is and merely described and compared in nondistortive philosophical language—there is no need for harmonization or evaluative assessments.

11.4.4. FIXED-DEGREE VERSUS MULTIGRADE PROPERTIES

Do we encounter a distinction between so-called fixed-degree and multigrade properties in representations of Yhwh in the Hebrew Bible? Many predicates of Yhwh can be shown to be multigrade or variably polyadic if it can be demonstrated that they are assumed to be true of various numbers of things.[24] For example, the predicate "is holy" is applied not only to Yhwh but also to Israel, religious artifacts, sacred spaces, cultic functionaries, and so on. In thisf sense, Yhwh's holiness is assumed to be a polyadic property.

Such multigrade predicates were very common (e.g., Yhwh as "personal"). While some of them can be analyzed as conjunctions of fixed-degree predicates, many of them cannot. "Standard logic does not accommodate multigrade predicates."[25] Given their commonality owing to anthropomorphisms in the god talk, however, if philosophical theologians

---

24. Swoyer, "Properties."
25. Ibid.

of the Hebrew Bible intend to use properties as semantic values of Hebrew predicates, then they need to use the notion of multigrade properties.

11.4.5. STRUCTURED VERSUS UNSTRUCTURED PROPERTIES

Is this distinction functional in the context of the Hebrew Bible's conception of Yhwh? Here biblical scholars might ask whether a given Hebrew Bible text assumes a distinction between what may be called simple and compound properties of Yhwh. Compound properties of Yhwh would be those properties of the divine which, if owned, imply the possession of other properties. In this regard, Yhwh's divinity might be seen as a compound property with some of his other properties being simple ones that are actually part of his being a god, for instance his immortality.[26]

11.4.6. FIRST-ORDER VERSUS HIGHER-ORDER PROPERTIES

Does the Hebrew Bible assume a hierarchy of properties arranged according to order? First-order properties and relations would be those that can only be instantiated by Yhwh *qua* individual. [27] For example, being spiritual can be instantiated by Yhwh and by other spiritual entities and phenomena. But the Hebrew Bible does not assume that the property of spirit is itself a spirit. It exists only as a trope (in its metaphysical sense of spiritual nature of something or somebody). "It is natural to suppose, however, that many first-order properties and relations can themselves have properties and relations."[28] Here again we might think of Yhwh's property of divinity (e.g., generic godhood). Thus the property of Yhwh's divinity is thought to exemplify the property of being a type of entity. And of course, once we think of second-order properties for Yhwh, it is natural to wonder whether there are third-order properties (properties of second-order or, perhaps in cumulative fashion, of second- and first-order properties), and so on up through ever higher orders.[29]

---

26. Ibid.
27. Ibid.
28. Ibid.
29. As the aforementioned resource notes, "this metaphysical picture finds a formal parallel in higher order logic. On one common system of classification, we move from familiar first-order logic to second-order logic by adding first-order variables, from second- to third-order logic by adding second-order constants, from

11.4.7. SUPERVENIENT VERSUS NONSUPERVENIENT PROPERTIES

Does the Hebrew Bible presuppose a distinction between supervenient properties of Yhwh and their opposite?[30] This can be said to be the case if in a given text a certain set of properties of Yhwh supervenes upon a second set, in the sense that no two things can differ with respect to the first set of properties without also differing with respect to the second set. In slogan form, "there cannot be an *A*-difference in Yhwh without a *B*-difference." In the Hebrew Bible, the property of Yhwh's generic divinity again provides an apt example of a supervenient property, inasmuch as many of his properties are what they are because he is assumed to be a god, and any hypothetical change in the property of generic godhood would imply that some of his other properties would not remain unaffected (e.g., his immortality). Thus the Hebrew Bible also assumes a distinction between absolute Godhood as a property and the properties of absolute Godhood, and assumes that a change in the former will of necessity involve a change in the latter. In this way, the property of absolute Godhood (Yhwh's haecceity) is believed to supervene on his properties of absolute Godhood.[31]

11.4.8. INITIAL VERSUS EMERGENT PROPERTIES

Because much of the Hebrew Bible knows nothing of the doctrine of divine simplicity, and because its variety of theism is often analogous to what might today be classified to as more similar to (though still different from) something like a combination of certain types of open and process theologies (albeit in prephilosophical primitive format), Yhwh's own character develops from a relatively simple state into a complex system over time (by analogy).[32] This represents the diachronic counterpart of the synchronic essential/accidental properties distinction, although the dis-

---

third- to fourth-order logic by adding third-order variables, and so on up, alternating constants and variables at successive steps" (ibid.).

30. For the concept, see Brian McLaughlin and Karen Bennett, "Supervenience," *SEP* [cited 14 December 2010]. Online: http://plato.stanford.edu/archives/fall2008/entries/supervenience/.

31. This distinction also comes from Swoyer, "Properties."

32. For specific treatment, see Timothy O'Connor and Hong Yu Wong, "Emergent Properties," *SEP* [cited 11 January 2010]. Online: http://plato.stanford.edu/archives/spr2009/entries/properties-emergent/.

tinction can be made on a synchronic level as well. Permanent properties are those durable characteristics that Yhwh is assumed to exhibit always and everywhere, whereas emergent properties arise over time as a result of interaction, role playing, relations, functions, and so on.[33]

Even so, most biblical theologies fail to draw the above distinctions. As a result they tend to be tempted—in their desire for system and closure—to paint a static and unified picture that is far more closely related to the philosophical distortions they decry than a descriptive application of philosophical property theory could ever be. From this it should again be readily apparent that the distortive element in utilizing philosophical theories comes not from their being philosophical, but from a habit biblical scholars have of looking to the wrong philosophical discussions either for terminology or for a scapegoat on which to blame their own philosophical and eisegetical misreadings. The often dogmatic and over-simplified discussion of the attributes of Yhwh in biblical theology would do well to take cognizance of property distinctions presupposed by the Hebrew Bible itself, but which become discernible to us only through the painstaking philosophical analysis of metaphysical assumptions within individual texts.

11.4.9 DIVINE PROPERTIES AS ESSENTIALLY FUZZY

Not only should different kinds of properties be distinguished and the nature of each be classified, but each property of Yhwh should itself also be subjected to philosophical analysis. This could be done with reference both to individual textual representations and with reference to the Hebrew Bible as a whole (in a comparative manner allowing for pluralism). On either account, it is *prima facie* apparent that the properties of Yhwh and the properties of absolute Godhood in the Hebrew Bible are inherently or intrinsically fuzzy.[34] We are never told the precise quality and quantities involved.[35]

---

33. An example of a literary-critical perspective on initial and emergent properties is found in Jack Miles, *God: A Biography.*

34. One Old Testament theologian who recognizes this time and again is Ludwig Köhler, who often asks questions concerning boundaries of properties in his *Old Testament Theology.*

35. In philosophy, it is common to make a distinction between fuzziness and vagueness. For an introduction to the latter as philosophical problem, see Roy

Among the so-called divine attributes examined by philosophers of religion proper, none has received more discussion in the literature than "omnipotence," defined by some as "perfect power." The Hebrew Bible knows no such word and divine power is always a fuzzy property. So while a few texts imply that nothing is impossible for Yhwh, even this idea itself belongs more to the rhetoric of the hyperbolic flattery of authority than to a philosophical-logical context of discourse suggesting that Yhwh is assumed to be able to do everything logically possible. Reading between the lines, there are many things that Yhwh cannot do, and different texts presuppose different limitations on the part of the deity. These are not only logical limitations—they also concern the fact that in some texts one might speak of divine weakness rather than limitation. Thus Yhwh can even, in some texts, be depicted as afraid of human potential (Gen 3:22, 11:7); defeated by technology (Judg 1:12); or in need of replenishing his vital powers (Exod 31:18). Again, I am not claiming that this view is found throughout the Hebrew Bible, since theological pluralism in the text involves the juxtaposing of traditions featuring Yhwh as a more or less powerful character.

What it comes down to in general is that while Yhwh is indeed said to be powerful (and holy, wise, merciful, etc.), we cannot say for sure just how much of this property is actually instantiated, or assume that possessing any given property means that its opposite is absent. Similarly, being merciful and good does not mean that Yhwh cannot at times be ruthless and evil. The same goes with reference to properties such as power and knowledge: many texts presuppose that Yhwh is not cognizant of something when it happens, does not expect it to happen and cannot do anything to prevent it, even though the text presupposes Yhwh has all the power possible at his disposal and the ability to know everything.

The exclusive categories of "perfect being" theology are thus completely out of place here, so that when it comes to determining what is assumed in the Hebrew Bible to make Yhwh *Yhwh*, we are left with a "sorites paradox."

The sorites paradox is the name given to a class of paradoxical arguments, also known as "little-by-little" arguments, which arise as a result of the indeterminacy surrounding limits of application of the predicates involved. For example, the concept of a heap appears to lack sharp

Sorensen, "Vagueness," *SEP* [cited 14 December 2010]. Online: http://plato.stanford.edu/archives/fall2008/entries/vagueness/.

boundaries and, as a consequence of the subsequent indeterminacy surrounding the extension of the predicate "is a heap," no one grain of wheat can be identified as making the difference between being a heap and not being a heap. Given then that one grain of wheat does not make a heap, it would seem to follow that two do not, thus three do not, and so on. In the end it would appear that no amount of wheat can make a heap. We are faced with paradox because, from apparently true premises and through seemingly uncontroversial reasoning, we arrive at an apparently false conclusion.[36]

The logic governing the representation of divine properties in the Hebrew Bible is therefore itself fuzzy, for it is not certain how much of a given property is assumed to make Yhwh who he is assumed to be, or how much less makes it seem odd to continue the identification.

11.4.10. Properties and Divine Complexity

Complexity in the divine condition is a *second-order* property, that is, a property of Yhwh's first-order properties such as wisdom, power, holiness, and the like. The notion of complexity may entail that Yhwh's (real) first-order properties are thought to be from his (real) second-order properties. But is it assumed that all of Yhwh's (real) second-order properties are different from his (real) first-order properties (and thus that Yhwh's complexity is different from whatever first-order properties sufficed for differentiation in the generic concept of divinity)?

Probably not. Since complexity and other divine second-order properties supervene on Yhwh's first-order properties, the latter is assumed to entail the former; nothing can instantiate each of Yhwh's (real) first-order properties without also instantiating such properties as complexity. But the converse may not be true. Is Yhwh not thought of as complex in the defined sense (namely, as having all first-order real properties different from each other and each with its own being)? If Yhwh is thought of in this way, then divine complexity is not assumed to be different from the real first-order properties that are assumed to suffice to make Yhwh a god.

In view of the above, and in view of biblical theologians' discussion of Yhwh's forms of manifestation and Yhwh as an entity with attributes, it

---

36. Dominic Hyde, "Sorites Paradox," *SEP* [cited 10 December 2010]. Online: http://plato.stanford.edu/archives/fall2008/entries/sorites-paradox/.

must be admitted that the Hebrew Bible often presupposes Yhwh's being to be a substance in the Aristotelean sense.

> In the millennia-old Aristotelian tradition, as well as some of the early modern traditions that follow it, substances are the things that instantiate properties. Substance theory, or substance attribute theory, is an ontological theory about objecthood, positing that a *substance is distinct from its properties*. This is part of essentialism, in that substance can also be a descriptor of an object's being (ontology) and/or nature.[37]

Yhwh's substance is therefore that permanent property without which he would no longer remain himself and therefore would become some other object (as opposed to being manifested in another object).

Thus the concept of substance, unpopular as it may be in contemporary philosophy, helps to explain, for instance, transitions in state such as theophanies. Let us take Yhwh appearing in a burning bush, in a cloud, in a dream, in person, and so on. Substance theory maintains that there is a "substance" within and behind the phenomena, which remains unchanged through the transitions and which is both the different manifestations of Yhwh and Yhwh himself. None of Yhwh's forms of manifestation would then be Yhwh's substance, as the god is assumed to be a bare particular behind it all. In other words, Yhwh's ability to change form means that he is seen as having a substance that exists independently of its properties (light, size, gender, etc.) and that his essential nature is assumed to be a bare particular.

11.5. The Philosophical Problem of Yhwh's Identity

Many Hebrew Bible scholars will be familiar with the concept of "identity" as it figures within the context of the social sciences. There it refers to a person's conception and expression of his or her individuality or group affiliations (such as national identity and cultural identity). In the study of ancient Israelite religion, the problem of identity has entered the discussion primarily with reference to the psychology of the stereotypical

---

37. "Substance Theory," *Wikipedia, The Free Encyclopedia* [cited August 13 2012]. Online: http://en.wikipedia.org/w/index.php?title=Substance_theory&oldid= 507106680.

Hebrew male[38] and the social-political matrix of "ancient Israel."[39] Absent in biblical scholarship is research that takes an interest in the philosophical problems related to personal identity, despite the fact that these have "been discussed since the origins of western philosophy and most major figures have had something to say about it."[40] Today, personal identity remains an issue for both Continental and analytic philosophy.

The basic problematic in philosophical research on personal identity concerns the question of what it takes for a person to persist from moment to moment—or, in other words, for the same person to exist at different moments. Usually the problem takes on diachronic dimensions in that what is sought is a set of necessary and sufficient conditions for the identity of persons over time. Yet there is also the synchronic problem of personal identity, which involves the question of what features or traits characterize a given person at any one time.[41] For the most part, what is of interest is human personhood.

In the present section, my concern lies with the identity of Yhwh in the Hebrew Bible. In the past, research on Yhwh's identity has been limited to literary, theological, religio-historical, and social-scientific readings.[42] What makes this study different is that its methodology is both philosophical and historical. Wary of the danger of imposing distortive philosophical categories onto biblical conceptual backgrounds, no attempt is made to construct any systematic or philosophically credible "biblical" perspective from the ancient prephilosophical texts. Rather, by asking the questions of philosophical identity theory in the context of the many and variable textual representations of Yhwh in the Hebrew Bible, this chapter aims only at an elucidation of their complexity. No normative metaphysical claims are made

---

38. Ludwig Köhler, *Hebrew Man* (London: SCM, 1956); and Clines: *Interested Parties*.

39. For instance Philip R. Davies, *In Search of Ancient Israel* (Sheffield: Sheffield Academic Press, 1992). Note also that postmodern social philosophy and philosophy of literature have been utilized in discussions of identity politics.

40. Eric T. Olson, "Personal Identity," *SEP* [cited 30 May 2011]. Online: http://plato.stanford.edu/archives/win2010/entries/identity-personal/.

41. Ibid.

42. For a literary example, see Miles, *God: A Biography*; and Carroll, *Wolf in the Sheepfold*. A theological example is Brueggemann, *Old Testament Theology*. Religio-historical examples include Patrick D. Miller, *Israelite Religion and Biblical Theology: Collected Essays* (Sheffield: Sheffield Academic Press, 2000); and Smith, *Memoirs of God*. For a social-scientific example, see Gottwald, *Tribes of Yahweh*.

with regard to the identity of any extratextual God, and all remarks pertain only to the literary character of Yhwh located within the world of the text.

While most accounts of personal identity in philosophy proper deal with *human* personhood, the same questions may be reframed and applied to the person represented by the character of Yhwh in the Hebrew Bible. Following the exposé of the philosophical problem of personal identity by Korfmacher and Olson, we may begin by noting that from a philosophical perspective there is no singular problem of Yhwh's personal identity in the text.[43] For this reason there can be only a wide range of loosely connected philosophical questions that can be asked with reference to the character of Yhwh, including the seven that follow.

11.5.1. BASIC QUESTIONS

First, who is the character of Yhwh's "I" in the world of the text assumed to be? Here we speak of Yhwh's "personal identity" in the sense of that which is assumed to make Yhwh the kind of person (in the philosophical sense) Yhwh is believed to be. Yhwh's identity consists roughly of what is assumed to make Yhwh unique as an individual and different from everything else. Of course, different texts offer different identity conditions for what makes Yhwh Yhwh, and no systematic account is possible. We may, however, by accepting theological pluralism, still look at how Yhwh is depicted as defining himself. Since in some contexts he lacks self-affirmations, we may look at the values and convictions the narrator uses to structure divine actions.

Yhwh's individual identity is a property (or set of properties) instantiated by the character Yhwh. Given the diachronic variability in characterization, however, the properties are those that Yhwh has only contingently: Yhwh's identity at t_1 (a point in time) might therefore be different from the one Yhwh has at t_2. Later representations of Yhwh may exchange Yhwh's earlier individual identity for a new one, while in texts with minimal characterization the narrator may get by without any explicitly defined identity for Yhwh's character. Second, there is Yhwh's godhood. We have dealt with this to some extent in the previous chapter, although there our focus was not on Yhwh per se. The question here is therefore more specific: What (as

---

43. Carsten Korfmacher, "Personal Identity," *IEP* [cited 30 May 2011]. Online: http://www.iep.utm.edu/person-i/; Olson, "Personal Identity."

opposed to who), according to a given text, is Yhwh assumed to be? What are the necessary and/or sufficient conditions for something to count as the kind of entity Yhwh is assumed to be? In other words, what was it about the character Yhwh that makes it seem meaningful to categorize Yhwh as a god as opposed to something else? What generic properties does Yhwh have to instantiate in order to be classified as a god? Also, what individual attributes does Yhwh have that other gods do not? Wherein lies Yhwh's uniqueness among the gods? At what point in the characterization does Yhwh's otherness become apparent? Note that what is required here is more than a theology of Yhwh's incomparability. A philosophical answer to the questions of what makes Yhwh divine would take the form: "Necessarily, Yhwh is a god, if and only if ... Yhwh ..." (with the blanks appropriately filled in).

Third, from a philosophical perspective there is the mystery of Yhwh's identity persistence. We have also touched on this matter in earlier remarks regarding modality in biblical god talk. The question to be asked here is the following: What does it take for Yhwh's character to persist from one span of narrated time to another—that is, for the same character to be recognizable as itself at different times within the world in the text? What sorts of changes can the characterization of Yhwh involve while nevertheless continuing to be about Yhwh? Conversely, we may also ask what boundaries must be crossed for Yhwh types of representation to come to an end? What determined which past or future version of Yhwh is considered to be more Yhwh-like? What is it about an earlier version vis-à-vis a later version of Yhwh, aside from the personal name, that makes it clear that one is dealing with Yhwh? These are the questions that can be asked about Yhwh's personal identity over time. An answer to them will take the form of an account of Yhwh's persistence conditions, or of a criterion of Yhwh's personal identity over time.[44]

Fourth, we may inquire about the epistemology in Yhwh's characterization in general, and evidence of Yhwh's personal identity in particular. How, according to the texts, can the reader know that Yhwh is appropriately characterized? What evidence bears on the question of whether Yhwh in one text is recognizable as the same Yhwh who was depicted

---

44. Based on the outline by Olson, "Personal Identity," one may say that historically this question frequently arises out of the belief that there is something essential and consistent in Yhwh's character. Whether this could happen depends on whether recharacterization necessarily brings Yhwh's earlier characterization to an end.

earlier? What does it mean if different kinds of evidence support opposing characterizations? One source of such evidence is, of course, first-person dialogue: if Yhwh refers to or remembers having done some particular action, then, according to that text, the deity in question is assumed to be Yhwh. Another source of evidence is phenomenal continuity: if Yhwh looks just like the one who appeared earlier or was in some sense spatio-temporally continuous with Yhwh, that might be another reason to think it is Yhwh one is dealing with. Which of these sources are assumed to be more fundamental? Moreover, given the fact that one is always dealing with a literary construct, did first-person memory by the character Yhwh count as evidence all by itself, or only insofar as it can be checked against other intertextual (source-critical) evidence?[45]

Fifth, there is the issue of a complex "population" within the character of Yhwh.[46] If we think of the persistence question as asking which of the characterizations of Yhwh introduced early in the history of Israelite religion have survived to become the ones at the end of it, we may also want to ask how many of these versions are embodied in the character in any given text. How does one determine the presence of a multiplicity of divine typologies? If there are, say, seven varieties of types of deity (typology of divinity being not an uncontroversial notion) in Yhwh's character in a particular representation, what facts—theological, literary, or other—made that the right number?

The question of population is not historical or literary; it does not ask what causes a certain number of divine profiles in Yhwh at a given time. The question is philosophical in its concern with what it means to be an entity constructed from a particular number of types. This is the problem of "synchronic identity," as opposed to the "diachronic identity" we encountered in the persistence question. In this case it is not about identity over time but about identity at a given moment in time. These are not separate, but it remains a fact that there are two kinds of situations in which we can ask how many profiles of Yhwh there are: synchronic situations

---

45. According to Olson, "Personal Identity," "The 'evidence question' dominated the philosophical literature on personal identity from the 1950s to the 1970s. It is important to distinguish it from the persistence question. What it takes for someone to persist through time is one thing; how we might find out whether they have is another."

46. See the section on "the Gods in Yahweh" in Miller, *The Religion of Ancient Israel*, 24–28.

involving just one representation of Yhwh, and diachronic ones involving many different historical contexts.

Sixth, what sort of thing, metaphysically speaking, is Yhwh assumed to be? This is not, as above, a question of genus, in other words what Yhwh's being a god entails. Rather, we are asking what is assumed about Yhwh's basic metaphysical nature. For instance, what, according to any given text, does Yhwh consist of? Is it spirit, matter, a mixture of the two, or something else? Where are Yhwh's spatial boundaries assumed to lie? More fundamentally, what is assumed to fix those boundaries? Is Yhwh assumed to be a substance—a metaphysically independent being—or is Yhwh assumed to be a state or an aspect of something else, or perhaps some sort of process or event? How variable in form can Yhwh be while still retaining his identity as Yhwh? Which properties does Yhwh have essentially, and which only accidentally or contingently?

Seventh, what matters in Yhwh's identity?[47] What, in the text, is the practical importance of facts about Yhwh's identity and persistence for the deity himself? Why does it matter to Yhwh? Why do the other characters or implied readers care about it? The only entity whose existence Yhwh cannot ignore is his own. Within the world in the text Yhwh has a special interest in his own life, unlike the interest he has in anyone else's. However, Yhwh's identity seems to matter practically both to himself and to those who worship him and create him as a character in their narratives and poetry. In this question, then, the problem pertains to the purpose of Yhwh's existence, that is, the meaning his character in the stories is assumed to experience in relation what is happening.

That completes our survey of some of the questions that have to be dealt with in the quest for a better understanding of Yhwh's personal identity in the Hebrew Bible. Though these seven questions are obviously related, "it is hard to find any important common feature" that makes them all questions about Yhwh's assumed personal identity.[48] They are different, and failing to keep them separate will only cause conceptual confusion. In the next section we shall take a closer look at some important distinctions with regard to Yhwh's personal identity, mainly in terms of the riddle of persistence.

---

47. See Derek Parfit, "The Unimportance of Identity," in *Personal Identity* (ed. R. Martin and J. Barresi; Malden, Mass.: Blackwell, 2003), 292–318.

48. Olson, "Personal Identity."

11.5.2. PERSISTENCE PROBLEMS VERSUS NUMERICAL/QUALITATIVE IDENTITY

The question of persistence in Yhwh's identity is one of the most pressing issues for any theological and philosophical discussions on the subject.[49] Yet, as in the case of the philosophy of mind proper, few concepts can be more prone to misunderstanding than Yhwh's identity over time. The reason for this is, as Olson observes, the fact that "the persistence question is often confused with other questions, or stated in a tendentious way."[50] The actual issue here concerns what, in the Hebrew Bible, is assumed to be necessary and sufficient for a past or future version of Yhwh's character to remain Yhwh. If we point to the character of Yhwh in a given text and then describe the deity as represented to exist at another time, we can ask whether we are referring to one character twice, or referring once to two characters. The persistence question asks what determines the answer to such questions (or what makes possible answers true or false).[51]

The persistence question should not be confused with the question of numerical identity. Yhwh (abbreviated to "Y") in text a (abbreviated to "a") and Yhwh in text b are numerically identical if and only if Y(a) and Y(b) are one entity rather than two. Technically, the personal identity of Yhwh is an instance of the relation of Yhwh's numerical identity, which is not the same as the persistence problem. Investigations into the nature of this identity must respect the formal properties that govern qualitative identity. Y(a) and Y(b) are qualitatively identical if and only if, for the set of nonrelational properties $P_1...P_n$ of Y(a), Y(b) only possesses $P_1...P_n$. ("A property may be called 'nonrelational' if its being borne by a substance is independent of the relations in which property or substance stand to other properties or substances."[52]) The concept of Yhwh's identity is thus uniquely defined by:

a. The logical laws of congruence: if Y(a) is identical with Y(b), then all nonrelational properties borne by Y(a) are borne by

---

49. See James Baillie, "Recent Work on Personal Identity," *Philosophical Books* 34/4 (1993): 193–206.

50. Olson, "Personal Identity."

51. Ibid.

52. Ibid.

Y(b), or formally "$\forall(Y(a), Y(b))[(Y(a) = Y(b)) \rightarrow (PY(a) = PY(b))]$; and

b. Reflexivity: every Y(a) is identical with itself, or formally "$\forall Y(a)(Y(a) = Y(a))$. (Note that congruence and reflexivity entail that identity be symmetric, "$\forall(Y(a), Y(b))[(Y(a) = Y(b)) \rightarrow (Y(b) = Y(a))]$, and transitive, "$\forall(Y(a), Y(b), Y(c))[((Y(a) = Y(b)) \& (Y(b) = Y(c))) \rightarrow (Y(a) = Y(c))]$).[53]

Philosophically speaking, nothing can make Yhwh numerically a different god from the one Yhwh is assumed to be. For Yhwh to be numerically different from himself is precisely for him not to be Yhwh. "This is not something that is the case with regard to personal identity in particular; it is simply a fact about the logic of identity."[54] To say that, after a certain event in the narratives of Israelite religion (the exodus or exile, for instance), Yhwh is a different god—or that Yhwh is no longer the god he once was—presumably means that, while Yhwh stills exists as a character in the world in the text, views about his nature have changed in some important ways. This kind of talk is actually thinking of Yhwh's individual identity in the sense of "Who is Yhwh's 'I'?" What is in view, therefore, is modality within the theological pluralism in the Hebrew Bible. It concerns the fact that in the history of Israelite religion Yhwh's character lost some of the properties that had made up its individual identity at a given time and acquired new ones. However, the question "Who is Yhwh's 'I'?" is not the persistence question.

Yhwh's numerical identity is, however, important for the Hebrew Bible's authors. Other characters cannot call on Yhwh without assuming that the entity called on is in fact Yhwh (1 Kgs 18; but see 1 Kgs 19). Of course, Yhwh's links to certain cultic places before the Deuteronomic centralization of the cult introduces some plurality within unity. The claim that Yhwh is one (Deut 6:4) presupposes a prephilosophical awareness of the problem of diffused numerical identity in the deity. However, in biblical narratives, the Yhwh who regrets his own actions and holds Israel accountable for breaking the covenant with him assumes numerical identity between multiple source characterizations. The question of what makes the many personas of Yhwh numerically the same given theological

---

53. See Korfmacher, "Personal Identity."
54. Ibid.

changes over time is therefore what constitutes the heart of the diachronic problem of Yhwh's personal identity.

Just as the persistence question must not be confused with the question of numerical identity, so too the problem of Yhwh's numerical identity should not be confused with the question of Yhwh's qualitative identity. Y(a) and Y(b) are qualitatively identical when they are exactly similar. Alternative versions of Yhwh are not qualitatively identical—one can usually tell them apart—even if in the tradition they are numerically identical. This is what makes Yhwh a variable character. In literary fiction, a past or future version of Yhwh need not be, at that past or future time, exactly like Yhwh at a given present point in order to be Yhwh (that is, in order to be numerically identical with Yhwh).[55] A character of fiction can be represented in many contradictory ways and be qualitatively different without losing its numerical identity.

This is one reason why Yhwh *qua* Yhwh need not remain qualitatively the same throughout the history of Israelite religion. Yhwh's characterizations definitely changed. For example, in general Yhwh became more distant and mediated; new interpersonal relationships were formed with new human characters while others became distant memories, and so on.[56] So the question regarding the persistence of Yhwh's character is not asking what it takes for a past or future version of Yhwh to be qualitatively just like Yhwh at any given time. It concerns what it takes for a past or future being to be Yhwh as opposed to someone or something other than Yhwh.

In the Hebrew Bible, it is thus numerical identity rather than qualitative identity that assures Yhwh's persistence over time. On this matter many historians of Israelite religion and biblical theologians have been essentialists and Platonists, eagerly distinguishing between text and world, between appearance and reality, and between orthodox/true types of characterization vis-à-vis foreign/inauthentic varieties. But while modern scholarship recognizes the fictitious nature of the literary character Yhwh, the question remains as to what the characters in the world in the text assumed. Surely in the world in the text Yhwh is not considered to be only a fiction. Despite the remarks about fictionalism and some implied authors made earlier, it cannot be denied that the biblical characters and many of the biblical authors were no doubt realists.[57]

---

55. Miles, *God: A Biography*, 2. See also Carroll, *Wolf in the Sheepfold*, 41.
56. Miller, *Israelite Religion*, 22; Smith, *Memoirs of God*, 12.
57. Thompson, *Bible in History*, 317.

In the metaphysics of the world in the text, what accounts for the continuity of Yhwh's person can be compared to what contemporary philosophers of mind refer to as "soul-centered" theories. Thus, according to ancient Israelite theological mereology, Yhwh too has a person (or נפשׁ) that anticipates, mourns, loves, abhors, is refreshed, is wearied, and so on (e.g., Lev 26:11–12; Isa 42:1; Jer 5:9; 6:8; 32:41; Zech 11:8). This is assumed to be some sort of core entity to whom thoughts and emotions occur. Yhwh's character may change in form and be revealed in or accompanied by natural phenomena. Yet, around all the variable forms and manifestations thereof, some inner essence of vitality was assumed to remain. And while neither philosophers nor Hebrew Bible scholars today may want to speak of Yhwh's "soul" (in the Neo-Platonic/Christian sense), the folk metaphysics in the world of the text often presupposes a rather similar notion as conceptually adequate.[58]

If the confusion of qualitative with numerical identity is one source of misunderstanding about the persistence question for Yhwh, another source of confusion is what it takes for Yhwh to remain the same kind of god over time (e.g., merciful, loving, just) The idea is that if Yhwh's nature were to alter in certain ways (i.e., through early dystheistic tendencies that made way for a more benign precursor to later proto-perfect-being theologies)—then historically critically one might wonder if Yhwh is really the god he was before. For example, if early in the history of Israelite religion Yhwh was credited with the actualization of metaphysical, moral, and natural evil, but later was perceived as almost omnibenevolent, the question becomes whether and how we are dealing with the same god—in other words, which one is the real Yhwh? Unless we consider severe mutability an option and stick with a literary ontology and fiction, this question is not easy to answer (but cf. Ps 77).

There is another type of identity change in the Hebrew Bible. It is seen when tradition criticism reveals how the depiction of Yhwh's memories about memorable events changed over time, for instance in reconfigurations of the Exodus tradition (see Jer 7:22; Amos 5:25 in relation to the book of Leviticus).[59] This also occurs when the depiction of Yhwh's personality changes dramatically via the introduction or conflation of multi-

---

58. James Barr, *The Garden of Eden and the Hope of Immortality* (London: SCM, 1993), 112.

59. For antirealist tendencies in the Hebrew Bible and the charge of reductionism, see Cupitt, *Taking Leave of God*, 43.

ple sources or the introduction of new mythological motifs, for instance in Hosea or Ezekiel). Then there are the results of redaction criticism, which show how Yhwh's character (or the divine will) underwent a profound moral makeover in postexilic editorial emendations of legal precepts.

Given these diachronic changes, the question of what it takes for Yhwh to remain the same kind of god is related, but not identical to, the persistence question. "It is not even a question about numerical identity."[60] If it were, it would answer itself: Yhwh necessarily remains numerically the same for as long as Yhwh exists. Questions about Yhwh's identity thus need to specify whether what is meant refers to numerical identity, qualitative identity, individual psychological identity, or something else. Otherwise, conceptual confusion is inevitable.

11.5.3. Reductionist Perspectives

Possible answers to the question of Yhwh's personal identity and the character's persistence over time are many. For similar reasons, contemporary personal identity theory in philosophy proper often works using reductionist perspectives, concentrating on the relative merits of different criteria of identity and related methodological questions.[61] Transposing the matter to the study of the Hebrew Bible, reductionist theories of Yhwh's personal identity will have in common the contention that facts about Yhwh's personal identity stood in an adequate reduction-relation to sets of subpersonal facts $SF_1.SF_n$ about property continuities, in such a way as to issue in biconditionals of the form "$Y(a)$ at t_1 is identical to $Y(b)$ at t_2 if and only if $Y(a)$ at t_1 and $Y(b)$ at t_2 stand in a continuity-relation fully describable by SF_x."

Thus, "any given set of subpersonal facts will impose demands, in forms of necessary and sufficient conditions, upon the kinds of adventures the character" of Yhwh can survive in persisting from t_1 to t_2.[62] The sets of necessary and sufficient conditions determined by these sets of subpersonal facts will constitute the various criteria of Yhwh's personal identity. "In a search for the necessary and sufficient conditions for the sustenance of personal identity relations between" representations of Yhwh, the ques-

---

60. Olson, "Personal Identity."

61. See Brian Garrett, "Personal Identity and Reductionism," *Philosophy and Phenomenological Research* 51 (1991): 361–73.

62. Korfmacher, "Personal Identity."

tion to be asked concerns which type of continuity relations *SF* could describe.[63] Almost all proposed answers to the persistence question will then fall into one of three categories.

First, most philosophers writing on personal identity since the early twentieth century have endorsed some version of what is called the "psychological approach." On this view some psychological relation is necessary or sufficient (or both) for Yhwh to persist. If we opt for psychological criteria of Yhwh's personal identity, we hold that psychological continuity relations in the text, that is, overlapping chains of direct psychological connections (beliefs, desires, intentions, experiential memories, character traits, and so forth) constitute the personal identity of the character Yhwh. There are three versions of the psychological criterion: the narrow version demands psychological continuity in Yhwh to be caused "normally," "the wide version permits any reliable cause, and the widest version allows any cause to be sufficient to secure psychological continuity."[64]

Many biblical theologians would regard as obvious the idea that the character of Yhwh's persistence is intrinsically related to the continuity in the character of the deity's memory and self-expression. Cashing out this conviction in theoretical terms, however, will be notoriously difficult. Tradition and redaction criticism show variation in the details of the character of Yhwh's memories such that accounts tend to differ in details (e.g., the different *ipsissima verba* in regarding the Sabbath commandment in Exod 20:8 and Deut 5:12). The question biblical scholars should ask is whether it makes sense to apply this criterion when any memory of Yhwh is involved. Surely Yhwh's psychological profile is relative to whatever the narrator of the mental life of this character makes it to be.

A second idea might be that Yhwh's identity through time consists in some brute physical relation. Yhwh is that past or future being that has Yhwh's body, or is the same divine being that he is.[65] This can be called a "somatic approach"[66] and should not be confused with the view that physical evidence has some sort of priority over psychological evidence in finding out if the character is Yhwh, which has to do with the "evidence

---

63. Ibid.

64. Ibid.

65. See Benjamin D. Sommer, *The Bodies of God and the World of Ancient Israel* (Cambridge: Cambridge University Press, 2011).

66. Olson, "Personal Identity."

question."[67] In the world of the text Yhwh is usually not assumed to be omnipresent in the technical sense, but appears to be located wherever his character's body shows up. Yhwh's body is not often referred to, but it tends to be presupposed in the character's appearance and movements, in references to divine body parts or the use of certain objects, and so on.[68]

A few biblical scholars endorse the somatic approach. Here, however, they are again Platonists, assuming that Yhwh's body is only human in appearance (Yhwh allegedly only "appears" in human form). These theologians like to speak of anthropomorphism and metaphor even when the texts clearly presuppose that Yhwh's original form is in fact humanoid (because humans were literally created in the divine image) and that religious language describing Yhwh's body can be univocally applied. Again the argument in favor of this claim is the way in which the character relates to itself and everything else. So while many biblical theologians would say that Yhwh is incorporeal in order to be philosophically vogue, this is anachronistic and not at all a historically descriptive assessment. In any case, wherever continuity in Yhwh's character is assumed to involve Yhwh's being a distinct embodied being (e.g., theophanies), the texts often assume that some sort of bodily criterion of Yhwh's personal identity was epistemologically sufficient.

There is a downside to this view. If Yhwh *qua* God can change form, using embodiment as a criterion is complicated. Moreover, aniconistic trajectories assume that there should not (cannot?) be a pictorial identity marker for Yhwh. That being said, elements of the somatic approach have the virtue of being compatible with related elements in ancient Israelite error theories of allotheism. The polemical critique which holds that idols do not display vital signs and actions actually presupposes divine embodiment, albeit with working senses and some fluidity in its forms of manifestation[69] (see also Ps 94; Isa 44).

Third, both the psychological and somatic approaches to Yhwh's personal identity would agree that in the world of the text it is assumed that there is something that it takes for Yhwh to persist—that Yhwh's identity through time consists in or necessarily follows from something other than itself. The third view, anticriterialism, would deny this. We see this whenever commentators imply that there were no informative, non-

---

67. Ibid.
68. See Sommer, *Bodies of God*, 3.
69. Ibid., 2.

trivial persistence conditions for Yhwh. That is, the character of Yhwh's personal persistence is assumed to be an ultimate and nonanalyzable fact operating according to the boundless rules of fiction.[70] While psychological and physiological continuities are evidential criteria, these do not constitute necessary and/or sufficient conditions for Yhwh's personal identity.

We may distinguish between two versions of anticriterialism.[71] In the first version it is nonreductive and wholly noninformative, denying that Yhwh's personal identity follows from anything other than itself. Here the label "identity mysticism" (*IM*)[72] is most appropriate: *IM*: $Y(a)$ at t_1 is identical to $Y(b)$ at t_2 if and only if $Y(a)$ at t_1 is identical to $Y(b)$ at t_2. The idea of identity mysticism will sound strange, given that Hebrew Bible theologians of the past have denied any mystical ideas in ancient Israelite religion. The view plays only an indirect role in contemporary personal identity theory, and is to be distinguished from a more popular version of the simple view, according to which personal identity relations are weakly reductive (*WR*) and in independence noninformative (*INI*): *WR-INI*: $Y(a)$ at t_1 is identical to $Y(b)$ at t_2 if and only if there is some fact F_1 about $Y(a)$ at t_1, and some fact F_2 about $Y(b)$ at t_2, and F_1 and F_2 are irreducible to facts about the subject's character, and $Y(a)$ at t_1 is identical with $Y(b)$ at t_2 in virtue of the fact that the propositions stating F_1 and F_2 differ only insofar as that "$Y(a)$" and "t_1" occur in the former where "$Y(a)$" and "t_2" occur in the latter. "*WR-INI* is weakly reductive in the sense that, while the identity relation in question can be reduced to a further domain, the further domain itself typically exhibits elements of nonreducibility and/or resistance to full physical explanation."[73]

In their most prominent variants, these elements are the result of references to spiritual or immaterial substances and/or properties. *WR-INI* may entail *IM* but does not do so necessarily: it is conceivable that personal identity relations for Yhwh in the Hebrew Bible consist of something that is itself neither identical with nor reducible to a spiritual substance; neither identical with nor reducible to aggregates or parts of character traits. If this is the case with Yhwh's characterization, however, then it is merely weakly reductive, because the identity of the phenomenon that

70. See Carroll, *Wolf in the Sheepfold*, 37; and Thompson, *The Bible in History*.
71. Korfmacher, "Personal Identity."
72. Ibid.
73. Ibid.

specifies the necessary and sufficient conditions for Yhwh's personal identity does not itself follow from anything other than itself. "While a weakly reductive criterion of personal identity relations is explicable in terms of the identities of phenomena" other than Yhwh's person, "the identities of these phenomena themselves are not explicable in other terms: their identity may have been, as we would suppose 'soul identity' to be, 'strict and philosophical' instead of merely 'loose and popular.'"[74]

11.5.4 NARRATIVE IDENITY?

Thus far we have been assuming that the criterion of personal identity involves a reidentification question: what were the conditions under which Yhwh as depicted in one text could be properly reidentified in another text? Answering this question calls for a criterion of numerical identity for Yhwh across time, a criterion of what makes Yhwh as characterized the same thing as itself at different times. However, according to Schechtman,[75] what is actually more appropriate is an attempt to answer the characterization question. In short, this approach asks about the conditions under which various psychological characteristics, experiences, and actions were properly attributable to Yhwh.

One reason for turning to this question may stem from recognizing the metaphysical difficulties various theories of numerical identity run into.[76] Here the concern aligns with the notion of divine action in the narrative: "What makes those actions, for which Yhwh is held responsible, Yhwh's?" And in each case, what makes some feature Yhwh's may actually be making reference to a nonnumerical type of identity, a type of identity encountered in the crises of belief in ancient Israel: "Who was Yhwh really?" "This is the question of identity as proper attributability," as providing an account of what is supposed to be Yhwh's true self and the various attributes genuinely belonging to it.[77]

---

74. Ibid.

75. Marya Schechtman, *The Constitution of Selves* (Ithaca, N.Y.: Cornell University Press, 1996).

76. Ibid., 26–70.

77. David Shoemaker, "Personal Identity and Ethics," *SEP* [cited 15 August 2012]. Online: http://plato.stanford.edu/archives/spr2012/entries/identity-ethics/.

In other words, "we are dealing with what can be called the narrative criterion of personal identity: what makes an action, experience, or psychological characteristic properly" attributable to Yhwh (and thus a proper part of Yhwh's true identity) is its correct incorporation into the stories featuring the character of the same name.[78] Narrative identity is thus really about a kind of psychological unity in the character" of Yhwh, "but not just an artless or random unity."[79] For Yhwh to have a personal identity,

> the character's experiences must have been actively unified, must have been gathered together into the life of one narrative ego by virtue of stories that weave them together, giving them a kind of coherence and intelligibility they wouldn't otherwise have. This is how the various experiences and events come to have any real meaning at all: rather than being merely isolated events, they are part of a larger collection of stories that relate them to one another.[80]

This may well be the case within the context of Yhwh's textual representations.

The narrative criterion of personal identity purports to account for the character of Yhwh's overridingly ethical concerns in a far more adequate way than accounts of numerical identity do. So it makes sense for Yhwh's character to anticipate via disclosure through prophetic revelation or intertextual allusion some future experiences that will fit coherently and accurately into the ongoing stories featuring Yhwh himself. By way of the popular distinction between narrated time and time of narration, Yhwh's character is depicted as constantly extending grand narratives into the future. The narrative criterion implies that what makes some past action Yhwh's (for which Yhwh becomes worthy of praise or blame) is that it flows from what is believed to be Yhwh's own central values, beliefs, and experiences, and that there is a coherent story uniting it to the other elements of his life.

However, there are problems with this account. For one thing, it is not entirely clear why on the level of the metaphysical assumptions of the world in the text a narrative is necessary to unite the various experiences

---

78. Ibid.
79. Ibid.
80. Ibid.

and events of Yhwh's life into a coherent whole. The character may have robust psychological unity without having any kind of story of the past attached to it (e.g., Gen 1). But even if we allow for biblical narratives to do this work, or for third-person narratives to count, it remains unclear just what role a narrative is playing here at all. For surely, given the theological pluralism in the text, we must allow that, depending on the point of view in the text we opt for, some narratives must have gotten it wrong, and if we allow for that, then it seems we must admit that it is not the narrative itself that makes the various events and experiences united with one another; rather, "they must be united with one another independently, and the (correct) narrative just serves as a kind of post hoc overlay, an articulation of the preexisting unity."[81]

"Perhaps the most serious worry comes from the fact that, as it stands, narrative identity depends on numerical identity."[82] What matters to the narrator is the necessary presupposition that Yhwh himself persists, but this is an issue of numerical identity. Another way to put this is that Yhwh cannot be a person, on the narrative view, unless the character of Yhwh gathers up the various experiences as a subject into a coherent narrative. But then the identity of Yhwh as subject of experiences must be preserved without changes across time for its experiences to be so gathered up. This is not the case, and yet the fact remains that narrative identity for Yhwh presupposes numerical identity.

11.5.5 The Trouble with a Literary Ontology

In order to discover what the Hebrew Bible's own prephilosophical or folk-philosophical attitudes are toward the issue of Yhwh's personal identity, we may raise the question of what an author had to do in order to re-create Yhwh in Yhwh's own image within a new historical, literary, or social context. We can examine how it could be ascertained whether the resulting character was indeed a candidate for being identical with Yhwh as represented long before. For there to have been a thing such as a stable and recognizable character for Yhwh, a number of conditions would have been necessary and sufficient for Yhwh to persist. Within the world in the text, those conditions would involve psychology, or brute physical continuity,

---

81. Ibid.
82. Ibid.

and so on; or they would be trivial and uninformative, as anticriterialism has it.

In research on Yhwh's identity in some larger overlapping parts of biblical literature, this is certainly the way to go. Within larger trajectories (e.g., the Deuteronomistic History), there is some sense of psychological continuity in the sense that the character of Yhwh tends to appeal to memories of his own earlier relations with Israel. In other postexilic combinations of preexilic sources, the character expressing Yhwh's current thoughts at the time of narration is assumed to be an aggregate of multiple previous character stages, each of which was "in some sense psychologically continuous with each of the others and not with anything else."[83] Here the personal identity of Yhwh's character does persist by virtue of psychological continuity, that is to say that Yhwh's temporal boundaries are determined by relations of psychological connectedness.

Overall, however, we may at last admit that, given the theological pluralism in the text, Yhwh's personal identity is simply indeterminate. There are prototypes and proxytypes for Yhwh's character in the sense of typicality effects for the category "God," thus making some characterizations seem more authentic than others to the mind of a modern reader. From a historical, descriptive and panbiblical perspective, however, it is more functional to use a model in which Yhwh is simply said to be identical to all his representations, no matter how diverse these may be. For the history of Israelite religion shows us that:

1. biblical authors can give Yhwh an appearance that bears no physical continuity or causal relation to the one he possessed before that text;
2. biblical authors can give new form or content to Yhwh's psychology, that is, that it is not necessary or sufficient for the new version of Yhwh to remember all of his own character's previous actions or experiences and that there do not have to be any causal connections between all the actions and experiences of Yhwh from before; and
3. the readerly question of whether or not the resulting version of Yhwh is "truly" or "purely" Yahwistic or, conversely, alien

---

83. Olson, "Personal Identity."

to orthodox Yahwism is, objectively speaking, essentially pejoratively ideological and/or meaningless.

This study's own suggestion, therefore, is that there is no unique right answer to the question of what it takes for the character Yhwh to persist as Yhwh. There are many "family resemblances" between different characterizations, but no essential properties or haecceities evident within the deity's multiple profiles. For example, the identity of the deity in Daniel and Qoheleth seems to presuppose two completely different sets of necessary and sufficient identity conditions. In every textual representation where Yhwh is depicted, there is a temporal part of Yhwh that exists only then. This gives us many likely character candidates for being Yhwh, all of which—depending on the context—may assume but not instantiate a combination of psychological, somatic and indefinable types of continuity in Yhwh's personal identity.

Because many mainstream Hebrew Bible scholars are Christians who accept pluralism yet remain Platonists at heart, theologically they will continue to make a distinction between Yhwh's absolute and relative identities. Others will assume the deity's character to be textually immanent, with no extratextual reference.[84] These critical and nonrealist views recognize that the personal identities of Yhwh in the Hebrew Bible take the form of a polythetic group with a spectrum of relative identities. Toward the near end of the spectrum, characterizations of Yhwh at t_1 are almost identical with characterizations of Yhwh at t_2; and toward the far end of the spectrum, characterizations of Yhwh at t_1 are not identical with characterizations of Yhwh at t_2 at all. There cannot be evidence for the existence of a sharp borderline between the cases in which characterizations of Yhwh at t_1 are, and the cases in which Yhwh at t_1 are not, identical with Yhwh at t_2. Hence, it is implausible to believe that such a borderline exists: Yhwh's absolute identity is indeterminate while relative identities have been fixed by way of representation and canonization.

The characterizations of Yhwh in the Hebrew Bible are as interlinked as are the components of a "rhizome," and his identity is a "becoming other" or "multiplicity."[85] Different utterances of the divine name will probably refer ambiguously to different candidates: to various sorts of

---

84. See Brueggemann, *Old Testament Theology*, 117 and *passim*.
85. For the meaning of these terms in Continental philosophy, see Deleuze and Guattari, *A Thousand Plateaus*, 9, 275.

psychologically interrelated aggregates, to a divine body, and perhaps to other phenomena as well. That would make it indeterminate which things, even which kinds of things, the multiplicity that is the character Yhwh is assumed to be. And insofar as the different candidates have different persistence conditions, it has always remained diachronically indeterminate what Yhwh's identity over time consists in. A nonessentialist approach to the matter is therefore best able to make sense of and do justice to the complexities and indeterminacy of the personal identity of the character Yhwh.

11.5.6. Yhwh's Identity across Possible Worlds

From a synchronic perspective (of theological pluralism), we exchange our thoughts on the problem of identity over time for the issue of identity across possible worlds.[86]

> The notion of transworld identity—"identity across possible worlds"—is the notion that the same object exists in more than one possible world (with the actual world treated as one of the possible worlds). It therefore has its home in a "possible worlds" framework for analyzing, or at least paraphrasing, statements about what is possible or necessary.[87]

Adapted to the context of literary fictionalism, to say that there is a transworld identity between God in Gen 1 and Yhwh in Gen 2 is to say that there is some possible world-in-the-text w_1, and some distinct possible world-in-the-text w_2, such that G_{Gen1} exists in w_1 and Y_{Gen2} exists in w_2, and G_{Gen1} is identical with Y_{Gen2}. In other words, to say that there is a transworld identity is to say that Yhwh exists in distinct possible worlds-in-the-text, or (more simply) that Yhwh exists in more than one possible world-in-the-text. In describing what is presupposed, biblical scholars can make use of descriptive philosophy of action to engage in a philosophical analysis of divine action in the biblical narratives.

Indeed, "the subject of transworld identity has been highly contentious, even among philosophers who accept the legitimacy of talk of pos-

---

86. Penelope Mackie, "Transworld Identity," *SEP* [cited 13 August 2009]. Online: http:// plato.stanford.edu/archives/fall2008/entries/identity-transworld/.
87. Ibid.

sible worlds."[88] Yet whether the metaphysics of modality has any real relevance for contemporary philosophy is for present purposes beside the point. Whatever the case may be, some of the stereotyped and adapted versions of the theory of transworld identity might still be considered to be useful as a way of modeling the theological pluralism deriving from the many "worlds-in-the-text." There is no unified or coherent "biblical" concept of Yhwh in the Hebrew Bible taken as a whole—there are only multiple conceptions of Yhwh. Nevertheless, it seems to be assumed that the entire Hebrew Bible is concerned with the same deity, and an interesting philosophical question is: how was this believed to be possible? How can the deity of the multiple worlds in the text have been considered to be the same entity when the properties instantiated by the many representations or personae of Yhwh differ to the point of incommensurability?

If perhaps it is said that the biblical authors were not cognizant of contradicting one another, and if on the level of redaction and canonization the matter cannot be settled to everyone's satisfaction, then granted a worst case scenario of complete deconstruction we shall have to opt for another form of modeling the ontology of the data. According to Francesco Berto, "David Hume and the empiricist tradition coined the slogan that the impossible cannot be believed, or even conceived."[89]

According to Berto,

> In *Positivismus und Realismus*, Moritz Schlick claimed that, while the merely practically impossible is still conceivable, the logically impossible, such as an explicit inconsistency, is simply unthinkable. Yet an opposite philosophical tradition argues that logical impossibilities are thinkable, but sometimes believable too. In *The Science of Logic*, Hegel already complained against one of the fundamental prejudices of logic as hitherto understood, namely that the contradictory cannot be imagined or thought. Our representational capabilities are not limited to the possible, for we appear to be able to imagine and describe impossibilities as well—perhaps without being aware that they are impossible. Hence the relatively young field called the logic of "impossible worlds."[90]

In philosophical logic,

---

88. Ibid.

89. Francesco Berto, "Impossible Worlds," *SEP* [cited 15 January 2010]. Online: http://plato.stanford.edu/archives/fall2009/entries/impossible-worlds/.

90. Ibid.

the concept of an impossible world (sometimes nonnormal world) is used to model certain phenomena that cannot be adequately handled using ordinary possible worlds. An impossible world, w, is the same sort of thing as a possible world (whatever that may be), except that it is in some sense "impossible." Depending on the context, this may mean that some contradictions are true at w, or that the normal laws of logic or of metaphysics fail to hold at w, or both.[91]

A survey of the literature on impossible worlds presents us with several different definitions. To put some order in the debate, Berto reduced them to four main items, ordered from the more to the less general, as explained here.[92]

The first definition has it that impossible worlds are worlds where the laws of logic are different. This is logic-relative: given some logic L, an impossible world is one in which the set of truths is not one that holds in any acceptable interpretation of L. A second, more restrictive, definition claims that impossible worlds are worlds where the set of things that hold is not the set of things that hold in any classical interpretation, that is, an acceptable interpretation of classical logic. A third still more specific definition has it that an impossible world is a world that realizes explicit contradictions, that is, where sentences of the form A and not A hold, against the law of noncontradiction.[93]

The possibilities this holds for describing the ontological rationale behind canonized pluralism for the ancient communities should be readily apparent. The logic of impossible worlds can offer the idea of the different worlds-in-the-texts as analogous to different intentional states.

Intentional states such as belief can be inconsistent—at least, covertly so—and not closed under (ordinary) logical consequence. Impossible worlds thus come as natural candidates to model such states: the content of a belief state can be analyzed as the set of worlds that make the beliefs true, that is, where things stand as they are believed to be, and this may include impossible worlds of various kinds.[94]

---

91. "Impossible World," *Wikipedia, The Free Encyclopedia* [cited 14 February 2010]. Online: http://en.wikipedia.org/w/index.php?title=Impossible_world&oldid =298964544.

92. Berto, "Impossible Worlds."

93. Ibid.

94. Ibid.

Independently of the analogy of psychological states, but in close connection with the issue of inconsistent information, one could be interested in using impossible worlds to model the ontology of inconsistent databases such as the ideological diversity of multiplex traditions in the Hebrew Bible. This is the case because the late redactors or communities would have known that the sets of data supplied by different sources they had to work with were inconsistent with one another, like incompatible evidence presented by different witnesses in a trial (to use Brueggemann's analogy for Old Testament theology).

> In this case, impossible worlds of the nonadjunctive kind are particularly useful. Intuitively, whereas one is allowed to draw the logical consequences of the data fed in by a single source, one should not conjoin data from distinct sources which could be inconsistent with each other. The database is "compartmentalized," so to speak: occasional inconsistencies are placed in separate sectors, not conjunctively asserted, and "sterilized" from an inferential point of view.[95]

In sum, working with "impossible worlds in the text" is perhaps the only way for a philosophical approach to be both synthetic and systematic—if that is what one is after at all costs. It can accommodate the entire Hebrew Bible and all its contradictions, thus making it possible to look at it as an impossibly unified whole. Note, however, that the aim of this discussion of theological pluralism in the context of the philosophy of identity is not harmonization along either fundamentalist or liberalist lines. Nor is it an atheological argument against realism as a result of biblical contradictions. Nor is it any scale of valuation of the various representations of Yhwh offered. The concern is not to end up with a unified or theologically relevant account of the properties of Yhwh. It is to provide a philosophical description of what we have in the text, to see what interesting philosophical problems arise and demand attention for their own sake.

11.6. Modeling Representational Theologics via an Oneirological Analogy

One way in which philosophers of religion use descriptive clarification is by way of analogical modeling. For example, the critical-realist philoso-

---

95. Ibid.

pher John Hick attempts to make sense of pluralism by way of a Kantian distinction. Hick interprets different beliefs and practices as different phenomenal perspectives of ultimate divine reality—the noumenal real.[96] This is for Hick a Copernican revolution in theology (although others would argue that Feuerbach did that). My own agenda is a bit more modest and purely descriptive. In this section, I wish to exchange critical realism for surrealism to show how the unity in diversity within the Hebrew Bible can be modeled, without of course making any claim regarding whether or how the worlds in the texts refer to those outside it.

What I would like to offer for consideration is an analogical model for the theological pluralism in the text, one that offers a concept grid for the paraconsistent reasoning of the Hebrew Bible as a whole, given its contradictory representations of Yhwh. In doing this I shall use the analogy of a dream (and the relation between the sleeping self "outside" the dream, the persona of the self within a dream, and the dream world) for what we have in ancient Israelite god talk's representation of how divinity vis-à-vis reality was (and could be) (re)configured. The parallels between religious realism and dreams were suggested in philosophy by Nietzsche (for example), when he wrote:

> *Misunderstanding dreams.* In ages of crude, primordial cultures, man thought he could come to know a *second real world* in dreams: this is the origin of all metaphysics. Without dreams man would have found no occasion to divide the world. The separation into body and soul is also connected to the oldest views about dreams, as is the idea of a spiritual apparition, that is, the origin of all belief in ghosts, and probably also in gods. "The dead man lives on, *because* he appears to the living man in dreams." So man concluded formerly, throughout many thousands of years.[97]

Whatever we make of this prodigious claim to explain religious belief, the core idea expressed here remains functional, given the logic of paradox in biblical god talk. I shall justify my suggestion by teasing out some interesting parallels between a surrealist ontology and representation of the divinity/reality relation in the Hebrew Bible as a whole. If we remember that in

---

96. See John Hick, *God and the Universe of Faiths* (London: Macmillan, 1973).

97. Friedrich Nietzsche, *Human, All Too Human: A Book for Free Spirits* (trans. Reginald J. Hollingdale; Cambridge: Cambridge University Press, 1996), 23–24.

the Hebrew Bible there was not assumed to be any difference in the onto-logical status of Yhwh appearing in the dream world and Yhwh appearing in waking life, recall the importance of dreams in divination, and consider Ernst Cassirer's philosophy of myth according to which such distinctions are out of place, it can be said that the concept of dreaming is in fact an intrabiblical category for modeling relations within biblical metaphysics and not something alien forced onto the discourse via the anachronistic frameworks in classical Christian systematic theology.

I am not sure what the following analogy's potency implies with regard to the relation between religious conceptions and dream worlds. All I can say is that the value of the oneirological analogy will become readily apparent when we observe the ways in which many age-old philosophi-cal-theological paradoxes generated by the transition from polytheistic to monotheistic conceptions are unexpectedly clarified, and this in a way that allows for a more nuanced and less distortively anachronistic reintroduc-tion of the metaphysical dichotomies mentioned earlier.

The noumenon–phenomenon relation: Yhwh was believed to be the thing-in-itself analogous to the way in which a dreamer is the body of the one dreaming. Yhwh was the thing-as-perceived analogous to the way in which the entity seen by others in the dream world is not the dreamer as he really is but only the projection of the self within the dream world. Yhwh as *noumenon* can never been seen without fatal consequences analogous to the way in which foreign entities in dreams can never see the dreamer's body as they cannot exist outside the dream world to look upon the dreaming subject. Yhwh as *phenomenon* can be seen analogous to the way in which entities in the dream world see the dreaming persona of the self with them in the dream without being thereby instantly destroyed. In biblical idiom, they are seeing the backside, and cannot see the face. This allows for a more appropriate retaining of the reality–appearance distinction and may also model a complex relation such as that between Yhwh and the angel of Yhwh.

Yhwh and ontological dependence: Yhwh was the source and sustainer of the world analogous to the way in which the dreamer is the source and sustainer of the dream world. Creatures are thus completely ontologically dependent on Yhwh analogous to the way in which entities in a dream world cannot exist without the dreamer. From this perspective the notion of divine aseity may also be understood.

Yhwh and identity: Many different and contradictory dream personas of the dreamer's self outside the dream can inhabit the dreamworld within the same and in different dreams. In the same way many incommersurable representations of Yhwh in the Hebrew Bible can all be said to refer to the same transcendental reality in the world outside the text.

Yhwh and substance: Yhwh is of a different substance than everything else analogous to the way in which the person dreaming is not of the same substance as the entities within the dream world. Yhwh is of the same substance as the rest of reality analogous to the way in which the dreaming persona of the self is part of the dream world and the dream world itself is substantially and inextricably a part of the dreamer. Thus Yhwh and reality are the same analogous to the way in which the dream is part of the dreamer. Yet Yhwh and reality are distinct in the way in which the dreamer sleeping is not her/himself the dream world. This also explains the distinction between Yhwh being a spirit and having a spirit. By analogy, Yhwh has a spirit body analogous to the way in which the dreaming self has a spirit body outside the dream. This also accounts for how Yhwh, being spirit, could interact with his creation, which is matter. In our analogy, Yhwh was assumed to be of a different substance as creation, yet could act within it analogous to the way a dreamer is actually a physical body but as dreaming persona can create and act in the dream world. In other words, a nonmaterial priorly existing Yhwh creates material reality analogous to the way in which a material dreamer creates a nonmaterial dream world.

Yhwh and time: Yhwh existed *before* time (the "beginning") analogous to the way in which a dreamer exists before dreamtime as a physical body. Yhwh exists since and *within* time analogous to the way in which the dreaming persona of the self world exists within dreamtime. Yhwh exists *outside* of time analogous to the way in which dreamtime and real-time are not identical—a day may be *as* a thousand years and vice versa (to *reinterpret* the biblical reference). As the dreaming subject is actually outside the dream world and simultaneously acts and experiences dreamtime's temporal succession and acts within it, the divine might be seen as both intra- and extratemporal to dreamtime. Yhwh is differently related to time analogous to the way in which real time and dreamtime differ (a day as a thousand years). Yhwh is the first and the last as the dream persona of the self is in a sense the first and the last—yet eternal in the sense that the dreamer exists beyond the duration of the dream world.

Yhwh and cognition: Yhwh knows all, analogous to the way in which a dreamer knows everything happening in the dream world. Yhwh knew the future analogous to how a dreamer on some level will always be the one whose mind actualizes the next particular state of affairs. Yet Yhwh could be cognitively limited too, analogous to the way in which the dreaming persona is often taken by surprise and cannot always consciously predict what will happen next.

Yhwh and space: Yhwh is *transcendent* analogous to the way in which the actual body of a dreamer is outside the dream. Yet Yhwh is also *immanent* just as the one dreaming has (and can be distinguished from) the dreaming persona which is the self present in the dream world. Everything is in Yhwh analogous to the way in which the entire dream world is in the dreamer. Yhwh is in everything analogous to the way in which the dreaming self is inside the entire dream world. In this sense Yhwh was assumed to relate to reality in quasi*panentheistic* ways, analogous to the way in which the dreaming self is both in the dream and the dream itself just is (in) the dreamer. He was omnipresent in the sense that the whole dream world is produced and controlled by the dreamer. Yet Yhwh is spatially limited in the sense of the limited space taken up by the dreaming self moving about within the dream world. Yhwh sits immovable on his throne in the transcendental realm analogous to the way in which the body of the dreamer lies inert on the bed. Yhwh is active and moving about in the world analogous to the way in which the persona of the dreaming self is constantly on the go within the dream world.

Yhwh and causality: Yhwh is a *material cause* of reality analogous to the way in which the dream world is part of the material of the dreamer's mind. Yhwh is the *formal cause* of reality analogous to the way in which a dream is in some sense the will and operates according to the rules of the dreamer's mind. Yhwh is the *efficient cause* of reality analogous to the way in which the dreamer is the agent initiating or ending the dream. Yhwh is the *final cause* of reality analogous to the way in which the dreamer is the persona for which the dream world exists. Yhwh is the *necessary and sufficient* cause of everything that happens in the world analogous to the ways in which the dreamer is the cause of everything that occurs in the dream world. No dreamer, no dream world. In this sense the divine is self-caused—the dreaming self outside the dream being the cause of the dreaming persona within the dream.

Yhwh and the moral order: Yhwh determines right and wrong analogous to the way the dreaming self plays a creative role in the moral order experienced in the dream world. Yhwh is independent from and subordinate to the moral order in that the dreaming persona is not the creator of but is experienced as noncausatively related to the moral order (i.e., *Euthyphro's Dilemma* becomes a false dichotomy).

Yhwh, goodness, and evil: Yhwh is believed to be purely good and not accountable (to be blamed) for everything bad analogous to the way in which the dreaming self is the cause of, but in some sense not really to be charged with, the evil which occurs in the dream world (despite the causal connections). In other words, Yhwh is behind whatever happens (also of evil) analogous to the way in which the dreamer is the source of everything in the dream, and yet Yhwh does not will the evil that happens in the dream analogous to the way in which a dreamer does not will nightmares in the dream world. This accounts for the logic operative in monistic theodicees.

Yhwh and free will: Analogous to the way in which the entities in a dream seem to have their own free will even though whatever they do is caused by the dreamer, so too Yhwh determined the thoughts and ways of humans even though they appear to have their own freedom of decision. This also solves the riddle of how the Yhwh himself can have free will given his attachment to the contents of divine foreknowledge, the divine nature, and predestination. Perhaps this can be seen as having been analogous to the way in which the one dreaming is not free to dream the contents that he/she does, yet experiences the appearance of free will within the dream world. So too could Yhwh be part of a predetermined process in which destiny and fate are fixed, yet where Yhwh can also repent and change his mind. The free will–determinism dichotomy is thus shown to be false and the paradox resolved (or maintained) by way of the analogy of oneirological compatabilism.

Yhwh and relation: Yhwh exists as a god only in relation analogous to the way the dreamer exists as dreaming persona only as long as the dream world exists. The entity which Yhwh is in himself exists independently without relations analogous to the ways in which the dreamer exists without relations to anything in the dream world when it is not dreaming.

Cognisance should be taken that in using the analogy I am neither committing to an analogical theory of the nature of religious language in the Hebrew Bible, nor claiming that it is all but a dream (in a pejorative sense). Rather, with the musings of this section I am asking whether a surrealist or oneirological analogy *might* be an improvement on the theory that biblical representations of divinity are metaphorical. Note, however, that in making use of this analogy I am not simply adopting the notion of reality as a dream, as in the Hindu conception of Maya or in the case of Dreamtime in the myths of the Aborigines. My analogical-oneirological modeling is merely aimed as a thought experiment put forward to show the possibility of sense and meaning in the paraconsistant logic of religious language in the Hebrew Bible. The logic was lost when philosophical monotheism divested itself of the analogy yet retained the anachronistic metaphysical dichotomies noted in chapter 9. Yet ultimately the value of the analogy becomes clear when we note that while in philosophy of religion there are many different analogies for modeling different philosophical mysteries, the dream analogy is able to make sense of virtually all the conceptual paradoxes put together.

11.7. The Nature of Divine Consciousness

The Hebrew Bible assumes that Yhwh has a mind (heart) and is conscious. This divine consciousness appears to many biblical scholars to be an unmysterious given. Yet perhaps no aspect of the divine mind is more puzzling than its conscious experience of itself and world. The nature of divine conscious awareness has been a matter of speculation for as long as there have been gods. "Preliterate cultures invariably embraced some form of spiritual or at least animist view that indicates a degree of reflection about the nature of conscious awareness."[98] In the context of the ancient Near East, ideas about the nature of divine consciousness are not found in overt philosophizing. Rather, they are implicit within the folk philosophy of mind presupposed in representations of divine cognition.

The problem of consciousness *per se* is arguably the most central issue in current philosophy of mind and is also importantly related to major traditional topics in metaphysics, such as the possibility of immortality and the belief in free will.

> Some philosophers have argued that consciousness as we know it today is a relatively recent historical development that arose sometime after the Homeric era. According to this view, earlier humans (including those who fought the Trojan War) did not experience themselves as unified internal subjects of their thoughts and actions, at least not in the ways we do today. Others have claimed that, as in the biblical Hebrew, even during the classical period there was no word in ancient Greek that corresponded to "consciousness." Though the ancients assumed a great deal

---

98. Robert van Gulick, "Consciousness," *SEP*. Online: http://plato.stanford.edu/archives/sum2011/entries/consciousness/.

about mental matters, it is less clear whether they had any specific concepts for or concerns about what we now think of as consciousness.[99]

"Since the 1980s there has been a major resurgence of philosophical research into the nature and basis of consciousness."[100] These developments have not received any real attention in biblical theology. We have already noted the contribution to related issues in Michael Carasik's *Theologies of the Mind*, but even here the concern is not divine consciousness in particular. So the question I wish to introduce to biblical philosophy in this section, and thereby to bring to the reader's attention, is as follows: What did the Hebrew Bible assume regarding Yhwh's consciousness? I shall try to offer a few preliminary remarks on the subject to give an indication of just how much can be inferred from data otherwise seemingly bereft of relevant speculation.

Let us begin by recognizing that Yhwh was regarded throughout the Hebrew Bible as conscious in a number of different senses. First of all, Yhwh was believed to be conscious in the generic sense of simply being a sentient entity, one capable of sensing and responding to its world. Second, Yhwh was assumed to be wakeful in that "he was exercising such a capacity rather than merely having the ability or disposition to do so."[101] Third, Yhwh was not only aware, but was also aware that he was aware, resulting in creature consciousness as a form of self-consciousness. Yet it was assumed that it was impossible to know divine consciousness completely, even through revelation.

So what was it assumed to be like to be a god? A few decades ago the philosopher of mind Thomas Nagel wrote a paper entitled "What Is It Like to Be a Bat?"[102] Nagel allegedly "chose bats instead of wasps or flounders because if one travels too far down the phylogenetic tree, people gradually shed their faith that there is experience there at all." Though more closely related to us than those other species, bats nevertheless present a range of activity and a sensory apparatus so different from ours that they make the problem exceptionally vivid." Nagel suggests that "anyone who has spent

---

99. Ibid.

100. Ibid.

101. Ibid.

102. Thomas Nagel, "What Is It Like to Be a Bat?" *Philosophical Review* 83/4 (1974): 435–50, following quotations from 436–37.

some time in an enclosed space with an excited bat knows what it is to encounter a fundamentally alien form of life."

Nagel noted that "bats perceive the external world primarily by sonar, or echolocation, detecting the reflections, from objects within range, of their own rapid, subtly modulated high frequency shrieks. Their brains are designed to correlate the outgoing impulses with the subsequent echoes, and the information thus acquired enables bats to make precise discriminations of distance, size, shape, motion, and texture comparable to those we make by vision." Nagel also challenged his readers to "imagine having webbing on one's arms, enabling one to fly around at dusk, and that, almost blind, one perceives the surrounding world by a system of reflected high frequency sound signals." For Nagel "this only goes so far: it tells only what it would be like to behave as a bat behaves." But as Nagel shows, "this is not the question." He wants to know "what it is like for a bat to be a bat."

In this section I would like to ask a similar if not stranger question: What it is like to be a god? I would agree with Nagel's argument, so in one sense I know my question is impossible to answer. But instead of trying to put forward any account of divine subjectivity with a transcendental pretense, I wish to prompt biblical scholars to investigate what some of texts in the Hebrew Bible assume it is like to be a god in general and the God Yhwh in particular. A god like Yhwh is assumed to be conscious, because there is something that it is like for this character to experience its world through its senses. The biblical authors were prephilosophical, and they were often naïve enough to assume that humans could indeed understand what it was like to be a god, and what consciousness was like from the god's own point of view. A philosophical approach to divine consciousness in the Hebrew Bible is exactly what is required to tease out these textual presuppositions pertaining to the folk philosophy of mind operative in the world in the text.

Based on insights from contemporary philosophy of consciousness, a comprehensive understanding of divine consciousness in the Hebrew Bible will likely require descriptive theories of many types. One might usefully and without contradiction accept a diversity of models that aim—each in its own respective way—to explain the physical, neural, cognitive, functional, representational, and higher-order aspects of divine consciousness as characterized in biblical discourse. "There is not likely to be any single theoretical perspective that will suffice to explain all the features of consciousness that we might wish to understand. Thus a synthetic and pluralistic approach may provide the best road to future progress."[103]

This, then, is a very brief note concerning a yet largely unexplored topic for a philosophical theology of the Hebrew Bible. Here the philosophy of religion intersects the philosophy of mind, a field that arguably dominates Anglo-Saxon analytic philosophy at present. The task of the biblical philosophical theologian would be to study the issues involved and to describe what, if anything, the Hebrew Bible assumed on each of these matters in relation to Yhwh himself.

11.8. Conclusion

In this chapter I have provided what I consider to be some preliminary proposals for the writing of a philosophical theology of the Hebrew Bible. Of course, what has been said here has hardly scratched the surface of the approach, yet I trust the reader will get the general idea of where such a project may be headed. Any limits to the number of philosophically interesting topics to be examined within this theology will be the result merely of the limits of our own imaginations.

---

103. Van Gulick, "Consciousness."

12

Natural A/theologies in Ancient Israel

What makes a subject difficult to understand—if it is significant, important—is not that some special instruction about abstruse things is
necessary to understand it. Rather it is the contrast between the understanding of the subject and what most people want to see. Because of
this the very things that are most obvious can become the most difficult
to understand. What has to be overcome is difficulty not of the intellect
but of the will.[1]

12.1. Introduction

In biblical theology, it is commonplace to suggest that the Hebrew Bible
does not attempt to argue for or prove the existence of Yhwh.[2] Scholarly
literature on the subject simply points to the biblical dictum that only fools
doubt Yhwh's reality and insists that the nature of "atheism" in ancient
Israel was at best practical, not theoretical (e.g., Ps 10:4; 14:1; 53:1; Zeph
1:12). The following example may be taken as typical:

> The thought of the Old Testament is centred in God. Yet it is nowhere
> attempted to prove God exists. For the God of the Old Testament is the
> God of experience and not of x speculation. It is not because some pos-
> tulate of thought led men to think of a first cause that they turned to
> the thought of God. They no more questioned his being than they ques-
> tioned the reality of the world around themselves. The philosopher may
> raise doubts about the reality of all things, but the plain man is content

---

1. Ludwig Wittgenstein, *Philosophical Occasions* (§§86–93 of the so-called "Big
Typescript") [cited 19 December 2010]. Online http://en.wikiquote.org/wiki/Ludwig_
Wittgenstein.

2. Kohler, *Old Testament Theology*, 19; Jacob, *Theology of the Old Testament*, 37;
Preuss, *Old Testament Theology*, 1:139.

> to base his belief in the reality of the world on his experience, however illusionary the philosopher may tell him it is. So the Hebrew was content to base his belief in the existence of God on what seemed to him to be his experience of God, granted to himself or to his people, and especially on the experience of God given to the nation in the great moments of its history.... He (God) was a postulate of experience rather than thought.... No man who hears the roar of the lion near him will turn to philosophy to ask whether there is any such objective reality as the lion, and no man who has had an experience of God is concerned to ask whether the philosopher will allow him to believe in God. Where we find atheism in the Old Testament it is a practical rather than theoretical atheism.[3]

The notion that actual natural a/theology is completely foreign to the Hebrew Bible has been accepted uncritically in philosophy of religion as well. Many assume that there is no such thing as concerns with the ontological status of divine reality in the Hebrew Bible. It is taken for granted that there were radical epistemological differences between Israelite religion and Greek philosophy:

> In contrast to Aristotle, the claims made by Genesis and the rest of the Scriptures of ancient Israel do not spring from a desire to discover the principles of nature's operation, nor even account for the existence of the universe. Belief in a Creator is not affirmed by the ancient Israelites because they desire to explain the world's existence and order. Its existence and order do not form the grounds for belief in God. On the contrary, they believed in God's self-revelation, first to Abraham, the founder of their race, and then to the other patriarchs, such as Isaac and Jacob, and then to the prophets. Their belief in the Divine is a response to God's initiative, rather than the result of their investigation of nature's order and origin.[4]

In the first section of this chapter I wish to suggest that the passionate denial by biblical theologians of natural theology in ancient Israelite religion is based on a theological reinterpretation rather than a historical appropriation of the textual data.[5] I am not the first to do so. Old Testament

---

3. H. H. Rowley, *The Faith of Israel: Aspects of Old Testament Thought* (London: SCM, 1956), 48–49.

4. Allen, *Philosophy for Understanding Theology*, 3.

5. For this section, see Jaco Gericke, "Natural A/Theologies in Ancient Israel: Descriptive Perspectives from Philosophy of Religion," *VE* 31/1 (2010).

theologians such as James Barr[6] and Rolf Knierim[7] identified traces of natural theology in the Hebrew Bible. Both recognized that the opposition to natural theology per se was not an example of a historical consciousness at work; it was biblical theologians speaking under the influence of certain trends in dogmatics and philosophy of religion.

In the mid-twentieth century, during the heyday of the Biblical Theology Movement's antiphilosophical sentiment, natural theology and philosophy of religion were closely related. The aversion to philosophy of religion then becomes understandable when we consider that much of that subject was concerned with natural theology. The problem was that natural theology was detested in Barthian dogmatics and in existentialist theologies and philosophies of the day, all of which had a profound influence on biblical theology. In philosophy of religion today, however, arguments for and against the existence of gods are no longer at the center of attention: they have made way for epistemological and linguistic turns in the field. Natural theology is still a subdivision in analytic philosophical theology and philosophy of religion, but in theory it can be viewed separately. As James Barr observed:

> Something more has to be said to define our theme in relation to two concepts, firstly the philosophy of religion … the philosophy of religion is not necessarily or absolutely linked with natural theology; for example, one might pursue a philosophical approach to religion while denying natural theology altogether. Nevertheless, it seems that there is a common tendency in the opposite direction; traditional natural theology has provided much interesting matter for the philosophy of religion, for example, traditional arguments for the existence of God. And conversely the denial of natural theology has commonly gone with a strong emphasis on revelation, and this in turn has been taken to mean that there are no adequate resources for a philosophical understanding of God. In extreme cases, the emphasis on revelation has been taken to mean that philosophical discussions of God and of religion have no relevance for Christian faith whatever.[8]

In practice, natural theology remains part of philosophy of religion. This means that if biblical scholars follow Barr and Knierim by granting

---

6. Barr, *Biblical Faith and Natural Theology, passim.*
7. Knierim, *Task of Old Testament Theology, passim.*
8. Barr, *Biblical Faith and Natural Theology,* 3.

the presence of natural theology in the Hebrew Bible, by implication they admit the presence of philosophical theology and philosophy of religion in the text as well. The location of natural theology is in the conceptual space presupposed behind biblical stories about creation and within the logic that governs the rationales behind biblical laws, prophetic discourse and practical wisdom. In fact, when it comes to being concerned about the existence of deity, no collection of ancient Near Eastern texts is more repressively obsessed with the (ir)reality of god(s) than the Hebrew Bible. In our case, however, what we are looking is all those presumed, unarticulated reasons for (dis)believing in the existence of Yhwh/the gods that now remain only as traces implicit in the biblical discourse.

12.2. Folk-Philosophical Arguments for the Existence of Yhwh

While most biblical theologians deny that the Hebrew Bible contains arguments for the existence of Yhwh, a few flirt with related philosophical concerns. Those that do are not necessarily descriptive and historical in orientation. For example, in his discussion of "The Reality of the Biblical God," Dale Patrick[9] claimed the presence of literary versions of three traditional philosophical arguments for the existence of God. These were the ontological argument (supposedly implicit in the suspension of disbelief to read the story), the cosmological argument (allegedly by rendering the world in the text as true life), and a moral-existential argument (implicit in the way the Hebrew Bible evokes an experience of the holy). Though interesting, Patrick's ideas stay on the level of narrative and rhetorical criticism, and never amount to a philosophical clarification of what is implicit in the texts themselves. The desire is to be theologically relevant at all costs rather than a mere concern for historical-philosophical elucidation.

In the remainder of this chapter I wish to approach the matter a bit differently. Many biblical theologians still assume that natural theology can only be a normative enterprise. As a result, they would agree with Brueggemann that biblical scholars as philosophers of religion can do without the ontological concerns philosophers worry about: "In a like manner we bracket out all questions of ontology which ask about the 'really real.'"[10]

---

9. Patrick, *Rendering of God in the Old Testament*, part 3.
10. Brueggemann, *Old Testament Theology*, 118.

However, it does not follow that ontology per se must be avoided. After all, there is something to be said for a descriptive ontology that seeks to identify and clarify the text's own assumptions about what is really real, and to ask why those assumptions seemed warranted to those who held them. So while biblical scholars cannot use the Bible to do natural theology proper, they can reconstruct in philosophical terms the rudiments of natural folk theologies implicit in the text. For while the Hebrew Bible does not argue extensively for the existence of Yhwh, it does assume the presence of sufficient reasons for believing that this God is real and that others are also such, or not.

12.2.1. IMPLICIT ARGUMENTS

On the level of implicit arguments, I would like to ask you, the reader, to imagine traveling to the biblical world in the text and, in the role of philosophical anthropologist, sitting in on a meeting of the elders at the city gate. Let us further suppose that your role is that of an analytic ordinary language African philosopher such as Barry Hallen, who was mentioned earlier.[11] Now imagine that you could ask these elders, concerning their belief in the reality of Yhwh: "Why do you believe that?" One is here looking for a reasoned justification of the sort where they might respond: "We believe x because y" (analogous to what in African philosophy is called "philosophical sagacity"). Of course, if x is "Yhwh exists," and the concept of existence is made clear, then "y" might be: "Because our fathers taught us that Yhwh delivered us with a strong hand from Egypt." This would amount to an "argument from tradition" which, while fallacious in natural theology as an appeal to authority, would have been part of the folk-philosophical rhetoric responsible for the apparent justification of the belief that Yhwh lives.

To be sure, biblical theologians might claim that an appeal to tradition amounts to "revealed" rather than natural theology. But is the distinction between revelation and nature not itself anachronistic here, and the product of Judeo-Christian philosophy of religion? For suppose that you could probe further and ask how the ancient believers in Yhwh's reality thought they knew that their belief was true. Or suppose one tried to understand what they meant when they said that Yhwh is a "living" god, and how they

---

11. Hallen, "Analytic Philosophy," 218–19.

knew this. Surely they would be able to answer that question. Prophetic polemics against the reality of other gods presuppose the ability for critical reflection about "identity conditions" for divinity. To be sure, the prephilosophical ancient Israelite responses forthcoming might satisfy neither philosophical nor theological orthodox sensibilities. However, to deny the presence of such folk philosophy in the text to divert attention from the Hebrew Bible's crudeness is not the way to go. What we need is a descriptive clarification of natural folk-theological arguments in ancient Israelite religion, whether they are valid and true or not.

12.2.2. EXPLICIT ARGUMENTS

There are bits and pieces of residual natural folk theologies in the folk philosophy of religion that we encounter in the Hebrew Bible. These appear in texts containing ideas on what were assumed to be sufficient reasons for holding certain beliefs about the nature and existence of Yhwh. These ideas are present also in poetry and song, since the Hebrew Bible did not distinguish philosophy from poetry as we do. This can be seen in the way wisdom motifs are found in the midst of lyrical texts and myths. One recognized instance of such quasiphilosophical thinking in Hebrew poetry comes from the Psalter. Thus, as has been recognized by biblical scholars for some time already,[12] we stumble upon natural theology in Ps 94:7–12:

ויאמרו לא יראה־יה	And they say: "Yah will not see,
ולא־יבין אלהי יעקב	neither will the God of Jacob give heed."
בינו בערים בעם	Understand brutish ones among the people;
וכסילים מתי תשכילו	and fools, when will you be clever?
<u>הנטע אזן הלא ישמע</u>	<u>The planter of the ear, will he not hear?</u>
<u>אם־יצר עין הלא יביט</u>	<u>Or the former of the eye, will he not see?</u>
היסר גוים הלא יכיח	The instructor of the nations, will he not correct?
המלמד אדם דעת	The one who teaches humans knowledge?
יהוה ידע מחשבות אדם	Yhwh knows the thoughts of humans,
כי־המה הבל	that they are vapor.

---

12. Andrew B. Davidson, *Theology of the Old Testament* (Edinburgh: T&T Clark, 1904), 33.

The question now concerns the nature of the reasoning in religious thought encountered in the underlined text above. This text clearly presupposes natural theological reflection as a state of affairs preceding the penning of the underlined ideas. After all, how did the author know (or think he knew) that these states of affairs were the case without some abstract contemplation regarding the nature of deity prior to composing the song? The phraseology presupposes that somewhere in the history of Israelite religion natural theology was at work. Can the argument presupposed here be described in extrabiblical philosophical categories that, though anachronistic, are not necessarily distortive of intratextual conceptual backgrounds? My answer is "yes," and in philosophical terms it may be said that the underlined section *presupposes* in embryo an abductive argument from design that argues from the world to Yhwh.

Abduction is a method of logical inference that is prescientific. In layman's terms it means "having a hunch" and arguing from the conclusion to the premises, that is, from the effects to a supposed cause. More formally stated, the psalm presupposes the validity of allowing the precondition a to be inferred from the consequence b. Of course, the implicit argument behind this particular piece of natural theology might be faulted for committing the fallacies of presumption; affirming the consequent; and anthropomorphism (there are multiple alternative possible explanations for b). Since David Hume's critique of the concept of causation and Kierkegaard's reminder that arguments from design already presuppose what they seek to prove, many philosophers would not argue along these lines anymore. But this is irrelevant for our purposes. We are interested in the reasoning used in ancient Israelite religious thought, whether the reasoning presupposed in the world behind the text of the psalm is invalid or not. The objective of the descriptive philosopher of Israelite religion should be to describe, clarify, and understand, rather than to adjudicate, explain or criticize.

Whatever the case may be, this instance of natural theology (which is surely the tip of the folk-philosophical iceberg in the world behind the text) clearly shatters the stereotype viewing Israelite thinking as not concerned to argue from the world to Yhwh. It furthermore confirms the words of Knierim:

> Because of limitation of space we can only allude to philosophical science in the Bible. The extent to which philosophy in modern times is acknowledged as scientific, not speculative but based on the empiri-

cal disciplines and logic is mirrored in the philosophical nature of
many of the biblical texts insofar as it alludes to God in the rationality
of thought. What is philosophical thereby depends much more on the
kind of thinking, the *Geistesbeshäftigung*, than on the format, especially
when compared with the format of treatises from Greek philosophy
on. Even there, the Socratic dialogue was an appropriate philosophical
form.[13]

Knierim went further, to suggest that Herder's comparisons between
Hebrew (biblical) and Greek (philosophical) thought rested on his own
philosophical assumptions, which were rooted in the anthropology of
romanticism. According to Knierim, what Herder did not realize was
that

> poetic intuition was by far not the only element in the mentality of
> the Hebrew literature and that systematization, logic and ration were
> very much intrinsic to the Hebrew mind, not only embryonically. They
> were even at work in the systematized generic structures of his beloved
> Hebrew poetry. The post-Herder evidence forces us to reconceptualise
> not only our understanding of the Hebrew mind but also the crite-
> ria of the philosophy of romanticism for determining authenticity or
> foreignness.[14]

This insight by Knierim suggests that biblical theology should take leave of
the Aristotelian dichotomy between philosophy and poetry and of Plato's
negative assessment of the philosophical value of the latter. Biblical scholars have anachronistically assumed that arguments for the existence of
God (i.e., reasons for believing that Yhwh lives) will only count as such if
they are found in the form of explicit systematic logical arguments riddled
with philosophical jargon. No wonder they conclude that no such thing is
present in the Hebrew Bible. But it is precisely because the Hebrew Bible is
not a textbook in Christian analytic philosophy of religion that we should
not expect it to look like one, and should go on to ask what it takes for
granted on matters related to that philosophical subdiscipline. The example mentioned above was just one instance, and there is a great deal of
research still to be done on the topic.

---

13. Knierim, *Task of Old Testament Theology*, 410.
14. Ibid., 51.

12.3. Descriptive Atheologies in the Hebrew Bible

It is an open question whether it is legitimate to speak of atheism in the Hebrew Bible. Research on the phenomenon of skepticism in ancient Israel has already borne this out to some extent.[15] However, hitherto the discussion seems to have dried up, and no attempt has been made to structure it according to the format of arguments against the existence of deity in philosophy of religion. In the discussion to follow, we do just that. In doing so, however, we are moving into controversial territory. In research on the Hebrew Bible, the concept of atheism is considered anachronistic.[16] In other words, discussions of radical unbelief in the reality of Yhwh (as opposed to skepticism about divine ways) are rare in scholarly literature. We need to bring some additional insight, order, and quality to the research. For this comparative philosophy of religion is required—not biblical theology repeating Barthian slogans against natural theology.

12.3.1. Varieties of Atheism and Atheology in Ancient Israel

The English term *atheist* in the sense of "one who denies or disbelieves the existence of God," is first attested from 1571 onward.[17] In ancient Greek the adjective *atheos* meaning "godless" or "impious" can be traced back to the sixth century B.C.E., when it referred only to impiety, eventually coming to denote a more intentional, active godlessness in the fifth century B.C.E. By then the term had acquired other meanings, such as "severing relations with the gods" or "denying the gods, ungodly."[18] Atheism in one form or another, however, predates Greek philosophy, and traces of it are found in elsewhere.[19] Biblical theologians discussing the phenomenon

---

15. William H. U. Anderson, "What Is Scepticism and Can It Be Found in The Hebrew Bible?" *SJOT* 13 (1999): 225–57; James L. Crenshaw, "The Birth of Skepticism in Ancient Israel," in *Divine Helmsman: Studies on God's Control of Human Events* (ed. James L. Crenshaw and Samuel Sandmel; New York: Ktav, 1980), 1–19; John F. Priest, "Humanism, Skepticism and Pessimism in Ancient Israel," *JAAR* 36 (1968): 311–26.

16. Gerhard von Rad, *Wisdom in Israel* (London: SCM, 1972), 65.

17. James Thrower, *Western Atheism: A Short History* (New York: Prometheus Books, 2000), 2.

18. Michael Martin, *The Cambridge Companion to Atheism* (Cambridge: Cambridge University Press, 2007), 1.

19. James Thrower, *The Alternative Tradition: Religion and the Rejection of Religion in the Ancient World* (Berlin: de Gruyter, 1980).

have failed to distinguish its many varieties. A quick perusal of the *Cambridge Companion to Atheism* reveals the following subtle distinctions:

1. *Implicit or negative* atheism is the absence of belief in gods, with explicit or *positive* atheism being the actual denial of a belief in gods.
2. Under explicit atheism *strong* atheism is the explicit affirmation that gods do not exist while *weak* atheism includes all other forms of nontheism, such as the belief that a specific deity does not exist or agnosticism, nontheism, and apatheism (but not antitheism).
3. *Narrow* atheism concerns particular gods, while *broad* atheism concerns all gods of whatever description.
4. *Hard* atheism is the proactive confession and promotion of atheism, while *soft* atheism entails silent personal disbelief.
5. *Theoretical* atheism is disbelief that has reasons for denying that a god exists, while *practical* or *pragmatic* atheism simply involves living as if there were no god, without necessarily being able to give grounds for the unbelief.[20]

These categories are functional even though they are postbiblical. Note that biblical theologians have only taken cognizance of the theoretical/practical distinction. This has resulted in an overly simplistic discussion within biblical theology of unbelief in ancient Israel. Not only theoretical or practical atheism, but also the other categories in the classification system, need to be brought to bear on the data. Far too little research has been done on why the existence of Yhwh and/or the gods was denied, and no one has yet bothered to write a descriptive atheology of the Hebrew Bible.[21]

Beside the concept of atheism, our second relevant term is *atheology*. The word was first used in seventeenth-century polemical literature, specifically to denote not so much antitheology or antagonism towards theology as arguments against the existence of God as conceived of in

---

20. Martin, *Cambridge Companion to Atheism*, 1–6.

21. For a comprehensive evaluative atheology of the Hebrew Bible, see Gericke, "Does Yahweh Exist?" This comes from a time in my research where my agenda was what could only be called militantly atheist. I have calmed down somewhat in the meantime.

a particular view of deity.[22] In this regard, the concern today is not as in the past evaluative atheological perspectives on the Hebrew Bible[23] but is rather to offer a purely historical and descriptive account of traces of atheology and atheism in the Hebrew Bible itself. My interests are antagonist discourse in the Hebrew Bible that denies the reality of Yhwh in some sense; and in protagonist polemical denials of the reality of other gods.

12.3.2. ANTAGONIST ATHEOLOGICAL ARGUMENTS

The presence of antagonist atheology in the Psalms is old news. In this regard, virtually all commentaries on the Psalms have noted the denial of god(s) in Pss 10 and 14, with the latter repeated in Ps 53. In Ps 10:4 we read:

רשע כגבה אפו בל־ידרש	The wicked, in the height of his nose, will not inquire;
אין אלהים כל־מזמותיו	"There are no gods," are all his thoughts.

A similar statement is found in Ps 14:1:

אמר נבל בלבו	The fool said in his heart:
אין אלהים	"There are no gods."

The paraphrase of the Targum Tehillim's rendering of Ps 14 and its twin, Ps 53, tried to downplay the nature of the atheological denial through the following elaborations:

> The fool said in his heart, "There is no *rule of* God *on the earth*."
> (Ps 14)
> The fool said in his heart, "There is no God *taking retribution*."
> (Ps 53)

---

22. Thomas Mautner, *The Penguin Dictionary of Philosophy* (London: Blackwell, 2000).

23. See Jaco Gericke, "Does Yahweh Exist? The Case against Realism in Old Testament Theology," *OTE* 17 (2004): 30–57.

Many biblical theologians have followed the targumic reading and have concluded that the masoretic version presupposes only "practical atheism." However, there are several problems with this classification.

First of all, the translation from Hebrew into English as "there is no God" might be wrong and could be read as a reference to a denial of the reality of generic divinity in general. In favor of the latter is the fact that the capitalization of the word "God" is the default option, given the translators' philosophical monotheism and their ideological interests. The popular classification of the atheology in the fool's words as involving a reference to Yhwh/God makes little sense when the denial is cast in the form of an indefinite description (no god = not a god). Personal names are out of place inasmuch as it seems incomprehensible why the fool would deny the existence of only one specific god.

Second, the classification of this as merely "practical atheism" was wittingly or unwittingly ideologically motivated by the need to deny the presence of natural atheology in the fool's words. This is partly the result of allegiance to a popular stereotype of "Hebrew thought" which insists that orthopraxy was more important than orthodoxy: despite many mid-twentieth-century biblical-theological discussions that sought to distance Hebrew (biblical) from Greek (philosophical) thinking, these are now known to have been riddled with fallacies including essentialism, generalization, stereotyping, oversimplification, and caricature.

Third, we should remember that the atheology of the "wicked" is not a firsthand account but a polemical caricature. What gives the game away is that the psalmist claims to know what the fool says "in his heart" (in secret)—the text itself implies that the psalmist has no access to such knowledge. In addition, the fool is depicted as oscillating inconsistently between atheism and antitheism when the existence of the gods is denied, and this denial is followed by rebellion against a specific god (Yhwh). The idea that the fool is a rebel rather than an unbeliever is practical atheism, to be sure, but it is a construct by the author, who cannot accept that a complete denial of the reality of Yhwh is possible. It serves no rhetorical purpose to present the fool as somebody who discovered that the same reasons for not believing in other gods could also be applied to belief in the God of Israel. Thus the conceptual inconsistencies in the view of the fool in the psalm (atheism vis-à-vis anti-Yahwism) are the result of the psalmist's projecting his own theistic frame of reference onto the mindset of the fool. With *ad hominem* arguments associating unbelief with immorality, the psalmist could discredit his opponent. This is a universal tendency in

religious apologetics to this day: atheists are depicted as willfully obsti-
nate immoral agents rejecting God when, from their point of view, there
is nothing to reject.

Fourth, a bit of deconstruction is in order, not deconstruction of the
textual meaning but metacommentary to aid in the clarification of what is
in fact there. Biblical theologians' dismissal of the possibility of theoretical atheism is the result of failure to recognize that the theoretical/practi-
cal distinction is partly superficial. All practice presupposes a minimum
amount of theory that acts as a rationale, even if it is subconscious or
unarticulated. No one in a religious culture is a practical atheist without
presupposing some sufficient reason, even if only vaguely conceived, for
being such. It becomes clear from reading between the lines of the descriptions of the wicked in the biblical text that there are in fact reasons for their
unbelief which are not spelled out. As we shall see, these concern arguments related to divine absence and evil.

Fifth, a more pedantic remark is in order to show the incompleteness
of "practical atheism" as a full classification for what we find in the fool's
denial. Aside from the theoretical/practical distinction, commentators will
have to indicate what other formats of atheism are present in the antagonist's atheology. For example, it may be said that from the description it
would seem that we are dealing with soft rather than hard atheism, in that
the denial is alleged to be private. Moreover, it is positive rather than negative atheism, in that the atheology is said to involve the actual denial that
gods exist and not merely the absence of belief in gods.

In sum, then, it would seem that the classification of the denial that
there are gods in Ps 14 is both oversimplified and incomplete. The question now is: if the atheism of the fool presupposes some theory (even if
unarticulated), what arguments against the existence of deity are taken for
granted in the psalm? Of course, it can hardly be expected that the psalmists would give their opponents a platform for their ideas—the latter must
be inferred from the secondhand caricature. In this regard, it is interesting
to note how the psalmists' references to antagonist atheological beliefs are
often coupled with charges of the absence of a belief in divine retribution. But why did some of the people not believe in divine retribution?
What was it about the world that offered what was assumed to be sufficient
reason for natural atheology?

We cannot say for sure, but additional inferences may be drawn from
other texts, in which antagonist atheology is associated with immorality.
One such example comes from Ps 55:20b, where we read of people:

אֲשֶׁר אֵין חֲלִיפוֹת לָמוֹ וְלֹא יָרְאוּ	Such as have no changes, and fear
אֱלֹהִים	no gods.

Consider also the reference to implicit antagonist natural atheological arguments in Ps 73:10–11, which reads:

יָמִיקוּ וִידַבְּרוּ בְרָע עֹשֶׁק	They scoff, and in wickedness utter oppression;
מִמָּרוֹם יְדַבֵּרוּ	they speak from the height.
שַׁתּוּ בַשָּׁמַיִם פִּיהֶם	They have set their mouth against the heavens,
וּלְשׁוֹנָם תִּהֲלַךְ בָּאָרֶץ	and their tongue walk through the earth.
לָכֵן יָשִׁיב עַמּוֹ הֲלֹם	Therefore he will let his people return here;
וּמֵי מָלֵא יִמָּצוּ לָמוֹ	and waters of fullness will be drained out by them.
וְאָמְרוּ אֵיכָה יָדַע אֵל	And they say: "How does a god know?
וְיֵשׁ דֵּעָה בְעֶלְיוֹן	And is there knowledge in the highest?"

From these texts it would seem that there were some people in ancient Israel who thought long and hard about the concept of deity and found certain divine attributes either conceptually incoherent or not instantiated in alleged divine governance of the world. Note that the skepticism noted in Ps 73:10–11 above, with regard to what Yhwh can know, need not be taken as the antagonist's admission that there is a god, but one that has no knowledge. Once again it may well be a reference to Yhwh for the sake of the argument—in the same way atheist philosophers of religion today speak of God only in the sense of referring to the concept. Whatever the reality behind the caricature of the antagonist's views may be, then, perhaps the following hypothetical antagonist atheological arguments might have been operational in the *vox populi*:

1. *An implicit argument from divine absence*, where the failure of any deity to act in certain events seemed to suggest that there is no god.
2. *An argument from amoral cosmic orders*, where the fact that evil—whether moral or natural—seemed to befall both the righteous and the wicked (thus an early argument from evil).

In sum, then, antagonist atheologies appear to have been motivated by appeals to irreligious experience and conceptual dilemmas in theistic truth claims.

12.3.3. PROTAGONIST ATHEOLOGICAL ARGUMENTS

Another way to discern what arguments against the reality of a god or gods were at least conceivable in ancient Israel is by inference from arguments against the existence of gods foreign to the cult of Yhwh. Surely these could have been applied by antagonists to Yhwh himself. However, by definition, Yahwism's own (protagonist) atheology can never amount to anything more than narrow atheism, that is, the denial of particular conceptions of godhood and not the denial of godhood absolutely. Most of it comes in the form of polemics against idols. Because the texts had no overt philosophical agenda, the reasons for disbelief in the reality of other gods are not spelled out. The texts do not present us with extensive discussions of the contents and reasoned arguments. Thus as with antagonist atheologies, the data we have to work with are limited to bits and pieces incidentally encountered in the course of individual psalms whose goals were not themselves atheological.

Apart from the familiar Pss 58 and 82, where the gods are charged with injustice and their death is proclaimed, several other psalms contain atheological motifs. For example, a word search of Hebrew terms translated "idols" leads one to a text such as Ps 115:4–7:

עצביהם כסף וזהב	Their idols are silver and gold,
מעשׂה ידי אדם	the work of men's hands.
פה־להם ולא ידברו	They have mouths, but they speak not;
עינים להם ולא יראו	eyes have they, but they see not;
אזנים להם ולא ישמעו	They have ears, but they hear not;
אף להם ולא יריחון	noses have they, but they smell not.
ידיהם ולא ימישׁון	They have hands, but they handle not;
רגליהם ולא יהלכו	feet have they, but they walk not;
לא־יהגו בגרונם	neither speak they with their throat.

It should not be overlooked that this passage assumes rather than denies the corporeality of deity. It simply denies that unreal gods are alive. Similar references to the gods of the nations as nonliving objects are also found in several other psalms with Yahwism's own atheological polemical claims:

כי כל־אלהי העמים אלילים	For the gods of the peoples are things of nought;
ויהוה שמים עשׂה	but Yhwh made the heavens. (Ps 96:5)
יבשׁו כל־עבדי פסל	Ashamed be all that serve graven images,
המתהללים באלילים	that boast themselves of things of nought. (Ps 97:7a)
עצביהם כסף וזהב	The idols of the nations are silver and gold,
מעשׂה ידי אדם	the work of men's hands. (Ps 135:15)

These are not just bold assertions. They presuppose a religious epistemology that takes for granted that one can know that other gods are not really gods. Given that ancient Israel came from a world filled with gods and represented a mediocre political entity, we can be sure the psalmists did not reach the above atheological conclusions without some serious folk-philosophical reflection. If this is not in the text, it is because the point of the text was not to discuss folk philosophy but to confess faith. This does not mean that there was no folk philosophy or that it is invalid for us to attempt to reconstruct it based on inferences from presuppositions. In other words, the absence of atheological arguments that are explicitly spelled out and systematically formulated here has nothing to do with any supposed practically orientated Hebraic thinking: it merely means that the arguments are taken for granted and presupposed. As such, the atheologies present in the text might to some extent be inferred from what is implicit. What is clear is that in the psalms the denial of the existence of other gods involves a narrow, explicit, positive, theoretical, and soft variety of atheism. From texts like those above, we discern the following implicit protagonist atheological arguments:

1. *An argument from alleged reification (hypostatization)*, charging the nations because of their alleged tendency to treat an abstraction (abstract belief or hypothetical construct) as if it were a concrete, real event or physical entity. In other words,

it exposes the error of treating as a "real thing" something that is not a real thing, and is merely an idea.

2. *An argument from the alleged pathetic fallacy*, where the nations are said to attribute to an inanimate object the characteristics of animate ones.

Yahwistic protagonist atheologies are therefore stereotypically *explicit/positive, narrow, strong, hard*, and *theoretical*. There is no reason to believe that antagonists could not have applied the same argument to the God of Israel. What is interesting in the above, however, is how in the Psalms (prayers from which many would like to exorcise all philosophical concerns) we find the core data clusters for ontological presupposition reconstruction. To be sure, many of the atheological arguments are nascent, and the atheism is narrow. Yet such ideas were to become the staple of atheologies in later deuterocanonical texts such as the Letter of Jeremiah (ch. 6) and the Wisdom of Solomon (chs. 12–15).

In sum, traces of natural a/theology are not altogether absent from the Hebrew Bible. Interestingly, the folk philosophy of religion seems to be best attested in poetic texts involving some or other polemical remark or reflection. These texts do not contain fully formulated arguments for or against the existence of deity, but they do provide bits and pieces of implicit folk philosophies of religion nascent in the presuppositions underlying sufficient reasons for holding to a specific ontological belief in the particular textual tradition. Atheological assertions are more frequent than natural theological claims. While in the past the biblical-theological evasion of this particular locus in analytic philosophy of religion has been popular, thanks to influence from Barthian dogmatics, the prospect of more thorough research involving a historical and descriptive ethnophilosophical clarification of ancient Israelite religion's own folk natural atheologies is now a real option.

12.4. YHWH AND THE MYSTERY OF EXISTENCE[24]

Why is there *something* rather than *nothing*? This question, properly understood, represents what the philosopher Martin Heidegger considered the

---

24. The "real" here is the "real" world in the text, not the world outside it. For a fuller discussion, see Jaco Gericke, "Why Is There Something Rather Than Nothing? Biblical Ontology and the *Mystery of Existence*," OTE 21 (2008): 329–44.

most fundamental problem of all philosophical inquiry.[25] It concerns the mystery of existence—a riddle that in some form or another has vexed thinkers in both Eastern and Western philosophy since its inception. Already in ancient Indian religious literature the puzzle concerning the origin of Being was acknowledged as essentially insoluble.[26] Since the time of Parmenides (fifth century B.C.E.), a related perplexity motivated philosophers to begin spending a substantial amount of time arguing whether nothingness is possible. By the time the modern era arrived (fashionably late), the question of why anything happens to exist asserted itself with a vengeance to such an extent that following its (re)formulation in the writings of Leibniz, other philosophers—including Hume, Kant, Schelling, Schopenhauer, Nietzsche, Wittgenstein, Heidegger, and Sartre—all felt compelled to say something in response to it. In the present postmodern period the question of why anything exists enjoys a somewhat ambivalent reputation. While some claim that it lies at the foundation of all metaphysical inquiry, others (typically dismissive of all metaphysics) insist that it is nothing more than language on holiday: why shouldn't things exist? Or is nothing considered the default condition (or even a sensible one)?

So what? Why is all of this important for a discussion of ancient Israelite ontological assumptions? According to James Crenshaw:

> Biblical sages never asked the question that is arguably the most divisive of all intellectual queries: "Does Being exist?" With one possible exception, the sayings of a non-Israelite named Agur in Proverbs 30:1–4, they joined their ancient Near Eastern counterparts in taking the existence of a supreme power as a given.[27]

It is not clear what Crenshaw means here. Technically philosophers never wondered whether Being exists, for being able to ask the question presupposes it. They did ask about the ontological status of Being or why there is something rather than nothing. So Crenshaw's question seems misconstrued, unless by Being he means God. This seems to be implied in the second part of the quote, where he identifies Being with a supreme power, which is in fact something neither Tillich nor Heidegger—from whom the concept is derived—would have been happy with. Being is not a power,

---

25. Long, *Twentieth-Century Western Philosophy of Religion*, 110.
26. Thrower, *Alternative Tradition*, 28.
27. Crenshaw, "Sipping from the Cup of Wisdom," 41–42.

not even the supreme power. It is something the existence of any power or beings whatsoever presupposes.

So Crenshaw seems to be trying to say that the most divisive question is whether God (Crenshaw's Being) exists, and that biblical texts do not, with one exception, presuppose such a concern. Note that he is doing comparative philosophy of religion on a minimalist scale, because to be able to deny ontological concerns in the text, one must first discern the metaphysical assumptions in the discourse. Anyhow, as we saw in the previous section, things are not so simple, and Agur is only the tip of the iceberg. In this section I wish to argue not only that the notion of God as Being is anachronistic in biblical ontology, but also that the biblical texts never addressed the mystery of existence in its philosophical form, since they had no conception of Being in the Heideggerian sense of the word.

In the Hebrew Bible itself, we find a certain inquisitive sense of mystery concerning beings. Adam marvels at Eve (Gen 2); Moses is perplexed at the durability of the burning bush (Exod 3); the psalmists gaze in awe at the wonders of creation (Pss 8, 104, etc.) and stand astounded by the incomprehensibility of the divine mind (Ps 139); a sage in Proverbs is dumbfounded by human and animal behavior (Prov 30); and so on. Even so, no biblical character is ever depicted as having any interest in ideas that presuppose the question, "Why is there something rather than nothing?" Biblical protological etiologies (creation myths/mythological motifs) seem to presuppose partial inquiries concerning what was perceived to be created phenomenal reality only. As such they presuppose the question, "Who configured contingent states of affairs?" This is an altogether different question from "Why is there any state of affairs to begin with?" Such a question is light-years away from what we have in the ontological assumptions presupposed in ancient Israelite metaphysical claims.

Of course, even if the ultimate question is never explicitly asked, many readers of the Hebrew Bible may still wonder whether biblical ontology did not provide an implicit if unintended solution to the mystery of existence via recourse to the "God hypothesis" (i.e., the notion of Yhwh as creator and necessary being). Several arguments may be put forward to show that this belief distorts both biblical ontology and the question of why things are the way they are, or why they are at all.

First of all, one possible reason why ontogenetic explanations are absent from biblical ontology is the fact that the concept of "existence per se," as an abstraction inferred from and vis-à-vis concrete instantiations of it in actual existents, is absent from ancient Israelite metaphysics. Thus we encounter the verb "to be" but not the generic noun "being." Even if we suppose that the Septuagint was correct in translating the divine name "Yhwh" to mean "he who is" (i.e., exists), the reference is not to existence per se, nor is the deity equated with Being itself. Even on that reading the focus is on the existing subject ("he who"), and the name is not a definition of reality or an equation of the deity with Being (i.e., the name is not "he who is existence"). It functions only as a polemical predication, not as a philosophical conclusion following ontological deliberation. Perhaps in this sense biblical theologians are right in denying that such philosophical abstraction as became evident in the Septuagint was possible in ancient Israelite religion.[28]

Second, let us take a closer look at the explanatory function of ancient Israelite varieties of the "God hypothesis" as represented in the belief in Yhwh as necessary being and creator. Here we find that the scope of the supposed answer is far too limited to deal with existence per se. Yhwh is assumed to exist, to be sure, but the "God hypothesis" does not pretend to explain *why* Yhwh happens to exist. Biblical ontology does not offer us some etiology of divine existence. Why Yhwh exists and why there is reality at all—so Yhwh could necessarily be—does not seem to have been something with reference to which an explanation is forthcoming (if one is possible at all). Ultimately, we are not told why the precreation reality characterized by the existence of Yhwh was assumed to be the way it was, or why it was at all.

Interestingly, even if one erroneously limits the mystery of existence to the created world, biblical ontology's "God hypothesis" actually increases rather than diminishes residual ontological mystery. For example, given Yhwh as creator it becomes a mystery as to why Yhwh created the things he did (rather than something else); in the manner he did (rather than by other means); or when he did (rather than sooner or later in eternity). In fact, why Yhwh as self-sufficient being would want to create anything in the first place is never explained. In other words, if the "God hypothesis" is taken to have represented an answer to the mystery of existence, it must be considered as extending and complicating the riddle rather than solving it (contra Edmund Jacob, who follows Karl Barth in the absurd claim that according to the text the world was created for the purpose of establishing a covenant).[29]

---

28. Preuss, *Old Testament Theology*, 1:141.
29. Jacob, *Theology of the Old Testament*, 137.

Of course, protological etiologies were not meant to be complete metaphysical explanations based on a rigorous and sustained application of the principle of sufficient reason. Of course, the biblical authors were not philosophers, and it would be unreasonable and anachronistic to expect them to have been such. But that is the point. In noting the absence of explanations I am simply describing the scope of residual ontological mystery in the text—not claiming that the presence of such mystery is a bad thing or the result of some oversight on the part of philosophical incompetents. Moreover, such observations are significant, since they suggest that biblical theologians and philosophers of religion defending biblical theism are mistaken if they assume that biblical ontology utilized the "God hypothesis" in protological etiologies, to account for the existence either of reality per se or of the reality of the created world.

Contrary to popular assumptions, therefore, in the Hebrew Bible the "God hypothesis" was never called upon to solve the riddle of the Real, and biblical ontology cannot be considered as having presented readers with any sort of attempted response to the mystery of existence in the philosophical-metaphysical sense. Even in the context of biblical ontology, why anything (including God) exists rather than nothing therefore remains an "Ultimate Unanswerable Unknown,"[30] if only for the reason that the problem of Being was not yet even conceivable in abstract philosophical terms. For this reason, Jewish and Christian philosophers of religion should not bracket the history of religion and assume that their metaphysical theories are grounded in biblical ontology, while Hebrew Bible scholars, for their part, should realize that the notion of Yhwh as creator did not arise from a utilization of the principle of sufficient reason in mythical guise and was never intended to be an answer to the question of why things are the way they are, or why they are at all.

12.5. Nonrealism, Fictionalism, and the Ontological Assumptions of the Implied Author

The following aphorism by Friedrich Nietzsche may prompt biblical scholars to consider the philosophical implications of literary criticism.

Irreligiosity of artists. Homer is so at home among his gods, and takes such delight in them as a poet that he surely must have been deeply

---

30. The term was formulated in Daniel Kolak, *In Search of God*, 447.

irreligious. He took what popular belief offered him (a paltry, crude, in part horrible superstition) and dealt as freely as a sculptor with his clay, that is, with the same openness Aeschylus and Aristophanes possessed, and which in more recent times has distinguished the great artists of the Renaissance, as well as Shakespeare and Goethe.[31]

In this regard, we may state the obvious: the human characters depicted in biblical narratives are definitely realists with reference to the ontological status of Yhwh in the world within the world in the text. That much cannot be denied. But what concerns us now is the ontological vantage point of the implied authors. Do we have any clue as to their ontological assumptions about referentiality, and about what they assumed about the relation between the worlds in the text and the world outside the text? Given that they knew what they were doing—that is, engaging in the creative construction of fictional scenarios—and irrespective of whether we think in terms of sources, traditions, redactions, or editorial comments, we have to ask whether realism was the default perspective of the authors as many biblical scholars seem to assume.

Reading between the lines of many books in the Hebrew Bible, it becomes readily apparent that the authors were very much aware of the fact that they were creating the persona of Yhwh as a character in a story. But if the authors were aware of their constructive role in the characterization of Yhwh in the world in the text, then some of the more radical claims of biblical scholars may not be all that anachronistic. For example, David Clines can feel justified in claiming that, when it comes to the way biblical scholars speak about the representation of God in the Pentateuch:

> God ... is a character in a novel. God in the Pentateuch is not a "person"; he is a character in a book. And there are no people in books, no real people, only fictions; for books are made, not procreated.... For if we were to imagine that the God of whom it speaks is identical to the "true God"—the God who is worshipped and theologised about—we might have some serious theological problems on our hands.[32]

Similarly, according to Robert Carroll, "the biblical God is a character in Hebrew narrative and therefore is, in a very real sense, a figure of fic-

---

31. Nietzsche, *Human, All Too Human*, 68 [par. 125].
32. Clines, *Interested Parties*, 190.

tion.[33] Moreover, Walter Brueggemann tells us that "even with reference to God, the imaginative generative power of rhetoric offers to the hearer of this text a God who is not otherwise known or available or even—dare one say—not otherwise 'there.'"[34]

Are these claims descriptive or evaluative? It is not clear. Some would say that they are evaluative in that this is the modern assessment, not that of the biblical authors themselves. According to James Crenshaw:

> The accusation of supernaturalism rests on a misunderstanding of descriptive analysis of biblical texts. These may give the impression of supernaturalism, for they accept the imaginary world of the authors, who definitely believed in an interventionalist deity. By no means does that openness to an alien world view suggest personal acceptance of it.[35]

Others are not so sure. Take, for example, Thomas Thompson, who insists that the nonrealism in respect to the ontological assumptions of both implied author and reader is not only evaluative but is also descriptive: "It is not a good idea to believe in a god when he is a character in story! Don't think for a moment that the narrator ... or his audience ever believed in ... that kind of god. This is the world that the teller has created for his representation of Old Israel."[36] To this can be added his claim that "[t]he Bible's language is not an historical language. It is a language of high literature, of story, of sermon and of song. It is a tool of philosophy and moral instruction."[37]

Now if the authors were self-consciously creating the deity as a character in a text, then the idea of an actual divine revelation in the past on which the details of the narratives are purportedly based is seriously problematic. It would also mean that the ontology of the world behind the text and of the possible worlds in the text may be best understood not via realism but by what is known as fictionalism. This means that statements in Israelite god talk should not be understood along descriptivist lines of referentiality but should rather be approached as intentionally useful fictions. In other words:

---

33. Carroll, *Wolf in the Sheepfold*, 38.
34. Brueggemann, *Old Testament Theology*, 51.
35. James Crenshaw, *Prophets, Sages, and Poets* (St. Louis: Chalice, 2006), 199.
36. Thompson, *Bible in History*, 332.
37. Ibid., 99.

1. Claims about Yhwh made within the Hebrew Bible are taken to be truth-apt; that is, true or false.
2. The Hebrew Bible's religious language is to be interpreted at face value—not reduced to metaphors for something else.
3. The aim of discourse in any given domain is not truth, but is rather some other virtue (e.g., simplicity, explanatory scope).

When we work with the representational pluralism, of the text it may be better to opt for what is called modal fictionalism, inasmuch as later redactors and those familiar with more than one tradition knew that alternative stories existed. Modal fictionalism, then, is the view which holds that biblical representations of possible worlds in the text are useful fictions, with no isomorphic referentiality beyond themselves. In this regard, modal fictionalism represents a further refinement of fictionalism proper. In the context of biblical theology, modal fictionalism involves a fictionalist approach to claims about possible worlds in the text. For instance, modal fictionalism in the mind of the implied author is not normally fictionalist about the claim that "It is possible that there is a god called Yhwh." Rather, it is fictionalist about the claim that "There is a possible world in which there is a god called Yhwh."

"The practice of regarding possible worlds merely as convenient fictions or of treating talk about possible worlds as being useful without being literally correct" is common in discussions of biblical authorship and canonization.[38] It is only recently, however, that philosophers and biblical scholars have seriously examined the implications of apprehending possible worlds merely as fictional objects. Modal fictionalism can therefore be interpreted as a descriptive theory of what biblical texts in fact amount to.

> If the theory is that we take possible worlds as no more than convenient fictions, and, in the case of strong modal fictionalism, that facts about the content and nature of the fiction of possible worlds explain and/or provide the basis of the analysis of our modal locutions, then the theory is descriptive.[39]

---

38. Daniel Nolan, "Modal Fictionalism," *SEP* [cited 15 August 2012]. Online: http://plato.stanford.edu/archives/win2011/entries/fictionalism-modal/.
39. Ibid.

In order to make convincing the hypothesis that the Hebrew Bible's ontology is fictionalist and that the hypothesis entails descriptive rather than evaluative philosophical clarification, it may help to demonstrate instances of metafiction in the discourse. Metafiction is fictional writing that selfconsciously and systematically draws attention to its status as an artifact by posing questions about the relationship between fiction and reality, usually through irony and self-reflection. Thus the question is: Are there parts of the Hebrew Bible that do not allow the reader to forget that he or she is reading a fictional work? Are there any metareferences in ancient Israelite god talk whereby fictional characters display an awareness that they are in a fictional work?

Several examples come to mind, both in prose and poetry. On the one hand, there are instances of texts where, reading between the lines, one can see that the authors were aware of their constructive role in creating a less than perfect deity in a universe in words. Such texts include Gen 1–11, Jonah, Job, and Ruth. It is hard to believe that, depicting Yhwh as he did, the author of Gen 2 actually believed that his character was identical to a real God outside the narrative. On the other hand, in juxtaposed instances of prose and poetry—for instance Exod 14 and 15, Judg 4 and 5, Jonah 1 and 2, and 2 Sam 21 and 22—the poetic *deus ex machina* recasting of the prosaic plot too obviously represents a colorful mythization that the redactors at least could not but be aware of.

But there is more, particularly from the perspective of source and redaction criticism. Do references to the book of Jeremiah in the book of Jeremiah count as an example of "breaking the fourth wall"? Or what about references to what Moses wrote down in the stories about Moses? Also, what about the juxtaposition of sources, the details of which contradict one another? If it is argued that ascribing this amount of critical reflection and distinction to editors, and using the very concept of fiction, are anachronistic, then the reply has to be that fictionalism is not distortive of the ontology of the implied authors, certainly no more so than applying the concept of history. For consider books such as Jonah and Job. The authors of these texts could not possibly have believed that the God Yhwh they themselves had deliberately created as a character in narratives and whose words they formed as poetry corresponded to an extratextual deity who corresponded fully to his persona in representation. Deities's private acts cannot be known from a third-person perspective, nor do they speak in poetry (as a rule). The narrator's perspective in Gen 1 is implied to be impossible by the story itself.

In these scenarios, the concept of modal fictionalism might not be an inappropriate descriptive ontology for the metaphysical assumptions operative in the world behind the text. In philosophy of religion itself the fictionalist option has been thoughtfully assessed by Victoria Harrison, in her *Fictionalism and Religious Diversity*.[40] One is also reminded of the ideas of Hans Vaihinger, who, in his *Philosophie des Als Ob* ("philosophy of as-if"),[41]

> argued that human beings can never really know the underlying reality of the world, and that as a result we construct systems of thought and then assume that these match reality: we behave "as if" the world matches our models. In the preface to the English edition of his work, Vaihinger expressed his "principle of factionalism," proposing that an idea whose theoretical untruth or incorrectness (and therewith also its falsity) is admitted is not for that reason practically valueless and useless. Such an idea, in spite of its theoretical nullity, may have great practical importance.[42]

The claim being made here is not that fictionalism is true or even correct in the context of contemporary metaphysics or semantics. There are many problems with the theory, and I am not basing my arguments on the assumption that it is beyond criticism. In the context of biblical scholarship, however, and given theological pluralism, historical change, and the presence of fiction in the Hebrew Bible, I am asking whether (not claiming that)—from pragmatic and functional perspectives—the notion of fictionalism might not itself be a useful fiction for describing issues concerning referentiality from the perspective of the biblical authors who knew they were being creative and constructive.

A question nevertheless remains for philosophers of biblical literature. How was it that the implied reader was expected to (and could) be moved by what he or she on some level might recognize was only a character in a

---

40. Harrison, "Metaphor, Religious Language and Religious Experience," 127–45; idem, "Philosophy of Religion, Fictionalism, and Religious Diversity," *IJPR* 68/1–3 (2010): 43–58.

41. Hans Vaihinger, *The Philosophy of As-If: A System of the Theoretical, Practical and Religious Fictions of Mankind* (London: Routledge, 1965).

42. "Hans Vaihinger," *Wikipedia, The Free Encyclopedia* [cited 16 August 2012]. Online: http://en.wikipedia.org/w/index.php?title=Hans_Vaihinger&oldid= 507113027

text, and in that sense did not exist? "The so-called "paradox of emotional response to fiction" is an argument for the conclusion that our emotional response to fiction is irrational."[43]

> The argument contains an inconsistent triad of premises, all of which seem plausible initially. These premises are (1) that in order for us to be moved (to tears, to anger, to horror) by what we come to learn about various people and situations, we must believe that the people and situations in question really exist or existed; (2) that such beliefs regarding existence ("existence beliefs") are suspended when we knowingly engage with fictional texts; and (3) that fictional characters and situations do in fact seem capable of moving us at times.[44]

A number of conflicting solutions to this paradox have been proposed by philosophers of art.

> While some argue that our apparent emotional responses to fiction are only "make believe" or pretense, others claim that "existence beliefs" are not necessary for us to have emotional responses (at least to fiction) in the first place. Still others hold that there is nothing especially problematic about our emotional responses to works of fiction, since what these works manage to do (when successful) is create in us the illusion that the characters and situations depicted therein actually exist.[45]

Of course, if one is going to claim nonrealism for biblical authors, then one needs an error theory to explain how and why people began to forget the fictional nature of biblical narrative. In the end, however, the claim being made here is not that fictionalism is true or even correct in the context of contemporary metaphysics or semantics. As I have already said, the theory presents many problems, and I am not basing my arguments on the assumption that it is beyond criticism. I simply wish to leave some food for thought based on a realization of what seems obvious once a fundamentalist perspective on the nature of the text and referentiality has been left behind.

---

43. Steven Schneider, "The Paradox of Fiction," *IEP* [cited 12 April 2010]. Online: http://www.iep.utm.edu/fict-par/.

44. Ibid.

45. Ibid.

12.6. Conclusion

In this chapter we have seen that, contrary to popular belief, there is much work to be done with regard to the question of the existence of deity. Biblical scholarship reveals a gap when it comes to research on biblical religious ontology. Perhaps a philosophical approach to ancient Israelite religion will be able to offer an official and independent platform for historical discussion (without interfering with Old Testament theologians, who are free to look the other way).

13
Epistemologies in Ancient Israelite Religion

Subsequently, the Old Testament is opposed to making an image of YHWH for reasons that were central to its faith in God, not for reasons having to do with philosophical epistemology, enlightened skepticism, or a general aesthetic criticism. At the heart of the prohibition was the recognition that YHWH's freedom was violated by an image.[1]

13.1. Introduction

Purely descriptive epistemological perspectives on ancient Israelite religion as encountered in the pluralist and dynamic traditions of the Hebrew Bible are rare.[2] To the extent that epistemology is a concern in biblical scholarship, the focus is on hermeneutics and metacommentary.[3] The interest typically lies with the epistemological assumptions of the readers of the Hebrew Bible, rather than with those implicit in the worlds in the texts themselves.[4] Exceptions exist, of course, particularly with reference to the study of wisdom literature[5] and with regard to research on the con-

---

1. Preuss, *Old Testament Theology*, 1:108.

2. Healy and Parry, *Bible and Epistemology*, ix. The contribution of Ryan O'Dowd ("A Chord of Three Strands: Epistemology in Job, Proverbs and Ecclesiastes," 65–82) is notable for its attempt to be concerned with the Hebrew Bible and epistemology.

3. Barr, *Concept of Biblical Theology*, 146–71.

4. Ferdinand Deist, *Ervaring, Rede en Metode in Skrifuitleg: 'n Wetenskapshistoriese Ondersoek na Skrifuitleg in die Nederduitse Gereformeerde Kerk 1840–1990* (Pretoria: Human Sciences Research Council, 1994).

5. For instance, Michael V. Fox, "Qoheleth's Epistemology," *HUCA* 58 (1987): 137–55. On the problem of knowledge in biblical literature from a philosophical perspective, see Annette Schellenberg, *Erkenntnis als Problem: Qohelet und die alttestamentlichen Diskussion um das menschliche Erkennen* (OBO 188; Fribourg: Universitatsverlag; Gottingen: Vandenhoeck & Ruprecht, 2002).

cept of revelation in ancient Israelite religion. In this regard it is noticeable that many biblical theologians interested in epistemology tend to be more attracted to Continental philosophy than to the concerns and concepts of the analytic traditions. Perhaps this is due to hermeneutical issues. In a relatively recent publication on biblical epistemology, one author remarked as follows:

> When I began working with epistemology in the Bible several years ago, I started with the Anglo-American tradition (justification, foundationalism, reliabalism, internalism, externalism, evidentialism and coherentism) and slowly lost confidence that I could connect these ideas with what I found in the Biblical text. Instead, I found the most profitable ideas among Continental philosophers like Hamman, Jacobi, Hegel, Kierkegaard, Levinas, Ricoeur and Gadamer whose attention to religion, ethics and ontology in their epistemological discussions provided concepts and vocabulary suitable to biblical and theological description. To my knowledge, these two traditions have very little interaction in the academy today. Consequently, most biblical scholars who attend to epistemology do so through the Continental tradition. I hope that these facts, implicit in the material here, will provoke philosophers-by-trade to help biblical scholars understand why this is so.[6]

If biblical scholars' concern is *descriptive* religious epistemology, I beg to differ from this view. Continental philosophy of religion and its constructive concerns are not really suitable to the historical task of describing the Hebrew Bible's folk epistemologies in philosophical language. However, if analytic epistemological concepts and categories are put into the service of descriptive historical inquiry, one is able to clarify the Hebrew Bible's own assumptions about the nature and justification of knowledge, truth, and belief. A similar quest has already begun with reference to the New Testament. One example is that of William Abraham who, in analyzing the Gospel of Mark, wrote as follows:

> Mark's Gospel is not, of course, an essay in epistemology. It is first and foremost an exercise in narration and proclamation.... Thus we must work indirectly by exploring the epistemological assumptions, insights,

---

6. O'Dowd, "A Chord of Three Strands," 65–82. See also O'Dowd's *The Wisdom of Torah: Epistemology in Deuteronomy and the Wisdom Literature* (FRLANT 225; Göttingen: Vandenhoeck & Ruprecht, 2009).

suggestions and proposals that show up *en route* to ends that are not directly epistemological.[7]

Substitute "Hebrew Bible" for "Mark's Gospel" and the hermeneutical legitimacy of an analytic epistemology of Israelite religion becomes perfectly obvious. Such a religious epistemology of ancient Yahwism, pursued within the context of biblical scholarship with its descriptive agenda, will be interested in discerning what were assumed to be the necessary and sufficient conditions of religious knowledge, what were assumed to be its sources, and what was taken for granted about its structure and its limits. As the study of allegedly justified belief, a descriptive epistemology of Israelite religion will moreover aim to understand the Hebrew Bible's concepts of belief justification, the conditions that were assumed to make justified beliefs justified, whether justification was assumed to be internal or external to one's own mind, and what reasoning (logic) was used in the religious thought of different epistemological perspectives in the text involved.[8]

13.2. Possible Concerns

13.2.1. Traces of Soft Evidentialism

In analytic philosophy of religion, religious epistemology has become very popular since the waning of the interest in natural theology.[9] The central obsession here has been the nature of justified true belief:

> Contemporary epistemology of religion may conveniently be treated as a debate over whether *evidentialism* applies to the belief-component of religious faith, or whether we should instead adopt a more permissive epistemology. Here by "evidentialism" we mean the initially plausible position that a belief is justified only if "it is proportioned to the evidence." … Evidentialism implies that full religious belief is justified only if there is conclusive evidence for it. It follows that if the arguments for there being a God, including any arguments from religious experience,

---

7. William J. Abraham, "The Epistemology of Jesus: An Initial Investigation," in Moser, *Jesus and Philosophy*, 149–68.

8. Matthias Steup, "Epistemology," *SEP* [cited 10 August 2010]. Online: http://plato.stanford.edu/archives/spr2010/entries/epistemology.

9. Philip L. Quinn and Christian B. Miller, *Essays in the Philosophy of Religion* (Oxford: Oxford University Press, 2006), 191.

are at best probable ones, no one would be justified in having a full belief that there is a God.[10]

What kind of evidence is supposed to count?

> Here several sorts of evidence are allowed. One consists of beliefs in that which is "evident to the senses," that is, beliefs directly due to sense-experience. Another sort of evidence is that which is "self-evident," that is, obvious once you think about it. Evidence may also include the beliefs directly due to memory and introspection.[11]

This may sound very modern, yet in ancient Israelite epistemologies the same demand is on occasion readily apparent. In such premodern folk epistemologies of religion, however, we are dealing with traces of "soft" or "narrow" (not applied to all deities) evidentialism as a sort of default setting in many polemical discourses within the Hebrew Bible. A classic example is Isa 41:21, 23.

קרבו ריבכם יאמר יהוה	Bring your arguments, says Yhwh;
הגישו עצמותיכם	Come with your reasons,
יאמר מלך יעקב	says the king of Jacob. ...
הגידו האתיות לאחור	Tell the signs of what comes after
ונדעה כי אלהים אתם	that we may know that ye are gods;
אף־תיטיבו ותרעו ונשתעה	also (do) good, or do evil,
ונרא (ונראה) יחדו	that we may be dismayed, and behold it together.

The entire passage makes sense only if there is some epistemological criteria for the justification of the belief in the instantiation of the property of generic אל-hood. That is, any person p is justified in believing that any entity x is a אל if there is evidence for it. Other texts with similar soft and narrow evidentialist assumptions are present, and one famous example involving Baal must suffice. In 1 Kgs 18:27 we read:

---

10. Peter Forrest, "The Epistemology of Religion," *SEP* [cited 2 April 2010]. Online: http://plato.stanford.edu/archives/sum2009/entries/religion-epistemology.

11. Ibid.

ויהי בצהרים	And it came to pass at noon
ויהתל בהם אליהו ויאמר	that Elijah mocked them and said:
קראו בקול־גדול כי־אלהים	"Cry aloud, for he is a god;
הואכי שיח וכי־שיג לו	either he is musing, or he is gone aside,
וכי־דרך לו	or he is in a journey,
אולי ישן הוא ויקץ	or perhaps he sleeps, and must be awaked."

This text is interesting given what it assumes gods do when not busy with the usual acts. The context of this contest on Mount Carmel also seems to presuppose an evidentialist motif represented in the request for "proofs" for who is really אלהים—Yhwh or Baal? Empirical evidence is demanded so that epistemic agents may know what state of affairs obtains in the actual world in the text. The evidentialist presuppositions taken for granted by the characters in the narrative allow for both verificationist and falsificationist criteria of meaningfulness in religious language, and may be formulated as follows:

1. Belief in x as not אלהים is rational, given the absence of empirical verification.
2. Belief in x as אלהים is rational, given empirical verification.
3. There is not any empirical verification for Baal as אלהים.
4. There is empirical verification for Yhwh as אלהים.
5. Therefore, a belief that Baal is אלהים is falsified.
6. Therefore, a belief that Yhwh is אלהים is verified.

The soft/narrow evidentialism is clearly visible, so there is a difference in scope from that of contemporary evidentialist epistemology. In no way was the evidentialist objection assumed by the implied speaker to be a disproof of the existence of אלהים per se. That is, the conclusion following the disproof was not broad atheism (i.e., that no אלהים exist whatsoever). The implicit religious epistemology is also very different from that of Christian philosophers such as Alvin Plantinga and William Alston ("Reformed epistemologians"), none of whom would agree to such a contest to test their own truth claims about God. The Carmel incident presupposes the possibility of verification and falsification, and in the world in the text also does not take perceiving divine reality as belonging to a doxastic practice different from any other form of empirical experimentation.[12]

Traces of soft evidentialist religious epistemology in the Hebrew Bible are everywhere evident, and are closely tied to the concept of divine revelation in ancient Israelite religion. Think of the evidentialist and verificationist assumptions presupposed in blessings and curses, signs and wonders ("so that they may know"), prophetic arguments about divine providence in history, verification and falsification in divination practices, abductive evidentialism in etiological legends, criteria for determining false prophecy, and so on. Notable specific examples of this kind of evidentialist epistemology include the ten plagues (evidence of "the finger of God"), Gideon's fleece (Judg 6), Samuel's predictions of signs to Saul (1 Sam 9), Hezekiah and the sundial (Isa 38), Ahaz being invited to ask for a sign from heaven or the underworld (Isa 7), apocalyptic signs (Joel, Dan), wisdom's natural theology's appeal to the cosmic and moral orders (Job 38–41), prophetic dramas (*passim*), symptoms of רוח-possession (miraculous powers), upheavals of nature in theophanies (Hab 3), and so on. All of these presuppose narrow and soft evidentialist motifs.

Also important to note is the fact that in the Hebrew Bible evidentialism is often found in association with foundationalist assumptions. Foundationalism is present in those texts that assume knowledge of Yhwh consisted of two levels of belief.[13] First, there were immediate and noninferential beliefs, which were assumed to be foundational or basic beliefs, because they provided a basis for other beliefs. Second, there were inferential or mediated beliefs, which were derived from other beliefs, and ultimately depended on basic beliefs for their justification.[14] Thus, while Walter Brueggemann may suggest that scholars of the Hebrew Bible are not drawn to foundationalist ideas of securing knowledge,[15] many texts in the Hebrew Bible have foundationalist assumptions inasmuch as religious knowledge was assumed to ultimately rest on a foundation of noninferential knowledge. The foundation, however, was not belief in Yhwh, who time and again had to reveal and prove himself to be the living God.

Of course, there might also be texts in the Hebrew Bible that are antifoundationalist and antievidentialist. I do not mean to claim that eviden-

---

12. Long, *Twentieth-Century Western Philosophy of Religion*, 392–97.

13. Ibid., 391.

14. Ibid.

15. Brueggemann, *Old Testament Theology*, 84.

tialism and foundationalism are the default religious epistemologies in all folk epistemological assumptions in ancient Israelite religion. Because the biblical authors were not a school of likeminded philosophers, we can expect that incommensurable religious epistemologies might well be found side by side, even juxtaposed in the same author's writings.[16]

13.2.2. Religious Experience and the Epistemological Problem of Divine Testimony

What kind of religious experiences were assumed to occur in the world in the text, and how did they differ from other experiences? Was a particular experience assumed to be ontic (internal) or noetic (external)? What so-called principles of credulity or incredulity were in place to establish that for any given experience of Yhwh as x by P, P could know that he was in fact experiencing Yhwh? Does a given text assume a descriptive or causal (or other) notion of reference for determining the identity of the entity experienced? (Was Yhwh positively identified by a set of essential properties, or via historical connection? [17]) These questions can be answered with reference to the assumptions in individual texts and are typical of issues discussed when analytic philosophers of religion discuss "God" and the justification of religious experience.[18] However, in philosophy the Hebrew Bible has for the most part been used only for illustrative purposes, as the following example shows:

> It does not seem that any rational subject S could ever be in an epistemic position to be confident of an internal justification of claiming to be appeared to by God. Suppose, for example, Yahweh appears to Moses as x and parts the Red Sea, and Moses then identifies his seeming appeared to by some x that parts the Red Sea as being appeared to by Yahweh. Parting the Red Sea is not an act that requires maximal power. It does not, for example, require as much power as creating or destroying a universe; therefore some lesser being might have parted the Red Sea—a being that is less than omnipotent. Moses has managed a successful identification of x as Yahweh, but completely unbeknownst to himself, and if Moses does not have the internal justification relative to his own epistemic situation to be confident that x is Yahweh, then no audience A would be

---

16. Gericke, "Fundamentalism on Stilts," 1–5.
17. Cf. Harris, *Analytic Philosophy of Religion*, 148–50.
18. Ibid., 141–92.

justified using POC, in attributing veracity to Moses' claim that Yahweh appeared to him as x. Indeed, it seems that any audience A should be suspicious of any such claim and remain incredulous.[19]

While there are interesting bits and pieces here that might account for some elements in the text, the concept of deity assumed by the author is anachronistic as it presupposes classic theism's "perfect being" theology. The biblical scholar would wish to ask, not whether the audience or Moses was ultimately in the right, but how the characters in the world in the text assumed their belief or doubt was justified (whether their reasons are now considered epistemologically sound or not). "Perhaps the justification most widely offered for religious belief concerns the occurrence of religious experience or the cumulative weight of testimony of those claiming to have had religious experiences."[20] Putting the latter case in theistic terms, the argument appeals to the fact that many characters in the biblical narrative testify that they have experienced Yhwh's presence. Was such testimony assumed to provide evidence that Yhwh exists as the living God? That depends on whether we can discern externalist or internalist assumptions operative in the religious discourse. In recent religious epistemology, there was great interest in the internalism-externalism debate.

> The internalism-externalism (I-E) debate lies near the center of contemporary discussion about epistemology. The basic idea of internalism is that justification is solely determined by factors that are *internal* to a person. Externalists deny this, asserting that justification depends on additional factors that are *external* to a person. A significant aspect of the I-E debate involves setting out exactly what counts as *internal* to a person.[21]

In the context of philosophy of religion and the justification of belief,

> internalism is best understood as the thesis that propositional justification, not doxastic justification, is completely determined by one's internal states. These include one's bodily states, one's state of mind, or one's reflectively accessible states. By contrast, externalism in this context is the view that there are environmental factors other than those

---

19. Ibid., 154.

20. Taliaferro, "Philosophy of Religion."

21. Ted Poston, "Internalism and Externalism in Epistemology," *IEP* [cited 11 November 2010]. Online: http://www.iep.utm.edu/int-ext/.

that are internal to the believer which can affect the justificatory status of a belief. The simple conception of the I-E debate as a dispute over whether the facts that determine justification are all internal or external to a person is complicated by several factors. First, some epistemologists understand externalism as a view that knowledge does not require justification, while others think it should be understood as an externalist view of justification. Second, there is an important distinction between having good reasons for one's belief (that is, propositional justification) and basing belief on the good reasons one possesses (that is, doxastic justification).[22]

If a text in the Hebrew Bible assumes an externalist view in its epistemological assumptions, it might take it for granted that testimony is a source of knowledge if and only if it comes from a reliable source. Internalist motifs will not assume such an answer to be satisfactory inasmuch as the reliability of a spokesman for the deity is unknown to others. On this latter view, someone's saying "Thus says Yhwh" would not put one in a position to know that Yhwh actually said it. Both views seem to be present in the Hebrew Bible, since both implicit arguments from authority and personal confirmation are attested. The epistemological problem of divine testimony, however, cannot be divorced from the question of meaning regarding what exactly is being said when the biblical text holds that "Yhwh said…" or that "The word of Yhwh came to x." One might think the question out of place, yet it is not so. Consider, for example, the perplexity of James Barr concerning Yhwh's alleged verbal communication:

> Central to the question, however, must be the way in which the divine word received by the prophet is supposed to have worked in relation to his (or her) own psyche and personality. It is difficult to obtain a clear idea of what most biblical theologians think about this…. None of them … takes the term quite literally, as if to say that in communicating with prophets God enunciated the precise sentences, in Hebrew and with correct grammar, vocabulary and phonetics necessary for intelligibility (and these would of course have to be synchronically correct!) and that the prophet merely repeated what he had audibly heard. But if not this, then what?[23]

---

22. Ibid.

23. Barr, *Concept of Biblical Theology*, 475.

Such questions, though rare in biblical scholarship given their association with positivism, are not unheard of. The last line above is paralleled in a related question of Walter Brueggemann regarding the meaning of the testimony in relation to the problem of historical reference (Lessing!).

> For example, in Exod. 15:21, perhaps one of Israel's oldest poems, Miriam and the other women sing, "horse and rider he threw into the sea." As a theological articulation, this lyrical statement is clear enough. But what could it mean historically? Does the statement mean that the Israelite women saw Yahweh in the water, pushing Egyptian soldiers off their horses? If not that, what?[24]

Back to Barr, who then goes on to speculate about the way such revelation might be understood, and indeed has been understood, by biblical scholars:

> Perhaps many think that the deity made some sort of nonauditory or subsonic communication, which the prophet "heard" and then passed on. The question then is how far the prophet's own mind, experience and perception of the contemporary situation entered into his rendering of the (originally nonarticulate) message. Or the possibility is that the message came from the prophet's experience and his perception about the situation in the first place, that he or she perhaps piled up a strong heap of violent reactions and sentiments and let them burst forth with the deep certainty that the resultant message was the Word of God. I suspect that most theologians hold this latter view but do not like to say so outright.[25]

Quite so; and the fact that very few scholars have been willing to say what they think about the ontological status of the divine *ipsissima verba* in the Hebrew Bible means that there is a great gap in the research on some philosophical aspects of Yhwh's verbal communication in the biblical texts. Many have thought that the question is only worth asking in the context of the world outside the text, and since the text is not history we need not try to understand it at all. But this is too extreme. While my concern is not "what actually happened" in the world outside the text, one can still inquire as to the epistemological assumptions in the text itself.

---

24. Brueggemann, *Old Testament Theology*, 35.
25. Barr, *Concept of Biblical Theology*, 475.

How does one, according to the text, know that Yhwh spoke? What epistemological criteria govern justified belief in the supposed authenticity of religious experience? Of course, normally one might well imagine the idea of a disembodied voice, but is this what the text itself assumes? Or might this reading be anachronistic and the result of the modern philosophical theological assumption that God is supposed to be incorporeal? Moreover, do all texts assume that the word of Yhwh involves a voice at all (as in 1 Sam 3)? Consider, for example, an interesting text that is often overlooked in the discussion on divine revelation, but which clearly illustrates an epistemological dilemma. One might even call the scenario "David's cave" (alluding to Plato's cave), where in 1 Sam 24:2–7 we read:

ויקח שאול שלשת אלפים	Then Saul took three thousand
איש בחור־מכל־ישראל	chosen men out of all Israel,
וילך לבקש את־דוד ואנשיו	and went to seek David and his men
על־פני צורי היעלים	upon the rocks of the wild goats.
ויבא אל־גדרות הצאן	And he came to the sheepcotes
על־הדרך ושם מערה	by the way, where was a cave.
ויבא שאול להסך את־רגליו	And Saul went in to cover his feet.
ודוד ואנשיו	Now David and his men
בירכתי המערה ישבים	were sitting in the depths of the cave.
ויאמרו אנשי דוד אליו	And the men of David said unto him:
הנה היום אשר־אמר יהוה	"Behold the day in which Yhwh had said
אליך הנה אנכי נתן	to you: Behold, I will deliver
את־(איבך) בידך	your enemy into your hand,
ועשית לו כאשר	and you shall do to him as
יטב בעיניך ויקם דוד	it shall seem good to you." Then David arose
ויכרת את־כנף־המעיל	and cut off the skirt
אשר־לשאול בלט	of Saul's robe.
ויהי אחרי־כן	And it came to pass afterward,
ויך לב־דוד אתו	that David's heart smote him,
על אשר כרת	because he had cut off

את־כנף אשר לשאול   Saul's skirt.

ויאמר לאנשיו   And he said to his men:

חלילה לי מיהוה אם־אעשׂה   "Yhwh forbid that I should do

את־הדבר הזה לאדני   this thing unto my lord,

למשיח יהוה   Yhwh's anointed,

לשלח ידי בו   to put forth my hand against him,

כי־משיח יהוה הוא   seeing he is Yhwh's anointed."

וישסע דוד את־אנשיו   So David checked his men

בדברים   with these words,

ולא נתנם לקום אל־שאול   and did not let them rise against Saul.

ושאול קם מהמערה   And Saul rose up out of the cave,

וילך בדרך   and went on his way.

Note "what happened" here in the world in the text, when Yhwh "said" something quite particular to David. From the perspective of the narrator it is a mistake to imagine that "Thus says Yhwh" meant that Yhwh spoke audible words. Here "Thus says Yhwh" is no more than a colorful way of saying that from a set of fortuitous circumstances can be inferred that the deity acted causally and thereby implicitly condones a certain line of action taking advantage of the state of affairs. The testimony is at first believed by David, suggesting his character assumed that this is the way one discerns a word of Yhwh; and that circumstances conducive to certain actions meet the epistemological criteria for knowledge of the divine will. David's reliance on his heart (the concept of which here overlaps with our notion of conscience) to settle the question of whether it was the word of Yhwh presupposes an internalist epistemology of belief justification. His subsequent change of mind implies that an appeal to theological tradition later epistemologically overrode an appeal to empirical experiences. This is different from divine speech in, say, 1 Sam 3, where there is literally a voice (so no generalization about revelation in the Hebrew Bible is possible).

Another good example of critical thinking and a more literal understanding comes from Jer 23:31–33:

הנני על־הנביאם	Behold, I am against the prophets,
נאם־יהוה הלקחים לשונם	says Yhwh, that use their tongues
וינאמו נאם	and say: "He said."
הנני על־נבאי	Behold, I am against them that prophesy
חלמות שקר נאם יהוה	lying dreams, says Yhwh,
ויספרום ויתעו את־עמי	and do tell them, and cause my people to err
בשקריהם ובפחזותם	by their lies, and by their wantonness;
ואנכי לא־שלחתים	yet I sent them not,
ולא צויתים	nor commanded them;
והועיל לא־יועילו לעם־הזה	neither can they profit this people at all,
נאם־יהוה	says Yhwh.

What was of interest was not so much the question of what is real as an epistemological concern about sources and meaning. The epistemology of dreaming proved problematic for the ancient Israelites, and a text like the one above shows that the epistemology of the ontological status of the word of Yhwh could be contested. Our concern with what actually happened in the story or with what is really real is, however, not vulnerable to the antipositivist and antiontological critiques of biblical theologians, since here the biblical scholar asks the questions with reference to the world in the text only. Moreover, our analysis is minimalist in that its findings pertain solely to the text in question. We are not making any hasty generalizations in claiming that this is the "biblical" view on the phenomenology of divine auditions. Pluralism in the texts makes all such claims obvious dogmatic distortions of what is there. Pluralism in theological language about divine revelation may well be shown to be underlain by further pluralism in the folk epistemologies implicit in the discourse.

13.2.3. The Justification of Religious Knowledge and Allotheism

Religious disagreement is a longstanding problem in philosophy of religion, but during this century there has great interest in disagreements between theists and atheists, and also in the disagreements between followers of various religions.[26] Our concern here is *public epistemic parity*. In

---

26. For examples of philosophical discussions on religious disagreement in epis-

this regard, the epistemological legitimacy of double standards in religious reasoning in the ancient Near East is well known, and the epistemology of ancient Israelite religion was no exception. That is, popular epistemological criteria of falsification for justifying atheological notions with reference to foreign gods were not consistently applied to Yhwh. Still, if the other gods did not exist or were worthless (according to some texts), there is need to discern error theories implicit in the text to account for allotheism, the belief in foreign gods. If Yhwh is the only God, how, according to the Hebrew Bible, was the phenomenon of idolatry possible at all?

One of the major issues that developed from a renewed interest in religious experience in philosophy of religion proper is the degree to which such an experience can be said to have epistemic value.[27] A fundamental matter in this regard concerns determining what was assumed to be the reference for referring expressions used to describe the objects of religious experience. If religious experience in the world in the text in the Hebrew Bible is held by the characters to have cognitive import, there must be implicit unformulated theoretical frameworks within which it is assumed one can explain how it is possible to identify those objects.

One of the most important issues to be determined in the worlds in the text is which ones are veridical and which ones are not. So whatever we can say about the veridical ones, when a divine being says, does, or appears, it seems crucial to be able to know that it is Yhwh, and not another divine, demonic, or human entity (Gen 17:1, 32; Exod 3; Judg 6; 1 Sam 3). Here we find the intersection between protagonist and antagonist error theories for allotheism in a culture where monolatrism was a real live option. So how does the text assume to account folk-epistemologically for the worship of other gods, if they are supposed to be weak or nonexistent? A classic example of such an attempt is Jer 44:18–23. The people have one explanation for their problems:

ומן־אז חדלנו לקטר   Since we left off offering

---

temological contexts, see Thomas Kelly, "The Epistemic Significance of Disagreement," in *Oxford Studies in Epistemology* (ed. Tamar Szabo; Oxford: Clarendon, 2005), 167–95; and Richard Feldman, "Epistemological Puzzles about Disagreement," in *Epistemology Futures* (ed. Stephen Hetherington; New York: Oxford University Press, 2006), 167–95.

27. Harris, *Analytic Philosophy of Religion*, 423.

למלכת השמים	to the queen of heaven,
והסך־לה נסכים	and pouring out drink offerings to her,
חסרנו כלו	we have lacked all things,
בחרב וברעב תמנו	and have been consumed by the sword and famine.

Pragmatic arguments have often been employed in support of theistic belief. These arguments are not arguments for the proposition that Yhwh exists; they are arguments for believing that divine providence is at work. The reasoning used in religious thought in such discourse clearly presupposes a counterfactual view of causation, in that "the meaning of causal claims is explained in terms of counterfactual conditionals of the form 'If A had not occurred, C would not have occurred.'"[28] If the people had not stopped their religious practices, misfortune would not have struck them. Jeremiah, however, is not convinced, and offers his own counterfactual theory for the justification of his own religious beliefs and experiences. Because the people did not obey Yhwh, disaster followed (44:21–23):

מפני אשר קטרתם	Because you have offered,
ואשר חטאתם	and because you have sinned
ליהוה ולא שמעתם	against Yhwh, and have not listened
בקול יהוה ובתרתו	to the voice of Yhwh, nor walked
ובחקתיו ובעדותיו	in his law, nor in his statutes,
לא הלכתם על־כן	nor in his testimonies; therefore
קראת אתכם הרעה הזאת	this evil is happened unto you,
כיום הזה	as at this day.

In the Jeremiah text we see the assumption that, though rational, the worshipers of other gods were not functioning properly as epistemic agents. The ones who have left Yhwh, though using the same form of arguments as a worshiper of Yhwh, could not produce reliable arguments. They were colored for the worse by inappropriate background beliefs, interests,

---

28. Peter Menzies, "Counterfactual Theories of Causation," *SEP* [cited 18 September 2010]. Online: http://plato.stanford.edu/archives/fall2009/entries/causation-counterfactual/.

desires, anxieties, and expectations.[29] The epistemic map that best makes sense of this particular instance of the phenomenon of allotheism is therefore clearly externalism. It is not that the people did not reason in a valid manner—their logical strategy is the same as that of Jeremiah. They are assumed to be malfunctioning as cognitive agents because their reasoning is affected by their alleged spiritual and moral vices. Hence they are depicted as being incapable of seeing the hand and will of Yhwh in what happens to them.

This creates an epistemic dilemma: if good and bad times during the worship of a god can no longer indicate whether the god is pleased or not, additional revelation is required to settle the question of what to infer from such events. This presents problems for any counterfactual empirical verification or falsification, a form of epistemological justification that the blessings and curses of Leviticus and the Hebrew Bible presuppose to be valid. This in turn complicates the metaphysics underlying the religious epistemology, since particular divine causality can no longer validly be inferred from *a posteriori* states of knowledge. A prophetic hermeneutic of reality is thus required, but it entails the potential for false prophecy and the attributing of this also to Yhwh. Hence the Nietzschean abyss the people are facing is staring right back at them (e.g., the horror story in 1 Kgs 13).

In the Hebrew Bible, giving divine honor to self-created objects of the mind is seen as the product of a cognitive mistake. One of the tasks for philosophical clarification of this locus is therefore to reconstruct the error theories for allotheism implicit in the worlds in the text of the Hebrew Bible. This is no anachronistic concern, since in the worlds in the text Yhwh himself wonders why the people have strayed from the way and followed other gods. However, we should go beyond the narrator's evaluative point of view and also seek to understand the error theories and justification procedures of the antagonists. The biblical authors did not mention these. Hence the philosopher of Israelite religion must try to understand the other side in order to see what the author and his audience took for granted. In other words, we also need to clarify the folk-philosophical assumptions that were part of the antagonists' justification of "idol" worship, in order to understand the worldview in which the text moves.

---

29. Abraham, "Epistemology of Jesus," 151.

13.2.4. DIVINE REVELATION AND THE PRINCIPLE OF SUFFICIENT REASON

The epistemology of divine revelation cannot be divorced from the metaphysical assumptions of the testimony and questions related to the principle of sufficient reason. In philosophy proper, the principle has a variety of expressions, all of which are perhaps best summarized as follows: "for every event e, if e occurs, then there is a sufficient explanation of why e occurs."[30] A philosophical analysis of the principle of sufficient reasons as operative in the metaphysical assumptions of ancient Israelite religious epistemology will need to attend to the question of whether there were assumed to be sufficient reasons for a particular methodology in Yhwh's ways of revealing himself. There remains the need to discover implicit assumptions about the rationale for the acts of Yhwh. Divine motivations can be subsumed under the rubrics found in the philosophy of action.

How little we know about this issue is readily apparent by asking a few simple yet profound questions about sufficient reasons for the particulars of divine communication. For example: Why, according to the text, is knowledge via divine revelation needed at all (and not, say, innate)? Why, according to the text, is knowledge via divine revelation given directly only to some people rather than to all (why mediation)? Why, according to the text, is divine revelation of religious knowledge offered so rarely rather than all the time? Why, according to the text, does knowledge disclosed in divine revelation often come across as obscure (lots, dreams, visions, etc.) rather than as straightforward?

Lest these questions be considered too abstract, speculative, and anachronistic, it should be noted that they are prompted by states of affairs and divine methodology in both possible and actual worlds in the text itself. With regard to alternative possibilities, one text (Num 12:5–8) assumes as much:

ויאמר יהוה פתאם אל־משה	And Yhwh spoke to Moses,
ואל־אהרן ואל־מרים	and unto Aaron, and Miriam:
צאו שלשתכם אל־אהל	"Come out, you three, to the tent

---

30. "Principle of Sufficient Reason," *Wikipedia, The Free Encyclopedia* [cited 17 August 2012]. Online: http://en.wikipedia.org/w/index.php?title=Principle_of_sufficient_reason&oldid=504690449.

מועד ויצאו שלשתם	of meeting." And the three came out.
וירד יהוה בעמוד ענן	And Yhwh came down in a pillar of cloud,
ויעמד פתח האהל	and stood at the door of the tent,
ויקרא אהרן ומרים	and called Aaron and Miriam;
ויצאו שניהם	and they both came forth.
ויאמר שמעו־נא דברי	And he said: "Hear now my words:
אם־יהיה נביאכם יהוה	if there be a prophet among you, I Yhwh
במראה אליו אתודע	make myself known to him in a vision,
בחלום אדבר־בו	I speak with him in a dream.
לא־כן עבדי משה:	My servant Moses is not so;
בכל־ביתי נאמן הוא	he is trusted in all my house;
פה אל־פה אדבר־בו	with him do I speak mouth to mouth,
ומראה ולא בחידת	even visible, and not in riddles;
ותמנת יהוה יביט	and the image of Yhwh does he behold.
ומדוע לא יראתם לדבר	Why then were you not afraid to speak
בעבדי במשה	against my servant, against Moses?"

Here we see that the deity does not have to use obscurities but can speak directly and in person to anyone he wants when he wants—so why not to everyone all the time? Of course, one could explain "what it means" with reference to the world outside the text via the history of religion and the psychology of religion, since of course we are dealing here with what humans made of dreams *ex post facto*. But this is not what is of interest at present. Our concern is with "what it meant" in the worlds in the text; and what we want to know is why, according to what is implicit in the world in the text, can the deity not be permanently visible, present, and speaking to all people one on one?

Frequently preferred answers—such as "sin," "divine holiness," or the argument that an ever-present deity would make faith redundant or compromise free will—seem at times overapologetic and anachronistic, as if to explain why no god presently appears to us. What we need here is presupposition reconstruction in combination with the history of Israelite religion's folk philosophy of religion. Answers to our earlier "why?" questions are present in the text, even though they are not overt. So it is not because the questions asked above were of no concern to ancient Israelites: they just took the answers for granted. That these things went without saying can be demonstrated with reference to texts that do show an interest in explaining the rationale for the particular divine strategies. Thus with reference to obscurity in revelation, we encounter the proposition in Prov 25:1, according to which the honor of the deity resides in concealment. Here then we have one possible answer that might have sufficed.

Ideally, however, one should not use one text to clarify another: this is a precritical interpretative strategy that has rightly fallen into disrepute since the rise of historical consciousness (today studies in intertextuality sometimes mask the same tendency). Instead, one should analyze the specific text to discern what can be ascertained from its own assumptions on the matter, whatever they are. So for our purposes it is irrelevant whether the answer is "all too human" or presupposing of honor and shame conventions that are now outdated. Our concern is not whether something is "really so," but what goes without saying in the worlds in the text.

13.2.5. PHILOSOPHICAL PERSPECTIVES ON PROPHECY

Philosophical perspectives on Hebrew Bible prophecy are rare.

> When philosophers discuss prophecy they are typically interested in predictions concerning the contingent future. A future event is assumed to be contingent if, and only if, it is assumed possible for it to happen and not happen.[31]

In other words, the events are not assumed to be determined to occur at all costs. Now imagine a text in the Hebrew Bible in which it is prophesied that some future contingent event will occur. Since in the ideology of the text it is assumed that Yhwh cannot be wrong, does it follow that the future contingent event is believed to be inevitable from the perspective of characters inside the world in the text? And if so, in what way is it assumed to be a contingent event cocreated by human free will?

From a historical-critical perspective aimed at reconstructions of the world behind the text, philosophical concerns such as these may seem anachronistic. First of all, prophecies are often *ex-eventu* postdictions, and so technically in such cases there is no real prediction about a future state

---

31. The structure and contents of this section are indebted to the outline by Scott Davison, "Prophecy," *SEP* [cited 4 August 2011]. Online: http://plato.stanford.edu/archives/sum2010/entries/prophecy/.

of affairs. Second, since the Hebrew Bible itself does not seem to show any overt concern for philosophical problems regarding prophecy, putting philosophical questions to the text might seem to be exegetically misplaced. Not so. While the Hebrew Bible is not philosophical in nature, its prophecies contain nascent metaphysical assumptions about the nature of divine foreknowledge, and the deity's relation to time and human freedom, whether the authors are aware of holding to them or not. These "folk-philosophical" presuppositions are in need of philosophical clarification if we are to understand the most fundamental building blocks of biblical worldviews.

An especially vivid example of interesting metaphysical assumptions in prophecy comes from Gen 15:12–16. We pick up the scene at the point where Yhwh reveals to Abraham what the latter can expect from the future:

ויהי השמש	And it came to pass that, when the sun
לבוא ותרדמה נפלה	was going down, a deep sleep fell
על־אברם והנה אימה	upon Abram, and behold, a dread,
חשכה גדלה נפלת עליו	a great darkness, fell upon him.
ויאמר לאברם ידע תדע	And he said to Abram: "Know for sure
כי־גר יהיה זרעך	that your seed shall be a stranger
בארץ לא להם	in a land that is not theirs,
ועבדום וענואתם	and shall serve them; and they shall afflict
ארבע מאות שנה וגם	them four hundred years; and also
את־הגוי אשר יעבדו	that nation, whom they shall serve,
דן אנכי ואחרי־כן יצאו	will I judge; and afterward shall they come
ברכש גדו ואתה	out with great substance. But you
תבוא אל־אבתיך בשלום	shall go to your fathers in peace;
תקבר בשיבה טובה	you shall be buried in a good old age.
ודור רביעי	And in the fourth generation
ישובו הנה כי לא־	they shall come back hither; for
שלם עון האמרי עד־הנה	the iniquity of the Amorite is not yet full."

The folk metaphysics behind this text is vague, ambiguous, and rather fascinating. What is interesting for our purposes is what is being predicted here:

1. Abraham will have descendants.
2. Abraham will live to a ripe old age and die in peace.
3. Abraham's descendants will go to and stay in Egypt.
4. Abraham's descendants will be oppressed.
5. His descendants will leave Egypt in the fourth generation.
6. The Amorites will have filled their iniquity only then.

Historically, of course, there is no philosophical problem in this, since we are dealing with a fictional construct. But given a fictionalist ontology and a literary-philosophical approach, it is hard to tell whether the outcomes are assumed to be wholly dependent on Yhwh or also partly on some cosmic moral order according to which nations are created and destroyed, and in relation to which Yhwh is portrayed as a catalyst (see vv. 14, 16). Indeed, it would seem that according to this text, Yhwh himself is constrained and has to wait for the scales of justice to tip before he can act (v. 16). This introduces the notion of a metaphysical moral order beyond the deity, upon which his actions are dependent, something familiar in the ancient Near East. It is hardly an orthodox idea, yet we must remember that also with regard to prophecy the Hebrew Bible might not always agree with what is believed about the deity/reality relation in modern Christian philosophical theology.

Particularly interesting from a philosophical perspective is the question of what the text of Gen 15:12–16 assumed about the relationship between divine foreknowledge and human free will, both of which seem to be taken for granted. Abraham and company are assumed to be free agents, yet their future seems fixed. Curiously, the narrative implies that Abraham has free will, yet is not free to commit suicide there and then, for otherwise he would not have children or grow old, and everything would prove to have been false. The text also seems to imply that Yhwh either knows a fixed future; or else he has to keep the descendants alive, has to get them to Egypt, has to get Pharaoh to oppress them, has to prevent them from leaving before the fourth generation, and has to get the Amorites to stay evil so that the extent of the evil can fit some sort of scale in an assumed moral order at exactly that time. All this may be something the text has no notion of, yet it follows logically from the discourse.

The question now is in what sense the text itself assumes the future to be fixed in relation to divine foreknowledge. Since Yhwh is not assumed to be mistaken (according to the theology of Gen 15), how are Abraham's and the other agents' actions assumed to be free? Clearly we are dealing with some form of compatabilism that affirms both divine determinism and human free will. But exactly what form does the folk theory behind Gen 15 take when reconstructed in philosophical terms? To answer this question, we may note that philosophers of religion have come up with a number of related perspectives that may allow us to clarify the text's own unspoken metaphysical presuppositions.

A first possible way of clarifying the folk-philosophical assumptions of Gen 15:12–16 is simply to play with the idea that in its folk metaphysics there are not assumed to be any future contingent events. What exactly does accepting this view mean for the understanding of the metaphysical presuppositions in Gen 15? Well, it would suggest that when Yhwh prophesies that Abraham's descendants will be oppressed in and then freed from Egypt, and will exterminate the Canaanites, there is no philosophical puzzle as long as the Israelites' actions are not assumed to be free. Of course, many exegetes would opt for another interpretation. Many Christian philosophers and biblical theologians will not find this idea to be acceptable, because they strongly believe in future contingent events, especially human free choices to, *inter alia*, account for the problem of evil.

A second possible reading involves interpreting the text as not assuming that Yhwh has any knowledge of the contingent future. On this reading, Gen 15 assumes that there might be future contingent events, but Yhwh is not assumed to actually know about them. But if this were the case, how is Yhwh assumed to be able to make the kind of predictions found in the text at all? On this, the so-called Open Future view, Yhwh does not actually foretell the future: technically, he merely reveals his own premeditated agenda. Yhwh knows what will happen not because he knows the future as such but because he knows what he himself wants to do. Since Yhwh's own actions in the future are assumed to be up to him, it is believed to be possible for Yhwh to know about them even though they are contingent; and hence it is possible for the prophecy to reveal them.

The up side of opting for this philosophical perspective is that it does not require the kind of "perfect being" theology alien to the prephilosophical metatheistic assumptions of the Gen 15 narrative. Also, the distinction between Yhwh's knowing the future because it is fixed and he is timeless, and knowing it because he knows what he wants to do even though he is within time, may be useful in avoiding anachronistic readings concerning the relation between Yhwh and time. The major problem with this view in the context of Gen 15, however, is that Yhwh is not only declaring his will. Rather, he seemed to be revealing a future state of affairs as though it were unconditional fate. Hence this perspective fails in that it is unable to deal with the more deterministic elements in the pericope. The Hebrew Bible in general is not that concerned with honoring human free will,' and has no problem with Yhwh's hardening hearts to achieve divine ends (e.g., Exod 7–12).

A third possible approach to explaining what is assumed about Yhwh's knowledge of the contingent future in Gen 15 involves suggesting that the text can be read as supposing that Yhwh exists outside of time altogether. If this idea is present, it would mean that, strictly speaking, Yhwh is not assumed to foreknow the future, since "foreknowledge is knowledge of an event that is possessed at a moment in time that occurs earlier than the moment in time at which the event foreknown occurs."[32] Instead, according to this reading the assumption of Gen 15 would be that Yhwh knows all events from the perspective of timeless eternity.

Supporting this view is that it offers an interesting approach to the metaphysical problems of the Gen 15 prophecy. In terms of the text, the defender of Yhwh's atemporal eternity would say that Yhwh is assumed by the author of Gen 15 to know from the perspective of eternity that the Israelites will be oppressed and freed at a certain time, and, on this basis, that Yhwh prophesied in time that the event in question would occur. The problem with this reading, whatever its philosophical efficiency, is the fact that the narrative of Gen 15 does not seem to assume Yhwh to be outside of time—the very idea is contradicted by the deity's timed actions relative to Abraham. Positing divine atemporality to account for Yhwh's foreknowledge is therefore historically suspect, because it presupposes a postbiblical picture derived largely from neoplatonic philosophical influences.

Fourth, long ago William Ockham (ca. 1285–1347) suggested what might by implication lead us to another interesting way of accounting for Yhwh's knowledge of the contingent future in Gen 15:12–16. Ockham claimed that what God revealed about the contingent future could have been and can be false, even though the existence of the prophecy in the past is ever afterwards necessary. In terms of our example involving Yhwh's prophecy concerning Israel's oppression, Ockham's idea would be that were Abraham to choose freely not to have children instead, then Yhwh would never have prophesied that his descendants would be oppressed in Egypt.

---

32. Ibid.

Some philosophers like to call this kind of proposition a "backtracking counterfactual," because it is a subjunctive conditional statement whose consequent refers to a time earlier than that of its antecedent. If Abraham were about to choose freely, then Yhwh would have known about it, and hence would have spoken accordingly.

The reason why philosophers of religion have expressed doubts about whether or not Ockham's approach is ultimately successful is that "Ockhamism commits one to having to choose between the Scylla of claiming that Yhwh can undo the causal history of the world and the Charybdis of claiming that divine prophecies might be deceptive or mistaken."[33] Our concern, fortunately, does not lie with what is philosophically credible, only with what the text of Gen 15 might assume or not. The Ockhamist perspective, if present in Gen 15, would suggest that for the text Abraham is implied to have a rather odd power over the past. Once Yhwh has said certain words with a certain intention, it does not seem coherent to say that Abraham is assumed to still have any choice about whether or not to procreate. Philosophically problematic as this may seem, if this view is present in Gen 15, it would be in need of further clarification. It is, however, unclear whether Gen 15 presupposes Ockhamism at all.

A fifth possible perspective on Gen 15 starts with the observation that once Yhwh knows that something definitely will happen, then it is assumed to be too late to do anything about it. This assumes that if Yhwh knows the future, then he himself has no free will, and thus there is a limit on divine power. Yhwh is not assumed to be free or able to do something other than what he himself has already predicted (by not letting Israel go down to Egypt, for example). What Yhwh needs, then, for the purposes of providence, "is not just knowledge about what will happen, but also knowledge about what can happen and what will happen in certain circumstances."[34] In other words, what Yhwh needs is "middle knowledge." On this reading, Gen 15 assumes that Yhwh knows what every possible person will do freely in every possible situation. So Yhwh decides which kind of future to actualize, including those situations in which free human persons should be placed, knowing how they will respond, and this results in Yhwh's free knowledge (contingent truths which are up to

---

33. Ibid.
34. Ibid.

Yhwh), which includes foreknowledge of the actual future, including all human actions.

If the text of Gen 15 does assume this account of Yhwh's knowledge (otherwise known as "Molinism"), the narrative presupposes that Yhwh knows (through middle knowledge) that if Abraham is placed in certain circumstances, then he will have descendants who will do as predicted. And that, for reasons not known to us, Yhwh decides to create those circumstances, place Abraham and Israel in them, and also prophesy what Israel will do. Such a middle-knowledge view also appears to have some biblical support, because there are verses which seem to attribute middle knowledge to Yhwh (e.g., 1 Sam 23:6–13). However, whether this view really helps us to understand the metaphysical assumptions of Gen 15 on its own terms must remain open to question. The middle-knowledge view arose out of the need to account for a philosophical problem the author of Gen 15 did not seem to presuppose in his compatibilist metaphysical assumptions. So while this theory is interesting as a possible lens through which to make sense of the philosophical puzzles of Gen 15, we should limit ourselves to what can be inferred from the textual evidence itself.

None of the above philosophical perspectives may fully do justice to the folkmetaphysics underlying a prophecy such as the test case from Gen 15:12–16. Nor can any possible conclusions simply be transposed onto other Hebrew Bible prophecies, as these might operate from different assumptions. Clearly, however, all Hebrew Bible prophecy is philosophically interesting because of its unspoken presuppositions about the nature of deity, divine foreknowledge, and human free will. That its author was not interested in asking the kinds of questions presented here is therefore not an argument against philosophical elucidation. On the contrary, the nonphilosophical nature of the textual discourse makes metaphysical clarification all the more urgent.

13.2.6. The History of Israelite Religion and the Logic of Belief Revision

Biblical criticism has demonstrated beyond a doubt the reality of "revision," "editing," "emendation," "reinterpretation," "redaction," "rethinking," "rewriting," and "reconstruction" in the Hebrew Bible. In logico-epistemological terms, belief revision has taken place, and the supporting data can be found in the findings of source, tradition, redaction, canonical, composition, ideological, and other types of biblical criticism. On a larger scale, historical, literary, sociological, theological, and psychological descriptions of how belief revision has occurred in Israelite religion are also available. The catalysts for belief change were several major events in the histories of Israel and Judah that brought about crises of belief and new ways of making sense of old ideas. Steinberg offers the following list, composed from a phenomenological perspective.[35]

Crisis	Impact
Philistine invasion (twelfth to eleventh centuries B.C.E.)	Development of Israelite consciousness and possible formation of a league of El and Yhwh worshipers identifying the two gods.
Imposition by Ahab of Tyrian Baal (mid-ninth century B.C.E.)	Demand by the prophetic movement to reject the native weather deity Baal-hadad (in likelihood with his consort, the native Ashtart/Ashtoreth) as un-Israelite and disloyal to Yhwh. Baal's characteristics are appropriated by Yhwh. (See Elijah on Carmel.)
Assyrian pressure (eighth and seventh centuries B.C.E.)	Crisis of confidence in Yhwh—was he weaker than the gods of Assyria? This may have led to the widespread worship of Astarte-Ishtar-Queen of Heaven and perhaps of astral deities.
Decline of Assyria (seventh century B.C.E.)	Demand by the Deuteronomic reformers for exclusive worship of Yhwh—all other deities are rejected as un-Israelite. To ensure uniformity of practice and concentration of resources, all sacrifice is centralized in Jerusalem. Outside of Jerusalem, prayer starts to replace sacrifice in popular worship.

35. Steinberg, *Israelite Religion to Judaism*.

Babylonian exile (sixth century B.C.E.)	Since Yhwh could not be said to have been defeated by the gods of Babylon, claim that he was lord of the world and author of the just destruction of Jerusalem. Prayer replaces sacrifice in popular worship.

Given all this, what is lacking is a descriptive philosophical clarification of the logic behind the cognitive processes involved in these major shifts in the belief systems within ancient Yahwism(s).

What makes such an exercise nontrivial is that different groups opted for different ways of coming to terms with the same historical events and theological developments. Some continued to hold on to traditional faith, others ventured to think of Yhwh in different ways, still others left faith in Yhwh behind altogether. We still do not know how exactly belief revision manifested itself or why. Since most biblical scholars are not familiar with the logic of belief revision, I shall give a short and utterly basic introduction to it in order to provide a foretaste of the clarifying possibilities this type of philosophical analysis may hold. The concern here is not to show that the reasoning was valid or invalid, or that belief revisions were justified and true or not. Our concern is merely to describe the logic behind the revisions in the Hebrew Bible and our logical criticism is simply a formalization of the findings of biblical criticism. We may begin by noting the following assumptions of belief revision logics:

1. *Quantity:* Beliefs were valuable, and so traditions did not change and texts were not edited without good reasons. So it may be safe to assume that in the process of belief change, the loss of existing beliefs was minimized.
2. *Quality:* The redactors edited the Hebrew Bible because of what they believed to be true. Beliefs were not adopted capriciously—there were assumed to be grounds for any gain in information.
3. *Categorial matching:* The result of the change was always going to be another belief state, whatever that involved.
4. *Success:* Changes were effected successfully, and this is why we still have a Hebrew Bible.

Two kinds of changes are usually distinguished:

1. *Updating:* The new information is about the situation at present, while the old beliefs refer to the past. Updating is the operation of changing the old beliefs to take into account the present situation.
2. *Revision:* Both the old beliefs and the new information refer to the same situation. An inconsistency between the new and old information is explained by the possibility of the old information being less reliable than the new. Revision is the process of inserting the new information into the set of old beliefs without generating an inconsistency.[36]

Various operations can be performed in this context:

1. *Contraction*—the removal of a belief without checking consistency;
2. *Expansion*—the addition of a belief without checking consistency;
3. *Revision*—the addition of a belief while maintaining consistency;
4. *Consolidation*—restoring the consistency of a set of beliefs; and
5. *Merging*—the fusion of two or more sets of beliefs while maintaining consistency.

In the logic of belief revision, there are also several so-called "rationality principles" (quantity, quality, etc.) These are codified via rationality postulates. The list below gives the ones for revision. K = knowledge; * = revision; x = old belief; y = new belief; Cn = consequences.

1. $K * x$ is closed under Cn
2. $x \in K * x$
3. $K * x \subseteq K + x$
4. $K + x \subseteq K * x$, if x is consistent with K
5. $K * x$ is inconsistent if x is (i.e., if $\neg x$ is a theorem)
6. If $Cn(x) = Cn(y)$, then $K * x = K * y$

---

36. "Belief Revision," *Wikipedia, The Free Encyclopedia* [cited 17 August 2012]. Online: http://en.wikipedia.org/w/index.php?title=Belief_revision&oldid=501423224.

7. $(K * x) + y \subseteq K * (x \wedge y)$

8. $K * (x \wedge y) \subseteq (K * x) + y$, if y is consistent with $K * x$

To show how these basic ideas in the field might be of use to the history of religion, consider the event that shook the faith of Israel's people *in extremis*: the exile. Though the event is indeed sometimes overrated as a catastrophe, it remains the greatest of all crises in Israelite religion, and it provided an impetus for the revision of history by Deuteronomists and by Priestly and other redactors. Core beliefs destroyed concerned the temple, the city, the land, the monarchy, prophecy, and so on. Histories of Israelite religion speak of "loss of faith" and "crisis of belief." According to Rainer Albertz, for example, as a result of the Babylonian captivity, "the feeling of having been dragged off against their will kept high their hope of a return and of a *revision* of the facts of history."[37] Albertz also speaks of a struggle for a theological interpretation of a failed history: "It says much for the high value which history acquired in the religion of Israel from its beginning as the medium of divine action that in the crisis of the exile there was a large scale theological revision of the previous history."[38] Regarding the Pentateuch he notes, "In addition to the brief references to the patriarchs in exilic prophecy of salvation, another large scale literary revision of the patriarchal tradition was undertaken during the exile."[39] He also says:

> The vital interests of the priest theologians in the temple cult also led at another point to a marked expansion and revision of the lay theological Pentateuch composition: in the creation stories and therefore in the question of the foundation of the Israelite relationship with god.[40]

As for postexilic Chronistic revision:

> The evaluation of the time of David and Solomon as the goal and climax of the Israelite foundation history with which the authors of Chronicles reacted to the challenge from Samaria amounted to no less than a revision of the canon. In their view, the decision taken in the Persian period, in the interest of opposition to domination and enthusiasm with a view to the emancipation of the priesthood, to end the foundation history of

---

37. Albertz, *History of Israelite Religion*, 2:373.

38. Ibid.

39. Ibid., 2:406.

40. Ibid., 2:489.

Israel with the death of Moses and thus largely exclude the old theology of kingship and the state cult from official Yahweh religion, needed revision. They felt that the canon should be urgently enlarged, that the historical tradition of DtrG which had been cut out and also the prophetic writings which brought out the special Jerusalem traditions of salvation should be accorded their due place in official theology.[41]

Revision is everywhere. With regard to the prophetic writings:

Though groups of prophets are known to have existed in older times, one may assume that in the course of the 8th century B.C.E. a nonconformist but literary elite gathered around these prophets and became responsible for the collection, *revision*, and transmission of their words.[42]

From the perspective of the logic of belief revision, all of the above references to "revision" in various sections of the Hebrew Bible are very interesting. With the aid of the logic of belief revision, the findings of the history of Israelite religion and of source, tradition, and redaction criticism regarding belief change can be described in formal philosophical terms to clarify the exact roads the faith took (and did not take). One possible way of doing this is via the so-called AGM model of the theory (named after its developers, Alchourron, Gardenfors, and Makinson). It assumes a static environment like a text, which in our case would involve a belief state in the form of a set of preexilic sentences in the text. It must be largely consistent and closed under a (classical) consequence operation Cn and the input is any (presumably self-consistent) redacted sentence. The nature of the state of the transformation of belief would be either contraction, expansion, or revision.

In *contraction*, a specified sentence x from preexilic belief set is *removed* by a Deuteronomistic or Priestly or other redactor. That is, a specific text's preexilic belief set $\aleph$ is superseded by a postexilic redacted belief set $\aleph(-x)$ that is a subset of $\aleph$ not containing x. When -x is the result of contracting $\aleph$ by x there is also belief suspension; so $x \notin \aleph$ -x if possible. Belief in x is lost; but this does not mean that belief in ¬x is gained, so that in terms of quality there is no capricious gain in information and it is ensured that $\aleph$ -x $\subseteq \aleph$. With regard to Categorial Matching it is ensured

---

41. Ibid., 547.

42. Meindert Dijkstra, "The Law of Moses: The Memory of Mosaic Religion in and after the Exile," in *Yahwism after the Exile: Perspectives on Israelite Religion in the Persian Era* (ed. Rainer Albertz and Bob Becking; Assen: Van Gorcum, 2003), 96.

that ℵ -x is closed under Cn and in terms of quantity, information loss was minimized, which is never easy. The question that remains is: What should Cn(a, a → b)-b be? Cn(a)? Cn(a → b)? or Cn(a ∨ b)? Because this creates a choice problem, an extralogical mechanism is necessary.

In *expansion* a redactional sentence x is *added* by a Deuteronomistic or Priestly redactor to the preexilic belief set ℵ *without checking for consistency*. That is, nothing is removed so that ℵ is replaced by a postexilic redacted set ℵ (+x), which is the smallest logically closed set that contains both ℵ and x. The construction or expansion may be formalized as ℵ + x = Cn(ℵ ∪ {x}) and the redaction was appropriate if x is consistent with ℵ and in terms of quantity. No information is lost, so that ℵ ⊆ ℵ + x. In terms of quality there is no capricious gain in information as ℵ + x ⊆ Cn(ℵ ∪ {x}), while with regard to categorical matching ℵ + x is closed under Cn and ℵ + x is the smallest (closed) set that contains the old knowledge and the new.

In *revision*, a redactional sentence x is *added* by the Deuteronomistic or Priestly redactor to the preexilic belief set ℵ, and at the same time other sentences are removed by him if this is needed to ensure that the resulting postexilic belief set ℵ (*x) is *consistent*. ℵ*x is the result of accommodating x into ℵ, even if x is not consistent with ℵ and it models belief accommodation, so x ∈ ℵ *x. ℵ*x must be consistent if possible, and again, in terms of quality there is no capricious gain in information. It is ensured that ℵ *x ⊆ ℵ + x, while it does not say much if x is inconsistent with ℵ. With regard to Categorial Matching it must be ensured that ℵ*x is closed under Cn, while the quantity should again mean that information loss will be minimized. The questions remaining are: What should be Cn(a, a → b) * ¬b? Cn(a, ¬b)? Cn(¬a, ¬b)? Or Cn(¬b)?

A different perspective on the matter is available from the KM model (named after Katsuno and Mendelzon), where one assumes a dynamic environment. Here one works not with a belief set of sentences but simply on the level of a single sentence.

> In the dominant belief revision theory, that is the so-called AGM model, the set representing the belief state is assumed to be a logically closed set of sentences (a *belief set*). In the alternative approach, the corresponding set is not logically closed (and is known as a *belief base*). In the KM model one speaks not of revision but of *updating*; and information is about *different situations*. The new information is concerned with the present, while the old beliefs refer to the past; updating is the operation of changing old beliefs to take into account change in the present Thus,

in contrast to the AGM model, in the KM model a belief state would be a sentence with the input being another sentence. The transformation involves erasure and updating, and the motive for belief change concerns the outdated nature of the beliefs within a dynamic environment.[43]

Of specific relevance for the discussion of the impact of the exile is the fact that

> one of the most interesting topics in belief revision theory is the recovery postulate. According to this postulate, all original beliefs can be regained if a specific belief with a major role in the system is first removed and then reinserted. The recovery postulate holds in the AGM model, but not in closely related models employing belief bases.[44]

Here we see the relevance of both models in representing synchronic and diachronic complexity in the Hebrew Bible. In our case, we wish to understand the logic behind repeated belief change in the history of ancient Israelite religious epistemology.

How does one revise beliefs with redaction? We can distinguish two cases. First, if the new belief x is consistent with beliefs already extant in the text, it seems reasonable for the redactor to add to the existing belief set. Second, if the redactional addition of x causes an inconsistency in the belief set (e.g., is ¬x), what should the agent do? Reject x in order to accept ¬x? Rejecting x may not be enough: Suppose that x necessarily implies y and z. Rejecting x and adding ¬ x to the agent's belief set would not remove the inconsistency, and y or z must be rejected as well. Was this always done in the postexilic redaction of the text?

> Logic alone is not sufficient to decide between which beliefs to give up and which to retain when performing a belief revision. What are the extralogical factors that determine the choices? One idea is that the information lost when giving up beliefs should be kept minimal. Another idea is that some beliefs are considered more important or entrenched than others and the beliefs that should be retracted are the least important

---

43. Sven O. Hansson, "Logic of Belief Revision," *SEP* [cited 10 January 2010]. Online: http://plato.stanford.edu/archives/spr2009/entries/logic-belief-revision/.
44. Ibid.

ones.... Again, the methodological rules chosen here are dependent on the application area.[45]

One can even involve modal logical representation, working with "possible worlds in the text." This would mean describing how the logic of belief revision played out against the backdrop of epistemic and hermeneutic plausibility conditions.

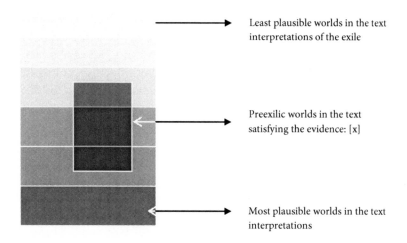

Least plausible worlds in the text interpretations of the exile

Preexilic worlds in the text satisfying the evidence: [x]

Most plausible worlds in the text interpretations

A sentence x is represented by the set [x] of worlds in the text that satisfy it. Together with the type of logical description mentioned earlier, this perspective on belief change in the history of Israelite religion might prove fruitful from a historical perspective. Such formal philosophical analysis will allow for a better understanding of the belief revision logics behind the religious developments and the redaction process. In this manner the logic of belief revision can contribute to our understanding of the nature of the beliefs and of the reasoning used in religious thought in pre-, intra- and postrevision contexts. Formal description is required if only for the clarity it is able to provide.

The above consideration suggests that it might someday be worth our while to write a history of Israelite religion from the perspective of the logic of belief revision that pays more attention to the diachronic dimen-

---

45. Peter Gardenförs, ed., *Belief Revision* (Cambridge: Cambridge University Press, 1992).

sion of justification in ancient Israelite religious epistemology.[46] The justification of new beliefs was as much diachronic as it was synchronic. It is not just a matter of the evidence currently available, but also one of coming to see things differently over time. Hence studies on beliefs in ancient Israelite religion should not focus narrowly on synchronic forms of justification. Once we bring externalist considerations into play, we are able to understand the mechanism behind belief change presupposed by the different redactors and historians of the ancient world. There is a necessary diachronic dimension, which fits naturally with an externalist reading of epistemology of and belief revision as a result of the exile. We see that in Yahwism(s) there was not the mere working out of abstract logic via sound reasoning; there was also a change of minds regarding how to read the relevant data; what counted as data; and how best to think of relevant warrants for beliefs and belief change.

13.3. CONCLUSION

In this chapter we touched on a number of epistemological issues of relevance to a philosophical study of religion. The discussion was by no means exhaustive. The aim was to provide a taste of what it might be worth our while to examine. The current obsession with epistemology in fundamentalist philosophy of religion and conservative biblical scholarship, though not wrong per se, cannot be our guiding frame of reference, since it is far too motivated by apologetics. What we need is a descriptive and historical religious epistemology that seeks to understand biblical folk epistemology on its own terms, and in all its diverse and primitive complexity. There is much work to be done, but for the moment it is time to move on to the next and last locus of this study: religion and morality.

---

46. For a related earlier assessment with reference to the New Testament to which the assessment in this paragraph is much indebted, see Abraham, "Epistemology of Jesus," 153.

14

RELIGION AND MORALITY IN ANCIENT ISRAEL

The study of Hebrew Bible ethics has sometimes suffered from an unwillingness on the part of scholars to contemplate "philosophical" questions at all, on the grounds that people of ancient Israel simply were not interested in, or could not have understood, questions of such a kind.[1]

14.1. INTRODUCTION

The word "ethics" does not appear in biblical Hebrew. Of course, this does not mean that there were no assumptions about the nature of morality in ancient Israel. This fact has been recognized, yet up to now, scholarly discussions on ethics in the Hebrew Bible have been primarily concerned with what philosophers call *substantive* theories of morality. These include *descriptive* ethics, which provides a supposedly unbiased account of the Hebrew Bible's moral beliefs; and *normative* ethics, which classifies the contents of moral beliefs in the Hebrew Bible via *ethical theory* and discerning the intricate operations of its *applied ethics* in reconstructed historical contexts. This emphasis on substantive theories of morality, however, has meant that issues related to *analytical* ethics (i.e., concerns with what moral philosophers call *metaethics*) have been neglected.

Almost three decades ago it was lamented that biblical scholars working on ethics tend to limit their interests to "rather specific, narrow topics, for instance social justice, the status of women, war, vengeance, property rights, ecological concern for nature, and the like."[2] Questions of metaethics were seldom raised in the secondary literature.[3] More recently,

---

1. Barton, *Understanding Old Testament Ethics*, 54.
2. Douglas Knight, "Old Testament Ethics," *ChrCent* 100 (20 January 1982): 55.
3. Eckart Otto, *Theologische Ethik des Alten Testaments* (TW 3/2; Stuttgart: Kohlhammer, 1994), 21.

the relative lack of interest in philosophical inquiry was also noted and ascribed to the influence of the Biblical Theology Movement.[4] Indeed, to my knowledge, no one has ever written a descriptive metaethics of the Hebrew Bible, something well worth doing in the context of a philosophical approach to ancient Israelite religion.

One of many possible reasons for the bracketing of metaethical issues in the study of biblical ethics may be the fact that metaethics is more abstractly philosophical in orientation than other branches of ethics.

> The range of issues, puzzles, and questions that fall within metaethics' purview are moreover consistently abstract, inviting an attempt to analyze the metaphysical, epistemological, semantic, and psychological presuppositions and commitments of moral thought, talk, and practice. As such, a descriptive metaethics proper counts within its domain a broad range of questions and puzzles, including: Is morality assumed to be a matter more of taste than truth? Are moral standards held to be culturally relative? Are there assumed to be moral facts? If there are moral facts, what is assumed to be their origin, and how is it that they set an appropriate standard for behavior? How are moral facts assumed to be related to other facts (about psychology, happiness, human conventions, etc.)? Also, is one assumed to have to learn such facts, or are they assumed to be innate? These questions lead naturally to puzzles about the meaning of moral claims as well as about moral truth and the justification of our moral commitments.[5]

14.2. What Is a Biblical Metaethics?

It is historical metaethics that we are interested in. What we wish to discover are not final answers to the above questions but rather what the texts of the Hebrew Bible presuppose in response to the aforementioned queries. These assumptions will be the concern of our descriptive metaethical inquiry. Like any comprehensive philosophical approach to metaethics, so our reading of the Hebrew Bible with reference to its metaethical assump-

---

4. John Barton, *Understanding Old Testament Ethics*, 54.

5. Geoff Sayre-McCord, "Meta-ethics," *SEP* [cited 25 February 2010]. Online: http://plato.stanford.edu/archives/fall2008/entries/meta-ethics/. See an introduction in "Meta-ethics," *Wikipedia, The Free Encyclopedia* [cited 25 February 2010]. Online: http://en.wikipedia.org/w/index.php?title=Meta-ethics &oldid=343298125.

tions will be constituted by the following three components already alluded to.

First, there is a semantic component, aimed at determining whether the moral assumptions in the Hebrew Bible presuppose, for instance descriptivism and/or nondescriptivism. That is, one should ask whether the Hebrew Bible contains

> prescriptive language (including ethical commands and duties) as a sub-division of descriptive language (and as having meaning in virtue of the same kinds of properties descriptive propositions have); and whether its ethical propositions are assumed to be irreducible in the sense that their meaning is not believed to be explicated sufficiently in terms of truth conditions.[6]

Second, a metaethics of the Hebrew Bible will have an epistemological component. This will involve deciding whether cognitivism and/or non-cognitivism are presupposed in the Hebrew Bible's metaethical assumptions. In so doing it should address the question of whether and to what extent moral discourse in the Hebrew Bible is understood as attempting to reach beyond the scope of human cognition; and should also ask whether the texts purport to be concerned with action rather than with knowledge. In other words, are the moralities encountered in the text essentially concerned with judgments of the same kind as knowledge judgments—namely about matters of fact—or not?[7]

Third and finally, there is an ontological component that will have to decide whether moral realism and/or nonrealism are operative. The focus will be on the Hebrew Bible's ideas about value-bearing properties, meaning the kinds of things that are assumed to correspond to or be referred to by ethical propositions. A nondescriptivist and noncognitivist perspective, if operative in the Hebrew Bible, will assume that ethics do not require a specific ontology, since ethical propositions do not refer to objects in the same way as descriptive propositions do (which would mean that its ontology was antirealist). If, however, the Hebrew Bible presupposes realism, then we need to explain what kinds of entities, properties or states the

---

6. Ibid.
7. Ibid.

Hebrew Bible assumes to be relevant for ethics, and why they are believed to have the normative status characteristic of ethics.[8]

As should be readily apparent, these components involve an adaptation of counterparts in metaethics proper so as to be suitable for use in the context of a descriptive study of metaethical assumptions in the Hebrew Bible.[9] Moreover, since no one has ever written a metaethics of the Hebrew Bible and there is no tradition of directly related philosophical research to fall back on, it might be prudent to devote the remainder of the chapter to offering a cursory introduction to a few of the stranger types of metaethical problems that might merit further research and future discussions.

14.3. A Few Neglected Metaethical Issues in Hebrew Bible Interpretation

There are several typically metaethical and religious philosophical issues biblical scholars have not yet paid sufficient attention to. The text that follows deals with six of them.

14.3.1. The Euthyphro Dilemma[10]

There seems to exist a popular consensus that the Hebrew Bible by default presents us with a historical precursor to what nowadays is known in moral philosophy and philosophy of religion as "Divine Command Theory" (DCT).[11] Not all biblical scholars classify the divinity–moral-

---

8. Ibid.

9. See also the section on metaethics at James Fieser, "Ethics," *IEP* [cited 25 February 2010]. Online: http://www.iep.utm.edu/.

10. This section is based on a paper read at the annual BSPR conference at Lady Margaret Hall Oxford 16–18 September 2009. The paper was published as Jaco Gericke, "Beyond Divine Command Theory: Moral Realism in the Hebrew Bible," *HTS* 65/1 (2009).

11. William B. Alston, "Some Suggestions for Divine Command Theorists," in *Christian Theism and the Problems of Philosophy* (ed. Norman Beaty; Notre Dame, Ind: University of Notre Dame Press, 1990), 303–26; Wes Morriston, "Must There Be a Standard of Moral Goodness Apart from God?" *Philosophia Christi* 2/3 (2001): 127–38; Philip L. Quinn, "Divine Command Ethics: A Causal Theory," in *Divine Command Morality: Historical and Contemporary Readings* (ed. Janine Idziak; New York: Mellen, 1979), 305–25; and idem, *Divine Commands and Moral Requirements* (Oxford: Clarendon, 1987); Eric Wierenga, "A Defensible Divine Command Theory," *Nous* 17

ity relation in the text using the concept of DCT, but in their theological claims they seem to imply that in ancient Israelite religion the divine will was assumed to be the ultimate foundation of morality (i.e., that human actions were considered morally good if and only if Yhwh willed or commanded them).[12] Hence one typically encounters prominent biblical theologians over the past fifty years insinuating that Yhwh and the moral order were inextricably related.

For example: "The power of the good rests entirely on the recognition of God as the one who is good. Of moral behavior for the sake of an abstract good there is none."[13] Consider also the following statements by three different authors:

> The ancient people, like many today, would not be prone to distinguish sharply between morality and religion. What is morally right to do is so because God wills it or because it is consistent with the divinely ordained structure of the world.[14]

> Also, the Old Testament is not familiar with the concept of doing good for the sake of the good; rather it is Yhwh's will that lays claim to human lives. Fixed orders are established by Yhwh.[15]

> To say that ethical obligation is obedience to the will of the national God, is to say that it is not the observation of ... universal human norms.[16]

Interestingly, many philosophers of religion (both theistic and atheistic) have uncritically followed suit and take it for granted that the historical precursor to Judeo-Christian versions of DCT is the Hebrew Bible itself.[17] Many introductory discussions on DCT assume as much, and even offer as illustration references to texts in the Hebrew Bible in which

(2003): 387–407; Linda Zagzebski, *Divine Motivation Theory* (New York: Cambridge University Press, 2004).

12. Otto, *Theologische Ethik des Alten Testaments,* 94; Knierim, *Task of Old Testament Theology,* 421.

13. Eichrodt, *Theology of the Old Testament,* 2:316.

14. Knight, "Old Testament Ethics," 55.

15. Preuss, *Theology of the Old Testament,* 2:291.

16. Barton, *Old Testament Ethics,* 46.

17. John Hare, "Religion and Morality," *SEP* [cited 13 October 2010]. http://plato.stanford.edu/archives/win2010/entries/religion-morality/.

moral norms are apparently acquired solely via divine commands, for example the giving of the Ten Commandments. Strong arguments for the presence of DCT in the text include the giving of seemingly nonnecessary commands (as to Adam and Eve, or the rituals of Leviticus) and even seemingly immoral commands (e.g., the command to Abraham to sacrifice Isaac, the order that the Israelites plunder the Egyptians and slaughter the Canaanites, and Hosea being told to marry a prostitute). In philosophical terms this would mean that the Hebrew Bible takes for granted a subjectivist yet universalist form of cognitivism, to be contrasted with other forms of ethical subjectivism, moral realism, error theory, and noncognitivism.

That the Hebrew Bible associates the right actions with what finds favor in the eyes of Yhwh cannot reasonably be denied. However, there is more than one way of interpreting the divinity/morality relation even given DCT (hence strong and weak versions of the theory).[18] This is also readily apparent from any attempt to answer Socrates' question to Euthyphro in Plato's dialogue,[19] which was subsequently adapted to become what is now called the "Euthyphro Dilemma" (ED). In the context of the Hebrew Bible it involves the following riddle: Did Yhwh command something because it is moral, or was something moral because it was commanded by Yhwh?

Owing to the problems both of the possible responses implied in this question are said to raise for DCT (e.g., moral relativism and redundant divine revelation), much has been written in an attempt to respond to the dilemma within the context of both fundamentalist and critical Christian philosophy of religion.[20] Curiously, however, I could not find any corresponding concern in biblical ethics, with someone trying to establish what a given text in the Hebrew Bible might imply in response to ED. Consequently, I would like to consider two questions as our research problem:

---

18. Wierenga, "A Defensible Divine Command Theory," 387–407.

19. Plato, *Five Dialogues: Euthyphro, Apology, Crito, Meno, Phaedo* (trans. George M. A. Grube; Indianapolis: Hackett, 1981), 1–20.

20. Wainright, *Religion and Morality*, 73–80; John Frame, *Euthyphro, Hume, and the Biblical God* [cited 13 February 2010]. Online: http://www.frame-poythress.org/frame_articles/1993Euthyphro.htm.

1. Is DCT the only or default metaethical perspective on the relation between divinity and morality in the Hebrew Bible?
2. Do some texts in the Hebrew Bible offer us any hints as to which (if any) of the two possible options presented by the ED they imply to be correct?

With these questions in mind, I wish to challenge the popular consensus by offering a hypothesis suggesting that the classification of the Hebrew Bible's metaethics as *in toto* a form of DCT involves the fallacies of anachronism and hasty generalization. I furthermore suspect that the errant reading resulted from prima facie assessments informed by postbiblical philosophical-theological reinterpretations of the essentially alien historical metatheistic assumptions of ancient Israelite religion. Moreover, it is possible to show that many texts in the Hebrew Bible presuppose moral goodness as not in fact something identical to to the divine will. Instead, in these texts both the deity and the divine commands were nontautologically predicated as "good," because they instantiated goodness as an accidental property that was ultimately assumed to be located in an independent and stable transworld moral order.

14.3.2. MORAL REALISM

Given the limitations of time and space applicable to this section, I shall offer only one or two illustrations from the biblical text for each argument. The quotations from the Hebrew Bible are not intended as proof-texts allowing for generalizations in order to prove that moral realism is the only biblical perspective on the deity/morality relation. Nor am I trying to argue that moral realism has biblical roots and is therefore philosophically credible. Conversely, I am not trying to prove that the basic idea of DCT is absent from the Hebrew Bible altogether or even that it is philosophically outdated. Rather, my aim is purely descriptive and historical, and I make a selective and cursory appeal to particular texts only to verify the presence of moral realist motifs in the biblical discourse in a way suggestive of the possibility that the same motifs might well be more pervasively attested than popular correlations to DCT would seem to imply.

A first argument for moral realism consists of instances of the nontautological predication of goodness. A useful point of departure would be to ask whether there are any examples in the Hebrew Bible of the nontautological predication of goodness as extrinsic property of Yhwh based on an alleged synthetic *a posteriori* religious epistemology. In Gen 1, when God creates the heavens and the earth, he looks at his work and then calls it good. The assumption is that he does not determine the nature of goodness, but judges his own work according to a presupposed universal standard already in existence. This also assumes that the word "good" is the same "good" humans call good (that no doctrine of analogy is presupposed). If so, it follows that moral goodness was indeed assumed to be something independent from the deity and with reference to which he could be called "good" (or not).

In this regard cognizance should be taken of the fact that we do indeed encounter many examples of nontautological predication, as in Ps 34:9:

טעמו וראו כי־טוב יהוה   Taste and see that Yhwh is good;

אשרי הגבר יחסה־בו   Happy is the man who takes refuge in him.

The above text assumes that the implied reader already has an idea of what goodness is, quite apart from Yhwh and with reference to which it could be determined whether the deity is in fact good or not. This means that the knowledge that Yhwh is good is not assumed to be the result of analytical a priori reasoning. To state, as the psalmist does, that Yhwh is good (and to presuppose that the claim is in theory open to falsification) would not even be considered meaningful were the goodness of Yhwh believed to be a logically necessary property of absolute Godhood. That is, if Yhwh is assumed to be good by definition—if goodness is assumed to be in the logical constitution of the concept of deity—the stating of the proposition that Yhwh is good is as superfluous as confessing that water is wet.

A second argument for moral realism concerns textual examples of instances where God and the gods are charged with moral wrongdoing within a case made by appealing to an objective moral order vis-à-vis deity. When we consider the relation between divinity and morality in the Hebrew Bible we should take cognizance that deity was not assumed to be moral by definition. In Ps 58:2 we read:

האמנם אלם צדק תדברון   Do you gods really speak justly,

מישרים תשפטו בני אדם   with uprightness judge humans?

Many translations have "judges" or "rulers" instead of "gods." Yet in this text (as in many others in the Hebrew Bible) the existence of divine beings other than Yhwh is taken for granted. It is also taken for granted that the gods are not by definition moral. This in turn presupposes the existence of a moral order vis-à-vis divinity and with reference to which divine acts can be judged. The gods may be able to do what they like because they have the power—but that still does not mean that whatever they do is by definition good. Might is not assumed to make right, and the appeal to the moral order in the charges against the gods suggests a form of moral realism where right and wrong are what they are irrespective of divine whim. A similar scenario is found in Ps 82:1–2:

אלהים נצב בעדת־אל   God stands in the divine assembly;
בקרב אלהים ישפט   in the midst of the gods he judges:
עד־מתי תשפטו־עול   "How long will you judge unjustly,
ופני רשעים תשאו   and lift the faces of the wicked?"

Again many translations try to evade the "theodiversity" of the "divine condition" (implicit in rendering "gods") with a host of more "orthodox" substitutes. The Hebrew, however, is clear: for it presupposes the entities to be immortal prior to the divine judgment (Ps 82:6). Moreover, that gods can be caught behaving badly suggests moral realism. And lest someone object by pointing out that in neither of the above instances is Yhwh himself being accused of doing wrong, the fact is that there are such texts, for example Pss 44 and 89, in which the psalmists blatantly accuse the God of Israel of betraying the covenant. In both these psalms Yhwh is at the receiving end of the critique, again presupposing the justification of the charges as coming from the appeal to what is given in the moral order. So it would seem that there are texts in the Hebrew Bible where even divinity can be judged with reference to a supposedly universal moral norm.

A third argument for moral realism takes its cue from the second, taking seriously the metaethical presuppositions underlying the Hebrew Bible's mythological motif of divinity as "judge." For consider the role of a judge vis-à-vis the law—a judge does not make the law, neither does a judge determine good or bad absolutely, nor can morality be defined with reference to the person of the judge. Rather, a judge acknowledges the law as it exists independent of him, without him being above the law. This is also often considered to be the case with the divine judge in the Hebrew Bible. A classic example comes from Gen 18:25, where Abraham appeals to the moral order to prevent Yhwh from what is understood to be an act of immoral retribution:

חללה לך	Far be it from you
מעשת כדבר הזה	to act in this way,
להמית צדיק עם־רשע	to slay the righteous with the wicked,
והיה כצדיק כרשע	that the righteous should be as the wicked.
חללה לך השפט	Far be it from you.
כל־הארץ לא יעשה משפט	Shall not the judge of all the earth do justly?"

Presupposing DCT, how can Abraham make a case? Can DCT explain why the divine judge can be "morally" taken to task through disobedience? Why does Abraham not modify his view of what is just? Surely it is because the text assumes that justice is a good thing and that its goodness is determined by the moral order independent of Yhwh. A similar scenario of corrective chutzpah is attested when Yhwh and Moses deliberate on an appropriate punishment for the "Golden Calf" incident. First there is the divine command (Exod 33:10):

ועתה הניחה לי	"Now leave me alone,
ויחר־אפי בהם ואכלם	so my anger burns and consumes them
ואעשה אותך לגוי גדול	and I will make of you a great nation."

Now in terms of DCT the "moral" thing to do would be for Moses to get the hell out of there. Moses, however, like Abraham, frustrates the divine will and convinces Yhwh qua divine judge what would be the moral thing to do. Thus in 33:11 we read:

ויחל משה את־פני	And Moses calmed the face

יהוה אלהיו	of Yhwh his God
ויאמר למה יהוה	and said, "Yhwh, why
יחרה אפך בעמך	does your anger burn against your people
אשר הוצאת מארץ מצרים	whom you took out of the land of Egypt
בכח גדול וביד חזקה	with great power and a strong hand?"

After Moses reminds his God that the latter's reputation will suffer among the foreign peoples should Yhwh destroy the Israelites and break the promise to Abraham, Moses' disobedience against the divine command to be left alone has the following result (Exod 33:14):

וינחם יהוה על־הרעה	And Yhwh repented of the evil
אשר דבר לעשות לעמו	which he said he would do to his people.

A scenario like this may be crude to the modern philosophical-theologian, and indeed apologists since the time of the Hebrew Bible itself have sought to reinterpret the idea of Yhwh's changing his mind. My concern here is not the postbiblical belief in divine immutability or its opposite, but rather the implication of the text that disobedience against the divine command can be a good thing for both the deity and humans in the vicinity. On DCT, Moses acted immorally, period. But if we presuppose that the meta-ethical assumptions of this text operated with a version of moral realism and a belief in a moral order independent of the deity, then the allowing of disobedience and debate—with an implicit appeal to what is right—makes perfect sense. Another good example of similar pious "back chatting" with fortuitous consequences can be found in Amos 7:1–3.

A fourth argument for moral realism concerns the stable actual worlds-in-the-text identity of the extension of the concept of goodness. Consider the moral status of the virtues vis-à-vis the deity as mentioned in Ps 15:1–3:

יהוה מי יגור באהלך	Yhwh, who shall dwell in your tent?
מי ישכן בהר קדשך	Who shall live in your holy mountain?
הולך תמים	He that walks uprightly,
ופעל צדק	and does righteousness

ודבר אמת בלבבו	and speaks truth in his heart.
לא רגל על לשנו	He does not slander with his tongue;
לא עשה לרעהו רעה	he does not do evil to his friend,
וחרפה לא נשא על קרבו	and does not heap insults on his neighbor.

In this text it seems that Yhwh is assumed to command these acts because they are moral and because Yhwh is assumed to be a moral god. To be sure, the psalm first intends to demonstrate Yhwh's moral requirements, yet it does not seem to imply that had Yhwh willed the opposite the divine will could have changed the moral status of the particular acts. Rather, what would change is the view of the deity as (only) moral, as was the case with Pss 44 and 89. Aside from Ps 15 (cf. Ps 24), the stability of the moral order vis-à-vis the possible vicissitudes of accidental divine moral properties are clearly assumed in the text (Ps 77:9–10) that reads:

השכח חנות אל	"Has God forgotten to be gracious?
אם־קפץ באף רחמיו	Did he shut up in anger his compassion?"
ואמר חלותי היא	And I say, "This is my illness,
שנות ימין עליון	the turn of the right hand of the Most High."

In this text the imaginary scenario of God ceasing to be "good" is assumed to occur in at least one possible world. Yet across all possible worlds compassion and mercy are considered virtues. Thus the entire psalm presupposes and depends on the idea of an objective moral order in relation to which Yhwh appears to have changed and with reference to which his nature may be described. Without this assumption there would be no reason for the psalmist's consternation.[21]

A fifth argument for moral realism relates to "bad" divine commands. In nonfundamentalist biblical theology, it is taken for granted that some texts in the Hebrew Bible do not assume Yhwh to be perfect in goodness, in that he is at times held responsible for the actualization of not only

---

21. Crenshaw, "Birth of Skepticism," 1–19; idem, *Theodicy in the Old Testament* (IRT4; Philadelphia: Fortress, 1983); idem, *A Whirlpool of Torment: Israelite Traditions of God as an Oppressive Presence* (Minneapolis: Fortress, 1984), 93–109.

natural but also moral evil.[22] In the context of ancient Israelite religion both philosophical theology's "perfect being" theology and the problem of evil in its classical formulation are anachronistic, since the Hebrew Bible often assumes good and evil to be complementary rather than incompatible properties of the divine nature (see Isa 45:7). In this regard, particularly relevant to our discussion are those texts depicting Yhwh issuing "bad" commands. On the one hand, this sometimes involves Yhwh's commands to spiritual entities to commit immoral acts, for instance in texts such as Job 1–2 and 1 Kgs 22:19–22. On the other hand, on occasion it also involves the divine commands to humans beings considered immoral, as in Ezek 20:25:

וְגַם־אֲנִי נָתַתִּי לָהֶם חֻקִּים	Therefore I gave them also statutes
לֹא טוֹבִים	that were not good,
וּמִשְׁפָּטִים	and ordinances
לֹא יִחְיוּ בָּהֶם	whereby they should not live.

To be sure, in the context of Ezek 20 these "bad" divine commandments are previously said to have been issued because of sin (Ezek 20:24). Yet the very possibility of divine commands being not good (irrespective of the motive for issuing them) certainly complicates DCT's equation of the good with whatever the deity commands. Even if Yhwh's act is assumed to be fair and just, this changes nothing about the fact that the divine command itself cannot be looked to in order to determine what is moral. So whatever we think about the nature of the deity himself implicit in this text, the divine commands themselves are not assumed to instantiate the property of goodness because they are issued by Yhwh. The good is therefore assumed to exist vis-à-vis the commands with reference to which the commands themselves can be judged to be either good or not.

A sixth and final argument pertains to the way in which the concept of goodness is predicated of the divine commands themselves. Good illustrations in this regard come from the so-called "Torah Psalms," especially Pss 19 and 119. In Ps 19:9 we read that:

---

22. Jaco Gericke, "Beyond Reconciliation: Monistic Yahwism and the Problem of Evil in Philosophy of Religion," *VE* 26 (2005): 64–92.

פקודי יהוה ישרים	The precepts of Yhwh are right,
משמחי־לב	rejoicing the heart;
מצות יהוה ברה	the commandment of Yhwh is pure,
מאירת עינים	lighting the eyes.

On what grounds and based on what criteria are the above claims made? Do they not presuppose that the concept of what is right and pure is already possessed and that the nature of the divine law fulfills all the necessary conditions for its application? If the divine ordinances determine what is right and pure, how does it make sense to add the superfluous detail predicating these qualities of the commands themselves? Surely there must be sufficient reason to assess the commands as such, other than this (again) being an allegedly tautological predication.

The same trend continues in Ps 119, where the divine commands are in the center of the psalmist's meditations. The ascription of the property of good to the commands and laws of Yhwh also presupposes that these are judged to be good with reference to the moral order itself and not because it goes without saying (Ps 119:39):

העבר חרפתי אשר יגרתי	Turn away my reproach, which I dread,
כי משפטיך טובים	for your ordinances are good.

Why would the psalmist need to imply that the reproaches are not good if whatever the deity does is good by definition? Why does he have to state that the divine ordinances instantiate the property of goodness if it is an essential and necessary property and if goodness is in the logical constitution of the concept of divine commands? To be sure, morality in the Psalms is often equated with, and discerned with reference to, the divine commands. Yet we often find the foundations for the good being deferred:

1. The divine commands are good because they reveal the divine will.
2. The divine will is good because it reveals the divine nature.
3. The divine nature is good because x.

On DCT assumptions the buck stop here and there is no sufficient reason as to why the divine nature is to be called good: it is good by definition, whatever it may happen to be in all possible worlds. However, on a moral realist sequence the equation of the good with the divine commands looks a little different, and x is the moral order itself. Not surprisingly, a closer inspection of the biblical data reveals the following subtle distinctions to be presupposed in many texts:

4. The divine commands mediate (but do not create) moral norms.
5. The divine will corresponds to (but does not cause) what is good.
6. The divine nature instantiates (but does not define) the property of goodness.

On this reading it would mean that in the metaethical assumptions of some texts it is not the deity or the divine commands that ultimately create the moral order—rather it is humans who, from their point of view, can determine what is good only by referring to the divine commands, which in turn are called good because they correspond to the moral order to which humans have no direct access except through divine revelation.

Together these arguments cumulatively demonstrate the presence of marked traces of moral realist assumptions in the Hebrew Bible, showing that DCT was not the only metaethical trajectory operative in the history of ancient Israelite religion. That the particular kind of moral realism involved has little in common even with a weak version of DCT (where the deity also has a mediatory function) should be readily apparent from the alien metatheistic assumptions on which the moral realist metaethical assumptions of ancient Israelite religion are based. Yet because DCT is anachronistic in the context of many passages in the Hebrew Bible, the upside is that the ED as dilemma is also not as problematic as it might otherwise be. For while the Hebrew Bible often implies that Yhwh commands something because it is good, the deity's commands are not made redundant thereby, as DCT implies happens when this divinity/morality relation is opted for. The reason for this is that, contrary to what is assumed in the Euthyphro Dilemma, the ancient Israelites were not optimists in their religious epistemology.

Even though the moral order is presented in the Hebrew Bible as existing independent of the divine, the divine will—if the deity is of the moral type—is still believed to be humanity's only access to that order. The deity is thus assumed to function in relation to the moral order as an instructor, a mediator, a judge, and an authority on right and wrong—not as its creator. From this it follows that, at least in the context of those texts in the Hebrew Bible where moral realism is presupposed, the ED indeed represents a false dilemma, not (as Aquinas suggested) because goodness is an essential part of the divine nature, but because the underlying moral epistemology assumes that humans need good gods to tell them what the good life is all about.

14.3.3. The Deity/Humanity Relation

A second related neglected metaethical concern not given its due in current and past research on ethics in the Hebrew Bible is the metaethical assumptions regarding the rationale for the particular divine/human relation assumed to be required by the moral order. In the discussion to follow in this section, my query is inspired by the strange audacity of David J. A. Clines in his two books, *Interested Parties: The Ideology of Writers and Readers of the Hebrew Bible* and *What Does Eve Do to Help and Other Readerly Questions to the Old Testament*.[23] And I begin by noting that the Hebrew Bible itself assumes that Yhwh is to be worshiped, and that most studies on the ethics of the Hebrew Bible take this for granted without batting an eye. In view of this, I would suggest that there are basic (postmodern) readerly questions to be asked in the spirit of innocent, childlike curiosity, questions that are invited by covert answers that seem to go without saying in the text. These answers are so much part and parcel of the setup that the questions themselves have never really been discussed philosophically by biblical scholars. For instance:

1. Why, according to the Hebrew Bible, does Yhwh want to be worshiped?
2. Why, according to the Hebrew Bible, does Yhwh want to be feared?

---

23. David J. A. Clines, *What Does Eve Do to Help? And Other Readerly Questions to the Old Testament* (Sheffield: JSOT Press, 1990); *Interested Parties*.

3.   Why, according to the Hebrew Bible, does Yhwh want to give laws?
4.   Why, according to the Hebrew Bible, does Yhwh want to judge?

The answers to these questions are implicit in the data, inasmuch as the texts assume some sufficient reason why such states of affairs obtain without logical necessity (as opposed to a theological one, perhaps) to explain why Yhwh would want to relate to humans in this manner.[24] That people in ancient Israel could be critical on this matter and did concern themselves with related questions can be seen in criticisms of the cultus. Of course, the actual justification for believing that Yhwh is and wants x and y because he is p and r was probably taken for granted by most ancient Israelites. However, the history of religion will contain answers to these assumptions.

In asking these questions, we are not concerned to provide a dogmatic-theological, naturalist-demythologizing, or social-psychological recon-struction of what we today might think the theopolitically correct reasons are as to why a god wants to be like this. We are concerned, rather, with the phenomenological aspect of our inquiry, in other words with philosophi-cal reflection on what the texts of the Hebrew Bible themselves presuppose regarding why the idea that Yhwh needs to exist in this way can go without saying. This explains why the obvious historical and sociological answers won't do, and why the popular apologetic response—which claims that Yhwh does not demand worship and that worship is instead a spontane-ous expression of human spirituality—misses the point and distorts the texts' own assumptions.

In view of the above, any objection to asking these questions that claims they are anachronistic confuses philosophical inquiry with theo-logical explication. Another misunderstanding confuses the texts taking these reasons for granted with the delusion that ancient Israelites were not interested in them—the two are not the same thing. Given that the bulk of the Hebrew Bible concerns prescriptive material regulating the worship of Yhwh, which change over time and which obtain variably in many different actual worlds in the text, the idea that there was no inter-

---

24. The validity but problematic nature of such questions is recognized in Jewish philosophy. See, for example, Samuelson, *Revelation and the God of Israel*, 14.

est in "why?" seems unwarranted. Just because the biblical authors neither ask nor answer these philosophical questions in so many words does not mean that the texts of the Hebrew Bible contain no presuppositions or implied ideas related to the matter. Even if the biblical authors do not concern themselves with answering these questions, their reference to related states of affairs presupposes some sufficient reason for the human belief or the divine act, whatever that might be (and whether they are aware of it or not).

Why have biblical scholars not asked these questions? Objection to them likely stems from motives that are essentially dogmatic and ideological. Perhaps there is the latent fear that a philosophical inquiry might uncover hopelessly crude and all-too-human answers in the Hebrew Bible, which might be an embarrassment to those contemporary lofty and sophisticated philosophical-theological conceptions of divine motives (conceptions which claim to be biblical but are nothing of the sort). In short, there is much work to be done, and one possible starting point for a philosophical clarification would be to reconstruct the divine needs in relation to three variations in the philosophical concept of the will, that is the will to life (Schopenhauer), the will to power (Nietzsche), and the will to knowledge (Foucault). These variations correspond neatly to what we learned the primary properties of generic godhood were assumed to be—knowledge, immortality, and power (see ch. 10).

14.3.4. The Axiology of Divine Intervention and the Philosophy of Action

In many texts in the Hebrew Bible, it is assumed that Yhwh does not want to live among humans on a permanent basis or in the manner of an extrovert. He does not talk to just anyone, and seems to keep his distance most of the time. The Hebrew Bible does not tell us why Yhwh wants to live in heaven or be hidden. To be sure, many historicoreligious and psychological explanations exist to account for the fact. They reveal that some texts in the Hebrew Bible presuppose Being to be hierarchically structured, with a cosmic apartheid between the world of the gods and that of humans. The reasons why humans are not allowed to come and go into and out of heaven as they please, but instead work through mediators that must be sent between domains, and why divine beings must always reside elsewhere, intervene selectively, and make either spectacular entrances or arrive virtually incognito, are based on a series of metaphysical assumptions and cannot be exhausted through the mechanism of sociomorphic projection.

Like the binary oppositions noted earlier about what gets privileged in constructing Yhwh's profile, these metaphysical assumptions are part of the folk-philosophical assumptions implicit in certain biblical world views. That these assumptions are not operative in some texts where much freer access to the divine realm is possible shows us that the set of presuppositions governing the *modus operandi* of divine intervention was fluid and variable over time and across possible worlds in the text.[25] The main assumptions are as follows:

1. There is something metaphysically wrong with the world (in the text).
2. The problem may or may not be a necessary state of affairs.
3. The problem is the result of some past divine and/or human action(s).
4. The problem is the result of a breach of the moral order.
5. The breach caused a systemic disruption in the cosmic order.
6. The cosmic order is threatened by a return to chaotic initial conditions.
7. The present condition reflects this disrupted state of affairs.
8. The state of affairs is a complex system that is riddled with anomalies.
9. The condition is not permanent and will terminate in the indefinite future.
10. The restoration will lead to a purification of the moral order.
11. The purging of the moral order will restore harmony to the cosmic order.
12. The restoration cannot be accomplished by human agency.
13. The restoration will come through the actions of divine intervention.
14. The divine methodology involves working through a significant person.
15. This person is fated to appear sometime in the future.

---

25. This is an adaptation of a related set of assumptions in the messianic mono-myth in Jaco W. Gericke, "Dividing One by Zero: Hyperreality in the Hebrew Bible and *The Matrix*," *JSem* 17 (2008): 344–66.

Inevitably, questions concerning the moral code that governs the deity's own actions will require much further research. On the one hand, we need more research on axiology and value theories implicit in ancient Israelite religion. In its metaphysical sense, "value theory":

> designates the area of moral philosophy that is concerned with theoretical questions about value and goodness of all varieties—the theory of value. The theory of value, so construed, encompasses axiology, but also includes many other questions about the nature of value and its relation to other moral categories.[26]

In other words, we need to know what values govern the text, and determine the characterization of the deity in his operations in the world in the text. We shall also have to attempt to discern what the metaethical assumptions in the text presuppose about intrinsic and extrinsic forms of value, and discuss the presupposed nature of the property of goodness, whether divine, abstract, or moral. Why, according to the text, are the divine and its will worth bothering with? And, perhaps most curiously, why is it assumed to be normal that religious value has to be taught by Yhwh? If it is because humans are ignorant and weak, why is it assumed laudable to create creatures with such little value? Moreover, why is it assumed to be imperative to know what is worthwhile (why is wisdom a good thing)? What is the axiological status of deity, of humanity, and of religion itself assumed to be? What is believed about the axiological status of religious texts?

Another thing that is needed in a discussion of sufficient reason for acts of deity would be to describe the divine *modi operandi* from the perspective of the philosophy of action. We do so not to judge but to clarify the motivation for and the nature of divine actions, according to whatever answers may be implicit in biblical narratives. In the philosophy of action, the focus is usually on human action, but we also need to account for the divine behavior that explains the acts of Yhwh from the perspective of issues in the philosophy of action. Such an inquiry will primarily be concerned with the moral structure of divine action, and will seek to distinguish between the rationale assumed for activity and passivity, voluntary, intentional, culpable, and involuntary divine actions, and related questions. The theory

---

26. Mark Schroeder, "Value Theory," *SEP* [cited 27 February 2010]. Online: http://plato.stanford.edu/archives/fall2008/entries/value-theory/.

of divine action will be pertinent to questions concerning divine freedom, intention, belief, responsibility, and other aspects. It is also related to the concept of causality and the issue of determinism in divine behavior.

If these concerns seem anachronistic, they are only such in the sense that the particular questions are not explicitly asked by the characters in the biblical texts themselves. But the reason for this cannot be that the concern is distortive or that there are no answers. Since a certain state of affairs obtains in at least one actual or possible world in the text, it means that there is data to work with even if it is implicit (because the supposed answers are taken for granted, and only for this reason are not spelled out). We therefore cannot limit our questions to those asked by ancient Israelites, for if this principle were consistently applied no exegesis would ever get done. Not many characters in the worlds in the text seem concerned to engage in biblical criticism or a study of religious texts themselves. None engaged in literary or historical or social-scientific criticism, or had a Bible as a canon of thirty-nine books. In the Bible, the word of Yhwh is not the Hebrew canon. Perhaps the people realized that a god created by ink on scrolls is no less of an idol and forbidden image than one made from wood and stone. Or perhaps not.

Ultimately the question about the value of the deity and divine action can indeed come to include philosophical reflection on the axiological status of whatever scriptures are alluded to in the worlds in the text. We may even ask ourselves the following: If these texts came into being as some sort of ethical answer, what were the metaethical questions assumed to have driven the characters in the text to construct a sacred body of literature in the first place? Why are there the beginnings of a Hebrew Bible, rather than nothing? We have historical, theological, and sociological answers; what we lack now is a philosophical clarification of the axiological assumptions that lie behind the creation of what eventually became a most delicious monster: a text within the worlds within the text.

14.3.5. IS THERE A PROBLEM OF EVIL IN THE HEBREW BIBLE?

While it is commonly treated separately in philosophy of religion, usually under the rubric of a/theology, the problem of evil can also be discussed in the consideration of the relation between religion and morality.[27] In bibli-

---

27. "Problem of Evil," *Wikipedia, The Free Encyclopedia* [cited 12 February

cal theology the problem of evil and theodicy has been no marginal concern.[28] It is also a great concern in philosophy of religion.[29] Major developments during the second half of the twentieth century have resulted in contemporary treatments of the problem of evil that incorporate new interpretations of the problem. Still, many Hebrew Bible scholars have been reluctant to admit to using philosophical concepts and categories for discussing the issues involved on a subject that is very controversial and in which trivialization and oversimplification are ever-present dangers. But sometimes biblical theologians dismiss the use of philosophical concepts and categories too readily. For instance, with reference to evil Brueggemann insists that "philosophy is never an adequate response ... for the crisis in the end demands face-to-face access to the raw holiness of God."[30] Ironically and deconstructively, however, theodicy is itself already philosophical. As John Levenson wrote with reference to the problem of evil:

> Why reality should be this way ... remains a crucial question in the *philosophy of religion*. I make no claim to have solved it or to have addressed it, nor have I attempted the Miltonic task of justifying the ways of God to man. For this reason I must decline both the praise of those who commend me for my theodicy and the censure of those who find it philosophically unpersuasive. My failure to address the problem of evil in the philosophical sense rests on more than my own obvious inadequacies. It rests also on a point usually overlooked in discussions of theodicy in the biblical context. The overwhelming tendency of biblical authors as they confront undeserved evil is not to explain it away but to call upon God to blast it away. This struck me as a significant difference between biblical and philosophical thinking.[31]

2010]. Online: http://en.wikipedia.org/w/index.php?title=Problem_of_evil&oldid=342626161.

28. No one has written more on the subject than James Crenshaw. See the bibliographical details and discussion in James L. Crenshaw, *Defending God: Biblical Responses to the Problem of Evil* (Oxford: Oxford University Press, 2005).

29. See Michael Tooley, "The Problem of Evil," *SEP* [cited 12 February 2010]. Online: http://plato.stanford.edu/archives/spr2010/entries/evil/. A more extensive overview is found in Joseph F. Kelly, *The Problem of Evil in the Western Tradition: From the Book of Job to Modern Genetics* (Collegeville, Minn.: Liturgical Press, 2002).

30. Walter Brueggemann, *Reverberations of Faith* (Louisville: Westminster John Knox, 2002), 214.

31. See Jon D. Levenson, *Creation and the Persistence of Evil* (San Francisco: Harper & Row, 1993), iv.

Note how "philosophical" thinking is here placed over and against "biblical" thinking. I wish to end this philosophy bashing and show how concepts and categories in philosophy of religion can aid the biblical scholar in the discussion of the relation between Yhwh and evil in the Hebrew Bible. Both the problem and the concept of theodicy derive from philosophy, so biblical theologians concerned with theodicy should know that it is already philosophical in terms of concepts, categories, and questions.

The term *theodicy* comes from Leibniz, while the logical formulation of the problem of evil is found in Hume, according to whom: "Epicurus' old questions are yet unanswered. Is he willing to prevent evil, but not able? then is he impotent. Is he able, but not willing? then is he malevolent. Is he both able and willing? whence then is evil?"[32] Actually, Epicurus left no written form of the argument, and similar questions attributed to the Greek philosopher can be traced back only as far as secondary Latin sources. What should be readily apparent is that no logical paradox arises for many ancient Near Eastern theologies that did not operate with classical theism's perfect-being theology and its idea that the divine is only benevolent.

Yet it is here as in few other places that philosophy of religion tends to bracket the history of religion and vice versa. In this section we try to use the format, concepts, and categories of philosophy of religion to clarify the situation in the Hebrew Bible, and to show that much of biblical scholarship on the subject has tended to be less than adequate, even as the intrusion of philosophy has been decried. What is conveniently forgotten is that the conception of maximal greatness in the ancient Near East often included the ability to cause evil as a greatmaking property and as instantiation of power in deities.

Let me state it at the outset of this section: what follows is not a moral critique of the God of the Hebrew Bible along the lines of militant writings as found in the antitheistic moral arguments of the New Atheism. It is ironic that people such as Richard Dawkins and Sam Harris use the argument from evil (and immorality) as an atheist disproof of the existence of God, when many people in the world of the text in the Hebrew Bible saw evil as traces of divine activity. As for myself, I choose not to enter that fray. My concern lies with offering a descriptive philosophical perspective

---

32. David Hume, *Dialogues concerning Natural Religion* (ed. Henry David Aiken; London: Forgotten Books, 1948), 133.

of worlds inside the text, whether the contents are real, orthodox, or politically correct or not. I seek to understand, and my explication is meant to be informative, not evaluative (in the sense of pejorative).

On the one hand, it cannot be denied that Yhwh was primarily worshiped as being a good God who disliked certain types of evil. Most texts describing the deity praise him for his moral qualities. On the other hand, dystheistic tendencies are rampant (even if not universal), and some charge Yhwh with injustice (e.g., Pss 44 and 89). By dystheism I understand the opposite of eutheism, which biblical theologians sometimes wish to force into the text by rationalizing and trivializing darker shades of the divine.

> Dystheism is the belief that God does exist but is not wholly good, or that he might even be evil. The opposite concept is eutheism, the belief that God exists and is wholly good. *Eutheism* and *dystheism* are straightforward Greek formations from *eu-* and *dys-* + *theism*, paralleling *atheism*; δύσθεος in the sense of "godless, ungodly" appearing e.g. in Aeschylus (*Agamemnon* 1590). The terms are nonce coinages, used by University of Texas at Austin philosophy professor Robert C. Koons in a 1998 lecture. According to Koons, "eutheism is the thesis that God exists and is wholly good ... [while] dystheism is the thesis that God exists but is not wholly good." However, many proponents of dystheistic ideas (including Elie Wiesel and David Blumenthal) do not offer those ideas in the spirit of *hating* God. Their work notes God's apparent evil or at least indifferent disinterest in the welfare of humanity, but does not express hatred towards him because of it.[33]

This is nothing novel: it represents the default view in ancient Near Eastern metatheistic assumptions. I use the term dystheism not in the sense of misotheism or antitheism, but in a purely descriptive sense in its more balanced connotations. Many texts in the Hebrew Bible show that associating the actualization of evil with the deity was an inextricable and ineradicable phenomenon in ancient Israelite spirituality. It makes for a concept of the divine that borders on how we speak of "nature" when we abstract and personify that concept.

The first controversial claim I wish to make in this section, therefore, is that there is no overarching traditional orthodox "problem of evil" in the

---

33. "Misotheism," *Wikipedia, The Free Encyclopedia* [cited 17 February 2010]. Online: http://en.wikipedia.org/w/index.php?title=Misotheism&oldid=334952842.

Hebrew Bible. By this, I do not deny that there is a conception of evil or that evil is something lamentable. I simply mean to suggest that, in ancient Israelite religion, evil was not a "problem" in the same sense it is in the classical version of the problem in Christian philosophy of religion. According to the latter there is a God, he is omnipotent and omnibenevolent, and yet evil exists. This is the typical problem of evil in Christian philosophy of religion in a very simplistic format. In many contexts in the Hebrew Bible it is a pseudo-problem, inasmuch as Yhwh is neither omnipotent nor omnibenevolent in the classical sense in a number of different representations of the God of ancient Israel.

But if in the Hebrew Bible some texts presuppose neither property for Yhwh—even as it admits the reality of divinity and evil—then the so-called argument from evil is itself also not applicable as part of an a/theology, as is typical of modern atheism. For unlike the modern believer, "spoiled" by "perfect being" theology, or the adorable entity of process/open theism who is only cognitively challenged, a god did not have to be either omnipotent or omnibenevolent before it was considered worthy of worship. No ancient Israelite lost his or her faith in God because of evil in the world—instead, evil was taken as the less congenial type of divine action, which included not only judgment but also hiding.

From a historical perspective, a reversed sociomorphism pervades the Hebrew Bible in this regard. The earth as a copy of the heavens is seen as functioning like a monarchy, with reality hierarchically structured and the highest personal reality (i.e., the deity) demanding subordination as a king would from his subjects, a master from his servants, a ruler from his covenant partners, shepherds from their sheep, or parents from their children. Even the covenant concept has little to do with what many modern evangelical Christians understand by the concept of a "personal relationship" with the deity. Concepts such as "fatherhood" also have very different elements from those considered normal in contemporary western folk philosophies of "family values." The fear of Yhwh does include a healthy dose of sheer terror before ultimate raw power.

In the ancient Near East, gods were worshiped for being superior beings, not for being user-friendly only. Being more powerful than humans, deities had the prerogative of doing what was right in their own eyes. Human servants might protest, but in the end, might made right. The idea of a deity at one's beck and call, who is subject to later philosophical stipulations of what a perfect god would be, is therefore virtually absent from the Hebrew Bible.

So how can philosophy of religion contribute to the discussion of theodicy in the text? First of all, it would provide some structure to the debate if we could adopt and adapt philosophy of religion's distinction between the *logical*, *evidential*, and *epistemological* forms of the problem. We already suggested that the logical form of the problem is a pseudo-issue, since a combination of open, process, and dystheistic theism is standard in biblical narratives. The absence of "perfect being" theology in many narrative representations of Yhwh's character means that the evidential form is also not on the same level as in the Christian tradition. The evidential form concerns not so much confessions of the nature of Yhwh as representations of evil acts or the neglecting of good acts in the actual world in the text. The epistemological issue concerns knowledge of good and evil.

The only place where the data of the texts approximate a modified version of the evidential problem is where Yhwh is charged with excessive cruelty. Here no attempt is made to explain away evil or to appeal to divine mystery—the authors of the Hebrew Bible call it as they see it. Hence, the epistemological issue of whether it is reasonable or rational to believe in God given the existence of evil is a pseudo-problem—or at least a problem of how to justify humans rather than the deity. The trouble lies in figuring out how the moral order is breached, not in how to reconcile evil with divine existence.

Second, the discussion can benefit by making the distinction philosophers of religion make between *metaphysical*, *natural*, and *moral* evil. This tripartite classification might be more functional than traditional theological discussion of biblical theodicy, where categories are haphazardly mixed. Many texts in the Hebrew Bible attribute all three kinds to Yhwh's fiat, even if a number of other texts present opposing views. In discerning Yhwh's relation to each type of evil in different texts, we would also do well to bring in philosophy in the form of the metaphysics of causality, to describe the deity's causal role in and relations to states of affairs classified as evil.

To give examples of texts in which Yhwh is called evil or is associated with the actualization of evil is beyond the scope of this chapter. Readers who may doubt the association should consult the existing mass of research literature that shows beyond all doubt (despite continuing apologetic detractions) how Yhwh is implicated in the realization of such evil.[34]

---

34. A good summary of the relevant textual data remains that of Crenshaw, *Prophetic Conflict*, 77–88.

Many biblical theologians' attempts to reinterpret, trivialize, or relativize the textual data still pervade biblical theology,[35] while many contemporary ideological critics err on the opposite side by overemphasizing the unpopular elements of Yhwh's dark side. Even feminist critics tend to be selective, and so do those who follow the approach of process or open theism. One of the latter is Terrence Fretheim, who can admit to an imperfect deity, yet refuses to allow for evil in the divine nature. All this is simply the result of anachronistic dogmatic expectations and the discomfort of wanting to be biblical while having to repress the fact that one does not believe in the kind of God some texts depict. The more cynical sections in Brueggemann's *Old Testament Theology* are perhaps the closest to an honest biblical theological assessment of the problem in that genre, while James Crenshaw's lifelong contribution is perhaps the point of departure for all future discussions.[36]

Another point of importance is to become aware of how not only the problem of evil but also philosophical responses in the form of popular theodicies in philosophy of religion have influenced discussions of evil in biblical theology. We have to become aware of the fact that many of our ideas are not biblical, but derive from philosophical contexts that distort the biblical data because the concept of divinity they embody is different. Ad hoc rationalizations and reinterpretations here would simply repeat what philosophers tried to do with Homer for having made his gods so immoral. Hence the challenge for us is to provide a philosophical description of what is there in the text, along phenomenological lines, bracketing all New Testament and postbiblical perspectives.

To give an example, one cannot offer freewill theodicy to describe the metaethical assumptions in all biblical contexts. In many of these the text is trying to show that there is no free will, as in scenarios where determinism rather than compatabilism is implied with regard to pawns of prophecy. In addition, on many occasions Yhwh is said to harden the hearts of the people, so that it actually becomes unbiblical to imagine that Yhwh has an intense respect for the free will of moral agents. On the contrary, the deity's ability to override the free will of moral agents is extolled in several texts. While many modern readers may find this offensive, ancient Israelites would simply have marveled.

---

35. Frederick Lindstrom, *God and the Origin of Evil: A Contextual Analysis of Alleged Monistic Evidence in the Old Testament* (Lund: Gleerup, 1983).

36. See ch. 3 regarding Crenshaw's relevance.

Not only is the freewill defense hardly biblical in the sense of being able to incorporate causality in biblical metaphysics, but other popular philosophical theodicies are equally distortively anachronistic. Included are Leibniz's idea of the best of all possible worlds, the consequences of sin, the idea of evil as a necessary complement to good, evil as illusion, the concept of soul-making, afterlife retribution, appeals to ignorance, and so on.[37] None of these is sufficient to account for how Yhwh relates to suffering in every context, even if many have some historical connection with a biblical motif. In addition, many so-called New Atheist moral critiques of the God of the Hebrew Bible are also riddled with anachronistic expectations and assumptions. Modern humans who believe only in user-friendly gods would have been considered hopelessly unrealistic in ancient Israel.

So while the argument from evil is fatal to "perfect being" theology, it does not even dent realism in dystheistic traditions in the biblical discourse, where evil in the world would simply be acknowledged as a result of divine action or hiddenness. Ancient peoples did not consider a god worthy of worship only for being perfect. Also, the intensions of the concepts of good and evil differed. This means that what modern people understand by love and goodness may not completely overlap with what the ancient Israelites understood by them. What seems currently like absurd forms of retribution, such as collective and transgenerational judgment, were less problematic for and variously viewed by different biblical authors.

In sum, then, in the Hebrew Bible, evil in relation to Yhwh's causal powers is not assumed to be as philosophically problematic as it later became, when concepts of divinity were upgraded and idealized in eutheism. The situation is complex in the Hebrew Bible, because different authors assume different relations between Yhwh and evil, and understand the concept of evil differently. This means that while in some texts it makes sense to speak of a problem of evil in the philosophical sense, in many it is a pseudo-problem, especially when dystheistic motifs are present. In certain traditions, accepting evil as coming from Yhwh is even part of a pious spirituality that does not serve the deity for any personal gain. The examples of Job (Job 1–2; 42) and Naomi (Ruth 1) come to mind.

---

37. "Theodicy."

In the end, the use of philosophy of religion in the study of evil in the Hebrew Bible has a clarifying rather than either a justifying or a condemnatory role to play. So indeed, perhaps the analogy of how modern people think of "nature" or "life" in the abstract, personified sense will help us get our heads around how the ancient Israelites could relate to, worship, and stand in awe of, a God who was responsible for the best and worst of all actual worlds. The only problems with the analogy are that Yhwh is assumed to be some*thing* rather than some*one*; and as not indifferent, but concerned. He has a will of his own, one that can be thwarted by negotiation in time. The "problem of evil" in the Hebrew Bible is thus a problem of justice based on the moral-realist assumptions of its dystheistic theologies.

14.3.6. ANCIENT ISRAELITE PERSPECTIVES ON THE MEANING OF LIFE

In the book *The Hitchhiker's Guide to the Galaxy*, by Douglas Adams,[38] a group of hyper-intelligent pandimensional beings demands to learn the Ultimate Answer to the Ultimate Question of "Life, the Universe, and Everything." For this they build a supercomputer they call Deep Thought. Deep Thought informs them that they should return for the answer after seven and a half million years. When the fateful day at long last dawns, a massive crowd awaits the moment of revelation with festivities and bated breath. With trepidation, Deep Thought tells them that the answer has been found but warns them that they are not going to like it. Undeterred, the beings tell the computer that it does not matter—they simply must know what it is. And so, in cold and clinical fashion, Deep Thought informs them that the Ultimate Answer to the Ultimate Question of Life, the Universe, and Everything is 42. After a moment of stunned silence the disillusioned and confused beings protest, demanding an explanation. Deep Thought remains unmoved by their disappointment, assures them that it has checked the answer quite thoroughly and that it is definitely 42. The real problem, according to Deep Thought, is that these beings never knew what the Ultimate Question was.

In biblical scholarship, the tendency is the search for final answers to old and often trivial questions rather than being concerned with the ultimate question. In this chapter, by contrast, the question of the meaning of

---

38. See Douglas Adams, *The Hitchhiker's Guide to the Galaxy* (London: Pan, 1979).

life will be the main focus. In this regard it should be clear that the meaning of life is not likely to be found in a dictionary. Neither are the meanings of life assumed in the Hebrew Bible something to be found in a biblical theology. The question itself, however, is everywhere as it is both popular[39] and philosophical[40] in nature.

> Many major historical figures in philosophy have provided an answer to the question of what, if anything, makes life meaningful, although they typically have not put it in these terms. Consider, for instance, Aristotle on the human function, Aquinas on the beatific vision, and Kant on the highest good.... Despite the venerable pedigree, it is only in the last 50 years or so that something approaching a distinct field on the meaning of life has been established in analytic philosophy, and it is only in the last 25 years that debate with real depth has appeared.[41]

When the topic of the meaning of life comes up in philosophical discussions, participants "often pose one of two questions: 'What are you talking about?' and 'So, what is the meaning of life?' The literature can be divided in terms of which question it seeks to answer."[42] The first question requires a systematic attempt to clarify what people mean when they ask what meaning life supposedly has. In other words, what is the meaning of the phrase "the meaning of life"? To which of the following does the word "meaning" refer: (the) origin, source, cause, reason, purpose, nature,

---

39. See Julian Baggini, *What's It All About? Philosophy and the Meaning of Life* (London: Granta, 2004); Raymond A. Belliotti, *What Is the Meaning of Human Life?* (Amsterdam: Rodopi, 2001); Christopher Belshaw, *Ten Good Questions about Life and Death* (Malden, Mass.: Blackwell, 2005); John Cottingham, *On the Meaning of Life* (London: Routledge, 2003); Michael Martin, *Atheism, Morality, and Meaning* (Amherst, N.Y.: Prometheus, 2002); Garret Thomson, *On the Meaning of Life* (South Melbourne: Wadsworth, 2003); and Julian Young, *The Death of God and the Meaning of Life* (New York: Routledge, 2003).

40. See David Benatar, ed., *Life, Death, and Meaning: Key Philosophical Readings on the Big Questions* (Lanham, Md.: Rowman & Littlefield, 2004); Peter Heinegg, ed., *Mortalism: Readings on the Meaning of Life* (Amherst, N.Y.: Prometheus, 2003); Elmer Daniel Klemke, ed., *The Meaning of Life* (2nd ed.; New York: Oxford University Press, 2000); and Joseph Runzo and Nancy M. Martin, eds., *The Meaning of Life in the World Religions* (Oxford: Oneworld, 2000).

41. Thaddeus Metz, "The Meaning of Life," *SEP* [cited 21 March 2011]. Online: http://plato.stanford.edu/archives/fall2008/entries/life-meaning/.

42. Ibid.

significance, value, content, or quality (of life)? What is assumed as the correct reference in this regard makes a world of difference in how one might recognize an answer to the question. Interestingly, in ordinary language the question regarding the meaning of life tends to revolve around a number of popular, albeit unproven, assumptions:

- that life is something that has meaning;
- that life can have only one meaning;
- that the meaning of life does not change;
- that the meaning of life can be known;
- that the meaning of life has to be given from outside it;
- that the meaning of life makes sense;
- that the meaning of life is good news and a cause for happiness;
- that the meaning of life has something to do with humans; and
- that one is obliged to learn what the meaning of life is.

None of these assumptions can be taken for granted in the philosophical debates. In philosophical discussion, several categories are typically found to constitute the bulk of classifications.[43] Answers include supernaturalist theories, which have in common the assumption that the meaning in life is be constituted by a certain relationship with a spiritual realm. Because both western and eastern philosophical traditions are included, there is no agreement on how the spiritual realm is constituted. Perspectives are subclassified as being either god-centered or soul-centered. A second category involves naturalist theories,[44] which hold that meaning can be obtained in a world known solely by empirical and rational probing. Here a distinction is made between subjectivist and objectivist accounts.[45] There is further-

---

43. See Metz, "The Meaning of Life." Metz has written about the topic elsewhere; see "Could God's Purpose Be the Source of Life's Meaning?" *RelStud* 36 (2000): 293–313; "The Concept of a Meaningful Life," *American Philosophical Quarterly* 38 (2001): 137–53; "The Immortality Requirement for Life's Meaning," *Ratio* 16 (2003): 161–77; and "Utilitarianism and the Meaning of Life," *Utilitas* 15(2003): 50–70.

44. When not religious, these views are usually atheist and humanist. See Kurt Baier, *Problems of Life and Death: A Humanist Perspective* (Amherst: Prometheus, 1997).

45. Arjan Markus, "Assessing Views of Life: A Subjective Affair?" *RelStud* 39 (2003): 125–43.

more also a logical space for a nonnaturalist theory that holds that meaning is a function of abstract properties that are neither spiritual nor physical.[46] Finally, an assorted variety of nihilistic perspectives can be found. They have in common that they all deny that life is the sort of thing that has any real meaning.

The question of the meaning of life is indeed probably on the mind of many biblical scholars at some point in their careers. Yet while many of our research concerns tend to involve autobiographical projections, no one has seemed very interested in exploring ancient Israelite assumptions about the meaning of life from a philosophical perspective. Perhaps the reason for this state of affairs is that many scholars have failed to notice that we do not actually know from face value what the biblical authors assumed about the matter. In the context of Christian philosophy of religion, the meaning of life is typically held to be the glorification of God, as the catechisms and confessions teach. But when asked for specifics on what the nonphilosophical texts of the Hebrew Bible assume about the ultimate question, one might be at a loss as to how to answer.

Because the Hebrew Bible is an ancient collection of prephilosophical texts, the basic concern of this study may seem anachronistic, as it is not explicitly treated by the Hebrew Bible authors. The fact is that while the Hebrew Bible is not philosophy, its texts contain a myriad of assumptions about what life's meaning is thought to be. So while in ancient Israel the question of life's meaning may not have been formulated in the modern existentialist sense, we can play it safe and state the assumptions of this study as being the following:

- that ancient Israelites assumed that life had meaning;
- that there were many meanings given different authors and characters; and
- that the meanings of life were not necessarily what they are today.

The philosophical methodology adopted in this study is based on an adaptation of a descriptive variety of ordinary language philosophy of religion as practiced by the philosopher of religion Don Cupitt. In the little book

---

46. Metz, "The Meaning of Life." For a more detailed outline of this view, see also Robert Audi, "Intrinsic Value and Meaningful Life," *Philosophical Papers* 34 (2005): 331–55.

The New Religion of Life in Everyday Speech, Cupitt, who is actually more Continental than analytic in approach, attempted to discern the presence of a folk philosophy of religion within ordinary language. He held that one could pick out all the phrases people actually use that are religiously or philosophically important and interesting.[47] For Cupitt, the philosophical contents of "religion" are built into the ordinary language that religious and nonphilosophical people actually use. This contradicts the popular belief that ordinary language philosophy is unsuitable for doing philosophy of religion.[48] Cupitt therefore suggests that the time has come to look at how ordinary people from different historical periods have looked at life in general, and in particular at their own lives in relation to it.[49]

In what follows I hope to make a contribution to this quest by showing how some texts in the Hebrew Bible fit in to these microhistories of the ordinary language philosophy of life. As suggested above, while the Hebrew Bible does not offer an explicit or unified philosophy of life, its texts contain implicit assumptions about the meaning of life in everyday affairs, whether those holding them are conscious of doing so or not. Let us now consider some of the textual evidence relevant to this topic.

Apparently the author of Gen 1:26–27 assumes that humans are here as substitute rulers of the earth:

ויאמר אלהים	And God said:
נעשה אדם בצלמנו	"Let us make man in our image,
כדמותנו	after our likeness;
וירדו	and <u>let them have dominion</u>
בדגת הים	over the fish of the sea,
ובעוף השמים	and over the fowl of the air,
ובבהמה ובכל־הארץ	and over the cattle, and over all the earth,
ובכל־הרמש הרמש על־הארץ	and over every creeping thing that creeps on the earth."

47. Cupitt, *Way to Happiness*, 2.
48. Mitchell, *Charts of Philosophy and Philosophers*, 68.
49. Don Cupitt, *Impossible Loves* (New York: Polebridge, 2007), 51.

As with ancient Egyptian theo-mythology, the human rulers are copies of the deity in representing his role in a particular created space. The meaning of human life according to the author of Gen 1:26 is therefore not as flattering as it may seem (or is often held to be). The idea is basically that humans are placed on earth to do the work of the deity so that the latter may repose. The implicit worldview is one of a cosmic society in which the divine world represents the upperclass populace who can afford to subcontract ruling the earth and to have humans acting on its behalf. In this view, human life means taking care of divine property.

This explains the theological debate about what the image of God in humans actually meant, and suggests that the idea that Gen 1:26 teaches intrinsic human value may be completely wrongheaded. It may be that reading Gen 1:26 as a compliment to human life is actually little more than an anachronistic projection of a liberal politics of human rights onto the ancient text. Humans are here to stand in for a God who is so aristocratic as to shift the responsibility of ruling the earth onto human representatives. Seen in this way, the point of the discourse is to compliment and elevate the deity, not to honor his human creatures. In comparative philosophical terms, this account is supernaturalist and god-centered rather than soul-centered. It is also subjectivist inasmuch as it presupposes that the meaning of human life is whatever it may mean for the deity.

In the second creation account there is a similar sort of cosmic apartheid at work. Here too a supernaturalist, god-centered, and divinely entertained subjectivist perspective on the meaning of human existence seems to be taken for granted. Thus the incidental remark in Gen 2:5 gives an answer to our question that is quite alien:

וכל שיח השדה	No shrub of the field
טרם יהיה בארץ	was yet in the earth,
וכל־עשב השדה	and no herb of the field
טרם יצמח	had yet sprung up,
כי לא המטיר יהוה אלהים	for Yhwh God had not caused it to rain
על־הארץ	on the earth,
ואדם אין לעבד את־האדמה	and there was no man to till the ground.

This verse assumes that humans are here to till the earth. In this perspective, therefore, it appears that the meaning of life is "gardening." The reason why the deity needs humans to protect and till his garden is the same as the theopolitical one that is found in Gen 1—it is beneath the god(s) to bother with such work. The sociomorphism is readily apparent as the story unfolds: Yhwh checks up on his laborers only when it is cool and more convenient to visit. So Gen 2, like Gen 1, assumes that, contrary to modern Christian ideas, human beings exist as the slaves of a master. According to Gen 2:5, at least, they have no use beyond that, since the entire cosmos is a hierarchy with the divine world as the highest natural kind.

In the rest of the Eden myth we see how the symbolism of the tree of life also bears witness to ancient Yahwistic assumptions about the meaning of life. Besides gardening and security work, the meaning of life in Eden is, as Kafka pointed out, that it stops. When the humans fail to eat from the tree of life, they fail to gain the immortality they never had.[50] From this it would seem that the deity is not assumed to value individual human life all that much. Humans are created as frail and mortal beings, lacking both wisdom and eternal life. Hence they are to reproduce and thereby be recycled at an alarming rate. Some lives have no meaning (e.g., Gen 4:2; Abel = *hbl*, cf. Qoheleth). The genealogies of Gen 1–11 assume that most people will be remembered only for the fact that they formed a link in the chain of "be and beget." The will to live—in Schopenhauer's sense of a blind striving for life for its own sake despite hardship—is clearly operative here.

Interestingly, the first time the question of the meaning of human life is explicitly asked by someone, it is in the voice of Isaac's wife Rebecca. In the narratives she not once but twice wonders what the point of life is in view of the suffering that accompanies it. In Gen 25:22 the context of her question is the pain she experiences giving birth to unruly twins.

ויתרצצו הבנים	And the children struggled together
בקרבה ותאמר	within her; and she said:
אם־כן <u>למה זה אנכי</u> ותלך	"If it be so, <u>why do I live?</u>"
לדרש את־ יהוה	And she went to inquire of Yhwh.

This text assumes that there should be reasons for living and that the deity has an answer to the question. Yet with so much physical discomfort

---

50. See Barr, *Garden of Eden*.

Rebecca seems to have felt that her life had lost whatever meaning it had. Then in Gen 27:46, Rebecca again wonders about the meaning of life. This time she wonders whether Esau should marry the women his mother does not approve of—so that unwanted family relations seem to be assumed as a source of meaninglessness:

תאמר רבקה אל־יצחק	And Rebecca said to Isaac:
קצתי בחיי	"I am weary of my life
מפני בנות חת	because of the daughters of Heth.
אם־לקח יעקב אשה	If Jacob takes a wife
מבנות־חת	of the daughters of Heth,
כאלה מבנות הארץ	such as these, of the daughters of the land,
למה לי חיים	what means life to me?"

These questions by Rebecca presuppose a quasinaturalist and subjective interpretation of the meaning of life. The text goes beyond the previous one in its subjectivism, in that it assumes that life has meaning if it means something to *Rebecca*, irrespective of what it means to the deity. In the rest of the Pentateuch's narratives and law codes, the promise of a long and happy life and the threats of death all assume that the meaning of life is, first, to survive, and second, to live in harmony with the deity and each other.[51] Here too the perspective is supernaturalist, god-centered, and subjectivist. Life is a task of serving and obeying in whatever ways finds favor in the eyes of Yhwh. The general focus on human subsistence is complemented in the cult with the care and feeding of the deity, which shows that a master/slave relationship is clearly at stake. Many biblical translations would tone down the oppressive wording to refer rather to a "Lord" and his "servants" (thereby recalling English colonialist status indicators). Humans, however, remain beings the meaning of whose lives is attributive.

Many texts in the Prophets presuppose that the meaning of life has much to do with the possession and cultivation of living space, namely, land issues. The deity has a land over which he rules, and the people of Israel are those who belong to him and whose lives he directs. The later

---

51. For the link between meaning and morality according to a number of philosophers, see Laurence Thomas, "Morality and a Meaningful Life," *Philosophical Papers* 34 (2005): 405–27.

utopian ideals of the eschatological visions in the prophets link up to this. No eternal life is envisaged as making this life meaningful. Even the vision of the new heavens and new earth in Isa 65 represents humans as growing old and dying, even though they will make it to at least a hundred before returning to dust.

In the Writings we find a variety of perspectives on what makes life meaningful. In the book of Daniel the characters of the friends of the prophet show contempt for any sort of life that does not allow for the worship of their God (see Dan 3). Later in the book we see that the meaning of earthly life is for the first time devalued, given the belief in a better afterlife. In the wisdom of Proverbs, on the other hand, the meaning of life seems to be the quest to gain wisdom so as to be able to live better and therewith longer (e.g., in Prov 3–4). However, in the more skeptical wisdom traditions of Job and Qoheleth, there is a return to pessimism and even nihilism as both figures struggle with the nightmare of injustice and futility.[52] For example, Job frequently asks the question why one should bother to live. It is assumed that the meaning of life is to be happy and that this can be taken away if one hits rock bottom. Hence the question in Job 3:20 (see also v. 23):

למה יתן לעמל אור   Why is light given to him that is in misery,
וחיים למרי נפש   and life unto the bitter in soul?

This text assumes that suffering robs life of its meaning, and that justice and happiness make life fulfilling. However, the discoveries that the deity is beyond good and evil (Nietzsche) and that the meaning of life is not exhausted in human existence were the first steps to Enlightenment (see Job 38–41). Ultimately (as in Nietzsche), however, death per se is not so much a problem as is dying at the wrong time (i.e., before one has lived a full life or after a point of diminished returns). Interestingly, and like Job many times, central biblical characters wish to be dead because, despite enjoying the favor of the deity, they no longer feel that life is worth living (e.g., Rebecca, Moses, Saul, Elijah, Jonah)

---

52. And as philosophers still do, See, for example, Brooke Alan Trisel, "Futility and the Meaning of Life Debate," *Sorites* (2001): 70–84.

As stated, the assumptions of Qoheleth about the meaning of life border on nihilism. In this he prefigures Schopenhauer, who thought of life as "a uselessly disturbing episode in the blissful repose of nothingness."[53] Yet a close reading reveals that Qoheleth's nihilism is Nietzschean "active nihilism." The persona of Qoheleth finds the courage to say "yes" to life as a gift, and his axiology has hedonistic tendencies, as in 8:15:

ושבחתי אני את־השמחה	So I commended joy,
אשר אין־טוב לאדם	that a man has no better thing
תחת השמש	under the sun
כי אם לאכל ולשתות	than to eat, and to drink, and to be merry,
ולשמוח והוא ילונו	and that this should accompany him
בעמלו ימי חייו	in his labor all the days of his life
אשר־נתן־לו האלהים	which God has given him
תחת השמש	under the sun.

However, both "hedonism" and "nihilism" are categories into which Qoheleth does not quite fit. What is important to note here is that while Qoheleth is at odds with other Hebrew Bible texts on many theological subjects, with regard to his axiology (or lack thereof), he stands in a long line of pessimists. While no biblical author is so nihilistic as to think of life as a "disease of matter" (Goethe), many authors would indeed admit that, as a popular slogan has it, "Life's a bitch and then you die." One example of just this sentiment is found in Ps 90:10:

ימי שנותינו בהם שבעים שנה	The days of our years are seventy years
ואם בגבורת שמונים שנה	and if strong eighty years,
ורהבם עמל ואון	and they are full of toil and injustice,
כי־גז חיש ונעפה	for it is over soon and flies away.

For the greater part of the Psalms, however, the desire to preserve life for

---

53. Arthur Schopenhauer, *Essays and Aphorisms* (trans. R. J. Hollingdale; London: Penguin, 1973), 21.

its own sake is paramount. The implication is that everyone wants to live, for example in Ps 34:13:

מי־האיש החפץ חיים   Who is the man that desires life,
אהב ימים לראות טוב   and loves days to see the good?

Of course, as always there are some very interesting exceptions to the rule, namely to the obsession with life above everything else. While some texts seem to assume that the significance of the deity revolves around his ability to give and sustain life, others, such as Ps 63:4, value the experience of Yhwh's care as better than life in itself:

כי־טוב חסדך מחיים   For your lovingkindness is better than life.

Other sections of the Writings that show little theological concern with the deity, such as Esther, Ruth, Lamentation, and Songs of Songs, are in some sense all nevertheless united in their attestation of a struggle for a meaningful life. Ruth and Esther focus on the preservation and continuation of life, both individual and communal. Song of Songs is concerned with love that is stronger than death (Song 8:6), and that goes along with and ultimately leads to a full life (and therewith sex). Indeed, for many Hebrew Bible texts the meaning of life is to have a passion for what one values (and therewith war).

But there is more. Discussions about Hebrew Bible axiological assumptions will have to go beyond a concern with human existence. The texts do not assume that the meaning of life is anthropocentric. Given the Hebrew Bible's god-centered subjectivist way of looking at things, one may well also attend to nonhuman existence, and here begin by asking what the texts presuppose about the purpose of Yhwh's own life. Even though, according to them, he is the living God, in biblical theologies the question of what the texts assume makes Yhwh's own existence meaningful to himself and to humans has not been given its due.

Even in philosophy proper, the notion of the assumed meaning of divine existence is seldom part of philosophy of religion.[54] The fact of the

---

54. Consider the absence of the question in those dealing with God-centered

matter is this: granted that in the world of the text the character of Yhwh is assumed to have reasons for doing what he does, it follows that what Yhwh's character does in fact do, and then feels about what he has done, both imply that there are states of affairs that are assumed to make Yhwh's existence more meaningful than others. That explains why the character Yhwh is made to act in certain ways rather than in others—because the narrators assume that this is what makes a god's existence meaningful. Here axiology overlaps with the philosophy of action (and divine motivation theory), and interesting questions arise. For example, *why*, according to different texts, does Yhwh want to create a heaven and an earth, kill and make alive, reveal and conceal himself, rule over and relate to people, be worshiped and served, fight and save, and so on?

A related question pertaining to the assumed purpose of divine existence from the perspective of the deity's character concerns the extent to which Yhwh is assumed to have free will in his decisions. Based on textual representations, it would seem that as a typical though often idiosyncratic Iron Age deity Yhwh is assumed to be engaging in "innate" divine behavior, acting out behavior attributed throughout the ancient Near East to any entity participating in "the divine condition." For all his uniqueness among the gods of yore, in terms of certain basic properties, functions, and relations, Yhwh seems to have been acting on "instinct" (for a god). Like other gods he cannot but create, reveal, bless or curse, save or destroy.[55] He cannot but want to be worshiped and feared.

Does this mean that these things are assumed in the Hebrew Bible to make the divine existence meaningful? Does it mean that Yhwh is assumed to be a slave to his own divine nature? In philosophy of religion, the discussion of divine freedom is a live topic. Yet this aspect of the supposed meaning of the divine life is less familiar to biblical theologians. It is a valid concern since, while some texts presuppose absolute divine freedom and sovereignty, others assume that Yhwh as character in the plot also acts pretty much according to how he already knows he will have to act, given the way the future of human actions will play out (e.g., Gen 15:12–16).[56]

---

views. One example is Paul Copan, "Morality and Meaning without God: Another Failed Attempt," *Philosophia Christi* Series 2/6 (2003): 295–304.

55. Miller, *The Religion of Ancient Israel*, 10.

56. William Rowe, "Divine Freedom," *SEP* [cited 13 February 2010]. Online: http://plato.stanford.edu/archives /fall2008/entries/divine-freedom/.

Not all texts assume determinism. Some assume dual causality, with both human and divine agents playing a role in actualizing possible states of affairs. In many Hebrew Bible narratives (e.g., the Joseph narrative in Gen 37–50), the divine existence is assumed to obtain meaning by controlling human affairs in order to further ultimate divine interests. Here the meanings of divine and human existence intersect, since the meaning of some people's lives in the Hebrew Bible appears as coterminous with what the lives in question meant to Yhwh, who is pulling the strings behind the scenes (e.g., see Isa 11; 45). In the end there is no one answer, because the narratives and poetry in the Hebrew Bible contain a complex array of diverse assumptions as to what makes the character of Yhwh's existence meaningful.

Aside from divine life, one might as well extend the scope of traditional philosophical curiosity to include textual presuppositions about the meaning of life also for other nonhuman agents (angels, demons, spirits of the dead, animals, plants, the sea, etc.). Take, for example, the life of the dead—what is assumed to be the point of this dreary postmortem existence? Nowhere is Yhwh said to have created the underworld, that is, Sheol. Early texts depict it as being out of his jurisdiction, while later ones have him in complete control of it. Given Sheol's intrusion into this life, the relationship between Yhwh and Sheol itself requires philosophical elucidation.[57]

14.4. Conclusion

In this chapter I have attempted to provide some sort of pioneering request that biblical scholars incorporate metaethics into their discussion of biblical ethics. Up to now, metaethical discussion has been inadvertent instead of an exclusive concern that is part of in-depth study. It is hoped that by way of a provocative (if not completely over the top) sort of introduction to some of the many possible issues that could come up for discussion, this chapter will contribute in some way to the introduction of metaethical inquiry in the near future. Whether this will happen and what exactly will be on the agenda, I do not wish to be prescriptive about. What I do wish

---

57. The Old Testament "saints" have to find meaning in a life that is not fair and that has no heaven or hell as incentives. On the issue in philosophy, see J. Jeremy Wisnewski, "Is the Immortal Life Worth Living?" *International Journal for Philosophy of Religion* 58 (2005): 27–36.

to do is to point out that the possibilities for metaethics are endless, and that the limits of the subject are nothing more than the limits of our own imagination.

15
Summary and Conclusion

I don't write a book so that it will be the final word; I write a book so that other books are possible, not necessarily written by me.[1]

The foregoing provocative romp through everything hitherto forbidden in the study of ancient Israelite religion barely touched the tip of the iceberg. There is a whole new world below this point, one that we have only begun to explore. There are more than enough issues of interest to keep those with an affinity for things philosophical busy for the remainder of their scholarly careers. Those who do follow this road will never again have to worry about new ideas for research when there is so much waiting to be done in countless unexplored realms under, inside, and above the worlds in the text.

I fully realize that many readers will not be convinced or excited by many of the ideas presented in this study. I welcome critique and am open to change my mind on many of the details. Yet if there is anything I would consider the heart of the matter, it is not so much the findings of my own idiosyncratic philosophical readings, but the general idea of this study, which pertains to the basic methodological proposal. I believe it offers nothing less than a catalyst for a "philosophical turn" in the way we study ancient Israelite religion as represented in the Hebrew Bible. In the end it all boils down to coming to terms with the following key assumptions or theses:

1. In the scientific study of religion it is generally accepted that a comprehensive perspective on, and an in-depth understanding of, any religion requires not only literary, histori-

---

1. Michel Foucault, quoted in Clare O'Farrell, *Michel Foucault* (New York: Sage, 2005), 9.

cal, comparative, phenomenological, sociological, psychological, and anthropological accounts of the data, but also a philosophical approach.

2. Even so, for a number of historical reasons, the study of ancient Israelite religion has been one of the few utterly lacking in a philosophical approach. There is currently no independent and officially recognized interpretive methodology available that allows biblical scholars to concern themselves exclusively with the provisioning of a philosophical account of the beliefs, concepts, and practices of ancient Israelite religion.

3. To be sure, given the nonphilosophical format of the Hebrew Bible, the philosophical distortions of the historical sense of the text in the precritical period and the popular equation of the task of philosophy of religion with propositional justification without recourse to revelation (natural theology), many reservations about recourse to a philosophical approach are quite justified.

4. However, there exist types of philosophical analysis that can be utilized solely for the purpose of conceptual clarification (narrow analysis); so that only rampant antiphilosophical sentiment, along with ignorance of recent developments in philosophy of religion and/or a lack of creativity, have prevented biblical scholars from recognizing the many opportunities that have been available for some time now for interdisciplinary research with philosophy of religion.

5. In ignorance of this, it has been assumed popularly that the question to be asked in relation to philosophy was: What could the biblical texts contribute to any contemporary philosophical discussions? This question was raised only to be dismissed. Now the question has been inverted, to become a concern with what philosophical analysis can contribute to a historical understanding of Israelite religion for its own sake.

6. Biblical scholars take essentialist views of historical inquiry and philosophical analysis, imagining the two to be incommensurable and mutually exclusive, primarily because they have insufficient conceptions of the descriptive tools available in philosophy and because they assume that the object of philosophical investigation must itself be philosophical in nature before philosophical questions can be asked. This is, of course, nonsense.

7. The biblical texts are not western philosophy; and yet their ordinary language in multiplex traditions of religious prose and poetry contain assumptions about existence, reality, being, truth, knowledge, reasoning, morality, and so on (i.e., philosophical assumptions), so that not only what the language means but also what it meant can be expressed in philosophical terms.

8. The Hebrew Bible's authors did not spell out these assumptions, as this would have been redundant. The authors were not concerned with them, precisely because they went without saying. In other words, the texts' fundamental presuppositions about the world were assumed to be common knowledge. Since we ourselves are not the implied readers, we cannot assume that we share this knowledge in biblical world views. This leads us to precisely why we need philosophical description: it is because the texts are not philosophy of religion, and because the assumptions of the text on such matters are not nonexistent, but are simply unarticulated and implicit.

9. A descriptive philosophical approach to ancient Yahwism is thus a philosophical clarification of the meaning of its nonphilosophical contents discourse and a reconstruction of the folk philosophies of religion in the text, that is, what texts in the Hebrew Bible took for granted about religion, the nature of religious language, the attributes and existence of deities, religious epistemology, the relation between religion and morality, religious pluralism, and so forth.

10. Philosophical categories allow for a clearer understanding of the conceptual content of a text, which was taken for granted because it constituted that text's fundamental assumptions. If alleged descriptive philosophical accounts end up distorting the data, this says more about the incompetence of the biblical scholar in choosing the correct approach, concepts, and categories than it says about the supposed distortive nature of philosophy.

11. Such a descriptive philosophical approach is not, as is popularly assumed, something over against the historical task. Rather, it is a compulsory subset thereof. And whereas other approaches bracket philosophical questions, philosophical

analysis allows interpreters to identify the assumptions in the
biblical discourse about issues on the agenda of philosophy
of religion.

12. Without this type of philosophical commentary on the text
as part of historical inquiry, we cannot even begin to understand the most basic elements of the Hebrew Bible's own
conceptions pertaining to fundamental religious phenomena. This allegedly hermeneutically justified bracketing of
philosophical concerns leaves us without the means to prevent ourselves from reading our own anachronistic philosophical-theological assumptions into and onto the biblical
discourse.

If these ideas seemed crazy initially, I hope that openminded readers have
now discovered to their delight or dismay that the contents of this study
have indeed proved to be "crazy enough." In the chapters that followed
I have both provided the theoretical base for the new approach (part 1)
and shown ways in which the theory may be fruitfully applied in practice,
with reference to a number of loci on the agenda of philosophy of religion
(part 2). In doing so, I hope that this study will go some way in showing
that philosophical reflection on ancient Yahwism(s) need not be distortive
or precritical, but can instead be immensely interesting, and can offer an
individually necessary and jointly sufficient condition for a comprehensive perspective on the religion. In all this, the rationale for the philosophical approach is always to supplement and learn from other approaches,
rather than to supplant any of them. What remains to be undertaken now
is discussion. In this, the debate regarding the viability of a descriptive
philosophical approach should ideally be distinguished from the debate
about philosophy in biblical theology.

Moreover, in utilizing an auxiliary discipline, there is always the danger
of not having sufficiently immersed oneself in the discipline to be able to
engage it in a manner that will satisfy its specialists. Any scholar of the
Hebrew Bible hoping to engage in philosophical reflection should go into
the practice feeling comfortable in the world of philosophy of religion.
To ensure quality work, the philosophical critic must also keep up with
what is happening in peer-reviewed accredited journals in philosophy of
religion proper. Often, much that features there may not be relevant, but
when methodological innovations are involved, we have to be there in the
thick of things. In fact, one should be so well versed in the auxiliary disci-

pline as to be able to read papers at conferences in philosophy of religion, with special attention to applying theory to the Hebrew Bible.[2]

I do realize, however, that my personal readerly ideology, manner of presentation, or imperfect application of a philosophical approach will not convince all readers that this new way of looking at the Hebrew Bible is a good thing. I understand that philosophy is not everybody's cup of tea, and all I ask is that the new approach be given a chance to prove itself. I do not expect everybody to jump onto the potential bandwagon it represents. I also realize that, instead of a single philosophical approach to the Hebrew Bible and ancient Israelite religion, there are many possible ways of engaging with these topics, and that therefore others might like to do things differently from what I have done. Though I have deliberately opted for a descriptive approach vis-à-vis an apologetic, atheological, or constructive format, others are free to develop their own philosophical agendas.

Because my concern is for the improvement of a descriptive and historical philosophical approach to ancient Israelite religion as represented in the Hebrew Bible—and not for the specifics of the findings of my own application of the theory—I therefore invite any and all critique with regard to both theory and practice. I do not think that the last word has been written on any of the matters discussed in this study and would be delighted if the approach can be improved, even at the cost of my own ideas concerning some of the details. I think it would be healthy for the discipline to accommodate different methodological and ideological points of view. I would therefore like to invite everyone interested in philosophical inquiry to do their own thing, so that no matter how much we differ in our concerns, assumptions, objectives, and findings, we at least start talking about all the philosophical questions we have bracketed for far too long.

As for further research, the sky is the limit. One only has to be creative to see that any Hebrew Bible text can be related to some issue in philosophy of religion or other, and that any philosophical (religious) locus can be brought to bear on the findings of any already extant approach. Those familiar both with the variety present in Hebrew Bible methods and with topics and issues of interest in philosophy will be able to provide a

---

2. I have been trying to do so and have read a paper at the British Society of Philosophy of Religion's annual conference.

philosophical perspective in any contribution to a book, a conference, a research interest group (e.g., at Society of Biblical Literature meetings), a local seminar, and so on. There is really no end to the ways in which philosophy of religion and the issues on its agenda can be brought to bear on whatever matter happens to be the subject of discussion at any particular time and place. All we need do is use our imagination.

BIBLIOGRAPHY

Abraham, William J. "The Epistemology of Jesus: An Initial Investigation." Pages 149–68 in *Jesus and Philosophy*. Edited by Paul K. Moser. Cambridge: Cambridge University Press, 2009.

———. *An Introduction to Philosophy of Religion*. Eaglewood Cliffs, N.J.: Prentice Hall, 1985.

Adams, Douglas. *The Hitchhiker's Guide to the Galaxy*. London: Pan, 1979.

Adinall, Peter. *Philosophy and Biblical Interpretation: A Study in Nineteenth-Century Conflict*. Cambridge: Cambridge University Press, 1991.

Albertz, Rainer. *A History of Israelite Religion in the Old Testament Period*. 2 vols. OTL. Louisville: Westminster John Knox, 1994.

Allen, Diogenes. *Philosophy for Understanding Theology*. Louisville: Westminster John Knox, 2007.

Allen, James P., ed. *Religion and Philosophy in Ancient Egypt*. New Haven: Yale University Press, 1989.

Alston, William B. "Some Suggestions for Divine Command Theorists." Pages 303–26 in *Christian Theism and the Problems of Philosophy*. Edited by Norman Beaty. Notre Dame, Ind.: University of Notre Dame Press, 1990.

Anderson, William H. U. "Philosophical Considerations in a Genre Analysis of Qoheleth." *VT* 48 (1998): 289–300.

———.What Is Scepticism and Can It Be Found in the Hebrew Bible?" *SJOT* 13 (1999): 225–57.

Aquino, Ranhilo C. "Existential Pessimism and the Affirmation of God: A Philosophical Reading of Qoheleth." Master's thesis, Saint Thomas Aquinas University, 1981.

Argall, Randall. *1 Enoch and Sirach: A Comparative and Conceptual Analysis of the Themes of Revelation, Creation, and Judgment*. Atlanta: Scholars Press, 1995.

Armstrong, Sharon Lee, Lila R. Gleitman, and Henry Gleitman. "What Some Concepts Might Not Be." Pages 225–59 in *Concepts: Core Readings*. Edited by Eric Margolis and Stephen Laurence. Cambridge: MIT Press, 1999.

Assmann, Jan. *The Price of Monotheism*. Translated by Robert Savage. Stanford, Calif.: Stanford University Press, 2009.

———. "Primat und Transendenz: Struktur und Genese der Ägyptischen Vorstellung eines 'Hochsten Wesens.'" Pages 117–36 in *Aspekten der spätägyptischen Religion*. Edited by Wolfhart Westendorf. Wiesbaden: Brill, 1979.

Audi, Robert. "Intrinsic Value and Meaningful Life." *Philosophical Papers* 34 (2005): 331–55.

Augé, Marc. *Non-places: Introduction to the Anthropology of Supermodernity*. Translated by John Howe. London: Verso, 1995.

Augustine, *The Confessions of St. Augustine*. Translated by Albert C. Outler. London: Courier Dover, 2002.

Baggini, Julian. *What's It All About? Philosophy and the Meaning of Life*. London: Granta, 2004.

Baier, Kurt. *Problems of Life and Death: A Humanist Perspective*. Amherst, N.Y.: Prometheus, 1997.

Baillie, James. "Recent Work on Personal Identity." *Philosophical Books* 34/4 (1993): 193–206.

Barr, James. *The Bible in the Modern World*. London: Trinity Press International, 1973.

———. *Biblical Faith and Natural Theology*. Oxford: Oxford University Press, 1994.

———. *The Concept of Biblical Theology: An Old Testament Perspective*. Philadelphia: Fortress, 1999.

———. *Fundamentalism*. London: SCM, 1977.

———. *The Garden of Eden and the Hope of Immortality*. London: SCM, 1993.

———. *History and Ideology in the Old Testament: Biblical Studies at the End of the Millennium*. Oxford: Oxford University Press, 2000.

———. *Old and New in Interpretation: A Study of the Two Testaments*. London: SCM, 1966.

———. *The Semantics of Biblical Language*. New York: Oxford University Press, 1961.

Barré, Michael L. "'Fear of God' and the World View of Wisdom." *BTB* 11 (1981): 41–43.

Barrett, Lee C., and Jon Stewart, eds. *The Old Testament*. Vol. 1 of *Kierkeg-aard and the Bible*. Edited by Lee C. Barrett and Jon Stewart. 2 vols. Kierkegaard Research: Sources, Reception, and Resources 1. Surrey, Eng.: Ashgate, 2009.

Bartholomew, Craig G. "Three Horizons: Hermeneutics from the Other End—An Evaluation of Anthony Thiselton's Hermeneutic Proposals." *European Journal of Theology* 5 (1996): 131–43.

Barton, John. "Alttestamentliche Theologie nach Albertz?" *JBT* 10 (1995): 25–32.

———. "Approaches to Ethics in the Old Testament." Page 114–31 in *Begin-ning Old Testament Study*. Edited by John W. Rogerson, John Barton, David J. A. Clines, and Paul Joyce. St. Louis: Chalice, 1998.

———. "The Basis of Ethics in the Hebrew Bible." *Semeia* 66 (1995): 11–22.

———. *Understanding Old Testament Ethics: Approaches and Explorations*. Louisville: Westminster John Knox, 2003.

Barton, John, and Julia Bowden. *The Original Story: God, Israel and the World*. Grand Rapids: Eerdmans, 2004.

Basinger, David. "Religious Diversity (Pluralism)." *SEP*. Cited 2 March 2010. Online: http://plato.stanford.edu/archives/fall2009/entries/reli-gious-pluralism/.

Beaney, Michael. "Analysis." *SEP*. Cited 22 July 2010. Online:http://plato.stanford.edu/archives/sum2009/entries/analysis/.

Bell, Richard H. *Understanding African Philosophy: A Cross-Cultural Approach to Classical and Contemporary Issues in Africa*. New York: Routledge, 2002.

Belliotti, Raymond. *What Is the Meaning of Life?* Amsterdam: Rodopi, 2001.

Belshaw, Christopher. *Ten Good Questions about Life and Death*. Malden, Mass.: Blackwell, 2005.

Benatar, David ed. *Life, Death and Meaning: Key Philosophical Readings on the Big Questions*. Lanham, Md.: Rowman & Littlefield, 2004.

Berto, Francesco. "Impossible Worlds." *SEP*. Cited 15 January 2010. Online: http://plato.stanford.edu/archives/fall2009/entries/impossible-worlds/.

Bertrand, Mark J. *Rethinking Worldview: Learning to Think, Live and Speak in This World*. Wheaton, Ill.: Crossway, 2007.

Bilimoria, Purushottama. "What Is the 'Sub-Altern' of the Comparative Philosophy of Religion?" *PEW* 53 (2003): 340–66.

Black, Max. *Models and Metaphor.* Ithaca, N.Y.: Cornell University Press, 1962.

Bloemendaal, Peter F. *Grammars of Faith: A Critical Evaluation of D. Z. Phillips's Philosophy of Religion.* Studies in Philosophical Theology. Leuven: Peeters, 2006.

Blumenberg, Hans. *Paradigm zu einer Metaphorologie.* Frankfurt: Suhrkamp, 1999.

Boer, Roland. *Marxist Criticism of the Bible.* London: Sheffield Academic Press, 2003.

————. "Philosophical Commentary." Pages 113–17 in *The Labor of Job: The Biblical Text as a Parable of Human Labor.* Edited by Antonio Negri. Durham, N.C.: Duke University Press, 2009.

Boman, Thorleif. *Hebrew Thought Compared with Greek.* Translated by Jules E. Moreau. 3rd ed. New York: Norton, 1970.

Botz-Bornstein, Thorsten. "Ethnophilosophy, Comparative Philosophy, Pragmatism: Toward a Philosophy of Ethnoscapes." *PEW* 56 (2006): 153–71.

Braun, Reiner. *Kohelet und die Frühhellenistische Popularphilosophie.* BZAW 130. Berlin: de Gruyter, 1973.

Brenner, Jeff. "Ancient Hebrew Thought." Cited 27 April 2010. Online: http://www.ancient-hebrew.org/12_thought.html.

Brett, Mark. *Biblical Criticism in Crisis? The Impact of the Canonical Approach on Hebrew Bible Studies.* London: Cambridge University Press, 2001.

Brink, Gijsbert van den, and Marcel Sarot, eds. *Understanding the Attributes of God.* Contributions to Philosophical Theology 1. Frankfurt: Lang, 1999.

Brown, Lee M. *African Philosophy: New and Traditional Perspectives.* Oxford: Oxford University Press, 2004.

Brueggemann, Walter. *An Introduction to the Old Testament: The Canon and Christian Imagination.* Louisville: Westminster John Knox, 2003.

————. *Isaiah 40–66.* IBC. Louisville: Westminster John Knox, 1998.

————. *Old Testament Theology: Testimony, Dispute, Advocacy.* Philadelphia: Fortress, 1997.

————. *Reverberations of Faith: A Theological Handbook of the Old Testament.* Louisville: Westminster John Knox, 2002.

Bultmann, Christoph. "Early Rationalism and Biblical Criticism on the Continent." Pages 875–901 in vol. 2 of *Hebrew Bible/Old Testament:*

The History of Its Interpretation. Edited by Magne Saebø. 2 vols. Göttingen: Vandenhoeck & Ruprecht, 1996–2008.

Burkert, Walter. "Prehistory of Presocratic Philosophy in an Orientalizing Context." Pages 55–85 in *The Oxford Handbook of Presocratic Philosophy*. Edited by Patricia W. Cord and Daniel W. Graham. New York: Oxford University Press, 2008.

Caputo, John D. *The Prayers and Tears of Jacques Derrida: Religion without Religion*. Bloomington: Indiana University Press, 1997.

Carasik, Michael. *Theologies of the Mind in Biblical Israel*. Studies in Biblical Literature 85. New York: Lang, 2006.

Carmy, Shalom, and David Shatz. "The Bible as a Source for Philosophical Reflection." Pages 13–38 in *History of Jewish Philosophy*. Edited by Daniel H. Frank and Oliver Learnman. Routledge History of World Philosophies 2. London: Routledge, 2003.

Carroll, Robert P. *When Prophecy Failed: Reactions and Responses to Failure in the Old Testament Prophetic Traditions*. London: SCM, 1979.

———. *Wolf in the Sheepfold: The Bible as Problem for Christianity*. London: SPCK, 1991.

Carson, D. A. *Exegetical Fallacies*. Grand Rapids: Baker, 1984.

Cassirer, Ernst. *Mythical Thought*. Vol. 2 of *The Philosophy of Symbolic Forms*. New Haven: Yale University Press, 1955.

Catto, Jeremy. "The Philosophical Context of the Renaissance Interpretation of the Bible." Pages 106–33 in vol. 1.2 of *Hebrew Bible/Old Testament: The History of Its Interpretation*. Edited by Magne Saebø. 2 vols. Göttingen: Vandenhoeck & Ruprecht, 1996–2008.

Chadwick, Owen. *Origen: Contra Celsum*. London: Cambridge University Press, 1980.

Charlesworth, Max J. *Philosophy of Religion: The Historic Approaches*. London: Macmillan, 1972.

Clines, David J. A. "From Copenhagen to Oslo: What Has (and Has Not) Happened at Congresses of the IOSOT." Pages 194–223 in vol. 1 of *On the Way to the Postmodern: Old Testament Essays 1967–1998*. 2 vols. JSOTSup 292. Sheffield: Sheffield Academic Press, 1998.

———. *Interested Parties: The Ideology of Readers and Writers of the Hebrew Bible*. Sheffield: Sheffield Academic Press, 1995.

———. *What Does Eve Do to Help? And Other Readerly Questions to the Old Testament*. JSOTSup 94. Sheffield: JSOT Press, 1990.

———. "Yahweh and the God of Christian Theology." *Theology* 83 (1980): 323–330.

Coackley, Sarah. "Feminism and Analytic Philosophy of Religion." Pages 494–525 in *The Oxford Handbook of Philosophy of Religion*. Edited by William Wainwright. Oxford: Oxford University Press, 2005.

Coetzee, Pieter H., and Andre P. J. Roux. *Philosophy from Africa: A Text with Readings*. 2nd ed. Cape Town: Oxford University Press, 2003.

Collins, John J. *Jewish Wisdom in the Hellenistic Age*. Louisville: Westminster John Knox, 1997.

Connolly, Peter, ed. *Approaches to the Study of Religion*. London: Continuum, 1999.

Copan, Paul. "Morality and Meaning without God: Another Failed Attempt." *Philosophia Christi* Series 2/6 (2003): 295–304.

Cottingham, John. *On the Meaning of Life*. London: Routledge, 2003.

Craig, Vincent M. *Charts of Philosophy and Philosophers*. Grand Rapids: Zondervan, 2007.

Creel, Richard E. *Thinking Philosophically: An Introduction to Critical Reflection and Rational Dialogue*. Oxford: Wiley-Blackwell, 2001.

Crenshaw, James L. "The Birth of Skepticism in Ancient Israel." Pages 1–9 in *The Divine Helmsman: Studies on God's Control of Human Events*. Edited by James L. Crenshaw and Samuel Sandmel. New York: Ktav, 1980.

———. *Defending God: Biblical Responses to the Problem of Evil*. Oxford: Oxford University Press, 2005.

———. *Prophetic Conflict: Its Effect upon Israelite Religion*. BZAW 24. Berlin: de Gruyter, 1971.

———. *Prophets, Sages, and Poets*. St. Louis: Chalice, 2006.

———. "Sipping from the Cup of Wisdom." Pages 41–62 in *Jesus and Philosophy: New Essays*. Edited by Paul K. Moser. Cambridge: Cambridge University Press, 2009.

———. *Theodicy in the Old Testament*. IRT 4. Philadelphia: Fortress, 1983.

———. *A Whirlpool of Torment: Israelite Traditions of God as an Oppressive Presence*. Minneapolis: Fortress, 1984.

Cupitt, Don. *Above Us Only Sky: The Religion of Ordinary Life*. Santa Rosa: California: Polebridge, 2008.

———. *After God: The Future of Religion*. London: Basic Books, 1997.

———. *Impossible Loves*. New York, Polebridge, 2007.

———. *Jesus and Philosophy*. London: SCM, 2009.

———. *The Meaning of the West: An Apologia for Secular Christianity*. London: SCM, 2008.

———. *The New Religion of Life in Everyday Speech*. London: SCM, 1999.

——. *Philosophy's Own Religion*. London: SCM, 2001.

——. *Sea of Faith*. London: SCM, 1984.

——. *Taking Leave of God*. London: SCM, 1980.

——. *The Way to Happiness*. London: Polebridge, 2005.

——. *What's a Story?* London: SCM, 1990.

Czachesz, István. "The Promise of the Cognitive Science of Religion for Biblical Studies." Cited 10 December 2010. Online: http://religionand-cognition.com/publications/czachesz_cssr.pdf.

Dafni, Evangelia. "Genesis 1–11 und Platos Symposion Überlegungen zum Austausch von hebräischem und griechischem Sprach- und Gedankengut in der Klassik und im Hellenismus." *OTE* 19 (2006): 584–602.

——. "Natürliche Theologie im Lichte des hebräischen und griechischen Alten Testaments," *ThZ* 57 (2001): 295–310.

DaGrazia, David. *Human Identity and Bioethics*. Cambridge: Cambridge University Press, 2005.

Dale, Erich M. "Hegel, Jesus, and Judaism." *Animus* 11 (2006): 4–12.

Davidson, Andrew B. *Theology of the Old Testament*. Edinburgh: T&T Clark, 1904.

Davies, Philip R. *In Search of Ancient Israel*. Sheffield: Sheffield Academic Press, 1992.

Davis, Stephen T. "Revelation and Inspiration." Pages 323–43 in *The Oxford Handbook of Philosophical Theology*. Edited by Thomas P. Flint and Michael Rea. Oxford: Oxford University Press, 2008.

Davison, Scott. "Prophecy." *SEP*. Cited 4 August 2011. Online: http://plato. stanford.edu/archives/sum2010/entries/prophecy/.

Deist, Ferdinand E. *Ervaring, Rede en Metode in Skrifuitleg: 'n Wetenskaps-historiese Ondersoek na Skrifuitleg in die Nederduitse Gereformeerde Kerk 1840–1990*. Pretoria: Human Sciences Research Council, 1994.

——. "Genesis 1:1–2:4a: World Picture and World View." *Scriptura* 22 (1987): 1–17.

Deist, Ferdinand E., with Robert Carroll. *The Material Culture of the Bible*. London: Continuum, 2000.

Deleuze, Gilles, and Félix Guattari. *A Thousand Plateaus*. Vol. 2 of *Capitalism and Schizophrenia*. Translated by Brian Massumi. New York: Continuum, 2004.

——. *What Is Philosophy?* Translated by Hugh Tomlinson and Graham Burchell. New York: Columbia University Press, 1994.

Dentan, Robert C. *Preface to Old Testament Theology*. New York: Seabury, 1963.

DeSmith, Felicia. "Frazer, Wittgenstein and the Interpretation of Religious Practice." *Macalester Journal of Philosophy* 14 (2005): 58–73.

Deuser, Hermann. *Religionsphilosophie*. Berlin: de Gruyter, 2008.

Dijkstra, Meindert. "The Law of Moses: The Memory of Mosaic Religion in and after the Exile." Pages 96–112 in *Yahwism after the Exile: Perspectives on Israelite Religion in the Persian Era*. Edited by Rainer Albertz and Bob Becking. Assen: Van Gorcum, 2003.

DiLella, Alexander. "An Existential Interpretation of Job." *BTB* 15 (1985): 49–55.

Drury, Maurice O'Connor. "Conversations with Wittgenstein." Pages 116–36 in *Recollections of Wittgenstein*. Edited by Rush Rhees. New York: Oxford University Press, 1984.

Dulls, Avery. "Response to Krister Stendahl's Method in the Study of Biblical Theology," in *The Bible in Modern Scholarship*. Edited by J. Philip Hyatt. New York: Abingdon, 1965.

Dunand, Francoise, and Christiane Zivie-Coche. *Gods and Men in Egypt: 3000 B.C.E. to 395 C.E.* Translated by David Lorton. New York: Cornell University Press, 2004.

Durrant, Michael, and Peter Geach. "The Meaning of 'God.'" Pages 71–90 in *Religion and Philosophy*. Edited by Martin Warner. Royal Institute of Philosophy Supplements 31. Cambridge: Cambridge University Press, 1992.

Dyrness, William A. *Themes in Old Testament Theology*. Downers Grove, Ill.: InterVarsity Press, 1979.

Earl, Dennis. "Concepts." *IEP*. Cited 12 April 2010. Online: http://www.iep.utm.edu/.

Efros, Israel I. *Ancient Jewish Philosophy: A Study in Metaphysics and Ethics*. Detroit: Wayne State University Press, 1964.

Eichrodt, Walter. *Theology of the Old Testament*. Translated by John A. Baker. 2 vols. OTL. Louisville: Westminster John Knox, 1961–1967.

Ellens, Deborah L. *Women in the Sex Texts of Leviticus and the Hebrew Bible: A Comparative Conceptual Analysis*. New York: T&T Clark, 2008.

Eskenazi, Tamara Cohn, Gary Allen Phillips, and David Jobling, eds. *Levinas and Biblical Studies*. SemeiaSt 43. Atlanta: Society of Biblical Literature, 2003.

Eze, Emanuel Chukwudi. *African Philosophy: An Anthology*. Blackwell Philosophy Anthologies. Oxford: Blackwell, 1998.

Fasiku, Gbenga. "African Philosophy and the Method of Ordinary Language Philosophy." *The Journal of Pan African Studies* 2/3 (2008): 1–17.

Feldman, Richard. "Epistemological Puzzles about Disagreement." Pages 167–95 in *Epistemology Futures*. Edited by Stephen Hetherington. New York: Oxford University Press, 2006.

Fieser, James. "Ethics." *IEP*. Cited 25 February 2010. Online: http://www. iep.utm.edu/.

Fischer, Rob. "Philosophical Approaches." Pages 105–26 in *Approaches to the Study of Religion*. Edited by Peter Connolly. London: Continuum, 1999.

Fitzgerald, Timothy. *The Ideology of Religious Studies*. Oxford: Oxford University Press, 2000.

Flannery, Kevin L. "Ancient Philosophical Theology." Pages 83–98 in *A Companion to Philosophy of Religion*. Edited by Charles Taliaferro, Paul Draper, and Philip Quinn. BCP 9. London: Wiley-Blackwell, 2010.

Flint, Thomas P., and Michael C. Rea. *The Oxford Handbook of Philosophical Theology*. New York: Oxford University Press, 2009.

Fohrer, Georg. *History of Israelite Religion*. Translated by David E. Green. Nashville: Abingdon, 1972.

Fontaine, Resianne. "Abraham Ibn Daud." *SEP*. Cited 22 September 2009. Online: http://plato.stanford.edu/archives/fall2008/entries/abraham-daud/.

Forrest, Peter. "The Epistemology of Religion." *SEP*. Cited 2 April 2010. Online: http://plato.stanford.edu/archives/sum2009/entries/religion-epistemology/.

Fox, Michael V. "Qoheleth's Epistemology." *HUCA* 58 (1987): 137–55.

———. *Qohelet and His Contradictions*. JSOTSup 71. Sheffield: JSOT Press, 1989.

Frame, John M. *Euthyphro, Hume, and the Biblical God*. Cited 13 February 2010. Online: http://www.frame- poythress.org/frame_articles/1993Euthyphro.htm.

Frank, Daniel H., Oliver Leaman, and Charles H. Manekin, eds. *The Jewish Philosophy Reader*. New York: Routledge, 2000.

Frankenberry, Nancy. "Feminist Philosophy of Religion." *SEP*. Cited 20 January 2010. Online: http://plato.stanford.edu/archives/fall2008/entries/feminist-religion/.

Frankfort, Henry, and Henrietta A. Frankfort. *Before Philosophy: the Intellectual Adventure of Ancient Man*. London: Penguin, 1949.

Fretheim, Terrence E. *The Suffering of God: An Old Testament Perspective.* OBT. Philadelphia: Fortress, 1984.

Froehlich, Karlfried. "Christian Interpretation of the Old Testament in the High-Middle Ages." Pages 531–54 in vol. 1.1 of *Hebrew Bible/Old Testament: The History of Its Interpretation.* Edited by Magne Saebø. 2 vols. Göttingen: Vandenhoeck & Ruprecht, 1996–2008.

Frydrych, Tomas. *Living under the Sun: Examination of Proverbs and Qoheleth.* VTSup 90. Leiden: Brill, 2002.

Gane, Laurence, and Kitty Chan. *Introducing Nietzsche.* Cambridge: Icon Books, 1999.

Gardenförs, Peter, ed. *Belief Revision.* Cambridge: Cambridge University Press, 1992.

Garrett, Brian. "Personal Identity and Reductionism." *Philosophy and Phenomenological Research* 51 (1991): 361–73.

Geivett, Douglas R., and Brendan Sweetman. *Contemporary Perspectives on Religious Epistemology.* Oxford: Oxford University Press, 1992.

Gericke, Jacobus W. "Beyond Divine Command Theory: Moral Realism in the Hebrew Bible." *HTS* 65/1 (2009).

———. "Beyond Reconciliation: Monistic Yahwism and the Problem of Evil in Philosophy of Religion." *VE* 26 (2005): 64–92.

———. "Brave New World: Towards a Philosophical Theology of the Old Testament." *OTE* 22 (2009): 321–45.

———. "Dividing One by Zero: Hyperreality in the Hebrew Bible and *The Matrix*." *JSem* 17/2 (2008): 344–66.

———. "Does Yahweh Exist? A Philosophical-Critical Reconstruction of the Case against Realism in Old Testament Theology." Ph.D. diss., University of Pretoria, 2004.

———. "Does Yahweh Exist? The Case against Realism in Old Testament Theology," *OTE* 17 (2004): 30–57.

———. "Fundamentalism on Stilts: A Response to Alvin Plantinga's Reformed Epistemology." *VE* 30/2 (2009): 1–5.

———. Natural A/Theologies in the Hebrew Bible: Perspectives from Philosophy of Religion." *VE* 31/1 (2010).

———. "The Nature of Religious Language in the Hebrew Bible: A Philosophical Reassessment." *JSem* 19 (2009): 78–97.

———. "Old Testament Studies and Philosophy of Religion: A Brief History of Interdisciplinary Relations." *OTE* 23 (2010): 652–87.

———. "The Quest for a Philosophical Yahweh (Part 1): Old Testament Theology and Philosophy of Religion." *OTE* 18 (2006): 579–602.

———. "The Quest for a Philosophical Yhwh (Part 2): Philosophical Criticism as Exegetical Methodology." *OTE* 19 (2006): 1178–92.

———. "The Quest for a Philosophical Yhwh (Part 3): Towards a Philosophy of Old Testament Religion." *OTE* 20 (2007): 669–88.

———. "What Is an אל? A Philosophical Analysis of the Concept of Generic Godhood in the Hebrew Bible." *OTE* 22 (2009): 21–46.

———. "What's a God? Preliminary Thoughts on Meta-theistic Assumptions in Old Testament Yahwism(s)." *VE* 27 (2006): 856–57.

———. "Why Is There Something Rather Than Nothing? Biblical Ontology and the Mystery of Existence." *OTE* 21 (2008): 329–44.

———. "Yahwism and Projection—A Comprehensive A/Theological Perspective on Polymorphism in the Old Testament." *Scriptura* (2007): 407–24.

———. "Yhwh and the God of Philosophical Theology." *VE* 27 (2006): 677–99.

Gerstenberger, Erhard. *Theologies in the Old Testament.* London: Continuum, 2002.

Gibson, Arthur. *Biblical Semantic Logic: A Preliminary Analysis.* New York: St. Martin's Press, 1981.

———. *Biblical Semantic Logic: A Preliminary Analysis.* 2nd ed. London: Continuum, 2001.

Gilkey, Langdon. "Cosmology, Ontology, and the Travail of Biblical Language." *JR* 41 (1961): 194–205.

Gnuse, Robert. Heilsgeschichte *as a Model for Biblical Theology: The Debate Concerning the Uniqueness and Significance of Israel's Worldview.* Lanham, Md.: University Press of America, 1989.

———. *The Old Testament and Process Theology.* St. Louis: Chalice, 2000.

Goodchild, Philip. "Continental Philosophy of Religion: An Introduction." Pages 1–39 in *Rethinking Philosophy of Religion: Approaches from Continental Philosophy.* Edited by Anthony P. Smith and Daniel Whistler. Perspectives in Continental Philosophy 29. New York: Fordham University Press, 2002.

Gottwald, Norman K. *The Tribes of Yahweh: A Sociology of the Religion of Liberated Israel, 1250–1030 BCE.* Maryknoll, N.Y.: Orbis, 1979.

Grau, Christopher. *Philosophers Explore* The Matrix. New York: Oxford University Press, 2005.

Griffiths, Paul. "Comparative Philosophy of Religion." Pages 718–24 in *A Companion to Philosophy of Religion.* Edited by Charles Taliaferro,

Paul Draper, and Philip Quinn. 2nd ed. BCP 9. London: Wiley-Blackwell, 2010.

Griffith-Dickson, Gwen. *The Philosophy of Religion*. London: SCM, 2005.

Gulick, Robert van. "Consciousness." *SEP*. Cited 25 September 2011. Online: http://plato.stanford.edu/archives/sum2011/entries/consciousness/.

Gupta, Anil. "Definitions." *SEP*. Cited 18 February 2011. Online:http://plato.stanford.edu/archives/spr2009/entries/definitions/.

Hacker, Peter M. S. "Beyond the Linguistic Turn." Pages 1–20 in *The Analytic Turn: Analysis in Early Analytic Philosophy and Phenomenology*. Edited by Michael Beaney. London: Routledge, 2007.

Hackett, Jeremiah, and Gerald Wallulis, eds. *Philosophy of Religion for a New Century: Essays in Honor of Eugene Thomas Long*. Studies in Philosophy and Religion 25. New York: Springer, 2004.

Hajek, Petr. "Fuzzy Logic." *SEP*. Cited 1 November 2009. Online: http://plato.stanford.edu/archives/fall2010/entries/logic-fuzzy.

Hallen, Barry. "Academic Philosophy and African Intellectual Liberation." *African Philosophy* 11/2 (1998): 93–97.

———. "Analytic Philosophy and Traditional Thought: A Critique of Robin Horton." Pages 216–28 in *African Philosophy: A Classical Approach*. Edited by Parker English and Kibujjo M. Kalumba. Upper Saddle River, N.J.: Prentice Hall, 1996.

———. "Does it Matter Whether Linguistic Philosophy Intersects Ethnophilosophy?" *APA Newsletters* 96 (1996): 136–40.

———. *The Good, the Bad, and the Beautiful: Discourse about Values in Yoruba Culture*. Bloomington: Indiana University Press, 2004.

———. *A Short History of African Philosophy*. Bloomington: Indiana University Press, 2002.

Hamori, Esther J. *When Gods Were Men: The Embodied God in Biblical and Near Eastern Literature*. Berlin: de Gruyter, 2008.

Hanna, Robert. "Conceptual Analysis." *REP* 2:518–22.

Hansson, Sven O. "Logic of Belief Revision." *SEP*. Cited 10 January 2010. Online: http: plato.stanford.edu/archives/spr2009/entries/logic-belief-revision/.

Hare, John. "Religion and Morality." *SEP*. Cited 13 October 2010. Online: http://plato.stanford.edu/archives/win2010/entries/religion-morality/.

Harris, Harriet. *Fundamentalism and Evangelicals*. Oxford: Oxford University Press, 2008.

Harris, Harriet, and Christopher Insole, eds. *Faith and Philosophical Analysis: The Impact of Analytical Philosophy on Philosophy of Religion.* London: Ashgate, 2005.

Harris, James F. *Analytic Philosophy of Religion.* London: Kluwer, 2002.

———. "The Causal Theory of Reference and Religious Language." *IJPR* 29 (1991): 75–86.

Harrison, Victoria S. "Metaphor, Religious Language, and Religious Experience." *Sophia* 46/2 (2007): 127–45.

———. "Philosophy of Religion, Fictionalism, and Religious Diversity." *IJPR* 68/1–3 (2010): 43–58.

———. "What's the Use of Philosophy of Religion?" Pages 29–45 in *God, Goodness and Philosophy.* Edited by Harriet Harris. Oxford: Ashgate, 2011.

Hartenstein, Friedhelm. "Personalität Gottes im Alten Testaments." Pages 19–46 in *Personalität Gottes.* Edited by Wilfried Härle and Reiner Preul. Marburg Jahrbuch, Theologie 19. Leipzig: Evangelische Verlagsanstalt, 2007.

Hasel, Gerhard. *Old Testament Theology: Basic Issues in the Current Debate.* 3rd ed. Grand Rapids: Eerdmans, 1985.

Hasker, William. "Analytic Philosophy of Religion." Pages 421–45 in *The Oxford Handbook of Philosophy of Religion.* Edited by William Wainwright. Oxford: Oxford University Press, 2005.

Haught, John F. *What Is God? How to Think about the Divine.* New York: Paulist, 1986.

Hayes, John, and Frederick Prussner. *Old Testament Theology: Its History and Development.* Atlanta: John Knox, 1991.

Hazony, Yoram. *The Philosophy of Hebrew Scripture.* New York: Cambridge University Press, 2012.

Healy, Mary, and Robin Parry, eds. *The Bible and Epistemology: Biblical Soundings on the Knowledge of God.* Colorado Springs: Paternoster, 2007.

Hebblethwaite, Brian. *Philosophical Theology and Christian Doctrine.* Oxford: Wiley-Blackwell, 2005.

Hecke, Pierre. *Metaphor in the Hebrew Bible.* New York: Peeters, 2005.

Heidegger, Martin. *Pathmarks.* Edited and translated by William McNeil. Cambridge: Cambridge University Press, 1998.

Heinegg, Peter, ed. *Mortalism: Readings on the Meaning of Life.* Amherst, N.Y.: Prometheus, 2003.

Helmer, Christine. "Open Systems: Constructive Philosophical and Theological Issues in Biblical Theology," *SBL Forum*. Cited 15 September 2004. Online: http://sbl-site.org/Article.aspx?ArticleID=310.

Hemmerle, Klaus. "Wandern mit deinem Gott—Religionsphilosophische Kontexte zu Mi 6, 8." Cited 18 June 2012. Online: http://www.klaus-hemmerle.de/cms-joomla/download/Wandern%20mit%20deinem%20Gott%20-%20religionsphilosophische%20Kontexte.pdf.

Hick, John. *God and the Universe of Faiths*. London: Macmillan, 1973.

Hirsch, Emil G. "Hegel, Georg Wilhelm Friedrich." *Jewish Encyclopedia*. Cited 19 August 2010. Online: http://www.jewishencyclopedia.com.

Hodgson, Peter C. "Hegel's Philosophy of Religion." In *The Cambridge Companion to Hegel and Nineteenth-Century Philosophy*. Edited by Frederick C. Beiser. Cambridge: Cambridge University Press, 2009. Cited 17 December 2009. Online: http://cco.cambridge.org/extract?id=ccol9780521831673_CCOL9780521831673A010.

Holder, R. Ward. "John Calvin." *IEP*. Cited 23 September 2009. Online: http://www.iep.utm.edu/.

Hume, David. *Dialogues concerning Natural Religion*. Edited by Henry David Aiken. London: Forgotten Books, 1948.

Hutto, Daniel. "Philosophical Clarification: Its Possibility and Point." *Philosophia* 37 (2009): 629–52.

Hyde, Dominic. "Sorites Paradox." *SEP*. Cited 10 December 2010. Online: http://plato.stanford.edu/archives/fall2008/entries/sorites-paradox/.

Ikuenobe, Polycarp. "The Parochial Universalist Conception of 'Philosophy' and 'African Philosophy.'" *PEW* 47 (1997): 189–90.

Imschoot, Paul van. *Theology of the Old Testament*. New York: Desclée, 1965.

Ingraffia, Brian D. *Postmodern Theory and Biblical Theology: Vanquishing God's Shadow*. Cambridge: Cambridge University Press, 1995.

Irwin, William. *The Matrix and Philosophy: Welcome to the Desert of the Real*. Chicago: Open Court, 2002.

Jacob, Edmund. *Theology of the Old Testament*. Translated by Arthur Heathcote and Peter Allcock. London: Hodder & Stoughton, 1958.

Jacobsen, Thorkild. *The Treasures of Darkness: A History of Mesopotamian Religion*. London: Oxford University Press, 1979.

Janowski, Bernd. "Das biblische Weltbild: Eine methodische Skizze." Pages 3–26 in *Das biblische Weltbild in seine altorientalischen Kontexte*. Edited by B. Janowski and B. Ego. FAT 32. Tübingen: Mohr Siebeck, 2001.

Janz, Bruce B. "African Philosophy." Cited 4 February 2010. Online: http://pegasus.cc.ucf.edu/~janzb/papers/37AfPhil.pdf.

Jones, Roger B. "Varieties of Philosophical Analysis." *History of Philosophy Overview*. Cited 12 May 2009. Online: http://www.rbjones.com/rbjpub/philos/history/his003.htm.

Jordan, Mark H. "Religion, History of the Philosophy of." Pages 759–63 in *The Oxford Companion to Philosophy*. Edited by Ted Honderich. New York: Oxford University Press, 1995.

Kaiser, Otto. *The Apocrypha: An Introduction*. New York: Hendrickson, 2004.

———. *Grundlegung*. Vol. 1 of *Der Gott des Alten Testaments: Theologie des Alten Testaments*. 3 vols. Göttingen: Vandenhoeck & Ruprecht, 2003.

———. *Zwischen Athen und Jerusalem: Studien zur griechischen und biblischen Theologie, ihrer Eigenart und ihren Verhältnis*. BZAW 320. Berlin: de Gruyter, 2003.

Kaiser, Walter C., Jr. *Toward an Old Testament Theology*. Grand Rapids: Zondervan, 1991.

Kass, Leon. *The Beginning of Wisdom: Reading Genesis*. New York: Free Press, 2003.

Katz, Claire E., and Lara Trout. *Emmanuel Levinas and the Question of Religion*. London: Routledge, 2005.

Kaufmann, Walter A. *Discovering the Mind: Kant, Goethe, Hegel*. Brunswick, N.J.: Transaction Publishers, 1991.

Keel, Othmar, and Christoph Uehlinger. *Gods, Goddesses, and Images of God in Ancient Israel*. Minneapolis: Fortress, 1998.

Kelly, John F. *The Problem of Evil in the Western Tradition: From the Book of Job to Modern Genetics*. Collegeville, Minn.: Liturgical Press, 2002.

Kelly, Thomas. "The Epistemic Significance of Disagreement." Pages 167–95 in *Oxford Studies in Epistemology*. Edited by Tamar Szabo. Oxford: Clarendon, 2005.

Kim, Wonil, Deborah Ellens, Michael Floyd, and Marvin A. Sweeny, eds. *Theological and Hermeneutical Studies*. Vol. 2 of *Reading the Hebrew Bible for a New Millennium: Form, Concept, and Theological Perspective*. 2 vols. Studies in Antiquity and Christianity. London: Continuum, 2000.

Kirch, Joy F. "Martin Luther: How One Man Responded." *Western Philosophy*. Cited 22 September 2009. Online: http://www.tamuk.edu/mcpe/kirch.htm.

Kittel, Rudolf. "Die Zukunft der alttestamentlichen Wissenschaft." *ZAW* 39 (1921): 84–99.

Klein-Braslavy, Sara. "The Philosophical Exegesis." Pages 302–20 in vol. 1.2 of *Hebrew Bible/Old Testament: The History of Its Interpretation.* Edited by Magne Saebø. 2 vols. Göttingen: Vandenhoeck & Ruprecht, 1996–2008.

Klemke, Elmer Daniel, ed. *The Meaning of Life.* 2nd ed. New York: Oxford University Press, 2000.

Knierim, Rolf P. *The Task of Old Testament Theology: Substance, Method, and Cases.* Grand Rapids: Eerdmans, 1995.

Knight, Douglas. "Old Testament Ethics." *ChrCent* 100 (20 January 1982): 55–59.

Köhler, Ludwig. *Hebrew Man.* London: SCM, 1956.

———. *Theology of the Old Testament.* Translated by Andrew S. Todd. LTT. London: Clarke, 1957.

Kolak, Daniel. *In Search of God: The Language and Logic of Belief.* London: Wadsworth, 1993.

Kolb, David. *New Perspectives on Hegel's Philosophy of Religion.* New York: State University of New York Press, 1992.

Köpf, Ulrich. "The Reformation as an Epoch of the History of Theological Education." Pages 348–59 in vol. 1.2 of *Hebrew Bible/Old Testament: The History of Its Interpretation.* Edited by Magne Saebø. 2 vols. Göttingen: Vandenhoeck & Ruprecht, 1996–2008.

Korfmacher, Carsten. "Personal Identity." *IEP.* Cited 30 May 2011. Online: http://www.iep.utm.edu/person-i/.

Kraft, Robert A. "Scripture and Canon in the Commonly Called Apocrypha and Pseudepigrapha and in the Writings of Josephus." Pages 199–216 in vol. 1.1 of *Hebrew Bible/Old Testament: The History of Its Interpretation.* Edited by Magne Saebø. 2 vols. Göttingen: Vandenhoeck & Ruprecht, 1996–2008.

Krailsheimer, A. J. *Pensées: Blaise Pascal.* London: Penguin Classics, 1995.

Kreeft, Peter. *The Philosophy of Tolkien: The Worldview behind* The Lord of the Rings. San Francisco: Ignatius Press, 2005.

———. *Three Philosophies of Life: Ecclesiastes—Life as Vanity, Job—Life as Suffering, Song of Songs—Life as Love.* San Francisco: Ignatius Press, 1989.

Kripke, Saul. *Naming and Necessity.* Oxford: Basil Blackwell, 1972.

Krueger, Thomas. "Einheit und Vielfalt des Gottlichen nach dem Alten Testament." Cited 10 March 2010. Online: http://www.theologie.uzh.

ch/faecher/altes-testament/thomaskrueger/ Krueger_1998_Einheit_
und_Vielfalt.pdf, 1998.

LaCocque, André, and Paul Ricœur. *Thinking Biblically: Exegetical and Hermeneutical Studies*. Translated by David Pellauer. Chicago: University of Chicago Press, 2003.

Lakoff, George, and Mark Johnson. *Metaphors We Live By*. Chicago: University of Chicago Press, 1980.

———. *Philosophy in the Flesh: The Embodied Mind and Its Challenges to Western Thought*. London: Basic Books, 1999.

Langer, Susanne K. *Philosophy in a New Key: A Study in the Symbolism of Reason, Rite, and Art*. 3rd ed. Cambridge: Harvard University Press, 1942.

Larrimore, Mark J. *The Problem of Evil: A Reader*. London: Wiley-Blackwell, 2001.

Laurence, Gane, and Kitty Chan. *Introducing Nietzsche*. Cambridge: Icon Books, 1999.

Lawrence, Matt. *Like a Splinter in Your Mind: The Philosophy behind* The Matrix Trilogy. Oxford: Wiley-Blackwell, 2004.

Leleye, Issiaka P. "Is There an African Philosophy in Existence Today?" Pages 86–106 in *Philosophy from Africa: A Text with Readings*. Edited by Pieter Coetzee and Andre P. J. Roux. Cape Town: Oxford University Press, 2002.

Levenson, Jon D. *Creation and the Persistence of Evil*. San Francisco: Harper & Row, 1993.

Levine, Michael P. "Contemporary Christian Analytic Philosophy of Religion: Biblical Fundamentalism, Terrible Solutions to a Horrible Problem, and Hearing God." *IJPR* 48 (2000): 89–119.

———. "Ninian Smart on the Philosophy of Worldviews." *Sophia* 36 (1997): 11–23.

Liddy, Richard M. "Symbolic Consciousness: The Contribution of Susanne K. Langer." *Proceedings of the American Catholic Philosophical Association* 44 (1971): 94–110. Online: http://www.anthonyflood.com/liddy-symbolicconsciousness.htm.

Lindstrom, Frederick. *God and the Origin of Evil: A Contextual Analysis of Alleged Monistic Evidence in the Old Testament*. Lund: Gleerup, 1983.

Littlejohn, Ronnie. "Comparative Philosophy." *IEP*. Cited 10 January 2010. Online: http://www.iep.utm.edu/.

Lloyd, Alan B., ed., *What Is a God? Studies in the Nature of Greek Divinity*. London: Duckworth, 1997.

Long, Eugene T., ed. *Issues in Contemporary Philosophy of Religion*. Studies in Philosophy and Religion 23. New York: Springer, 2002.

———. *Twentieth-Century Western Philosophy of Religion, 1900–2000*. HCPR 1. Dordrecht: Kluwer, 2003.

Ludwig, T. M. "Gods and Goddesses." *ER* 6:67–78.

Macarthur, John, Richard Mayhue, and John J. Hughes. *Think Biblically! Recovering a Christian Worldview*. Wheaton, Ill.: Crossway, 2003.

MacDonald, Scott. "What Is Philosophical Theology?" Pages 17–29 in *Arguing about Religion*. Edited by Kevin Timpe. New York: Routledge, 2009.

MacIntyre, Alasdair, and Anthony Flew, eds. *New Essays in Philosophical Theology*. London: SCM, 1955.

Mackie, Penelope. "Transworld Identity." *SEP*. Cited 7 August 2010. Online: http:// plato.stanford.edu/archives/fall2008/entries/identity-transworld/.

Maffie, James. "Aztec Philosophy." *IEP*. Cited 25 August 2010. Online: http://www.iep.utm.edu/.

———. "Ethnoepistemology." *IEP*. Cited 29 January 2010. Online: http://www.iep.utm.edu/.

Margolis, Eric, and Stephen Laurence. "Concepts." *SEP*. Cited 18 February 2010. Online: http://plato.stanford.edu/archives/fall2008/entries/concepts/.

Marion, Jean-Luc. *God without Being*. Chicago: University of Chicago Press, 1991.

Markus, Arjan. "Assessing Views of Life: A Subjective Affair?" *RelStud* 39 (2003): 125–43.

Marshall, Taylor. "Thomas Aquinas on Plato Reading the Old Testament." *Canterbury Tales*. Cited 17 February 2010. Online: http://cantuar.blogspot.com/2008/04/thomas-aquinas-on-plato-reading-old.html.

Martin, Michael. *Atheism, Morality, and Meaning*. Amherst, N.Y.: Prometheus, 2002.

———. *The Cambridge Companion to Atheism*. Cambridge: Cambridge University Press, 2007.

Masolo, Dismas A. *African Philosophy in Search of Identity*. Edinburgh: University of Edinburgh Press, 1994.

Mautner, Thomas. *The Penguin Dictionary of Philosophy*. London: Blackwell, 2000.

Mayes, Andrew D. H. "Deuteronomy 14 and the Deuteronomic World View." Pages 165–81 in *Studies in Deuteronomy: In Honour of C.J.*

Labuschagne on the Occasion of His 65th Birthday. Edited by F. García Martínez. Leiden: Brill, 1994.

Mbiti, John. *African Religions and Philosophy*. Rev. ed. London: Heinemann International Books, 1990.

McCartney, Dan C. "Literal and Allegorical Interpretation in Origen's *Contra Celsum*." *WTJ* 48 (1986): 281–301.

McFague, Sallie. *Metaphorical Theology: Models of God in Religious Language*. Philadelphia: Fortress, 1982.

McInerny, Ralph, and John O'Callaghan. "Saint Thomas Aquinas." *SEP*. Cited 16 September 2010. Online: http://plato.stanford.edu/archives/fall2008/entries/aquinas/.

McKenzie, John L. *A Theology of the Old Testament*. Garden City, N.Y.: Doubleday, 1976.

McLaughlin, Brian, and Karen Bennett. "Supervenience." *SEP*. Cited 14 December 2009. Online: http://plato.stanford.edu/archives/fall2008/entries/supervenience/

Mead, Hunter. *Types and Problems of Philosophy*. New York: Henry Holt & Co., 1962.

Meister, Chad, and Paul Copan, eds., *The Routledge Companion to Philosophy of Religion*. London: Taylor & Francis, 2010.

Menzies, Peter. "Counterfactual Theories of Causation." *SEP*. Cited 18 September 2010. Online: http://plato.stanford.edu/archives/fall2009/entries/causation-counterfactual/.

Merk, Otto. *Biblische Theologie des Neuen Testaments in Ihrer Anfangszeit*. Marburg: Elwert, 1972.

Metz, Thaddeus. "The Concept of a Meaningful Life." *American Philosophical Quarterly* 38 (2001): 137–53.

———. "Could God's Purpose Be the Source of Life's Meaning?" *RelStud* 36 (2000): 293–313.

———. "The Immortality Requirement for Life's Meaning," *Ratio* 16 (2003): 161–77.

———. "The Meaning of Life." *SEP*. Cited 21 March 2011. Online: <http://plato.stanford.edu/archives/fall2008/entries/life-meaning/.

———. "Utilitarianism and the Meaning of Life," *Utilitas* 15 (2003): 50–70.

Miles, Jack. *God: A Biography*. New York: Knopf, 1995.

Miller, Patrick. *Israelite Religion and Biblical Theology: Collected Essays*. Sheffield: Sheffield Academic Press, 2000.

———. *The Religion of Ancient Israel*. Library of Ancient Israel. Louisville: Westminster John Knox, 2000.

Mills, Mary E. *Images of God in the Old Testament*. New York: Glazier, 1998.

Mitchell, Craig Vincent. *Charts of Philosophy and Philosophers*. Grand Rapids: Zondervan, 2007.

Moore, Megan Bishop. *Philosophy and Practice of Writing a History of Israel*. London: Continuum, 2005.

Morgan, Kathleen A. *Myth and Philosophy from the Presocratics to Plato*. New York: Cambridge University Press, 2000.

Morris, Thomas V. *Our Idea of God: An Introduction to Philosophical Theology*. Contours of Christian Philosophy. London: Regent College Publishing, 2002.

Morriston, Wes. "Must There Be a Standard of Moral Goodness apart from God?" *Philosophia Christi* 2/3 (2001): 127–38.

Moseley, Alan N. *Thinking against the Grain: Developing a Biblical Worldview in a Culture of Myths*. Grand Rapids: Kregel, 2003.

Müller, Hans-Peter. "Alttestamentliche Theologie und Religionswissenschaft." Pages 20–31 in *Wer Ist Wie Du, Herr, unten den Göttern?* Edited by Ingo Kottsieper and Otto Kaiser. Studien zur Theologie und Religionsgeschichte Israels. Göttingen: Vandenhoeck & Ruprecht, 1994.

———. "Bedarf die Alttestamentliche Theologie einer philosophischen Grundlegung." Pages 342–51 in *Alttestamentlicher Glaube und biblische Theologie*. Stuttgart: Kohlhammer, 1994.

———. *Glauben, Denken und Hoffen: Alttestamentliche Botschaften in den Auseinandersetzungen unserer Zeit*. Berlin: LIT, 1998.

Murphy, Nancey. *Beyond Liberalism and Fundamentalism: How Modern and Postmodern Philosophy Set the Theological Agenda*. Valley Forge, Pa.: Trinity Press International, 1996.

Nagel, Thomas, "What Is It Like to Be a Bat?" *Philosophical Review* 83/4 (1974): 435–50.

Nadler, Steven. "Baruch Spinoza." *SEP.* Cited 16 September 2010. Online: http://plato.stanford.edu/archives/win2009/entries/spinoza/.

Nasr, Seyyed Hossein, and Mehdi Aminrazavi, eds. *From Zoroaster to 'Umar Khayyam*. Vol. 1 of *An Anthology of Philosophy in Persia*. London: Tauris, 2008.

Naugle, David K. *Worldview: A History of the Concept*. Grand Rapids: Eerdmans, 2002.

Negri, Antonio. *The Labor of Job: The Biblical Text as a Parable of Human Labor*. Translated by Matteo Mandarini. Durham, N.C.: Duke University Press, 2009.

Neumark, David. *The Philosophy of the Bible*. Cincinnati: Ark, 1918.

Nielsen, Kai. "Philosophy and '*Weltanschauung*.'" *Journal of Values Inquiry* 27 (1993): 179–86.

Nietzsche, Friedrich. *The Anti-Christ*. Translated by Henry Louis Mencken. London: Nu Vision, 2007.

———. *Beyond Good and Evil*. Translated by Helen Zimmern. Project Gutenberg. Cited 8 August 2010. Online: http://www.gutenberg.org/etext/4363.

———. *Human, All Too Human: A Book for Free Spirits*. Translated by Reginald J. Hollingdale. Cambridge: Cambridge University Press, 1996.

———. On the Genealogy of Morality. Edited by Keith Ansell-Pearson. Translated by Carol Diethe. Cambridge: Cambridge University Press, 1995.

———. *The Will to Power*. Translated by Gordon Kaufman and Reginald Hollingdale. London: Vintage Books, 1968.

Noebel, David, and Chuck Edwards, eds. *Thinking Like a Christian: Understanding and Living a Biblical Worldview*. New York: B & H, 2002.

Nolan, Daniel "Modal Fictionalism." *SEP*. Cited 15 August 2012. Online: http://plato.stanford.edu/archives/win2011/entries/fictionalism-modal/.

O'Connor, Timothy, and Hong Y. Wong. "Emergent Properties." *SEP*. Cited 11 January 2010. Online: http://plato.stanford.edu/archives/spr2009/entries/properties-emergent/.

Odera Oruka, Henry. "Four Trends in Current African Philosophy." Pages 1–7 in *Philosophy in the Present Situation of Africa*. Edited by Alwin Diemer. Wiesbaden: Steiner, 1981.

O'Dowd, Ryan. "A Chord of Three Strands: Epistemology in Job, Proverbs and Ecclesiastes." Pages 65–82 in *The Bible and Epistemology: Biblical Soundings of the Knowledge of God*. Edited by Mary Healy and Robin Parry. Carlisle, U.K.: Paternoster, 2007.

———. *The Wisdom of Torah: Epistemology in Deuteronomy and the Wisdom Literature*. FRLANT 225. Goettingen: Vandenhoeck & Ruprecht, 2009.

Oeming, Manfred. *Gesamtbiblische Theologien der Gegenwart*. Stuttgart: Kohlhammer, 1985.

Oesterley, William O. E., and Theodore H. Robinson. *Hebrew Religion: Its Origin and Development*. London: SPCK, 1952.

O'Farrell, Clare. *Michel Foucault*. New York: Sage, 2005.

Okafor, Fidelis U. "In Defense of Afro-Japanese Ethnophilosophy." *PEW* 47 (1997): 363–81.

Ollenburger, Ben C. *Old Testament Theology: Flowering and Future.* 2nd ed. SBTS 1. Winona Lake, Ind.: Eisenbrauns, 2004.

Olson, Eric T. "Personal Identity." *SEP.* Cited 30 May 2011. Online: http://plato.stanford.edu/archives/win2010/entries/identity-personal/.

Orr, James. "Philosophy." *ISBE.* Cited 30 April 2010. Online: http://www.bible-history.com/isbe/P/PHILOSOPHY/.

Otto, Eckart. *Mose: Geschichte und Legende.* Munich: Beck, 2006.

———. *Theologische Ethik des Alten Testaments.* TW 3/2. Stuttgart: Kohlhammer, 1994.

Otto, Rudolph. *The Idea of the Holy: An Inquiry into the Non-rational Factor in the Idea of the Divine and Its Relation to the Rational.* Galaxy Books 14. Oxford: Oxford University Press, 1968.

Owen, Huw P. *Concepts of Deity.* New York: Macmillan, 1971.

Paget, James N. B. Carleton. "The Christian Exegesis of the Old Testament in the Alexandrian Tradition." Page 478–542 in vol. 1.1 of *Hebrew Bible/Old Testament: The History of Its Interpretation.* Edited by Magne Saebø. 2 vols. Göttingen: Vandenhoeck & Ruprecht, 1996–2008.

Pailin, David. *Groundwork of Philosophy of Religion.* London: Epworth, 1986.

Pallesen, Carsten. "Philosophy of Reflection and Biblical Revelation in Paul Ricoeur." *ST* 62 (2008): 44–62.

Pangle, Thomas L. *Political Philosophy and the God of Abraham.* Baltimore: Johns Hopkins University Press, 2003.

Panikkar, Raimundo. "Deity." *ER* 4:274–76.

Parfit, Derek. "The Unimportance of Identity." Pages 292–318 in *Personal Identity.* Edited by R. Martin and J. Barresi. Malden, Mass.: Blackwell, 2003.

Parpola, Simo. "The Assyrian Tree of Life: Tracing the Origins of Jewish Monotheism and Greek Philosophy." *JNES* 52 (1993): 161–208.

Patrick, Dale. *The Rendering of God in the Old Testament.* OBT 10. Philadelphia: Fortress, 1982.

———. *The Rhetoric of Revelation in the Hebrew Bible.* OBT 22. Minneapolis: Fortress, 1999.

Patterson, Charles. "The Philosophy of the Old Testament." *JNABI* 2 (1934): 60–66.

———. *The Philosophy of the Old Testament.* New York: Ronald Press, 1953.

Pattison, Andrew S. P. *Essays in Philosophical Criticism.* New York: Longmans, Green, 1883.

Pattison, George. *A Short Course in the Philosophy of Religion.* London: SCM, 2001.

Pearcey, Nancy. *Total Truth: Liberating Christianity from Its Cultural Captivity.* Wheaton, Ill.: Crossway, 2005.

Pedersen, Johannes. *Israel: Its Life and Culture.* Translated by Auslag Moller and A. I. Fausbell. 4 vols. London: Oxford University Press, 1926–1940.

Perdue, Leo G. *The Collapse of History: Reconstructing Old Testament Theology.* Minneapolis: Fortress, 1994.

———. "Cosmology and the Social Order in the Wisdom Tradition." Pages 457–78 in *The Sage in Israel and the Ancient Near East.* Edited by John Gammie and Leo G. Perdue. Winona Lake, Ind.: Eisenbrauns, 1990.

———. *Reconstructing Old Testament Theology: After the Collapse of History.* OBT. Minneapolis: Fortress, 2005.

Phillips, Dewi Zephaniah. *The Concept of Prayer.* 2nd ed. Oxford: Blackwell, 1981.

———. *Religion and the Hermeneutics of Contemplation.* Cambridge: Cambridge University Press, 2001.

———. "Wittgensteinianism: Logic, Reality and God." Pages 448–54 in *Oxford Handbook of Philosophy of Religion.* Edited by William Wainwright. Oxford: Oxford University Press, 2005.

Planck, Max K. *Scientific Autobiography and Other Papers.* Translated by Frank Gaynor. New York: Philosophical Library, 1949.

Plantinga, Alvin. "Advice to Christian Philosophers." Pages 14–40 in *Christian Theism and the Problems of Philosophy.* Edited by Michael D. Beaty. Notre Dame, Ind.: University of Notre Dame Press, 1990.

———. *Warranted Christian Belief.* New York: Oxford University Press, 2000.

Plantinga, Richard J., ed. *Christianity and Plurality: Classic and Contemporary Readings.* BRMT. Oxford: Blackwell, 1999.

Plato. *Five Dialogues: Euthyphro, Apology, Crito, Meno, Phaedo.* Translated by G. M. A. Grube. Indianapolis: Hackett, 1981.

Poijman, Louis, and Michael Rea. *Philosophy of Religion: An Anthology.* 5th ed. London: Thomson/Wadsworth, 2008.

Porter, Barbara N., ed. *What Is a God? Anthropomorphic and Non-anthropomorphic Aspects of Deity in Ancient Mesopotamia.* Transactions of the Casco Bay Assyriological Institute 2. Winona Lake, Ind.: Eisenbrauns, 2009.

Poston, Ted. "Internalism and Externalism in Epistemology." *IEP*. Cited 17 February 2010. Online: http://www.iep.utm.edu/.

Preuss, Horst D. *Old Testament Theology*. 2 volumes. OTL. Louisville: Westminster John Knox, 1996.

Priest, John F. "Humanism, Skepticism, and Pessimism in Ancient Israel." *JAAR* 36 (1968): 311–26.

Procopé, John F. "Greek Philosophy, Hermeneutics and Alexandrian Understanding of the Old Testament." Pages 453–76 in vol. 1.1 of *Hebrew Bible/Old Testament: The History of Its Interpretation*. Edited by Magne Saebø. 2 vols. Göttingen: Vandenhoeck & Ruprecht, 1996–2008.

Pyysiäinen, Ilkka "God: A Brief History with a Cognitive Explanation of the Concept." Pages 1–35. Cited 12 November 2009. Online: http://www.talkreason.org/articles/god.pdf.

Quinn, Philip L. "Divine Command Ethics: A Causal Theory." Pages 305–25 in *Divine Command Morality: Historical and Contemporary Readings*. Edited by Janine Idziak. New York: Mellen, 1979.

———. *Divine Commands and Moral Requirements*. Oxford: Clarendon, 1987.

———. *Philosophy of Religion A–Z*. Edinburgh: Edinburgh University Press, 2006.

Quinn, Philip L., and Christian B. Miller. *Essays in the Philosophy of Religion*. Oxford: Oxford University Press, 2006.

Rad, Gerhard von. *The Theology of Israel's Historical Traditions*. Vol. 1 of *Old Testament Theology*. OTL. Louisville: Westminster John Knox, 2001.

———. *Wisdom in Israel*. London: SCM, 1972.

Ramsey, Ian. *Religious Language*. London: SCM, 1957.

Rapp, Christoph. "Aristotle's Rhetoric." *SEP*. Cited 2 October 2010. Online: http://plato.stanford.edu/archives/win2008/entries/aristotle-rhetoric/.

Rea, Michael C., ed. *Providence, Scripture, and Resurrection*. Vol. 2 of *Oxford Readings in Philosophical Theology*. Edited by Michael C. Rea. Oxford: Oxford University Press, 2009.

———. *Trinity, Incarnation, Atonement*. Vol. 1 of *Oxford Readings in Philosophical Theology*. Edited by Michael C. Rea. Oxford: Oxford University Press, 2009.

Reimer, Marga. "Reference." *SEP*. Cited 12 October 2010. Online: http://plato.stanford.edu/archives/spr2010/entries/reference/.

Reventlow, Henning G. "English Deism and Anti-Deist Apologetic." Pages 851–74 in vol. 2 of *Hebrew Bible/Old Testament: The History of Its Interpretation*. Edited by Magne Saebø. 2 vols. Göttingen: Vandenhoeck & Ruprecht, 1996–2008.

———. *From the Old Testament to Origen*. Vol. 1 of *History of Biblical Interpretation*. 4 vols. Translated by Leo G. Perdue. Atlanta: Society of Biblical Literature, 2009.

———. "Immanuel Kant: The Impact of His Philosophy on Biblical Hermeneutics." Pages 1034–40 in vol. 2 of *Hebrew Bible/Old Testament: The History of Its Interpretation*. Edited by Magne Saebø. 2 vols. Göttingen: Vandenhoeck & Ruprecht, 1996–2008.

———. *Problems of Old Testament Theology in the Twentieth Century*. London: SCM, 1985.

———. "Towards the End of the Century of Enlightenment." Pages 1041–50 in vol. 2 of *Hebrew Bible/Old Testament: The History of Its Interpretation*. Edited by Magne Saebø. 2 vols. Göttingen: Vandenhoeck & Ruprecht, 1996–2008.

Reynolds, Frank, and David Tracy. *Myth and Philosophy*. New York: State University of New York Press, 1990.

———. *Religion and Practical Reason: New Essays in Comparative Philosophy of Religions*. New York: State University of New York Press, 1994.

Richardson, Alan. *Genesis 1–11: The Creation Stories and the Modern Worldview*. London: SCM, 1953.

———. *Religion and Practical Reason: New Essays in Comparative Philosophy of Religions*. New York: State University of New York Press, 1994.

Rickman, Hans P. "Wilhelm Dilthey." Page 403 in vol. 2 of *Encyclopedia of Philosophy*. Edited by Paul Edwards. New York: Macmillan, 1967.

Ricœur, Paul. *The Rule of Metaphor: Multi-disciplinary Studies of the Creation of Meaning in Language*. Translated by Robert Czerny, with Kathleen McLaughlin and John Costello, S.J. London: Routledge, 1978.

———. *Symbolism of Evil*. Translated by Emerson Buchanan. New York: Harper & Row, 1967.

Ringgren, Helmer. *Israelite Religion*. Translated by David E. Green. Philadelphia: Fortress, 1966.

———. "אֱלֹהִים." *TDOT* 1:267–84.

Riordan, Peter. "Religion as *Weltanschauung*: A Solution to a Problem in the Philosophy of Religion." *Aquinas* 34 (1991): 519–34.

Rissler, James. "Open Theism." *IEP*. Cited 25 January 2010. Online: http://www.iep.utm.edu/.

Robertson, Teresa, "Essential vs. Accidental Properties." *SEP*. Cited 12 January 2010. Online: http://plato.stanford.edu/archives/fall2008/entries/essential-accidental/.

Rogerson, John W. *Old Testament Criticism in the Nineteenth Century: England and Germany*. London: SPCK, 1984.

———. *A Theology of the Old Testament: Cultural Memory, Communication, and Being Human*. Philadelphia: Fortress, 2010.

Rorty, Richard. *The Linguistic Turn: Essays in Philosophical Method*. Chicago: University of Chicago Press, 1992.

Rossi, Philip. "Kant's Philosophy of Religion." *SEP*. Cited 15 April 2010. Online: http://plato.stanford.edu/archives/win2009/entries/kant-religion/.

Rowe, William. "Divine Freedom." *SEP*. Cited 25 August 2010. Online: http://plato.stanford.edu/archives/fall2008/entries/divine-freedom/.

Rowley, H. H. *The Faith of Israel: Aspects of Old Testament Thought*. London: SCM, 1956.

Rudavsky, Tamar. "Gersonides." *SEP*. Cited 24 September 2009. Online: http://plato.stanford.edu/archives/fall2008/entries/gersonides/.

Runzo, Joseph, and Nancy M. Martin, eds. *The Meaning of Life in the World Religions*. Oxford: Oneworld, 2000

Russell, Bertrand. *History of Western Philosophy*. Rev. ed. London: Allan & Unwin, 1961.

Russell, Paul. "Hume on Religion." *SEP*. Cited 6 December 2009. Online: http://plato.stanford.edu/ archives/win2008/entries/hume-religion/.

Ryle, Gilbert. "Abstractions." *Dialogue (Canadian Philosophical Review)* 1 (1962): 5–16. Repr. as pages 435–45 of vol. 2 in Gilbert Ryle, *Collected Papers*. 2 vols. London: Hutchinson, 1971.

———. *The Revolution in Philosophy*. London: Macmillan, 1957.

———. "Systematically Misleading Expressions." Pages 85–100 in Richard M. Rorty, *The Linguistic Turn*. Chicago: University of Chicago Press, 1992.

Saebø, Magne. "From the Renaissance to the Enlightenment—Aspects of the Cultural and Ideological Framework of Scriptural Interpretation." Pages 21–45 in volume 2 of *Hebrew Bible/Old Testament: The History of Its Interpretation*. Edited by Magne Saebø. 2 vols. Göttingen: Vandenhoeck & Ruprecht, 1996–2008.

———, ed. *Hebrew Bible/Old Testament: The History of Its Interpretation*. 2 vols. Göttingen: Vandenhoeck & Ruprecht, 1996–2008.

Saggs, Hallo W. *The Encounter with the Divine in Mesopotamia and Israel.* London: Athlone, 1978.

Samuelson, Norbert M. *Jewish Philosophy: An Historical Introduction.* London: Continuum, 2006.

———. *Revelation and the God of Israel.* Cambridge: Cambridge University Press, 2002.

Sandys-Wunsch, James. *What Have They Done to the Bible?* New York: Liturgical Press, 2005.

Sandys-Wunsch, James, and L. J. P. Eldredge. "Gabler and the Distinction between Biblical and Dogmatic Theology: Translation, Commentary and Discussion of His Originality." *SJT* (1980): 133–58.

Sayre-McCord, Geoff. "Meta-Ethics." *SEP.* Cited 25 February. 2010. Online: http://plato.stanford.edu/archives/fall2008/entries/meta-ethics/.

Scarborough, Milton. "Myth and Phenomenology." Pages 46–64 in *Thinking through Myths: Philosophical Perspectives.* Edited by Kevin Schilbrack. London: Routledge, 2002.

Schaeffer, Francis. *How Should We Then Live? The Rise and Decline of Western Thought and Culture.* Wheaton, Ill.: Crossway, 2005.

Schatz, David. "Judaism." Pages 54–64 in *The Routledge Companion to Philosophy of Religion.* Edited by Chad Meister and Paul Copan. London: Taylor & Francis, 2010.

Schechtman, Marya. *The Constitution of Selves.* Ithaca, N.Y.: Cornell University Press, 1996.

Schellenberg, Annette. *Erkenntnis als Problem: Qohelet und die altestamentlichen Diskussion um das menschliche Erkennen.* OBO 188. Freiburg: Universitatsverlag; Gottingen: Vandenhoeck & Ruprecht, 2002.

Schilbrack, Kevin, ed. *Thinking through Myths: Philosophical Perspectives.* London: Routledge, 2002.

Schmidt, Werner H. "אֱלֹהִים."*TLOT* 1:115–26.

———. *The Faith of the Old Testament: A History.* Translated by John Sturdy. Philadelphia: Westminster, 1983.

Schneider, Steven. "The Paradox of Fiction." *IEP.* Cited 12 April 2010. Online: http://www.iep.utm.edu/fict-par/.

Schopenhauer, Arthur. *Essays and Aphorisms.* Translated by Robert J. Hollingdale. London: Penguin Classics, 1970.

———. *The World as Will and Representation.* 2 vols. Translated by Eric F. J. Payne. New York: Courier Dove Publications, 2005.

Schroeder, Mark. "Value Theory." *SEP*. Cited 27 February 2010. Online: http://plato.stanford.edu/archives/fall2008/entries/value-theory/.

Schultz, Hermann. *Old Testament Theology: The Religion of Revelation in its Pre-Christian State of Development.* Edinburgh: T&T Clark, 1892.

Seeskin, Kenneth. "Maimonides." *SEP*. Cited 16 September 2009. Online: http://plato.stanford.edu/archives/fall2008/entries/maimonides/.

Segal, Robert. "Myth as Primitive Philosophy: The Case of E. B. Tylor." Pages 18–45 in *Thinking through Myths: Philosophical Perspectives.* Edited by Kevin Schilbrack. London: Routledge, 2002.

———, ed. *The Blackwell Companion to the Study of Religion.* BCR. New York: Wiley-Blackwell, 2006.

Sekine, Seizo. *Transcendency and Symbols in the Old Testament: A Genealogy of the Hermeneutical Experience.* BZAW 275. Berlin: de Gruyter, 1999.

Shank, Carl H. "Qoheleth's World and Life View as Seen in His Recurring Phrases." *WTJ* 37 (1974): 57–73.

Sharma, Arvind. "Hinduism." Pages 5–15 in *The Routledge Companion to Philosophy of Religion.* Edited by Chad Meister and Paul Copan. London: Routledge, 2007.

Shoemaker, David. "Personal Identity and Ethics." *SEP*. Cited 15 August 2012. Online: http://plato.stanford.edu/archives/spr2012/entries/identity-ethics/.

Sicker, Martin. *Reading Genesis Politically: An Introduction to Mosaic Political Philosophy.* Westport, Conn.: Praeger Publishers, 2002.

Siegert, Folker. "Early Jewish Interpretation in Hellenistic Style." Pages 130–98 in vol. 1.1 of *Hebrew Bible/Old Testament: The History of Its Interpretation.* Edited by Magne Saebø. 2 vols. Göttingen: Vandenhoeck & Ruprecht, 1996–2008.

Simkins, Ronald. *Creator and Creation: Nature in the Worldview of Ancient Israel.* Peabody, Mass.: Hendrickson, 1994.

Skarsaune, Oscar. "The Development of Scriptural Interpretation in the Second and Third Centuries–Except Clement and Origen." Pages 389–417 in vol. 1.1 of *Hebrew Bible/Old Testament: The History of Its Interpretation.* Edited by Magne Saebø. 2 vols. Göttingen: Vandenhoeck & Ruprecht, 1996–2008.

Smart, Ninian. "The Philosophy of Worldviews, or the Philosophy of Religion Transformed." Pages 22–39 in *Religious Pluralism and Truth: Essays on Cross-Cultural Philosophy of Religion.* Edited by Thomas Dean. Albany: State University of New York Press, 1995.

——. "The Philosophy of Worldviews: That Is, the Philosophy of Religions Transformed." *Neue Zeitschrift fur Systematische Theologie und Religionsphilosophie* 23 (1981): 212–24.

——. *World Philosophies.* Edited by Oliver Leaman. New York: Routledge, 2008.

Smart, Ninian, and John T. Shepherd. *Ninian Smart on World Religions: Selected Works.* Oxford: Ashgate, 2009.

Smend, Rudolph. "The Interpretation of Wisdom in Nineteenth-Century Scholarship." Pages 257–86 in *Wisdom in Ancient Israel.* Edited by John Day, R. P. Gordon, and Hugh R. Williamson. New York: Cambridge University Press, 1998.

Smith, Mark. *God in Translation: Deities in Cross-Cultural Discourse in the Biblical World.* FAT 57. Tübingen: Mohr Siebeck, 2008.

——. *The Memoirs of God: History, Memory, and Experience of the Divine in Ancient Israel.* Augsburg: Fortress, 2004.

——. *The Origins of Biblical Monotheism: Israel's Polytheistic Background and the Ugaritic Texts.* New York: Oxford University Press, 2001.

Soames, Scott. "What Is Philosophical Analysis?" *Encyclopedia of Philosophy.* Cited 12 August 2010. Online: http://www-rcf.usc.edu/~soames/sel_pub/Philosophical_Analysis.pdf.

——. *The Dawn of Analysis.* Vol. 1 of *Philosophical Analysis in the Twentieth Century.* Princeton: Princeton University Press, 2003.

Sommer, Benjamin D. *The Bodies of God and the World of Ancient Israel.* Cambridge: Cambridge University Press, 2011.

Sorensen, Roy. "Vagueness." *SEP.* Cited 14 December 2010. Online: http://plato.stanford.edu/archives/fall2008/entries/vagueness/.

Soskice, Janet M. *Metaphors and Religious Language.* Oxford: Oxford University Press, 1985.

Soulen, Richard N., and Kendall R. Soulen. *Handbook of Biblical Criticism.* Louisville: Westminster John Knox, 2001.

Stacey, David. *Prophetic Drama in the Old Testament.* London: Epworth, 1990.

Staerk, Willy. "Religionsgeschichte und Religionsphilosphie und ihrer Bedeutung für die biblische Theologie des Alten Testaments." *ZTK* 4 (1923): 289–300.

Steinberg, David. *Israelite Religion to Judaism: The Evolution of the Religion of Israel.* Cited 19 July 2009. Online: http://www.adath-shalom.ca/israelite_religion.htm.

Stendahl, Krister. "Biblical Theology, Contemporary." Pages 418–32 in vol. 1 of *Interpreter's Dictionary of the Bible*. Edited by George A. Buttrick. 4 vols. Nashville: Abingdon, 1962.

Steuernagel, Carl. "Alttestamentliche Theologie und Alttestamentliche Religionsgeschichte." Pages 266–73 in *Vom Alten Testament*. Edited by Karl Budde. BZAW 41. Giessen: Töpelmann, 1925.

Steup, Mark. "Epistemology." *SEP*. Cited 10 August 2010. Online: http://plato.stanford.edu/archives/spr2010/entries/epistemology/.

Stevenson, James. *A New Eusebius: Documents Illustrating the History of the Church to AD 337*. London: SPCK, 1987.

Stigen, Anfinn. "Philosophy as World View and Philosophy as Discipline." Pages 313–30 in *Contemporary Philosophy in Scandinavia*. Edited by Raymond E. Olson and Anthony M. Paul. Baltimore: Johns Hopkins University Press, 1972.

Stiver, Dan R. *The Philosophy of Religious Language: Sign, Symbol, and Story*. Oxford: Wiley-Blackwell, 1996.

Stump, Eleanore. "Modern Biblical Scholarship, Philosophy of Religion and Traditional Christianity." *Truth Journal* 1 (1985). Cited 8 October 2009. Online: http://www.leaderu.com/truth/1truth20.html.

———. "Religion, Philosophy Of." Cited 12 November 2009. Online: http://www.rep.routledge.com/article/K113.

Stump, Eleanore, and Thomas P. Flint, eds. *Hermes and Athena: Biblical Exegesis and Philosophical Theology*. Notre Dame, Ind.: University of Notre Dame Press, 1993.

Sullivan, L. E. "Supreme Beings." *ER* 6:166–81.

Sutherland, Robert. *Putting God on Trial: The Biblical Book of Job*. Victoria: Trafford, 2004.

Swartz, Norman. *Definitions, Dictionaries, and Meanings*. Cited 18 November 2009. Online: http://www.sfu.ca/~swartz/definitions.htm.

Swoyer, Chris. "Properties." *SEP*. Cited 19 July 2010. Online: http://plato.stanford.edu/archives/fall2008/entries/properties/.

Taliaferro, Charles. *Evidence and Faith: Philosophy and Religion since the Seventeenth Century*. New York: Cambridge University Press, 2005.

———. "Philosophy of Religion." Pages 123–45 in *The Blackwell Companion to the Study of Religion*. BCR 45. Edited by Robert A. Segal. New York: Wiley-Blackwell, 2006.

———. "Philosophy of Religion." *SEP*. Cited 16 January 2010. Online: http://plato.stanford.edu/archives/spr2009/entries/philosophy-religion/.

Taliaferro, Charles, Paul Draper, and Philip Quinn, eds. *A Companion to Philosophy of Religion*. BCP 9. London: Wiley-Blackwell, 2010.

Taliaferro, Charles, and Paul Griffiths, eds. *Philosophy of Religion: An Anthology*. Oxford: Wiley-Blackwell, 2003.

Taliaferro, Charles, and Chad Meister, eds. *The Cambridge Companion to Christian Philosophical Theology*. Cambridge: Cambridge University Press, 2010.

Tanney, Julia "Gilbert Ryle." *SEP*. Cited 16 March 2010. Online: http://plato.stanford.edu/archives/win2009/entries/ryle/.

Tarnas, Richard. *The Passion of the Western Mind: Understanding the Ideas that Have Shaped Our World View*. New York: Ballantine, 1991.

Tempels, Placide. *Bantu Philosophy*. Translated by A. Rubbens. Paris: Présence Africaine, 1959.

Thiselton, Anthony. *The Two Horizons: New Testament Hermeneutics and Philosophical Description with Special Reference to Heidegger, Bultmann, Gadamer and Wittgenstein*. Grand Rapids: Eerdmans, 1980.

Thomas, Laurence. "Morality and a Meaningful Life." *Philosophical Papers* 34 (2005): 405–27.

Thompson, Thomas L. *The Bible in History: How Writers Create a Past*. London: Jonathan Cape, 1999.

Thomson, Garrett. *On the Meaning of Life*. South Melbourne: Wadsworth, 2003.

Thrower, James. *The Alternative Tradition: Religion and the Rejection of Religion in the Ancient World*. Berlin: de Gruyter, 1980.

———. *Western Atheism: A Short History*. New York: Prometheus Books, 2000.

Tillich, Paul. *Biblical Religion and the Search for Ultimate Reality*. Chicago: University of Chicago Press, 1964.

Tooley, Michael. "The Problem of Evil." *SEP*. Cited 12 February 2010. Online: http://plato.stanford.edu/archives/spr2010/entries/evil/.

Toorn, Karel van der. "God (1)." *DDD*, 911–19.

Trakakis, Nick. *The End of Philosophy of Religion*. London: Continuum, 2008.

———. "Meta-Philosophy of Religion: The Analytic-Continental Divide in Philosophy of Religion." *AD* 7 (2007): 1–47.

Trisel, Brooke Alan. "Futility and the Meaning of Life Debate" *Sorites* (2001): 70–84.

Tsevat, Mattitiahu. "An Aspect of Biblical Thought: Deductive Explanation." *Shnaton* 3 (1978): 53–58 [Hebrew with English summary].

Vaihinger, Hans. *The Philosophy of As-If: A System of the Theoretical, Practical and Religious Fictions of Mankind*. London: Routledge, 1965.

Vallicella, William F. "Divine Simplicity." *SEP*. Cited 12 November 2009. Online: http://plato.stanford.edu/archives/fall2008/entries/divine-simplicity/.

Van Leeuwen, Raymond C. "Liminality and Worldview in Proverbs 1–9." *Semeia* 50 (1990): 111–44.

Vanhoozer, Kevin. *Biblical Narrative in the Philosophy of Paul Ricœur: A Study in Theology and Hermeneutics*. New York: Cambridge University Press, 1990.

Vawter, Bruce. "The God of Hebrew Scriptures." *BTB* 12 (1982): 1–8.

Wainwright, William. "Monotheism." *SEP*. Cited 12 May 2010. Online: http://plato.stanford.edu/archives/win2009/entries/monotheism/.

———. *Philosophy of Religion: An Annotated Bibliography of Twentieth-Century Writings in English*. New York: Garland Publishing, 1978.

———. *Religion and Morality*. Ashgate Philosophy of Religion Series. London: Ashgate, 2005.

———, ed. *The Oxford Handbook of Philosophy of Religion*. Oxford: Oxford University Press, 2005.

Wallmann, Johannes. "Scriptural Understanding and Interpretation in Pietism." Pages 902–25 in vol. 2 of *Hebrew Bible/Old Testament: The History of Its Interpretation*. Edited by Magne Saebø. 2 vols. Göttingen: Vandenhoeck & Ruprecht, 1996–2008.

Ward, Keith. *Concepts of God: Images of the Divine in Five Religious Traditions*. Oxford: Oneworld, 1998.

———. *God: A Guide for the Perplexed*. Oxford: Oneworld, 2005.

———. *Religion and Creation*. Oxford: Oxford University Press, 1996.

———. *Religion and Human Nature*. Oxford: Oxford University Press, 1998.

———. *Religion and Revelation: A Theology of Revelation in the World's Religions*. Oxford: Oxford University Press, 1994.

Weatherson, Brian. "Intrinsic vs. Extrinsic Properties." *SEP*. Cited 12 January 2010. Online: http://plato.stanford.edu/archives/fall2008/entries/intrinsic-extrinsic/.

Weed, Jennifer H. "Religious Language." *IEP*. Cited 11 November 2009. Online: http://www.iep.utm.edu/.

Westphal, Merold. "Continental Philosophy of Religion." Pages 472–93 in *The Oxford Handbook of Philosophy of Religion*. Edited by William Wainwright. Oxford: Oxford University Press, 2005.

———. *God, Guilt, and Death: An Existential Phenomenology of Religion.* Studies in Phenomenology and Existential Philosophy. Bloomington: Indiana University Press, 1984.

———. *Kierkegaard's Critique of Reason and Society.* Macon, Ga.: Mercer University Press, 1987.

———. "Phenomenology of Religion." *REP* 7:352–55.

———. "Phenomenology of Religion." Pages 661–71 in *The Routledge Companion to Philosophy of Religion.* Edited by Chad Meister and Paul Copan. London: Routledge, 2007.

———. "Traditional Theism, the AAR and the APA." Pages 21–28 in *God, Philosophy and Academic Culture.* Edited by William Wainwright. Atlanta: Scholars Press, 1996.

Wetzel, J., editorial adviser. *Journal of Philosophy and Scripture.* Cited 10 April 2010. Online: http://www.philosophyandscripture.org/index. html.

Wheeler-Robinson, Henry. *The Philosophy of Revelation.* Oxford: Clarendon, 1938.

White, Morton. *The Age of Analysis.* New York: Mentor Books, 1955.

Whybray, Norman. *Ecclesiastes.* Grand Rapids: Eerdmans, 1989.

Wierenga, Eric. "A Defensible Divine Command Theory." *Nous* 17 (2003): 387–407.

Wilcox, John T. *The Bitterness of Job: A Philosophical Reading.* Ann Arbor, Mich.: University of Michigan Press, 1994.

Williams, Thomas. "Saint Anselm." *SEP.* Cited 22 September 2009. Online: http://plato.stanford.edu/archives/fall2008/entries/anselm/.

Williamson, Raymond K. *Introduction to Hegel's Philosophy of Religion.* New York: State University of New York Press, 1984.

Wilson, Andrew N. *God's Funeral: The Decline of Faith in Western Civilization.* London: Abacus, 1999.

Wiredu, Kwasi. "African Philosophical Tradition: A Case Study of the Akan." *The Philosophical Forum* 24/1–3 (1992–1993): 35–62.

———. "African Religions from a Philosophical Point of View." Pages 34–55 in *A Companion to Philosophy of Religion.* Edited by Charles Taliaferro, Paul Draper, and Philip Quinn. BCP 9. London: Wiley-Blackwell, 2010.

———. "On Defining African Philosophy." Pages 87–110 in *African Philosophy: The Essential Readings.* Edited by Tsenay Serequeberhan. New York: Paragon House, 1991.

———, ed. *A Companion to African Philosophy.* Oxford: Blackwell, 2004.

Wisnewski, J. Jeremy "Is the Immortal Life Worth Living?" *International Journal for Philosophy of Religion* 58 (2005): 27–36.

Wittgenstein, Ludwig. *Philosophical Investigations.* Translated by Gertrude Elizabeth Margaret Anscombe. New York: Wiley-Blackwell, 2001.

———. *Philosophical Occasions.* Sections 86–93 of the so-called "Big Typescript." Cited 19 December 2010. Online http://en.wikiquote.org/wiki/Ludwig_Wittgenstein.

———. *Tractatus Logico-Philosophicus.* Translated by Gertrude Elizabeth Margaret Anscombe. New York: Wiley-Blackwell, 2001.

Wolde, Ellen van. *Reframing Biblical Studies: When Language and Text Meet Culture, Cognition, and Context.* Winona Lake, Ind.: Eisenbrauns, 2009.

Wolfle, Dael Lee, ed. *Symposium on Basic Research.* American Association for the Advancement of Science 56. Washington, D.C., 1959.

Wolterstorff, Nicholas. "How Philosophical Theology Became Possible in the Analytic Tradition of Philosophy." Pages 155–69 in *Analytic Theology: New Essays in the Philosophy of Theology.* Edited by Oliver D. Crisp and Michael C. Rea. Oxford: Oxford University Press, 2009.

Wong, David. "Comparative Philosophy: Chinese and Western." *SEP.* Cited 25 February 2010. Online: http://plato.stanford.edu/archives/win2009/entries/comparphil-chiwes/.

Wright, David F. "Augustine: His Exegesis and Hermeneutics." Pages 701–30 in vol. 1.1 of *Hebrew Bible/Old Testament: The History of Its Interpretation.* Edited by Magne Saebø. 2 vols. Göttingen: Vandenhoeck & Ruprecht, 1996–2008.

Wright, G. Ernest, *The Old Testament against Its Environment.* Chicago: Regnery, 1950.

Yandell, Keith E. *Philosophy of Religion: A Contemporary Introduction.* RCIP 5. London: Routledge, 1999.

Young, Julian. *The Death of God and the Meaning of Life.* New York: Routledge, 2003.

Zagzebski, Linda. *Divine Motivation Theory.* New York: Cambridge University Press, 2004.

Index of Biblical References

Hebrew Bible/Old Testament

Genesis
1:26–27	438
2:5	439
2–3	105
3:5	279
3:22	279
15:12–16	390–91
18:25	414
25:22	440
27:46	446

Exodus
3:14	105, 216
33:10	414
33:11	414
33:14	415

Numbers
12:5–8	387–88

Deuteronomy
32:21	262

1 Samuel
16:7	109 n. 77
24:2–7	381–82

1 Kings
18:27	375

2 Kings
19:18	262

Isaiah
41:21–24	280, 374
43:10	262

Jeremiah
2:11	262
16:20	262
23:31–33	382–83
44:18–19	384
44:21–23	385

Ezekiel
20:25	417
28:2–3	282
28: 9	282

Hosea
8:6	262

Habakkuk
1:11	262

Psalms
10:4	353
14:1	262, 353
15:1–3	415
19:9	417
22:1	105
34:9	412
34:13	443
53:1	353
55:20	356
58:2	412
63:4	443

73:10–11	356
77:9–10	416
82:1–2	413
90:10	443
94:7–12	348
96:5	358
97:7	358
115:4–7	357
119:39	418
135:15	358

Job
3:20	442

Ecclesiastes
8:15	442

Index of Modern Authors

Abraham, William J.   24 n. 27, 373 n. 7, 386 n. 29, 404 n. 46

Adams, Douglas   433 n. 38

Adinall, Peter   73 n. 144

Albertz, Rainer   270 n. 16, 399 nn. 37–40, 400 n. 41

Allen, Diogenes   193 n. 119, 344 n. 4

Allen, James P.   164 n. 25

Alston, William B.   408 n. 11

Anderson, William H. U.   78 n. 164, 351 n. 15

Aquino, Ranhilo C.   78 n. 162

Argall, Randall   211 n. 24

Armstrong, Sharon L.   280 n. 32

Assmann, Jan   164 n. 26, 274 n. 24

Audi, Robert   436 n. 46

Augé, Marc   13 n. 13

Augustine   48 n. 31, 49 n. 33

Baggini, Julian   434 n. 39

Baier, Kurt   435 n. 44

Baillie, James   317 n. 49

Barr, James   5 nn. 5–6, 6 n. 6–7, 7 n. 8, 41 n. 2, 41 n. 4, 48 n. 27, 58 n. 71, 63 nn. 98–99, 65 nn. 110–11, 66 nn. 115–16, 71 nn. 135–39, 99 n. 52, 115 n. 1, 129 n. 37, 144 nn. 64–65, 145 n. 66, 146 nn. 71–73, 149 n. 78, 151 n. 80, 155 nn. 1–2, 191 n. 115, 192 n. 116, 193 n. 118, 199 n. 1, 269 n. 12, 278 n. 31, 293 n. 3, 320 n. 58, 345 nn. 6 and 8, 371 n. 3, 379 n. 23, 380 n. 25, 439 n. 50

Barré, Michael L.   189 n. 110

Barrett, Lee C.   86 n. 19, 87 n. 20

Bartholomew, Craig G.   140 nn. 56–57

Barton, John   76 nn. 155–57, 144 n. 63, 194 n. 120, 195 n. 121, 298 n. 15, 405 n. 1, 406 n. 4, 409 n. 16

Basinger, David   38 n. 74

Beaney, Michael   202 nn. 6–8, 203 n. 9

Bell, Richard H.   166 n. 31

Belliotti, Raymond   434 n. 39

Belshaw, Christopher   434 n. 39

Benatar, David   434 n. 40

Bennett, Karen   307 n. 30, 331 n. 76, 78

Berto, Francesco   331 nn. 89–90, 332 nn. 92–94, 333 n. 95

Bertrand, Mark J.   186 n. 98

Bilimoria, Purushottma   131 n. 41

Black, Max   251 n. 15

Bloemendaal, Peter F.   125 n. 25

Blumenberg, Hans   252 n. 22

Boer, Roland   86 n. 18, 203 n. 10

Boman, Thorleif   65, 66 n. 116, 190

Botz-Bornstein, Thorsten   169 nn. 43–44, 170 n. 45

Bowden, Julia   76 n. 157

Braun, Reiner   77 n. 161

Brenner, Jeff   191 n. 115

Brett, Mark   76 n. 154

Brink, Gijsbert van den   302 n. 18

Brown, Lee M.   166 n. 31

Brueggemann, Walter   75 nn. 148–49, 146 n. 69, 204 n. 11, 209 n. 20, 250 n. 12, 312 n. 42, 329 n. 84, 346 n. 10, 365 n. 34, 376 n. 5, 380 n. 24, 426 n. 30

Bultmann, Christoph   41 n. 4, 56 n. 66, 57 nn. 67–69

Burkert, Walter   162 n. 20

Carasik, Michael   191 n. 114, 210 n. 22

Carmy, Shalom   158 nn. 5–6, 159 n. 7

Carroll, Robert P.   68 n. 123, 95 n. 41, 147 n. 76, 148 n. 77, 237 n. 12, 250 n. 11, 297 n. 10, 312 n. 42, 319 n. 55, 324 n. 70, 365 n. 33

Carson, David A.   278 n. 37

Cassirer, Ernst   180 n. 77

Catto, Jeremy   52 n. 50

Chadwick, Owen   42 n. 6

Charlesworth, Max J.   23 n. 26, 24 nn. 30–32, 25 nn. 33–34, 141 n. 58

Clines, David J. A.   72 n. 140, 270 n. 14, 364 n. 32, 420 n. 23

Coackley, Sarah   31 n. 56

Coetzee, Pieter H.   174 n. 49

Collins, John J.   189 n. 107

Connolly, Peter   8 n. 9

Copan, Paul   231 n. 8, 444 n. 54

Cottingham, John   434 n. 39

Craig, Vincent M.   123 n. 18

Creel, Richard E.   205 n. 14, 206 n. 15

Crenshaw, James L.   69 n. 129, 70 n. 131, 298 n. 14, 351 n. 15, 360 n. 27, 365 n. 35, 416 n. 21, 426 n. 28, 430 n. 34

Cupitt, Don   11 n. 12, 16 n. 3, 17 n. 9, 18 n. 15, 30 n. 52, 95 n. 41, 107 n. 69–70, 108 nn. 71–76, 109 n. 77, 123 nn. 19–20, 205 n. 13, 225 n. 3, 275 n. 26, 320 n. 59, 437 n. 47 and 49

Czachesz, István   196 n. 123

Dafni, Evangelia   44 n.11, 12

Dale, Erich M.   85 nn. 14 and 16–17

DaGarcia, David   326 n. 70

Davidson, Andrew B.   349 n. 12

Davies, Philip R.   312 n. 39

Davis, Stephen T.   102 n. 58

Davison, Scott   389 n. 31, 393 n. 32, 394 nn. 33–34

Deist, Ferdinand E.   189 n. 110, 237 n. 12, 371 n. 4

Deleuze, Gilles   229 n. 5, 329 n. 85

Dentan, Robert C.   41 n. 4, 66 n. 117

DeSmith, Felicia   120 n. 13

Deuser, Hermann   111 n. 81

Dijkstra, Meindert   400 n. 42

DiLella, Alexander   180 n. 76

Drury, Maurice O'Connor   92 n. 33

Dulls, Avery   67 n. 118

Dunand, Francois   274 n. 23

Durrant, Michael   274 n. 26

Dyrness, William A.   64 n. 108, 196 n. 122

Earl, Dennis   214 n. 29

Edwards, Chuck   186 n. 98

Eichrodt, Walter   63 n. 100, 64 nn. 101–6, 207 n. 15, 253 n. 24, 268 n. 7, 409 n. 13

Ellens, Deborah L.   212 n. 24

Eldredge, Laurence J. P.   59 n. 76

Eze, Emanuel C.   173 n. 54

Ezkenazi, Tamara K.   106 n. 66

Fasiku, Gbenga   172 n. 51

Feldman, Richard   384 n. 26

Fieser, James   408 n. 9

Fischer, Rob   21 n. 23, 24 n. 29

Fitzgerald, Timothy   35 n. 64

Flannery, Kevin L.   296 n. 8

Flew, Anthony   94 n. 36

Flint, Thomas P   99 n. 53, 294 n. 7

Fohrer, Georg   216 n. 33, 268 n. 8, 270 n. 16

Fontaine, Resianne   50 nn. 36–38

Forrest, Peter   375 n. 10

Foucault Michel D.   447 n. 1

Fox, Michael V.   77 n. 159, 371 n. 5

Frame, John M.   410 n. 21

Frank Daniel H.   159 n. 8, 176 n. 60

Frankenberry, Nancy   32 nn. 57–58, 55

Frankfort, Henriette A. 66 n. 113
Frankfort, Henry 66 n. 113
Fretheim, Terrence E. 69 n. 128, 177 n. 66, 243 n. 2, 250 n. 10, 297 n. 11
Froehlich, Karlfried 51 n. 44, 52 n. 47
Frydrych, Tomas 77 n. 160, 189 n. 108
Gardenförs, Peter 403 n. 45
Garrett, Brian 321 n. 61
Gauttari, Felix 229 n. 5, 329 n. 72
Geach, Peter 274 n. 26
Geivett, Douglas R. 37 n. 71
Gericke, Jacobus (Jaco) W. 3 n. 2, 41 n. 3, 79 nn. 172–73, 160 n. 16, 201 n. 4, 223 n. 1, 243 n. 1, 253 n. 25, 259 n 1, 276 n. 28, 293 n. 1, 297 n. 12, 344 n. 5, 352 n. 21, 353 n. 23, 359 n. 24, 377 n. 16, 408 n. 10, 417 n. 22, 423 n. 25
Gerstenberger, Erhard 142 n. 60
Gibson, Arthur 68 nn. 124–25
Gilkey, Langdon 97 n. 47
Gleitman, Henry 280 n. 32
Gleitman, Lila R. 280 n. 32
Gnuse, Robert 76 n. 153, 189 n. 109
Goodchild, Philip. 26 n. 36
Gottwald, Norman K. 269 n. 13
Grau, Christopher 177 n. 62
Griffiths, Paul 17 n. 7, 22 n. 24
Griffith-Dickson, Gwen 28 nn. 41–43, 30 n. 49, 34 nn. 61 and 63, 37 n. 74, 252 n. 21
Guattari, Félix 229 n. 5, 329 n. 85
Gulick, Robert van 339 n. 98, 340 nn. 99–101, 342 n. 103
Gupta, Anil 290 n. 38, 291 n. 42
Hacker, Peter M. S. 16 n. 3
Hackett, Jeremiah 23 n. 15
Hajek, Petr 289 n. 37
Hallen, Barry 166 n. 31, 171 n. 50, 348 n. 11
Hamori, Esther J. 230 n. 7, 256 n. 27
Hanna, Robert 214 n. 30
Hansson, Sven O. 402 nn. 43–44

Hare, John 409 n. 17
Harris, Harriet 100 n. 55, 118 n. 10
Harris, James F. 26 n. 36, 116 n. 3, 118 n. 9, 246 nn. 5–6, 256 nn. 28–29, 377 nn. 17–18, 378 n. 19, 384 n. 27
Harrison, Victoria S. 21 n. 22, 251 n. 20, 368 n. 40
Hartenstein, Friedhelm 237 n. 10
Hasel, Gerhard 41 n. 3, 4, 59 n. 77, 60 n. 83, 61 n. 84, 83, 65 n. 112, 145 n. 67
Hasker, William 30 n. 51
Haught, John F. 274 n. 21
Hayes, John 41 n. 3, 55 nn. 60–61, 56 nn. 64–65, 61 n. 87, 62 n. 91, 269 n. 12
Hazony, Yoram 162 n. 19
Healy, Mary 78 n. 170, 210 n. 23, 371 n. 2
Hebblethwaite, Brian 103 n. 60, 150 n. 79
Hecke, Pierre 250 n. 14
Heidegger, Martin 275 n. 27
Heinegg, Peter 434 n. 40
Helmer, Christine 212 n. 26, 213 nn. 27–28
Hemmerle, Klaus 91 n. 31
Hick, John 334 n. 96
Hirsch, Emil G. 84 n. 13, 85 n. 15
Hodgson, Peter C. 84 nn. 11–12
Holder, Ward R. 54 n. 55
Hughes, John J. 186 n. 98
Hume, David 427 n. 32
Hutto, Daniel 115 n. 2
Hyde, Dominic 310 n. 36
Ikuenobe, Polycarp 167 n. 39
Imschoot, Paul van 67 n. 121
Ingraffia, Brian D. 74 n. 147
Insole, Christopher 118 n. 10
Irwin, William 178 nn. 70–71
Jacob, Edmund 49 n. 34, 343 n. 2, 362 n. 29
Jacobson, Thorkild 274 n. 20

Janz, Bruce B.   167 nn. 37–38, 170 n. 47, 171 n. 48

Janowski, Bernd   185 n. 97

Jobling, David   106 n. 66

Johnson, Mark   251 n. 17

Jones, Roger B.   121 n. 15

Jordan, Mark H.   16 n. 2, 5, 17 n. 25

Kaiser, Otto   44 n. 13, 14, 70 n. 132, 71 n. 134, 268 n. 8

Kaiser, Walter C., Jr.   67 n. 119

Kass, Leon   78 n. 167

Katz, Claire E.   106 n. 67

Kaufmann, Walter A.   83 n. 8, 84 nn. 9–10

Keel, Othmar   270 n. 16

Kelly, John F.   426 n. 29

Kelly, Thomas   384 n. 26

Kim, Wonil   73 n. 143

Kirch, Joy F.   53 nn. 51–52

Kittel, Rudolph   62 n. 93

Klein-Braslavy, Sara   50 n. 40

Klemke, Elmer D.   434 n. 40

Knierim, Rolf P.   58 n. 71, 59 n. 75, 72 n. 141, 73 nn. 142–43, 179 n. 73, 193 n. 118, 208 n. 17, 223 n. 2, 237 n. 11, 268 n. 9, 269 n. 10, 293 n. 4, 345 n. 7, 350 nn. 13–14, 409 n. 12

Knight, Douglas   405 n. 2, 409 n. 14

Köhler, Ludwig   65 n. 109, 193 n. 118, 268 n. 7, 308 n. 34, 312 n. 38, 343 n. 2

Kolak, Daniel   36 n. 69, 363 n. 30

Kolb, David   58 n. 73

Köpf, Ulrich   53 n. 53

Korfmacher, Carsten   313 n. 43, 316 n. 48, 318 nn. 54–54, 321 n. 62, 322 nn. 63–64, 324 nn. 71–73, 325 n. 74

Kraft, Robert A.   44 n. 14

Krailsheimer, A. J.   54 n. 57

Kreeft, Peter   78 n. 163, 190 n. 113

Kripke, Saul   257 n. 30

Krueger, Thomas   269 n. 11

LaCocque, Andre   105 n. 63

Lakoff, George   251 n. 17

Langer, Susanne K.   181 n. 80, 182 nn. 84 and 87–88

Larrimore, Mark J.   36 n. 70

Lawrence, Matt   177 n. 62

Laurence, Stephen   214 n. 29, 262 n. 4

Le Roux, Andre P J.   174 n. 49

Leleye, Issiaka P.   174 n. 55

Levenson, Jon D.   426 n. 31

Levine, Michael P.   100 n. 56, 101 n. 57, 132 n. 43

Liddy, Richard M.   181 n. 83, 182 nn. 85–86

Lindstrom, Frederick   431 n. 35

Littlejohn, Ronnie   133 n. 46, 134 n. 47

Lloyd, Alan B.   274 n. 22

Long, Eugene T.   29 n. 46, 30 n. 50, 31 nn. 53–55, 82 n. 2, 92 n. 32, 105 n. 65, 118 n. 9, 126 n. 29, 130 nn. 38–39, 360 n. 25, 376 nn. 12–14

Ludwig, Theodore. M.   273 n. 19

Macarthur, John   186 n. 98

MacDonald, Scott   136 n. 49–50, 137 n. 51–52

MacIntyre, Alasdair   94 n. 36

Mackie, Penelope   330 nn. 86–87, 331 n. 88

Maffie, James   157 n. 4, 209 n. 21

Margolis, Eric   214 n. 29, 262 n. 4

Marion, Jean L.   107 n. 68

Markus, Arjan   435 n.45

Marshall, Taylor   52 n. 48

Martin, Michael   351 n. 18, 352 n. 20, 434 n. 39, 435 n. 45

Martin, Nancy M.   434 n. 40

Masolo, Dismas A.   168 n. 39

Mautner, Thomas   353 n. 22

Mayes, Andrew D. H.   189 n. 109

Mayhue, Richard L.   186 n. 98

Mbiti, John   171 n. 49

McCartney, Dan C.   42 n. 5, 7

McFague, Sallie 251 n. 18
McInerny, Ralph 52 n. 49
McKenzie, John L. 67 n. 120
McLaughlin, Brian 307 n. 30
Meister, Chad 231 n. 8
Mead, Hunter 187 n. 103
Menzies, Peter 385 n. 28
Merk, Otto 200 n. 3
Metz, Thaddeus 434 nn. 41–42, 435 n. 43, 436 n. 46
Miles, Jack 270 n. 15, 308 n. 33, 312 n. 42, 319 n. 55
Miller, Christian B. 374 n. 9
Miller, Patrick D. 271 n. 16, 312 n. 42, 315 n. 46, 319 n. 56, 444 n. 55
Mills, Mary E. 250 n. 13
Mitchell, Craig Vincent 123 n. 21, 437 n. 48
Moore, Megan B. 79 n. 171
Morgan, Kathleen A. 183 n. 89
Morris, Thomas V. 36 n. 68, 143 n. 61, 275 n. 26, 294 nn. 5–6
Morriston, Wes 408 n. 11
Moseley, Alan N. 186 n. 98
Müller, Hans-Peter 71 n. 131, 74 n. 146
Murphy, Nancy 6 n. 4
Nadler, Steven 55 n. 62, 56 n. 63
Nagel, Thomas 340 n. 102
Nasr, Seyed H. 164 n. 29
Naugle, David K. 186 n. 98
Negri, A. 203 n. 10
Neumark, David 159 n. 10
Nielsen, Kai 187 n. 100
Nietzsche, Friedrich 88 n. 24, 89 nn. 25–27, 90 nn. 28–29, 91 n. 30, 334 n. 97, 364 n. 31
Noebel, David 186 n. 98
Nolan, Daniel 366 nn. 38–39
O'Callaghan, John 52 n. 49
O'Connor, Timothy 307 n. 32
Odera Oruka, Henry 168 n. 40
O'Dowd, Ryan 372 n. 6

Oeming, Manfred 74 n. 146, 268 n. 8
Oesterley, William 271 n. 16
O'Farrell, Clare 447 n. 1
Okafor, Fidelis U. 168 n. 41
Ollenburger, Ben C. 41 n. 3, 4, 58 n. 72, 59 n. 74, 60 nn. 79–82, 61 n. 85–86, 62 n. 89, 74 n. 147, 269 n. 12
Olson, Eric T. 312 nn. 40–41, 314 n. 44, 315 n. 45, 316 n. 48, 317 nn. 50–52, 321 n. 60, 322 n. 66, 323 n. 67, 328 n. 83
Orr, James 143 n. 62
Otto, Eckhart 164 n. 27, 180 n. 74, 405 n. 3, 409 n. 12
Otto, Rudolph 126 n. 31
Owen, Huw P. 273 n. 19
Paget, James N. B. C. 48 n. 28, 29
Pailin, David 24 n. 28, 25 n. 35, 37 n. 73
Pallesen, Carsten 65 n. 104
Pangle, Thomas L. 78 n. 169
Panikkar, Raimundo 273 n. 19
Parfit, Derek 316 n. 47
Parpola, Simo 163 n. 21
Parry, Robin 78 n. 170, 210 n. 23, 371 n. 2
Patrick, Dale 69 nn. 126–27, 346 n. 9
Patterson, Charles 94 nn. 37–39, 95 n. 40, 95 n. 42, 96 nn. 43–45
Pattison, George 18 n. 16
Pearcey, Nancy 186 n. 98
Pedersen, Johannes 191 n. 114
Perdue, Leo G. 74 n. 145, 77 n. 160, 189 n. 108
Phillips, Dewi Zephaniah 120 n. 14, 124 n. 22 and 22
Planck, Max K. 1 n. *
Plantinga, Alvin 99 nn. 50–51
Plantinga, Richard J. 46 n. 23
Poijman, Louis 17 n. 7
Porter, Barbara N. 274 n. 25
Poston, Ted 378 n. 21, 379 n. 22

Preuss, Horst D.   142 n. 59, 146 n. 68, 343 n. 2, 362 n. 28, 371 n. 1, 409 n. 15

Priest, John F.   351 n. 15

Procopé, John F.   45 n. 15, 19, 21, 46 n. 22, 48 n. 30

Prussner, Frederick   41 n. 3, 55 nn. 60–61, 56 nn. 64–65, 61 n. 87, 62 n. 91, 269 n. 12

Purushottma, Bilimoria   131 n. 36

Pyysiäinen, Ilkka   247 n. 9

Quinn, Philip L.   34 n. 62, 373 n. 9, 408 n. 11

Rad, Gerhard von   64 n. 107, 351 n. 14

Ramsey, Ian   274 n. 26

Rapp, Christoph   254 n. 26

Razavi, Mehdi Amin   164 n. 29

Rea, Michael C.   38 n. 75, 294 n. 7

Reimer, Marga   257 n. 30

Reventlow, Henning G.   43 n. 8, 54 n. 56, 57 n. 70, 60 n. 78, 83 n. 6, 269 n. 12

Reynolds, Frank   183 nn. 90–91

Rickman, Hans P.   188 n. 104

Richardson, Alan   189 n. 110

Ricoeur, Paul   105 nn. 62–63, 251 n. 16

Ringgren, Helmar   267 n. 6, 271 n. 16

Riordan, Peter   187 n. 100

Rissler, James   103 n. 59

Robertson, Teresa   303 n. 21

Robinson, Henry   271 n. 16

Rogerson, John W.   54 n. 54, 77 n. 158

Rorty, Richard   117 n. 7

Rossi, Philip   58 n. 73, 83 n. 7

Rowe, William   444 n. 56

Rowley, H. H.   268 n. 7, 344 n. 3

Rudavsky, Tamar   51 nn. 42–43

Runzo, Joseph   434 n. 40

Russell, Bertrand   112 n. 83

Russell, Paul   82 nn. 3–4, 83 n. 5

Ryle, Gilbert   117 n. 6, 121 n. 16

Saebø, Magne   41 n. 3, 55 n. 59

Saggs, Hallo W.   271 n. 17

Samuelson, Norbert   159 nn. 9 and 11–13, 421 n. 24

Sandys-Wunsch, James   41 n. 3, 59 n. 76

Sarot, Marcel   302 n. 18

Sayre-McCord, Geoff   406 n. 5, 407 nn. 6–7, 408 n. 8

Scarborough, Milton   184 n. 96

Schaeffer, Francis   186 n. 98

Schatz, David   158 n. 6, 159 n. 7, 160 nn. 14–15

Schechtman, Marya   325 nn. 75–76

Schellenberg, Annette   371 n. 5

Schilbrack, Kevin   184 n. 94

Schmidt, Werner H.   267 n. 6, 271 n. 16

Schneider, Steven   369 nn. 43–45

Schopenhauer, Arthur   87 nn. 21–22, 88 n. 23, 442 n. 53

Schroeder, Mark   424 n. 26

Schulz, Hermann   45 n. 18

Seeskin, Kenneth   50 n. 39, 51 n. 41

Segal, Robert   8 n. 9, 9 n. 10, 184 n. 95

Sekine, Seizo   76 n. 152

Shank, Carl H.   189 n. 110

Shepherd, John T.   132 n. 44

Shoemaker, David   325 n. 77, 326 nn. 78–80, 327 nn. 81–82

Sicker, Martin   78 n. 168

Siegert, Folker   42 n. 7, 5 n. 20

Simkins, Ronald   189 n. 109

Skarsaune, Oscar   46 n. 22

Smart, Ninian   132 nn. 42 and 44, 133 n. 45, 156 n. 3, 187 n. 100

Smend, Rudolph   61 n. 88, 62 n. 89–90

Smith, Mark   147 nn. 74–75, 164 n. 27, 167 n. 35, 208 nn. 18–19, 259 n. 2, 271 n. 18, 312 n. 42, 319 n. 56

Soames, Scott 201 n. 5
Sommer, Benjamin D. 322 n. 65, 323 nn. 68–69
Sorensen, Roy 308–9 n. 35
Soskice, Janet M. 251 n. 19
Soulen Kendall n. 3, 180 n. 75
Soulen, Richard N. 4 n. 3, 180 n. 75
Stacey, David 190 n. 112
Staerk, Willy 63 nn. 94–96
Steinberg, David 129 n. 36, 396 n. 35
Stendahl, Krister 269 n. 12
Steuernagel, Carl 63 n. 97
Steup, Mark 373 n. 8
Stevenson, James 47 n. 26
Stigen, Anfinn 187 n. 100
Stiver, Dan R. 35 n. 65
Stump, Eleanor 81 n. 1, 98 nn. 48–49, 99 n. 53, 135 n. 48
Sullivan, L.E. 273 n. 19
Sutherland, Robert 78 n. 166
Swartz, Norman 291 n. 43, 292 n. 45
Sweetman, Brendan 37 n. 71
Swoyer, Chris 283 n. 34, 285 n. 35, 305 nn. 24–25, 306 nn. 26–29, 307 n. 31
Taliaferro, Charles 9 n. 10, 17 n. 7, 1 n. 8, 20 n. 21, 34 n. 60, 133 n. 45, 378 n. 20
Tanney, Julia 122 n. 17
Tarnas, Richard 112 n. 83
Tempels, Placide 166 n. 33–34
Thiselton, Anthony 139 nn. 54–55, 146 n. 70, 192 n. 117
Thomas, Laurence 440 n. 51
Thomas, Louis V. 174 n. 55
Thompson, Thomas L. 75 nn. 150–51, 178 nn. 67–68, 319 n. 57, 324 n. 70, 365 nn. 36–37
Thomson, Garrett 434 n. 39
Thrower, James 351 n. 17, 19, 360 n. 26
Tillich, Paul 97 n. 46
Tooley, Michael 426 n. 29

Toorn, Karel van der 267 n. 6
Trakakis, Nick 26 n. 36, 27 n. 37, 28 n. 40, 30 n. 47, 101 n. 61
Tracy, David 183 nn. 90–91
Trisel, Brooke A. 441 n. 52
Trout, Lara 106 n. 67
Tsevat, Matitiahu 191 n. 114
Uehlinger, Christoph 270 n. 16
Vaihinger, Hans 368 n. 41
Vallicella, William 247 n. 9
Van Leeuwen, Raymond C. 189 n. 110
Vanhoozer, Kevin 105 n. 64
Vawter, Bruce 268 n. 7
Wainright, William 17 n. 9, 18 nn. 12–14, 18 n. 17, 19 nn. 18–20, 29 n. 44, 37 n. 72, 70 n. 130, 234 n. 9, 410 n. 20
Wallmann, Johannes 53 n. 54
Wallulis, Gerald 23 n. 25
Ward, Keith 35 n. 67, 36 n. 68, 50 n. 35, 109 n. 78, 110 n. 79, 126 n. 30, 128 n. 35, 275 n. 26, 293 n. 2
Weatherson, Brian 304 n. 22
Weed, Jennifer H. 35 n. 66, 245 n. 4, 246 n. 7, 247 n. 8
Wetzel, James 112 n. 82
Westphal, Merold 26 n. 36, 27 n. 39, 29 n. 45, 110 n. 80, 126 n. 27, 127 nn. 32–33, 128 n. 34, 138 n. 53
Wheeler-Robinson, Henry 68 n. 122
White, Morton 117 n. 8
Whybray, Norman 189 n. 107
Wiredu, Kwasi 166 n. 31, 171 n. 52, 172 n. 53
Wierenga, Eric 408 n. 11, 410 n. 18
Wilcox, John T. 78 n. 165
Williams, Thomas 51 n. 44
Williamson, Raymond K. 58 n. 73
Wilson, Andrew N. 85 n. 18
Wiredu, Kwasi 165 n. 29, 167 n. 39, 172 nn. 46–47
Wisnewski, J. Jeremy 445 n. 57

Wittgenstein, Ludwig   3 n. 1, 93 n. 34, 118 n. 11, 119 n. 12, 343 n. 1

Wolde, Ellen van   196 n. 124

Wolfle, Dael L.   241 n. 1

Wolterstorff, Nicholas   93 n. 35

Wong, David   133 n. 40, 175 nn. 57–58, 176 nn. 59 and 61–62

Wong, Hong Yu   307 n. 32

Wright, David F.   49 n. 32

Wright, G. Ernest   66 n. 114

Wisnewski, J. Jeremy   445 n. 60

Yandell, Keith   34 n. 61

Young, Julian   434 n. 39

Zagzebski, Linda   409 n. 11

Zivie-Coche, Christiane   274 n. 23

Index of Subjects

AAR, 29
APA, 29
African philosophy, 165–74
allegory, 42–43
allotheism, 383–86
analogies, 154–98
analytic philosophy of religion, 26, 30, 97–103, 118–25
analytic-Continental divide, 26–29
ancient Near Eastern philosophy, 162–65
antiphilosophical sentiment, 62–68
atheism, 351–59
    and atheology, 351–59
axiology, 422–25
Babylonian philosophy, 163
biblical criticism, 3, 199–223
biblical theology movement, 65–66
binary oppositions, 299–300
Chinese philosophy, 175
Christian philosophy of religion, 27, 233–40
cognitive science, 195–97
comparative philosophy of religion 31, 129–34
conceptual analysis, 211–14
consciousness, divine 338–40
Continental philosophy of religion, 103–13
critical theory, 6, 31
deconstruction, 13, 30
descriptive philosophy of religion, 8–10
divine command theory, 411–41

divine complexity, 300–302
divine condition, 264
dystheism, 425–33
Egyptian philosophy, 163
epistemology of Israelite religion, 370–404
ethnophilosophy, 168–69
Euthyphro dilemma, 408–10, 419
evidentialism, 377–83
existence, mystery of, 359–63
expository philosophy, 205–7
false dichotomies, 254–56
feminist philosophy of religion, 31–32
fictionalism, 363–69
folk-philosophical assumptions
    epistemological, 209
    logical, 210
    metaphysical, 206–9
    moral, 210
folk philosophy, 154–57
fundamentalism, 97–104
God
    existence of, 36
    nature of, 35
godhood,
    generic concept of, 259–93
Greek philosophy, 42–43
Hebrew Bible
    in early modern philosophy, 80–97
    in analytic philosophy, 97–104
    in continental philosophy, 104–14
Hebrew Bible studies
    as interdisciplinary, 3–4
    essence of, 3

Hebrew Bible studies (cont.)
  philosophy and, 4–5
  philosophy of religion and, 41–80
Hebrew thought, 190–92
hermeneutics, 30
history of Israelite religion, 227–31, 395–403
hypermodernity, 13, 13 n. 13
impossible worlds, 331–32
Israelite religion
  philosophical approach to, 4, 8–10
Jewish philosophy of religion, 157–63
logic of belief revision, 395–403
meaning of life, Israelite perspectives on, 434–46
metaethics, 402–8
metaphor, 251–54
metaphilosophy of religion, 15–41
metatheistic assumptions, 265, 267, 276, 277, 279, 280, 282
moral realism, 411–22
myth and philosophy, 179–284
necessary and sufficient conditions, 265
nonrealism, 363–65
objections to philosophy, 142–54
Old Testament ethics, 194–95
Old Testament theology, 192–93
oneirological analogy, 332–38
perfect being theology, 296–301
Persian philosophy, 164
phenomenology of religion, 129–34
philosophical analysis, 201–3
philosophical approaches to religion, 4, 8–10, 16–21, 21
philosophical commentary, 203–21
philosophical criticism, 6, 199–223
  pros and cons, 219–21
philosophical definition, 289–91
philosophical description, 139–41
philosophical theology, 38, 104–8, 292–342
philosophical translation, 214–17

philosophical turn, 68–80
philosophy, 6, 15, 16
  as analysis, 24
  as handmaid of religion, 24
  as making room for faith, 24
  as religion, 25
  as study of reasoning, 25
philosophy in literature, 174–79
philosophy of history, 58, 64, 75, 84
philosophy of Israelite religion, 6, 17, 222–40
philosophy of religion, 6, 7, 16–22
  currents in, 30–32
  issues in, 33–38
philosophy of science, 71, 79
Plato, 410 n. 20
pluralism, 3–4, 22
polytheism, 247–50
possible worlds, 329–32
postmodernism, 13
presupposition analysis, 204–10
principle of sufficient reason, 386–88
problem of evil, 36, 425–33
prophecy, philosophical perspectives on, 389–95
realism, 363–70
reference, 256–58
religion, nature of, 17, 35, 233
religion and history, 37, 237
religion and morality, 37, 236, 405–47
religion and science, 37, 237
religious epistemology, 37, 237
religious experience, 236, 377–383
religious language, nature of, 35, 244–47
religious pluralism, 37
religious studies, 4
revelation, 35, 386–88
social philosophy, 6
supermodernism, 12–13
theodicy, 425–33
theodiversity, 261
Wittgensteinian philosophy, 119–23

worlds in the text, 204
worldview, 185–89
Yhwh
 existence of, 342–51
 identity of, 311–32
 ontological status of, 363–70
 properties of, 303–11

Lightning Source UK Ltd.
Milton Keynes UK
UKOW040304180613

212395UK00001B/8/P